MEDIEVAL HISTORY AND ARCHAEOLOGY

General Editors
John Blair   Helena Hamerow

Charlemagne and Rome is a wide-ranging exploration of cultural politics in the age of Charlemagne. It focuses on a remarkable inscription commemorating Pope Hadrian I who died in Rome at Christmas 795. Commissioned by Charlemagne, composed by Alcuin of York, and cut from black stone quarried close to the king's new capital at Aachen in the heart of the Frankish kingdom, it was carried to Rome and set over the tomb of the pope in the south transept of St Peter's basilica not long before Charlemagne's imperial coronation in the basilica on Christmas Day 800. A masterpiece of Carolingian art, Hadrian's epitaph was also a manifesto of empire demanding perpetual commemoration for the king amid St Peter's cult. In script, stone, and verse, it proclaimed Frankish mastery of the art and power of the written word, and claimed the cultural inheritance of imperial and papal Rome, recast for a contemporary, early medieval audience. Pope Hadrian's epitaph was treasured through time and was one of only a few decorative objects translated from the late antique basilica of St Peter's into the new structure, the construction of which dominated and defined the early modern Renaissance. Understood then as precious evidence of the antiquity of imperial affection for the papacy, Charlemagne's epitaph for Pope Hadrian I was preserved as the old basilica was demolished and carefully redisplayed in the portico of the new church, where it can be seen today.

Using a very wide range of sources and methods, from art history, epigraphy, palaeography, geology, archaeology, and architectural history, as well as close reading of contemporary texts in prose and verse, this book presents a detailed 'object biography', contextualising Hadrian's epitaph in its historical and physical setting at St Peter's over eight hundred years, from its creation in the late eighth century during the Carolingian Renaissance through to the early modern Renaissance of Bramante, Michelangelo, and Maderno.

MEDIEVAL HISTORY AND ARCHAEOLOGY

General Editors
John Blair   Helena Hamerow

The volumes in this series bring together archaeological, historical, and visual methods to offer new approaches to aspects of medieval society, economy, and material culture. The series seeks to present and interpret archaeological evidence in ways readily accessible to historians, while providing a historical perspective and context for the material culture of the period.

FRONTISPIECE The epitaph of Pope Hadrian I (d. 795).
Photo: By kind permission of the Reverenda Fabbrica di San Pietro in Vaticano, Rome.

Charlemagne and Rome

Alcuin and the Epitaph of Pope Hadrian I

JOANNA STORY

Great Clarendon Street, Oxford, OX2 6DP,
United Kingdom

Oxford University Press is a department of the University of Oxford.
It furthers the University's objective of excellence in research, scholarship,
and education by publishing worldwide. Oxford is a registered trade mark of
Oxford University Press in the UK and in certain other countries

© Joanna Story 2023

The moral rights of the author have been asserted

All rights reserved. No part of this publication may be reproduced, stored in
a retrieval system, or transmitted, in any form or by any means, without the
prior permission in writing of Oxford University Press, or as expressly permitted
by law, by licence or under terms agreed with the appropriate reprographics
rights organization. Enquiries concerning reproduction outside the scope of the
above should be sent to the Rights Department, Oxford University Press, at the
address above

You must not circulate this work in any other form
and you must impose this same condition on any acquirer

Published in the United States of America by Oxford University Press
198 Madison Avenue, New York, NY 10016, United States of America

British Library Cataloguing in Publication Data
Data available

Library of Congress Control Number: 2022948813

ISBN 978–0–19–920634–6

DOI: 10.1093/oso/9780199206346.001.0001

Printed in the UK by
Bell & Bain Ltd., Glasgow

Links to third party websites are provided by Oxford in good faith and
for information only. Oxford disclaims any responsibility for the materials
contained in any third party website referenced in this work.

For Martin, Julia, and Edward

PREFACE AND ACKNOWLEDGEMENTS

A project that has taken this long to come to fruition carries with it many debts of gratitude, not least to the series editors, John Blair and Helena Hamerow, and the editors at Oxford University Press who have waited patiently. This book grew out of small project devised to find a way to do some research in Rome. Having written an article investigating the unique manuscript copy of a letter to Charlemagne, written by Cathwulf in 775, I thought that focusing on another 'unicum' that had also been composed by another English scholar in the service of the Frankish king would be a logical next step. I had come across a reference to Pope Hadrian's epitaph in an entry in an early Northumbrian chronicle and was intrigued to find that the original inscription still existed in St Peter's basilica. Donald Bullough had published a plate of it, and he encouraged me to find out more.

Many have helped me over the years, and, in different ways, I am very grateful to Olof Brandt; Claire Breay; Leslie Brubaker; Judith Bunbury; Lida Lopes Cardozo Kindersley; Erin T. Dailey; David Ganz; Richard Gem; Eric Groessens; Florian Hartmann; Ulrike Heckner; David Howlett; Michael Lapidge; Paolo Liverani; Rosamond McKitterick; Paul Meyvaert; Lawrence Nees; Janet L. Nelson; Jennifer O'Reilly; Andy Orchard; John Osborne; Mario Piacentini; Susan Rankin; Carol M. Richardson; Sebastiano Sciuti; Julia M. H. Smith; Roey Sweet; Francis Tourneur; Chris Wickham; Ian Wood and, most particularly, to Pietro Zander who granted permission to examine the epitaph and who has been unfailingly helpful with the project that ensued. Without his help, none of this work could have happened and I am greatly indebted to him and his colleagues at the Reverenda Fabbrica di San Pietro in Vaticano.

Aspects of this research has been supported with generous grants from the Arts and Humanities Research Council (AHRC), the British Academy and the Leverhulme Trust, as well as the University of Leicester especially through its support for study leave. I am most grateful to colleagues at the British School at Rome, principally Maria Pia Malvezzi, Stefania Peterlini, and Valerie Scott, for their help in securing permissions and access to archives and sites. Ulrike Heckner, Gregor Kalas, Tom Knott, Paolo Romiti (via Alamy), and Lacey Wallace have all supplied images that they have created. Numerous libraries, archives, and museums have granted rights to reproduce images of manuscripts and objects in their collections and to them I am most grateful: Archives e Bibliothèque patrimoniale, Abbeville; Archivio Fotografico dei Musei Capitolini, Rome; Bayerische Staatsbibliothek, Munich; Bergerbibliothek, Bern; Biblioteca Apostolica Vaticana, Rome; Bibliothèque nationale de France; Bibliothèque Royale de Belgique, Brussels; Bildarchiv Preußischer Kulturbesitz, Berlin; The British Library Board; Domkapitel, Aachen; Fitzwilliam Museum,

Cambridge; Istituzione Biblioteca Classense, Ravenna; Leiden University Libraries; the Ministero della Cultura, via the Parco archeologico del Colosseo, the Istituto Centrale per il Catalogo e la Documentazione (ICCD) and the Uffizi Galleries, Florence; Musées Royaux d'Art et d'Histoire, Brussels; National Museum of Fine Arts, Stockholm; Österreichische Nationalbibliothek, Vienna; Pontificio Istituto de Archeologia Cristiana, Rome; Stiftsbibliothek, Einsiedeln; Reverenda Fabbrica di San Pietro in Vaticano; Rijksmuseum van Oudheden, Leiden; Romisch-Germanisches Museum, Köln; Utrecht University Library; Universitätsbibliothek, Würzburg.

The names of churches and saints are given in the linguistic style of the country in which they are located. Thus, I refer to churches in Rome by the names that they are known in Italian (e.g. S. Adriano, Sta. Maria Maggiore, San Paolo fuori le Mura). Likewise, churches in France are called by their familiar French names, normally hyphenated to differentiate between the saint and a church dedication (e.g. Saint-Germain-des-Près, Saint-Riquier). The exception is St Peter's in the Vatican. Here I use the English name throughout for saint and church.

Finally, this book is dedicated to Martin, Julia, and Edward, with much love and appreciation of their tolerance and patience. The last word, however, I leave to Alcuin, the author of Pope Hadrian's epitaph:

> Pippin: *Quid est littera?* | What is lettering?
> Alcuin: *Custos historiae* | The guardian of history.
>
> *Disputatio regalis et nobilissimi iuvenis Pippini cum Albino scholastico*
> The debate of the regal and most noble youth Pippin with the scholar, Alcuin

CONTENTS

List of Figures	xiii
List of Abbreviations	xix
Edition and Translation: Alcuin's Epitaph for Pope Hadrian I (by David R. Howlett)	xxii
Introduction: Charlemagne and Italy	1
1. Renaissance Rome: Hadrian's Epitaph in New St Peter's	29
2. The 'Life' and Death of Pope Hadrian I	85
3. Alcuin and the Epitaph	111
4. Recalling Rome: Epigraphic *Syllogae* and Itineraries	143
5. Writing on the Walls: Epigraphy in Italy and Francia	185
6. Black Stone: Materials, Methods, and Motives	227
7. Aachen and the Art of the Court	257
8. Charlemagne, St Peter's, and the Imperial Coronation	311
List of Manuscript Sources	343
Bibliography	347
Index	389

LIST OF FIGURES

Frontispiece The epitaph of Pope Hadrian I (d. 795). Photo: By kind permission of the Reverenda Fabbrica di San Pietro in Vaticano, Rome. iv

0.1 Jean Fouquet, 'The Coronation of the Emperor Charlemagne', *Grandes Chroniques de France* (1455–60); Paris, BnF, Fr. 6465, fol. 89v. Reproduced by permission of the Bibliothèque nationale de France, Paris. xxiv

1.1 Charlemagne's epitaph for Pope Hadrian I in the portico of St Peter's in the Vatican with its seventeenth-century frame. Photo: Author, with kind permission of the Reverenda Fabbrica di San Pietro in Vaticano, Rome. 28

1.2 Detail of the apse and south transept of the old basilica at St Peter's from the 1590 engraving of Alfarano's plan. Hadrian's chapel is marked as no. 15, the Leonine chapel is no. 14 and the remains of S. Martino are labelled 'a'. Photo: By kind permission of the Reverenda Fabbrica di San Pietro in Vaticano, Rome. 31

1.3 Reconstruction of Old St Peter's. Drawing: © Lacey Wallace. 32

1.4 Detail of Raphael's 'Coronation of Charlemagne' from the *Stanza dell'Incendio* in the Vatican palace. Photo: Reproduced with permission of Bildarchiv Preußischer Kulturbesitz, Berlin. 37

1.5 The tomb of Pope Hadrian VI in S. Maria dell'Anima. The outer pair of columns are made of *africano* marble, the rarest and most expensive coloured marble in antiquity. Photo: Author. 41

1.6 Donato Bramante (1505–6), 'Sketches for the basilica of St Peter's' showing the outline of the new structure superimposed over the old. Notice that the eastern piers stand within the nave of the old basilica. Florence, Uffizi Galleries, Gabinetto dei Disegni e delle Stampe degli Uffizi, Inv. GDSU n. 20 A. Photo: Reproduced by permission of the Ministero della Cultura. 47

1.7 The Porta del Popolo (built 1563–5). The four antique columns were taken from the exedra screens in the transept of the old basilica at St Peter's. Photo: Author. 48

1.8 'View of St Peter's from the south west', BAV, Collezione Ashby no. 329. Photo: Reproduced by kind permission of the Biblioteca Apostolica Vaticana, Rome. 51

1.9 Maerteen van Heemskerck (*c*.1536), 'View of St Peter's under construction from the south'. Berlin, Kupferstichkabinett, 79 D 2a, fol. 54r. Photo: Reproduced with permission of the Bildarchiv Preußischer Kulturbesitz, Berlin. 52

1.10 Maerteen van Heemskerck (*c*.1536), 'View of St Peter's under construction from the south-east'. Berlin, Kupferstichkabinett, 79 D 2a, fol. 51r. Reproduced with permission of the Bildarchiv Preußischer Kulturbesitz, Berlin. 53

1.11 Maerteen van Heemskerck (*c*.1536), 'The new crossing and Bramante's tegurium seen from within the north transept of Old St Peter's'. Stockholm, National Museum, coll. Anckarsvärd 637. Photo: Courtesy of the National Museum of Fine Arts, Stockholm. 54

1.12 Giovanni Antonio Dosio (*c*.1564), 'Sketch of the interior of St Peter's basilia', shown under construction, with Bramante's *tegurium* and the ancient apse, seen from within the south transept; Florence, Uffizi Galleries, Gabinetto dei Disegni e delle Stampe degli Uffizi, Inv. GDSU n. 91 A. Photo: Reproduced by permission of the Ministero della Cultura. 56

1.13 Battista Naldini (?) (*c*.1564), 'St Peter's, view from the nave towards the apse and Bramante's *tegurium*'. Note the stubs of the western transept wall on either side of the *tegurium*. Hamburg, Kunsthalle, Inv. Nr 21311. Photo: Reproduced with permission of the Bildarchiv Preußischer Kulturbesitz, Berlin. 57

1.14 A watercolour by Domenico Tasselli (*c*.1611) for Giacomo Grimaldi's *Album di San Pietro*, showing the interior of the eastern part of the nave of St Peter's, looking towards the *muro divisorio*. Note the numerous altars and monuments, and the door closing the arch in the *muro divisorio* with steps leading up to the door and to the raised floor level in the new basilica beyond. BAV, Arch. Cap. S. Pietro, A.64.ter, fol. 12r. Photo: Reproduced by kind permission of the Biblioteca Apostolica Vaticana, Rome. 59

1.15 The doorway in the western wall of the south transept, showing the marble threshold and door jamb, the paving of the old basilica and, on the far left, the projecting wall of the tomb structure that fills the space between the doorway and the exedra pier. Photo: By kind permission of the Reverenda Fabbrica di San Pietro in Vaticano, Rome. 62

1.16 The face of the western pier that marked the boundary of the southern exedra. Abutting it to the right are two walls, both with painted decoration, which project slightly beyond the pier into the space of the transept. Photo: By kind permission of the Reverenda Fabbrica di San Pietro in Vaticano, Rome. 62

1.17 Engraving of Alfarano's plan of St Peter's, 'Almae urbis Divi Petri veteris novique Templi descriptio', by Martino Ferrabosco, in G. B. Costaguti, *Architettura della basilica di San Pietro in Vaticano. Opera di Bramante Lazzari, Michel'Angelo Bonarota, Carlo Maderni, e altri famosi Architetti...*(Rome, 1684). Photo: By kind permission of the Fabbrica di San Pietro in Vaticano, Rome. 66

1.18 View of the façade of St Peter's and its atrium by G. A. Dosio, engraved by Giambattista Cavalieri to show the opening of the Porta Santa by Gregory XIII on 24 December 1574; from, Ehrle and Egger, *Piante e Vedute*, tav. 31. Roma, ICCD, Fototeca Nationale, F8245, reproduced with permission of the Ministero della Cultura. 71

1.19 Drawing of the oratory of Pope John VII, from Grimaldi's *Instrumenta autentica*. Hadrian I's 783 inscription is labelled as Item *M*; the porphyry tomb of Pope Hadrian IV (1154–9) stands to the left, BAV, Barb. Lat. 2733, fols 94v–95r. Reproduced by kind permission of the Biblioteca Apostolica Vaticana, Rome. 80

2.1 Detail from the *Sta Maria Regina* fresco, from the atrium of Santa Maria Antiqua, Rome (right-hand side), showing Pope Hadrian I on the left with a square nimbus. Photo: Roberto Sigismondi (2011), reproduced by concession of the Ministero della Cultura, Parco archeologico del Colosseo. 84

2.2	Denarius of Hadrian I (issued 781–95); *EMC* 1: no. 1032 (enlarged, x2). Obverse: CN[or H] ADRIANUS PAPA | IB reverse: VICTORIA DNN CONOB|H[adrianus]|R[o]M[a]. Photo: Courtesy of the Fitzwilliam Museum, Cambridge.	88
2.3	The *Annales Laureshamenses*, showing last part of the annal for 795 and beginning of the entry for 796; Vienna, ÖNB, Cod. 515, fol. 2r, detail. Photo: Courtesy of the Österreichische Nationalbibliothek, Vienna.	103
3.1	Detail of Hadrian's epitaph, line 17. Photo: Author.	110
3.2	Denarius of Charlemagne (issued 772–93). *EMC* 1: no. 730 (PG 202) (enlarged, x2). Photo: Courtesy of the Fitzwilliam Museum, Cambridge.	123
3.3	The colophon recording Charlemagne's instruction to make this copy of Paul the Deacon's *Liber de diversisi quasticunculis* 'from the original'; Brussels, Bibliothèque Royale de Belgique, MS II 2572, fol. 1r. Photo: Courtesy of the Bibliothèque Royale de Belgique, Brussels.	124
3.4	'Epitaphium Caroli', Munich, Bayerische Staatsbibliothek, Clm 14641, fol. 31v (detail). Photo: Courtesy of the Bayerische Staatsbibliothek, Munich.	126
3.5	A ninth-century copy of Alcuin's 'Epitaph for Pope Hadrian'; BnF, Lat. 2773, fol. 23v. Photo: Courtesy of the Bibliothèque nationale de France, Paris.	128
3.6	A twelfth-century copy of the *Liber Pontificalis*, showing the end of the *Life* of Stephen II and the first twelve lines of Hadrian's epitaph, which is completed on the next folio; BnF, Lat. 16897, fol. 33v (detail). Photo: Courtesy of the Bibliothèque nationale de France, Paris.	129
4.1	The final ten lines of Hadrian's epigram and the full text of the verses for Hildegard's altar cloth; BAV, Pal. Lat. 833, fol. 29v. Photo: Courtesy of the Biblioteca Apostolica Vaticana, Rome.	142
4.2	Illustration showing the interior of a church with a 'hanging crown' over a draped altar. The Utrecht Psalter, Ps. 42: *Iudica me*; Utrecht, Rijksuniversiteitsbibliothek MS 32, fol. 25r (detail). Photo: Courtesy of Utrecht University Library.	165
4.3	The Ravenna *mappa*, showing woven bands of text. Reproduced from M. Mazzotti, 'Antiche stoffe liturgiche ravennati', *Felix Ravenna*, 3rd ser., 53.ii (1950), 43. Photo: Courtesy of the Istituzione Biblioteca Classense, Ravenna.	167
4.4	The opening of the appendix to the *Notitia ecclesiarum urbis Romae* with the pilgrim's itinerary of St Peter's basilica. The first line on the page is the last of the account of cult sites in Milan; Vienna, ÖNB, Cod. 795, fol. 187r. Photo: Courtesy of the Österreichische Nationalbibliothek, Vienna.	172
4.5	Plan of St Peter's and its oratories, *s.* viii/ix. © Lacey Wallace.	174
4.6	*Descriptio Urbis Romae*. The Einsiedeln Itineraries, No. 1; Einsiedeln, Stiftsbibliothek, Cod. 326 (1076), fols 79v–80r. Photo: Courtesy of the Stiftsbibliothek, Einsiedeln.	181
5.1	Detail of Hadrian's epitaph showing coral fossils on the edges of the letter E. Photo: Author.	184

5.2	Detail of Hadrian's epitaph showing the ornamental border with golden coloured pigment overlain by white lead in and around the vine scroll. Photo: Author.	188
5.3	Detail of the central motif in the lower ornamental border of Hadrian's epitaph. Photo: Author.	189
5.4	Detail of Hadrian's epitaph showing engraved ruling lines. Photo: Author.	190
5.5	Detail of Hadrian's epitaph, showing part of lines 14–16. Photo: Author.	191
5.6	Hadrian's epitaph: detail of letter T, showing traces of chisel marks. Photo: Author.	191
5.7	The epitaph of Pippin of Italy, d. 810, in Sant'Ambrogio, Milan (detail and complete text). Photo: Author.	196
5.8	The epitaph of Bernard of Italy, d. 817, in Sant'Ambrogio, Milan (detail and complete text). Photo: Author.	196
5.9	The *Lex de imperio Vespasiani*, Musei Capitolini, Rome. Photo: Courtesy of Archivio Fotografico dei Musei Capitolini, Rome.	199
5.10	Maerteen van Heemskerck (*c*.1536), details of two drawings of the Lateran (conjoined here) showing the equestrian statue of Marcus Aurelius in front of the loggia of Boniface VIII (*c*.1300) that projects from the southern end of the polyconch triclinium (the *Sala del concilio*) built by Leo III (795–814); Berlin, Kupferstichkabinett, 79 D 2a, fol. 12r and fol. 71r. Photo: Reproduced with permission of the Bildarchiv Preußischer Kulturbesitz, Berlin.	201
5.11	Pope Damasus' eulogy at Sant'Agnese fuori le Mura. The text is not in any extant *sylloge*. Photo: Author.	203
5.12	Pope Damasus' eulogy for S. Eutychius, at S. Sebastiano. This text was copied into the fourth Lorsch *sylloge* (L$_4$). *MEC* I, V.2. Photo: Reproduced by kind permission of the Pontificio Istituto de Archeologia Cristiana, Rome.	204
5.13	Pope Damasus' verses for the font at St Peter's. Photo: By kind permission of the Reverenda Fabbrica di San Pietro in Vaticano, Rome.	204
5.14	Part of an inscription from a pluteus at S. Pudenziana, naming Pope Siricius (385–98). Photo: Author.	206
5.15	Mosaic dedication inscription at Sta. Sabina (442–32). Pope Celestine's name is in the top line, with the donor's name, Peter, centrally placed in the middle of the text. Photo: Paolo Romiti, Alamy Stock Photo.	206
5.16	Inscription by Sixtus III for the Lateran Baptistery (the fifth of eight distiches). Photo: Author.	207
5.17	Verse inscription by Pope Leo I commemorating the restoration of the roof at S. Paolo fuori le Mura. *MEC* I, X.5. Photo: Reproduced by kind permission of the Pontificio Istituto de Archeologia Cristiana, Rome.	209
5.18	Inscription for Pope Vigilius after the Goths' siege of Rome in 537/8. *MEC* I, XI. 7/8. Photo: Reproduced by kind permission of the Pontificio Istituto de Archeologia Cristiana, Rome.	209
5.19	Inscription for Pope John II (533–5) in S. Pietro in Vincoli. John's name before his election (Mercurius) and his ties to S. Clemente are recorded in lines 2–3. Photo: Author.	210
5.20	Fragments from the epitaph of Pope Gregory I (d. 604). Photo: Author, with kind permission of the Reverenda Fabbrica di San Pietro in Vaticano, Rome.	211

5.21	The Column of Phocas, dedicatory inscription, 1 August 608. Photo: Gregor Kalas.	212
5.22	The epitaph of Theodore, d. 619, at Sta. Cecilia (detail). Photo: Author.	213
5.23	Inscription on a screen from the Oratory of Mary at St Peter's dedicated by John VII (705–7). Photo: By kind permission of the Reverenda Fabbrica di San Pietro in Vaticano, Rome.	215
5.24	A diploma of Pope Gregory II (715–31), recording a gift of lights to St Peter's, as displayed in the portico in its seventeenth-century frame. Photo: Author, with kind permission of the Reverenda Fabbrica di San Pietro, Rome.	216
5.25	Pope Gregory III, record of the Council of 732 regarding the enactment of the offices to be said in his new oratory. Photo: By kind permission of the Reverenda Fabbrica di San Pietro in Vaticano, Rome.	217
5.26	Prayers for Pope Gregory III, from the oratory of All Saints: Photo: By kind permission of the Reverenda Fabbrica di San Pietro in Vaticano, Rome.	218
5.27	Verses by Gregory, cardinal priest of S. Clemente, describing a gift of books during the pontificate of Zacharias (741–52). Photo: Reproduced by kind permission of the Pontificio Istituto de Archeologia Cristiana, Rome.	219
5.28	List of the feast days of male saints buried at S. Silvestro by Pope Paul I (757–67). Photo: Author.	220
5.29	A list of saints, from the pontificate of Paul I (757–67), at St Peter's. Photo: By kind permission of the Reverenda Fabbrica di San Pietro in Vaticano, Rome.	221
5.30	Record of gifts of land by Eustathius and George, Sta. Maria in Cosmedin (s. viii med.) (detail). Photo: Author.	222
5.31	Inscription of Pope Hadrian I, 783, from the Chapel of John VII, St Peter's. Photo: By kind permission of the Reverenda Fabbrica di San Pietro in Vaticano, Rome.	223
6.1	The black marble inscription of Verus, *moritex*, from Cologne (dimensions: 104cm × 82cm × 8cm; CIL XIII.8164a = ILS 7522). Photo: Courtesy of the Romisch-Germanisches Museum, Köln.	226
6.2	Map showing key places and the underlying geology of eastern Francia. © Tom Knott.	234
6.3	The modern quarry at Salet, Belgium (lower Viséan). Photo: Author.	236
6.4	Octagonal itinerary column from Tongeren, Belgium, made of black Mosan marble (36cm × 38cm). Brussels, Musées Royaux d'Art et d'Histoire, Inv. No. B000189-001. Photo: CC BY–MRAH/KMKG.	238
6.5	Altar to the goddess Nehalennia, from Colijnsplaat, Netherlands, made of black Mosan marble. Photo: Courtesy of the Rijksmuseum van Oudheden, Leiden.	239
6.6	*Blaustein* blocks in the masonry of the NNW exterior wall of the Carolingian chapel at Aachen. Note the large block with clamp and lewis holes showing likely reuse from a Roman structure. Photo: Author.	246
6.7	Opus sectile from the upper floor at Aachen. Photo: Courtesy of Ulrike Heckner.	248
6.8	Black porphyry columns in Aachen. Reproduced by permission of the Domkapitel Aachen. Photo: Ann Münchow/Pit Siebigs.	249
6.9	Black porphyry column from the chapel of S. Zeno, Sta Prassede, Rome. Photo: Author.	251

xviii LIST OF FIGURES

6.10 Upper-level columns and arcading in the interior of the Aachen chapel. Photo: Author. 254
7.1 The Easter Table for the years 779–97 with marginal annotations recording the death of Pope Hadrian against the entry for 796 in the left-hand margin, and in the right-hand margin the places where Charlemagne celebrated Easter in the years 787–97. Würzburg, Universitätsbibliothek, M.p.th.f.46, fols 14v–15r. Photo: Reproduced with permission of Würzburg Universitätsbibliothek. 258
7.2 Dedicatory verses in Godesscalc's Evangelistary. Charlemagne and Hildegard are named at the foot of the second column; Paris, BnF, NAL 1203, fol. 126v. Photo: Courtesy of the Bibliothèque nationale de France, Paris. 271
7.3 Dedicatory verses from Charlemagne to Pope Hadrian in the Dagulf Psalter; Vienna, ÖNB, Cod. 1861, fol. 4r (detail). Photo: Courtesy of the Österreichische Nationalbibliothek, Vienna. 273
7.4 The Dagulf Psalter showing the Incipit facing the Beatus; Vienna, ÖNB, Cod. 1861, fols 24v–25r. Photo: Courtesy of the Österreichische Nationalbibliothek, Vienna. 276
7.5 The title page of a copy of the *Collectio Canonum Quesnelliana*; Einsiedeln, Stiftsbibliothek, Cod. 191, fol. 3r. Photo: Courtesy of the Stiftsbibliothek, Einsiedeln. 279
7.6 Opening to the gospel of St John in the Abbeville Gospels; Abbeville, Bibliothèque municipale, MS 4, fol. 154r. Photo: Courtesy of the Archives e Bibliothèque patrimoniale, Abbeville. 281
7.7 The Lorsch Gospels, *Incipit* to the gospel of Luke. BAV, Pal. Lat. 50, fol. 7v. Photo: Reproduced by kind permission of the Biblioteca Apostolica Vaticana, Rome. 285
7.8 The Lorsch Gospels, *Incipit* to the gospel of John. BAV, Pal. Lat. 50, fol. 70v. Photo: Reproduced by kind permission of the Biblioteca Apostolica Vaticana, Rome. 286
7.9 The title page to the four gospels; London, British Library, Harley MS 2788, fol. 12v. Photo: Reproduced with permission of The British Library Board. 288
7.10 *Incipit* to the Gospel of John; London, British Library, Harley MS 2788, fol. 162r. Photo: Reproduced with permission of The British Library Board. 290
7.11 The second set of bronze railings in the Aachen Chapel. Reproduced by permission of the Domkapitel Aachen. Photo: Ann Münchow/Pit Siebigs. 291
7.12 'Bertcaud's alphabet'; Bern, Burgerbibliothek, Cod. 250, fol. 11v. Photo: Courtesy of the Bergerbibliothek, Bern. 292
7.13 The dedication verses for the palace chapel, Aachen. The first two lines are at the foot of fol. 19r and the text continues with six lines at the top of the first column of fol. 19v; Leiden, Universiteitsbibliotheek, Voss. Lat. 69, fol. 19 r/v. Photo: Courtesy of Leiden University Libraries. 297
8.1 Einsiedeln, Stiftsbibliothek, Cod. 326 (1076), fol. 68r, detail showing the correction of the first word in line 5, from *hinc* to *hanc*. Photo: Courtesy of the Stiftsbibliothek, Einsiedeln. 310
8.2 The Lateran Triclinium mosaic, as recreated in 1743. Photo: Author. 338

LIST OF ABBREVIATIONS

AASS	*Acta Sanctorum.*
AFSP	L'Archivio della Fabbrica di San Pietro.
Alfarano, *DBV*	Tiberius Alpharanus, *De Basilicae Vaticanae Antiquissima et Nova Structura*, ed. C. M. Cerrati (Vatican City, 1914).
ALMA	*Archivum Latinitatis Medii Aevi.*
AMPr	*Annales Mettenses Priores*; B. de Simson, ed., MGH, SS rer. Germ (Hanover and Leipzig, 1905).
Arch. Cap.	Archivio Capitolare.
ARF	*Annales regni francorum unde ab a. 741 usque ad a. 829, qui dicuntur Annales laurissenses maiores et Einhardi*; F. Kurze, ed., MGH, SS rer. Germ. 6 (Hanover, 1895).
BAV	Vatican City, Bibliotheca Apostolica Vaticana.
Bischoff, *Katalog*	B. Bischoff, *Katalog der festländischen Handschriften des neunten Jahrhunderts (mit Ausnahme der wisigotischen)*, 4 vols (Wiesbaden, 1998–2017).
Bischoff, *MS*	B. Bischoff, *Mittelalterliche Studien: Ausgewählte Aufsätze Zur Schriftkunde Und Literaturgeschichte*, 3 vols (Stuttgart, 1966–81).
BL	London, British Library.
BnF	Paris, Bibliothèque nationale de France.
BSPV	*Basilica Sancti Petri Vaticani/The Basilica of St Peter in the Vatican*, ed. A. Pinelli, M. Beltramini and A. Angeli, 4 vols (Modena 2000), I.i–ii (*Atlas*), II.i (*Essays*), II.ii (*Notes*).
CBCR	*Corpus basilicarum Christianarum Romae: The early Christian basilicas of Rome (IV–IX Centuries)*, ed. R. Krautheimer, S. Corbett, and A. K. Frazer, 5 vols (Vatican City, 1937–77).
CC	*Codex Carolinus*, ed. W. Gundlach, MGH, Epp. III, *Epistolae Merowingici et Karolini aevi*, I (Hanover, 1892), 469–657 (see also *CeC*).
CCCM	Corpus Christianorum Continuatio Mediaevalis.
CCSL	Corpus Christianorum Series Latina.
CD	S. de Blaauw, *Cultus et Decor. Liturgia e architettura nella Roma. tardoantica e medieval. Basilica Salvatoris, Sanctae Mariae, Sancti Petri*, 2 vols (Rome, 1994).
CeC	*Codex epistolaris Carolinus. Frühmittelatlerliche Papstbriefe an die Karolingerherrscher*, ed. and German tr. F. Hartmann and T. B. Orth-Müller, Ausgewählte quellen zur Geschichte des Mittelalters Freiherr-vom Stein-Gedächtnisausgabe, 49 (Darmstadt, 2017); *Codex epistolaris Carolinus. Letters from the popes to the Frankish rulers, 739–791*, English tr. R. McKitterick, D. van Espelo, R. Pollard, and R. Price, Translated Texts for Historians, 77 (Liverpool, 2021). Both volumes put the letters in the order that they are found in the unique manuscript copy; thus, *CeC* 49 is the same as *CC* 60, using Gundlach's well-established reference system.

CIL	*Corpus Inscriptionum Latinarum*, 17 vols (Berlin, 1871–1986).
CLA	*Codices Latini antiquiores: a palaeographical guide to Latin manuscripts prior to the ninth century*, 12 vols (Oxford, 1934–72).
CLLA	K. Gamber, *Codices liturgici latini antiquiores*, Spicilegii friburgensis Subsidia, 1, 2 vols (Fribourg, 1963–4).
CSASE	Cambridge Studies in Anglo-Saxon England.
CSLMA	*Clavis des auteurs latins du Moyen Age. Territoire français 735–987*, ed. M.-H. Jullien and F. Perelman, Corpus Christianorum Continuatio. Mediaevalis (Turnhout, 1994–).
ChLA	*Chartae Latini Antiquiores: Facsimile Edition of the Latin Charters prior to the Ninth Century*, 49 vols, ed. A. Brucker and R. Marichal (Olten and Lausanne, 1954–).
ED	Ferrua, A., *Epigrammata Damasiana*. Sussidi allo studio delle antichità cristiane, 2 (Vatican City, 1942).
EHR	*The English Historical Review.*
Einhard, *VK*	Einhard, *Vita Karoli*; O. Holder-Egger, ed., *Einhardi Vita Karoli Magni*, MGH, SS rer. Germ. (Hanover and Leipzig, 1911). Translated by P. E. Dutton, *Charlemagne's Courtier: The Complete Einhard*, Readings in Medieval Civilizations and Cultures, 2 (Peterborough, ON, 1998) and D. Ganz, *Einhard and Notker the Stammerer: Two Lives of Charlemagne* (London, 2008).
EMC 1	P. Grierson and M. A. S. Blackburn, eds, *Medieval European Coinage, with a catalogue of the coins in the Fitzwilliam Museum, Cambridge. Vol. 1, The early Middle Ages (5th–10th centuries)* (Cambridge, 1986).
Ep./Epp.	*Epistola/ae*, cited by edition number.
Facs.	*Facsimile.*
Fredegar Cont.	J. M. Wallace-Hadrill, ed. and tr., *The Fourth Book of the Chronicle of Fredegar with its continuations* (London, 1960).
ICUR II.i	G. B. de Rossi, ed., *Inscriptiones Christianae Urbis Romae septimo saeculo antiquiores*, II.i: *pars prima ab originibus ad saeculum XII* (Rome, 1888), cited by item number.
ICUR n.s.	*Inscriptiones Christianae Urbis Romae septimo saeculo antiquiores: nova series*, 10 vols (Rome, 1922–92), i: A. Silvagni, ed., *Inscriptiones incertae originis*; ii: A. Silvagni, ed., *Coemeteria in viis Cornelia Aurelia, Portuensi et Ostiensi*.
KdG	W. Braunfels and P. E. Schramm, eds, *Karl der Grosse. Lebenswerk und Nachleben*, 5 vols (Düsseldorf, 1967), i: *Persönlichkeit und Geschichte*, ed. H. Beumann; ii: *Das geistige Leben*, ed. B. Bischoff; iii: *Karolingische Kunst*, ed. W. Braunfels and H. Schnitzler; iv: *Das Nachleben*, ed. W. and P. E. Schramm; v: *Registerband*, ed. W. Braunfels.
LP	*Liber Pontificalis* (cited by biography number and chapter); *Le Liber Pontificalis*, ed. L. Duchesne, 3 vols (Paris, 1886–1957), i–ii: *texte, introduction et commentaire*; iii: *Additions et corrections*.

MEC	Silvagni, A., ed., *Monumenta epigraphica christiana saeculo XIII antiquiora quae in Italiae finibus adhuc exstant iussu Pii XII pontificis maximi*, 4 vols in 7 (Rome, 1943); i: *Roma*; ii.1: *Mediolanum*; ii.2: *Comum*; ii.3: *Papia*; iii.1: *Luca*; iv.1: *Neapolis*; iv.2: *Beneventum*.
MGH	Monumenta Germaniae Historica.
—DD	Diplomata.
DD. Kar. 1	Diplomata Karolinorum 1.
—Epp.	Epistolae.
Epp. sel.	Epistolae selectae.
—Fontes	Fontes Iures Germanici Antiqui in usum scholarum separatim editi.
—Leges	Leges.
Capit.	Capitularia reges Francorum.
Conc.	Concilia.
—Poetae	Poetae Latini medii aevi.
PLAC	Poetae Latini ævi Carolini I–III.
—SS	Scriptores (in Folio).
—SS rer. Germ.	Scriptores rerum germanicarum in usum scholarum separatim editi.
—SS rer. Lang.	Scriptores rerum Langobardicarum et Italicarum saec. VI–IX.
—SS rer. Merov.	Scriptores rerum Merovingicarum.
ÖNB	Vienna, Österreichische Nationalibliothek.
OSPR	*Old St Peter's, Rome*, ed. R. McKitterick, J. Osborne, C. M. Richardson, and J. Story (Cambridge, 2013).
PBSR	*Papers of the British School at Rome*.
PL	J.-P. Migne, ed., *Patrologiae cursus completus: sive biblioteca universalis, integra, uniformis, commoda, oeconomica, omnium SS. Patrum, doctorum scriptorumque ecclesiasticorum qui ab aevo apostolico ad usque Innocentii III tempora floruerunt*, 221 vols (Paris, 1844–64).
Rev.	Revised version of the Annales regni Francorum; *Annales regni francorum unde ab a. 741 usque ad a. 829, qui dicuntur Annales laurissenses maiores et Einhardi*, ed. F. Kurze, MGH, SS rer. Germ. 6 (Hanover, 1895).
RFSP	Reverenda Fabbrica di San Pietro.
RIB	Roman Inscriptions of Britain, https://romaninscriptionsofbritain.org/.
SSCI	Settimane di studio del Centro Italiano di studi sull'alto Medioevo.
SW, *799*	C. Stiegemann and M. Wemhoff, eds, *799. Kunst und Kultur der Karolingerzeit. Karl der Große und Papst Leo III in Paderborn*, 3 vols (Mainz, 1999), i–ii: *Katalog der Ausstellung, Paderborn 1999*; iii: *Beiträge*.
YP	*Alcuin; The Bishops, Kings, and Saints of York*, ed. P. Godman, Oxford Medieval Texts (Oxford, 1982), cited by line number.
UB	Universitätabibliothek/Universiteitsbibliotheek.
VZ	R. Valentini, and G. Zucchetti, eds, *Codice topografico della città di Roma*, 4 vols, Fonti per la Storia d'Italia 81, 88, 90 (Rome, 1940-53), i: *Scrittori secoli I–IV*; ii: *Scrittori secoli IV–XII*; iii; *Scrittori secoli XII–XIV*; iv: *Scrittori XV*.

EDITION AND TRANSLATION: ALCUIN'S EPITAPH FOR POPE HADRIAN I
(by David R. Howlett)

HIC PATER ECCLESIAE ROMAE DECVS INCLYTVS AVCTOR
    HADRIANVS REQVIEM PAPA BEATVS HABET
VIR CVI VITA DEVS PIETAS LEX GLORIA CHRISTVS
    PASTOR APOSTOLICVS PROMPTVS AD OMNE BONVM
NOBILIS EX MAGNA GENITVS IAM GENTE PARENTVM   5
    SED SACRIS LONGE NOBILIOR MERITIS
EXORNARE STVDENS DEVOTO PECTORE PASTOR
    SEMPER VBIQVE SVO TEMPLA SACRATA DEO
ECCLESIAS DONIS POPVLOS ET DOGMATE SANCTO
    IMBVIT ET CVNCTIS PANDIT AD ASTRA VIAM   10
PAVPERIBVS LARGVS NVLLI PIETATE SECVNDVS
    ET PRO PLEBE SACRIS PERVIGIL IN PRECIBVS
DOCTRINIS OPIBVS MVRIS EREXERAT ARCES
    VRBS CAPVT ORBIS HONOR INCLYTA ROMA TVAS
MORS CVI NIL NOCVIT CHRISTI QVAE MORTE PEREMPTA EST   15
    IANVA SED VITAE MOX MELIORIS ERAT
POST PATREM LACRIMANS KAROLVS HAEC CARMINA SCRIBSI
    TV MIHI DVLCIS AMOR TE MODO PLANGO PATER
TV MEMOR ESTO MEI SEQVITVR TE MENS MEA SEMPER
    CVM CHRISTO TENEAS REGNA BEATA POLI   20
TE CLERVS POPVLVS MAGNO DILEXIT AMORE
    OMNIBVS VNVS AMOR OPTIME PRAESVL ERAS
NOMINA IVNGO SIMVL TITVLIS CLARISSIME NOSTRA
    HADRIANVS KAROLVS REX EGO TVQVE PATER
QVISQVE LEGAS VERSVS DEVOTO PECTORE SVPPLEX   25
    AMBORVM MITIS DIC MISERERE DEVS
HAEC TVA NVNC TENEAT REQVIES CARISSIME MEMBRA
    CVM SANCTIS ANIMA GAVDEAT ALMA DEI
VLTIMA QVIPPE TVAS DONEC TVBA CLAMET IN AVRES
    PRINCIPE CVM PETRO SVRGE VIDERE DEVM   30
AVDITVRVS ERIS VOCEM SCIO IVDICIS ALMAM
    INTRA NVNC DOMINI GAVDIA MAGNA TVI
TVNC MEMOR ESTO TVI NATI PATER OPTIME POSCO
    CVM PATRE DIC NATVS PERGAT ET ISTE MEVS
O PETE REGNA PATER FELIX CAELESTIA CHRISTI   35
    INDE TVVM PRECIBVS AVXILIARE GREGEM
DVM SOL IGNICOMO RVTILVS SPLENDESCIT AB AXE
    LAVS TVA SANCTE PATER SEMPER IN ORBE MANET
SEDIT BEATAE MEMORIAE HADRIANVS PAPA
    ANNOS XXIII MENSES X DIES XVII OBIIT VII KALENDS IANVARIAS   40

Here the father of the Church, the glory of Rome, the renowned author,
    Hadrian the blessed pope has rest,
a man for whom [there was] life, God, piety, law, glory, Christ,
    an apostolic shepherd, prompt at all good,
noble, born from a great race of forebears, 5
    but nobler by a long way in sacred merits,
a shepherd being eager with a devout breast to adorn
    always and everywhere temples consecrated to his own God;
churches with gifts and peoples with holy teaching
    he imbues, and for all he opens the way to the stars; 10
to paupers generous, to no man second in piety,
    and for the common people always thoroughly vigilant in sacred prayers,
doctrines, with resources he had erected your fortresses on the walls,
    he [your] honour, renowned Rome, city, head of the world,
for whom death, which was destroyed by the death of Christ, brought no harm, 15
    but was soon the gate of a better life.
Weeping after the father, I Charles have written these songs.
    You, for me sweet love, you now I lament, father.
You be mindful of me; my mind follows you always.
    With Christ may you hold the blessed realms of the pole. 20
You the clergy, the people loved with great love;
    you were one love for all, best bishop;
I join our names, together with titles, most clearly
    Hadrian, Charles, I the king and you the father.
You whoever may read the verses, suppliant with a devout breast, 25
    say of both men, 'Gentle God, be merciful'.
May this rest now hold your members, dearest one;
    with the holy ones of God may [your] holy soul rejoice,
until indeed the last trumpet may call to your ears,
    'With the prince Peter rise to see God'. 30
You will be bound to hear, I know, the holy voice of the Judge,
    'Enter now into the great joys of your Lord'.
Then be mindful of your son, best father, I ask,
    and with the Father say 'May this my son proceed'.
O seek, happy father, the celestial realms of Christ. 35
    Thence aid your flock with prayers.
While the sun glowing red shines splendidly from the fiery-haired axis
    your praise, holy father, remains always in the world.
Hadrian the pope of blessed memory sat
    23 years, 10 months, 17 days; he died on the 7th kalends of January. 40

FIGURE 0.1 Jean Fouquet, 'The Coronation of the Emperor Charlemagne', *Grandes Chroniques de France* (1455–60); Paris, BnF, Fr. 6465, fol. 89v. Reproduced by permission of the Bibliothèque nationale de France, Paris.

Introduction

Charlemagne and Italy

CHARLEMAGNE IN ST PETER'S BASILICA

The next time you go to the Vatican in Rome, look down as you cross the threshold of St Peter's basilica. Set into the floor, inside and quite close to the central door on the axis of the nave, is a very large stone disc made of red porphyry.[1] This is the *rota porphiretica* where popular tradition claims that Charlemagne was crowned emperor by Pope Leo III during the celebration of mass at the Christmas feast in the year 800, and acclaimed 'by all the faithful Romans'.[2] The scene is shown in a mid-fifteenth-century manuscript painting by the French miniaturist Jean Fouquet in a copy of the *Grandes Chroniques de France* made not long after 1458 (Figure 0.1).[3] Here the events of Christmas Day 800 are shown in a setting which is plausibly that of the old basilica of St Peter as it appeared in the later middle ages; Charlemagne kneels on a coloured *rota* in front of the pope, surrounded by an entourage of late medieval cardinals, laymen, and acolytes carrying the symbols of his office—a sword, an orb, and banners that anachronistically combine the heraldic devices of the French crown and the high medieval Holy Roman Empire. Behind them, in the nave, is the canons' choir, and beyond the triumphal arch gothic windows can be seen set into the walls of the apse.[4] Early evidence associating the porphyry disc with the events of Charlemagne's imperial coronation is scant; the contemporary sources say that he was crowned by the pope as he rose from prayer in front of the shrine of St Peter, but say nothing of a *rota*

---

[1] M. Andrieu, 'La "Rota porphyretica" de la basilique Vaticane', *Mélange d'Archeologie et d'Histoire*, 66 (1954), 189–218; M. Gani, 'Rota porphiretica', *BSPV*, rad, 741, no. 1207. The *rota* was moved into its present position in 1650; H. Brandenburg, A. Ballardini, and C. Theones, *Saint Peter's. The Story of a Monument*, Monumenta Vaticana Selecta (Vatican City, 2017), 25, and fig. 22.

[2] *LP* 98.23, 'universi fideles Romani'; R. Davis, tr., *Lives of the Eighth-Century Popes* (Liber Pontificalis), Translated Texts for Historians, 13 (Liverpool, 1992), 190–1.

[3] BnF, Fr. 6465, fol. 89v; Andrieu, 'Rota', 195.

[4] C. M. Richardson, 'St Peter's in the fifteenth century: Paul II, the archpriests and the case for continuity', in *OSPR*, 324–7, at 330.

in the pavement.[5] But by the twelfth century, the books that recorded the rituals and liturgies of the basilica noted that during an imperial coronation ceremony the new emperor would receive a papal blessing at the doors of the basilica and then process into the church to the *rota*, where he knelt to receive a second blessing.[6] In the centuries that followed thereafter, drawing on the medieval legends that had grown up around Charlemagne, the *rota* became an important element in the liturgical rituals of the coronation of an emperor, and—indeed—of the late medieval popes as well.

Just outside, on the external wall of the basilica within the portico, is another large stone monument that has a much more secure connection with Charlemagne than the *rota* that lies inside. High up, to the left of the main door, is a long inscription cut onto a large slab of black marble. This is the epitaph that commemorates the life and achievements of Pope Hadrian I, who died in late 795 after a pontificate lasting nearly 24 years (1 February 772–26 December 795).[7] Charlemagne commissioned the inscription, which names him twice, and the surviving stone slab is the epigraphic masterpiece of the Carolingian Renaissance. Hadrian's long pontificate was concurrent—quite by chance—with Charlemagne's exceptionally long reign in Francia (9 October 768–28 January 814). After his death, Hadrian was buried in St Peter's basilica, in a tomb near the high altar, and this monumental inscription marked the site throughout the Middle Ages. The inscription was preserved when the old basilica was torn down in the sixteenth century and it was subsequently redisplayed in the portico of the new structure.[8]

Contemporary eighth-century sources record that Charlemagne had 'ordered an epitaph, written in gold letters on marble, to be made in Francia so that he might send it to Rome to adorn the sepulchre of the supreme pontiff Hadrian'.[9] The text of the epitaph is a poem, composed by Alcuin (d. 804), an Anglo-Saxon scholar from the kingdom of Northumbria who spent the latter part of his life working for Charlemagne in Francia. In these verses Alcuin took on the voice of his patron the king, and so it is in the first person that *Karolus* laments the death of Hadrian, invoking readers of the poem to pray for the donor as well as the deceased; 'You, whoever may read the verses, suppliant with a devout breast, say of both men, "Gentle God, be merciful"'. The meaning of the verses, their sophisticated metrical structure, the form of the script, the layout of the inscription, its ornamentation, and the black stone on which

---

[5] *ARF s.a.* 801; *LP* 98.23–24.

[6] *CD* ii, 679, 702–9, 735–6.

[7] *LP* 97.2. The length of Hadrian's pontificate and the date of his death are also recorded in the last two lines of the epitaph.

[8] For a contrary view, see E. Caldelli, 'Sull'iscrizione di Adriano I', *Scrineum Rivista*, 13 (2016), 49–91, who tentatively suggests that because quality of the lettering is so good, the existing slab could be a mid-fifteenth-century replica and thus should not be regarded as evidence for the revival of Roman square capitals in the age of Charlemagne. I respectfully disagree with this suggestion, based on the multiplicity of evidence for its contemporaneity, as described below.

[9] *Annales Laureshamenses, s.a.* 795; G. H. Pertz, ed., MGH, SS I, 36. See below, Chapter 2, 102–3.

it was cut, all point to an object that was of the highest cultural value when it was made in the late eighth century. What is more, its prominent location at the threshold of the renewed, Renaissance basilica of St Peter's shows that the significance of the epitaph was recognised by the seventeenth-century architects of the portico who had it set up beside the main door to the church. Hadrian's epitaph, and the story of its commission, display and preservation across the centuries, provides us with a way into the cultural and political history of the early Middle Ages, and also to the legacy of Charlemagne and his age to later European history.

The chapters that follow examine the early medieval evidence for the making and reception of Hadrian's epitaph, and the later medieval motives for its preservation. The questions are multi-layered: many relate to the minutiae of the manufacture and display of the artefact—who wrote the verses; what are the parallels for the epigraphy and ornamentation; where was the stone from; when did the inscription reach Rome; where was it placed in St Peter's; why did it survive in the new basilica when so much else was lost from the old? Other questions concern the motives for the creation of the inscription: when was it made; how does it compare to other Carolingian gifts to St Peter's; why was a king of the Franks involved in the creation of an epitaph for a pope in Rome; how did it interact with other symbolic representations of secular power, not least concerning the Emperor Constantine I (306–37) who by Carolingian times was remembered as the first Christian emperor and founder of the basilica at St Peter's shrine? Yet more questions focus on the bigger issues of geopolitics and cultural history: what does an inscription like this reveal about the renewal of scholarship and art that flourished under royal patronage in Carolingian Francia in the late eighth and early ninth centuries; how does it contribute to our understanding of Frankish involvement in Italy, the Carolingian devotion to St Peter, the evolution of the temporal lordship of the papacy and its institutional powers, and the relationship between the Carolingian kings and the popes who were rulers of Rome and increasingly large tracts of land in central Italy?

Hadrian's death at Christmas 795 makes these questions especially pointed. Exactly five years later, Charlemagne was crowned emperor in St Peter's basilica by Hadrian's successor, Leo III (795–816). Charlemagne thus became the first emperor in the west since the late fifth century, reviving a title that was to endure as a political force in Western Europe for a thousand years until it was dissolved in 1806. With the benefit of considerable hindsight, Charlemagne's imperial coronation in Rome in 800 has long been regarded as a pivotal moment in European history, when the balance of power tilted northwards from its traditional Mediterranean axis in favour of the Germanic kingdoms of northern Europe. The historiography on this topic is enormous, as is that discussing the consequences of the pope's role in effecting this transformation, and how it affected the long-term balance of power between spiritual and secular authorities. On the back of this event—more than any other in his long reign—Charlemagne's cultural and political legacy has been contested by successive generations, especially in the Carolingian heartlands of France and Germany, each one eager to appropriate a Charlemagne for its own ends.[10] Recent scholarship has tended to see the events of 800 rather differently; not so much as a grand plan to reintroduce empire to western Europe but as rather more contingent on the volatile politics of the day. These revisionist views note—for example—the claim made by the Frankish sources that Charlemagne took the title only because there was at that time no emperor in the East; from 797 to 802 the imperial title in Constantinople was claimed by the Empress Irene, but her sex rendered the imperial throne vacant in the eyes of the Frankish commentators.[11] Michael I (811–13) acknowledged Charlemagne's right to use the title of emperor in 812, and only then, it is argued, did Charlemagne issue his iconic imperial portrait coins.[12]

Pope Hadrian's epitaph has an important part to play in this story. It came out of particular political circumstances and reflects the Frankish nexus of culture and wealth in the late eighth century. But when transported to Rome and displayed in the basilica of St Peter, it went further, and forcefully projected, through word, stone, and script, a message of Carolingian confidence and ambition to the Roman elites who saw it, shaping contemporary and later perceptions of Charlemagne and the Franks. In Francia it came out of an intensely productive phase of reflection at the court about Carolingian identity and purpose, and at a time when the king was investing considerable intellectual and material resources in the construction of a palace and chapel at Aachen.[13] Its text spoke to that courtly audience of the centrality of Rome and its Church, the intimacy of the bond between king and pope, and the eternal destiny and triumph of the Christian Franks and their king. It was received in Rome, however, in a period of transition from the stability of an exceptionally long-lived papal regime to one that quickly challenged the vested interests of an established elite. Unlike Hadrian, Leo III was not of noble Roman stock and, despite the evidence presented by his biographer of universal support for his candidacy and rapid confirmation in office, conflict between Leo and the Roman establishment was not slow in coming. The silence of Leo's biographer on the earliest years of his pontificate is frustrating but

---

[10] On Charlemagne's reputation and legacy, see *KdG* iv; M. Becher, *Charlemagne* (New Haven, CT, and London, 2003), 135–9; R. Morrissey, *Charlemagne and France: A thousand years of mythology*, tr. C. Tihanyi (Notre Dame, IN, 2003).

[11] *Annales Laureshamenses*, *s.a.* 801; Pertz, ed., MGH, SS I, 38.

[12] J. Lafaurie, 'Les monnaies impériales de Charlemagne', *Comptes rendus des séances de l'Académie des Inscriptions et Belles-Lettres*, 122.i (1978), 154–76; P. Grierson and M. A. S. Blackburn, *Medieval European Coinage with a catalogue of the coins in the Fitzwilliam Museum, Cambridge, i: The Early Middle Ages (5th–10th centuries)* (Cambridge, 1986), 209–10; S. Coupland, 'The Formation of a European Identity: Revisiting Charlemagne's Coinage', in E. Screen and C. West, eds, *Writing the Early Medieval West: Studies in Honour of Rosamond McKitterick* (Cambridge, 2018), 213–29.

[13] See below, Chapter 7, 257–60.

telling.[14] In 799 a botched attempt to mutilate, silence, and depose Leo precipitated his escape from Rome, flight to Francia, and Charlemagne's journey to Rome the following year. This attempted coup was led by relatives of Hadrian and men who had been nurtured by him, fuelled by accusations of adultery and perjury against Leo that seemed worryingly plausible to the ears of some Frankish writers.[15] It was in these early, fractious, years of Leo's pontificate that Hadrian's epitaph arrived in Rome. There, Leo's allies could have read it as a statement of Carolingian support for the institution of the papacy; his detractors, however, will have seen in it an emotional statement of regret at the passing of Hadrian's regime. All who saw the epitaph will have noted its monumentality, the dark-coloured marble, and the expert application of unadorned old-style square capitals, the golden lettering, and restrained rinceau border. This Frankish inscription was better than anything made in contemporary Rome, and it eloquently proclaimed the Carolingian mastery of the materials, techniques, and graphic authority of an older, Classical aesthetic.

Hadrian's epitaph also fits into a longer discourse between the popes and the Carolingians that had been shaped by the exchange of envoys, letters, and gifts since the early decades of the eighth century. This longer-term perspective puts the epitaph in a different kind of context, and there it can be seen as part of a series of gifts to St Peter's basilica that amplified and secured the perpetual presence of the Carolingian dynasty at the very heart of the basilica that was the *domus* of Christ's chief apostle. Even more importantly from the point of view of the popes, was the gradual accumulation of territory in central Italy from the 730s onwards, which gave the papacy the wealth, independence, and power that came from the control of land with all its men, settlements, resources, and produce. The development of the temporal lordship of the papacy in central Italy ran parallel to the emergence of the Carolingian dynasty as a political and landowning force in Francia. In some respects the two phenomena were symbiotic, although modern studies see the connection as less direct and less synchronous than earlier scholarship, which perceived an intimate link between the birth of the papal Republic and the dawn of the Carolingian monarchy in the 750s.[16] Nevertheless, the accrual of land, plus the power and wealth that came with it, was a fundamental component of the diplomacy that brought the Franks and the papacy

---

[14] *LP* 98.2; T. F. X. Noble, *The Republic of St. Peter: The Birth of the Papal State 680–825* (Philadelphia, PA, 1984), 187–8. The absence of information other than his donations to Roman churches in the years 795–8 is in striking contrast to the opening section of Hadrian's 'Life' which dealt in detail with his campaign to suppress the factional politics of his predecessors.

[15] *LP* 98.11, 13; Paschal the *primicerius* or chief notary was Hadrian's nephew (*CC* 61/*CeC* 73) and Campulus had been promoted to notary by Hadrian by 781 (*CC* 67/*CeC* 72) and was by 799 the *sacellarius* or treasurer of the papal court. See below, Chapter 8, 314.

[16] For summaries of the historiography, see Noble, *Republic*, xxii–xxix and R. McKitterick, 'The Franks and Italy, 739–791', in R. McKitterick, D. van Espelo, R. Pollard, and R. Price, tr., *Codex Epistolaris Carolinu: Letters from the Popes to the Frankish Rulers, 739–791*, Translated Texts for Historians, 77 (Liverpool, 2021), 102–25.

onto parallel tracks in the eighth century, and was a topic raised frequently in correspondence between the two. All this secular pragmatism ran alongside the efforts made by successive eighth-century popes to nurture and strengthen a 'sacred alliance' with the Carolingian dynasty.[17] The context for the emergence of this alliance and the confluence of Franco-papal interests is to be found in the volatile geopolitics of Italy in the earlier eighth century.

POWER AND POLITICS IN ITALY IN THE EARLIER EIGHTH CENTURY

Through late summer and winter of 773 Charlemagne's armies besieged the Lombard capital at Pavia. In June the following year the city capitulated and Desiderius, the king of the Lombards, was forced into submission and lifelong exile in Francia. His deposition signalled the end of an independent Lombard kingdom in Italy; Charlemagne claimed the Lombard crown with all its territories in the north, and by the summer of 774 had incorporated the title *rex Langobardorum*, 'king of the Lombards', into his own.[18] Charlemagne's conquest of the Lombard kingdom was his first major military success beyond Frankish borders, and it marked the beginnings of Carolingian government in Italy. This campaign, however, was the culmination of sporadic diplomatic and military activity by the Franks in Italy over several decades, and in all that time the Franks had been but minor players, one force among many in the volatile and fast-flowing factional politics of Italy in the earlier eighth century.

Two powers dominated Italy at that time: the Lombard kingdom and the Roman Empire, then with a single capital and emperor in Constantinople.[19] The third actor was the pope, whose temporal authority in Italy around the turn of the century was underpinned by his role as bishop of Rome and landlord of the many Church-owned estates that comprised the papal patrimonies, although his spiritual reach was already very much more extensive.[20] Imperial interests in Italy derived from Justinian's efforts

---

[17] A. Angenendt, 'Das geistliche Bündnis der Päpste mit den Karolingern (754–796)', *Historisches Jahrbuch*, 100 (1980), 1–94.

[18] MGH, DD. Kar. 1, nos 80–4, 114–22.

[19] For useful summaries, see the essays by P. Delogu on 'Lombard and Carolingian Italy' and T. S. Brown on 'Byzantine Italy c.680–c.876', in *New Cambridge Medieval History*, ii: *c.700–c.900*, ed. R. McKitterick (Cambridge, 1995), 290–319 (esp. 294–303) and 320–48 (esp. 322–7).

[20] It is these *patrimonia* that supplied the wealth. The *Register* of Gregory the Great enables detailed analysis of the estates *c.*600; there is also a fragment of what may have been a register compiled during the pontificate of Gregory II preserved in the late eleventh-century *Collectio Canonum* of Deusdedit (calendared by P. F. Kehr, ed., *Regesta Pontificum Romanorum. Italia Pontificia*, ii: *Latium* (Berlin 1907), xiv–xv, 3–12, 34, 49, 139, 183, 190). See E. Spearing, *The Patrimony of the Roman Church in the Time of Gregory the Great* (Cambridge, 1918); V. Recchia, *Gregorio Magno e la società Agricola*, Verba Seniorum, n.s., 8 (Rome, 1978); F. Marazzi, *I 'Patrimonia Sanctae Romanae Ecclesiae' nel Lazio (secoli IV–X). Struttura amministrativa e prassi gestionali*, Nuovi studi storici, 37 (Rome 1998). There is a useful summary in Noble, *Republic*, 243–9.

to re-conquer the peninsula in the mid-sixth century and were led thereafter by an exarch who ruled from Ravenna on the Adriatic coast. A second imperial patrician, based in Sicily, governed Naples and Calabria in the far south. The Ravenna exarchate controlled a series of duchies that governed much of coastal Italy, including the duchy of Rome that was overseen by an imperially appointed duke, documented from the later seventh century.[21] However, by the early eighth century centralised imperial influence in Italy had waned as the duchies became increasingly autonomous; by 730 the exarch could not rely on the loyalties of the aristocratic militaries of Ravenna, Venice, or the five cities of the Pentapolis (Rimini, Pesaro, Fano, Senigallia, and Ancona) on the eastern flank of the Apennines. Elsewhere, imperial power was contingent on the effectiveness and loyalty of the duke, especially in Rome. In 751, the exarch Eutychios died in battle defending Ravenna against a Lombard army; he was not replaced, and the Ravenna exarchate effectively died with him. After this, imperial interests in Italy prospered only in the heavily Hellenised areas of Calabria and Sicily, and, despite protestations from Constantinople, the north was no longer part of the empire in any legal or practical sense. Many would argue that, in fact, centralised imperial authority had ceased to function in northern Italy long before this moment of crisis, and that it was the gradual decline in imperial influence in the early decades of the eighth century which had created space for the temporal power of the papacy to grow and for a substantial, sovereign papal state to begin to emerge in central Italy.[22]

The decline in imperial influence in Italy in the earlier eighth century was the result of many factors, not least pressures caused by the military advance of Arab armies which had besieged Constantinople in 717. The most important factor, however, was the increasingly onerous demand from Constantinople for tax revenues from imperial possessions in Italy, including the lands of the papal patrimonies that previously had been exempt.[23] The growing resentment of imperial citizens in Italy to the emperor and his representatives was exacerbated by the effect of iconoclasm on the politics and stability of the regime in Constantinople itself. The debate over the role of images in Christian worship had surfaced in the late 720s during the reign of Emperor Leo III, the Isaurian (717–41), and was institutionalised under his successor Constantine V (741–75).[24] It was, in essence, a theological dispute about the role of images in Christian worship, contemporary with but separate from Islamic aniconism that was

---

[21] A. Guillou, 'Inscriptions du duché de Rome', *Mélanges de l'école française de Rome: Moyen Âge*, 83 (1971), 149–58.

[22] This is the thesis put forward by Noble, *Republic*. The older view is that the papal states emerged in the 750s, in the wake of intervention by Pippin, Charlemagne's father; see below.

[23] *LP* 91:12,16 (relating to events in 725) and Davis, tr., *Lives of the Eighth-Century Popes*, 10, n. 44. See also, F. Marazzi, 'Il conflitto fra Leone III Isaurico e il papato fra il 725 e il 733, e il "definitive" inizio del medioevo a Roma: un'ipotesi in discussione', *PBSR*, 59 (1991), 231–57; L. Brubaker and J. Haldon, *Byzantium in the Iconoclast Era, c.680–850: A History* (Cambridge, 2011), 80–6, where they stress the priority of the resistance to fiscal demands over opposition to imperial religious policy.

[24] For a summary, see Brubaker and Haldon, *Byzantium*, 121–3.

also evolving at this time.[25] For a century and more afterwards, adherence to either the iconoclast (anti) or iconodule (pro) stance on the orthodox theology of images was an important element in the rivalry between political and dynastic factions in Constantinople.[26] What all this meant for Italy before 750 was that the exarch in Ravenna could no longer rely on the prospect of substantive assistance (military or financial) from Constantinople, and this was sufficient weakness to shift fundamentally the balance of power in the region. The untethering of established political and cultural ties created opportunities for other actors, such as the papacy, to expand their reach.

Iconoclasm was rejected wholesale by the emperor's subjects in Italy, and resistance to increasingly heavy taxation imposed by Constantinople prefigured open rebellion in 727 in opposition to the promulgation of an imperial decree ordering the destruction of images. The voice leading opposition in Italy to the emperor's fiscal and theological demands was that of Pope Gregory II (715–31); his official biography records (with the benefit of hindsight) that he 'armed himself against the emperor as against an enemy, denouncing his heresy and writing that Christians everywhere must be on their guard wherever such impiety might arise'.[27] Even the armies of the Ravenna exarchate rose in armed revolt, proclaiming defence of the pope against forces loyal to the exarch, Paul, who was killed in ensuing skirmishes.[28] Eutychios, the new exarch sent from Constantinople, met stiff resistance when he landed in Naples apparently demanding Pope Gregory's assassination. In the meantime, Italians elected dukes without imperial mandates, and the duchies of Ravenna and Venice made a decisive bid for autonomy from central imperial authority.[29]

The primary beneficiary of the disintegration of imperial control in Italy was the Lombard kingdom. The Lombard king's power was centred on Pavia and the rich lands of the Po valley as well as the region of Tuscia, which lay to the south, on the western side of the Central Apennines and to the north-west of Rome. His writ was not absolute, however, as two mighty Lombard duchies controlled inland areas further south, around Spoleto and Benevento. These duchies had a long history of independence partly because they had been cut off from royal territories in the north by a corridor of imperial lands that traversed the Apennines, linking Ravenna in the north-west with the duchy of Rome on the eastern coast. The Lombard dukes of Spoleto and Benevento guarded their autonomy jealously and were far from being automatic or loyal supporters of the Lombard king. They could act independently and

---

[25] Brubaker and Haldon, *Byzantium*, 106.
[26] 'The politicisation of religious art impinged upon every area of thought and action', R. Cormack, *Byzantine Art* (Oxford, 2000), 87, also 79–81, 90–2.
[27] *LP* 91.16–17, 23–4; Brubaker and Haldon, *Byzantium*, 80; R. Price, tr., *The Acts of the Second Council of Nicaea (787)*, Translated Texts for Historians, 68, 2 vols (Liverpool, 2018), I, 64–5.
[28] *LP* 91.18; Noble, *Republic*, 30.
[29] *LP* 91.17; Davis, tr., *Lives of the Eighth-Century Popes*, 11–12, n. 51; Noble, *Republic*, 32–4.

aggressively in their own interests; in 717, Beneventan forces captured the *castrum* at Cumae, north-west of Naples, and the following year the duke of Spoleto seized Narni. Both fortresses were on the borders of imperial and Lombard duchies, and their capture by Lombard troops compromised the integrity of the imperial duchy of Rome.[30] Imperial vulnerability thus provided great opportunities not just to the Lombard dukes but also to the Lombard king who entertained the prospect of extending his power not only over imperial lands to the east (attacking Ravenna and Classe in 717–18) but also over the Lombard duchies in central Italy that were increasingly exposed by the removal of the imperial buffer zone that had separated them from royal lands in the north and which had protected them from direct royal interference in local affairs.[31] The tension between the Lombard king and the Lombard dukes in the south thus added another dimension to the factional politics and meant that the dukes of Spoleto or Benevento were available as potential military allies to the pope, who lacked significant manpower resources of his own.[32]

The Lombard king Liutprand (712–44) took advantage of renewed imperial unpopularity catalysed by the emperor's tax demands and promulgation of iconoclast policies to embark on an expansionist campaign, proclaiming his support for the pope against imperial aggression. He focused initially on imperial territory in central Italy, taking the strategic fortress at Sutri, on the border of Tuscany and the duchy of Rome. In 728, at the entreaty of Pope Gregory II, Liutprand gave up Sutri, handing it over to 'the Apostles Peter and Paul'—in other words, into the control of the pope.[33] This was the first occasion that the papacy had gained sovereign rights to territory outside the duchy of Rome; a decade earlier, Gregory had also intervened decisively to reassert imperial control of Cumae, which lay to the south of Rome.

The other beneficiary of waning imperial power in Italy was, therefore, the papacy, although the long-term effects of this change were far from obvious at the time. Fear of domination by Lombard kings (who were Arian until the mid-seventh century) had been a central factor in shaping papal domestic policy ever since the pontificate of Gregory I (d. 604), and so the relative rise in the power of the Lombard king at imperial expense in the early eighth century was a matter of real concern for the incumbents of St Peter's chair. Broadly speaking, the popes' political interests were aligned with those of the empire; the pope was the bishop of Rome, and the city was at the heart of a duchy controlled by a duke who owed his rank and position to the emperor in the east. Likewise, each pope announced his election to the exarch, and

---

[30] *LP* 91.7, 13; Noble, *Republic*, 25–62 arguing for the opportunism of these attacks against imperial territory while the Arabs were at the walls of Constantinople.

[31] *LP* 91.13.

[32] See, for example, the papal–ducal alliances of 725 and 728/9; *LP* 91.16, 19, 22; Noble, *Republic*, 29, 34; J. T Hallenbeck, 'The Roman–Byzantine Reconciliation of 728: Genesis and Significance', *Byzantinische Zeitschrift*, 74 (1981), 29–41.

[33] *LP* 91.21; Noble, *Republic*, 31–2.

was confirmed in office by him; the last pope to do this was Gregory III, in 732.[34] In the century before the accession of Hadrian in 772, eleven out of the seventeen popes whose consecration was approved by imperial mandate were Greek (or Greek-speaking) from families that hailed from Syria or Sicily.[35] Papal correspondence with Constantinople in the first half of the eighth century is remarkable for the unswerving loyalty of pope to emperor, despite strident disagreements over matters of economics, theology, and politics. The character of papal landholdings within the dispersed patrimonies meant that there were limitations on the resources that the papacy could draw on to sustain and defend itself, and thus the popes relied for political and physical protection on the resources of the empire in the form of either the distant exarch in Ravenna or (more practically) the duke of Rome. In practice, this meant that the popes of the earlier eighth century had to negotiate short term, pragmatic political and military alliances to keep hostile Lombard armies away from the gates of Rome and, throughout the eighth century, popes strove to provide the city and its bishop with its own resources of land and men, persisting with claims to legal control of resources, estates, and rights within the *patrimonia*, and to extend sovereign control over lands that had previously been under imperial rule.

The popes' accumulation of territories in central Italy and the legal rights that accompanied them is a phenomenon of the long eighth century; it came into being at the expense of the empire as successive popes took on increasingly decisive political roles. The transition that we can see with the benefit of hindsight was not—it seems—a defined policy from the outset but a cumulative and opportunistic one. Gregory II played an especially important part skilfully negotiating increased papal autonomy all the while avoiding the imposition of new imperial authority or Lombard lordship. His successor, Gregory III (731–41), extended papal autonomy in Italy still further; shortly after his accession he is reported to have articulated Italian opposition to iconoclasm at a synod held in Rome in November 731.[36] His personal patronage of images was demonstrated a few months later by the establishment of an oratory in St Peter's dedicated to Christ, Mary, the Apostles, and All Saints, replete with an image of the Virgin and marble inscriptions recording the liturgical arrangements for the oratory.[37] When sent a gift of six twisted columns by the exarch of Ravenna, he set

---

[34] Noble, *Republic*, 49–50 for discussion of the evidence against Zacharias having performed these obsequies, and Davis, tr., *Lives of the Eighth-Century Popes*, 41, n. 46 and 45, nn. 73–4.

[35] A. J. Ekonomou, *Byzantine Rome and the Greek Popes: Eastern Influences on Rome and the Papacy from Gregory the Great to Zacharias, AD 590–752* (Lanham, MD, 2007), 199.

[36] *LP* 92.3–4. Excerpts of the *Acta* of this synod are found in the proceedings of the synod held in Rome in 769. See Brubaker and Haldon, *Byzantium in the Iconoclast Era*, 84–5 for scepticism about the contemporaneity of these records.

[37] *LP* 92.6. On the inscriptions, see *MEC* I, XIII.1a–b; *ICUR* II.i, 423, no. LXVI.41; Davis, tr., *Lives of the Eighth-Century Popes*, 23, n. 23; H. Mordek, 'Rom, Byzanz und die Franken im 8. Jahrhundert: ur Überlieferung und kirchenpolitischen Bedeutung der Synodus Romana papst Gregors III. vom Jahr 732 (mit Edition)', in G. Althoff, ed., *Personen und Gemeinschaft im Mittelalter: Karl Schmid zum fünf und sechsigsten Geburtstag*

these up as a screen in front of the *confessio*, and placed silvered beams on top of them with images in relief of Christ, the apostles, the Mary, and the holy virgins.[38] At around the same time, and perhaps as a consequence of Gregory's objections to imperial iconoclasm, the wealthy ecclesiastical provinces of southern Italy, Sicily and Illyricum, including the papal patrimonies, were transferred into direct imperial control. It is this that may have triggered papal estrangement from the empire, although the exact chronology and sequence of events remains obscure.[39] The years 727–33 were a tipping point; thereafter, the duchy of Rome came under papal control and ultimately its dukes were papal appointees.[40]

ITALY, ROME, AND THE EARLY CAROLINGIANS

By the end of Gregory III's pontificate in 741, the issue had become not so much about a break with the emperor, whose sovereign influence in northern and central Italy had effectively ceased, as freedom from the threat of Lombard oppression. Two crucial things had changed; firstly, a critical mass of territories was now in papal hands and secondly, there had emerged the potential of a new military and political alliance with the Franks.

Gregory III made the first formal approach to the Franks in 738; he may have been prompted to do so by Boniface, the West Saxon missionary, who was in Rome in 737 and who understood the internal politics of the Frankish realm through his role as archbishop in eastern Francia.[41] Two letters survive from Gregory III to Charles

(Sigmaringen, 1988), 123–56; T. F. X. Noble, *Icons, Iconoclasm, and the Carolingians* (Philadelphia, PA, 2013), 125–6; C. Smith and J. F. O'Connor, *Eyewitness to Old St. Peter's: A Study of Maffeo Vegio's 'Remembering the ancient history of St. Peter's basilica in Rome'* (Cambridge, 2019), 275–6.

[38] *LP* 92.5. On the columns, see J. B. Ward-Perkins, 'The Shrine of St Peter and Its Twelve Spiral Columns', *Journal of Roman Studies*, 42 (1952), 21–33, and J. Toynbee and J. Ward-Perkins, *The Shrine of St Peter and the Vatican Excavations* (London, 1956), 215–16; Brandenburg, Ballardini and Theones, *Saint Peter's*, 57–9, fig. 27. For an overview of papal patronage of art in Rome in the eighth century, see X. Barral I Altet, 'L'VIII secolo: da Giovanni VI (701–705) ad Adriano I (772–795)', in M. D'Onofrio, ed., *La committenza artistica dei papi a Roma nel Medioevo* (Rome, 2016), 181–212.

[39] M. V. Anastos, 'The Transfer of Illyricum, Calabria and Sicily to the Jurisdction of the Patriarchate of Constantinople in 732–33', *Studi bizantini e neoellenico*, 9 (1957), 14–31; V. Prigent, 'Les empereurs isauriens et la confiscation des patrimoines pontificaux d'Italie du Sud', *Mélanges de l'école française de Rome: Moyen Âge*, 146 (2004), 557–94 (which argues that the transfer occurred at a later date, in the 740s). Brubaker and Haldon, *Byzantium*, 86; Price, tr., *Acts of the Second Council*, I, 65.

[40] E. Ewig, 'The Papacy's Alienation from Byzantium and the Rapprochement with the Franks', in H. Jedin and D. Dolan, eds, *The Church in the Age of Feudalism* (New York, NY, 1969), 3–25 at 7; Noble, *Republic*, 38–9, and n. 125, and 53 for the situation in 743 (arguing that this was the case from 728); Davis, tr., *Lives of the Eighth-Century Popes*, 21, n. 13. See also *CC* 60, 61/*CeC* 49, 73 for Theodore 'our duke'.

[41] *LP* 92.14; Noble, *Republic*, 46, 61–2 suggests that Boniface who was in Rome in 737 might have been the instigator of the letters and provided Gregory with the inside information about power politics in Francia. Boniface's personal links with Rome are likely also to have been a factor in the promotion of papal authority

Martel (Charlemagne's grandfather, namesake, mayor of the palace, and de facto ruler of the Franks). These are preserved in the collection of papal letters known as the *Codex Carolinus* that was compiled in Francia on Charlemagne's orders in 791.[42] The two letters, written several months apart, requested Frankish aid for 'defending the Church of God and his [St Peter's] peculiar people [i.e. the Romans] which are now suffering persecution and oppression by the Lombards'. A comment added to the *Liber Pontificalis* says that Liutprand's army had camped outside the gates of Rome, plundering Campania.[43] Charles Martel chose not to raise an army in support of the pope, probably because Liutprand had been a valued ally first against Bavaria and again in 738–9 against Arab raiders in Provence.[44] But it is clear that Martel did respond to Gregory's approach; the pope sent his second letter to Francia via one of Martel's *fideles*, named Anthat, who must have been in Rome on some form of official business.[45] What is more, Frankish sources reveal that potent gifts had accompanied the pope's letters to Francia—the keys to St Peter's tomb and a link from his chains, no less. 'Such a thing had never been seen or heard of before', say the Frankish sources, which add that Martel had sent his own embassy back to Rome led by two Frankish clerics (Grimo, abbot of Corbie, and Sigebert, a monk from Saint-Denis), with gifts of his own for the pope.[46] Significantly, the Frankish sources also claimed that the pope, 'in consultation with the Romans' (*romano consulto*) had offered to desert the imperial cause and join with Martel.[47]

Gregory's letters to Charles Martel are an interesting reflection of papal realpolitik in the late 730s. They show that Gregory had recognised the reality of Carolingian power in Francia, even though the dynasty was not yet a royal one, and that he realised that the forces of the empire could offer Rome neither practical nor rapid assistance against Lombard aggression. Gregory may have been overly optimistic in his request for Frankish military support and the Frankish sources are a touch melodramatic in their reporting of his negotiating stance, but Gregory's request was a percipient one, and—as the archiving of these letters right at the beginning of the *Codex Carolinus* indicates—it was seen with hindsight by the Carolingians as the beginning of the

---

within the Frankish Church in the mid-eighth century. On the interpolation into this chapter of the *Liber Pontificalis*, and the letters from Gregory in the *Codex Carolinus*, see R. McKitterick, *Rome and the Invention of the Papacy: The* Liber Pontificalis (Cambridge, 2020), 208–10.

[42] CC 1, 2/*CeC* 2, 1; F. Unterkircher, ed., *Codex Epistolaris Carolinus. Österreichische Nationalbibliothek Codex 449*, Codices Selecti, 3 (Graz, 1962), fols 1v–2v. See A. T. Hack, *Codex Carolinus: Päpstliche Epistolographie im 8. Jahrhundert, Päpste und Papsttum*, 35, 2 vols (Stuttgart, 2007). The letters describe Martel as *subregulus* of the Franks (compare *LP* 93.21 and 94.15 where he is described as *rex*).

[43] *LP* 92.14; McKitterick, *Rome and the Invention*, 209–10.

[44] Noble, *Republic*, 31, 45.

[45] CC 2/*CeC* 1, dated late 739/40. Hack, *Codex Carolinus*, ii, 1074.

[46] *Fredegar Cont.*, ch. 22; *AMPr s.a.* 741; *Chronicon Moissacense s.a.* 734, G. H. Pertz, ed., MGH, SS I, 291–2; *Annales Iuvavenses breves s.a.* 739, G. H. Pertz, ed., MGH, SS III, 123.

[47] See Noble, *Republic*, 47 for the long-running historiography of the debate on this point.

political, military, and spiritual alliance between Rome and the Franks that would prove to be so important for both the papacy and the Carolingian dynasty.

Modern scholarship accepts a symbiotic connection between the establishment of the Carolingians as a royal dynasty and the consolidation of a papal republic in Italy. The early 750s are regarded as the formative period, when a series of events brought the pope and the Carolingians into closer contact than they had ever been before.[48] The key events are well known and the sources (and the relative significance of each) have been much discussed: the Frankish accounts say that in 751 Pope Zacharias sanctioned the deposition of the last Merovingian monarch and elevation of Pippin III (Charlemagne's father) to the kingship by agreeing to Pippin's enquiry that 'he who held the power should also wear the crown'; in late 753 Zacharias' successor Pope Stephen II (752–7) crossed the Alps—the first pope to do so—and met Pippin at Ponthion in the heart of Francia, begging him to come to the aid of St Peter against the Lombards; in April 754, Pippin gathered an assembly at Quierzy and, with the backing of the Frankish magnates, agreed to come to the pope's assistance, drawing up a document that outlined what lands the pope might receive in the event of the capitulation of the Lombards.[49] In July that year Pope Stephen anointed Pippin and his young family at a solemn ceremony in Saint-Denis and conferred on him the title *patricius romanorum*. These powerfully symbolic events in Francia were followed in late 754 or early 755 by a campaign into northern Italy.[50] A second expedition followed in 756 after Aistulf, the Lombard king (749–56), reneged on his promises and laid siege to Rome itself.[51] Both times the Franks forced the Lombards to capitulate and agree treaties that assigned to the pope large tracts of once-imperial territory that lately had come under Lombard control.

The 'Second Treaty of Pavia', drawn up in the aftermath of the 756 campaign, has long been referred to as the 'Donation of Pippin'. Despite protestations from Constantinople, an agreement was apparently made to transfer most of the exarchate of Ravenna into papal control, along with the cities of the Pentapolis and Emilia,

---

[48] The literature is vast and includes the work of many of the great names of early medieval historiography (Duchesne, Halphen, Ullmann, Ewig, Schramm, Angenendt); for a summary, see Noble, *Republic*, xxii–xxvi, 67–98, 256–61; R. McKitterick, *History and Memory in the Carolingian World* (Cambridge, 2004), 137–50 for doubts about the Frankish accounts of the approach to Zacharias.

[49] P. E. Schramm, *Kaiser, Könige, und Päpste*, 4 vols (Stuttgart, 1968–71), i, 170–4. This 'Donation of Quierzy' referred to a vast swathe of central Italy comprising Lombard and imperial lands south of a line from Montselice in the north-east, to Luni on the west coast. It was described in the 'Life' of Hadrian, in the context of Charlemagne's visit to Italy in 774; see *LP* 97.41–2.

[50] *LP* 94.31–7; *Fredegar Cont.*, ch. 37; *ARF s.a.* 755. Doubt about the precise date is summarised by Noble, *Republic*, 88. On the document drawn up after the first campaign, known as the First Treaty of Pavia, see also the *AMPr s.a.* 754, de Simson, ed., MGH, SS rer. Germ. X, 47–8 and *CC* 6–7/*CeC* 7, 9; for discussion, see Davis, *Lives of the Eighth-Century Popes*, 68, n. 75–6 and Noble, *Republic*, 89–90.

[51] *CC* 8, 9, 10/*CeC* 6, 4, 3; *LP* 94.43 and 46; *Fredegar Cont.*, ch. 38; *ARF s.a.* 756.

as well as the city of Narni that had been captured by the duke of Spoleto in 718.[52] The 'Donation' engendered great debate—at the time as well as in subsequent historiography—because of the scale of the lands in question and the historic, economic, and symbolic importance of the cities involved, as well as the practicalities of seeing the agreement implemented. The document recording the detail of the agreement does not survive, although it was summarised in the *Vita* of Stephen II, which says that a copy was deposited at the tomb of St Peter (with the keys to the cities that had been gathered by Pippin's legate, Abbot Fulrad of Saint-Denis) and 'is kept safe in the archive of the holy church'.[53] For centuries, historians regarded Pippin's 'Donation' as the foundation treaty of the papal states and the temporal suzerainty of the papacy. However, the Donation obliged Aistulf to hand over parcels of land that were less extensive than the territory of the former imperial exarchate, and much more limited than had been outlined in the earlier agreement made at Quierzy, itself but a 'contingent' treaty laying out what would happen if and when the Lombard kingdom was definitively conquered.[54] Pippin did not do this, assenting to the petition of his own nobility to leave Aistulf in possession of his life and crown; thus the so-called 'Donation of Pippin' in 756 fell short of the Quierzy agreement which remained (in Frankish eyes) a theoretical statement rather than the binding commitment that the papacy had desired.[55]

From the late sixteenth century, humanist and antiquarian scholars discussed a monumental inscription that seemed to confirm Pippin's Donation with the words, *Pipinvs pivs primvs amplificandae ecclesiae viam apervit ex exarcatvm ravennae cum amplissimis*...('Pious Pippin first opened the way to the enlargement of the Church from the exarchate of Ravenna with the most ample . . .').[56] These early modern sources say that the marble slab bearing the inscription was broken, and, since no trace of the stone survives today, we cannot know if it was an early medieval inscription independently recording the Donation or one put up later under the instruction of a patron working from other written records. The epithet 'pious' is an unusual one for Pippin and its reference to him as the first to act in this way suggests that the wording of the inscription cannot have been strictly contemporary with him; but how long after that

---

[52] *LP* 94.37; the list also includes Narni (between Otricoli and Terni), which had been captured from the duchy of Rome by the duke of Spoleto in 718. See Noble, *Republic*, map 2, and 101–2 for the *civitates reliquias* which were later promised (but not delivered) to Stephen by Desiderius in return for his help in claiming the Lombard throne; Davis, *Lives of the Eighth-Century Popes*, 77–8.

[53] *LP* 94.46–7.

[54] For the interpretation of the Quierzy agreement as a 'contingent treaty', see P. Kehr, 'Die sognenante karolingische Schenkung von 774', *Historische Zeitschrift*, 70 (1893), 335–441.

[55] *Fredegar Cont.*, ch. 38; *AMPr.* 755.

[56] See, for example, the editions of the *LP* and *CC* in *PL* 128, col. 1118C (n. 254) and *PL* 98, col. 0115D. F. Pagi, *Breviarum historico-chronologico-criticum, illustriora pontificum romanorum gesta, conciliorum generalium acta* (Antwerp, 1717), 564; G. Daniel, *Histoire de France depuis l'établissement de la monarchie françoise dans les Gaules, i: 486–768* (Paris, 1729), 549.

it was composed is not clear.[57] Most antiquarian sources followed Jean-Papire Masson (1544–1611), writing in France for Henry III in 1578, who had said that the inscription could be seen in Ravenna and that it was 'a marble tablet of ancient work'.[58] But before this, in 1566, Marc Antoine Muret had quoted the inscription in an address to the French king Charles IX (1550–74) and Pope Pius V (1566–72). Muret says it was to be seen in the Borgia Tower in the Vatican.[59] Muret was one of the most renowned Latinists of the Renaissance, and from 1563 was based in Rome; his account is therefore important. What is more, not far from the Borgia Tower, in the apartments that had been made for Julius II (1503–13), the Pippin inscription was quoted in a painted scroll, placed beneath the fresco showing the Battle of Ostia in the *Stanza del Incendio* ('The Fire in the Borgo') that had been painted by Raphael and his school for Leo X (1513–21). This room is replete with allusions to Carolingian history, and to events recorded in the *Liber Pontificalis* concerning the lives of Leo III (795–816) and Leo IV (847–55).[60] Here, however, the last part of the Pippin inscription was amended to supply a complete sentence; *Pipinvs pivs primvs amplificandae ecclesiae viam apervit exarcatvm ravennate et aliis plvrimis ei oblatis* ('…having presented to it [i.e. the Church] the Ravenna exarchate and many others').[61] The difference between the wording of the painted inscription and the broken marble slab implies that Muret saw and quoted the latter rather than the painted version in Raphael's *stanza*, and makes it possible that the *tabula marmorea* (of whatever date) was, as he says, to be seen in the Vatican in Rome during the mid-sixteenth century.

Inscriptions were central to the development of the bond between the nascent Carolingian dynasty and the basilica and cult of St Peter. The *Vita* of Paul I (757–67) describes the discovery of relics of Petronilla in an extra-mural cemetery and their translation into an oratory in St Peter's basilica. This was the beginning of a long-term link between Petronilla and the kings of France; in time her oratory at St Peter's became known as the *Cappella del Re di Francia* and throughout the Middle Ages

---

[57] *Pius* is occasionally used as an epithet for Charlemagne's son, Pippin of Italy (781–810); see, for example, *Laudes Vernonensis Civitatis*, ed. E. Dümmler, MGH, PLAC I, 122, line 32 (also, a forged diploma purporting to date to 784, E. Mühlbacher, ed., MGH, DD. Kar. I, 480, no. 317). It is used for Charlemagne's father only by Ademar of Chabannes (988–1037) writing in the early eleventh century.

[58] J.-P. Masson, *Annalium libri quatuor: Quibus res gestae Francorum explicantur. Ad Henricvm Tertium Regem Franciae et Poloniae* (Paris, 1578), 93.

[59] 'Exstat adhuc tabula marmorea in ea turri, cui Borgia nomen est, in qua haec omnia olim honoris ergo incisa et praescripta fuisse constat. Ita enim in ea adhuc legitur: *Pipinus pius primus amplificandae ecclesiae viam apervit et exarchatum Ravennae cum amplissimis*. Pars tabulae, in qua reliqua scripta errant, aut casu aliquo, aut temporum, aut hominum injuria confracta est. At aenea quidem et marmorea monumenta conficere ac consumere longinquitas temporis potuit'; M. A. Muret, *Orationes XXIII* (Venice, 1575), 218 (Oratio XIII, 1566).

[60] See below, Chapter 1, 36.

[61] Raphael's version of the inscription was recorded in 1643 by H. Coring, 'De Germanorum Imperium Romano', *Varia scripta ad historiam et ius publicum imperii germanici* (Brunswick, 1730), 42, note a.

Petronilla was regarded as the French king's special patron in Rome.[62] Petronilla's relics were first identified because they had been enshrined in a marble sarcophagus:

> …on which were carved letters [*sculptum litteris*] reading 'To Aurea Petronilla, sweetest daughter'. There is no doubt that the carving of these letters is set apart as having been drawn out [*designata esse*] by St Peter's own hand, out of love for his sweetest child.[63]

This information, along with an account of the translation of the relics from an extramural cemetery, and a description of Paul's adornment of the basilica, is recorded in only the Frankish redaction of the *Liber Pontificalis*, and may have been added some time after the events it describes.[64] Nevertheless it corroborates other early sources, which show that the new relics were believed to be those of Peter's daughter.[65] Paul, acting on his predecessor's initiative, had these relics translated into the rotunda that stood adjacent to the south transept of the basilica. This rotunda had been constructed as an imperial mausoleum by the emperor Honorius (384–432) in the early fifth century; it received the remains of the Empress Maria (d. 407/8) as well as other members of the imperial dynasty, probably including Honorius himself.[66] The translation of Petronilla's relics there in 757 transformed that building from a focus of imperial patronage to one of overt Petrine devotion. This realignment of the devotional function of the building was given added force by its physical location; the mausoleum was aligned not only with the southern arm of basilica's transept, providing privileged access to the sanctuary and shrine, but also on the axis of another rotunda just to the east that had been erected in the late second or early third century hard up against the obelisk that had once been the *spina* of the circus at the foot of

---

[62] P. Dangelfort, *Sainte Pétronille, fille de St. Pierre, patronne et auxiliatrice de la France* (Avignon, 1911); K. Weil-Garris Brandt, "Michelangelo's Pietà for the Cappella del Re di Francia", in C. L. Frommel and M. Winner, eds, *"Il se rendit en Italie": Etudes offertes à Henri Chastel* (Rome, 1987), 77–119.

[63] *LP* 95.3; Davis, tr., *Lives of the Eighth-Century Popes*, 81 and n. 6; C. Goodson, 'To Be the Daughter of Saint Peter: S. Petronilla and the Forging of the Franco-Papal Alliance', in V. West-Harling, ed., *Three Empires, Three Cities: Identity, Material Culture and Legitimacy in Venice, Ravenna and Rome, 750–1000* (Turnhout, 2015), 159–82.

[64] The Frankish recension was classified as Group B by Duchesne, ed., *Le Liber Pontificalis*, clxxi–clxxxix and 464; it was used by Ademar of Chabannes, *c.*1030: see Davis, tr., *Lives of the Eighth-Century Popes*, xvii. Also, R. McKitterick, *Perceptions of the Past in the Early Middle Ages* (Notre Dame, IN, 2006), 48; McKitterick, *History and Memory*, 146–8.

[65] Duchesne, ed., *Le Liber Pontificalis*, I, 466, with reference to de Rossi's research on the excavation of the tomb in 1474 and the misreading of this inscription; *AVR* is an abbreviation for *Aurelia* not *aurea*, and thus the text refers to the tomb of an otherwise unknown woman called Aurelia Petronilla.

[66] H. Koethe, 'Zum Mausoleum der weströmischen Dynastie bei Alt-Sankt-Peter', *Römische Mitteilunge*, 46 (1931), 9–26; M. J. Johnson, *The Roman Imperial Mausoleum in Late Antiquity* (Cambridge, 2009), 167–74; F. Paolucci, 'La tomba dell'imperatrice Maria e altre sepolture di rango di età tardoantica a San Pietro', *Temporis Signa: Archeologia della tarda antichità e del medioevo*, 3 (2008), 225–52; M. McEvoy, 'The Mausoleum of Honorius: Late Roman Imperial Christianity and the City of Rome in the Fifth Century', in *OSPR*, 119–37; Brandenburg, Ballardini and Theones, *Saint Peter's*, 29.

the Vatican hill.[67] This eastern rotunda had been remodelled inside by Pope Symmachus (498–514) to serve as an oratory for the cult of St Andrew, Peter's brother.[68] The appropriation of the Honorian rotunda for Peter's daughter complemented the earlier dedication of the adjacent building to Andrew, and effectively proclaimed the whole basilican complex on the Vatican hill as a mausoleum for St Peter's family.

This complemented the practice of papal burial; from the mid-fifth century, following the death of Leo I in 461, St Peter's became the papal necropolis.[69] This development may have arisen precisely because the emperor's family had built and was using a mausoleum so close to the shrine of St Peter, but it was not the obvious choice, since it was the Lateran, not St Peter's, that was the pope's cathedral.[70] By commandeering this imperial space for Peter's 'daughter', Paul I reinforced the place of the bishops of Rome as part of the Petrine dynasty, in life and in death. It was no coincidence that Paul arranged his own burial place in the oratory that he set up in honour of Mary, *Genetrix Dei*, in the southern exedra of the transept, just to the right of the doors that led from the exedra into the Oratory of Santa Petronilla recently established in the rotunda.[71] There he erected a gilded silver effigy of the Virgin weighing 150lb, which has to be seen as an overt rebuttal of eastern iconoclasm.[72] Paul was also responsible for the decoration of this oratory with 'beautiful pictures' (*picturis miro*), perhaps the scenes from the life of the Emperor Constantine I ('the Great') (306–37) that were reported there by fifteenth-century observers and described by them as 'ancient'.[73] If so, the choice of that theme, for this decorative cycle in this place, would have underlined once again papal appropriation of the narrative of the imperial past and, in conjunction with the re-dedication of the once-imperial mausoleum, depleted yet again the relationship between contemporary Constantinople and St Peter's basilica.

Paul's actions on behalf of Petronilla had been prefigured by his elder brother, Pope Stephen II (752–7), whose *Vita* implies that he had been the one to dedicate the

---

[67] On this building, see R. Gem, 'The Vatican Rotunda: A Severan Monument and its Early History, *c*.200 to 500', *Journal of the British Archaeological Association*, 158 (2005), 1–45. See also E. Thunø, 'The Pantheon in the Middle Ages', in T. A. Marder and M. Wilson Jones, eds, *The Pantheon from Antiquity to the Present* (Cambridge, 2015), 231–54, at 242–4.

[68] J. D. Alchermes, 'Petrine Politics: Pope Symmachus and the Rotunda of St Andrew at Old St. Peter's', *The Catholic Historical Review*, 81 (1995), 1–40. See further, Chapter 3, 133–4.

[69] M. Borgolte, *Petrusnachfolge und Kaiserimitation. Die Grablegen der Päpste, ihre Genese und Traditionsbildung* (Göttingen, 1995), 343–60; R. McKitterick, 'The representation of Old St. Peter's Basilica in the *Liber Pontificalis*', in *OSPR*, 95–118, at 106–7.

[70] McKitterick, 'Representation of Old St. Peter's', 116–17.

[71] *LP* 95.6–7. It is recorded in many later sources, not least the appendix to the late eighth-century *Notitia ecclesiarum urbis Romae*, on which, see below, Chapter 4, 173.

[72] A. Angenendt, 'Der römische und gallisch-fränkische Anti-Ikonolasmus', *Frühmittelalterlich Studien*, 35 (2001), 201–25; Noble, *Icons, Iconoclasm*, 128.

[73] *LP* 95.3; Davis, tr., *Lives of the Eighth-Century Popes*, 81, n. 6. The decoration was described in 1458; *CD* ii, 639, n. 127 and J. Emerick, 'Charlemagne: A new Constantine?', in M. Shane Bjornlie, ed., *The Life and Legacy of Constantine: Traditions through the Ages* (London and New York, 2017), 135.

rotunda to Petronilla. It also notes that when Stephen had been in Francia, 'he had promised the most bountiful king Pippin that it was there he would place Petronilla's body'.[74] The translation and reburial of Petronilla's relics took place after Stephen's death and was overseen by Paul, probably in the first few months of his pontificate. It is probably relevant that the feast of Petronilla's translation is recorded in later calendars as 8 October; this was the vigil of the feast of St Denis, whose cult site was in Paris and who was a special patron of the Frankish kings, especially Pippin III.[75] Stephen had stayed at Saint-Denis in 754, and when back in Rome had turned his own house into a monastery dedicated to St Dionysius, probably (under the circumstances) the Parisian saint rather than the third-century pope of the same name.[76] These details—again—are recorded only in the Frankish redaction of the *Liber Pontificalis*, but concur with other records such as letters in the *Codex Carolinus* from Paul to Pippin showing that the Carolingians were keen partners in the cultivation of Peter's daughter. In 758 Pippin sent to Paul the cloth that had been used to wrap his newborn daughter, Gisela, after her baptism, and asked Paul to be her *compater* ('godfather'). Paul replied that he had received the cloth with great joy and had placed it in the oratory of Petronilla—a daughter's oratory for a daughter's gown.[77] Paul says that the oratory, 'now dedicated', is distinguished *pro laude*, 'with the eternal memory of your name'.

Paul also took possession of a precious altar table that Pippin had earlier sent to Stephen.[78] Paul's letter says that the table was brought within the basilica (*aula*) to the singing of hymns, holy canticles, and the *laetaniae laude* ('litanies of praise') and that Pippin's *missi* had presented it, in the king's stead, in front of the *confessio*. This was the space beneath the high altar and apse that contained the shrine where Peter's body was believed to be buried. Gregory the Great had modified this area, raising the floor level of the apse, with steps leading up either side in front of the altar which stood directly over the holy tomb. A niche beneath the altar enabled a supplicant who

---

[74] *LP* 94.52.

[75] On the calendars, see Duchesne, ed., *LP*, 466, n. 5. On the importance of the basilica at Saint-Denis to the early Frankish kings, see S. McKnight Crosby, *The Royal Abbey of St.-Denis from Its Beginnings to the Death of Suger, 475–1151* (New Haven, CT, and London, 1987), 8–9. On the burial of Pippin III there, see *Fredegar Cont.*, ch. 53, 120–2.

[76] *LP* 94.27; *Fredegar Cont.*, ch. 36, 104. On the dedication of the monastery in Rome to St Denis, see Davis, tr., *Lives of the Eighth-Century Popes*, 51 and 82, n. 9.

[77] *CC* 14/*CeC* 27. See also. A. M. Voci, '"Petronilla auxiliatrix regis Francorum". Anno 757: sulla "memoria" del re dei Franchi presso San Pietro', *Bullettino dell'Istituto Storico Italiano per il Medio Evo e Archivio Muratoriano*, 99 (1993), 1–28; R. Schieffer, 'Charlemagne and Rome', in J. M. H. Smith, ed., *Early Medieval Rome and the Christian West: Essays in Honour of Donald A. Bullough* (Leiden, 2000), 279–296, at 287.

[78] *CC* 21/*CeC* 14; A. Angenendt, 'Mensa Pippini Regis. Zur liturgischen Präsenz der Karolinger in Sankt Peter', in E. Gatz, ed., *Hundert Jahre Deutsches Priesterkolleg beim Campo Santo Teutonico 1876–1976. Beiträge zu seiner Geschichte* (Rome, 1977), 52–68, reprinted in his *Liturgie im Mittelalter: ausgewählte Augsätze zum 70. Geburtstag* (Münster, 2005), 89–110; Borgolte, *Petrusnachfolge und Kaiserimitation*, 107–9; Hack, *Codex Carolinus*, ii, 843–7.

was standing, kneeling, or lying on the floor of the basilica to look downwards at the tomb or upwards to the altar above it. A passageway (ring crypt) that followed the semicircle of the apse beneath the raised floor could be entered by staircases on either side, permitting access to the *confessio* at the lower level.[79] This was thus the focal point and final objective for pilgrims to the shrine of the Apostle and the most sacred part of the basilica. Paul sanctified Pippin's offertory table with holy oil in front of the *confessio* and then celebrated mass over it, praying for the enduring stability of Pippin's kingship in Francia and the eternal reward of his soul, before issuing a solemn anathema that it should never be removed from the church of St Peter.

The basilica and its apostolic shrine thus play a prominent role in the descriptions of the ceremonies that accompanied the reception and installation of both of Pippin's gifts. They are brought *infra aulam* to the witness of a crowd and liturgical thanksgiving. But the building is more than just a theatrical backdrop: through these gifts the structure itself contains and bears witness to the eternal remembrance of the Carolingian king: 'Look, your *memorale* in that same apostolic hall, gleaming, endures for eternity' and, again, *pro laude*, the oratory of Petronilla 'is distinguished with the eternal *memoria* of your name'.[80] Over and over, Paul emphasised the importance of the repeated commemoration of the Carolingian king's name at the basilica.[81] Angenendt has referred to the 'liturgical presence' of the Carolingians at St Peter's, and it is important to notice that even in Pippin's time this was being done in multidimensional, immersive ways—aurally through liturgy, visually via objects of devotion, and spatially within significant architectural zones in the basilica.[82]

Pope Paul's final illness and death precipitated a coup in Rome, and the installation of Constantine II, a nobleman-turned-cleric, whose election as pope was forced through by his brother Toto, the duke of Nepi. Constantine's brief tenure of the papal throne is described in the *Vita* of his successor, Stephen III, where he is referred to consistently as a *transgressor* or 'intruder'.[83] This episode arose from local politics, and it reflects the fact that by now the secular aristocracy knew that to control the city of Rome they had to control the papacy. But—in a significant indication of the

---

[79] See Toynbee and Ward Perkins, *Shrine of St Peter*, 215 (fig. 22) and 226 (fig. 25). See also Smith and O'Connor, *Eyewitness to Old St. Peter's*, 8–11, figs 1–3; Brandenburg, Ballardini, and Theones, *Saint Peter's*, 55; C. B. McClendon, *The Origins of Medieval Architecture* (New Haven, CT, and London, 2005), 29–31.
[80] *CC* 21/*CeC* 14 and *CC* 14/*CeC* 27.
[81] See, for example, *CC* 14, 22, 30/*CeC* 27, 19, 34 (Paul I); *CC* 69/*CeC* 56 (Hadrian I).
[82] Angenendt, 'Mensa Pippini Regis', 52. On the central role of prayer for the king in Hadrian's relationship with Charles, see S. Scholz, *Politik—Selbstverständnis—Selbstdarstellung. Die Päpste in karolingischer und ottonischer Zeit* (Stuttgart, 2006), 86–9.
[83] *LP* 96.3–22. K. Herbers, 'Konkurrenz und Gegnerschaft. "Gegenpäpste" im 8. und 9. Jahrhundert', in H. Müller and B. Hotz, eds, *Gegenpäpste. Eine unerwünschtes mittelalterliches Phänomen* (Vienna, 2012), 55–70, at 56–8; R. McKitterick, 'The *Damnatio Memoriae* of Pope Constantine I (767–768)', in R. Balzaretti, J. Barrow, and P. Skinner, eds, *Italy and Early Medieval Europe*, Past and Present Book Series (Oxford, 2018), 231–48.

changing geo-politics of the age—both Pope Constantine's accession and his subsequent demise demanded rapid contact with the Franks. Constantine wrote quickly to Pippin after Paul's death, announcing his own election using formulae that popes had previously used to contact the exarch.[84] This could have been a matter of scribal reflex in stressful times rather than diplomatic innovation or faux pas, but it nevertheless reflected how far Frankish interests had become embedded in the practices of the papal writing office. The letter announced Constantine's election and begged Pippin to honour the promises and friendship that he had made to Stephen II and Paul I. This letter, and a second one composed a few months later, is preserved in the *Codex Carolinus*, as part of the collection of papal letters which Charlemagne thought might be useful for posterity. It is significant that in the unique manuscript of that collection these two letters were placed out of chronological sequence, right at the end of the book.[85] This arrangement suggests that the compiler of the collection and the scribe of the manuscript recognised that these two letters were anomalous because they had come from a man later judged to have been an interloper into the see of Rome. But the preservation of papyrus originals in Francia and the decision to include them in the Frankish register of papal letters implies that the Carolingian archivist regarded them as both legitimate and useful for future readers, fulfilling Charlemagne's instruction recorded at the front of the volume to transcribe the papal correspondence 'so that no testimony whatsoever of the holy Church that will be of use in the future should be found wanting to his successors'.[86] In Rome, by contrast, documents from Constantine's year in office were publicly consigned to a bonfire.[87]

Constantine's 'intrusion' lasted just over a year. He was replaced by Stephen III (768–72) and tried at a Council held in Rome in April 769.[88] The council was attended by forty-nine bishops, including twelve from Francia. Like his predecessors Stephen had quickly written to Pippin, and had sent his envoy to Francia to announce his election and to request the assistance of Frankish bishops 'who were skilled, learned in the divine scriptures and the teachings of the Holy Canons, and thoroughly expert'.[89] Pope Stephen's envoy arrived in Francia only to find that Pippin had died (24 September 768). So he consulted Pippin's sons, Charles (Charlemagne) and Carloman, who are called the *reges Francorum et patricios Romanorum* in Stephen's *Vita*, and they readily agreed that Frankish bishops should travel to Rome. Thus it was

---

[84] *CC* 98–9/*CeC* 98–9.

[85] Letters 98 and 99 (out of 99) in ÖNB, Cod. 449, fols 96–8.

[86] 'Ut nullum penitus testimonium sanctae ecclaesiae profuturm suis deesse successoribus videatur'; 'preface', ed. Gundlach, MGH, Epp. I, 476 (lines 17–18). The preface to the *Codex Carolinus* says that the project was driven by the need to transfer the letters onto the enduring medium of parchment because the existing copies, presumably the originals as sent from Rome, were degraded by age and negligence; McKitterick, van Espelo, Pollard, and Price, tr., *Codex Epistolaris Carolinus*, 23, 50–1 (on Pope Constantine), 147.

[87] *LP* 96.20.

[88] *LP* 96.16–18; Davis, tr., *Lives of the Eighth-Century Popes*, 95–9. See also Noble, *Republic*, 117–19.

[89] *LP* 96.16; Stephen's first letter does not survive, but is referred to in a later letter, *CC* 45/*CeC* 45.

that the bishops of Amiens, Meaux, Mainz, Tours, Lyons, Bourges, Narbonne, Worms, Würzburg, Langres, Reims, and Noyon witnessed, confirmed, and participated in the decrees of the 769 synod in Rome alongside thirty-seven bishops from the Lombard kingdom as well as the lands of the old exarchate, Pentapolis, and duchy of Rome, that were now subject to papal control.[90]

The function of the 769 Council was to condemn both Constantine and the means by which he had been falsely elected; thereafter, popes could be chosen only from among the cardinal deacons and priests, and only clerics could participate in the election of a new pope; laymen were explicitly excluded.[91] These restrictions undoubtedly reflected the fact that Stephen's promotion (and the ejection of the 'layman' Constantine) had been masterminded by Christopher, the *primicerius notariorum* or 'chief secretary' to the papal court and leader of the clerical faction in Rome; hereafter, the institution of the papacy and the choice of incumbent would be controlled by the clergy alone. Then (as now), this had the effect of focusing attention on the continuity of the institution rather than on the person of the pope. The fact that the *primicerius* of the Lateran notaries was the political force behind both the new pope and the gathering of this international synod to approve the new procedures, makes the order to burn publicly the registers of Constantine's *acta* and the council that had confirmed him doubly significant, sanctioning as it did the destruction of records and a public *damnatio memoriae* of the *transgressor*. Similarly, the use of a novel formula by the notaries to date the acts of the 769 synod must have been deliberate; for the first time in Rome a document was dated not by the regnal years of the eastern emperor, as had been the traditional practice of Roman diplomatic, but 'in the reign of our Lord Jesus Christ'.[92] The public participation of the Frankish bishops in this 'constitutional' synod bound the Frankish bishops to the legitimation of Stephen III as pope, and to the agreements on the procedures for future papal elections. It also involved the Frankish Church in another formal denunciation of iconoclasm, distancing Rome further still from the eastern emperor.[93]

CHARLEMAGNE AND ROME BEFORE 774

Stephen III's troubles were not solved by the 769 synod. The remainder of his short pontificate was complicated by Frankish domestic politics which spilled over into foreign policy through the ambitions of Pippin's widow, Bertrada, for her elder son,

---

[90] MGH, Conc. II.1, 75–6, 80–1 and *LP* 96.17. For comments on the transmission of the lists, see Duchesne, *Le Liber Pontificalis*, i, 473–5, 482–3, nn. 28–45 and Davis, tr., *Lives of the Eighth-Century Popes*, 96, nn. 43–4.
[91] *LP* 96.20.
[92] See below, Chapter 2, 93–5.
[93] Noble, *Icons, Iconoclasm*, 145–9; Price, tr., *Acts of the Second Council*, I, 65.

Charles, against the interests of his younger brother, Carlomann.[94] The brothers had fallen out; Stephen's first extant letter to them written in 769–70 urged them to make peace so that they could pursue St Peter's rights against the Lombards.[95]

Bertrada came to Rome in 770. She was the first royal Carolingian to make this trip, albeit as a dowager-queen.[96] Both Bertrada and her objectives were formidable; en route she negotiated peace between Charles and Tassilo, the duke of Bavaria, and arranged for Charles' marriage to a daughter of the Lombard king, Desiderius (756–74). Another Lombard princess was already married to Tassilo, so this new marriage alliance with Francia promised a three-way bloc that was greatly to Desiderius' benefit but detrimental to both Carloman in Francia and also—at first sight—to the pope in Rome. Desiderius had won the Lombard crown in 756 with the support of Stephen II, and in return had promised to hand over control of several Italian cities. He had never fulfilled his promised donation, and papal letters thereafter pressed the Frankish kings to demand restitution of what the pope thought Desiderius still owed to St Peter. The new marriage alliance with Charles in Francia made it even less likely that Desiderius would hand over these lands and called into question the bond between the papacy and the Carolingians that had been cultivated so carefully in recent years.

Understandably Stephen was aghast at the prospect of this marriage, complaining in a long, bilious letter addressed to both brothers (perhaps because he did not know which of the two was to be married off to the Lombard princess) that 'this infiltration is the devil's own work' (*haec propriae diabolica est immisio*).[97] He urged them not to pollute their kingship by joining it to the 'horrible', 'stinking', and 'leprous race' of the Lombards.[98] A second letter followed addressed to Carloman alone, in which Stephen praised Carloman's queen and offered to baptise their new son, Pippin. Perhaps by then he had more information and knew that the 'diabolical' and 'polluting' union with the Lombards was intended for Charles, and so chose to contrast it with

---

[94] The causes, chronology, and consequences of this episode has generated much debate; a useful summary is in Noble, *Republic*, 120–7 and J. L. Nelson, 'Women at the Court of Charlemagne: A Case of Monstrous Regiment?', *Studies in Church History*, 27 (1990), 53–78 reprinted in her collected essays, *The Frankish World 750–900* (London, 1996), 223–42, at 231–4.

[95] *Fredegar Cont.*, ch. 53; *ARF s.a.* 770; *CC* 44/*CeC* 47; Einhard, *VK*, ch. 3.

[96] In 747 Bertrada's brother-in-law, also called Carloman, had come to Rome 'devoutly with some of his loyal followers', to become a monk at Monte Cassino; he returned to Francia (as a monk) in 754, to argue the Lombard case to Pippin (or so says the *LP*); *LP* 93.21 and 94.30; Davis, tr., *Lives of the Eighth-Century Popes*, 46–7 and 65. Noble, *Republic*, 66–7 and *Annales Laureshamenses s.a.* 746, ed., G. H. Pertz, MGH, SS I, 27.

[97] In *CC* 45/*CeC* 45, the pope refers to the Frankish wives of both kings as *nobilissima* and *pulchrissima*; clearly one of these virtuous women was to be repudiated in favour of the Lombard princess. Doubt was later cast on the legitimacy of Charles' first marriage to Himiltrude, who is thus often listed as one of his (many) concubines; Nelson, 'Women at the Court of Charlemagne', 232–3; W. Pohl, 'Why Not to Marry a Foreign Woman', in V. L. Garver and O. M. Phelan, eds, *Rome and Religion in the Medieval World: Studies in Honor of Thomas F. X. Noble* (Farnham, 2014), 47–63.

[98] *CC* 45/*CeC* 45.

Carloman's fruitful marriage to a Frankish wife who was 'most excellent', 'most Christian', and 'most sweet'.[99]

On arriving in Rome, Bertrada was able to reassure Pope Stephen that her diplomatic initiative would not damage existing Frankish obligations to St Peter's see, nor threaten the survival of the papal Republic. Partisan Frankish annals claim that she persuaded Desiderius to 'hand back many cities in various places to St Peter', and other sources show that Charles fulfilled her promises to Stephen that lands in Benevento would be restored, and that recent problems in Ravenna would be solved.[100] Returning home, she collected the Lombard princess and delivered her to be married to her elder son.

For Stephen, this turn of events precipitated further political upheavals in Rome, causing the alienation and downfall of Christopher and his faction whose position in Rome had been based on the strength of the anti-Lombard stance of the Franks and the pope's fear of Lombard domination. The pope's rapprochement with Desiderius, forced by the new Frankish marriage alliance, meant that Christopher's influence in Rome was supplanted by another aspirant 'king/pope-maker', Paul Afiata, who worked to promote Desiderius' interests in Rome.

Barely a year later, however, Charles had repudiated his new Lombard queen and sent her back to her father in Italy. This action, Einhard said later, had caused the only row that anyone could remember between Bertrada and her favourite son.[101] Einhard didn't know the reason for Charlemagne's rejection of his new bride and it was certainly a gamble—scholarly opinion is divided whether it was taken from a position of political fragility or confidence.[102] Either way, the king's volte-face turned the tables on Desiderius, humiliating him and re-establishing the Franco-papal alliance on more traditional anti-Lombard terms. This was reinforced when Carloman died at the end of 771, and his wife and sons fled for protection (quite unnecessarily, thought Einhard) to Desiderius who now had two women wronged by Charlemagne at his court, and the sons of one of them to use against him.[103]

HADRIAN'S ACCESSION

Stephen died on 24 January 772, and was replaced within a fortnight by Hadrian I. Hadrian's accession thus coincided with the beginning of Charlemagne's

---

[99] *CC* 47/*CeC* 48.
[100] *Annales Laureshamenses s.a.* 770; G. H. Pertz, ed., MGH, SS I, 30. *Chronicon Moissacense s.a.* 770; G. H. Pertz, ed., MGH, SS I, 295. *LP* 96.26; *CC* 46/*CeC* 46. Also, Noble, *Republic*, 123–4 with notes on the contested historiography.
[101] Einhard, *VK*, ch. 18.
[102] See, for example, the views of Nelson, 'Women at the Court of Charlemagne', 233 and Noble, *Republic*, 127.
[103] *LP* 97.9; Einhard, *VK*, ch. 18.

period of sole rule in Francia, and he was plunged immediately into a domestic and foreign policy crisis that culminated in the invasion and conquest of Lombard Italy by Charlemagne's armies in the autumn and winter of 773–4.[104] But from such unpromising and tense beginnings developed one of the most important and influential pontificates of the early Middle Ages.

Hadrian was a Lateran cleric who came from the ranks of the Roman aristocracy; he was therefore acceptable to a powerful section of the secular elite in Rome as well as fulfilling the new criteria for the election of a pope as laid down in the acts of the 769 synod.[105] The opening sentence of his biography in the *Liber Pontificalis* emphasises his status as a native of Rome and a member of its nobility, with roots in the *regio* of the Via Lata at the heart of the ancient city.[106] Hadrian had been raised by his uncle, Theodotus, who was doubtless a driving force in establishing and consolidating his nephew's career. Theodotus, the *Liber Pontificalis* said, was 'formerly consul and duke and, afterwards, *primicerius* of our holy Church'.[107] He was described similarly in an inscription at Sant'Angelo in Pescheria, which may date to 755; *Theodotus holim dux nunc primicerius s[an]c[t]ae sedis apostolicae*.[108] This has led many to argue that Theodotus was promoted to the rank of *primicerius notariorum* in charge of the papal chancery, and thus that he had set aside his secular status to become the most powerful cleric in the pope's administration.[109] But another near contemporary text from Santa Maria Antiqua, which stood not far away in the Forum at the foot of the

---

[104] Scholz, *Politik*, 78–89.

[105] *LP* 97.1–2. On the extent of aristocratic control of the papacy and its key offices in the mid and later eighth century, see T. S. Brown, *Gentlemen and Officers: Imperial Administration and Aristocratic Power in Byzantine Italy, AD 554–800* (London, 1984), 185–6; F. Hartmann, *Hadrian I (772–795). Frühmittelalterliches Adelspapsttum und die Lösung Roms vom Byzantinischen Kaiser,* Päpste und Papsttum, 34 (Stuttgart, 2006), 37–79, esp. 38–9; F. Marazzi, 'Aristocrazia e società (seculi VI–XI)', in A. Vauchez, ed., *Roma medievale* (Bari, 2001), 41–69.

[106] *LP* 97.1. On the seven urban *regions*, see L. Duchesne, *Scripta minora. Etudes de topographie romaine et d géographie ecclésiastique* (Rome, 1913); P. Toubert, ' "Scrinium" et "Palatium": la formation de la bureaucratie romano-pontificale aux VIIIe–IXe siècles', in *Roma nell'alto Medioevo*, SSCI, 48.1 (Spoleto, 2001), 57–118, at 69–70; L. Pani Ermini, 'Forma Urbis: lo spazio urbano tra VI e IX secolo', *Roma nell'alto Medioevo*, 48.1 (2001), 255–324, tav. I, and L. Pani Ermini, ed., *Christiana loca: lo spazio cristiano nella Roma del primo millennio*, 2 vols (Rome, 2000), ii, 174–7. The exact boundaries are not known for sure, but the 'region of the via Lata' may have been Regio VI where Sant'Angelo in Pescheria, and San Marco (for which Hadrian held a special affection (*LP* 97.2 and 97.94–5)) are located. On Hadrian's rural estates in Tuscia, at *Capracorum*, see *LP* 97.54 and 69.

[107] *LP* 97.2 says that Theodotus had been 'dudum consule et duce, postmodum vero primicerio sanctae nostrae ecclesiae'.

[108] The inscription is dated 'Anno ab initio mundi 6263' in the time of Stephen *iunioris*, referring probably to 755. For the inscription, see *MEC* I, no. XIV.3. Discussion: Duchesne, ed., *LP* I, 524, n. 2 (arguing the case for 770); *CBCR* ii, 65, 73; O. Bertolini, 'Per la storia delle diaconie romane', *Archivio della Società romana di Storia patria*, 70 (1947), 1–145, at 26; Hartmann, *Hadrian I*, 41; M. Maskarinec, *City of Saints: Rebuilding Rome in the Early Middle Ages* (Philadelphia, PA, 2018), 94, 181–2, and fig. 3 (all arguing for 755).

[109] Bertolini, 'Per la storia delle diaconie romane', 25. See also Davis, *Lives of the Eighth-Century Popes*, 52, 123, n. 3, and Noble, *Republic*, 197, 219–22.

Palatine, suggests that—initially at least—Theodotus held a different office in the service of the Church, retaining all the while his status as a layman.[110] The text is painted around a donor portrait of Theodotus, who is shown offering a model of the church.[111] He is paired on the same panel with a portrait of Pope Zacharias (741–52) demonstrating his closeness to the incumbent pope; each man sports a square nimbus, probably indicating that he was alive when the donation was made and the portraits commissioned. The inscription around the head of Theodotus says that he was *prim[iceri]o defensorum et dispensatore*.[112] At this point, then, Theodotus was the senior lawyer in the papal curia and chief among the seven regional *defensores* charged with protecting the legal rights of Church properties as well as the poor, widows, and orphans of the city, judging cases, concluding wills and contracts, and administering

---

[110] There is debate about whether there was one high ranking official called Theodotus in Rome at this time, or two, because the *primicarius notariorum* was a clerical official and the *primicerius defensorum* a secular one: see G. Savio, *Monumenta onomastica romana medii aevi (X–XII sec.)*, 5 vols (Rome, 1999), ii, no. 035908–9 (s.v. Deodatus); Toubert, ' "Scrinium" et "Palatium" ', 73 (with bibliography); Brown, *Gentlemen and Officers*, 172, n. 14. Hartmann squares the circle by arguing that there was a single man of this name who held these offices in sequence, becoming a cleric and *primicerius* of the notaries only in 755 ('nunc', as per the inscription at Sant'Angelo), holding that office until Christopher took over some time before 765; Hartmann, *Hadrian I*, 40, n. 16, and 56–8. Brown argued that, '[given] the secular outlook of many church administrators it is misleading to posit a rigid division between clergy and laity. Rather the lay aristocracy came to see its infiltration of this powerful ecclesiastical corporation as the best way of retaining its leadership'; *Gentlemen and Officers*, 186. The other, more economical, possibility is that the single-word designation—*primicerius*—in the *LP* and at Sant'Angelo referred only to the secular role of *primicerius defensorum* and that Theodotus only ever held that office (see below, n. 112, for the reading of the key word in the inscription at Santa Maria Antiqua). The title *primicerius defensorum* is attested also in the first of the Roman *ordines* (late seventh century) which has many references to the *primicerius defensor* working alongside the *primicerius notariorum*; M. Andrieu, *Les ordines Roman du Haut Moyen Âge*, ii: *Les Textes (Ordines I–XIII)* (Louvain, 1948), 41 (and n. 11 for a discussion of the inscription) and *Ordo* I, chs 32, 68, 69, 74, 79, 81, 98, 113.

[111] E. Tea, *La basilica di S. Maria Antiqua* (Milan, 1937), 222; *CBCR* ii, 250; J. Osborne, *Rome in the Eighth Century: A History in Art* (Cambridge, 2020), 95–136. The best reproduction is in W. de Grüneisen, *Sainte Marie Antique avec le concours de Huelsen, Giorgis, Federici, David* (Rome, 1911), pl. IC.xxxviii, and for the text, 118–21, 419 (fig. 334) and 446, no. XI.1.

[112] + [...t]HEODOTVS PRIM[iceri]O DEFENSORVM/ET D[isp]ENSATORE S[an]C[ta]E D[e]I/GENETR[ic]IS SENPERQVE/BIRGO MARIA QVI APPELLATVR/ANTIQ<u>A. This painted inscription is now faded, but was legible and photographed when uncovered; the sharpest image is in Grüneisen, *Sainte Marie Antique*, Pl. IC.xxxviii, but see also the plate in the supplement to Grüneisen's volume by V. Federici, *Album Epigraphique. Supplément au chapitre: 'Epigraphie de l'Eglise Sainte-Marie-Antique'* (Rome, 1911), pl. IX.1 and *MEC* I, tav. XXXIV.3. The reading of the key word is contested: there is a contraction line above the whole of the word PRIMO (it lies just above the frame of the painting) suggesting that the word should be expanded, just as over the letters SCE DI in the line below, but there are also medial punctus points on either side of the word which in other contexts would indicate a numeral. See also S. J. Lucey, 'Art and Socio-Cultural Identity in Early Medieval Rome: The Patrons of Santa Maria Antiqua', in E. Ó Carragáin and C. L. Neuman de Vegvar, eds, *Roma Felix—Formation and Reflections of Early Medieval Rome* (Aldershot, 2007), 139–59, fig. 6.2–3 and M. Costambeys, 'Pope Hadrian I and Santa Maria Antiqua: Liturgy and Patronage in the Late Eighth Century', in E. Rubery, G. Bordi, and J. Osborne, eds, *Santa Maria Antiqua: The Sistine Chapel of the Early Middle Ages* (London, 2021), 373–83, at 375 and fig. 1.

vacant bishoprics and patrimonial lands.[113] As *dispensator* he oversaw the distribution of welfare at the *diaconia* of Santa Maria, and may well have had the same role at Sant'Angelo, where the dedication inscription goes on to describe him as 'father (*pater*) of that venerable deaconry', noting too that he had built that church *a solo*, 'for the sake of his soul and the redemption of all his sins'. There are two other portraits of Theodotus in the chapel at Santa Maria Antiqua, leaving viewers in no doubt about his patronage of that place; once he is shown kneeling and offering candles to saints Julitta and Quirinus, and once more, clearly depicted as a layman, he is accompanied by his wife and two children (one a boy, the other a girl) standing either side of the Virgin and Child, emphasising both his secular status as well as the aspiration of his donation.

Theodotus' nephew, Hadrian, had entered the ranks of the clergy under Paul I, and was promoted by him to the key office of notary of one of Rome's *regiones* and to the rank of subdeacon; Stephen III promoted him again, to the duties of a deacon. It is possible that in all three offices he served the same *regio* of the city, and, if this had been the same as where his uncle had been *primicerius defensor*, the family would have been able to consolidate a very significant local powerbase within the city with local control of the urban interests of the Church and effective oversight of the secular rule of the city. What is more, the synod of 769 granted the seven regional deacons the right to participate in papal elections, and—crucially for Hadrian—eligibility for election to the papacy itself.[114]

Hadrian's background as a native of Rome and a member of the city's aristocracy gave him considerable advantages when dealing with the complex factional politics that preceded his election and which dogged his first two years in office. The opening section of his *Life* in the *Liber Pontificalis* provide a very detailed but partisan account of Hadrian's actions in 772 and his efforts to destroy the faction of Paul Afiarta which had weakened Stephen's hand in his dealings with Desiderius.[115] Desiderius continued to apply military pressure on Roman territories and tried to force Hadrian to baptise the sons of Carloman and to anoint them as kings. This was a direct challenge to Charles and his dynastic ambitions which he could not ignore. Combined with the threat of an imminent of a Lombard attack on the city of Rome itself, Hadrian wrote in secret to Charles to ask for military support from the Franks. When two embassies failed to persuade Desiderius to comply, 'God-protected Charles, great king (*a Deo protectus Carolus magnus rex*)' mustered his armies and set out for Italy late in the summer of 773.

---

[113] Toubert, '"Scrinium" et "Palatium"' 73, n. 41, 99, n. 11, 104–5 (referring to this role as *primus defensor*); L. Nees, *Early Medieval Art* (Oxford, 2002), 147–9, and Noble, *Republic*, 221–2, 233.

[114] By the late eighth century, the seven regional deacons were known as 'cardinal deacons'; Noble, *Republic*, 218.

[115] *LP* 97.4–44; Davis, tr., *Lives of the Eighth-Century Popes*, 124–42.

Charlemagne's assault on the Lombard kingdom and the siege of Pavia, which lasted through the winter of 773, precipitated the capitulation of many northern cities to Hadrian.[116] The military campaign also had a strong dynastic motive; as Charlemagne's forces approached Pavia, Desiderius sent Carloman's widow and young sons to Verona which was 'the strongest of the Lombard cities' and out of the direct line of the Frankish assault. Charlemagne's response was unambiguous. According to the *Liber Pontificalis*, he sent for his new young queen, Hildegard, and their sons to join the besieging army at Pavia, and then went himself to Verona with a battalion to capture his nephews. The presence of Charlemagne's queen, Hildegard (who was pregnant again) and her children was a calculated insult; Charles was parading his fecund, favoured wife and her legitimate offspring in front of those who had been ejected from the fold of the Carolingian dynasty.

These, then, were the circumstances of Hadrian's election and early months in office: Rome was restless following the messy, factional struggles that had spilled over in the aftermath of the downfall of the *transgressor* Constantine, and Lombard armies threatened the city. At Hadrian's request, Frankish warriors crossed the Alps in unprecedented numbers. But Hadrian could not have been entirely certain of the intentions of the young and ambitious warrior king who led them, especially when—leaving his armies encamped outside the walls of Pavia—he turned south and headed for Rome, ostensibly to pray at the shrine of the apostle, St Peter.[117]

---

[116] *LP* 97.32–3; Davis, tr., *Lives of the Eighth-Century Popes*, 136–8.
[117] Scholz, *Politik*, 80.

Figure 1.1 Charlemagne's epitaph for Pope Hadrian I in the portico of St Peter's in the Vatican with its seventeenth-century frame. Photo: Author, with kind permission of the Reverenda Fabbrica di San Pietro in Vaticano, Rome.

1

Renaissance Rome

Hadrian's Epitaph in New St Peter's

INTRODUCTION

Charlemagne's epitaph for Pope Hadrian I is found today inside the portico of the basilica of St Peter's in the Vatican.[1] It is placed high up on the exterior of the façade, between the Door of Death and the Door of Good and Evil that open into the nave (Figure 1.1). The inscription was placed there in October 1619 to decorate Carlo Maderno's atrium that completed the enormous new church. This new building was begun in 1506 when Pope Julius II (1503–13) started work to renew the ancient, fourth-century basilica thought, by long tradition, to have been commissioned by Constantine I (306–37), the first Christian Roman emperor, over an earlier shrine to St Peter.[2] The placement of this eighth-century inscription at the entrance to the new church at St Peter's is one that demands close attention in terms of the symbolic architecture of that Renaissance building. Hadrian's epitaph is a piece of textual *spolia* and Maderno's decision to redisplay it in such a prominent location should be understood

---

[1] C. Franzoni, 'Epitaph of Hadrian I (795)', in *BSPV* I.i (*Atlas*), 204–5 (no. 262), 233–5 (fig. 191–6), 286, II.ii (*Notes*), 494–6 (no. 262); G. Cascioli, *Epigrapfi Cristiane nell'area vaticana VI–X secolo*, Quaderno d'archivio 9 (Vatican City, 2014), 94–6.

[2] *CBCR* v, 165–279; A. Arbeiter, *Alt-St. Peter in Geschichte und Wissenschaft: Abfolge der Bauten, Rekonstruktion, Architekturprogramm* (Berlin, 1988), 75–192; G. Grimaldi, *Descrizione della basilica antica di S. Pietro in Vaticano: codice Barberini latino 2733*, ed. R. Niggl, Codices e Vaticanis Selecti, 32 (Vatican City, 1972), 395–6. For a summary of the arguments against Constantine as *auctor* of the basilica, see G. W. Bowersock, 'Peter and Constantine', in W. Tronzo, ed., *St. Peter's in the Vatican* (Cambridge, 2005), 5–15; Bowersock's arguments in favour of Constans (337–50), finds some support in R. Gem, 'From Constantine to Constans: The Chronology of the Construction of Saint Peter's Basilica', in *OSPR*, 35–64 and A. Logan, 'Who Built Old St Peter's? The Evidence of the Inscriptions and Mosaics', *Vigiliae Christianae*, 75 (2020), 1–27. An argument for Constantius II (337–61) as the prime instigator of St Peter's basilica has been proposed by R. Westall, 'Constantius II and the Basilica of St Peter in Vatican', *Historia. Zeitschrift für Alte Geschichte*, 64.2 (2015), 205–42. Restating the case for Constantine's initiative, see P. Liverani, 'Saint Peter's, Leo the Great and the Leprosy of Constantine', *Papers of the British School at Rome* 76 (2008), 155–72, and 'Old St Peter's and the Emperor Constans? A Debate with G. W. Bowersock', *Journal of Roman Archaeology*, 28 (2015), 485–504. A useful synthesis is in Brandenburg, Ballardini, and Theones, *Saint Peter's*, 9–35.

alongside his use of architectural *spolia*, carefully salvaged from the remains of the old basilica.[3] Like Filarete's great bronze doors or the antique columns from the old nave that Maderno reused in the new portico, Hadrian's epitaph symbolised the institutional stability of the papacy as well as the physical continuity of the ancient basilica into the new building.

Originally, however, the epitaph had stood elsewhere, deep within the fourth-century basilica against the western wall of the south transept. The orientation of St Peter's basilica is eccentric: the Vatican hill lies on the west bank of the Tiber and, since the basilica faces the city, it is thus orientated with the apse and high altar at the west and the main entrance at the east. The southern arm of the transept is, therefore, on the left as the visitor enters the church. Hadrian's epitaph is first described *in situ* in the twelfth century by Peter Mallius who wrote a description of the basilica for Pope Alexander III (1159–81). Mallius, a canon of the basilica, composed his account in the form of an itinerary, leading his readers on a journey around the sights of the basilica.[4] He said that 'the oratory of the Lord Pope Hadrian I of blessed memory' was between that dedicated to the first four popes named Leo and that of Urban II (1088–99). Urban's tomb stood next to the oratory of Pope Paul I (757–67), dedicated to the Virgin, which was itself adjacent to a bronze door leading to the oratories for saints Petronilla and Andrew that were in the two late antique rotundas named after them just to the south of the basilica. This sequence makes it clear that Hadrian's oratory stood midway down the southern arm of the transept.

Mallius also quoted the first part of the text of Hadrian's epitaph, implying that it could be read at the oratory. His work informed all later descriptions of the basilica including the late sixteenth-century account of the antique basilica by Tiberio Alfarano who wrote when much of the old building had been destroyed.[5] Alfarano's description was written between *c*.1570 and 1582. It is also arranged as a tour around the liturgical sights of the basilica and was complemented by a plan that was drawn up in

---

[3] L. Bosman, *The Power of Tradition: Spolia in the Architecture of St. Peter's in the Vatican* (Hilversum, 2004); D. Kinney, 'Spolia', in Tronzo, ed., *St. Peter's*, 16–47. On Maderno's portico, see H. Hibbard, *Carlo Maderno and Roman Architecture 1580–1630* (London, 1971), 162–3. On Filarete's doors, see M. Beltramini, 'Porta (1433–45)', in BSPV I.i (Atlas), 252–71 and II.ii (Notes), 483–90, and R. Glass, 'Filarete's Renovation of the Porta Argentea at Old St. Peter's', in *OSPR*, 348–70. On Maderno's epigraphic programme, including the reuse of ancient inscriptions, see also F. De Rubeis, 'Verba volant, scripta manent. Epigrafia e fama', in I. Lori Sanfilippo and A. Rigoni, eds, *Fama e Publica Vox nel Medioevo, Atti del convegno di studio svoltosi in occasione della XXI edizione del Premio internazionale Ascoli Piceno, Palzzo dei Capitani, 3–5 dicembre, 2009* (Rome, 2011), 191–210.

[4] Peter Mallius, 'Historia Basilicae antiquae S. Petri Apostoli in Vaticano', *AASS* Iunii vii, col. 34A–52, at 40B or 'Opusculum Historiae Sacrae ad Beatissimum Patrem Alexandrum III Pont. Max.'; VZ, iii, 382–442, at 393.

[5] Tiberius Alpharanus, *De Basilicae Vaticanae Antiquissima et Nova Structura*, ed. C. M. Cerrati (Vatican City, 1914). For Alfarano's knowledge of the sylloge of Mallius and Vegio, see F. Della Schiava, 'Per la storia della basilica Vaticana nel '500: una nuova silloge di Tiberio Alfarano a Catania', *Italia Medioevale e Umanistica*, 48 (2007), 257–82.

1571 and engraved in 1590.[6] Alfarano's measured plan showed both the outline of the new church and, in more detail, the old basilica and its oratories (Figures 1.2 and 1.3). This plan, and his description that accompanied it, placed Hadrian's oratory (no. 15) against the west wall of the south transept, in the space next to the marble columns that screened the outer room, known as the exedra, from the main body of the transept. The Leonine oratory was a little to the north (no. 14), and Urban II's tomb (no. 16), and Paul I's oratory to the Virgin (no. 17) stood further south, within the exedra.[7]

This plan accords with the eighth- and ninth-century accounts of St Peter's basilica. The biography of Pope Paul I (757–67) in the *Liber Pontificalis* and an independent, late eighth-century account of the internal arrangement of this part of the basilica that was probably compiled during Hadrian's lifetime, confirm this as the location of the Leonine oratory and Paul I's altar to the Virgin, as does a bull of Hadrian himself dated December 781.[8] A bull issued in 854 by Pope Leo IV (847–55) noted that an

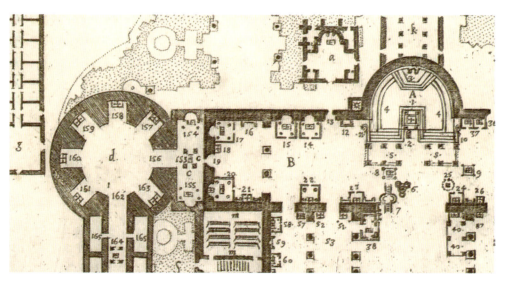

FIGURE 1.2 Detail of the apse and south transept of the old basilica at St Peter's from the 1590 engraving of Alfarano's plan. Hadrian's chapel is marked as no. 15, the Leonine chapel is no. 14 and the remains of S. Martino are labelled 'a'. Photo: By kind permission of the Reverenda Fabbrica di San Pietro in Vaticano, Rome.

---

[6] Brandenburg, Ballardini, and Theones, *Saint Peter's*, 38–43, fig. 7–8 (where the oratories are numbered differently to Alfarano's original).

[7] R. McKitterick, J. Osborne, C. M. Richardson, and J. Story, 'Introduction', in *OSPR*, 1–20, at 18–20 and foldout. J.-C. Picard, 'Étude sur l'emplacement des tombes des papes du III au Xe siècle', *Mélanges d'archeologie et d'histoire*, 81 (1969), 725–82, at 767; Borgolte, *Petrusnachfolge und Kaiserimitation*, Abb. 7.

[8] *LP* 95.6; Davis, tr., *Lives of the Eighth-Century Popes*, 84; G. B. de Rossi, *La Roma sotterranea cristiana*, 3 vols (Rome, 1864–77), i, 138–40; 'Notitia ecclesiarum urbis Romae'; VZ, ii, 67–99, at 94–9 and P. Geyer and O. Cuntz, eds, *Itineraria et alia Geographica. Itineraria Hierosolymitana. Itineraria Romana. Geographica*,

32 CHARLEMAGNE AND ROME

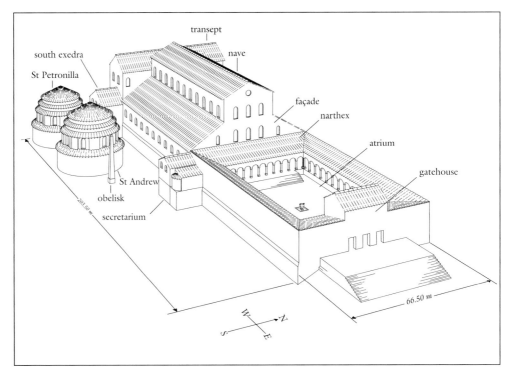

FIGURE 1.3 Reconstruction of Old St Peter's. Drawing: © Lacey Wallace.

oratory dedicated to Sant'Adriano stood next to that of Leo I with a doorway between them leading out of the basilica.[9] The biography of Leo IV in the *Liber Pontificalis* also records the donation of rich textiles to the individual oratories in the south

---

CCSL 175 (Turnhout, 1965), 303–11, at 310–11 (also called the *Enchiridion de sacellis et altaribus basilicae vaticana* in *ICUR* II.i, 224–8), on which see below, Chapter 4, 170–5. Hadrian's bull for Fulrad is in the ninth-century letter book of the abbots of Saint-Denis, BnF, Lat. 2777, fols 46v–47r, see A. Stoclet, 'Les établissements francs à Rome au VIIIe siècle: "Hospitale intus basilicam beati Petru, domus Nazarii, schola Francorum" et palais de Charlemagne', in M. Sot, ed., *Haut moyen âge. Culture, éducation et société: Études offertes à Pierre Riché* (Nanterre, 1990), 231–47, at 245–6, and Bischoff, *Katalog*, no. 4229. On this manuscript, see also R. Grosse, 'La Collection de formules de Saint-Denis (Bibl. nat. Fr., Lat. 2777): un dossier controversé', *Bibliothèque de l'École des chartes*, 172 (2014), 185–97.

[9] The extant copy of the 854 bull dates to 1053 and the pontificate of Leo IX; G. Marini, *I Papiri Diplomatici* (Rome, 1805), 14–16, 221–2 (no. 13); L. Schiaparelli, 'Le carte antiche dell'Archivio Capitolare di S. Pietro in Vaticano', *Archivio della Reale Società Romana di Storia Patria*, 24 (1901), 393–496, at 432–7; G. Ferrari, *Early Roman Monasteries: Notes for the History of the Monasteries and Convents at Rome from the V through the X Century* (Vatican City, 1957), 230–40, at 236; Stoclet, 'Les établissements francs', 235; R. Davis, tr., *The Lives of the Ninth-Century Popes* (Liber Pontificalis), Translated Texts for Historians, 20 (Liverpool, 1995), 156–7, n. 156. For the translation of Leo I's relics in 688, see *LP* 86.12; R. Davis, tr., *The Book of Pontiffs (Liber Pontificalis): The Ancient Biographies of the First Ninety Roman Bishops to AD 715*, Translated Texts for Historians, 6 (Liverpool, 1989), 88. For its refurbishment in the mid-ninth century, see *LP* 105.31; Davis, tr., *Lives of the Ninth-Century Popes*, 123 and n. 53. For its refurbishment under Paschal II in the early twelfth century, and its excavation by Gregory XIII in 1580, see Grimaldi, *Descrizione*, ed. Niggl, 232–9.

transept, including a cloth decorated with wheels, human figures, chevrons, and a gold studded cross to the oratory of Sant'Adriano.[10] Perhaps during his lifetime Pope Hadrian had endowed an oratory at St Peter's dedicated to his patronymic saint, the martyr Sant'Adriano of Nicomedia (as he had done elsewhere in the city)[11] and intended this also to be his own burial place: this was certainly how later commentators interpreted the arrangement of the oratory and the epitaph.[12] An alternative explanation is that by Leo IV's pontificate the dedication had mutated from commemorating the pope to a saint of the same name; Leo's *Vita* similarly records an oratory nearby dedicated to a martyr named St Pastor, although it had been known previously as the *Oratorium Pastoris* (the Altar of the Shepherd), that is, of St Peter himself.[13]

For the Carolingian patrons of the inscription, Hadrian's oratory was in a powerfully symbolic part of the basilica, standing between the *confessio* of the Apostle Peter at the high altar and the oratory of Petronilla in the early fifth-century imperial mausoleum immediately to the south of the transept.[14] Petronilla was believed to have been the daughter of St Peter and, ever since the discovery and translation of her relics to the rotunda in 757, the Carolingians had claimed her as their special patron in Rome.[15] Late in the Middle Ages her chapel was known as the *Cappella del Re di Francia*.[16] Beyond Petronilla's rotunda was another dedicated to St Peter's brother, Andrew (the rotunda of Sant'Andrea). Hadrian's oratory, therefore, stood amid the places commemorating the relics of St Peter's family.

In both old and new St Peter's the significance of the Hadrian's epitaph was enhanced by its location, firstly in the south transept and later at the main entrance to the church. It was, however, highly unusual among monuments from the ancient basilica in being translated from the old building and redisplayed within the superstructure of

---

[10] *LP* 105.36–37; Davis, tr., *Lives of the Ninth-Century Popes*, 125.

[11] For Hadrian's gifts to the church of Sant'Adriano (dedicated to the third-century martyr by Pope Honorius 625–38), see *LP* 97.51, 73, 81; Davis, tr., *Lives of the Eighth-Century Popes*, 145–6, 160, 165, the latter recording the establishment of a deaconry there. For the identification of the deaconry of Sant'Adriano with the ancient *Curia* in the forum, see R. Lanciani, 'L'aula e gli uffici del senato Romano', *Atti della reale accademia dei Lincei, Memorie della classe di scienze morali, storiche e filologiche*, 3rd ser., 11 (1882–3), 13–14. See also, Picard, 'Études', 767, n. 3.

[12] In 1192, Romanus, also a canon at St Peter's, amplified Mallius' description of Hadrian's tomb by adding that the oratory contained an altar to the martyr St Hadrian; *AASS* Junii vii, col. 40B; Davis, tr., *Lives of the Ninth-Century Popes*, 125, n. 58; Della Schiava, 'Per la storia', 265–6.

[13] *LP* 105.43; Davis, tr., *Lives of the Ninth-Century Popes*, 129, n. 73. See also J. Story, 'The Carolingians and the Oratory of Peter the Shepherd', in *OSPR*, 257–73 and below, Chapter 4, 175–7.

[14] On the fifth-century mausoleum, see McEvoy, 'Mausoleum of Honorius', 119–36.

[15] Alfarano, *DBV*, 135–7; *LP* 95.3; Davis, tr., *Lives of the Eighth-Century Popes*, 81, where he notes that some later calendars record the date of the translation as 8 October, that is the day before the feast of St Denis, the Carolingians' patron saint in Paris; Borgolte, *Petrusnachfolge*, 109; P. Liverani, *La topografia antica del Vaticano* (Vatican City, 1999), 135–6, no. 60; *CD* ii, 467–8, 576–7. See also Weil-Garris Brandt, 'Michelangelo's *Pietà*', 78.

[16] *CD* ii, 577.

the new one. In the early seventeenth century, many other inscriptions from the old basilica—mostly fragmentary—were inserted into the walls of the papal grotto beneath the new building. The construction of the grotto was not part of any of the early designs of that structure and was proposed only in 1590 as a response to the decision to raise and pave the nave floor, and to remodel below it the sacred space around the tomb of the Apostle. The decision to use these new underground spaces as a place to display sepulchral and epigraphic remains from the old basilica arose as a consequence of a subsequent decision made by Pope Paul V (1605–21) at the beginning of his pontificate to dismantle what was left of the fourth-century basilica and to finish the new church on a longitudinal plan with another nave and portico.[17] The grotto provided an appropriate resting-place for human and artistic relics from the ancient basilica that was both practical and symbolic, underpinning the new church physically and spiritually.

Charlemagne's epitaph for Pope Hadrian was treated differently. It is remarkable that this Carolingian monument survived the protracted and contentious demolition of old St Peter's complete and largely undamaged. When so much else was displaced, destroyed, or broken, the survival of this early medieval inscription, as well as the decision to redisplay it in the upper part of the church rather than the grotto, requires explanation. It reveals much about the evolution of papal attitudes through the sixteenth century towards the authority of the old basilica and the means by which its heritage might assist contemporary spiritual, political, and artistic objectives.[18] The story of the process by which Hadrian's epitaph came to be removed from its original location in the south transept of old St Peter's and redisplayed in the portico of the new church reflects the long-drawn out sequence of decisions about the design of the new basilica, as well as the changing attitudes of papal patrons and their architects to the significance of the fourth-century building and its contents. More broadly, the actions taken to preserve Hadrian's epitaph also fit into the upsurge of Counter Reformation interest in textual and archaeological relics that could support papal claims to temporal lordship and spiritual authority over Christendom.[19]

RECALLING CHARLEMAGNE

Charlemagne's epitaph for Pope Hadrian I was translated into new St Peter's because it reflected the aesthetic, spiritual, and political needs of the Renaissance and Counter Reformation popes; it was a thing of beauty that also demonstrated unambiguously

---

[17] V. Lanzani, *The Vatican Grottoes*, Roma Sacra. Guide to the Churches in the Eternal City, Itineraries 26–7 (Vatican City, 2003), 12–15.
[18] De Rubeis, 'Verba volant', 200–10.
[19] As discussed by S. Ditchfield, *Liturgy, Sanctity and History in Tridentine Italy: Pietro Maria Campi and the Preservation of the Particular* (Cambridge, 1995).

the antiquity of royal and imperial devotion to the papacy. Charlemagne's reputation had long since become the stuff of legend and his eulogy to Pope Hadrian was thus a powerful exemplar for later rulers who found themselves at St Peter's shrine. It is no surprise therefore that kings and popes often recalled Charlemagne's history to suit their own contemporary circumstances. On at least two occasions in the early sixteenth century, the papacy invoked Charlemagne's reputation and his links with Italy in a way that may have contributed to the preservation of Hadrian's epitaph in this formative (and destructive) phase of the St Peter's project.

Between 1515 and 1519, the relationship with France was the major concern of the papacy's foreign policy; it was no coincidence, therefore, that this was also the period when design and construction work at St Peter's was focused on the new *Cappella del Re di Francia* that was to be incorporated into the south arm of the new basilica.[20] In 1515 Francis I had succeeded his cousin Louis XII as king of France and inherited the complex diplomacy that had characterised French foreign policy in Italy in the late fifteenth and early sixteenth centuries.[21] Charles VIII's invasion of Italy in 1494, laying claim to the kingdom of Naples, had unbalanced the dynastic and political equilibrium of the region. The Borgia pope, Alexander VI, and his cardinals were complicit in the ever-changing network of alliances that eventually saw the Medici thrown out of Florence and the French army out of Italy. As cardinal, Julius II had cultivated the French in opposition to Alexander, and on his accession to the papal throne in 1503 he initially allied the papacy with France before campaigning to restore papal territory that had been alienated under Borgia rule. Once papal rule had been consolidated Julius turned against the French, and by the end of 1512 drove them out of Italy. Francis I revived French claims to Naples and Milan, defeating papal and imperial forces at Marignano in September 1515. But later that year he reached agreement with Julius' successor, Leo X who ceded Parma and Piacenza to the French and established a concordat at Bologna that settled the contentious issue of control of French ecclesiastical offices, extending royal control over the Church in France. The years between 1516 and 1519 saw an unprecedented level of co-operation between the two powers, since Francis needed papal support to settle French dynastic claims in Italy and Leo looked to Francis as the potential leader of a crusade that he proclaimed in 1518 against Selim I and the resurgent forces of the Ottoman Turks.

This was the geopolitical context for Leo X's grandiose ambitions at St Peter's. He had appointed Raphael as chief architect in 1514, and reportedly met with him daily to discuss the project that Raphael estimated would cost more than a million gold

---

[20] Liverani, *Topografia antica*, 135, n. 8; A. Brodini, 'Michelangelo e la volta della cappella del re di Francia in San Pietro', *Annali di architettura*, 17 (2005), 115–26, at 116.

[21] For what follows, see J. Guillaume, 'François Ier en Charlemagne. Réflexions sur un portrait', in Frommel and Winner, eds, *"Il se rendit en Italie"*, 159–62, at 159–60; Weil-Garris Brandt, 'Michelangelo's *Pietà*', 78–80.

ducats.[22] Financial constraints meant that little progress was made on actual construction and the talents of his architects were manifest mainly in the myriad of plans drawn up for the site. Nevertheless, the entente with France precipitated the demolition of the imperial mausoleum that had been built by the Emperor Honorius for his wife Maria (d. 408) that had contained the shrine of St Petronilla (and latterly also, for a time, Michelangelo's *Pietà*) at the southern end of the south transept, and focused attention on the design and construction of the southern arm to act as a new, improved *Cappella del Re di Francia*.[23]

Raphael's creative energies were focused in these years on embellishment of the Vatican palace; especially relevant is the decorative programme executed between 1514 and 1517 for the papal dining room known now as the *Stanza dell'incendio*.[24] The walls depict four scenes of events from the ninth century derived from accounts in the *Liber Pontificalis*: the oath of Leo III (800), the coronation of Charlemagne (800), the fire in the Borgo (847), and the battle of Ostia against the Saracens (849).[25] The key actor in these scenes is the pope, either Leo III (795–816) or Leo IV (847–55) each time thinly disguised as Leo X, and each of the historical events was an allegory for a recent incident. Thus, the 'battle of Ostia' referred to Leo X's attempts to organise a new crusade against the Turks, and the 'Fire' scene showed the pope in the *loggia* at St Peter's extinguishing the flames with the sign of the cross, reminding viewers of the defeat of heretics and schismatics.[26] An inscription underneath the 'Oath' dates that fresco to 19 March 1517 and reminded viewers that *Dei non hominum est episcopos iudicare* ('God, not man, is judge of bishops'). This alludes to the principle of papal supremacy that had been reiterated by the eleventh Lateran Council, which had met three months earlier in December 1516.[27] The 'Coronation' scene recalls the Concordat of Bologna of October 1515 in which Francis I had committed himself to the protection of the Church (Figure 1.4). An inscription labels Charlemagne as 'the sword and shield of the Church' and he is shown kneeling before Leo III with his head bowed in submission; the king's face is unmistakably that of Francis I.[28]

---

[22] C. Theones, 'Renaissance St. Peter's', in W. Tronzo, ed., *St. Peter's in the Vatican* (Cambridge, 2005), 64–93, at 83.

[23] Weil-Garris Brandt, 'Michelangelo's *Pietà*', 87; *CD* ii, 467, with reference to the discovery of Empress Maria's tomb in 1544 during the demolition of the pavement in the rotunda.

[24] D. G. Cavallero, F. D'Amico, and C. Strinati, *L'Arte in Roma nel secolo XVI*, ii: *Le pittura e la scultura* (Bologna, 1992), 83–6, and pl. LI–LIV. Letters to Simone Ciarla and Alfonso d'Este provide the date parameters.

[25] *LP* 98.21–2 (the 'Oath') *LP* 98.23 (the 'Coronation'); *LP* 105.20 (the 'Fire') and *LP* 105.51–2 (the 'Battle').

[26] Another scene in the adjoining Stanza di Elidoro shows the meeting of Pope Leo I and Attila in 452, which was probably substituted for Leo X's benefit after his accession; Cavallero et al., *L'Arte in Roma*, 84 and pl. XLIX.2.

[27] Cavallero et al., *L'Arte in Roma*, 86.

[28] Guillaume, 'François Ier en Charlemagne', 160; F. Mancinelli, 'L'incoronazione di Francesco I nella stanza dell'incendio di borgo', in Frommel and Winner, eds, *"Il se rendit en Italie"*, 163–72, esp. pl. LVI–VII.

FIGURE 1.4 Detail of Raphael's 'Coronation of Charlemagne' from the *Stanza dell'Incendio* in the Vatican palace. Photo: Reproduced with permission of Bildarchiv Preußischer Kulturbesitz, Berlin.

These frescos portray Leo X in idealised contexts, and served to reassure him of several things: that he was answerable to no one except God (the 'Oath'); that great princes obeyed him (the 'Coronation'); that he was a protector of Rome and all it symbolised (the 'Fire'); that he was conqueror of the infidel and heretics (the 'Battle'). The coincidence of Leo's name with that of two ninth-century predecessors provided a useful set of historical precedents and a convenient if contrived link with Charlemagne. A real connection with these ninth-century forebears, however, would have taken Leo to the south transept of the old basilica, where the oratory to popes Leo I–IV stood adjacent to that of Hadrian I (see Figure 1.2).

The idealised association that Leo X contrived with Charlemagne was trumped in 1522 when a new pope was elected under very different political circumstances. After the death of Leo X in December 1521, the Curia elected the cardinal bishop of Utrecht, Adrian Florensz Dedal, under pressure from a new Holy Roman Emperor, Charles V. Unusually, Dedal retained his baptismal name and became Hadrian VI.[29] He was the first non-Italian pope for generations, and the last 'German' to hold the office until the election of Benedict XVI in 2005. Hadrian had been tutor to the young Charles, and when elected was absent in Spain on the emperor's business. Once again, an Emperor Charles worked alongside a Pope Hadrian.

But this Hadrian's pontificate was short, unlike his eighth-century namesake, and he died in September 1523, twelve months after returning to Rome, and only eighteen months after his election. He was unpopular in Rome as a reform-minded foreigner and inquisitor, who cared little for patronage of the arts.[30] During his pontificate he paid scant attention to the progress of the new basilica, throwing his energies into combating Luther and the threat to Catholicism caused by the demands for Reformation, which had been catalysed in part by Leo X's issue of indulgences to pay for the rebuilding of St Peter's.[31] Hadrian VI had been Charles' chief inquisitor in Spain before his election, and as pope his energies were focused on combating the Lutheran heresy and initiating reforms to the Curia, whose abuses he recognised as a major cause of Protestant complaints. The papal bulls attributed to him are revealing, citing eighth-century precedents: just as Charlemagne and Hadrian I had conquered the pagan Saxons and brought right religion among them, so too would Charles V

---

[29] M. Verweij, ed., *De Paus uit de Lage Landen Adrianus VI, 1459–1523: catalogus bij de tentoonstelling ter gelegenheid van het 550ste geboortejaar van Adriaan van Utrecht*, Supplementa humanistica Lovaniensia, 27 (Leuven, 2009); M. Verweij, *Adrianus VI (1459–1523), de tragische paus uit de Nederlanden* (Antwerp, 2011).

[30] S. Bauer, *The Invention of Papal History: Onofrio Panvinio between Renaissance and Catholic Reform* (Oxford, 2020), 152–5.

[31] There are scant references in the records to work done at St Peter's during Hadrian VI's pontificate: e.g. AFSP, Arm. 24. F. 1, fol. 95r (recording repairs to a door by Guiliano Leno); see also the design for a fireplace bearing Hadrian's name, in Frommel and Adams, eds, *Architectural Drawings*, 111, 324 (Uff. 170A); also, S. Benedetti and G. Zander, eds, *L'Arte in Roma nel secolo XVI*, I: *L'architettura* (Bologna,1990), 169–75 and R. Lanciani, *Storia degli scavi di Roma e notizie intorno le collezioni romane di antichità*, 4 vols (Rome 1902), i, 214–19. On Hadrian VI's response to Luther, see S. H. Hendrix, *Luther and the Papacy: Stages in a Reformation Conflict* (Philadelphia, PA, 1981), 142.

and Hadrian VI fight the contagion of schism and Lutheran heresy amid the Saxons of their own day. An angry letter to Frederick III, Elector of Saxony, attributed to Hadrian VI, appealed directly to historical precedent, comparing the papal–imperial alliance of the eighth century with that of the sixteenth.[32]

> II.2 Et quid dicemus vobis, quam quod Galatis suis Paulus, O insensati, quis vos fascinavit veritati non obedire? currebatis bene: interrogate patres vestros, ac dicent vobis, maiores vestros et annuntiabunt vobis quod ab ea aetate quo uno eodemque tempore vixere Hadrianus Romanus Pontifex et Carolus ille Magnus Imperator, Saxoniae fidei plantatores, ad nostra usque et carissimi in Christo filii nostri Caroli tempora, avi et proavi vestri, atque adeo Saxones omnes, semper habiti estis veluti pacis amatores, fidei propugnatores et per omnia obedientiae pacifici filii, talesque ut non immerito Gregorius V, natione Saxo, olim Romanus Pontifex, Saxoniae ducem in Romani imperatoris constituerit electorem.

> And this we say to you, as Paul said to his Galatians, 'O senseless ones, who has bewitched you that you do not obey the truth? You have run well'. Question your forefathers, and they say to you; your elders, and they will remind you, that from that age when at one and the same time lived the Roman Pope Hadrian and Charles that Great Emperor, planters of the Saxons' faith, even up to our time and that of our Charles, most beloved son in Christ, and of your grandfather and great-grandfather, indeed truly all the Saxons have always been regarded as lovers of peace, fighters for the faith, and obedient peace-loving sons; such that it was not without cause that Gregory V [996–9], a Saxon by birth, once he was Roman pontiff, organised the election of a Saxon duke as Roman Emperor [Otto III].

> II.13 Vivunt una Pontifex Hadrianus et religiosissimus imperator Carolus, meus carissimus in Christo filius et alumnus... Non committemus ut, quos olim cum magno Carolo Hadrianus Pontifex in Christo genuerunt, nunc Hadrianus Pontifex et imperator Carolus, sub schismatico ac haeretico tyranno, haeresum ac schismatum sinamus interire contagione. Quare revertimini ad cor et resipiscite tu tiuque misere seducti saxones, nisi utrumque gladium, apostolicum simul et caesareum, velitis experiri.

> Pope Hadrian and the most religious Emperor Charles, my most beloved son in Christ and protégé, whose true Christian edict against the Lutheran treachery you have not been afraid to violate with grave offence and contempt for the imperial majesty, are living now. We will unite so that those [Saxons] whom Pope Hadrian with Charlemagne once brought to Christ we, Pope Hadrian and emperor Charles today, will not allow to die by the contagion of heresy and schism under a schismatic and heretical tyrant. Therefore return to your heart and recover your senses, you and your miserably seduced Saxons, unless you wish to feel both the apostolic sword and that of Caesar.

---

[32] A. Tomassetti, ed., *Bullarum Diplomatum et Privilegiorum Romanorum Pontificum*, 24 vols (Rome, 1857–1972), vi, 3–10: 'Satis et plus', ch. 2 and 13 (quoted here). The intemperate tone of the letter led some contemporaries of Frederick, as well as later Catholic historians, to consider it to have been the work of another individual, writing in the pope's name; see L. von Pastor, *The History of the Popes from the Close of the Middle Ages*, tr. R. F. Kerr, 17 vols (London 1908–33), ix, 132.

This bull makes no mention of the epitaph of Hadrian's namesake, but there is every reason to suppose it was known in Rome in the early 1520s; the coincidence of names of patron and pope, as well as his appreciation of historical precedent of their military and spiritual campaigns against the heretical Saxons, is far too great for it to have gone unnoticed. The new Hadrian might even have intended his namesake's epitaph to adorn his own tomb. But the enmity that he faced within Rome and the Curia meant that after his unexpected death in September 1523 he was given temporary burial in St Peter's in a modest brick tomb in the south-eastern corner of the nave, between the burials of Pius II and Pius III; *hic iacet impius inter pios* quipped a contemporary satirist.[33] Now recognised as the first 'Counter Reformation' pope, Hadrian VI was quickly forgotten in the haste to elect another Medici pope, Clement VII, who had more refined Renaissance tastes. Hadrian's remains were moved on 11 August 1533 to Santa Maria dell'Anima, the German national church in Rome, into a tomb commissioned from Baldassare Peruzzi by Cardinal van Enckevoirt, the only cardinal that he created during his pontificate.[34] The magnificent tomb, which reuses antique columns made from strikingly coloured *africano* and *rosso antico* marble, has a sculpted relief of Hadrian entering the city in August 1522 with a senator representing the city kneeling before him and cardinals following behind (Figure 1.5). The inscription laments the lost opportunity of Hadrian's pontificate; 'Alas, how much depends upon the age in which even the most virtuous of men is placed'.[35] At a time when so much else from St Peter's was being destroyed or dispersed, Hadrian's short pontificate provides a compelling political context for the preservation of one of the most important monuments of an earlier, Carolingian, Renaissance.

REBUILDING ST PETER'S: THE DEMOLITION OF OLD ST PETER'S AND THE FATE OF HADRIAN'S ORATORY

Scholars of architectural history have rightly regarded the project to renew St Peter's in the Vatican as one of the most important building projects of the Italian Renaissance, and the critical history of the various intersecting projects for the new church is as

---

[33] 'Here lies the impious between the pious'. Alfarano, *DBV*, 86, 191, no. 83; Borgolte, *Petrusnachfolge*, 295–6; Grimaldi, *Descrizione*, ed. Niggl, 407.

[34] F. Gregorovius, *The Tombs of the Popes: Landmarks in Papal History* (London, 1903), 104–6; J. Schmidlin, *Geschichte der deutschen Nationalkirche in Rom. S. Maria dell'Anima* (Freiburg, 1906), 279–90; C. L. Frommel, *Baldassare Peruzzi als Maler und Zeichner* (Vienna and Munich, 1967–8), 119–21, no. 86, and pl. LXIV–LXV; Cavallero et al., *L'Arte in Roma*, 356–8 and pl. CCXXVII; N. Hegener, '"VIVIT POST FVUNERA VIRTUS" Albrecht von Brandenburg, seine römischen Prokuratoren und Francesco Salviati in er Markgrafenkappel von S. Maria dell'Anima', in M. Matheus, ed., *S. Maria dell'Anima: Zur Geschichte einer 'deutschen' Stiftung in Rom*, Bibliothek des Deutschen Historischen Instituts in Rom, 121 (Berlin, 2010), 137–214, at 149.

[35] Verweij, ed., *De Paus uit*, 407–11, Ill. 54–5; 'Proh Dolor. Quantum refert in quae tempora cuiusque virtus incidat'.

FIGURE 1.5 The tomb of Pope Hadrian VI in S. Maria dell'Anima. The outer pair of columns are made of *africano* marble, the rarest and most expensive coloured marble in antiquity. Photo: Author.

complex as it is voluminous.[36] Consequently, the treatment of the old basilica during the construction of the new one is given less attention than it deserves, particularly in the early phases of the rebuilding project. But recent research, particularly on the use of architectural *spolia*, has shown that the architects who worked on the St Peter's project during the sixteenth and early seventeenth centuries had always to consider the physical, liturgical, and symbolic constrictions that the fabric and topography of the ancient building imposed on the design of the new. And although the architects' responses to these issues varied, there was never a period when they could disregard completely the extensive physical remains of the old building or the symbolic resonance of Constantine's temple to Christ's chief apostle. The old basilica was physically present throughout most of the sixteenth century while the construction of the new church was underway. The eastern end of the nave remained intact and functional, and even at the western end around the *confessio*, where the new construction work was focused initially, substantial portions of the fabric of the old building remained upright until at least the 1560s, and the apse and *confessio* itself were not demolished until 1592.[37] Indeed, there is now a consensus that it was not until very late in the St Peter's project that the complete removal of the ancient church became inevitable, that is, after the accession of Paul V in 1605. There are also good reasons to believe that the *muro divisorio*, constructed across the nave of the old basilica in 1538 to separate the construction site to the west from the intact eastern portion of the nave, was regarded by many as a permanent structure connecting the remains of the old edifice with the new one that was rising up over the shrine of the Apostle.[38]

Fifteenth-century plans

The building project that was initiated by Julius II in 1506 was one of the most important of the Renaissance both in architectural and in political terms: it consumed the attention of some of the most important artists of the era—Bramante, Raphael, Sangallo, and Michelangelo—and its exorbitant cost was such a drain on papal coffers that it became a political sore throughout the courts of Europe and an important trigger for the demands of many for a reformation of the Church.[39] But Julius was not the first pope to have realised the constraints of the antique basilica and to have attempted

---

[36] Useful summaries of the complex evidence can be found in C. L. Frommel, 'St. Peter's: The Early History', in H. A. Millon and V. Magnago Lampugnani, eds, *The Renaissance: From Brunelleschi to Michelangelo: The Representation of Architecture* (London, 1994), 398–423 and C. Thoenes, 'Renaissance St. Peter's', in Tronzo, ed., *St. Peter's in the Vatican*, 64–93, and the richly illustrated essay by Theones in Brandenberg, Ballardini, and Theones, *Saint Peter's*, 165–299.

[37] L. Rice, 'La coesistenza delle due basiliche', in G. Spagnesi, ed., *L'architettura della basilica di San Pietro: storia e costruzione* (Rome, 1997), 255–60.

[38] Bosman, *Power of Tradition*, 95.

[39] Thoenes, 'Renaissance St. Peter's', 83.

structural renewal. In the mid-fifteenth century Pope Nicholas V (1447–55) initiated a radical plan to modernise the basilica to fit the needs of the papacy, recently returned to Rome from its long exile in Avignon, and to transfer the Curia from the Lateran to residence at St Peter's.[40] Maffeo Vegio, an accomplished scholar and canon of St Peter's, talked of Nicholas' desire to create a *novum et ingens aedificium*, a 'new and huge building', that would serve contemporary ceremonial needs.[41] In order to create the space needed by a greatly extended papal entourage and clergy, Nicholas planned to replace the whole of the western end of the old basilica with a massive new choir and a transept that was as wide as the ancient church was long. From 1452 to 1454, substantial progress was made behind the old apse on the 'very high foundation walls' for the new choir, although construction work ceased before Nicholas' death in March 1455.[42] These substantial foundations remained in place for decades and were an important influence on later architects who had to decide whether to incorporate them into their own plans or to remove them altogether.[43]

The new choir and transept were intended to be a radical, long-term solution to the problem of overcrowding in St Peter's. But in the short-term, Nicholas ordered that the interior of the existing basilica be cleared out to create more space. This included the removal of many medieval chapels and monuments in the nave and transepts, including it seems the oratory of Hadrian that stood against the west wall of the south transept. Vegio, writing in about the mid-1450s, says that the oratory:

> Nam nunc prorsus evanuit, cujus nec apparet aliud, nisi tantum affixum lateri basilicæ insigne quoddam marmor quadratum cum insculptis ei versibus, qui ostendunt, ipsum ibi curante Carolo Magno sepultum esse... Est sane marmor ipsum Numidicum & atrum, ac quale quidem rarum habeatur.
>
> ...is now totally vanished, and nothing of it can be seen except only the remarkable hewn marble fixed to the wall of the basilica with verses inscribed on it showing that he himself [Hadrian] had been buried there with the careful attention of Charles the Great... The marble itself to be sure is Numidian and black and is indeed as rare as may be had.[44]

---

[40] Thoenes, 'Renaissance St. Peter's', 65–70; A. Pinelli, 'The Old Basilica', in *BSPV* II.i (*Essays*), 9–51, at 37–40; Richardson, 'St. Peter's in the Fifteenth Century', emphasises the role of Cardinal Pietro Barbo (later Paul II, 1464–71) in longer-term efforts to transform the basilica in the mid-fifteenth century.

[41] Maffeo Vegio, 'De antiqua S. Petri apostoli Basilica in Vaticano, *c*.1455', *AASS* Junii vii (Paris and Rome, 1867), col. 57A–85D or 'De rebus antiquis memorabilibus basilicae S. Petri Romae', VZ, iv, 375–98. For an English translation and commentary, see Smith and O'Connor, *Eyewitness to Old St. Peter's*. On Vegio's antiquarian role, see T. Foffano, 'Il *De rebus antiquis memorabilibus Basilice Sancti Petri Rome* di Maffeo Vegio e i primordi dell'archeologia cristiana', in L. Secchi Tarugi, ed., *Il sacro nel Rinascimento*. Atti del XII Convegno inter-nazionale (Chianciano-Pienza, 17–20 July 2000) (Florence, 2002), 719–29; F. Della Schiava, ' "Sicuti traditum est a maioribus" Maffeo Vegio antiquario tra fonti classiche e medievali', *Aevum*, 84 (2010), 617–39.

[42] Thoenes, 'Renaissance St. Peter's', 71.

[43] Thoenes, 'Renaissance St. Peter's', 72, 78–9.

[44] *AASS* Junii vii, ch. 122 (col. 81D), quoted also by Grimaldi, *Descrizione*, ed. Niggl, 396.

His description suggests that Hadrian's oratory fell victim to Nicholas's modernisation plans for the basilica. His statement implies that any structure that stood on the floor was removed but the epitaph itself survived because it was fixed to the back wall of the chapel, that is, to the western wall of the south transept. Vegio's statement about the chapel needs to be compared with the archaeological evidence (discussed below), but it is likely that he described the original location of the epitaph; from that position visitors to the tomb would have been able to read the text, and it would have been easily visible from the body of the transept to those passing by. There is no reason to suppose that it had been moved between Charlemagne's time and when Vegio saw it six and a half centuries later; its sheer size would have made it very difficult to shift, and its good condition today suggests that it was not manhandled often, arguably not before the western wall of the transept was eventually taken down in the mid-sixteenth century. Giacomo Grimaldi, in his important account of the ancient basilica and its contents, completed in 1619, copied out the whole text, and noticed that it had been cut using *litteris maiusculis Romanis*.[45] He quoted Vegio on the epitaph, and added a comment about the condition and size of the epitaph, noting that 'the marble is of great thickness, and intact and solid'.[46] Grimaldi's words very likely record his own observation of the inscription made just before October 1619 when it was raised into its current location in the wall of the new portico.

Nicholas V's scheme therefore proposed a radical remodelling of the most important sacramental spaces around the *confessio* of the Apostle and it had an aggressive and destructive impact on medieval monuments and chapels within that part of the ancient basilica, including Hadrian's oratory. However, it left the superstructure of the old basilica intact since the footprint of the new choir lay outside the apse, to the west of the building, and the project was aborted before it impinged on the fabric of the old church. Only the late fourth-century mausoleum of the Anicii, built by the family of Sextus Petronius Probus against the external wall of the apse, was removed at this time.[47] Hadrian's epitaph, placed as it was on the western wall of the south transept, thus survived this initial attempt to modernise St Peter's and remained intact and in what was probably its original location.

Hadrian's epitaph continued to attract attention despite the apparent loss of the attendant oratory and was mentioned again before the end of the fifteenth century. Peter Sabin, a doctor of Latin literature at the College of Rome, compiled a *sylloge* of

---

[45] BAV, Barb. Lat. 2733, fols 355r–356r.

[46] BAV, Barb. Lat. 2733, fol. 356r (marginal note), 'Est multae crassitudinis marmor istud et integrum solidumque'; Grimaldi, *Descrizione*, ed. Niggl, 396. See also *CBCR* v, 212–14.

[47] It was seen and described by Vegio before demolition, 'De antiqua S. Petri apostoli Basilica', *AASS* Junii vii, 107–9 (col. 79A); Smith and O'Connor, tr., *Eyewitness to Old St Peter's*, 190–3, IV.106–10; *CD* ii, 468; Pinelli, 'The Old Basilica', 25–6; Theones, 'Renaissance St. Peter's', 74. The mausoleum is marked 'k' on Alfarano's plan. For the early fifth-century ivory diptych commissioned by Ancius Petronius Probus for the Emperor Honorius, now in Aosta Cathedral, see F. Crivello and C. Segre Montel, *Carlo Magno e le Alpi. Viaggio al centro del Medioevo* (Milan, 2006), 108–9, no. IV.1.

significant Christian inscriptions from Rome and its environs that he presented to the French king, Charles VIII, in 1494.[48] Charles came to Rome in that year at the head of an army en route to claim his wife's title to the kingdom of Naples. Despite the tense relationship with the Borgia pope, Alexander VI, it is said that Charles attended Mass at St Peter's shrine, and afterwards went from the high altar down the south transept (i.e. past Hadrian's epitaph) to the oratory of Petronilla.[49] There he performed the ritual of Touching for the King's Evil, done normally only at the coronation of a French king. Copious donations, alongside this display of sacramental wonder working, were calculated to strengthen the image and authority of the French monarchy before his Italian audience. Charles gave thanks to St Petronilla for his recovery from illness as a youth, which he and his parents had put down to the miraculous intervention of St Peter's daughter.

Hadrian's epitaph was the sixth item in Sabin's anthology for Charles VIII, included there for obvious reasons since it featured his patron's illustrious Frankish namesake so prominently. Sabin said that:

> The epitaph of Pope Hadrian, who flourished in the time of the august Charles the Great, is in that same church in the next chapel with the *cathedra* of St Peter, incised on a porphyry slab with very elegant letters.

Sabin's use of the descriptor porphyry to describe the marble slab suggests that he had not personally inspected the inscribed version in St Peter's. Furthermore, as de Rossi noted, Sabin's transcription was lax and contained multiple errors, including transposing the words *post mortem* for the inscription's *post patrem* in line 17.[50] Sabin's description and transcription of the epitaph are thus distinctly second-rate.

Julius II and Bramante

The western end of the old basilica was also the focus of the construction programme initiated by Pope Julius in 1506; but his project differed from the earlier work in its ambition and scale, and in its impact on old St Peter's. The stimulus for Julius may have been his egocentric concern for the construction of his own tomb, which he had commissioned from Michelangelo in 1505.[51] Alighting on Nicholas' half-built choir as a suitable venue for the tomb, he gave permission for building work to resume. Immediately, however, it became apparent that in order for the choir to be completed,

---

[48] *ICUR* II.i, 407–52, no. LXVI; R. Favreau, *Épigraphie Médiévale* (Turnhout, 1997), 141.
[49] Weil-Garris Brandt, 'Michelangelo's *Pietà*', 79.
[50] 'Epitaphium Hadriani pontificis in eodem templo iuxta sacellum Cathedre sancti Petri incisum in tabula porphiretica litteris ellegantissimis qui floruit temporibus Caroli magni augusti', *ICUR* II.i, 411; de Rossi refused to print Sabin's version of the epitaph because of its copious errors.
[51] C. L. Frommel, 'Die Peterskirche unter Papst Julius II. im Lichter neuer Dokumente', *Römisches Jahrbuch für Kunstgeschichte*, 16 (1976), 57–136.

a new transept would be required to articulate it with the main church. The architect eventually chosen for the task was Donato Bramante, although other prominent architects were canvassed for opinions that proved to be influential in the early design and construction phases.[52] Bramante's scheme was radical, iconoclastic, and rapidly initiated. Construction work began with the four colossal piers that were to support a dome spanning the sacred heart of the basilica, centred on the entrance to the *confessio*.[53] On this plan it was the suppliant before the shrine who would be at the centre of the structure, with the shrine itself left untouched in its original location a little to the west.[54]

The foundation stone for the south-west pier was laid on 18 April 1506 immediately behind the south transept. The building of this pier necessitated the destruction of a small structure, marked '*a*' by Alfarano and identified on the printed version of his plan as the monastery of S. Martino that had been founded in the early seventh century (see Figure 1.2).[55] Barely a year later work started on the south-east pier. As one of Bramante's own plans shows, this pier lay within the fourth-century basilica, and its construction thereby required the demolition of a substantial part of the eastern wall of the south transept—opposite Hadrian's oratory—and large parts of the western end of the nave, including the triumphal arch (Figure 1.6).[56] The oratory of Petronilla in the early fifth-century rotunda to the south of the transept was also demolished, sometime around 1514.[57]

The speed and decisiveness with which Bramante tackled the fabric of the old church in pursuit of his new building earned him the epithet *maestro ruinante* ('the master wrecker'), coined by Paris de Grassis (d. 1528), the papal master of ceremonies. This nickname stuck fast, in part because it shifted blame for the damage done to old St Peter's away from Julius; it certainly served the interests of Counter Reformation historians later in the century to argue that the architect rather than the pope had been the driving force behind the demolition of the ancient basilica.[58] Michelangelo, when he took over as architect in 1546, also criticised Bramante's

---

[52] Bosman, *Power of Tradition*, 66.

[53] *CBCR* v, 214 and fig. 193.

[54] For Michelangelo's architectural sleight of hand that seems to place the celebrant at the high altar over the tomb under the "centre" of the dome, see H. A. Millon, 'Michelangelo to Marchionni, 1546–1784', in Tronzo, ed., *St. Peter's in the Vatican*, 93–110, at 100–1.

[55] Bede, *HE* IV.18, ed. and tr. B. Colgrave and R.A.B. Mynors, *Bede's Ecclesiastical History of the English People* (Oxford, 1986), 388–9; *CD* ii, 518; Ferrari, *Early Roman Monasteries*, 239. The autograph drawing of the plan shows that this small structure was part of a much large complex, which was doubtless the monastery of S. Martino; Afarano *DBV*, tav. II.

[56] On the inscription at the arch and the debate about the mosaic image above it, see below, Chapter 8, 327–33; *ICUR* II.i, no. II.6 and no. X.1. See also BAV, Barb. Lat. 2733, fol. 164v where Grimaldi notes that the arch perished during the time of Julius II; he quoted Maffeo Vegio for this inscription and that at the apse.

[57] Frommel, 'St. Peter's: The Early History', 419; *CBCR* v, 180.

[58] Theones, 'Renaissance St. Peter's', 74; B. Kempers, 'Diverging Perspectives – New St. Peter's: Artistic Ambitions, Liturgical Requirements, Financial Limitations and Historical Interpretations', *Mededelingen van het Nederlands Instituut te Rome*, 55 (1996), 213–51, at 237–8.

RENAISSANCE ROME: HADRIAN'S EPITAPH IN NEW ST PETER'S   47

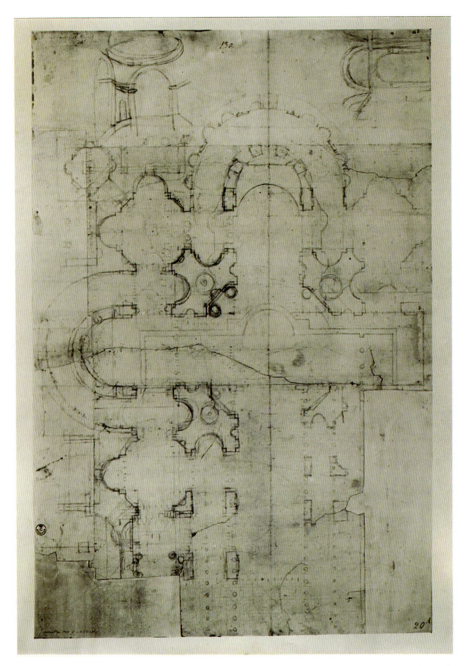

FIGURE 1.6 Donato Bramante (1505–6), 'Sketches for the basilica of St Peter's' showing the outline of the new structure superimposed over the old. Notice that the eastern piers stand within the nave of the old basilica. Florence, Uffizi Galleries, Gabinetto dei Disegni e delle Stampe degli Uffizi, Inv. GDSU n. 20 A. Photo: Reproduced by permission of the Ministero della Cultura.

attitude to the old building implying that Bramante had recklessly pulled down precious marble columns and let them be broken. In practice, however, forty-four of the forty-eight large marble columns from the old nave were reused whole and undamaged within the new basilica, suggesting that quite the opposite was true.[59] The four columns from the transept exedra screens were reused in 1563–5 in the new gate leading into the Piazza del Popolo from the Via Flaminia (Figure 1.7).[60]

Egidio da Viterbo, writing during the pontificate of Julius' successor, Leo X (1513–21), regaled a story of an argument between Bramante and Julius concerning the location of the shrine. Julius had vetoed a plan by Bramante to relocate the saint's tomb to a more convenient location, with the words that *nihil ex vetere templi situ inverti*,

FIGURE 1.7 The Porta del Popolo (built 1563–5). The four antique columns were taken from the exedra screens in the transept of the old basilica at St Peter's. Photo: Author.

---

[59] Bosman, *Power of Tradition*, 90, 123; Kinney, 'Spolia', 39.
[60] Alfarano, *DBV*, 8; *CD* ii, 460; Bosman, *Power of Tradition*, 122 and fig. 44. The columns must have been stored for around twenty years before being reused.

that is, 'nothing from the old temple may be removed from its site'.[61] This anecdote alludes to the general tensions caused by the demands of the new architecture overriding the integrity of old, rather than any particular scheme, and it undoubtedly refers to the special status of the *locus* of the Apostle's tomb. It is, however, interesting to consider whether the sentiment attributed to Julius might be applied more widely to other elements from the old basilica, including inscriptions such as Hadrian's epitaph. The story reflects an appreciation, during the pontificate of Leo at least, that objects from the old basilica were imbued with particular significance by virtue of their specific, traditional location.

When Bramante died in 1514 the four massive dome piers and the arches that connected them had been completed, as well as a western choir that was a modified form of the structure begun by Nicholas V with a square choir bay, polygonal apse, and coffered vault.[62] He had also constructed a *tegurium* to surround, ornament, and protect the *confessio*, since the central area of the old church was now a building site open to the skies.[63] The *tegurium* was attached to the ancient apse, thereby preserving that part of the old building. The impact of Bramante's work was fundamental, not just because it dictated that the defining feature of the final structure would be a massive central dome but also because it began the demolition of the old basilica. It also ensured that the Apostle's shrine was to remain in its traditional location and would be the focal point of the new building.

Demolishing the south transept

A series of fine drawings done in the 1520s and 1530s enable us to establish the sequence and chronology of the destruction of particular parts of the old basilica after Bramante's interventions. Despite the lapse of a decade and more, these drawings reflect the situation at St Peter's more or less as it was after the deaths of Julius in 1513 and Bramante in 1514. Leo X employed Raphael to continue the project, but the increasing difficulty of raising funds and the fact that Raphael was preoccupied with work in the adjacent Vatican Palace meant that little of real substance was done on the new basilica. Antonio da Sangallo restarted construction on the ambulatory of the apse for a new southern transept in 1519 and, after he was promoted to chief architect in 1520 following Raphael's death, he composed a detailed critique (known as the *Memoriale*) of the structure thus far completed and as projected by the existing plans. He was particularly critical of the proportions of the nave that he thought

---

[61] Da Viterbo, *Historia viginti saeculorum*, cited in Theones, 'Renaissance St. Peter's', 75.
[62] Theones, 'Renaissance St. Peter's', 78–9, and fig. 74; W. Tronzo, 'Il tegurium di Bramante', in Spagnesi, ed., *L'architettura della basilica*, 161–6.
[63] Bosman, *Power of Tradition*, 105–18.

would be like 'a long, narrow and high alley'.[64] But Sangallo's attempt to impose his own vision onto the project was dealt a severe blow when Leo died in December 1520. Leo was succeeded by Hadrian VI who showed little interest in the St Peter's project and concerned himself with tackling both the overdue reform of the papal Curia and the threat posed to the Church in his homelands north of the Alps by the popularity of Luther's Reformation.

As noted above, in many respects, Hadrian VI was the first of the Counter Reformation popes, arguing as he did that 'the sins of the people have their origins in the sins of the clergy'.[65] Unsurprisingly, his short reign was unlamented by Rome's artistic elite. His successor, Clement VII (1523–34), was a patron of art in true Renaissance style, although the 'Sack of Rome' in May 1527, when imperial troops devastated the city, forced all work at St Peter's to stop.[66] It was not until the mid 1530s that Sangallo was able to resume work on the plans for St Peter's with any prospect of seeing them come to fruition.[67]

Throughout this period the area that saw most activity was the southern end of the south arm of the new basilica.[68] Bramante had designed a transept with matching ambulatories at either end (see Figure 1.6 for an early version of this idea). It was a version of this design that Antonio da Sangallo took on in 1518/19, and which he elaborated in a series of extant sketches.[69] This area of the St Peter's building site is also shown in contemporary drawings that permit analysis not just of the progress of the new building, but also the decline of the old. The earliest drawing showing a view of St Peter's from the south dates to the early 1520s and depicts the western choir and southern transept from the south-west.[70] At the far left of the drawing is the polygonal, vaulted exterior of Bramante's choir, built over the fifteenth-century foundations. Rising above it to the right (i.e. to the east) are the south-western and south-eastern piers for the dome, and the coffered crossing-arch that joins them together. Beneath this high arch can be seen the vault of the transverse arch (supported by scaffolding) linking the south-western dome pier to the secondary pier in the arm of the new

---

[64] Frommel, 'St. Peter's: The Early History', 419–20; C. L. Frommel and N. Adams, eds, *The Architectural Drawings of Antonio da Sangallo the Younger and his Circle, ii: Churches, Villas, the Pantheon, Tombs and Ancient Inscriptions* (New York, 2000), 65–7 (U 33A: the text of the Memoriale).

[65] S. Benedetti, 'The Fabric of St. Peter's', in *BSPV*, II.i (*Essays*), 53–128, at 68.

[66] Benedetti, 'The Fabric of St. Peter's', 71. A contemporary account of the assault on the city was recorded by Luigi Guicciardini, *The Sack of Rome*, tr. J. H. McGregor (New York, NY, 1993).

[67] C. Theones, 'St. Peter's, 1534–1546', in Frommel and Adams, eds, *Architectural Drawings*, ii, 33–44.

[68] Benedetti, 'The Fabric of St. Peter's', 68–9. C. Frommel, 'S. Pietro. Storia della sua costruzione', in Frommel et al., eds, *Raffaello architetto* (Milan, 1984), 241–310, on Raffael's plans for the south transept.

[69] A. Bruschi, 'The Drawings of Antonio da Sangallo the Younger at St. Peter's under Leo X', in Frommel and Adams, eds, *Architectural Drawings*, ii, 23–3. See also U34A; U35A; U37A; U45A–U48A; U51A; U54A–U57A; U59A; U79A; U122A; U252A; U718A; U1780 as reproduced in Frommel and Adams, eds, *Architectural Drawings*, 67–9, 72–3, 77–84, 97–8, 108, 121–2, 144, 256.

[70] BAV, Coll. Ashby no. 329; Spagnesi, ed., *L'architettura della basilica*, 621–2, no. 323; A. Carpiceci, 'La basilica Vaticana vista da Martin van Heemskerck', *Bollettino d'arte*, 44 (1987), 67–128, at 86–8, no. 11.

southern transept, and the external and internal faces of that transept-pier itself. Lower down and further to the right in the picture, are the half-built walls of the new southern apse, with a number of columns for the ambulatory on the far right-hand side (Figure 1.8).

Of the old basilica, much was still upstanding. Most obvious is the later medieval bell tower, or campanile, with its pointed spire, and the roof of the nave to its left, surmounted by a cross. At the far right of the drawing, the second-century rotunda can be seen clearly with the pinnacle of the stadium obelisk (the 'Needle') emerging just behind it.[71] At the western end, part of the old south transept was still extant; the gabled end wall that rose above the colonnaded exedra screen stands full height. This can be seen in the middle of the drawing, between the high crossing-arch and the campanile, and can be identified by a tiny belfry on top of the pitched-roof of the gable. The artist has also drawn the top of the western wall of the old transept, before it is hidden by the vault of the new transept-pier. Thus, the corner of the old south transept that had contained Hadrian's chapel was preserved, full height but roofless (*pandit ad astra viam*, as the epitaph says), while the construction work of the massive new crossing and southern transept carried on around it.

FIGURE 1.8 'View of St Peter's from the south west', BAV, Collezione Ashby no. 329. Photo: Reproduced by kind permission of the Biblioteca Apostolica Vaticana, Rome.

---

[71] It was dedicated to St Andrew, the brother of Peter, by Pope Symmachus (498–514), and was later known as Santa Maria della Febbre. It remained standing until 1776, serving in its final phase as the basilica's sacristy; *CBCR* v, 180–1; *CD* ii, 466–8; Millon, 'Michelangelo to Marchionni', 109–10; Liverani, *Topografia antica*, 131–4, no. 58; Gem, 'The Vatican Rotunda'. On the stairs leading up to the new entrance created by Symmachus and repaired by Leo III, see below, Chapter 3, 133–4.

A further series of drawings show the same area about a decade later. Maerteen van Heemskerck's masterful drawings were done in the mid 1530s, certainly before 1538 (Figure 1.9). His focus is the new church but invariably he also shows the upstanding portions of the old basilica. His view of the new southern ambulatory from the south shows that more of that part of the building had been completed in the decade since the earlier illustration.[72] The south-eastern transept-pier had been completed, rising to the cornice at the top of the entablature. In the centre of the image, beneath the high arch of the crossing vault, is the gable-end of the old southern transept with its small belfry standing out against the shadow of the high arch, just as before. In this illustration we can see more of the western wall of the old transept, stretching back into the centre of the building. In this image it stands about two-thirds full height. Here, the artist used the remnants of the old basilica to sharpen the perspective of the view, and to demonstrate graphically the fantastic scale of the new building in comparison to the old.

The same wall can be seen in another van Heemserck drawing, this time of the southern flank of the entire complex (Figure 1.10).[73] The gable-end wall of the south transept can be made out in the shadow of the south-eastern transept-pier, under the

FIGURE 1.9 Maerteen van Heemskerck (c.1536), 'View of St Peter's under construction from the south'. Berlin, Kupferstichkabinett, 79 D 2a, fol. 54r. Photo: Reproduced with permission of the Bildarchiv Preußischer Kulturbesitz, Berlin.

---

[72] Millon and Lampugnani, eds, *Renaissance*, 630, no. 342; Carpiceci, 'La basilica Vaticana', 91–2, no. 14; *CBCR* v, 228 and fig. 208; J. H. Jongkees, *Studies on Old St. Peter's* (Groningen, 1966), 55 and pl. 4.

[73] Carpiceci, 'La basilica Vaticana', 89, no. 13; Jongkees, *Studies*, 54–5 and pl. 3; F. Ehrle and H. Egger, *Piante e vedute di Roma e del Vaticano dal 1300 al 1676* (Vatican City, 1956), tav. xiv.

FIGURE 1.10 Maerteen van Heemskerck (c.1536), 'View of St Peter's under construction from the south-east'. Berlin, Kupferstichkabinett, 79 D 2a, fol. 51r. Reproduced with permission of the Bildarchiv Preußischer Kulturbesitz, Berlin.

high crossing-arch at the left-hand side of the drawing. The particular value of this illustration for our study is that it enables a comparison of the height of the transept wall with the extant portion of the old nave that can be seen, still roofed, in the centre of the drawing. This makes it clear that the extant south transept wall is that which rose above the exedra screen, to almost the full height of the nave walls, rather than the exedra itself that projected south beyond the columns of the screen and which was not as tall as the main portions of the basilica.[74]

Elements of the southern arm of the old transept can also be seen in another drawing by van Heemskerck, this time done from within the basilica (Figure 1.11). The artist sat in the northern part of the transept beyond the columns of the north exedra screen. His focus in this drawing was Bramante's *tegurium* surrounding the *confessio*, which he framed with the marble columns and architrave of the north exedra. In the distance, beyond the *tegurium*, is the eastern-most of the two columns

---

[74] The height of the transept at St Peter's has been much discussed: *CBCR* v, 223, 257–61 and figs 201 and 229; Pinelli, 'The Old Basilica', 18–19; G. H. Forsyth, 'The Transept of Old St. Peter's at Rome', in K. Weitzmann, ed., *Late Classical and Mediaeval Studies in Honor of Albert Mathias Friend, Jr* (Princeton, NJ, 1955), 56–70; C. Bozzoni, 'L'immagine dell'antico San Pietro nell rappresentazioni figurate e nella architettura costruita', in Spagnesi, ed., *L'architettura della basilica*, 63–72. The wall over the north exedra was raised to the height of the transept by Pope Hadrian IV (1154–9); *CBCR* v, 176, 278; Carpiceci, 'La basilica Vaticana', 82–4, no. 9; Jongkees, *Studies*, 55, pl. 5.

Figure 1.11 Maerteen van Heemskerck (c.1536), 'The new crossing and Bramante's tegurium seen from within the north transept of Old St Peter's'. Stockholm, National Museum, coll. Anckarsvärd 637. Photo: Courtesy of the National Museum of Fine Arts, Stockholm.

of the south exedra screen, with its composite capital, entablature and a high wall above it. The outline of four square-shaped panels can just be made out on the wall above the column, indicating that some of the internal decoration still survived. Other decorative elements, including a coat-of-arms and the aedicule of a shallow oratory, can be seen on the far right of the drawing, on the western wall of the north transept.[75]

This drawing shows that substantial structural and decorative elements of the transept, north and south, survived, especially around the exedra screens that separated these outer chambers from the main body of the transept. The significance of this should be obvious since, according to Alfarano, Hadrian's oratory had stood just inside the exedra screen of the south transept, next to its western pier (see Figure 1.2). The internal face of this western wall of the south transept is not shown on van Heemskerck's drawings, but enough of the transept and its decoration is visible to be confident that the wall bearing Hadrian's epitaph was also upstanding in the mid-1530s. The survival of fresco or mosaic images on the inner face of the south exedra

---

[75] R. Krautheimer, 'Some Drawings of Early Christian Basilicas in Rome: St. Peter's and S. Maria Maggiore', *The Art Bulletin*, 31 (1949), 211–15; Millon and Lampugnani, eds, *Renaissance*, 631, no. 345; Carpiceci, 'La basilica Vaticana', 78, no. 6; Jonkees, *Studies*, 55–6 and pl. 6.

wall indicates that interior decorations still survived intact in this area, including, in all likelihood, Hadrian's epitaph.

By the mid-1560s all this had gone. A drawing of new St Peter's by Giovanni Antonio Dosio, made around 1564, shows the crossing and the dome under construction from a viewpoint within the south transept.[76] The *tegurium* and the ancient apse are in the centre of the image, in deep shadow, while a large block of stone for the new dome—hanging like a wrecking ball—is being raised into place above it. Dosio's drawing shows that by *c.*1564 most of the western wall of the southern transept had been demolished, and only a stub of it remained between the apse and the *tegurium* (Figure 1.12). Another drawing, usually attributed to Battista Naldini and dating to around the same time, shows the *tegurium* from the viewpoint of the nave, with the truncated western wall of the transept on either side (Figure 1.13).[77]

The date of the demolition of the old transept is disputed, but its fate had been sealed by a key decision made by Antonio da Sangallo to raise the floor level of the new basilica by about 3.70m to 'correct' what he had long considered to be the unsatisfactory proportions of the existing structure.[78] This new, higher level is shown in the drawing of the crossing attributed to Naldini (Figure 1.13). The human figure in the foreground and Bramante's *tegurium* are shown at the old floor level but on the far left of the drawing, the base of the aedicule on the east face of the south-east crossing pier is shown at the new, raised level. The same is true of the bases of the crossing pier and aedicule shown on the left of Dosio's drawing. Significantly, however, these drawings show that although the decision had been taken to raise the floor level, and the aedicules had been built for that level, the nave and transept pavements were not actually laid at the new height for many years.

The decision to raise the floor of the new building followed the construction of a dividing wall, the *muro divisorio*, across the nave in the summer of 1538, and was associated with the finalisation of the design of the aedicules for the altars of the new church using columns from the old nave.[79] The erection of this dividing wall and the aedicule design reflected important conceptual changes at St Peter's that signalled a new resolve to bring the project to a conclusion, and to do so—in the short term at least—by articulating the remains of old structure with the new. After the politically and financially disastrous pontificate of Clement VII, Paul III (1534–49) was elected determined to complete the job that Julius II had started; like Julius, Paul thought of

---

[76] Millon and Lampugnani, eds, *Renaissance*, 666, no. 401; *CBCR* v, 169, 228–9, fig. 209.
[77] Millon and Lampugnani, eds, *Renaissance*, 666, no. 400, dating the drawing *c.*1563.
[78] Theones, 'St. Peter's, 1534–46', 37. A lower figure of 3.24m is given in *CBCR* v, 184.
[79] B. Apollonj Ghetti, A. Ferrua, E. Josi, and E. Kirschbaum, eds, *Esplorazione sotto la confessione di san Pietro in Vaticano, eseguite negli anni 1940–49* (Vatican City, 1951), 207–16; Bosman, *Power of Tradition*, 79–80, 92–9, fig. 28–30; Frommel and Adams, eds, *Architectural Drawings*, 86–7, 123 on Sangallo's drawings U64A and U253A.

FIGURE 1.12 Giovanni Antonio Dosio (*c*.1564), 'Sketch of the interior of St Peter's basilia', shown under construction, with Bramante's *tegurium* and the ancient apse, seen from within the south transept; Florence, Uffizi Galleries, Gabinetto dei Disegni e delle Stampe degli Uffizi, Inv. GDSU n. 91 A. Photo: Reproduced by permission of the Ministero della Cultura.

FIGURE 1.13 Battista Naldini (?) (c.1564), 'St Peter's, view from the nave towards the apse and Bramante's *tegurium*'. Note the stubs of the western transept wall on either side of the *tegurium*. Hamburg, Kunsthalle, Inv. Nr 21311. Photo: Reproduced with permission of the Bildarchiv Preußischer Kulturbesitz, Berlin.

himself as a new Solomon, building the Temple.[80] His architects, Sangallo and Peruzzi, competed with plans and models for the completion of the building, albeit on a reduced scale to that envisaged under Leo X.

Actual construction, however, concentrated on consolidating and repairing the old structure and joining it to the new one, as well as the completion and underpinning of the great crossing piers.[81] Sangallo oversaw the erection of the *muro divisorio* in 1538, which was designed to stabilise the outer walls of the old basilica and to ensure that the remnants of the old church could continue to function as a coherent liturgical space. The large arch in the centre of the new wall was given columns and an architrave to match those in the old nave, and it remained open for several years, providing a clear line of sight through to the *tegurium* and *confessio*. In 1544–5 Sangallo built an eastern arm for the new church to connect it with the remaining part of the old nave, and it was probably about this time that the central arch of the *muro divisorio* was closed with a door. This was a pragmatic solution that rendered the site more useable, but it also mollified those who opposed on ideological grounds the destruction of the basilica believed to have been built by Constantine and whose views were becoming increasingly influential.[82] Thus the 'dividing' wall in fact ensured a stay of execution for the antique church and its atrium, and acted as a means of uniting the old and new parts of St Peter's. This was reinforced by the decision to use the columns from the ancient nave as the defining unit of measure for the aedicules for the altars in the new building. The reuse of the columns in this way expressed visual and physical continuity between the two buildings, as well as being an economic reuse of valuable resources.

This phase of the project also saw the relocation of many tombs, altars, and monuments from the western part of the old nave into the eastern portion, now protected by the *muro divisorio*, serving to concentrate the liturgical *memorie* of St Peter's within the remaining part of the old church.[83] What is more, new monuments were constructed in the old basilica and old ones—such as the altar of saints Simon and Jude—were restored, and clerics, laymen, and popes continued to be buried there.[84] The fact that St Peter's continued in use as a place of burial until the early seventeenth century

---

[80] Theones, 'Renaissance St. Peter's', 73–4, 85; Theones, 'St. Peter's, 1534–1546', 33.

[81] Theones, 'Renaissance St. Peter's', 85–9; Theones, 'St. Peter's 1534–1546', 39–40; Benedetti, 'The Fabric of St. Peter's', 71, 78–9.

[82] Theones, 'Renaissance St. Peter's', 83; G. Miarelli Mariani, 'L'antico San Pietro, demoliro o conservarlo?', in Spagnesi, ed., *L'architettura della basilica*, 229–42; Kinney, 'Spolia', 16.

[83] Bosman, *Power of Tradition*, 14–15; Kempers, 'Diverging Perspectives', 238–9. See also the drawing by Tasselli from the viewpoint of the old nave looking towards the *muro divisorio*, Figure 1.14.

[84] On Paul III's restoration of the altar of saints Simon and Jude, see Alfarano, *DVB*, 63, no. 44; G. Miarelli Mariani, 'L'antico San Pietro, demoliro o conservarlo?', in Spagnesi, ed., *L'architettura della basilica*, 229–42, at 234–5; Borgolte, *Petrusnachfolge*, 358–9; Pinelli, 'The Old Basilica', 45.

is, as Rice has argued, 'the single most compelling piece of evidence that its destruction was considered by many to be neither imminent nor inevitable'.[85] Although it may not have been Sangallo's intention, the *muro divisorio* survived until March 1615 and, as the voices calling for the conservation of the basilica as a relic from the age Constantine grew louder within the Curia, so the temporary wall may have seemed to many to be a permanent solution enabling part of the old building to be preserved (Figure 1.14).[86] Indeed, when the new, raised floor was finally laid in the western part

FIGURE 1.14 A watercolour by Domenico Tasselli (*c*.1611) for Giacomo Grimaldi's *Album di San Pietro*, showing the interior of the eastern part of the nave of St Peter's, looking towards the *muro divisorio*. Note the numerous altars and monuments, and the door closing the arch in the *muro divisorio* with steps leading up to the door and to the raised floor level in the new basilica beyond. BAV, Arch. Cap. S. Pietro, A.64.ter, fol. 12r. Photo: Reproduced by kind permission of the Biblioteca Apostolica Vaticana, Rome.

---

[85] L. Rice, *The Altars and Altarpieces of New St. Peter's: Outfitting the Basilica, 1621–1666* (Cambridge, 1997), 23.

[86] Bosman, *Power of Tradition*, 95; C. Theones, 'Alt und Neu St. Peter unter einem dach. Zu Antonio da Sangallo *Muro divisorio*', in M. Jansen and K. Winands, eds, *Architektur und Kunst im Abenland* (Rome, 1992), 51–61.

of the nave in the early 1590s, the threshold of the doorway in the arch was also raised, and steps were inserted leading up from the original floor level in the eastern end of the old basilica to the higher level in the new part of the church.[87]

The decision to raise the floor within the church disrupted the plans for the ambulatory of the southern arm, and forced considerable adjustments to be made to its design.[88] In the late 1540s Michelangelo removed the outer part of the southern ambulatory in its entirety, preserving only the inner apse from the earlier design.[89] By 1548 he had removed the remaining sections of the ancient northern transept.[90] It is possible that the floor had been laid at the new, higher level in the southern arm of the new church as early as 1543–4 and, if Krautheimer is right in that argument, this action would also have 'required the razing of the remaining portions of the old south transept'.[91] However, there are some physical and textual grounds for arguing that the section of the south transept around the exedra screen may have survived until about 1560. The exedra columns were not reused for the construction of the new Porta del Popolo until 1563–5 and comments by Onofrio Panvinio in 1560 about Hadrian's epitaph and its location suggest that the transept was still partially extant (see below), suggesting that the floor had not yet been laid across the whole of the new southern arm.

MOVING HADRIAN'S EPITAPH: TIBERIO ALFARANO AND CONTINUITY AT ST PETER'S IN THE LATE SIXTEENTH CENTURY

Krautheimer's preferred chronology implies that Hadrian's epitaph was taken down from the western wall of the southern transept by the mid-1540s when many of the monuments from that area were translated into the eastern end of the old nave. From the south transept, for example, the altar of Santa Maria de Praegnantibus and the oratory of the holy martyrs, saints Processus and Martinianus, was probably moved from the

---

[87] Frommel and Adams, eds, *Architectural Drawings*, 107–8; Lanzani, *Vatican Grottoes*, 7–10. These steps and part of the base of the wall were seen in excavation; Apollonij Ghetti et al., eds, *Esplorazioni* I, 213–14 and fig. 103, and II, tav. LXXXVI and CIX.

[88] Theones, 'St. Peter's 1534–1546', 37. The tomb of Maria, wife of the Emperor Honorius, who had died in 407/8 and buried in the rotunda later dedicated to Santa Petronilla, was excavated in February 1544: Liverani, *Topografia antica*, 60; *CD* ii, 467; Alfarano, *DBV*, 136.

[89] Benedetti, 'The Fabric of St. Peter's', 68, 77, 85; Theones, 'St Peter's, 1534–1546', 41–2.

[90] *CBCR* v, 184; Millon, 'Michelangelo to Marchionni', 93–5. For the continuation of the work on the north transept in 1564–7 by Michelangelo's successor as architect at St Peter's, see D. R. Coffin, *Pirro Ligorio: The Renaissance Artist, Architect and Antiquarian* (Pennsylvania, PA, 2004), 67–9.

[91] *CBCR* v, 184; Bosman, *Power of Tradition*, 80; Carpicei, 'La basilica Vaticana', tav. vi.

south exedra to the inner face of the *muro divisorio* at around this time.[92] The Leonine oratory that had stood between the site of Hadrian's oratory and the *confessio* was also dismantled in 1544 (see Figure 1.2); payments are recorded for the removal of its columns, although it seems that the new floor was not fully installed at that place until after 1580 because excavations were done at the old floor level in that year to discover the relics of Leo I.[93]

Substantial parts of the west wall of the south transept, its superstructure and its foundations, have been exposed through excavation and are visible in two chambers that were excavated to the south of the *Cappella della Bocciata* in the grotto.[94] The floor of the *Cappella* is some 70cm lower than the fourth-century pavement, and so here and in the next chamber to the south, the foundations of the western wall of the old transept can be seen. Within the next, southernmost chamber the original paving of the first basilica is preserved, with the west wall exposed above it for a length of 7.12m, including the opening for a doorway, 2.40m wide, complete with a marble threshold and one door jamb (Figure 1.15).[95] In total, about 20m of the western wall of the southern arm of the transept has been seen in excavation, from near its junction with the apse up to the pier that projects 3m from it to demarcate the line of the columnar screen of the southern exedra. The whole face of that pier has been exposed, showing it to be 1.28m wide and about 3m in depth. The survival of the western wall of the transept shows that here the sixteenth-century workmen had only to demolish that part of the old wall that rose above the new floor level; the lower part was left and the voids filled with rubble to form the packing for the pavement of the new basilica at the new, higher level.

This space, between the exedra pier and the doorway, is exactly where Alfarano says that Hadrian's oratory was located. The excavators did not comment on this, nor on the two projecting walls that are plastered and painted with a simple linear design and a flower motif, which stand hard up against the exedra pier on its northern side (Figure 1.16). Nor do they comment on the substantial, rectangular, brick structure with a central void that fills the corner between these decorated walls and the doorway. This structure is 3m long and 2m wide and has walls up to 93cm thick that rise about 40cm above the pavement of the old basilica. Krautheimer thought that these

---

[92] Alfarano, *DVB*, 42–4, 62–3 (no. 18, 20, 42–3); Miarelli Mariani, 'L'antico San Pietro', 234; Lanzani, *Vatican Grottoes*, 4–5.

[93] Alfarano, *DVB*, 38–40, n. 4. Lanzani, *Vatican Grottoes*, 5, 93–4; Grimaldi, *Descrizione*, ed. Niggl, 232–9. For the tomb of Popes Leo II, III, and IV within the Cappella della Madonna della Colonna, and that of Leo I in the new basilica, see *BSPV* I.i (*Atlas*), 552–61, figs 712–15.

[94] Apollonij Ghetti et al., eds, *Esplorazioni*, i, 156–8, ii, tav. LXII–III; *CBCR* v, 193–5, figs 158–9 and 165–7.

[95] This doorway is not shown on Alfarano's plan; instead, he showed one (no. 13) further north between the Leonine oratory (no. 14) and the *confessio*, for which there is no excavated evidence; Apollonij Ghetti, *Explorazioni*, 158; *CBCR* v, 193–4, fig. 165–6. I am most grateful to Professor Zander for facilitating access to these areas.

FIGURE 1.15 The doorway in the western wall of the south transept, showing the marble threshold and door jamb, the paving of the old basilica and, on the far left, the projecting wall of the tomb structure that fills the space between the doorway and the exedra pier. Photo: By kind permission of the Reverenda Fabbrica di San Pietro in Vaticano, Rome.

FIGURE 1.16 The face of the western pier that marked the boundary of the southern exedra. Abutting it to the right are two walls, both with painted decoration, which project slightly beyond the pier into the space of the transept. Photo: By kind permission of the Reverenda Fabbrica di San Pietro in Vaticano, Rome.

remains were 'presumably the tomb of the chapel of Hadrian I'.[96] But de Blaauw has argued that, although the remains probably reflect the ancient form of Hadrian's oratory, the extant brick structure is more likely to date to the mid-fifteenth-century remodelling of this part of the basilica, when the oratory was modified—perhaps for the Jubilee of 1450—to house the *cathedra Petri*. Alfarano later reported that this petrine relic—the second most important in the basilica after the corporeal remains of the Apostle himself—was set 'in a marble covering of the highest workmanship...[and] guarded with honour'.[97] This accommodates Vegio's description of the clearance work undertaken during the pontificate of Nicholas V (1447–55). Writing after Nicholas' death, Vegio claimed that Hadrian's oratory had 'vanished totally' except for the 'remarkable' marble inscription set on the wall. But he also said that 'where formerly the altar of Sant'Adriano had been, there is now another space, excellently ornamented, where the *cathedra* is set, on which blessed Peter had been accustomed to sit while overseeing solemnities'.[98] This being so, from the mid-fifteenth century at least, the *cathedra Petri* was kept within the oratory where Hadrian's epitaph was displayed, affixed to the back wall.[99] It is a notable coincidence that the *cathedra*, known now to have been of Carolingian manufacture, was located in the oratory which also housed the Carolingian epitaph for Hadrian.

There is no clear record of the removal of the epitaph from the western wall of the south transept. The records of the Fabbrica di San Pietro reveal that many old inscriptions were kept in the storeroom next to the limekiln. Some were recovered from there and moved to the new grotto under the church in 1619–20 but many others could have been lost to the furnace next door.[100] It is possible that, like several other monuments from the western end of the basilica, the epitaph was not put into storage at this stage but was moved into the remaining part of the old church.

Our next 'view' of the epitaph is in around 1560, slightly before Dosio made his drawing from the south transept. Onophrio Panvinio (1529–1568), a prolific antiquarian scholar of great skill, wrote an account in that year of the 'ancient things'

---

[96] *CBCR* v, 194–5.

[97] *CD* ii, 570–1; Smith and O'Connor, tr., *Eyewitness to Old St. Peter's*, 23–4.

[98] 'Porro in ipso altari S. Adriani factus est nunc alius locus, egregie ornatus, ubi collocata est cathedra, super quam sedere B. Petrus, dum solennia ageret, consueverat'; Vegio, 'De antiqua S. Petri apostoli Basilica', *AASS* Junii vii, ch. 124 (col. 82B); Smith and O'Connor, tr., *Eyewitness to Old St. Peter's*, 203–4 (IV.124).

[99] The *Cathedra Petri* has been shown to be of Carolingian manufacture. The ivory panels, some of which display images of the labours of Hercules, incorporate a portrait of Charles the Bald, Charlemagne's grandson. It is likely to have been made and brought to Rome for his imperial coronation in 875. M. Guarducci, *La Cattedra di San Pietro nella scienza e nelle fede* (Rome, 1982); M. Zalum, 'La Cattedra Ligena di San Pietro (sec. IX)' in *BSPV*, I.1 (Atlas), 616–19, and M. Maccarrone and D. Rezza, *La cattedra lignea di San Pietro*, Archivum Sancti Petri, Bolletino d'archivio (Vatican City, 2010). On the *cathedra*'s Carolingian context, see especially, L. Nees, *A Tainted Mantle: Hercules and the Classical Tradition at the Carolingian Court* (Philadelphia, PA, 1991).

[100] Lanzani, *Vatican Grottoes*, 13–15. On the structure of the archive, see I. Jones, 'L'archivio della Fabbrica di San Pietro', in *BSPV,* II.i (*Essays*), 399–407.

at St Peter's.[101] He provided a very accurate transcription of the inscription and noted the location of Hadrian's burial in the oratory 'close to the main altar of St Peter, and near the oratories of [Pope] Paul and the four Leos'. Nothing he says suggests that the inscription had been moved from its original place, and the accuracy of his transcription (far superior to any that had preceded it) is compelling evidence that the epitaph itself was accessible, and that he had seen it and transcribed it himself. He does not repeat errors introduced to the text by Vegio, and his version is very much more accurate than that produced by Sabin.[102] Panvinio gives instead the text almost exactly as it is found on the stone, with only a couple of minor variants. His edition was printed in 1562 as an appendix to his revision of Bartolomeo Platina's popular *History of the Popes*, published originally in Venice in 1479. Platina had not included the text of Hadrian's epitaph in the original version; it is, however, to be found in the printed editions made after 1562 that contain Panvinio's revisions.[103]

The next explicit reference to the epitaph is by Tiberio Alfarano, a 'beneficed cleric' of St Peter's, in his tract *De Basilicae Vaticanae antiquissima et nova structura* that he composed between 1570 and 1582.[104] This is a comprehensive description of the old basilica by a contemporary witness; his primary interest however was the internal liturgical topography of old St Peter's (that is, the location of the oratories and tombs) rather than its architectural details. Alfarano's text is supplemented by a famous, large-scale plan that was engraved in 1589–90 from his original drawing done in 1571 (see Figure 1.2).[105] Alfarano wrote, therefore, after the western half of the old basilica had been demolished but while the eastern end of the nave was still standing and in use. His detailed account is thus very useful for reconstructing the internal layout of

---

[101] Onofrio Panvinio, 'De rebus antiquis memoratu dignis basilicae S. Petri Vaticanae libri VII', 6.22, 'De Romanis Pontificibus, qui in basilica Vaticana sepulti sunt': BAV, Arch. Cap. S. Pietro, G.10, fols 385v–86v and Arch. Cap. S. Pietro, H.87, fol. 177v (digital facsimiles available on DigiVatLib). The text was edited by A. Mai, ed., *Spicilegium Romanum*, 10 vols (Rome, 1843), ix, 94–328, at 353–4. See also *CBCR* v, 207, n. 8. On Panvinio's contribution to Christian archaeology, see I. Herklotz, 'Historia sacra und mittelalterliche Kunst wahrend der zweiten Halfte des 16. Jahrhunderts in Rom', in R. De Maio, ed., *Baronio e l'arte. Atti del convegno internazionale di Studi. Sora 10–13 ottobre 1984* (Sora, 1985), 21–74, at 25–39. For Panvinio's career and antiquarianism, see W. Stenhouse, *Reading Inscriptions and Writing Ancient History: Historical Scholarship in the Late Renaissance* (London, 2005), 1–6, 169, and Bauer, *Invention of Papal History*, 7–8, 51–61.

[102] Vegio has *carissime* for *clarissime* in line 23, and *gratissima* for *carissime* in line 27. These two lines are not in Mallius' version, which finishes at line 14.

[103] B. Platina, *Historia de vitis pontificum Romanorum: a D.N. Iesv Christo usque ad Paulum Papam II. Cvi Onvphrii Panvinii Veronensisfratris Eremitæ Augustiniani opera, reliquiorum quoque pontificium uitæ usque ad Pium IIII pontificiem maximum adiunctæ sunt* (Venice, 1562), 92–4. On the Counter-Reformation censorship of Platina's work, see S. Bauer, *The Censorship and Fortuna of Platina's 'Lives of the Popes' in the Sixteenth Century* (Turnhout, 2006), 110; Bauer, *Invention of Papal History*, 150–3; A. Petrucci and C. Romeo, *Scriptores in urbibus: Alfabetisimo e cultura scritta nell'Italia altomedievale* (Bologna, 1992), 11.

[104] Alfarano, *DVB*, 41–2, 116, 184, 195; Pinelli, 'The Old Basilica', 15. Alfarano's autograph copy is now BAV, Arch. Cap. S. Pietro, G.4 (fols 23r, 53v–54r for the references to Hadrian's epitaph).

[105] *CBCR* v, 218–19 and fig. 195. Alfarano's autograph drawing is reproduced by Cerrati, in Alfarano, *DVB*, tav. II.

the basilica, not least because it records two phases; the old church as Alfarano's contemporaries thought it had been before anything was demolished, and the situation in the later sixteenth century after the *muro divisorio* had been built, the western end demolished, and some of its monuments moved into the eastern section of the nave. The notes to the plan identify not only new locations of monuments that had been moved *ex priori loco* into the western end of the basilica but also those in the eastern end of the building that had been moved to accommodate them. Unsurprisingly, therefore, the eastern half of the nave is the most densely occupied part of his plan (Figure 1.17).

For the western part of the basilica, Alfarano necessarily relied on his own memory and those of others still living, as well as earlier written descriptions of the fabric of the building and its internal fittings. He had been in Rome since 1544 around the time that Michelangelo restarted work on the southern ambulatory and the north transept, so his personal memories could have contributed to his description of that part of the old basilica.[106] He certainly knew the ancient apse that was attached to Bramante's *tegurium* because it was not until 1592 that the sanctuary area was cleared to make way for the new high altar; Alfarano noted details about it that are unrecorded elsewhere and which have since been substantiated by excavation.[107]

A particularly important source for Alfarano was Giacomo Hercolano (d. 1573), his mentor at St Peter's, a canon, and *altarista* to the high altar, who, Alfarano says, 'taught me about all of the memorable antiquities before they were dismantled in order to make the church one sees today'.[108] Many of Hercolano's recollections were recorded by Alfarano in another work that complements *De Basilicae Vaticanae*.[109] Hercolano had been at St Peter's since the days of Julius II and so had witnessed many changes. Some years earlier he had recalled the disruption to life at the basilica caused by the building work; 'As far as I know and can remember since I entered this church as a cleric in 1505 until the present in 1554, regarding the small part of the old church that had been left for the holy offices and the divine cult, it was reduced to a public street with carts and beasts of burden, introduced without any respect, buffaloes and other animals, and used as a workshop for sculptors and carpenters. It was never reported to His Holiness because of the difficulties made by the men from the *fabbrica*'.[110]

Alfarano is an eye-witness, therefore, to the eastern portion of old St Peter's including the atrium, and his description of the layout of the church to the east of the *muro divisorio* is of the highest value. His account of the western end around the sanctuary is marginally less reliable, relying as it did on oral and written testimonies as well as his

---

[106] Alfarano, *DVB*, xiii–xiv.
[107] *CBCR* v, 184, 218–19; Millon, 'Michelangelo to Marchionni', 104.
[108] Alfarano, *DVB*, xvi–xix, xxiv, 1.
[109] Alfarano, *DVB*, xlviii–l and 151–77 for transcriptions of select extracts; the manuscript is BAV, Arch. Cap. S. Pietro, G.5. See also Della Schiava, 'Per la storia della basilica vaticana', 258–9.
[110] AFSP 4. 258, f. 258r; cited in Lanzani, *Vatican Grottoes*, 3.

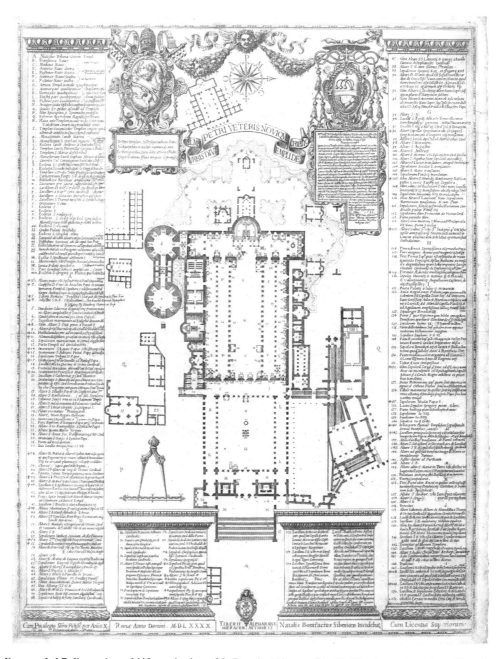

Figure 1.17 Engraving of Alfarano's plan of St Peter's, 'Almae urbis Divi Petri veteris novique Templi descriptio', by Martino Ferrabosco, in G. B. Costaguti, *Architettura della basilica di San Pietro in Vaticano. Opera di Bramante Lazzari, Michel'Angelo Bonarota, Carlo Maderni, e altri famosi Architetti*…(Rome, 1684). Photo: By kind permission of the Fabbrica di San Pietro in Vaticano, Rome.

own memories from the site in his youth. Occasionally his plan of the old building can be shown to be inaccurate. It omits the columns between the side aisles and the transepts, for example, and misrepresents the form of the narthex between the rotundas dedicated to St Andrew and to St Petronilla. Importantly also, the door in the south transept that led outside towards the monastery of San Martino is known by excavation to have been further south than indicated on his plan: that is, this doorway lay between the oratories of Hadrian (no. 15) and the Leonine popes (no. 14), and not between the Leonine oratory and the apse as shown on the plan (see Figures 1.2 and 1.16).[111] But, as noted already, the structural details of the basilica were of less importance to Alfarano than the arrangement of its oratories, altars, and tombs.

THE OLD BASILICA AND THE COUNCIL OF TRENT

Alfarano's work on the old basilica is symptomatic of a much wider phenomenon in the history of the later sixteenth century. Paul III, who had restarted the St Peter's project in the mid-1530s after the hiatus caused by the Sack of Rome, was also responsible for calling a general council of the Catholic Church. The Council of Trent, which eventually met between 1545 and 1563, promulgated a series of decrees on the fundamental principles of Catholic faith. These provided a doctrinal basis for the 'Counter' or Catholic Reformation and sought to modernise the Church in order to confront the twin challenges of Protestantism in Europe and mission to the New World. Underpinning all this was an appeal to tradition and history, especially in support of the cult of saints and the hierarchy of the Church, both of which had been comprehensively challenged by the Protestant reformers and which had little authority in Scripture.[112] This theologically inspired revision of sacred history was exemplified on a grand scale by the fourteen-volume history of the Church by Cardinal Cesare Baronio. His *Annales ecclesiastici* were published in Rome between 1588 and 1607 in direct response to the first major Protestant history known as the *Magdeburg Centuries* that were published in Basel in 1559–74 by Matthias Flacius Illyricus. There evidence had been marshalled for a Protestant version of the Christian past intended to demonstrate the extent of the deviation of Catholicism from the ideals of the early Church.[113]

At a local level, the enforcement of the universal decrees of the Council of Trent created anxiety among the Catholic faithful, not least because the decrees insisted upon the regularisation of devotional practices at local cult sites where traditional

---

[111] *CBCR* v, 193–5, fig. 165. This door had been blocked off by the time that Vegio was writing in the mid-fifteenth century; *AASS* Junii vii, ch. 120 (col. 81B); Alfarano, *DVB*, 37, n. 3.
[112] See, especially, Ditchfield, *Liturgy, Sanctity and History*, 10, 273–85.
[113] P. Polman, *L'Élément historique dans la controverse religieuse du XVIe siècle* (Gembloux, 1932), 213–34 on Flacius Illyricus, and 527–38 on Baronio.

habits did not always conform to the newly defined, centralised orthodoxy. And yet, the 'wave of devotional nostalgia' unleashed by the Tridentine decrees fed widespread enquiries into the antiquity—and thus the legitimacy—of such local cults as a means of getting local liturgical practices approved by the central authorities in Rome.[114]

Alfarano's *De Basilicae Vaticanae* documented the heritage of his own 'local' cult—that of St Peter himself—by tracing the antiquity of the fourth-century building, and the physical and epigraphic evidence of the centuries of pious devotion that it had attracted. Alfarano's work on the basilica had a much wider application because his local cult was that of Christ's chief apostle. As such, it supported the literal claims of St Peter's successors in Rome to spiritual overlordship of Christendom by documenting the antiquity and continuity of devotion to St Peter at the site of his grave. *Tu es Petrus*, Christ had said, 'and upon this Rock I will build my Church and the gates of Hell shall not prevail against it'.[115] The project to rebuild St Peter's basilica thus encapsulated the challenge facing the post-Tridentine Church at both a universal and local level: renewal springing from continuity. At St Peter's that task was all the more urgent because the ancient building that housed this collective memory was being destroyed. The challenge that had faced Bramante and all his successors was to find a way of expressing continuity of form, function, and institutional memory within a new architectural idiom that nevertheless reflected the aesthetic of the Constantinian age. The exploration of this theme was key to the protracted design process at St Peter's as successive architects rose to the challenge of developing designs that fulfilled their patrons' demands for a building that was fabulous and new, yet affordable and resonant with the heritage of the structure they were replacing. The new building had to reflect the ambition of the modern papacy and to capture the centuries of institutional and theological authority that the old one embodied.

By the latter part of the sixteenth century, attitudes towards the old basilica had changed. The Counter-Reformation had generated intense interest in the physical and spiritual remains of the early Church, and the old basilica was now revered as a relic of the age of Constantine.[116] In his *Annales ecclesiastici*, Baronio—who championed the cause to preserve the remnants of the old church—claimed 'to demonstrate for every age that the visible monarchy of the Catholic Church was instituted by Christ our Lord and founded upon Peter and his true and legitimate successors, the true Roman pontiffs, and that it is preserved inviolate, religiously guarded neither broken nor

---

[114] For Rome itself, see Herklotz, '*Historia Sacra* und mittelalterliche Kunst', 21–72; Miarelli Mariani, 'L'antico San Pietro', 236–7; A. Van Dijk, 'The Afterlife of an Early Medieval Chapel: Giovanni Battista Ricci and Perceptions of the Christian Past in Post-Tridentine Rome', *Renaissance Studies*, 19.5 (2005), 686–98.
[115] Matt. 16:18.
[116] Hibbard, *Carlo Maderno*, 66; Rice, *Altars and Altarpieces*, 23; Kempers, 'Diverging Perspectives', 238–40.

interrupted but continuous, for ever'.[117] What Baronio did for the Catholic Church at large, Alfarano did for the basilica of St Peter.

ALFARANO AND HADRIAN'S EPITAPH

The inscription is mentioned twice in Alfarano's text: once when he described the arrangement of the south transept (no. 15), and again when he recorded the inscription's second home in the portico of the atrium of the old basilica (no. 132).[118]

> (No. 15) Sed iuxta praedictum sancti Leonis Oratorium sequebatur sancti Adriani primi Oratorium in quo Beati Petri Sedes sive Cathedra in marmoreo operculo egregie fabre summo cum honore custodiebatur, in quo etiam quidem Adrianus Pontifex requiescit, ut ex epitaphio a Carolo Magno numidico lapidi insculpto liquet, qui quidem postea lapis ante Basilicae ianuas anno 1574, Gregorii XIII Sum. Pont. iussu translatus est, et in parietibus affixus ut ab omnibus fidelibus in argumentum fidei Catholicae legi possit.

> But next to the aforementioned oratory of St Leo was found the Oratory of St Hadrian I, in which the Chair or *Cathedra* of Blessed Peter in a marble covering of the highest workmanship was guarded with honour. In that place lies Pope Hadrian, as is evident from the epitaph by Charles the Great cut in Numidian stone, indeed that stone was later translated before the doors of the basilica by the order of Gregory XIII, highest pontiff, in 1574 and affixed to the walls so that it might be read for proof of the Catholic faith by all the faithful.

> (No. 132) Nostris vero temporibus parietibus Basilicae fuit affixus magnus lapis numidicus in quo est sepulcri Adriani primi epitaphium insculptum, a Carolomagno compositum, ex Basilicae ruinis eiusque sepulcri loco avulsus.

> In our times the great Numidian stone was fixed to the walls of the basilica, on which is cut the epitaph from the tomb of Hadrian I, composed by Charlemagne, wrenched from the ruins of the basilica and the place of his burial.

Both of these locations are also labelled on the plan and described in the appendix to it.[119] Alfarano notes first of all that the oratory had been the place where the *cathedra* or chair thought to have been used by St Peter himself was kept; this he knew from Vegio (and doubtless too from local memory). Regarding the inscription itself, for Alfarano as for Vegio and Sabin before him, its association with Charlemagne was its

[117] Baronius, 'Ad lectorem', as cited by Ditchfield, *Liturgy, Sanctity and History*, 283.
[118] Alfarano, *DVB*, 41–2, 116.
[119] Alfarano, *DVB*, 184, 195: No. 15. 'Oratorium sancti Adriani primi ubi Cathedra sancti Petri honorifice custodiebatur, et in pavimento sub lapide numidico a carlomagno versibus elegantissimis insculpto ipse sanctus Adrianus requiescit'; No. 132, 'Olim sepulchrum Sergii promi eximium, nunc in parietibus est affixus lapis Numidicus cui inest insculptum Epitaphium sepulchri Adriani primi a Carolo Magno aeditum, ex priori loco translatus'.

key feature and, like them, he attributed authorship of the text to Charlemagne himself. He also noted the unusual marble of the inscription, copying Vegio in saying that it is a *magnus lapis numidicus*; in other words, that it was black.[120] Both authors, in fact, had conflated Pliny's descriptions of the rare marble from Numidia, which was bright yellow, with the 'mainly black' marble named after Lucullus.[121] Unlike Vegio and Sabin, however, Alfarano did not cite the text of the inscription in *De Basilicae Vaticanae*, although he did quote it elsewhere, in another work that set out to amplify the *syllogae* of inscription-texts collected by Mallius in the later twelfth century and Vegio in the mid-fifteenth.[122]

Alfarano records details about the relocation of the inscription to the narthex. This was done in 1574 by order of Pope Gregory XIII Boncompagni (1572–85).[123] The traditional interpretation of the demolition history of the old basilica assumes that—apart from the apse that was protected by the *tegurium*—the western end of the basilica had gone entirely by this date, in which case Gregory could not have been responsible for removing the inscription from the south transept. The comment in the notes to the plan that the inscription was removed from 'the ruins of the basilica', however, recalls Panvinio's description of the epitaph, which implies that the transept may still have been partially extant *c*.1560, not long before Alfarano wrote his account. These are slim grounds for arguing that parts of the ruinous transept was still extant as late as 1574, and Dosio's drawing from the interior of the south transept showing the stub of the western wall would seem conclusive. Rather, the emphasis of Alfarano comments is to credit Gregory XIII with the instruction to move the displaced inscription to safety in front of the eastern doors of the basilica and to fix it to the wall there in 1574 'in our time' (Figure 1.18).

The date is important: 1575 was a Holy Year, a Jubilee, when hundreds of thousands of pilgrims were expected to come to St Peter's to take part in the devotions at the shrine which would enable them to claim the plenary indulgence for the remission of their sins that was customarily granted on such occasions. Unprecedented efforts were made for the 1575 Jubilee, to prepare the city and its churches for the vast crowds that were expected to participate in the rituals at the city's major basilicas and the processions between them.[124] This Holy Year was an important weapon in the armoury

---

[120] Vegio says it is *numidicum et atrum* ('Numidian and black'); 'De antiqua S. Petri apostoli Basilica', *AASS* Junii vii, ch. 122 (col. 81D).

[121] See further below, Chapter 6, 230–1.

[122] Arch. Cap. S. Pietro, G.5. This miscellany contains numerous texts including a text in Italian in Alfarano's hand, entitled, 'Delle pierre antiche', on pp. 147–226. On the complex structure of this codex, see Della Schiava, 'Per la storia della basilica vaticana', 258–9, n. 6.

[123] Alfarano *DBV*, 152–3; BAV, Arch. Cap. S. Pietro, G.5, pp. 13–14 (nineteenth-century transcription) and p. 154 (marginal note adding a reference to Charlemagne) and p. 159, in Alfarano's hand, which refers the reader to copies of Mallius and Vegio for the text of the epitaph.

[124] Pastor, *History of the Popes*, xix, 197–215; C. Bandini, *Gli Anni Santi* (Turin, 1934), 65–84 on the Jubilee of 1575.

RENAISSANCE ROME: HADRIAN'S EPITAPH IN NEW ST PETER'S

FIGURE 1.18 View of the façade of St Peter's and its atrium by G. A. Dosio, engraved by Giambattista Cavalieri to show the opening of the Porta Santa by Gregory XIII on 24 December 1574; from, Ehrle and Egger, *Piante e Vedute*, tav. 31. Roma, ICCD, Fototeca Nazionale, F8245, reproduced with permission of the Ministero della Cultura.

of Catholic renewal, since the act of mass pilgrimage would nourish and consolidate popular piety and focus the devotional energies of Catholics worldwide on the city of Rome and its relic-filled churches. A contemporary English writer, Gregory Martin, noted that this was 'the time wherein true Catholiks and the obedient Children of the Church ought to shew their zele of faith and pietie, in following and renewing the ancient devotion of former ages'.[125] Another account notes the number of pilgrims who attended mass at the great festivals at St Peter's during the 1575 Jubilee: a total figure of 354,400 is given for the year, with nearly 70,000 attending during Advent.[126]

GREGORY XIII AND THE 1575 JUBILEE

The installation of Hadrian's epitaph in the portico of St Peter's was part of the wide-ranging programme of works ordered by Gregory XIII throughout the city and its primary basilicas—St Peter's, S. Maria Maggiore, S. Paulo fuori le Mura, and S. Giovanni in Laterano—to accommodate the spiritual and physical needs of the Holy Year pilgrims.[127] At St Peter's, extensive work was done on the pavement around the *confessio*, and Gregory ordered the floor of the old basilica to be cleared of rubble and repaired so that pilgrims could access the shrine of St Peter within the new basilica. 'From the central gate up to the high altar [the pavement] was found intact' overlying many tombs, some whole and others in ruins; in repairing the floor, they also installed new burials 'with inscriptions and titles of cardinals and others'.[128] He restored and re-consecrated altars in the old nave, such as that dedicated to saints Philip and James, and commissioned a new ceiling for the portico bearing his coat of arms.[129] He also made plans for the massive red granite obelisk that stood to the south of the basilica to be moved to the piazza in front of the church for the Holy Year celebrations, *per maggior commodità della vista delle persone che veranno l'anno santo a Roma* ('for the greater convenience of viewing by the people who will come to Rome for Holy Year').[130] This echoes Gregory's motive for fixing Hadrian's epitaph to the wall of the portico.

---

[125] Gregory Martin, *Roma Sancta (1581)*, ed. and tr. G. Bruner Parks (Rome, 1969), 224–55.

[126] BAV, Arch. Cap. S. Pietro, G.5, pp. 207, 354, cited in Alfarano, *DVB*, 164.

[127] On the restoration of the Constantinian baptistery at the Lateran, see J. Freiburg, 'The Lateran Patronage of Gregory XIII and the Holy Year 1575', *Zeitschrift für Kunstgeschichte*, 57 (1991), 66–87.

[128] Alfarano, *DVB*, 153, Appendix 6; Lanzani, *Vatican Grottoes*, 4; *CD* ii, 551, n. 10; Weil-Garris Brandt, 'Michelangelo's *Pietà*', 88.

[129] Alfarano, *DVB*, 67, 69, 153; Rice, *Altars and Altarpieces*, 24, n. 44. On the preparations for Holy Year, including the portico at St Peter's, see the contemporary account by G. P. Maffei, *Degli annali di Gregorio XIII pontefice massimo*, 2 vols (Rome, 1742), i, 107.

[130] S. F. Ostrow, 'Piazza San Pietro: the Obelisk', in *BSPV* II.ii (*Notes*), 445–7; P. Jacks, 'A Sacred Meta for Pilgrims in the Holy Year 1575', *Architectura*, 19 (1989), 137–65. The Vatican obelisk was eventually moved in 1586; see B. A. Curran, A. Grafton, P. O. Long, and B. Weiss, *Obelisk: A History* (Cambridge, MA, 2009), 103–38.

He wanted it there 'so that it might be read for proof of the Catholic faith by all the faithful'.[131] Gregory thought that the pilgrims' journey to the shrine of St Peter should incorporate the viewing of sacred objects in and around the basilica, each of which would offer reassurance about the antiquity of the cult and illustrate the centuries of devotion that it had inspired. The Apostle's shrine was the ultimate goal of the pilgrims, but the journey to and through the basilica had much to enlighten them.

Gregory expected pilgrims to read Hadrian's epitaph, and to draw conclusions from it about devotion to the papacy in ancient times. This suggests that the inscription was set into the wall of the portico relatively low down, presumably at about the same level as it had been in the south transept (and lower certainly than it is in its current setting, where it is too high to be read easily). The text of the epitaph had much to edify the faithful: the first section extols the nobility, piety, and generosity of Pope Hadrian, *pastor apostolicus*. He was 'a man for whom [there was] life, God, piety, law, glory, Christ' (line 3). Furthermore, Hadrian 'always and everywhere' consecrated temples to God and endowed 'churches with gifts and peoples with holy teaching' (lines 8–9). These strictures sat well with the objectives of the Catholic reformers, especially the dual emphasis on the beautification of churches and the instruction of the faithful. More particularly, and echoing the St Peter's project itself, 'with resources he had erected your fortresses on the walls, he [your] honour, renowned Rome, city, head of the world [*urbs caput orbis*]' (lines 13–14).

The literary echoes here are important. The expression, *Roma caput orbis* was a rhetorical commonplace used by both Ovid and Livy, the latter in relation to the deification of Romulus.[132] In the mid-fifth century, Pope Leo the Great had transformed the same expression by applying it specifically to the see of St Peter rather than the wider city as part of his campaign to enforce the primacy of Rome and the apostolic succession of the papacy. In a sermon for the feast of the Apostles Peter and Paul in 441, he addressed Rome, and compared the victories that the Apostles had brought the city with the glories that followed its foundation under Romulus and Remus:

> These [Apostles] are they who advanced you [Rome] to this glory so that, as a sacred nation, a chosen people, a priestly and royal city, made head of the world (*caput orbis*) by the blessed Peter through the sacred see, you should obtain wider sway by divine worship than by earthly dominion.[133]

---

[131] Alfarano, *DVB*, 42. In Alfarano's autograph, BAV, Arch. Cap. S. Pietro, G.4, fol. 23r these words are added in the margin.

[132] Livy, 1.16.7 and Ovid: *Amores* I.15.26 and Ovid, *Fasti*, 2.684. See below, Chapter 8, 323, n. 56.

[133] 'Isti sunt qui te ad hanc gloriam provexerunt, ut gens sancta, populus electus, civitas sacerdotalis et regia, per sacram beati Petri sedem caput orbis effecta, latius praesideres religione divina quam dominatione terrena'; Leo the Great, *Sermon* 82.1, 'In natale apostolorum Petri et Pauli', *PL* 54, col. 422; P. Brown, 'Aspects of the Christianization of the Roman Aristocracy', *Journal of Roman Studies*, 51 (1961), 1–11; M. Roberts, 'Rome Personified, Rome Epitomized: Representations of Rome in the Poetry of the Early Fifth Century', *The American Journal of Philology*, 122 (2001), 533–65, at 560; D. A. Bullough, 'Empire and Emperordom from Late

Two poets at Charlemagne's court, Alcuin and Theodulf (bishop of Orléans, c.798–818, archbishop from 801), applied the expression to Hadrian and his successor Leo III.[134] For a Counter-Reformation audience, the expression *urbs caput orbis* was resonant not just with late antique arguments for the primacy of the See of St Peter, but also with contemporary efforts to ensure the dominance of the Catholic form of Christianity across the world. More obviously, it reflected the expression *urbi et orbi* ('to the City and to the World') that came to be used as part of the papal blessing that prefaced documents proclaimed after the enthronement of a pope or those granting a plenary indulgence such as that issued in a Holy Year.

The next section of Hadrian's epitaph was perhaps even more valuable to Gregory XIII and his pilgrims. Lines 17 to 38 are spoken in the first person and the speaker is named as *Karolus*: 'Weeping after the father, I Charles have written these songs' (line 17). The poem eulogises the intimacy of the relationship between the Frankish king and pope, and links them in death as they had been in life. Charlemagne petitions Hadrian to intercede with St Peter on Judgement Day, so that he might enter Heaven with the pope. This display of devotion to the papacy by Charlemagne, soon to be emperor of the Romans, was a very powerful exemplar and a reminder to all that even kings and emperors would need the intercession of a priest at the final hour. Charlemagne addresses the reader directly, putting words into the mouth of the reader; 'You whoever may read the verses, suppliant with a devout breast, say of both men, "Gentle God, be merciful"' (lines 25–6). Thus the reader—whether in the early ninth century or in the later sixteenth (or, indeed, right now)—becomes an active participant in the commemoration of the king and the pope.

The text of Hadrian's epitaph was, therefore, one that fitted well with Counter-Reformation concerns. It was evidence of the antiquity of papal authority at St Peter's and of the devotion of powerful kings to Peter's successors, who accepted the ultimate supremacy of priestly over secular power. That the poem was spoken in the voice of Charlemagne—first of the medieval emperors—made the message especially powerful. The beauty of the epigraphy and the oddity of the black stone made the object all the more remarkable and especially worthy of display to the 1575 Jubilee pilgrims and those who came after them. It is probably no coincidence that Gregory also arranged for the monumental bronze inscription that preserved part of the *Lex de imperio Vespasiani* to be moved from the Lateran to the Capitoline in 1576.[135] As discussed

---

Antiquity to 799', *Early Medieval Europe*, 12 (2003), 377–87, at 383. Arator developed Leo's concept when he described the Church as the personified city, whose head was 'crowned with turrets', casting out to the edge of the earth ('Haec turrita caput mundi circumtulit oris'); R. Hillier, tr., *Arator, Historia Apostolica*, Translated Texts for Historians, 73 (Liverpool, 2020), 67–98 and 223, lines 1225–6.

[134] See below, Chapter 8, 323, also Alcuin's poems to Theophylact and to Leo III, MGH, PLAC I, 242 (no. XXI, line 5) and 245 (no. XXV, line 3).

[135] Master Gregorius, *The Marvels of Rome*, tr. J. Osborne, Mediaeval Sources in Translation, 31 (Toronto, ONT, 1987), 97.

below, the bronze ground of that inscription was also burnished black and, like Hadrian's epitaph, it represented the continuity of the authority of Rome to present times (see Figure 5.9).[136]

INSCRIPTIONS IN THE PORTICO

Alfarano says that there were two other early inscriptions in the portico of the old basilica. Like the epitaph, these also served a didactic purpose as demonstrations of the antiquity and munificence of the papacy in that place. The earlier of these inscriptions dates from the pontificate of Gregory II (715–31) and is cut onto two grey rectangular marble slabs.[137] Originally there had been a third slab, but this had been lost before the mid-fifteenth century when Vegio was writing, and he recorded only two.[138] The full text from all three slabs is known, however, from the twelfth-century account of the basilica by Peter Mallius who said that it was fixed 'to the wall in front of the basilica'; the last slab reveals that the inscription had been cut during the reign of the emperor, Leo III (717–41).[139] John the Deacon had seen it there in the later ninth century, but he like Mallius, Vegio, Sabin, and others attributed it to Pope Gregory the Great (590–604).[140]

The text of this inscription records a grant by Gregory II of thirty-nine olive groves for the supply of oil for lighting the lamps at St Peter's (see Figure 5.24). Apart from its practical value, the grant had an obvious spiritual resonance since the oil would provide a perpetual 'light in the temple' and, indeed, the *Liber Pontificalis* claimed that Constantine had made similar grants when the basilica was founded.[141] This inscription would have appealed to Gregory XIII both for its Christological and

---

[136] C. Nardella, *Il fascino di Roma nel Medioevo. Le 'Meravglie di Roma' di maestro Gregorio* (Rome, 1997), 94–6, pl. 9; Krautheimer, *Rome, Profile of a City, 312–1308* (Princeton, NJ, 1980), 192–3; H. L. Kessler and J. Zacharias, *Rome 1300: On the Path of the Pilgrim* (New Haven, CT, and London, 2000), 21–2 and fig. 16.

[137] Cascioli, *Epigraffi Cristiane nell'area vaticana VI–X secolo*, 72–6; C. Franzoni, 'Diploma of Gregory II Referring to the Donation of Olive Trees for the Supply of Oil to the Lamps of the Old Basilica (711–730)', in *BSPV* II.ii (*Notes*), 493–494; *MEC* I, tav. XIV.1; N. Gray, 'The Palaeography of Latin Inscriptions in the 8th, 9th and 10th Centuries in Italy', *PBSR*, 16 (1948), 38–162, at 49–50, no. 4. A transcription by Alfarano is in BAV, Arch. Cap. S. Pietro, G.5, pp. 150–2.

[138] Vegio, 'De antiqua S. Petri apostoli Basilica', *AASS* Junii vii, ch. 70 (col. 0070D–E).

[139] 'In pariete ante Ecclesiam fixis'; Mallius, 'Historia basilicae antiquae S. Petri Apostoli in Vaticano', *AASS* Junii vii, ch. 56–8 (col. 43D–F); *ICUR* II.i, 209–10, no. XIX.39.

[140] Franzoni, 'Diploma of Gregory II', 494; *ICUR* II.i, 209, no. XIX.39 and 411–13, no. LXVI.7, and tab. 134; John the Deacon, 'Vita S. Gregorii', II.20, *AASS* Mar. ii, col. 150E.

[141] Matt. 5.14; John 8:12 and 9:5. C. Savettieri, 'The Atrium', in *BSPV* II.i (*Essays*), 321–4; *LP* 34.12 (for lights at the Lateran), *LP* 34.19 (for St Peter's). On this inscription, see J. Story, 'Lands and Lights in Early Medieval Rome', in R. Balzaretti, J. Barrow, and P. Skinner, eds, *Italy and Early Medieval Europe: Papers for Chris Wickham* (Oxford, 2018), 315–38 and P. Fouracre, *Eternal Light and Earthly Concerns: Belief and the Shaping of Medieval Society* (Manchester, 2021), 19, 25–31. De Rubeis, 'Verba volant', 206, linking this inscription to the continued interest c.1570 in the 'Donation of Constantine' (see, further, below, Chapter 8, 331–7).

Constantinian connotations, as well as the fact that the grant had been made by his namesake, *Gregorius indignus servus*. Gregory XIII himself gave a gift of twelve lights for the apse of St Peter's in 1574, in preparation for the forthcoming Jubilee.[142]

Despite the fact that the inscription in the portico was cut in the earlier eighth century to commemorate a donation by Gregory II, the epigraphy of the inscription does in fact bear close comparison with a genuine inscription of a diploma of Gregory I extant in S. Paulo fuori le Mura. The epigraphic parallels between the early seventh-century inscription of Gregory I for S. Paulo and that of Gregory II cut a century or so later for St Peter's is probably deliberate; both were cut in classical 'Roman' capitals with the first two lines larger than those that follow, although the lettering of the earlier inscription is more consistent, has fewer abbreviations, and is of higher quality overall.[143] Moreover, both inscriptions record the donation of land in the *patrimonium Appiae* for the purpose of supplying oil for the lamps of the two fourth-century basilicas. It is little wonder therefore that Gregory II's donation to St Peter's was widely attributed by later writers to Gregory I, since the epigraphy and the text recalled quite intentionally the earlier donation recorded at S. Paulo.

Gregory I had been buried at St Peter's in front of the sacristy (*secretarium*) at the southern end of the narthex at St Peter's. His tomb had been noted as a place of pilgrimage from at least the eighth century, and this may account for the decision to locate Gregory II's inscription in the south end of the narthex.[144] Gregory XIII's veneration of all things Gregorian is well known. He planned for himself a burial place in new St Peter's, in a chapel in the new north aisle which was the first to be decorated in the new building, called the *Cappella Gregoriana*, and he wanted the chapel to be consecrated with the bones of a suitable predecessor. He was not able to translate the body of Gregory the Great from old St Peter's (which says much about attitudes towards maintaining the integrity of the remaining part of the old church), and so settled for the remains of St Gregory of Nazianus (329–389) who had played a key role in the Council of Constantinople (381) and was one of the four great doctors of the

---

[142] *CD* ii, 552, n. 210. See also Grimaldi's discussion of the terminology of different types of lamps given to St Peter's by Hadrian I and Leo III, *Descrizione*, 412–15, fig. 245–252.

[143] *MEC* I, tav. XII.1; S. Morison, *Politics and Script: Aspects of Authority and Freedom in the Development of Graeco-Latin Script from the Sixth-Century BC* (Oxford, 1972), 104–7, pl. 73; Gray, 'Palaeography of Latin Inscriptions', 49–50 (no. 4); W. Koch, *Inschriftenpaläographie des abendländischen Mittelalters und der früheren Neuzeit. Früh- und Hochmittelalter* (Vienna and Munich, 2007), 83, fig. 56. The parallel is explored in detail in Story, 'Lands and Lights'.

[144] The location of Gregory's tomb and his epitaph was recorded by Bede (*HE*, II.1) in 731, that is, during Gregory II's pontificate; Colgrave and Mynors, ed. and tr., *Bede's Ecclesiastical History*, 130–3. See also the later eighth-century pilgrim itinerary appended to the 'Notitia ecclesiarum urbis Romae'; VZ, ii, 95–9, at 99 (also called the *Enchiridion de sacellis et altaribus basilicae vaticana* in *ICUR* II.i, 224–8, ch. 23). See also, Picard, 'Étude', 758, 762–3; Borgolte, *Petrusnachfolge*, 76–8, Abb. 7 places it in the vestibule of the *secretarium* (i.e. Alfarano's 'ee').

Eastern Church.[145] The relics were installed in June 1580, translated from Santa Maria in the Campo Marzio. He also installed in the new chapel in February 1578 a venerated image of the Madonna, called the *Madonna del Soccorso*, which had come from the oratory of St Leo in the south transept of the old basilica and placed latterly in an altar against the *muro divisorio*, and had the interior of the new chapel decorated in coloured marble *opus sectile*, evoking late antique decoration.[146] All of this expressed continuity with the old basilica and conformed to Counter-Reformation doctrines on the power of sacred images and relics.[147]

The other early inscription noted by Alfarano in the old narthex dates to 1300 and the pontificate of Boniface VIII (1294–1303).[148] It is a copy of part of his bull, *Antiquiorum habet fida relatio*, proclaiming a plenary indulgence for pilgrims to Rome during the very first Holy Year Jubilee in 1300.[149] This *privilegium* had been pronounced at mass on the Feast of the *Cathedra* of St Peter, 22 February 1300, and a copy of the bull placed on the high altar. It symbolised the confidence of the papacy during Boniface's pontificate, and was an explicit statement of his belief in the supremacy of spiritual over temporal power. As a record of the first Jubilee, this inscription was obviously of historic importance for St Peter's and was of great material significance to pilgrims visiting in 1575, since it set in stone the provision for the remission of all their sins if proper devotions were made to the Apostles' shrines in Rome during a Jubilee. Alfarano says it was placed there for the perpetual commemoration of the faithful who had come in 1300 and to ensure maximum exposure of its message to those who would come to the shrine in the future.

Gregory XIII's decision to display Hadrian's epitaph in the narthex of the old basilica thus reflected the needs of the imminent Holy Year celebrations, as well as wider intellectual concerns of the Counter Reformation Church. The three inscriptions in the narthex attested to the antiquity of the institution of the papacy, and to the centrality of the Apostle and of the basilica of St Peter's to its ministry in Rome and beyond. Pilgrims coming to St Peter's for the 1575 Holy Year celebrations would have approached the shrine of the Apostle by passing through the courtyard of the

---

[145] Alfarano, *DVB*, 94, no. 96; S. F. Ostrow, 'The Gregorian Chapel and Its Adjacent Spaces', in *BSPV* II.ii (*Notes*), 666–8; Rice, *Altars and Altarpieces*, 24.

[146] Alfarano, *DVB*, 38–40 (no. 14), 89, 191–192 (no. 90). The image had been translated to an altar against the *muro divisorio* (Alfarano's no. 90) in 1543/4. Apollonij Ghetti et al., eds, *Esplorazioni*, i, 212–13; Rice, *Altars and Altarpieces*, 24, n. 46. On the marble walls, see N. Courtright, *The Papacy and the Art of Reform in Sixteenth-Century Rome: Gregory XIII's Tower of the Winds in the Vatican* (Cambridge, 2003), 250, n. 93; *BSPV* I.ii (*Atlas*), 701–15, esp. fig. 951–3.

[147] On this issue, see also Van Dijk, 'Afterlife of an Early Medieval Chapel', 696.

[148] Alfarano, *DVB*, 116 and 195, no. 129. See also Grimaldi, *Descrizione*, ed. Niggl, 418–20, and fig. 253–4 for a 'facsimile' of the inscription.

[149] C. Franzoni, 'Inscription with the Bull *Antiquiorum habet fida relatio* regarding the Jubilee of Boniface VIII (22 February 1300)', in *BSPV* II.ii (*Notes*), 496–7 (no. 263), II.i, 287; Alfarano, *DVB*, 116, 152 (Appendix 4) and 195.

atrium, to the narthex, and nave of the old basilica before passing through the door in the *muro divisorio* into the shell of the new building. They walked on the floor of the old basilica, now cleared of rubble and repaired. On the right was the *Cappella Gregoriana*, nearing completion and, ahead of them, the *confessio* still within the fourth-century apse, fronted and covered by Bramante's *tegurium*. This journey symbolised the transition from the old to the new, but true to Counter Reformation principles it demonstrated continuity; everywhere the pilgrims turned they were reminded that the old remained at the heart of the new.

GIACOMO GRIMALDI, CARLO MADERNO, AND THE DEMOLITION OF THE REMAINING PARTS OF THE OLD BASILICA

The inscription is mentioned once again before the end of the sixteenth century. Philippe de Winghe, writing in 1590, copied the text in its entirety and noted its new location to the left of the central door in the narthex of the old church. He refers to its elegant letters and notes that the inscription was made of black marble and that it was 'girded with a vine scroll'.[150] In June 1605, shortly after the election of Paul V, an *avviso* from the Congregation responsible for St Peter's records that, 'building work is to continue and the old basilica is to be pulled down'.[151] In September 1605 a decision was made to demolish what remained of the nave and portico of the old basilica on the grounds that the structure had become dangerously unsafe; a block had fallen from the cornice during mass at the altar of the Madonna of the Column—hitting the altar but miraculously, it was believed, missing the celebrant and the worshippers.[152] Another *avviso* of 17 September 1605 records the decision, and a third dated 26 September noted the pope's approval.[153]

The canons of St Peter's protested vociferously in a long letter to the pope.[154] But their emphasis was not on the fabric of the building, for which they made no claim. Their primary concern was for the 'ancient veneration and adornment of that church, and [thus] of the devotion of the people and of all Christianity, since it is an example to which all the others turn, the remnants being looked after'. The canons considered themselves the custodians of the institutional memories of the community and centuries

---

[150] G. B. de Rossi, 'L'inscription du tombeau d'Hadrien I, composée et gravée par ordre de Charlemagne', *Mélanges d'archéologie et d'histoire*, 8 (1888), 478–501, at 482–3.
[151] Hibbard, *Carlo Maderno*, 156–7.
[152] Grimaldi, *Descrizione*, ed. Niggl, 241.
[153] Millon, 'Michelangelo to Marchionni', 104.
[154] BAV, Reg. Lat. 2100, fol. 104v; C. M. Richardson and J. Story, 'Letter of the Canons of St Peter's to Paul V Concerning the Demolition of the Old Basilica, 1605', in *OSPR*, 404–15. See also Kempers, 'Diverging Perspectives', 239 and n. 99.

of devotion by countless pilgrims that had focused on and accumulated within the oratories, altars, and ornamentation of the church; the building itself was secondary, the vessel for this collected *memoria*. As such, the canons urged the seamless translation not just of altars and their associated traditions but of the sacred space where these acts of devotion had occurred. Thus, in the final paragraph of their letter, they urged the pope to enclose within the new building all of the spaces that had lain within the old one including the narthex, which they called the 'portico of the pontiffs' by virtue of the burials in the sacristy and the ancient inscriptions on its walls, including Hadrian's epitaph.

The canons' request was heeded, and so the building was completed by a nave of exceptional length that enveloped completely the footprint of the old narthex. Ironically, by emphasising the need to embrace the sacred spaces of the old church, the canons colluded in the complete destruction of its superstructure. The nave of the new church resembled the form of the old one, but to the canons this was of secondary significance to their desire to see the sacred spaces of the old completely enclosed within the new. Their concerns go a long way to explaining why new St Peter's was completed by a basilican nave rather than, for example, the fourth arm of a Greek Cross, as is shown on the autograph drawing of Alfarano's plan.[155] The fundamental principle behind the canons request was repeated in the monumental inscription set over counter-façade in 1615. There, Paul V proclaimed that he had finished the basilica 'with a mighty annex' comprising 'the whole extent of Constantine's basilica [that was] august with sanctity'.[156] In the last resort, the power of the place was embodied not by the ancient building itself but in the innumerable acts of devotion that had taken place within its walls.

Between October 1605 and early the following year, solemn ceremonies were held to dismantle the old altars and to translate their relics into new St Peter's. As part of this process, Paul V ordered that, 'everything was to be diligently recorded with designs and writings', and a careful record was to be made of the tombs, altars, and reliquaries as they were demolished. Giacomo Grimaldi, a canon, notary, and archivist at St Peter's, and Domenico Tasselli were commissioned to compile the *Instrumenta autentica* to describe and illustrate 'above all the oratory of John VII, the Ciborium of the Holy Veil of Veronica, the paintings of Pope Formosus, the façade mosaic of Gregory IX, and other ancient *memoria*'.[157] Grimaldi's work provides the sort of record that was never made when the demolition of the western end of old St Peter's

---

[155] Alfarano, *DBV*, tav. 2.

[156] '…uniuersum constantinianae basilicae ambitum religione uenerabilem…': translation from T. Lansford, *The Latin Inscriptions of Rome: A Walking Guide* (Baltimore, MD, 2009), 512–13, no. 15.4B, esp. n. 1. Paul V's inscription was removed and replaced in 1631 with another by Urban VIII, who toned down some of his predecessor's more exuberant claims. On the latter, see also M. Gani, 'Plaque with Inscription of Paul V', in *BSPV* II.ii (*Notes*), 739, no. 1194.

[157] Grimaldi, *Descrizione*, ed. Niggl, 148; Lanzani, *Vatican Grottoes*, 13.

had begun so many decades before. His account is an important work of history, but it was also recognised at the time as a key part of the process of *translatio memoriae* legitimising the replacement of 'Constantine's basilica' with the new building (Figure 1.19).

Grimaldi records the full text of Hadrian's epitaph and its location in the old narthex where it had been placed for the 1575 Holy Year. Much of his description is based on earlier writers such as Mallius, Vegio, and Alfarano (especially concerning the derivation of the black marble) but he also comments on the great thickness of the inscription, suggesting that he had witnessed it in the round when it was taken down from the narthex wall.[158] Elsewhere he revealed the location of another Hadrianic inscription, showing it to have been set on the internal wall of the north aisle, below a window and between ornate early third-century pilasters that decorated the oratory built by

FIGURE 1.19 Drawing of the oratory of Pope John VII, from Grimaldi's *Instrumenta autentica*. Hadrian I's 783 inscription is labelled as Item *M*; the porphyry tomb of Pope Hadrian IV (1154–9) stands to the left, BAV, Barb. Lat. 2733, fols 94v–95r. Reproduced by kind permission of the Biblioteca Apostolica Vaticana, Rome.

[158] Grimaldi, *Descrizione*, ed. Niggl, 395–6.

John VII (705–7) for the Virgin and which had later become venerated as the shrine of the Sudarium, or Veronica (the Holy Veil).[159]

This inscription is cut on a piece of marble which is set within a neat frame on two sides but roughly hewn on the others. It dates to November 783 and records the translation of the relics of a number of unnamed saints. The difference in the quality of the epigraphy of this inscription with that of Hadrian's epitaph is startling (see Figure 5.31)—Grimaldi said that it was as if it had been cut with a club rather than a chisel—although the quality of the marble is superlative.[160] This earlier inscription was preserved partly because of its position in the eastern end of the basilica, out of the way of the building work, but partly also because it was interpreted as early evidence for the presence of the relic of the Veronica in the oratory of John VII, otherwise first attested c.1000.[161] The Veronica was central to Counter Reformation arguments supporting the miraculous origins and ancient veneration of holy images, and the 783 inscription was read as evidence supporting arguments for the presence there of the Veronica in the eighth century.[162] Grimaldi's drawing also shows that just to one side of the inscription stood the antique porphyry tomb of another Pope Hadrian (Hadrian IV, 1154–9), moved there from its original location in the southern part of the transept just to the left of the oratory of Constantine's pope, Sylvester I (314–35).[163]

Despite the rapidity with which altars were deconsecrated and relics removed, the final design for the last part of St Peter's was not confirmed until 1608. The choice between a centralised structure or one with an extended nave was not simply one of aesthetic preference; the former design might allow for the preservation of some of the ancient fabric but the latter mirrored the plan of the ancient basilica. Ironically, therefore, those who had argued for the preservation of old St Peter's argued in support of the un-traditional, centralised plan whereas those who wanted to hold true to the fourth-century plan ended up supporting the destruction of the remaining part of the old nave.[164] Paul V equivocated about the scheme, choosing first a centralised plan but changing his mind in September 1607 to back the longitudinal plan proposed by

---

[159] Grimaldi, *Descrizione*, ed. Niggl, 126–7, and also, BAV, Vat. Lat. 6438, fol. 57; D. Dufresne, *Les Cryptes Vaticanes* (Paris and Rome, 1902), 20–1, no. 27; Gray, 'Palaeography of Latin Inscriptions', 53–4, no. 12; Kinney, 'Spolia', 30–2, figs 23–4. It had been noted also by Sabin in the late fifteenth century; *ICUR* II.i, 431, no. LXVI.70.

[160] Grimaldi, *Descrizione*, ed. Niggl, 106. Brandenburg, Ballardini, and Theones, *Saint Peter's*, 70–1. For an analysis of the quality of the marble, see A. Ballardini and P. Pogliani, 'A Reconstruction of the Oratory of John VII (705–707)', in *OSPR*, 190–213, at 200–4. For a note by Alfarano, see BAV, Arch. Cap. S. Pietro, G.5, p. 153.

[161] Dufresne, *Les Cryptes Vaticanes*, 21; Van Dijk, 'Afterlife of an Early Medieval Chapel', 686. Grimaldi's note reads, 'Inscriptio Hadriani papae primo de qua latius dixi in libro sanctiss. sudarii Veronicae'; *Descrizione*, ed. Niggl, 127, fig. 42.

[162] Van Dijk, 'Afterlife of an Early Medieval Chapel', 696–7.

[163] Alfarano, *DBV*, 46, 185 (no. 23).

[164] Pinelli, 'The Old Basilica', 43–5.

Carlo Maderno, under whose direction the remains of old St Peter's were finally removed and the new basilica completed.[165]

The three 'ancient inscriptions' from the old narthex were translated into their new, and final, positions in October 1619, shortly before Grimaldi completed his text. He says of Hadrian's epitaph that it was, 'placed in the magnificent new portico by the order of Paul V in the month of October in the year 1619'.[166] Maderno signed off the accounts of the *Fabbrica* for that year, recording that Leone Garvo had been paid 65 *scudi* for work on the 'ancient inscriptions' in the portico in late September. By late October, Garvo was working on the ornamental surrounds for the three inscriptions, and between 12 October and Christmas he was paid 120.20 *scudi* for this job. By way of contrast, Giovanni Casalano was paid 2,175 *scudi* for the stucco on the vault of the new portico, and for gilding in the portico Anibale Durante was paid 1,450 *scudi*, plus 376.65 *scudi* for his gold and mordent.[167] Matteo Albertini, *scarpellino* (stone worker) and later maestro of the *Fabbrica*, was paid 319 *scudi* between late March and late September that year for work on cutting inscriptions (*epitaffi*) for the new grotto beneath St Peter's.[168] Albertini provided small marble labels for the fragmentary artefacts from the old basilica, and set these objects wherever they would fit in the walls of the *peribolos* and adjoining chapels, focusing especially on the rooms around the Leonine altar that had been uncovered in the southern arm of the old transept in 1580.[169]

These payments show that considerable care and expense was taken over the decoration of the entrance to the newly completed basilica and reveal that the three 'antique inscriptions' were considered to be an essential element in the decorative register of the portico. By placing them in the new portico in the same positions as they had been in recent times, Maderno was recreating the visual references that had meant so much to the canons of St Peter and echoing Leo X's fundamental stricture that 'nothing from the old temple may be moved from its site'. Furthermore, all bar one of the ten pairs of columns in the portico were reused from the old nave.[170] At the front of the main entrance to the new portico, Maderno set the huge, fabulously rare, and expensive

[165] Millon, 'Michelangelo to Marchionni', 104. See also Theones, 'St Peter's 1534–1546', 39 for the argument that it was actually the work on the Cappella Paolina in the Vatican palace that forced the issue, requiring an extended nave to articulate it with the basilica.

[166] Grimaldi, *Descrizione*, ed. Niggl, 396. On the chronology of the decorative design of the portico, see A. Bortolozzi, 'Two Drawings by Giovanni Battista Ricci da Novara for the Decoration of the Portico of new St Peter's', *The Burlington Magazine*, 153 (2011), 163–7. See also De Rubeis, 'Verba volant', 204.

[167] On the stucco decoration and its iconography see, I. Herklotz, 'Francesco Barberini, Nicolò Alemanni, and the Lateran Triclinium of Leo III: An Episode in Restoration and Seicento Medieval Studies', *Memoires of the American Academy in Rome*, 40 (1995), 175–96, at 181.

[168] AFSP, Arm. 26 C. 227 (Spesi 1619), fols 10r–12r. See also the summary accounts produced every fortnight for 1619 in AFSP, Arm. 26 C. 229. For Casalano's work on the stucco ceiling, see *BSPV* I.i (*Atlas*), 290–1, fig. 286–70, and Bortolozzi, 'Two drawings', 163. Also, De Rubeis, 'Verba volant', 205.

[169] Lanzani, *Vatican Grottoes*, 13–14.

[170] Bosman, *Power of Tradition*, 149, fig. 57 and appendix B.

africano columns that had been the first pair in the old nave and which had 'sustained the church like the Apostles Peter and Paul', in order to 'finally make present the substance of the old basilica in all parts of new St Peter's'.[171] Garvo's setting of Hadrian's inscription high up in the portico wall makes it hard for modern viewers to read but, by this stage, the symbolism of the site was such that the power of the object lay as much in the historical associations of place as in the meaning of its verses.

[171] *BSPV*, I.i (*Atlas*), 86, fig. 41; Bosman, *Power of Tradition*, 136–8 and fig. 53.

Figure 2.1 Detail from the *Sta Maria Regina* fresco, from the atrium of Santa Maria Antiqua, Rome (right-hand side), showing Pope Hadrian I on the left with a square nimbus. Photo: Roberto Sigismondi (2011), reproduced by concession of the Ministero della Cultura, Parco archeologico del Colosseo.

2

The 'Life' and Death of Pope Hadrian I

The evidence from later medieval and Renaissance sources shows that the Hadrian's epitaph was treasured in Rome as an object of considerable significance and symbolism long after it had been created. It was particularly valuable as a statement of the devotion of kings-of-old to the papacy, especially in the sixteenth century when Catholicism was challenged. That the king in question was Charlemagne—recalled as the first of the German emperors and ruler of the lands that had spawned the Protestant heresy—made its message all the more resonant to later readers at St Peter's. Politics aside, medieval and Renaissance commentators clearly also valued the inscription as a remarkable artefact; time and again they referred to the oddity of the stone and the quality of its epigraphy, as well as the meaning of its verses.

The cultural value of the inscription in later centuries reflects the original investment in its creation and the care taken over its composition, design, and eventual display in St Peter's basilica. Visually and textually, the inscription proclaimed Carolingian mastery of both the form of inscriptional lettering and the function of epigraphic display on a grand scale, and it was an overt statement of Carolingian *Romanitas*. It should also be seen as part of a pattern of patronage at the basilica whereby secular rulers, Carolingians among them, sought to maintain political influence and spiritual longevity at St Peter's shrine through the donation of gifts—be they physical objects for use in the ritual life of the church, or documents that enshrined a decision or preserved the promise of action and the transfer of privilege or property. The basilica itself was a very important element in these transactions. It was not just a passive architectural setting for the display and use of an object; that setting could influence the form, reception, perception, and remembrance of both the gift and the donor. The symbolism of the site conditioned both the character of the gift itself and subsequent responses to it. The motives behind this particular gift were multiple. The immediate circumstances of its commission after news of Hadrian's death had reached Francia are known from various sources, but reports of Charlemagne's tearful response in early 796 was conditioned both by acknowledgements of Hadrian's unprecedented period of rule as well as the complex relationship that had developed between the two men over the twenty-four years of his pontificate.

HADRIAN'S LIFE

The preservation in Francia of so many of Hadrian's letters within the *Codex Carolinus* has encouraged a Franco-centric analysis of his pontificate. The historiography on Hadrian is dominated by analysis of his relationship with the Frankish king, albeit often shaped by foreknowledge of the events that took place in 800 and a retrospective perception that his pontificate had played midwife to Charlemagne's empire. It used to be argued that, under Hadrian, the cumulative transfer of the trappings of power in Italy away from the emperor in Constantinople was such that his successor's actions in 799/800 were simply a 'recognition' of the reality of the Frankish king's imperial position.[1] This old view is balanced by others that argue for the importance of Hadrian's pontificate in the development of the territorial integrity and institutional independence of the papacy as a temporal power within Italy, suggesting that the markers of authority lost by the eastern emperors at this time were assumed not so much by the Frankish king as by the pope himself.[2] Hadrian's many letters trace efforts to negotiate the transfer of considerable tracts of land in the aftermath of the Frankish conquest of the Lombard kingdom as well as attempts to secure protection for Rome from the remaining Lombard duchies and from Constantinople. However, the formulaic diplomatic niceties of his letters cannot hide the tensions inherent in these negotiations, and the correspondence shows that communication with the pope was often fractious on questions of land and politics as well as theology. Indeed, recent analysis has argued that Hadrian's pontificate was characterised not so much by collaboration with the Frankish king as by tension and conflict, and that his admonitions to Charlemagne on matters of sovereignty as well as theology were frequently frustrated.[3] A more specifically Roman perspective on Hadrian's career shows that his achievements were grounded in his capacity to control the city of Rome as a secular ruler, rooted in his wealthy, aristocratic background and reinforced through strategic patronage of buildings, people, ceremony, and art. Criticism of the quality of Latin texts emanating from the papal office have suggested to some the increasing secularization of the clergy in Hadrian's Rome.[4]

Hadrian oversaw the restoration and embellishment of the city; the *Liber Pontificalis* lists in detail the huge sums of money, bullion, and material resources that he made available for the restoration of churches across the city, as well as civic projects such as

---

[1] P. E. Schramm, 'Die Anerkennung Karls des Grossen als Kaiser. Ein Kapitel aus der Geschichte der mittelatlerlichen "Staatsymbolik"', in *Kaiser, Könige, und Päpste*, i, 215–63. D. S. Sefton, 'The Pontificate of Hadrian I (772–795). Papal Theory and Political Reality in the Reign of Charlemagne', PhD thesis, Michigan State University, East Lansing (1975).

[2] Bullough, 'Empire and Emperordom', 384–5; Scholz, *Politik*, 79, 144–6.

[3] Hartmann, *Hadrian I*, 197–265; Scholz, *Politik*, 100–7.

[4] Marazzi, 'Aristocrazia e società', 49–51; Hartmann, *Hadrian I*, 292–3; C. Wickham, *Medieval Rome: Stability and Crisis of a City, 900–1150* (Oxford, 2015), 15; J. L. Nelson, *King and Emperor: A New Life of Charlemagne* (London, 2019), 347.

the repair of aqueducts, the city walls, and the embankments of the Tiber.[5] Extant buildings and decorative schema are testimony to this patronage. At Santa Maria Antiqua, for example, Hadrian adorned the atrium with a fresco of *Maria Regina* enthroned, surrounded by six nimbed figures. One of these figures—on the left of the scene—is Hadrian himself, holding a large book held tight shut with two clasps. He is shown with a square nimbus, and the portrait is labelled […]ISSMVS [had] RIANVS; the Virgin's right hand, robed in black, extends towards him (Figure 2.1).[6] At St Peter's itself, a puzzling inscription, very roughly cut into a piece of precious Phrygian marble of immense value, records that 'in the time of our lord Hadrian' a relic of the 'holiest of holies' was enclosed in an altar.[7] His patronage of liturgy and liturgical processions in the city incorporating churches such as Santa Maria Antiqua and S. Adriano in Foro (both located within the *Forum Romanum*) reinforced papal articulation of the ancient urban space, reinterpreted for contemporary times.[8]

Hadrian's association with the city was shown also on his coins, which are the first true papal issues and a statement of independence since they were minted in the name of the pope without reference to the emperor in Constantinople.[9] The earlier of Hadrian's two types (minted 772–81) pairs his name and title on the obverse with the legend SCI|PET|RI on the reverse. The later type (781–95) uses the traditional mint mark of Rome—RM—around a stepped cross which incorporates a large letter H on the reverse, matched on the obverse by a facing portrait bust of the pope, sporting a tonsure, and an inscription that read HADRIANVS PAPA (Figure 2.2).[10]

Hadrian also extended the networks of *domuscultae* (church-run estates) in the vicinity of Rome that had been established by Pope Zacharias (741–52) to secure the provision of agricultural produce for the churches, including oil for lights, and the

---

[5] R. Coates-Stephens, 'Dark Age Architecture in Rome', *PBSR*, 65 (1997), 177–232; F.A. Bauer, 'Die Bau- und Stiftungspolitik der Päpste Hadrian I (772–795) und Leo III (795–816)', in SW, *799*, iii, 514–28; T. F. X. Noble, 'Topography, Celebration, and Power: The Making of a Papal Rome in the Eighth and Ninth Centuries', in de Jong and Theuws, eds, *Topographies of Power*, 45–91; Barral I Altet, 'L'VIII secolo', 204–7. On the walls, see especially H. W. Dey, *The Aurelian Wall and the Refashioning of Imperial Rome, AD 271–855* (Cambridge, 2011), 265–6.

[6] Grüneisen, *Sainte-Marie-Antique*, 436 (no. 126, pl. IX.9), 492–3; Maskarinec, *City of Saints*, pl. 6; Costambeys, 'Pope Hadrian I', 379 and fig. 3.

[7] For a discussion of this inscription and its association with the relic of the Veronica, see Ballardini and Pogliani, 'A Reconstruction', 200–3, and this volume, Chapter 5, 222–4, fig. 5.31.

[8] Hartmann, *Hadrian I*, 81–114; Costambeys, 'Pope Hadrian I', 373.

[9] Schramm, 'Die Anerkennung', 225–9; Scholz, *Politik*, 95.

[10] On Hadrian's coins, see Grierson and Blackburn, *Medieval European Coinage*, i, 10, 560 (nos 1031–2), and 638, discussing the possible meaning of the letters IB on the obverse (perhaps a Greek numeral, immobilising an indiction date with reference to the year 783/4, or the initials for 'King Jesus' in Greek). The legend on the reverse fossilises imperial elements (*DN* for Dominus noster, 'our lord', and *CONOB*, used since the fifth century to refer to the production of solidi at the mint of Constantinople). See also I. Garipzanov, *The Symbolic Language of Authority in the Carolingian World (c.751–877)* (Leiden, 2008), 174–5.

Figure 2.2 Denarius of Hadrian I (issued 781–95); *EMC* 1: no. 1032 (enlarged, x2). Obverse: CN[or H] ADRIANUS PAPA | IB reverse: VICTORIA DNN CONOB|H[adrianus]|R[o]M[a]. Photo: Courtesy of the Fitzwilliam Museum, Cambridge.

diaconiae (such as at Sant'Adriano) founded to provide relief for the poor of the city.[11] His own family estates at *Capracorum*, 15km north of Rome, became the centre of a new *domusculta*, which he dedicated to the service of the poor in perpetuity; its revenue and produce were to be used to feed one hundred paupers daily at the steps of the Lateran palace.[12] Hadrian was proactive in matters of theology too; robustly condemning both Iconoclasm and Adoptionism, he sent legates to both Nicaea in 787 and Frankfurt in 794 to uphold papal orthodoxy. These achievements and virtues—his nobility, his patronage of building projects and liturgical spaces, his support of theological orthodoxy, and his care for the poor and vulnerable in Rome—were lauded in the opening paragraph of his 'Life' in the *Liber Pontificalis* and summarised in the closing chapter, written after his death. The first section of the epitaph composed in Francia highlights the same attributes (lines 5–9). This striking parallel between the Roman texts about Hadrian's virtues and the Frankish-produced epitaph reflects the dissemination of an official, papally sanctioned summary of Hadrian's life and legacy.

SOURCES FOR THE LIFE OF HADRIAN: THE *LIBER PONTIFICALIS* AND *CODEX CAROLINUS*

The major sources for studying Hadrian's pontificate are the biographical account in the *Liber Pontificalis* and a substantial corpus of letters.[13] Written in Rome, these sources preserve the papal perspective but both have a distinct Frankish preservation

---

[11] F. Marazzi, 'Il *Liber Pontificalis* e la fondazione delle Domuscultae', in H. Geertman, ed., *Atti del Colloquio Internazionale Il* Liber Pontificalis *e la storia material (Roma, 21–22 febbraio 2002)*, Mededelingen van het Nederlands Instituut te Rome, deel 60/61 (Rome, 2003), 167–88, argues that the earliest *domuscultae* were founded by Zacharias. See also Davis, tr., *Lives of the Eighth-Century Popes*, 31–4. On gifts of oil for lights, see Story, 'Lands and Lights', and Fouracre, *Eternal Life and Earthly Concerns*.

[12] *LP* 97:54, 69. See Marazzi, 'Il *Liber Pontificalis* e la fondazione delle Domuscultae', 176–7; Brown, *Gentlemen and Officers*, 172.

[13] Hartmann, *Hadrian I*, 13–36.

bias. The letters were preserved only because the recipient copies of Hadrian's letters were transcribed in Francia in 791, under Charlemagne's orders, into a collection known now as the *Codex Carolinus*.[14] The *Liber Pontificalis* too, has an important Frankish dimension.[15] The redaction of the text that circulated in Francia is the most diffuse, to judge by the number of extant manuscripts made there before *c*.900. The additions to this redaction were of particular interest to a Frankish readership and may reflect eye witness accounts as relayed to the Frankish court, augmenting, for example, the description of the dedication by Stephen II and Paul I of the imperial mausoleum on the southern flank of St Peter's basilica to St Petronilla, and noting Stephen's renewal of the night office and monastic duties at St Peter's.[16] Details were added to one mid-ninth-century Frankish manuscript of the names of the twelve Frankish bishops who attended the Synod of Rome in 769, alongside a list of bishops from sees in Italy.[17] Two early manuscripts of this redaction, written in the 820s, include the 'Life' of Hadrian, but give him a reign of only twenty years, which may point to the date of the compilation of their exemplar.[18]

The *Liber Pontificalis* is a compilation of biographies of the bishops of Rome down to the death of Stephen V in AD 891; the earliest entries are short, and, from the fourth century, concentrate on lists of endowments of treasure and land made to Roman churches. The brevity of these early entries belies the radical agenda of the text which efficiently re-framed Roman history within a Christian chronology and re-shaped it as a Christian narrative using the Roman genre of serial biography.[19] An important formulaic element of each biography was the closing statement, compiled posthumously, that listed the ordinations conducted by a pope, the date and place of his burial, and a calculation of the length of time that the bishopric was vacant. Thus, each *vita* concludes by focusing on the continuity of the institution. The first edition

---

[14] D. B. van Espelo, 'Rulers, Popes and Bishops: The Historical Context of the Ninth-Century Cologne *Codex Carolinus* Manuscript (Codex Vindobonensis 449)', in R. Meens et al., eds, *Religious Franks. Religion and Power in the Frankish Kingdoms: Studies in Honour of Mayke de Jong* (Manchester, 2016), 455–71; F. Hartmann and T. B. Orth-Müller, eds, *Codex Epistolaris Carolinus: Frühmittelalterlich Papstbriefe an die Karolingerherrscher* (Darmstadt, 2017), 1–30; McKitterick et al., tr., *Codex Epistolaris Carolinus*, 1–13.

[15] M. Buchner, 'Zur Überlieferungsgeschichte des Liber Pontificalis und zu seiner Verbreitung im Frankenreich im 9. Jh.', *Römische Quartalschrift für christliche Altertumskunde und Kirchengeschichte*, 34 (1926), 141–65; McKitterick, *Perceptions of the Past*, 50–1; McKitterick, *Rome and the Invention*, especially 206–20 suggesting that the Frankish additions to the *Liber Pontificalis* and the production of the *Codex Carolinus* may have been contemporary projects.

[16] *LP* 94:40 and 52; 95:3; 96:17; McKitterick, *History and Memory*, 32–3, 142–8.

[17] Duchesne, *Le Liber Pontificalis*, I, ccxxix; Leiden, UB, Voss. Lat. Q. 41, probably copied in western Francia, between 827 and 844 (Bischoff, *Katalog*, no. 2218). On these manuscripts, see McKitterick, *Rome and the Invention*, 216–18.

[18] BnF, Lat. 13729, probably copied at Saint-Denis during Hilduin's abbacy, between 824 and 827 (Bischoff, *Katalog*, no. 4929) and Laon, Bibliothèque Municipale, MS 324, Reims, s. ix[med] (Bischoff, *Katalog*, no. 2109); Duchesne, *Le Liber Pontificalis*, I, clxxvi–vii (nos 19–20); Davis, tr., *Lives of the Eighth-Century Popes*, xv.

[19] R. McKitterick, 'Roman Texts and Roman History in the early Middle Ages', in C. Bolgia, R. McKitterick, and J. Osborne, eds, *Rome across Time and Space, c.500–c.1400: Cultural Translation and the Exchange of Ideas* (Cambridge, 2011), 19–34.

of the *Liber Pontificalis* was compiled shortly after 530 making use of earlier, brief lists and summaries, and contained an account of each pope down to Felix IV (526–30). It was soon revised, and a brief continuation was added in the 540s. The principal early phases of composition can thus be dated to the first half of the sixth century (*c*.520–*c*.550), during a period of political transition, from the domination of Italy and Rome by Arian Ostrogothic rulers to reconquest by eastern emperors.[20] After this, the project was neglected for about a century, until work began again probably around the time of Pope Honorius (625–38). At that point the strategy changed and the biographies of the popes that followed were closely contemporary compositions. A copy of the *Liber Pontificalis* arrived in Northumbria in the early 720s where it was used by Bede. His knowledge of the opening elements of the *Life* of Gregory II (715–31) shows that by the early eighth century writing commenced during the lifetime of the pope, and that the text could be disseminated before the final version was released.[21] This contemporaneity means that the *vitae* of the eighth-century popes are both longer and more overtly topical than those that had come before. The content of each one reflects both the personal interests of the various compilers as well as the formulaic conventions of the genre; not every author was interested in the big issues of contemporary geo-politics, and some preferred to focus more intently on the details of factional rivalry, or papal patronage within the city of Rome.

The *Life* of Hadrian was by far the longest in the *Liber Pontificalis* to date. But its coverage of Hadrian's pontificate is uneven; the first forty-four chapters describe in detail the politics of the first two years of Hadrian's rule that culminated in the summer of 774 with the Frankish invasion and conquest of Lombard Italy and the banishment of the Lombard king Desiderius to permanent exile in Francia. The next fifty-two chapters change tack and focus on Hadrian's enrichment of churches in Rome (especially St Peter's) and the construction of the network of estates—known as *domuscultae*—in the countryside surrounding the city.[22] This shift of emphasis is probably due to a change of author. But the two parts of the account can be linked, seeing in Hadrian's largess evidence of the stability engendered by the new politics that saw Frankish control of the Lombard territories in northern Italy.[23] The *Life* finishes in conventional style with a chapter summarising Hadrian's virtues, the number of ordinations he performed, and the date of his burial in the basilica of St Peter's. The *Life* tells us that this *beatissimus et praeclarus pontifex* was buried

---

[20] Davis, tr., *Book of the Pontiffs*, xiii–xv, xlii–xlvii; McKitterick, *Rome and the Invention*, 15–19.

[21] Duchesne, *LP* I, ccxxii–iii; J. Story, 'Bede, Willibrord and the Letters of Pope Honorius I on the Genesis of the Archbishopric of York', *English Historical Review* 127 (2012), 783–818, at 787.

[22] F. A. Bauer, 'Il rinnovamento di Roma sotto Adriano I alla luce del Liber Pontificalis. Immagine e realtà', in Geertman, ed., *Atti del colloquio internazionale il* Liber Pontificalis *e la storia materiale. Roma* (Rome, 2003), 189–203 and Marazzi, 'Il Liber Pontificalis e la fondazione delle Domuscultae', Geertman, ed., *Atti*, 167–88.

[23] H. Geertman, 'Gli spostamenti di testo nella vita di Adriano I', in Geertman, ed., *Atti*, 155–66 and H. Geertman, *More Veterum. Il Liber Pontificalis e gli edifici ecclesiastici di Roma nella tarda antichita e nell'alto medioevo* (Groningen, 1975) for the phasing of the second part of the *Vita*.

[*depositus*] on 26 December. This, according to the epitaph, was the day that he had died. His rapid burial shows that his tomb had been prepared in advance.

The partial and partisan account from the *Life* of Hadrian is complemented by the evidence of a substantial group of letters from Hadrian, including forty-five addressed to Charlemagne that have been preserved, as noted above, because they were copied in Francia on the instructions of the king in 791.[24] These letters begin when the political section of the *Liber Pontificalis* stops, dating from 774 after the fall of Pavia.[25] The latest among them was probably written in 791, leaving largely silent the closing years of his pontificate.[26] The *Codex Carolinus* not only symbolises the importance which Charlemagne attached to his correspondence with Rome but also demonstrates the existence of some form of centralised archive in Francia where the recipient collection had been gathered and was recopied.[27] The extant manuscript is a late ninth-century copy of the original, made probably in Cologne for Archbishop Willibert (870–89).[28] It retains a copy of the original preface to the collection, set out with red ink in rustic capitals. The preface opens with a chrismon and 'Regnante' invocation followed by a dating clause that records the Anno Domini date (791) plus Charlemagne's full title and regnal year. The preface describes how Charlemagne had issued an instruction to 'restore and recopy' (*renovare ac rescribere*) those letters that had been sent 'from the highest apostolic throne of the blessed Peter, prince of the apostles, or even from the emperor, in the time of his grandfather the lord Charles of good memory and also in the times of his most glorious father Pippin and his family'.[29] Age and neglect had meant that papyrus originals sent from Rome were badly damaged, so the king had commanded that they should be copied anew onto parchment (*membrana*) that was more robust, 'so that no testimony whatsoever of the Holy Church that will be of use in the future should be seen wanting to his successors'.[30]

---

[24] There are forty-five letters from Hadrian to Charlemagne (*CC* 49–94/*CeC* 49–94). There are three others letters from Hadrian that relate to Spain. These were addressed to the Spanish bishops (*CC* 95/*CeC* 97), to Bishop Egila and Johannes the priest (*CC* 96/*CeC* 96), and to Egila alone (*CC* 97/*CeC* 95). On dating, and the inclusion of this Spanish group in the Carolingian collection, see D. A. Bullough, 'The Dating of the Codex Carolinus nos. 95, 96, 97, Wilchar and the Beginnings of the Archbishopric of Sens', *Deutsches Archiv*, 18 (1962), 223–30; Hack, *Codex Carolinus*, i, 76; J. C. Cavadini, *The Last Christology of the West: Adoptionism in Spain and Gaul, 785–820* (Philadelphia, PA, 1993), 13–14, 73–l; D. B. van Espelo, 'A Testimony of Carolingian rule? The *Codex Epistolaris Carolinus*, its Historical Context and the Meaning of *Imperium*', *Early Medieval Europe*, 21 (2013), 254–82, at 267–8.
[25] *CC* 49–50/*CeC* 54–5.
[26] *CC* 93/*CeC* 94 (as dated by Hartmann and Orth-Muller).
[27] Hack, *Codex Carolinus*, i, 74, and ii, 1077–9.
[28] ÖNB, Cod. 449, s. ix$^{3/4}$ (Bischoff, *Katalog*, no. 7121); Unterkircher, ed., *Codex Epistolaris Carolinus* (Graz, 1962); Espelo, 'Rulers, Popes and Bishops', 457–60.
[29] Hack, *Codex Carolinus* i, 60–9. The preface on fol. 1r supplies an Anno Domini date of 791; 'Praefatio', *Codex Carolinus*, ed., Gundlach, 476.
[30] 'Ut nullum penitus testimonium sanctae ecclesiae profuturm suis deesse successoribus videatur' (tr. Espelo, 'A Testimony', 255).

The *Codex Carolinus* comprises ninety-nine letters that had been sent from Rome to Francia, including a summary of one too badly damaged to be recopied in full.[31] Its earliest elements are a pair of letters from Gregory III, sent in 739 or 740 to Charles Martel, Charlemagne's grandfather.[32] These are followed by letters from Zacharias (1), Stephen II (8), Paul I (31) and Stephen III (5). Also included is a letter sent in 757 in the name of 'the senate and all the people of the city of Rome', allegedly from St Peter himself. Two more were added to the end of the manuscript; these had been sent to Pippin in late 767 by Constantine II (June 767–August 768) announcing his election and begging Pippin to maintain the promises that he had made to previous pontiffs.[33] The filing of these two letters at the end of the collection shows that, despite the later *damnatio memoriae* against Constantine in Rome (as described in the *Life* of his successor), the Franks recognised a residual value in his correspondence. The sequence of Hadrian's letters begins in mid to late 774, after Charlemagne had returned from Italy to Francia, and continues until 790.[34] Their distribution clusters unevenly within these years; about a dozen can be dated probably to the eighteen-month period from mid-774 to early 776, another ten in the two years from May 781 to April 783, and seven more in the year-or-so from April 787.[35] Each of these peaks follows one of Charlemagne's visits to Rome. Not all the letters are closely datable, however, since the dating clauses were omitted from the manuscript copy and the order of the letters within the manuscript is only loosely chronological, so it may be that the distribution is more evenly spread than present understanding allows.

It is certain that more correspondence once existed than was transcribed into the *Codex Carolinus*: the letters themselves reveal that Hadrian had written at least another four (now lost) to Frankish correspondents, and that at least twenty-seven had gone the other way, from Francia to Rome.[36] Also, fragments survive of three original letters, none of which was copied into the collection: two of these were written in Italy and are on papyrus (which was the normal support for papal letters throughout this period), and both were sent to Francia early in 788. One was from Hadrian and the other from Maginar, abbot of Saint-Denis and royal envoy to Italy;

---

[31] Hack, *Codex Carolinus*, ii, 1074–9. The summary letter is no. 15 (from Paul I to Pippin).

[32] CC 1–2/*CeC* 2, 1; Noble, *Republic*, 45, n. 151, dates letter 2 to the end of 739 or early 740.

[33] The letter from St Peter and 'the Romans' is CC 13/*CeC* 36. Constantine II's letters are CC 98–9/*CeC* 98–9; he held the see from 5 July 767 to 6 August 768; his fate was recorded in the biography of his successor, *LP* 96: 3–14.

[34] CC 82–5/*CeC* 92, 88, 86, 71 can be dated through internal references to 788 (like the extant papyrus letters discussed below) and no. 94 to 790/1. The dates of CC 86–97/*CeC* 74, 77, 82–5, 87, 89, 94–7 are less secure, and any of these might be dated as late as 791 which is the date supplied by the preface to the collection. See also McKitterick, 'The *Damnatio Memoriae*', 231–48.

[35] CC, nos 49–58, 66–74, 79–84/*CeC* 50–6, 58–60, 63, 67–70, 72, 76, 78–9, 81, 86, 88, 90, 92–3; Hack, *Codex Carolinus*, ii, 1077–8.

[36] Hack, *Codex Carolinus*, ii, 952–82.

both letters concerned Franco-papal policy in Benevento.[37] A third letter—this time on parchment and surviving only in palimpsest—is from Charlemagne to Hadrian; it too discussed Italian affairs including the elevation of Waldo to the bishopric of Pavia, and dates to *c*.791, that is, around the time the *Codex Carolinus* was compiled.[38] Yet more letters are certain to have been exchanged in the last four years of Hadrian's pontificate, after the recopying project had been commissioned.[39] Hadrian's letter-treatise of autumn 793 concerning the Frankish response to the iconodule synod of Nicaea, is unlikely to have been the only correspondence between Rome and Aachen in these years.

Diplomatic innovation

The text opening the *Codex Carolinus* deploys a distinctive dating formula.[40] Its use here was more than a pious invocation, and in the context of a collection of papal (and perhaps originally also imperial) letters was politically pointed.

> + Regnante in perpetuum domino et salvatore nostro Iesu Christo, anno incarnationis eiusdem domini nostri DCCXI, Carolus excellentissimus et a deo electus rex Francorum et Langobardorum ac patricios romanorum, anno felicissimo regni XXIII.

> + Reigning forever Our Lord and Saviour Jesus Christ, in the year of the incarnation of that same Lord 791, Charles most excellent and by-God-elected king of the Franks and Lombards and Patrician of the Romans, in the 23rd year of his most favoured reign.

The 'Regnante' formula had been used in the opening statement of the *acta* of the synod convened in Rome in April 769 by Stephen III, 'thrice-blessed and co-angelic', which had condemned Constantine II and established new rules for the election of

---

[37] Both were preserved in the archive of Saint-Denis. This letter from Pope Hadrian I is now Paris, Archives Nationales, K. 7. No. 9², see *ChLA*, XVI, no. 630, and *Codex Carolinus*, Appendix 1, ed., W. Gundlach, MGH, Epp. III (Berlin, 1892), 654–5. The letter from Maginarius is Paris, Archives Nationales, K. 7 No. 9¹; *ChLA*, XVI, no. 629; *CC*, Appendix 2, 655–7. On these letters, see Hack, *Codex Carolinus*, i, 615–21, and ii, 1011.

[38] The palimpsest letter is now in Munich, Bayerische Staatsbibliothek, Clm 6333, fols 90v and 87r; *ChLA*, xii, no. 543; see also M. Mersiowsky, 'Preserved by Destruction: Carolingian Original Letters and Clm 6333', in G. Declercq, ed., *Early Medieval Palimpsests*, Bibliologia, 26 (Turnhout, 2007), 73–98; Hack, *Codex Carolinus*, ii, 947.

[39] See also Wolfenbüttel, HAB, Cod. Guelf. 254 Helmst. which include a quire (labelled XIII, now fols 1–8v) containing ten of Leo's letters to Charlemagne (808–13) alongside another quire (XII, now fols 9r–16v) containing the *Brevium Exemplar* and the *Capitulare de villis*. A digital facsimile is available, and see also C. Brühl, ed., *Capitulare de villis. Cod. Guelf. 254 Helmst. der Herzog August Bibliothek Wolfenbüttel*, 2 vols (Stuttgart, 1971).

[40] For its use in synodal proceedings in Britain, e.g. Clofesho in 747, see A. W. Haddan and Stubbs, eds, *Councils and Ecclesiastical Documents Relating to Great Britain and Ireland*, 3 vols (Oxford, 1869–78), iii, 362–76, at 362, and J. Story, *Carolingian Connections: Anglo-Saxon England and Carolingian Francia, c.750–c.870*, Studies in the Early History of Britain, 2 (Aldershot, 2003), 76–7.

future popes.[41] Its use there has been explained as an explicit rejection of imperial authority over Rome, both political and theological.[42] The proceedings of 769 synod broke with a convention that had been followed in Rome since the time of the Emperor Justinian (527–65), who had insisted on documents being dated by a formula that stressed imperial authority and divine confirmation of the emperor's rank; *Imperante domino piisimo augusto N., a Deo coronato, magno imperatore* ('By the most pious august lord *N* commanding, by God crowned, great emperor').[43] Now, however, the pope ruled in Rome during the reign of Christ the king, rather than any temporal, imperial power. Charlemagne's use of the 'Regnante' invocation at the opening of the *Codex Carolinus* similarly stressed the priority of the kingship of Christ and the fact that he, Charles, had been selected (*electus*) by God Himself to be king of the Franks, Lombards, and patrician of the Romans; God had chosen Charles to rule as king, in contrast to the emperors who were 'crowned by God' after selection by mortal men.

Although not new, the 'Regnante' formula began to be used systematically in Italy from the early 770s. The Lombard duke of Spoleto, Hildeprand, who had been installed by Hadrian in Spoleto in 774 began to date documents for the abbey of Farfa by papal era, *temporibus ter beatissimus et coangelici domni adriani et universalis papae*, and then—once Charlemagne's conquest was assured—by the regnal years of his new overlord, *Regnante domno nostro Karolo excellentissimo rege Francorum atque Langobardorum, anno regni eius in Italia deo propitio ii*.[44] Pope Hadrian did likewise, and after the Frankish conquest of Lombardy he rejected imperial-style dating clauses, preferring the 'Regnante' formula combined with the years of his own pontificate. In 781 (following Charlemagne's visit to Rome) he issued a privilege for Saint-Denis in Paris, which contained a dating clause that cited the day (*Kal. Dec.*), his pontifical year, and the indiction, and which used the phrase, *Regnante domine et salvatore nostro Iesu Christo*. The same expression is used in papal privileges throughout the 780s

---

[41] The text is given by Duchesne, ed., *Le Liber Pontificalis* i, 483, n. 46. The term 'ter beatissimus et coangelicus' had been used earlier in a letter sent by the Roman 'senate' to Pippin III in 757 in support of Paul I; *CC* 13/*CeC* 36. In a letter to Boniface, datable 746–7, Archdeacon Theophylact (whose challenge for the papacy after the death of Stephen II in 757 lay behind the letter to Pippin), had referred to Zacharias as the 'holy co-angelic father'; M. Tangl, ed., MGH, Epp. sel. 1 (Berlin, 1916), 189–91, no. 85; E. Emerton, trans., *The Letters of Saint Boniface*, Records of Civilization. Sources and Studies, 31 (New York, NY, 1940), 156–7, no. 69.

[42] Schramm, 'Die Anerkennung', 223–4; E. H. Kantorowicz, *The King's Two Bodies. A Study in Medieval Political Theology* (Princeton, NJ, 1957), 334; Noble, *Papal Republic*, 133–4. See also A. Bellinger and P. Grierson, eds, *Catalogue of the Byzantine Coins in the Dumbarton Oaks Collection and in the Whittemore Collection*, 3.i (Washington, DC, 1993), 90.

[43] 'Concilium Romanum, 769', ed. A. Werminghoff, MGH, Conc. 2.1 *Concilia aevi Karolini*, I, (Hannover, 1906), no. 14, 74–92, at 79; Noble, 'Topography, Celebration, and Power', 75–7. For an English translation of the text of Justinian's 47th *novella*, and its general application over the 'provinces over which God has granted us to rule', see D. J. D. Miller and P. Sarris, *The Novels of Justinian: A Complete Annotated English Translation*, 2 vols (Cambridge, 2018), i, 405–8.

[44] 'In the time of thrice blessed and co-angelic lord Hadrian and universal father' and 'Reigning by our lord Charles, most excellent king of the Franks and Lombards, the second year of his reign in Italy by God's grace', Noble, 'Topography, Celebration, and Power', 78–9. *LP* 97.33; Davis, tr., *Lives of the Eighth-Century Popes*, 137, n. 47.

and is reflected also in the legends on the first, overtly papal coins produced for Hadrian in Rome. The parallel with the preface to the *Codex Carolinus* composed in 791 is thus especially striking, not least because it is otherwise so rare in Carolingian sources.

It was used in only two other extant texts from Francia in the late 780s, both with connections to the pope. It is found at the head of the *Admonitio generalis*, Charlemagne's great reform capitulary of 789, which made use of the collection of canon law and decretals that Hadrian had sent to Francia in 774, known as the *Dionysio-Hadriana*.[45] It is also used twice in the report written by the papal legates who had been sent to Britain by Hadrian in late 786.[46] A report was sent back to Rome by one of the two legates, George, bishop of Ostia and Amiens (who had been a prominent signatory of the 769 Synod of Rome).[47] As befitting his dual role as bishop of a Frankish see as well as a Roman one, the Legates' Report combined the new-style papal and Carolingian dating protocol in its proem:

> Synodus que facta est in anglorum saxnia temporibus ter beatissimi et coangelici domini Hadriani summi pontificis et universalis papae, regnante gloriosissimo Karolo excellentissimo rege Francorum et Langobardorum seu patricio Romanorum, anno regni ipsius XVIII, missis a sede apostolica Georio [*sic*] Ostiensi episcopo, et Theophylacto, venerabili episcopo sancte Tudertine ecclesie, regnante domino nostro Iesu Christo in perpetuum, anno incarnationis eiusdem domini nostri DCCLXXXVI, indictionis X.[48]

> The synod which was held in English Saxony in the time of thrice blessed and coangelic Lord Hadrian, highest pontiff and universal father, with the most glorious Charles reigning, most excellent king of the Franks and Lombards, or Patrician of the Romans, the 18th year of his rule, George bishop of Ostia and Theophylact, venerable bishop of the holy church at Todi sent by the apostolic see, our Lord Jesus Christ reigning forever, in the year of the incarnation of that same Lord 786, in the 10th indiction.

A few manuscripts of Hadrian's canon law collection, the *Dionysio-Hadriana,* open with a dedicatory poem that contains another intriguing innovation which seems to

---

[45] *Die Admonitio generalis Karls des Grossen*, ed. H. Mordek et al., MGH, Fontes XVI (Wiesbaden, 2013), 180–239, at 180, 250. Duchesne, ed., *LP* I, 516; D. A. Bullough, 'Roman Books and Carolingian *renovatio*', in his *Carolingian Renewal: Sources and Heritage* (Manchester, 1991), 1–38, at 14; L. Kéry, *Canonical Collections of the Early Middle Ages (ca. 400–1140), A Bibliographical Guide to the Manuscripts and Literature*, History of Medieval Canon Law, ed. W. Hartmann and K. Pennington (Washington, DC, 1999), 13–20; H. Mordek, 'Dionysio-Hadriana', *Lexikon des Mittelalters*, 9 vols (Stuttgart, 1999), 1074–5.

[46] George of Ostia and Amiens, 'Legates' Report'; E. Dümmler, ed., MGH, Epp. IV, 19–29, at 20. On the Legates' Report, see C. Cubitt, *Anglo-Saxon Church Councils, c. 650–c. 850*, Studies in the Early History of Britain (London, 1995), 166–90, and Story, *Carolingian Connections*, 55–92.

[47] Hack, *Codex Carolinus*, ii, 1001–4.

[48] See J. Story, 'Insular Manuscripts in Carolingian Francia', in C. Breay and J. Story, eds, *Manuscripts in the Anglo-Saxon Kingdoms: Cultures and Connections* (Dublin, 2021), 67 (fig. 5.1) for a plate of the unique manuscript (Wolfenbüttel, HAB, Cod. Guelf. 454, fol. 114r), which emphasises in larger letters the opening phrase 'Regnante domino nostro Iesu Christo in perpetuum'.

reflect these developments in diplomatic protocol and was one that proved enduring. It has long been thought that this legal collection was compiled following a request made by the Frankish king during his visit to Rome at Easter 774. The poem that prefigures the collection in some ninth- or early tenth-century manuscripts anticipates the destruction of Lombard independence—'you will crush underfoot the neck of the perfidious king Desderius'—and attributes the king's victory directly to St Peter who provides honour and victory in exchange for the Lombard territories that are the *sacra dona* promised to the church (*aula*) of Peter.[49] The poem seems very likely to have been composed in Rome in the later eighth century, and may be as early as 774.[50] It is difficult to interpret and date securely because the Latin of the poem is corrupt and the metre stilted because the structure is artificially constrained by the device of an acrostic.[51] The first letter of each line spells out the name of the donor and recipient: *Domino excell(entissimo) filio Carulo, magno regi, Hadrianus papa*; 'Pope Hadrian to his most excellent son, the lord Charles, great king'. This seems to be the first time that the epithet *magnus* had been associated with Charles, although it modifies the word *rex* rather than the king's personal name. It occurs here twice, in the acrostic and again in the body of the poem, *In hanc sanctam sedem rex magnus Carolus splendit* (line 16). It was used in the same way four times in the section of the *Life* of Hadrian in the *Liber Pontificalis* that described Charlemagne's advance on Rome at Easter 774. There *Carolus magnus rex* was also *excellentissimus*, *christianissimus*, or *benignissimus* too, as well as *a Deo protectus* or *a Deo institutus*.[52] The tone of these triumphal epithets is rather different to the formal epistolary and diplomatic protocol that was observed in the letters that came from Hadrian's office after the summer of

---

[49] Duchesne, *Le Liber Pontificalis*, i, 516; E. Dümmler, ed., MGH, PLAC I, 90–1; 'Nefa perfidi regis calcabis Desiderii colla / Vires eius prosternens mergis barathrum profundi. / Septus Languvardorum regnum munus reddis tuum, / Pollicita sacra dona clavigeri aulae Petri / Amplius donans tibi victoriam simulque honorem'; 'You will crush underfoot the neck of the perfidious king Desiderius / You destroy his powers and sink them into the depths of the abyss / You restore the captured Lombard kingdom as your gift / The sacred offerings promised to the church of the key-bearer Peter / Who gives to you greater victory and also honour' (lines 39–43). On the epithet 'clavigerus', and its use in *tituli* in St Peter's, see Chapter 3, 134 and J. Story, 'Aldhelm and Old St. Peter's Rome', *Anglo-Saxon England*, 39 (2010), 7–20, at 18–19.

[50] On the difficulties of these lines, see A. Firey, 'Mutating Monsters: Approaches to "Living Texts" of the Carolingian Era', *Digital Proceedings of the Lawrence J. Schønberg Symposium on Manuscript Studies in the Digital Age*, 2 (2010), 1–14, at 6–9. For a German translation of the verses and analysis of their connection with Hadrian's rhetoric in other letters, see Scholz, *Politik*, 82–5.

[51] For damning criticism of the Latinity and metrical quality of the poem, see Hartmann, *Hadrian I*, 271–2, 292. The poem is found in six of the extant ninety-one medieval copies of the *Dionysio-Hadriana*: the earliest is BnF, Lat. 11710, f. 1 (*c.*805 from Burgundy) which lays out the poem as prose in two columns, thereby missing the effect of the acrostic on the first letter of each verse; Bischoff, *Katalog*, no. 4707. The acrostic can best be seen in Munich, Bayerische Staatsbibliothek, Clm 6355, fol. 1b, s. ix$^{2/4}$ from Freising; Bischoff, *Katalog*, no. 3059. The other manuscripts are Munich, Bayerische Staatsbibliothek, Clm 6424, s. ix$^{2/4}$ (Bischof, *Katalog*, no. 3000); Paris, BnF, Lat. 1452, s. ix$^{4/4}$ or s. ix/x (Bischoff, *Katalog*, no. 4012); Paris, BnF, Lat. 3182, s. x$^{2/2}$; Paris, BnF, Lat. 3844, s. ix$^{2/4}$ (Bischoff, *Katalog*, no. 4283); Paris, BnF, Lat. 4278, s. ix$^{3/4}$ (Bischoff, *Katalog*, no. 4295).

[52] *LP* 97: 23, 27, 29, 37.

774 and which avoided such hyperbole. In those letters Charles was invariably addressed as *rex Francorum et Langobardorum et patricius Romanorum*.[53] But innovation seems to have been possible in literary contexts such as the acrostic dedication poem and the *Liber Pontificalis*. *Carolus magnus rex* was thus, it seems, a papal invention, self-consciously recalling the old-style imperial invocation that had styled Justinian and his successors, *a Deo coronato, magno imperatore*, 'crowned by God, great emperor'.

HADRIAN'S DEATH

The *Liber Pontificalis*, which is so detailed for the opening years of Hadrian's pontificate, is silent on the last years of his life and on the reactions to news of his death. His death is recorded in formulaic fashion, with a summary of his achievements (giving alms to the poor, endowing churches, maintaining orthodox faith), notice of the ordinations that he had made, and the date of his burial in St Peter's on 26 December. Missing is a calculation of the period that the apostolic see lay vacant. An explanation for this is found in the opening chapters of the next *vita*, which reveal that Leo was elected on St Stephen's Day, that is, the same day that Hadrian was entombed. The speed of Leo's election was doubtless due to the coincidence of his predecessor's death during the Christmas feast when the electoral college was present in Rome but suggests also that Leo's faction was ready to act.

Beyond Rome, however, several sources recorded the death of Hadrian and Charlemagne's reaction to the news. The king wept. His response was personal and emotional and is recorded over and again, often in the first person, using the king's voice. In Alcuin's verses, Charles cried as he composed the verses of the epitaph.[54] His first letter to the new pope, Leo, opens with reference to the 'tearful wound of grief inflicted on our soul by the death of the most beloved father and faithful friend'. 'I cannot speak of it', Charles continued, 'without grief, nor think of it without tears for my sadness'.[55] The king's letter is preserved in the basic Tours collection of Alcuin's correspondence and this, along with the parallel diction of the epitaph plus other characteristic rhetorical devices, strongly suggests that Alcuin also drafted the letter. Subsequently, Theodulf and Einhard used similar language, comparing the loss of the pope to the deaths of members of the king's close family. Theodulf's verses for

---

[53] M. McCormick, *Eternal Victory: Triumphal Rulership in Late Antiquity, Byzantium and the Early Medieval West*, Past and Present Publications (Cambridge, 1986), 378; Hack, *Codex Carolinus*, i, 118–23. The earliest letter from Hadrian postdates the fall of Pavia in July 774; *CC* 49, 50/*CeC* 54, 55.

[54] Hadrian's epitaph, line 17; POST PATREM LACRIMANS KAROLVS HAEC CARMINA SCRIBSI | weeping after the father, I Charles have written these songs.

[55] Charlemagne, 'Letter to Leo III'; Alcuin, *Ep.* no. 93. For Alcuin's authorship, see Bullough, *Alcuin*, 455–8.

Hadrian 'intone the words of weeping' (*verba tonat...lacrimosa*), taking on the voice of the king better to convey the intimacy of his grief:

> Protinus agnovi veteris vestigia luctus,
> Morsque parentum oculis est revocata meis.
> Taedia Pippini sensi venientia morte,
> Bertradamque dolor, pro dolor, iste refert.
> Cumque tui aspectus, sanctissime papa, recordor
> Corque oculosque meos nil nisi luctus habet.
>
> Immediately I recognised the traces of old grief,
> And the death of my parents was revealed to my eyes.
> I felt the weariness that came with the death of Pippin
> And that sorrow, alas, brings back to my mind Bertrada.
> And when I recollect your appearance (*aspectus*), most holy pope,
> Nothing but grief seizes my heart and my eyes.[56]

This tearful response is echoed in Einhard's biography of the king;

> Nuntiato etiam sibi Hadriani Romani pontificis obitu, quem in amicis praecipuum habebat, sic flevit, asci fratrem aut carissimum filium amisisset.
>
> When he was informed of the death of Hadrian, the Roman pontiff, he cried so much that it was as if he had lost a brother or a deeply loved son, for he had thought of him as a special friend...[57]

This passage is placed in the midst of Einhard's chapter about Charlemagne's family, which discusses his affection for his own children, his attention to their education and their place at his court, as well as his grief when two of his sons and a daughter died in their youth. The discussion of Hadrian's death in this domestic, personal context reinforces the impression of a special bond between Charlemagne and the pope, as one that went beyond the normal ties of political diplomacy or friendship between men of the world; theirs, implied Theodulf and Einhard, was a deeper connection that bordered on family.

The 'major' sets of Frankish annals note none of this emotion. Hadrian's death is reported at the opening of the entry for 796, but the writers of both the *Annales regni Francorum* and the Revised version of that text quickly moved on to discuss the election of the next pope, Leo III, and his decision to announce his election by dispatching envoys to Charles carrying extraordinary gifts: the keys to St Peter's *confessio* and the banner (*vexillum*) of the city of Rome.[58] These symbolised the king's rights in

---

[56] Theodulf of Orléans, 'Super sepulchrum Hadriani papae', ed. E. Dümmler, MGH, PLAC I (Berlin, 1881), 489–90, lines 13–18; Andersson, tr., *Theodulf of Orléans*, 73–5.
[57] Einhard, *VK*, ch. 19; Dutton, tr., *Charlemagne's Courtier*, 28–9.
[58] *ARF and Rev. s.a.* 796; Schramm, 'Die Anerkennung', 239–42.

Rome as *patricius Romanorum* as well as his duties, and the Frankish annalists were clearly impressed by this symbolic presentation of Charlemagne's clout in Rome. The Revised version alone says that Leo also asked Charlemagne to send one of his *optimates* to Rome 'so that the Roman people might declare its loyalty and submission through an oath of allegiance'.[59] Angilbert, abbot of Saint-Riquier, was duly sent for this purpose, along with some of the vast Avar treasure recently won by the Frankish armies in Pannonia.[60] A year after his accession, Hadrian had also sent an embassy to Francia but, in contrast to Leo's supplications in 796, Hadrian's objective in 773 had been to remind Charlemagne of his duty as *patricius Romanorum* to defend Rome against the encroachments of the Lombards, 'for the service of God, the rights of St Peter and the relief of the Church'.[61] Leo's several acts of deference on his accession in 796 demonstrate how much the Frankish king's authority had grown in the intervening twenty-five years and just how much the balance of power was shifting in his favour now that Hadrian was dead. Leo's insistence on a Frankish witness to a ritualised oath of allegiance from the *populum Romanorum* cleverly triangulated the bonds of obligation between king, pope, and people.

Charlemagne's letter to Leo reveals that a high-level Frankish embassy, led by Angilbert, had intended to visit Hadrian early in the year. Planning was at an advanced stage—including the preparation of special gifts for the pope—when papal envoys arrived in Aachen bearing news of Hadrian's death and the election of Leo. The gifts intended for Hadrian may have included some part of the Avar treasure, recently acquired, that Angilbert subsequently delivered to the new pope. Another sumptuous royal gift certainly meant for Hadrian, and which was probably also intended for inclusion in Angilbert's luggage, was the Dagulf Psalter, so called after its primary scribe who also composed and copied two poems that were added to the front of the book. The first of these (on fol. 4r), yet again, was in Charlemagne's voice, dedicating the codex: 'To Hadrian highest pope and blessed father / I, King Charles, send greetings and good wishes, father'.[62] The ivory covers made for the psalter depict in four panels the story of the production of the psalms: King David is first shown instructing scribes to copy down the verses and then enthroned, playing the harp,

---

[59] *Rev. s.a.* 796, 'qui populum Romanum ad suam fidem atque subiectionem per sacramenta firmaret'.

[60] *ARF s.a.* 796.

[61] *ARF s.a.* 773. The earliest letter from Hadrian in the *Codex Carolinus* dates to the second half of 774; *CC* 50/*CeC* 55.

[62] Dagulf, 'Verses to Hadrian', 'Hadriano summo papae patrique beato / Rex Carolus salve mando valeque, pater'; Dümmler, ed., MGH, PLAC I, 91–2, lines 1–2; *CSLMA* I, 287–9 (DAGU 2). K. Holter, ed., *Der goldene Psalter 'Dagulf Psalter': Vollständige Faksimile-Ausgabe im Originalformat von Codex 1861 Der Österreichischen Nationalbibliothek*, Codices selecti phototypice impressi, 69 (Facsimile) and 69* (Commentarium) (Graz, 1980), 48 and L. Nees, *Frankish Manuscripts: The Seventh to the Tenth Century*, Survey of Manuscripts Illuminated in France, I (London, 2022), no. 35. On the debate over the date of the manuscript, see Chapter 7, 272–5.

surrounded by animated musicians.[63] On the other side, St Jerome is depicted first receiving a letter from Pope Damasus (366–84) with instructions to translate the psalms, and then dictating the improved verses to his scribes. In the second poem (on fol. 4v), this time addressed to the king himself, Dagulf described these ivory tablets on the covers of the book as having been 'marvellously sculpted by an ingenious hand'. Here, he picks up on the nickname, David, by which Charles was known at court, eliding the Frankish king's piety and wisdom (*rex pie, dux sapiens*) with that of the Old Testament ruler, who is *rex doctiloquax* and sings with the choir.[64] This was a gift that emphasised royal wisdom, religious devotion, biblical authenticity, and the cultural prowess of the court.

Written throughout in golden letters, Dagulf's verses to Charlemagne begin, *Aurea Daviticos en pingit littera cantus* ('Golden lettering paints the chant of David, Behold!').[65] This line was known to Theodulf, who reused its diction and tight metrical structure in the opening words of his verses on the death of Hadrian: *Aurea funereum complectit littera carmen* ('Golden lettering embraces the funereal song'). Theodulf also borrowed the epithets 'pious' and 'wise', but this time applied them to the pope, who had been *vir pie, vir sapiens*. His verses refer directly to the gifts (*munera grata*) that Charlemagne was preparing to send to Rome 'while you were alive'. But now that Hadrian is dead, says Theodulf (using Charlemagne's voice), 'I prepare sorrowful gifts from a mournful breast / Marble in place of clothing, a tearful song (*flebile carmen*) in place of gold / Borne on the capacious urn (*urna capax*) which is now your little home'.[66] Thus, says Theodulf, a marble stone carrying a verse lament was being sent in place of the gifts that had been so carefully planned for the pope. Golden lettering on the black stone replaced the golden words of the purple psalter, and Theodulf's reworking of Dagulf's opening line skilfully references both. This poetic description and the two lines directly addressing Leo (lines 29–30), as well as the shared metaphor of the defended walls, suggest that Theodulf's verses were

---

[63] Paris, Louvre, Département des Objets d'art, MR370 and MR371; Holter, ed., *Der goldene Psalter*, Commentarium, 48.

[64] Dagulf, 'Verses to Charlemagne', 'Haec merito tabulis cultim decorantur eburnis / quas mire exculpsit ingeniosa manus. / Illic psalterii prima ostentatur origo / et rex doctiloquax ipse canere choro'; E. Dümmler, ed., MGH, PLAC I, 92, lines 5–8; Holter, ed., *Der goldene Psalter*, Commentarium, 47; *CSLMA* I, 287–9 (DAGU 1). This is probably the earliest manuscript that can be securely linked to an extant luxury cover. On the association of the name of King David with Charlemagne, see M. Garrison, 'The Social World of Alcuin: Nicknames at York and the Carolingian Court', in L. Houwen and A. A. MacDonald, eds., *Alcuin of York: Scholar at the Carolingian Court* (Groningen, 1998), 59–79.

[65] See also Chapter 7, 272, 278. This metrical structure is often called a 'golden line' where the two adjectives are separated by a verb from the two substantive nouns (abVAB).

[66] 'Tristia numc maesto pectore dona paro / Marmora pro tunicis, proque auro flebile carmen / Quae gerat urna capax iam tua parva domus'; Theodulf, 'Super sepulchrum Hadriani papae'; Dümmler, ed., MGH, PLAC I, 489–90, lines 20–2.

written in response to, rather than in competition with, Alcuin's epitaph for Hadrian.[67] It seems highly likely, as Bullough suggested, that Theodulf's verses were composed to accompany the finished Alcuinian inscription when it was taken to Rome.[68] In a nice touch, the metaphor of the *capax urna*, from which the lot of each man's destiny was drawn and which bore words of the *flebile carmen*, was a metaphor especially favoured by the Roman poet Horace, whose cognomen, Flaccus, was Alcuin's courtly nickname.[69]

Another set of annals, now called the *Annales Laureshamenses* ('The Lorsch Annals') because of frequent references to that monastery in the early section of the text, provides valuable details of Charlemagne's actions after Hadrian's death.[70] The witness of this set of annals is especially important as it is generally agreed to be a closely contemporary record of events of the years 794 to 803, and survives in two manuscripts, the earlier of which was copied very close in date to the events being described, and may be contemporary.[71] This fragmentary manuscript, now in Vienna, contains a set of annals that begin half way through an entry for 794 and finishes with a brief account of events in 803. Two scribes worked on the entry for 795, changing over from one to the other halfway through the account of the year's events. The scribe who completed the 795 entry incorporated the information about the death of Hadrian and went on to write out the annals for 796 (on the Avars) and 797 (on the Saxons). A change in the ink colour between the closing sentences for 795 and the opening words of the entry for 796, and again at the start of 797, suggests that the scribe paused for a time between annals. The other scribe returned to write the entry

---

[67] Bullough, *Alcuin*, 460–1; S. Scholz, 'Karl der Große und das Epitaphium Hadriani. Ein Beitrag zum Gebetsgedenken der Karolinger', in R. Berndt, ed., *Das Frankfurter Konzil von 794. Kristallisationspunkt karolingischer kultur*, 2 vols (Mainz, 1997), i, 373–94. See also this volume, Chapter 8.

[68] On the timing of the composition of Alcuin's epitaph for Hadrian, see Bullough, *Alcuin*, 439–40 n. 24, 460–1, and further in this volume, Chapter 8, 312–14.

[69] Quintus Horatius Flaccus [Horace], *Odes* III.1: 'omne capax movet urna nomen'. The phrase 'flebile carmen' derives from Ovid, who used it twice (*Heroides*, 15, 5; *Tristia*, V.1, 5).

[70] G. H. Pertz, ed., MGH, SS I, 22–39; tr., P. D. King, *Charlemagne: Translated Sources* (Kendal, 1987), 137–45. Another version of the text also contributed to the *Chronicon Moissiacense*, written in southern Gaul containing annals up to 818; G. H. Pertz, ed., MGH, SS I, 282–313, at 302 for the entry interpolating the data on the death of Hadrian and the commission of the epitaph. See also R. Collins, 'Charlemagne's Imperial Coronation and the Annals of Lorsch', in J. Story, ed., *Charlemagne: Empire and Society* (Manchester, 2005), 52–70, at 60.

[71] ÖNB, Cod. 515, fols 1–5; CLA X.1483; Bischoff, *Katalog*, no. 7132 ('Upper Rhine, ?Alemannia area)', s. VIII/IX. For a facsimile and commentary on this manuscript, see F. Unterkircher, ed., *Das Wiener Fragment der Lorscher Annalen [Annales Laureshamenses], Christus und die Samariterin, Katechese des Niceta von Remesiana: Codex Vindobonensis 515 der Österreichischen Nationalbibliothek*, Codices selecti phototypice impressi, 15 (Graz, 1967). The complete text of the Lorsch Annals is found in Sankt Paul in Kärnten, Stiftsbibliothek St. Paul im Lavanttal, MS 8/1 (25.4.9a); Bischoff, *Katalog*, no. 5939 (s. ix[in], Reichenau), on which see SW, 799, ii.3. The entries for 795–800 (first part) in this manuscript are re-written over an extensive erasure. Both manuscripts are discussed by Collins, 'Charlemagne's Imperial Coronation', 55–9, and digital facsimiles are available via 'Biblioteca Laureshamenses–Digital'.

for 798, before someone else took over to write the entry for 799, and the first part of the entry for 800. A similar change of ink colour is observable at the head of each of these annals, and halfway through the entry for 800 revealing the different scribal stints. The copying out of this group of annals more or less year-by-year by a small number of scribes leaves open the possibility that these entries were copied annually and could be contemporary with events they describe. Even if the scribes were not themselves the authorial voices, this manuscript must be close in both time and place to the person responsible for compiling the report for each year.[72] Following Fichtenau, many have thought that the author or patron of this section of these annals was Richbod, a writer of charters at Lorsch before 778 and abbot there after 784, as well as archbishop of Trier from around 791.[73] It is commonly supposed that he spent the years immediately before 784 at the royal court where he would have seen the new minuscule book hand in use, and could have been a member of the chapel staff, headed at that time by Fulrad.[74] Richbod died in 804, the year after the last annal was written into the Vienna manuscript, a few months after his friend and teacher, Alcuin. Whether or not Richbod was directly involved in the production of the text, the form of the script and date of the manuscript (which Bischoff thought, on the basis of script type, was probably Alemannian rather than Franconian) as well as the contents of the annals supplies a view of the years around 800 that was written much closer in time to events than any other surviving account, and one which did not suffer from reworking by annalists revising entries with the benefit of hindsight.[75] The Lorsch Annals are thus a crucial independent and closely contemporary witness (Figure 2.3).

The Lorsch Annals for 795 indicate four distinct stages to Charlemagne's *memoria* for the pope: first, Charlemagne went into mourning for Hadrian; secondly, he issued instructions that prayers be said for the pope's memory throughout the Christian peoples 'within his boundaries'; thirdly, he issued an abundance of alms in this cause; fourthly, he ordered an epitaph to be made in Francia that would be taken thence to Rome to adorn Hadrian's tomb.

> ...Et in ipso hieme, id est viii Kal[ends] Ianuar[ii], sanctae memoriae domnus Adrianus summus pontifex Romanus obiit, pro quo domnus rex, postquam a planctu eius cessavit, orationes per universum christianum populum infra terminos suos fieri rogavit, et aelimosina

---

[72] McKitterick, *History and Memory*, 106.

[73] H. Fichtenau, 'Karl der Grosse und des Kaisertum', *Mitteilungen des Instituts für Österreichische Geschichtsforschung*, 61 (1953), 257–334, at 287–303 and 'Abt Richbod und die Annales Laureshamenses', *Beiträge zur Geschichte des Klosters Lorsch*, Geschichtsblätter für den Kreis Berstrasse, Sonderband 4 (Lorsch, 1978) 277–301, at 286–9. Collins was more skeptical: see 'Charlemagne's Imperial Coronation', 56–7.

[74] Bullough, *Alcuin*, 317, 345–6, 371–2, 399–400.

[75] Bischoff, *Die Südostdeutschen schreibschulen und bibliotheken in der Karolingerzeit, i: Die Bayrischen Diözesen* (Wiesbaden, 1960), 145–6; Bischoff, *Die Abtei Lorsch im Spiegel ihrer Handschriften* (Lorsch, 1989), 61, 87. See also Collins, 'Charlemagne's Imperial Coronation', 62, fig. 6, and McKitterick, *History and Memory*, 105–6, and this volume, Chapter 8, 317–18.

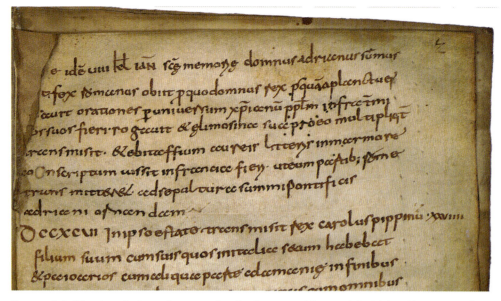

FIGURE 2.3 The *Annales Laureshamenses*, showing last part of the annal for 795 and beginning of the entry for 796; Vienna, ÖNB, Cod. 515, fol. 2r, detail. Photo: Courtesy of the Österreichische Nationalbibliothek, Vienna.

sua pro eo multipliciter transmisit, et ebitaffium aureis litteris in marmore conscriptum iussit in Francia fieri, ut eum partibus Romae transmitteret ad sepultura summi pontificis Adriani ornandam.

…And that same winter, that is on 25th December, the supreme Roman pontiff the lord Hadrian of holy memory died, for who the lord king, after he had ceased his mourning, asked that prayers be said throughout the whole Christian people within his boundaries, and sent an abundance of alms for him, and ordered that an epitaph be made in Francia written in gold letters on marble, so that he might send it from that place to Rome to adorn the sepulchre of the supreme pontiff Hadrian.[76]

This account of a period of formal mourning and co-ordinated commemoration is very unusual, particularly as it was organised from a distance by a patron who was neither a member of the pope's kin nor a member of the Roman clergy.[77] Funeral and mourning rituals are pivotal moments in both the transition of power and to the development of a memorial cult; as such, they often reveal rather more about the ambitions of those left behind than the wishes of the deceased.[78] Distant in Francia, Charlemagne would not ordinarily expect to have any role in a pope's burial. But his extraordinary efforts to co-ordinate the liturgical *memoria* for the pope and to set up

---

[76] *Annales Laureshamenses*, s.a. 795; Pertz, ed., MGH, SS I, 36; King, tr., *Charlemagne*, 142.

[77] Borgolte, *Petrusnachfolge*, 114; Schieffer, 'Charlemagne and Rome', 290; Hartmann, *Hadrian I*, 257.

[78] J. L. Nelson, 'Carolingian Royal Funerals', in F. Theuws and J. L. Nelson, eds, *Rituals of Power from Late Antiquity to the Early Middle Ages*, The Transformation of the Roman World, 8 (Leiden, 2000), 131–84.

a large monument at his tomb in St Peter's reflects an ability to transcend local custom and a wish to control the way that the bond between king and pope was remembered in Rome by the noble families that had supported Hadrian, by the rival factions that backed the new pope, and by future generations.

Other sources corroborate the evidence of the Lorsch Annals and imply also that the English (and perhaps the British and Irish too) were part of this contemporary audience for the *memoria* of the pope. A letter by Alcuin, 'son of the holy church of York', to all the bishops of Britain repeated the instruction of the Lorsch Annals, that Charlemagne, 'greatly desires your prayers . . . for the soul of the most blessed Pope Hadrian', and requested that additional prayers be said for, 'the king himself, for the stability of his kingdom, and for the spread of Christianity'.[79] The bearers of this letter were a group of monks and fellow-priests or bishops, carrying gifts from Charlemagne to ensure that his instructions were fulfilled. Alcuin's expectation that the bishops would enact Charlemagne's command and organise public prayer throughout the bishoprics of Britain is significant; such demands were made by Frankish kings in times of spiritual stress (as here) or military crisis, and were used by them as a liturgical tool to bind the service and loyalty of their subjects to the Carolingian cause. So much so that the proper performances of these litanies were considered 'acts of loyalty towards the monarch' and 'failure to perform them was ground for an accusation of *infidelitas*'.[80] Such liturgical instructions from the centre harnessed the power of prayer for the ruling elite and bound distant regions to the political, spiritual, or military projects of the court. Alcuin's extension of Charlemagne's command to the bishops of Britain suggests that towards the end of the eighth century some elements of the political élite in Francia thought that Anglo-Saxon kingdoms lay within the boundaries (*termini*) of Charlemagne's influence.

This group of messengers may also have delivered another letter from Charlemagne with gifts from the Avar treasure hoard for the rulers of the kingdoms of Mercia and Northumbria and the metropolitan bishops of Britain (Canterbury, York, and Lichfield—an archdiocese from 787 to 803). This letter from Charlemagne to Offa of Mercia also refers to a gift of alms for the sake of the soul of the pope, repeating the request that the Mercian king, 'orders intercession for [Hadrian's] soul, not that we doubt that his blessed soul is at rest but to show our faithful love for our dear friend'.[81] A further letter from Alcuin, sent early in the summer after the return of these

---

[79] '...pro se ipso et sui stabilitate regni, etiam et pro dilatatione christiani nominis, seu pro anima beatissimi patris Adriani pape'; Alcuin, *Ep.* no. 104; Allott, tr., *Alcuin of York*, no. 25; Bullough, *Alcuin*, 458–9.

[80] M. McCormick, 'The Liturgy of War in the Early Middle Ages', *Viator*, 15 (1984), 1–24.

[81] Charlemagne, 'Letter to Offa', 'In elimosinam domni Adriani apostolici, patris nostri et amatoris vestri, direximus; deprecantes ut diligenter iubeatis intercedere, pro anima illius, nullam habentes dubitationem beatam ilius animam in requie esse, sed ut fidem et dilectionem ostendamus in amicum nobis carissimum'; Dümmler, ed., MGH, Epp. IV, 144–6, no. 100; Allott, tr., *Alcuin*, no. 40. Bullough, *Alcuin*, 643–5. Offa died on 29 July 796.

Carolingian envoys, indicates that Charlemagne was sending more gifts to Offa and alms to the bishoprics, this time 'for Pope [Leo] and for himself, for you to have prayers said for them'.[82] This is good evidence for the presence in England of at least two formal gift-laden Carolingian legations in the first half of 796, both with instructions for liturgical offerings for the Frankish king, the recently dead pope, and his successor in Rome. In 796 the Carolingian diplomatic machine was hard at work.

It was doubtless through Alcuin's network of connections with Northumbria that news of Hadrian's death came to be recorded in some Latin annals, perhaps in York. These annals are embedded within a longer text known as the *Historia Regum*, which was compiled in its final form by Symeon of Durham in the early twelfth century.[83] These Latin annals are closely related to the vernacular entries in the northern recension of the Anglo-Saxon Chronicle, and, interpolated into them very early in their history was a set of fourteen high-quality entries concerned with events in Francia and Rome. Although the annals (including these Frankish entries) were subsequently modified by a tenth-century editor, the core of the material is genuine and the entry for 796 preserves a record of the epitaph, which is closer to that in the Lorsch Annals than any other source. Like Theodulf's poem and the Lorsch Annals, the *Historia Regum* entry says that the inscription was inscribed in gold letters, but the *Historia Regum* alone notes that the epitaph was in verse. It also says that the verses were fixed to the wall; this observation is important because placement on the vertical plane of the wall would have made the inscription much easier to read than had it been placed on the floor or on the flat upper surface of a tomb.[84]

> …Adrianus papa venerandus eodem anno sublevatus est ad Dei visionem vii kal[ends] Ianuarii, qui sedit annos xxvi menses decem dies xii. Est quoque in ecclesia sancti principis apostolorum Petri sepultus, et super sepulchrum platoma <id est marmor> parieti infixa, gesta bonorum eius aureis litteris et versibus scripta. Hoc marmor ibi Karolus rex ob amorem et memoriam praedicti patris facere iussit, regali fretus diademate.
>
> …The venerable Pope Hadrian was raised to the sight of God in the same year on 26 December, having ruled 26 years, ten months, and 12 days. And he was buried in the church of the chief apostle, Peter, and over his tomb a slab <that is, marble> was fixed to

---

[82] Alcuin, 'Letter to Offa', 'Etiam et per episcopales sedes in elemosinam sui et domni apostioloci benedictiones transmittit, ut iubeatis orationes fieri pro illis', Alcuin, *Ep.* 101, Dümmler, ed., MGH, Epp. IV, 146–8, no. 101; Allott, tr., *Alcuin*, no. 41. The letter followed news from the Carolingian envoys of the assassination of King Æthelred of Northumbria on 18/19 April 796, rousing Charlemagne's fury; Bullough, *Alcuin*, 645–6.

[83] T. Arnold, ed., *Symeonis Monachis Opera Omnia*, Rolls Series 75, 2 vols (London, 1885), ii, 2–283, at 56–7; P. Hunter Blair, 'Some Observations on the *Historia Regum* Attributed to Symeon of Durham', in N. K. Chadwick, ed., *Celt and Saxon: Studies in the Early British Border* (Cambridge, 1963), 63–118; M. Lapidge, 'Byrhtferth of Ramsey and the Early Sections of the *Historia Regum* Attributed to Symeon of Durham', *Anglo-Saxon England*, 10 (1982), 97–122; Story, *Carolingian Connections*, 104–10, discussing the phrase 'regali fretus diademate' as a typical example of Byrhtferth's diction.

[84] See Chapter 1, 43, for Vegio's observation in *c*.1450 of the epitaph fixed to the wall of the basilica.

the wall, inscribed in verse with his good deeds in golden letters. This marble, King Charles, strengthened by the royal diadem, ordered to be made for the love and memory of the aforementioned father.

The error in the calculation of the length of Hadrian's reign is easily explained by miscopying Roman numerals: transposing xxvi (26) for xxiii (23) in the original, and xii (12) for xvii (17). The rare word *platoma* was glossed (*id est marmor*) in the unique twelfth-century manuscript.[85] The earliest uses of that word are significant since they occur in the *Liber Pontificalis*. It was used in the account of the inscription erected by Pope Damasus (d. 384) at the *Basilica Apostolorum* on the Via Appia and again in the 'Life' of Sixtus III (d. 440) to describe slabs made of porphyry installed around the *confessio* and for the transenna at S. Lorenzo.[86] The word was also used to describe an inscription that Sixtus commissioned at the cemetery of Callixtus 'where the names of bishops are recorded'.[87] The next use of the word *platoma* is in the 'Life' of Leo III where it is used for the marble architraves that replaced decayed wooden beams over the columns surrounding the presbyterium in S. Paolo fuori le Mura.[88] In the *Liber Pontificalis*, therefore, the word *platoma* was used invariably for a marble slab of high worth, often inscribed, and installed by papal command close to the tomb of a martyr. Its use in the *Historia Regum* carries the same connotations, here describing a prestige inscription set up near the tomb of St Peter.

BURYING THE POPE

The Frankish involvement in spreading the news of Hadrian's death and in organising rites of mourning on his behalf was a novel intervention in papal conventions. It seems that the death of a pope was not normally a cause for extended rituals of mourning in Rome itself; rather, the focus moved rapidly to the election of the next pontiff and the seamless continuation of the office—at least, this is the impression that the official accounts in the *Liber Pontificalis* sought to create. The eighth-century papal biographies in that text rarely mentioned the circumstances of the death of a pope, or anything about his burial other than the date; but they always concluded with a statement

---

[85] Cambridge, Corpus Christi College, MS 139, fol. 66r/v (*c*.1160, Durham).
[86] LP 39:2 and 46:5; Trout, *Damasus of Rome*, 121.
[87] *LP* 46:7, 'et platoma in cymiterio Calisti, ubi conmemorans nomina episcoporum'. The inscription does not survive, only its frame (contra Davis, tr., *Book of Pontiffs*, xl) although de Rossi reconstructed a possible text that has been widely accepted; de Rossi, *La Roma sotteranea christiana*, ii, 48. Duchesne, *Le Liber Pontificalis*, 235, n. 16; *ICUR* n.s. iv, no. 9516.
[88] *LP* 98.97; Davis, tr., *Lives of the Eighth-Century Popes*, 225, n. 187; C. du Cange, *Glossarium Mediae et Infimae Latinitatis*, 10 vols (Niort and London, 1886), v, 296; Story, *Carolingian Connections*, 109. On Hadrian and Leo III's interventions at S. Paolo, see N. Camerlenghi, *St. Paul's Outside the Walls: A Roman Basilica, from Antiquity to the Modern Era* (Cambridge, 2018), 127–33, esp. figs 4.8–10.

about the place where a pope was buried and a calculation of the exact length of his pontificate. An exception is the reference in the *Life* of Gregory III to the funeral of his predecessor in February 731; Gregory was noticed at the front of the bier and 'by divine inspiration' was picked out by the crowd to be the next pontiff.[89] In September 767, also, we are told of the spectacle and ceremony that accompanied the removal of the body of Paul I from the basilica of S. Paolo where he had died three months before. His body was transferred, 'by the citizens of Rome and those of other origin...across the river Tiber on boats...with the honour of psalmody to St Peter's; and they buried it in the chapel which he had constructed'.[90]

We know nothing of the circumstances of Hadrian's death in December 795, whether it was sudden or slow in coming (although he must have been comparatively elderly). As is usual, the date supplied by the *Liber Pontificalis*, 26 December, is that of his burial rather than his death, and it makes nothing of the coincidence with the Christmas feast.[91] It is the epitaph that reveals that he had in fact died on 26 December (*obiit vii kl. Ian.*). Even by eighth-century standards, the election of Leo III was rapid: Hadrian was buried in St Peter's on the day that he died, and Leo was elected the same day and ordained as pope the day after that (27 December). The fact that Hadrian had died during the Christmas festivities may have meant that the electoral college was on hand to proceed with the selection of a successor but his rapid election smacks of a firm grip on the reins of power and the procedural technicalities of papal elections by those who moved Leo's candidacy.[92]

Charlemagne's intervention in the aftermath of Hadrian's death was an innovation in many respects, not least because the means by which a pope was honoured in Rome was usually a Roman affair. The actual circumstances of the burial of a pope might be determined by unpredictable factors, but it is clear that an eighth-century pope could plan his own tomb. Paul I, for example, had died on 28 June 767 at S. Paolo where he had gone to escape the oppressive heat of the summer. The heat meant that he was buried there, but his body was translated across the Tiber three months later in September, and interred in St Peter's in the chapel that he had constructed for that purpose in the south exedra (see Figure 1.2).[93] The *Liber Pontificalis* describes this chapel saying that Paul had already adorned it with mosaics, precious metals, and a silver statue of the Virgin (weighing 150lbs), adding that, 'in this chapel he also constructed his own tomb'. Paul's tomb-chapel was an important precedent for Hadrian's

[89] *LP* 92:1.

[90] *LP* 95:7. The chapel of Paul I was in the exedra of the south transept 'close to Pope St Leo's oratory, alongside the entrance to Santa Petronilla' and Sant'Andrea'; *LP* 95.6. This translation took place during the early months of the rule of Constantine who (it was later argued) had been elected pope uncanonically, on which, see McKitterick, 'Damnatio Memoriae'.

[91] *LP* 97:97.

[92] On the decrees of the synod of 769 which set out a new procedure for election to the papacy, see *LP* 96.20 and Noble, *Republic*, 195–202, esp. 199, and above, pp. 93–4.

[93] It is no. 17 on Alfarano's plan; Alfarano, *DBV*, 42 and 184.

oratory a little further along the south transept, and it provides a contemporary model for understanding how a pope might try to determine the locus of his own tomb and thus to influence his own posthumous commemoration. In Paul's case it was the veneration of the miraculous image of the Virgin that ensured the care of his oratory in the long term (known later as Santa Maria in Cancellis).[94] But the circumstances of Paul's death at S. Paolo and subsequent translation to St Peter's also remind us that, despite best-laid plans, it is the living who determine the interment of the dead.

It seems very likely that, like Paul's oratory in the south exedra, Hadrian had planned his own tomb-chapel in the south transept of St Peter's.[95] Hadrian's oratory is not mentioned before the mid-ninth-century when Leo IV's bull of 854 and biography in the *Liber Pontificalis* noted its dedication to Hadrian's patronymic saint, the martyr Adriano. Pope Hadrian had favoured other foundations in the city dedicated to Adriano.[96] It is likely that he was also responsible for constructing an oratory for the saint at St Peter's, and that this was where he intended to be buried. This is inferred partly by the subsequent placement of the epitaph in that place, but also by what else is known of the pattern of patronage at St Peter's, which shows that the south transept was especially favoured in the eighth century.

If we accept that the oratory of Sant'Adriano was constructed in the later eighth century under Pope Hadrian's patronage, it would imply that some thought had been given to the locus of his tomb *pre-mortem* and to the management of the memory of his pontificate. The Carolingian gift of the epitaph was in this respect much more than a contribution to the decorative schema of the oratory. Charlemagne's decision to commission an inscription for Hadrian's tomb was an extension of his instruction for commemorative litanies to be said for the pope *infra terminos suos*. The litanies functioned as a method of uniting Frankish prayers in the present moment in the immediate aftermath of Hadrian's death. They focused the minds of participants on the life of the pope and also on Charlemagne who had issued the instructions and had provided alms for the ceremonies throughout his own kingdoms and even in Anglo-Saxon England. For the longer term, the epitaph functioned in exactly the same way, extolling future readers to contemplation and prayers for the memory of both pope and king. In this way, the epitaph appropriated Hadrian's tomb-chapel as a space for commemorating Frankish kingship and the Carolingian relationship with Rome, as well as the memory of the pope himself. Given what is known of the sacred topography of the basilica in the late eighth century, it is likely that the epitaph was commissioned and made in full knowledge of the location of the oratory of Sant'Adriano in the south transept of St Peter's, half way between the oratory of Santa Petronilla and the entrance to the *confessio* of the Apostle.

---

[94] Alfarano, *DBV*, 42; *CD* ii, 569.
[95] See Chapter 1, 31–3, and Hartmann, *Hadrian I*, 257.
[96] *LP* 98: 77 (Santi Adriano e Lorenzo in praesepe) on which, see Ferrari, *Early Roman Monasteries*, 179–81; the deaconry of Sant'Adriano in Foro, *LP* 98: 45, 77.

FIGURE 3.1 Detail of Hadrian's epitaph, line 17. Photo: Author.

3

Alcuin and the Epitaph

The Lorsch Annals' account of the death of Hadrian says that Charlemagne instigated the acts of memorial for the pope and commissioned the production of his epitaph that was to be made in Francia and taken to Rome. But we know that the author of the epitaph was Alcuin, the Northumbrian scholar who had met Charlemagne in 781 at Parma and later came to Francia to join his court. He was made abbot of the prestigious monastery of Saint-Martin at Tours and died there in 804. The confident attribution of the poem to Alcuin is made on grounds of style, with a great many correspondences of diction, syntax, and structure between Hadrian's epitaph and Alcuin's other compositions in verse and prose.[1] The poem itself is anonymous; Alcuin's name is not on the inscribed version in St Peter's and does not appear with it in any of the extant early copies. However, the poem was included within collections of Alcuin's verse in two early manuscripts, perhaps from Saint-Bertin and Salzburg, that are now lost, and early readers might thereby have linked it with Alcuin by association with the other texts in those books.[2]

Medieval commentators on the epitaph, like Mallius and Romanus, were unaware of, or uninterested in, the identity of its author: they focused instead on the location of the inscription within St Peter's, citing it as evidence of the richness of the heritage of the basilica and its papal patrons.[3] These twelfth-century accounts quote only the opening section that describes Hadrian's piety and generosity and stop at the end of line 14, when the focus shifts from the dead pope to the poem's patron. Maffeo Vegio in the mid-fifteenth century noted the change of voice in the middle section of the

---

[1] D. Schaller and E. Könsgen, eds, *Initia carminum Latinorum saeculo undecimo antiquiorum: bibliographisches Repertorium für die lateinische Dichtung der Antike und des früheren Mittelalters* (Göttingen, 1977), no. 6573; L. Wallach, 'Alcuin's Epitaph of Hadrian I: A Study in Carolingian Epigraphy', *The American Journal of Philology*, 72 (1951), 128–44; L. Wallach, 'The Epitaph of Hadrian I Composed for Charlemagne by Alcuin', in *Alcuin and Charlemagne: Studies in Carolingian History and Literature*, Cornell Studies in Classical Philology, 32 (Ithaca, NY, 1959), 178–97; D. Howlett, 'Two Latin Epitaphs', *ALMA* 67 (2009), 235–47. Ernst Dümmler, the MGH editor of the epitaph, did not include it within the edition of Alcuin's compositions, but within a separate group of texts entitled, 'Tituli saeculi VIII', MGH, PLAC I, 99–115, at 113–14 (no. 11).

[2] For these lost manuscripts of Alcuin's poems, see Bullough, *Alcuin*, 11, 24, 406 and Dümmler, ed., MGH, PLAC I, 101, 165–6. For the editions based on these manuscripts by André Duchesnse (1617) and Frobenius Forster (1777) which used these manuscripts, see below, 129, n. 77.

[3] Peter Mallius, 'Historia Basilicae antiquae S. Petri Apostoli in Vaticano', *AASS* Iunii vii, col. 34A–52, at 40B or 'Opusculum Historiae Sacrae ad Beatissimum Patrem Alexandrum III Pont. Max.'; VZ, iii, 382–442, at 393.

poem (lines 17–24), and connected the verses with Charlemagne.[4] Here, the 'author' of the epitaph speaks directly to the reader, saying:

POST PATREM LACRIMANS KAROLVS HAEC CARMINA SCRIBSI
Weeping after the father, I Charles, have written these songs.

Alfarano, writing in the 1570s, took this line to its natural conclusion and assumed that Charlemagne had composed the epitaph. Grimaldi (1619) and others followed Alfarano in this attribution, and it was not until 1717 when the Bollandist scholar Conrad Janning published and commented on Vegio's work on St Peter's in *Acta Sanctorum* that Alcuin was resurrected as the author of Pope Hadrian's epitaph.[5]

ALCUIN AND FRANCIA

Alcuin's reputation and extensive intellectual legacy was sealed through his connection with Charlemagne in Francia. He was, however, a Northumbrian, born in the southern province of Deira *c.*740 to a family of middling social rank that controlled some land and monastic estates to the east of York, on the north bank of the Humber estuary towards Spurn Head.[6] Alcuin had entered the service of the archbishops of York during the episcopacy of Ecgberht (732–66) and it was at York that he spent the greater part of his career and where his fame as a scholar was established. He was ordained only to the rank of deacon (there is no contemporary evidence that he was ever professed a monk) but his abilities ensured that he rose to prominence under Archbishop Ælberht (767–78), and eventually became master of the York school and keeper of the remarkable library that Ælberht had created there.[7]

York in the later eighth century was a cosmopolitan city that was linked to the wider world by sea routes that took merchants, pilgrims, missionaries, and scholars down the east coast to northern Francia and southern Scandinavia. To judge by the many literary allusions in Alcuin's writing, and by the list of authors that he cites in his *York Poem*, the York library was extensive and its resources had been amplified by Ælbert.[8] A single letter survives in Ælberht's name, addressed to and preserved in the letter

---

[4] Vegio, 'De antiqua S. Petri apostoli Basilica', *AASS* Junii vii, ch. 124 (col. 82B).
[5] *AASS* Juni vii, cols 110–11. The attribution to Alcuin was not doubted by de Rossi, *ICUR* II.i, xlviii.
[6] Alcuin, *Vita Willibrordi*, 1.1, 1.31; W. Levison, ed., MGH, SRM VII (Hannover and Leipzig, 1920), 81–144, at 116; partial tr., Whitelock, *EHD* 1, no. 151. See also, Bullough, *Alcuin*, 129, 164–5.
[7] Bullough, *Alcuin*, 165–8; M. Garrison, 'The Library of Alcuin's York', in R. Gameson, ed., *The Cambridge History of the Book in Britain, i: c.400–1100* (Cambridge, 2012), 633–64.
[8] P. Godman, ed. and tr., *Alcuin: The Bishops, Kings, and Saints of York* (Oxford, 1982), lxv–xxv and 122–7 (vv. 1536–1562); M. Lapidge, *The Anglo-Saxon Library* (Oxford, 2006), 228–32.

collection of Archbishop Lul of Mainz (754–86).[9] It concerns books; Lul was seeking information on the age of the earth and seas that Ælberht was unable to supply. He did though have access to books of cosmography which he offered to have copied for Lul. As a young man Alcuin had travelled to Francia with Ælberht, who, he says, 'more than once took the pilgrim's route to foreign lands...led by...hope of finding new books and studies there to bring back with him'.[10] Ælberht's travels are recalled elsewhere, not least in a letter that Alcuin wrote years later to the monks of Murbach in Alsace recalling his visit there with Ælberht many years before. In the epitaph that Alcuin composed for his master, c.780, he remembered their journeys together to Rome and to the 'flourishing kingdom of the Franks'.[11]

Alcuin's letter-poem *Cartula, perge cito*, composed no later than 778–80, is evidence for another early journey to Francia. The poem describes the route that the letter was to take around the Frankish Rhineland: from Utrecht to Cologne, Echternach, Mainz, and Speyer, and describes the people that the letter would encounter en route.[12] Alcuin intended the poem to be read aloud at these places by men of power, and the verses imply that Charlemagne and his court would be among its audience. The context strongly suggests that the primary audience comprised men who were known to Alcuin, and that the route the letter-poem was to take retraced a journey already taken by its author. This echoes a comment made by Alcuin's ninth-century biographer that when Charlemagne met Alcuin at Parma in 781, he asked him to return to Francia 'for he had become acquainted with him earlier, when his master [Ælberht] had sent Alcuin to him'.[13]

At York, Alcuin had acquired a considerable reputation as a scholar and teacher, attracting students like Liudger from Frisia to study with him. Liudger's *Vita* says that he stayed in York for three years, returning home in 773 with copies of many books. But despite Alcuin's importance within the York community, the most influential part of his career lay ahead of him in Francia. When Ælberht decided to retire from the archbishopric in 778, he bequeathed control of the library to Alcuin, and the metropolitan see to Alcuin's colleague, Eanbald.[14] The Anglo-Saxon Chronicle for

---

[9] Ælberht, 'Letter to Lul', ed., Tangl, MGH, Epp. sel. 1, 261–2, no. 124; on Alcuin's possible authorship of the letter (or its influence on his style), see Bullough, *Alcuin*, 296–8.

[10] *YP*, 1454–7.

[11] Alcuin, 'Letter to monks of Murbach', Dümmler, ed., MGH, Epp. IV, 429–30, no. 271; Bullough, *Alcuin*, 166 (the letter was composed in the early 790s).

[12] Alcuin, 'Cartula, perge cito'; MGH, PLAC I, 220–3, no. 4; P. Godman, *Poets and Emperors: Frankish Politics and Carolingian Poetry* (Oxford, 1987), 44–6; L. Sinisi, 'From York to Paris: Reinterpreting Alcuin's Virtual Tour of the Continent', in H. Sauer and J. Story, with G. Waxenberger, eds, *Anglo-Saxon England and the Continent*, Essays in Anglo-Saxon Studies, 3 (Tempe, AZ, 2011), 275–92.

[13] Anon., *Vita Alcuini*, ch. 9; ed., W. Arndt, MGH, SS XV.1 (Hannover, 1887), 182–97, at 190; Bullough, *Alcuin*, 316–18.

[14] *YP*, 1521–30. Ælberht retired two years and four months before he died (*YP*, 1565) on 8 November in the fourteenth year of his rule (*YP*, 1583–4) in 780 (*HReg*).

780 records that King Ælfwald sent a man to Rome to collect the pallium for the new archbishop.[15] Alcuin's *Vita*, written in the 820s, says that it was he who had been commissioned with this task. The *Vita* goes on to say that on his return journey Alcuin met Charlemagne at Parma, who was travelling south to have two of his young sons consecrated as kings of Aquitaine and Lombard Italy by Pope Hadrian, and for Pippin, the younger of the two, to be baptised during the Easter feast. 'With great exhortations and prayers', the *Vita* says, Charlemagne 'expressed his desire that when [Alcuin] had completed his mission he should return to Francia' to join his court. The *Vita* adds that Alcuin 'did what was asked of him, with the approval of his own king and archbishop, on the condition that he would come back to them in due course'.[16]

It is traditionally assumed that Alcuin left almost at once for Francia, and that he was at the Carolingian court early as 782. There is no definitive evidence, however, to place him there before late 786; nothing in the extant Frankish sources proves that he was a member of the court group of scholars in the early 780s.[17] Certainly, Alcuin was in Northumbria and Mercia in 786 for a series of councils held there by Pope Hadrian's legates. Charlemagne was represented at these meetings primarily by a Frankish abbot named Wigbod, but also by the senior papal legate, Bishop George, who held the Frankish see of Amiens as well as that of Ostia outside Rome. Given his experience of foreign courts, it is probable that Alcuin also had some sort of intermediary role in the councils, but if so the extant portion of Bishop George's report to Pope Hadrian concerning the mission to England says nothing.[18] Bishop George noted simply that Alcuin and his assistant Pyttel were representatives of the Northumbrian king and archbishop, and had escorted the legates' party south to the second Mercian council. Subsequent letters from Francia show that Alcuin had met many of the Mercian court, very likely during this meeting with the papal legates. Furthermore, not long after the legates' synod (and perhaps a consequence of it) Offa's son Ecgfrith was consecrated as king.[19] This ceremony was an innovation in England but Alcuin had witnessed the preparations for just such an event in Rome some six years before, and it is possible that his knowledge of the consecration of the Carolingian princes informed events in Mercia.

A few extant letters show that Alcuin was in Francia in the late 780s, and others sent from England in the early 790s refer to friendships he had already made at the Frankish

---

[15] ASC DE, s.a. 780; G. P. Cubbin, ed., *The Anglo-Saxon Chronicle. A Collaborative Edition, vi: MS D* (Cambridge, 1996), 16; S. Irvine, ed., *The Anglo-Saxon Chronicle. A Collaborative Edition, vii: MS E* (Cambridge, 2004), 41. *Historia Regum s.a.* 780 records that Archbishop Eanbald received the pallium; Arnold, ed., *Symeonis Monachis*, ii, 47. On the difficulties of the chronology of these years, see Bullough, *Alcuin*, 331–6.

[16] Anon., *Vita Alcuini*, c.9; ed., Arndt, MGH, SS XV.1, 190.

[17] Bullough, *Alcuin*, 343–6, 356.

[18] Bullough, *Alcuin*, 346–7 and 350–6 for doubts about Alcuin's role in the formulation of the Legates' decrees. See also Cubitt, *Anglo-Saxon Church Councils*, 166–90, and Story, *Carolingian Connections*, 61–4.

[19] ASC s.a. 785 (*recte* 787).

court.[20] There is also indirect evidence for associating Alcuin with the production of the decrees of Charlemagne's great reform capitulary known as the *Admonitio generalis* that was promulgated at Aachen in March 789, and perhaps also with the royal letter, *De litteris colendis*, that was sent out to the monasteries of Francia calling, among other things, for the establishment of schools and the accurate copying of texts, both of which had been mentioned in the *Admonitio* and were subjects dear to Alcuin's heart.[21] One of his letters to Paulinus of Aquileia may have been written in 787, and another to an unnamed recipient in north-east Francia must have been written before the end of 789 since it conveys Alcuin's wish to be remembered to Bishop Willehad who had been made bishop of Bremen in July 787 and died in November 789.[22] This same letter also asked for information about Charlemagne's campaign against the Slavs, and about his plans for combating the Avars who had invaded Northern Italy the year before (i.e. in 788).[23] Another letter, this time addressed to his friend Colcu, an Irish priest, shows that Alcuin was still in Francia early in 790. He wrote about the gifts of olive oil and silver that he was sending with the letter, of Charlemagne's campaign in the past year against the Slavs, and of a row that had escalated between Charlemagne and Offa, adding that, 'some think we [i.e. Alcuin] should be sent there [to England] in the interests of peace.'[24]

Later in 790 Alcuin was back in Northumbria at the start of Æthelred's second reign (790–6). He wrote from there to his one-time pupil, Joseph, back in Francia, asking for money and supplies to be sent to him, and for news of Charlemagne.[25] He wrote also to Adalhard at Corbie and to Arn, bishop of Salzburg and abbot of Saint-Amand, asking for news from Francia; he asked Adalhard to remember him to Bishop George of Amiens/Ostia and Angilbert at Saint-Riquier.[26] Other letters that are addressed to Charlemagne's family—his daughters Rotrude and Bertha, to his son Pippin and his sister Gisela—may also have been written during his stay in Northumbria

---

[20] On the evidence of letters and poems of Alcuin's presence at the court in Francia in the late 780s, see Bullough, *Alcuin*, 363–76, 379–85.

[21] *Admonitio generalis*, ed., Mordek et al., MGH, Fontes XVI, 47–55 for arguments supporting Alcuin's leading authorial role in the composition of that text. See also *De litteris colendis*, ed. A. Boretius, MGH, Capit. I (Hannover, 1883), 78–9, no. 29 and T. Martin, 'Bemerkungen zur "Epistola de litteris colendis"', *Archiv für Diplomatik*, 31 (1985), 227–72 (on the copy of the letter written, c.800, on the front flyleaf of Oxford, Bodleian Library MS Laud 126, fol. 1r) and D. Mairhofer, *Medieval Manuscripts from Würzburg in the Bodleian Library, Oxford: A Descriptive Catalogue* (Oxford, 2014), 401–2, 408, fig. 64.

[22] Alcuin, *Epp.* 6 and 28; Dümmler, ed., MGH, Epp. IV, 31 and 69–71.

[23] *ARF s.a.* 788; Bullough, *Alcuin*, 364, 390.

[24] Alcuin, *Ep.* 7; Dümmler, ed., MGH, Epp. IV, 31–3; Allott, tr., *Alcuin*, no. 31.

[25] Alcuin, *Ep.* no. 8; Dümmler, ed., MGH, Epp. IV, 33–4; Allott, tr., *Alcuin*, no. 9. See also Bullough, *Alcuin*, 343, 363, 397–8.

[26] Alcuin, *Epp.* nos 9–10; Dümmler, ed., MGH, Epp. IV, 34–6; Allott, tr., *Alcuin*, nos 10 and 135; Bullough, *Alcuin*, 398.

in an attempt to maintain his status at the Carolingian court while far away.[27] A short letter to a friend who may have been the royal scribe Dagulf, hinting at jealousies and rumours circulating against him at the court, may also be part of this group of letters that date from his visit to Northumbria in the early 790s.[28]

Alcuin was able to return to Francia only in late 792 or early 793. The evidence for this comes from a Northumbrian annal for 792, embedded in the *Historia Regum*, which records that Charlemagne had sent Alcuin a copy of the Latin translation of the decrees from the synod of Nicaea in 787 that had re-established the authority of icons in the Eastern Church. Alcuin was instructed to compose a response and the annal records that, after having discussed his text with the Northumbrian lay and clerical elite, Alcuin took it to Charlemagne in Francia.[29] He was certainly in Francia when news came of the disastrous viking raid on St Cuthbert's monastery on Lindisfarne in June 793. Among his many letters to English recipients in the aftermath of the raid, he wrote to Bishop Higbald of Lindisfarne to say that he would ask Charlemagne to intercede on behalf of the captives taken by the pirates. Aside from implying the existence of active diplomatic channels between Charlemagne's court and those in Scandinavia, Alcuin's response also shows that he was confident about access to the king at this time even though he was distant, on campaign with the army.[30]

Alcuin seems to have remained at court and close to Charlemagne's family for the next couple of years. In June 794, at the synod of Frankfurt, Charlemagne recommended that Alcuin be 'received into its religious fellowship and prayers since he was a man learned in ecclesiastical doctrines'.[31] The synod had dealt, among many other things, with the Iconodule decrees from Constantinople and the heresies of Felix of Urgel; both were subjects that Charlemagne had commissioned Alcuin to refute. It was around this time that Charlemagne began to invest heavily in his new palace in Aachen; Frankish annals indicate that from 794 onwards Aachen was Charlemagne's preferred residence for the great Christian feasts of Easter and Christmas. Alcuin's 'Aachen years' which so dominate his reputation and legacy, were in fact very short, and only a part of this period was spent in company of the king, most usually during the winter months. This was probably the period recalled by Einhard in his biography of Charlemagne when Alcuin had been in charge of instructing the king in all of the subjects of the seven liberal arts, except grammar which he had learned from Peter of Pisa. Einhard says that Charlemagne spent a great deal of time with Alcuin studying

---

[27] Alcuin, *Epp.* 15, 29, 72; Dümmler, ed., MGH, Epp. IV, 40–2, 71, 114–15; Allott, tr., *Alcuin*, no. 87 (to Gisela) and no. 92 (to Rotrude and Berta).

[28] Alcuin, *Ep.* 73; Dümmler, ed., MGH, Epp. IV, 115; Bullough, *Alcuin*, 365–6, 391.

[29] *Historia Regum*, s.a. 792; Arnold, ed., *Symeonis Monachis*, ii, 53–4; Bullough, *Alcuin*, 402–3.

[30] Alcuin, *Ep.* no. 20 (also nos 19, 21–2); Dümmler, ed., MGH, Epp. IV, 56–8; Allott, tr., *Alcuin*, no. 26, and 27–9; Bullough, *Alcuin*, 411, argued that this letter might better be dated to the summer of 794, after the synod of Frankfurt.

[31] *Synodus Franconfurtensis*, Boretius, ed., MGH, Capit. I, 73–8 (no. 28.56); tr. King, *Charlemagne*, 224–30.

rhetoric, dialectic, and astronomy, 'as well as the art of calculation'.[32] In a later letter to his student, Fridugis, Alcuin recalled a conversation on the beauty of numbers that he had held with Charlemagne whilst they were bathing in the hot springs at Aachen; 'I know you were there too', he reminded Fridugis.[33]

Charlemagne rewarded Alcuin's service with several abbacies, at Troyes and Ferrières, as well as the cell at Saint-Josse near Quentavic, and the prestigious monastery of Saint-Martin at Tours. Alcuin left the court for Tours in mid- to late summer 796 and died there on 19 May 804. The Tours phase of his career was fundamental to the survival of his reputation. Not only did he encourage a school of biblical scholarship and a scriptorium that was to become one of the most influential in all Francia but, because he was now absent from the king's court, he was obliged to write frequent letters to his network of friends to keep in touch with the affairs of the kingdom. About 280 of his letters survive, the majority written after 796. Although he had begun to collect copies of his letters before this date, after 796 this was done more systematically than before and, as a result, the decade of the 790s is among the most closely documented of the Carolingian era.[34]

Alcuin's long-term reputation rests on the survival of his compositions from these Carolingian years. A few works from his time at York survive—most notably his letter poem, *Cartula, perge cito* (778–80), his epitaph for his master, Archbishop Ælberht (*c.*780), and perhaps also his *York Poem*—but even these survive only in Frankish manuscripts, notably those from Reims. There is precious little evidence for the preservation of his writing in early England. The exception is a substantial set of letters, mainly to English recipients, which was evidently preserved and copied there in the early eleventh century for Archbishop Wulfstan of York.[35] The *York Poem*, which is customarily dated *c.*782 to reflect the traditional narrative of his move to Francia, circulated in Francia and was preserved in manuscripts at Reims. Its epic structure fits well with the output of the Carolingian court poets in the later years of the century; perhaps Alcuin revised and 'published' the poem only after he had joined Charlemagne's court.[36]

---

[32] Einhard, *Vita Karoli*, ch. 25; Dutton, tr., Charlemagne's *Courtier*, 32.

[33] Alcuin, *Ep.* no. 262; Dümmler, ed., MGH, Epp. IV, 419–20; Allott, tr., *Alcuin*, no. 73.

[34] On the transmission of the letter collections, see Bullough, *Alcuin*, 43–120. On the density of the chronology of the letters, see D. A. Bullough, 'Alcuin, Arn and the Creed in the Mass', in M. Niederkorn-Bruck and A. Scharer, *Erzbischof Arn von Salzburg*, Veröffentlichungen des Instituts für Österreichische Geschichtsforschung, 40 (Munich, 2004), 128–38, at 129.

[35] BL, Cotton MS Vespasian A XIV. Another unusually elaborate English-made manuscript, containing part of the Tours collection including many letters to Charlemagne was made in southern England in the early tenth century, perhaps for a secular patron; London, Lambeth Palace Library, MS 218. On these manuscripts, see C. Breay and J. Story, eds, *Anglo-Saxon Kingdoms: Art, Word, War* (London, 2018), nos 48 and 140.

[36] Godman, ed., *Alcuin*, xlii–vii; Godman, *Poets and Emperors*, 41–2. Lapidge, *Anglo-Saxon Library*, 229 argues that the final section (vv. 1596–657) are a supplement to the main text and proposes a date of 790–3 for this concluding section.

ALCUIN AND ROME

Rome—past and present, real and imagined—was a constant theme in Alcuin's life. He knew that York had been 'first built by Roman hands...an ornament to the Empire'.[37] There he had read the late antique Christian poets such as Caelius Sedulius, Juvencus, Prudentius, Prosper, Fortunatus, Arator, and Paulinus (of Nola) among others, and learned the works of classical authors such as Lucan, Pliny, Cicero, and— especially—the epic verses of Vergil. The *York Poem*, among others, shows that the influence of Vergil on Alcuin's poetry was all pervasive and, as he recorded later in a letter to Richbod, the works of this pagan poet could be a powerful distraction from the more edifying works of scripture.[38] At York, Alcuin also had access to collections of metrical inscriptions or *tituli*, many concerning altars, oratories, and churches in Rome.[39] Collections of these short poems had been available in England since the late seventh century, and had deeply influenced the verse compositions of Aldhelm (d. 709/10), Bede (d. 735), Cuthbert of Canterbury (d. 760), and Milred of Worcester (d. 774) before Alcuin. More than one epigraphic collection had been made by northern pilgrims to Rome in the late seventh or early eighth century (perhaps Aldhelm himself among them), and had been brought back to England where they acted as sources of inspiration for Anglo-Latin verse composition and an *aide memoire* to the Christian heritage and topography of the city's churches.[40]

Alcuin also knew Rome from first-hand experience, having travelled there at least twice. His own verse *tituli* may thus have been influenced by first-hand exposure to the inscriptions of Rome. He made one journey with his master Ælberht probably in the mid 760s. Alcuin's epitaph for Ælberht recalls his debts to his master, remembering especially their travels together to Francia and to 'Rome, universally honoured'.[41] In the *York Poem* he says that Ælberht had 'travelled devoutly to the city of Rome...visiting holy places far and wide'. Ælberht, he said, had been fêted by foreign kings who 'wished to keep him with them', but he chose to return to Northumbria and became archbishop there in 767. If the internal chronology of the *York Poem* can be trusted, this dates Ælberht's journey to Rome to the mid-760s when Alcuin was in his twenties. This is probably the journey that Alcuin later mentioned in a letter to Charlemagne written early in 799, where he says that he had visited the Lombard capital of Pavia while on a journey to Rome as a young man; if so, it might have been

---

[37] *YP*, 19–26.
[38] Godman, ed., *Alcuin*, lxxi–iii; Bullough, *Alcuin*, 371–2.
[39] W. Levison, *England and the Continent in the Eighth Century* (Oxford, 1946), 162; Bullough, *Alcuin*, 278.
[40] M. Lapidge, 'The career of Aldhelm', *Anglo-Saxon England*, 36 (2007), 15–69, at 52–64; M. Lapidge, 'Some Remnants of Bede's Lost Liber Epigrammatum', *English Historical Review*, 90 (1975), 798–820, reprinted in his *Anglo-Latin Literature, 600–899* (London and Rio Grande 1996), 357–81; P. Sims-Williams, 'Mildred of Worcester's Collection of Latin Epigrams and its Continental Counterparts', *Anglo-Saxon England*, 10 (1982), 21–38; A. Orchard, *The Poetic Art of Aldhelm* (Cambridge, 1994), 203–12; J. Story, 'Aldhelm and Old St. Peter's Rome', *Anglo-Saxon England*, 39 (2010), 7–20.
[41] Alcuin, 'Epitaphium Ælberhti'; ed. Dümmler, MGH, PLAC I, 206–7, no. 2.

Desiderius, king of the Lombards, who had tried to persuade Ælberht to stay with him to 'water their fields with his stream of divine learning'.[42]

Alcuin travelled again to Rome in 780 when he went to collect the *pallium* for Eanbald, Ælberht's successor as archbishop in York and Alcuin's friend since youth. Alcuin alludes to this journey in a letter written to King Offa of Mercia in 792/3 explaining the proper procedure for the consecration of English archbishops, 'as very knowledgeable men in Rome informed me'.[43] As the official representative of the new Northumbrian king and archbishop, it is conceivable that he met Pope Hadrian on that visit.

There is a single extant letter from Alcuin to Hadrian, written shortly before Hadrian's death, but in it Alcuin makes no claim to personal acquaintance with the pope.[44] Traditionally dated to the summer of 794, after the synod of Frankfurt, Bullough has suggested that it should be dated about a year later than this.[45] He argued that the letter was one of several that Alcuin wrote to accompany a Frankish embassy to Hadrian led by Angilbert that intended to leave for Rome in the early spring of 796, but which was aborted when news came through of Hadrian's death at Christmas time and the rapid election of Leo III as his successor. Alcuin's letter, which survives as part of the collection of his letters made at Tours, is a formal petition for confession and the forgiveness of sins, details of which were to be communicated verbally to the pope by 'my most beloved son', Angilbert, the king's emissary. Bullough suggested that the sins which drove Alcuin to seek papal absolution rather than from his metropolitan may have been sufficiently serious (perhaps even sexual in character) to bar his appointment to high ecclesiastical office—specifically, Bullough speculates, the archbishopric in York. Whatever the real motives for Alcuin's letter, Bullough's re-dating implies that the letter was never received by Hadrian, and in fact may never have been sent. That no action was taken is reinforced by another letter along similar lines that was addressed to Hadrian's successor, Leo.[46]

CONTENT AND POETIC FORM OF HADRIAN'S EPITAPH

The forty lines of Alcuin's poem consist of nineteen distiches and a two-line prose dating clause that gives the length of Hadrian's pontificate (23 years, 10 months, and 17 days) and the day on which he died (26 December). The poem is symmetrical in

---

[42] Alcuin, *Ep.* 172; Dümmler, ed., MGH, Epp. IV, 284–5; Allott, tr., *Alcuin*, no. 75. *YP*, 1464. See also Alcuin, *Ep.* 143; Dümmler, ed., MGH, Epp. IV, 224–7 (partial Allott, tr., *Alcuin*, no. 81) for another possible reference to this journey in a letter to Charlemagne written in 798; on which, see Bullough, *Alcuin*, 243–6, where he notes the coincidence of Ælberht's absence from Northumbria during the reign of Æthelwald (759–66), and his retirement on the accession of Æthelwald's son, Æthelred, in 778.

[43] Alcuin, 'Letter to Offa'; Levison, ed., *England and the Continent*, 245–6; Bullough, *Alcuin*, 332.

[44] Alcuin, *Ep.* 27; Dümmler, ed., MGH, Epp. IV, 68–9.

[45] Bullough, *Alcuin*, 116–17, 452–4.

[46] Alcuin, *Ep.* 94; Dümmler, ed., MGH, Epp. IV, 138–9.

structure and consists of three sections of sixteen, eight, and sixteen lines. The name of BEATVS HADRIANVS PAPA appears in the second line and is repeated in the penultimate one, at line 39. This is matched by the placement of the name of KAROLVS in the first and last lines of the central section of the poem, at lines 17 and 24. This elementary patterning of the proper names demonstrates that the two prose lines that close the poem are integral to the structure of the poem, despite the fact that the early manuscript copies omit them (see below). By omitting the closing lines, those copies disrupt the tightly constructed internal framework of the piece.

As a whole, the poem is subtly crafted.[47] Each of the three sections is internally structured with parallel statements and chiastic patterning of words and phrases. This also occurs across the whole poem, so that all three sections are interwoven by parallel and chiastic patterns that cross the entire text. This demonstrates that the poet who produced these verses understood the complex rules of classical Latin poetry and could apply them with confidence to his own compositions. This analysis is reinforced by the high quality of the orthography and prosody of the poem that conform to classical standards.

Each of the three sections has a distinct subject and voice: the opening sixteen-line section is written in the third person, and focuses on the merits of the late pope; the second section switches to the first person and takes on the voice of Charlemagne himself; the third part uses the second person and addresses the reader directly on the subject of the entrance of both men into Heaven on Judgement Day. In the mid-twelfth century, Mallius and Romanus copied only the first fourteen lines, leading later to speculation that the remainder of the inscription had been cut on a separate stone. Mallius in fact rarely copied texts in their entirety and, since the purpose of his text was to embellish the papal credentials of St Peter's over the claims of the Lateran, it made sense for him to use just the section of the poem that concentrated on Hadrian's achievements as *pater ecclesiae*, as the first line proclaims.

The first part draws inevitably on epigraphic convention (*hic…requiem habet*) linking the inscription with the locus of Hadrian's burial. Echoing a line of the *Te Deum* hymn, it lists the things he valued most in life (l. 3),[48] discusses Hadrian's readiness to do good deeds (l. 4), his unparalleled piety, and his generosity to the poor (l. 11). His noble lineage is emphasised, surpassed only by the nobility of his holy virtues (ll. 5–6). The poem then moves on to discuss more specific aspects of Hadrian's achievements, notably his enhancement of the reputation and physical environment of Rome through the patronage of learning (*doctrina*), the construction of walls (*muri*), and the accumulation of wealth (*opes*) (ll. 13–14). In terms of doctrine, Rome had long been considered the source of authentic liturgical practices, and Hadrian had sent to Francia

---

[47] For the following, I am grateful to David Howlett; see Howlett, 'Two Latin Epitaphs', 235–47.
[48] Compare the *Te Deum* (line 14): 'Tu rex gloriae christe' with Hadrian's epitaph (line 3): 'Vir cui vita deus pietas lex gloria christus'.

the collection of canon law known later as the *Dionysio-Hadriana* (in 774), a copy of the Gregorian sacramentary designed for papal use, known as the *Hadrianum* (*c.*790), and the Latin translation of the acts of the 787 synod of Nicaea (in 792).[49] He had also repaired the city walls between 774 and 776, and continued to refurbish and restore buildings throughout the city. Analysis of Hadrian's biography in the *Liber Pontificalis* shows that there was a genuine boom in construction during the early 780s and that, barring the years 790–2 when none is recorded, as many as twenty projects were initiated annually throughout his pontificate.[50]

The first part of the epitaph finishes with a distich proclaiming that death was not harmful to Hadrian but was 'soon the gate of a better life'.[51] Here Alcuin followed a familiar Anglo-Saxon theology of the afterlife. Following Dryhthelm's vision, as reported by Bede and repeated by Alcuin, those who had lived a perfect life would migrate directly to Heaven after death, without having to wait for the Final Judgement in the resting place that was Paradise.[52] As Alcuin said in his *York Poem*, 'Those who are wholly perfect will enter the heavenly palace immediately after death', whereas those who have done good 'but less than holy Faith requires, gaze upon the Kingdom of Heaven' from Paradise.[53]

This thought leads naturally to the theme in the remainder of the poem in which Charlemagne himself entreats Hadrian to act his intercessor before the heavenly Judge; 'say, "May this my son proceed"' (l. 34). Charlemagne is named twice (ll. 17, 24) and is the primary actor of these verses. What is more, this central part of the poem is written in the first person, in Charlemagne's voice; it is he who has 'written these songs' (l. 17). 'You be mindful of me', the king says, 'my mind follows you always' (l. 19)—a phrase paralleled later in line 33.[54] Hadrian is not just *pater ecclesiae* but is *pater* to Charles, his *natus* (ll. 33–4). All this talk of familial ties echoes closely the reports of Charlemagne's reaction on hearing the news of Hadrian's death.

This bond is stressed in an elegant and powerful couplet that completes the central section of the epitaph: 'I join our names, together with titles, most clearly / Hadrian, Charles, I the king and, you, the father' (ll. 23–4). The word order and structure of the verses reflects this union graphically: the personal names are adjacent and the

---

[49] Bullough, 'Roman books', 14–17; D. Ganz, '"Roman Books" Reconsidered: The Theology of Carolingian Display Script', in Smith, ed., *Early Medieval Rome*, 297–316.

[50] T. F. X. Noble, 'Paradoxes and Possibilities in the Sources for Roman Society in the Early Middle Ages', in Smith, ed., *Early Medieval Rome*, 55–83, at 61–3.

[51] *Mors* ('death') is given in place of *mox* ('soon') in Paris, Lat. 16837 (line 16) and other later editions of the epitaph, including Dümmler's.

[52] For Dryhthelm's vision, see Bede, *HE* V.12; ed. and tr. Colgrave and Mynors, *Bede's Ecclesiastical History*, 490–3; *YP*, 876–1007. For analysis of these lines and Alcuin's use of *requies* ('a resting place'), see Bullough, *Alcuin*, 460. See also S. Foot, 'Anglo-Saxon "Purgatory"', in P. D. Clarke and T. Claydon, eds, *The Church, The Afterlife and the Fate of the Soul*, Studies in Church History, 45 (Woodbridge, 2009), 87–96.

[53] *YP*, 995–8.

[54] Hadrian's epitaph: line 19, 'tu memor esto mei' and line 33, 'tunc memor esto tui nati'.

words *Hadrianus…pater* buttress the words *Karolus rex ego*, embracing the king's name and persona.[55] Furthermore, as Howlett has observed, the alphanumeric value of the two names is identical (that is, the value of the letters in both names add up to ninety-one), illustrating a further level of metrical sophistication and mastery of a compositional technique common in Insular Latin poetry.[56] It is important to note that this alphanumeric bravado works only in the epigraphic not the manuscript form of the poem where *capitalis v* is used for *u*, and *k* is used for the initial letter of the king's name. This is a key piece of evidence that square capitals were intended by the author, Alcuin, as the script for the inscribed version of the epitaph. The superiority of the inscribed version of the epitaph is reinforced by further wordplay with the word TITVLVS, meaning 'inscription' as well as 'title', and the double meaning is doubtless intentional, hinted perhaps by the word *simul* that precedes it.[57] This alternative reading, 'I join our names together, most clearly in these inscribed lines' underscores the fact that the poem was designed for monumental display, and that the extant inscription is the *ur*-text for Hadrian's epitaph.

It is *Karolus rex*, however, who is at the centre of this relationship both literally and figuratively. A longstanding tradition in Insular poetry used the golden section ratio to refer to the author: here the golden section divides the poem in the middle of line 23 at the words *Karolus rex ego*.[58] The inscribed form of the name *Karolus* in line 17 reinforces this sense of *ego* and the immediacy of Charlemagne physical presence. Line 17 is the longest line in the poem, and the letter-cutter had to use numerous ligatures and smaller letters nested inside adjacent ones to save space. This enabled the letter-cutter not only to get all forty-four letters onto the line but also to place the word KAROLVS right at its centre (Figure 3.1). The king's name was carefully done; the AR is ligatured with the small O embedded in the angle of the R. This is identical with the early, epigraphic form of the king's name used, for example, on a legend from a 'pre-reform' coin (*c*.772–93) (Figure 3.2).[59] The king's name was similarly treated in line 6 of the colophon to a copy of Paul the Deacon's *Liber de diversis quaestiunculus* made *c*.800, which 'the lord king Charles ordered to be copied from the original (*ex authentico*) of Archdeacon Peter', perhaps held in the king's library (Figure 3.3).[60]

[55] See Chapter 8, 312–13.
[56] HADRIANVS: 8+1+4+17+9+1+13+20+18 = 91 and KAROLVS: 10+1+17+14+20+18 = 91. For this and other examples in the inscribed version of the poem, see Howlett, 'Two Latin Epitaphs'.
[57] I owe this observation to Shane Bobrycki. A parallel can be found in the use of 'similes' in the text for the *Basilica Apostolorum*; see Chapter 3, 136, n. 106.
[58] Howlett, 'Two Latin Epitaphs', 247.
[59] S. Coupland, 'Charlemagne's Coinage: Ideology and Economy', in J. Story, ed., *Charlemagne: Empire and Society* (Manchester, 2005), 211–29, at 213 and fig. 7a. On the date of the reform, I. Garipzanov, 'Regensburg, Wandalgarius, and the *novi denarii*: Charlemagne's Monetary Reform Revisited', *Early Medieval Europe*, 24 (2016), 58–73.
[60] IUSSIT DOMNVS REX|CAROLVS TRANSCRIBE|RE EX AVTENTICO PE|TRI ARCHIDIACONI: Brussels, Bibliothèque Royale de Belgique, MS II 2572; Bullough, *Katalog*, no. 755. See D. A. Bullough, 'Reminiscence and Reality: Text, Translation

Figure 3.2 Denarius of Charlemagne (issued 772–93). *EMC* 1: no. 730 (PG 202) (enlarged, x2). Photo: Courtesy of the Fitzwilliam Museum, Cambridge.

Here again, King Charles is the subject of the clause and the instigator of the action, giving permission for the text to be transcribed and 'published'.[61] The monogram thus used was more than just epigraphic convenience; it signified publicly the authority of the king and his sanction to act.

One of the decrees of the synod of Frankfurt, promulgated in June 794, discussed the sanctions that would be imposed on anyone who rejected 'the coin with our name' (*nomini nostri nomisma*).[62] These coins were the new, heavy pennies, introduced perhaps in late 793 or 794, and which had the other form of the king's monogram on the reverse with the letters KRLS arranged around a central lozenge that embedded the vowels AOV.[63] The monogram was literally the stamp of royal authority, signifying the virtual presence of the king—to reject the coin bearing the king's name was tantamount to rejecting the king and instructions. The graphic echo of the king's early monogram in the inscription sent to Rome was thus deliberate; it appears in the line that opens the central section in which Charlemagne 'speaks' to the reader, and the epigraphy of that line is modified to ensure that the monogram is centred in the

---

and Testimony of an Alcuin letter', *Journal of Medieval Latin*, 5 (1995), 174–201, suggesting that the manuscript may reflect the debate between Peter of Pisa and a Jewish scholar that Alcuin had heard discussed during an early visit to Italy. Also, B. Bischoff, 'The Court Library of Charlemagne', in *Manuscripts and Libraries in the Age of Charlemagne*, ed., M. Gorman (Cambridge, 1994), 56–75 at 58, n. 15. The membrane used to make this book is Insular-style vellum, on the use of which in manuscripts associated with court patronage see T. J. Brown, 'On the Distribution and Significance of Membrane prepared in the Insular Manner', in J. Glenisson and C. Sirat, eds, *La Paléographie Hébraïque Médiévale*, Colloques Internationaux du CNRS 547 (Paris, 1974), 127–35, reprinted in J. Bately, M. Brown, and J. Roberts, eds, *A Palaeographer's View: Selected Writings of Julian Brown* (London, 1993), 125–40 at 132–3. For other similar colophons referring to an 'authentic exemplar' (the *Hadrianum* Sacramentary and the *Dionysio-Hadriana* collection of canons), see C. Vogel, *Medieval Liturgy: An Introduction to the Sources* (Washington, DC, 1986), 81.

[61] A. Freeman and P. Meyvaert, 'The meaning of Theodulf's apse at Germigny-des-Prés', *Gesta*, 40 (2001), 125–39, at 137, n. 21.

[62] Wallach, 'The Epitaph', 180. *Synodus Franconofurtensis*, ch. 5; ed., Boretius, MGH, Capit. I, 73–8, at 74 (no. 28.5).

[63] Coupland, 'Charlemagne's Coinage', 218.

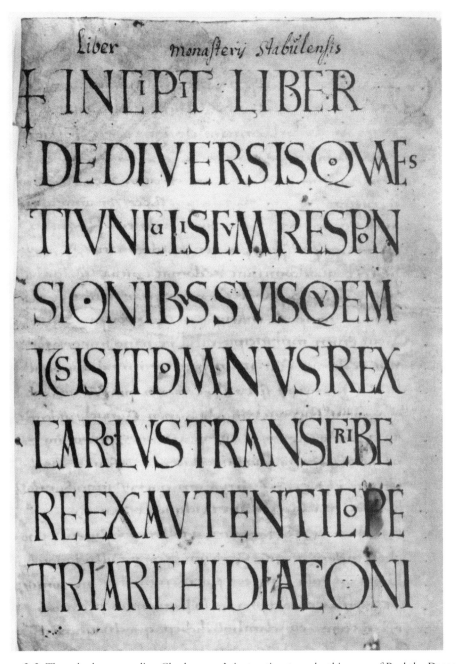

FIGURE 3.3 The colophon recording Charlemagne's instruction to make this copy of Paul the Deacon's *Liber de diversisi quasticunculis* 'from the original'; Brussels, Bibliothèque Royale de Belgique, MS II 2572, fol. 1r. Photo: Courtesy of the Bibliothèque Royale de Belgique, Brussels.

middle of the verse. What follows is thus not just the personalisation of the king's emotion, but also carries the weight of his direct instruction. All this is a product of the graphic design of the inscription (which is lost in the manuscript copies), and once again reinforces the point that Alcuin's verses were composed for inscription on stone. The visual presentation of the verses gives graphic expression to their content.

The inscribed version of the king's name does not affect its pronunciation or the poetic metre of the line even though the diminution of the medial *o* suggests the Germanic form of the king's name, *Karlus*, rather than the Latinised *Karolus*. The metre demands that the 'a' of *Karolus* is short both here and in line 24, and the alphanumeric play requires initial κ. The use of the hard κ rather than the c (as in the coin) is also notable but is not as chronologically significant as Wolfram has argued through analysis of charters, arguing that *Karolus* was the post-800, imperial form of the king's name.[64] The spelling of the king's name was evidently not standardised, although over time the form *Karolus* seems to have become more common than earlier in his reign when *Carolus* is the form found more often in charters and on coins, and throughout the papal correspondence.[65] The KRLS form of the king's monogram is found in diplomata from the very beginning of the reign but is usually glossed *signum Caroli gloriosissimi regis*.[66] Similarly, many of the heavy *denarii* issued after 793/4 had the legend CARLVSREXFR(*ancorum*) around the central KRLS monogram.[67] The choice of κ over c in the monogram probably reflects knowledge of Greek practices.[68] Manuscripts copied around the turn of the century can show both spellings of the name within the same text. A pertinent example is the copy of Charlemagne's own epitaph that was copied at Fulda after 814 in Insular script and which may be independent of Einhard's rendition in the *Vita Karoli*.[69] The rubric refers to the *Epitaphium Caroli* (Figure 3.4), but the next line tells of the *corpus karoli magni*. Of the several scribes who worked on the Vienna fragment of the Lorsch Annals that was copied in the opening years of the ninth century, one used *Karolus* when writing the entry for 799 and part of that for 800, another alternated between the two spellings of the king's name, using both *Karolus* and *Carolus* within the annal for 801, and

---

[64] H. Wolfram, A. Scharer, and H. Kleinschmidt, eds, *Intitulatio*, 3 vols, Mitteilungen des Instituts für Österreichische Geschichtsforschung, 21, 24, 29 (Vienna, 1967–88), i, 239.
[65] Hack, *Codex Carolinus*, i, 92.
[66] See, for example, ChLA XV 608 (769 Aachen); 612 (772 Herstal); 616 (775 Quierzy).
[67] Coupland, 'Charlemagne's Coinage', 218 and fig. 7b. On the graphic power of monograms, see I. H. Garipzanov, 'Metamorphoses of the Early Medieval Signum of a Ruler in the Carolingian World', *Early Medieval Europe*, 14 (2006), 419–64.
[68] Garipzanov, *Symbolic Language*, 175–6.
[69] Munich, Bayerische Staatsbibliothek, Clm 14641, fol. 31v. The first part of this manuscript (fols 1–31) is one of the earliest examples of Carolingian minuscule from Fulda, although Charlemagne's epitaph is added on fol. 31v in an Insular script of a type written at Fulda during the abbacy of Raban Maur (822–41); Bischoff, *Die Südostdeutschen schreibschulen*, i, 252; Bischoff, *Katalog*, II, no. 3235.

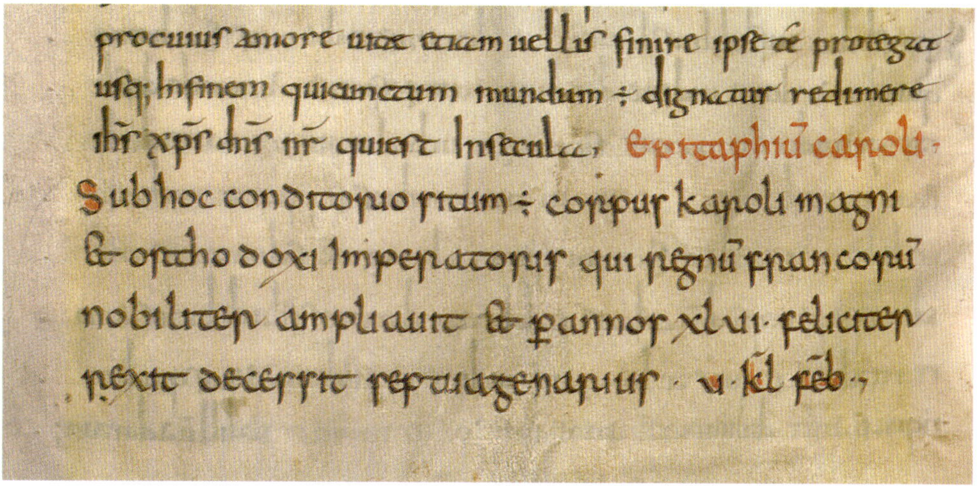

Figure 3.4 'Epitaphium Caroli', Munich, Bayerische Staatsbibliothek, Clm 14641, fol. 31v (detail). Photo: Courtesy of the Bayerische Staatsbibliothek, Munich.

another, who took over for the 802 entry preferred *Carolus* throughout.[70] The scribe of the *laudes regiae* that were added to a manuscript (now in Montpellier) before 794 refers to *Karolus*, both father and son, in its acclamation of Hadrian and the Carolingian royal family.[71] Such variation might be as much a reflection of the linguistic background of a scribe as of the exemplar.

The sense of personal immediacy that is generated by the use of the first-person voice and the monogram form of Charlemagne's name is further reinforced by the use of direct speech in the third and final section of the epitaph (lines 24–40, at 25–6 and 34). In the first instance the poet engages the reader directly. Referencing the penitential psalm sung in the funerary liturgy (*Miserere mei, Deus*, Ps. 50 (51)), the poet calls out to the reader: 'You whoever may read the verses, suppliant with a devout breast / Say of both men, "Gentle God, be merciful"'. Just as the names of king and pope were bound together on Earth, so also they would be bound in Heaven. The epitaph thus not only makes Charlemagne the central actor in the *memoria* for the pope but also makes him a direct beneficiary of those acts, whose memory and presence would be invoked whenever prayers were prompted by the reading of the verses.[72]

---

[70] See Chapter 2, 101–3.

[71] Montpellier, Bibliothèque interuniversitaire de Montpellier, section Médecine, H 409, fo. 344r/v. The *laudes* include the names of Hadrian and Fastrada and were composed for use, and likely copied, before the queen's death during the synod at Frankfurt in 794. The main body of the manuscript is linked to Tassilo's dynasty and shares a scribe with others known to have been written at Mondsee. On the basis of its script, the last quire including the *laudes* was added in northern Francia; *CLA* VI.795; *CLLA*, ii, no. 161, 580; Bischoff, *Katalog*, no. 2871a; SW, *799*, ii, IX.18. See also Chapter 8, 319.

[72] Hartmann, *Hadrian I*, 259. See also Alcuin's own epitaph which he composed himself; 'Epitaphium Alchuuini', ed. Dümmler, MGH, PLAC I, 350–1 (no. 123); L. Wallach, 'The Epitaph of Alcuin: A Model of Carolingian Epigraphy', *Speculum*, 30 (1955), 367–73 and C. A. M. Clarke, *Writing Power in Anglo-Saxon England: Texts, Hierarchies, Economies* (Cambridge, 2012), 49–51.

Here it is the reader who acts as intercessor for the dead, generating penitential prayers for Charlemagne and Hadrian together, each and every time the poem is read (as you too have just done).

MANUSCRIPT COPIES OF HADRIAN'S EPITAPH

Alcuin's poem to the memory of Pope Hadrian survives almost complete in two ninth-century manuscripts now in Paris: BnF, MS Lat. 9347, fol. 49r (s. ix^1) and BnF, MS Lat. 2773, fol. 23v (s. ix^2) (Figure 3.5). Both omit the prose dating clause that comprise the last two lines on the inscription. These manuscripts contain copies of late antique Christian poetry that constituted the core of the Carolingian 'school canon'. *Ex libris* notae shows that the earlier and more impressive of the two belonged to the monastery of St Remigius at Reims and was undoubtedly made there, dating in large part probably to the second quarter of the ninth century.[73] The second book is slightly later and was—on the basis of its textual filiations as well as its script—also made at Reims, probably during the rule of Archbishop Hincmar (845–82).[74] These two books have a number of items in common and they are closely related, sharing an exemplar if not copied one from another. The contents of these two books overlap with that of a third (now BnF, MS Lat. 10307) but this third book does not contain Hadrian's epitaph, despite the claims made for it by de Rossi and in the commentary to the MGH, edition of the text.[75]

A fourth Paris manuscript, dating from the later twelfth century, also contains Hadrian's epitaph but here the verses are appended to a copy of the *Liber Pontificalis* which recites the papal biographies up to and including Stephen II (d. 757) (Figure 3.6).[76] Unlike earlier ninth-century manuscript copies, this version does includes the two-line prose date clause that completes the inscribed poem. Hadrian's epitaph is also reported by seventeenth- and eighteenth-century editors of Alcuin's works to have been included in two other manuscripts that probably dated from the

---

[73] Bischoff, *Katalog*, no. 4570; G. Glauche, *Schullektüre im Mittelalter: Entstehung und Wandlungen des Lektürkanons bis 1200* (Munich, 1970), 32; Carey dates it 900–50 without explanation: F. M. Carey, 'The Scriptorium of Reims during the Archbishopric of Hincmar (845–882 A.D.)', in *Classical and Mediaeval Studies in Honour of Edward Kennard Rand*, ed. L. W. Jones (New York, 1938), 41–60 at 58. See also, Story, 'Aldhelm', 7–20.

[74] Bischoff, *MS* III, 247 who dates it s. ix$^{3/4}$; Bischoff, *Katalog*, no. 4227; Glauche, *Schullektüre*, 33. Bullough agrees, *Alcuin*, 459 n. 87, but says that this is the earliest manuscript copy. See Story, 'Aldhelm', 11 (Pl. 1).

[75] Bischoff, *Katalog*, no. 4627, 'no later than 875'; Both have confused BnF, Lat. 2773, fol. 23v with BnF, Lat. 10307, fol. 23v; *Epitaphium Hadriani Papae*, ed. Dümmler, MGH, PLAC I, 101, 113–14; de Rossi, 'L'inscription du tombeau', 481, where he compounds the confusion by saying that BnF, Lat. 10307 contains only the first twenty-four lines of the epitaph.

[76] BnF, Lat. 16897 (s. xii$^{4/4}$), fols 33v–34r. The *Liber Pontificalis* is followed in this volume by the canons of Isidore; a list of provinces and cities of Gaul, and a list of popes up to and including Agapitus II (946–55) with the lengths of their reigns. The first quire of this book (fols 1–8) was remade, s. xiv.

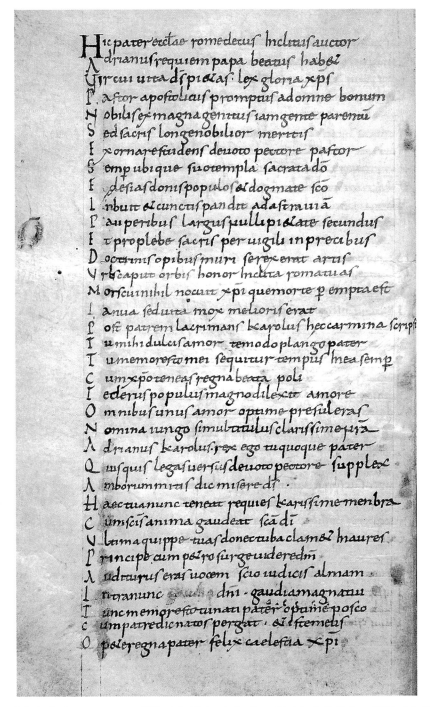

FIGURE 3.5 A ninth-century copy of Alcuin's 'Epitaph for Pope Hadrian'; BnF, Lat. 2773, fol. 23v. Photo: Courtesy of the Bibliothèque nationale de France, Paris.

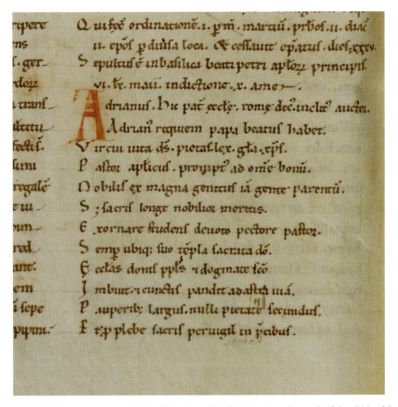

FIGURE 3.6 A twelfth-century copy of the *Liber Pontificalis*, showing the end of the *Life* of Stephen II and the first twelve lines of Hadrian's epitaph, which is completed on the next folio; BnF, Lat. 16897, fol. 33v (detail). Photo: Courtesy of the Bibliothèque nationale de France, Paris.

ninth century but which are now lost: one from Saint-Bertin and another that by the eighteenth century was in the library at St Paul's, Regensburg and which carried an inscription claiming that it had made by order of Liutpram, bishop of Salzburg from 836 to 859.[77] Finally, the first section (lines 1–16) of Hadrian's epitaph was also copied into a late medieval continuation to Paul the Deacon's *Historia Langobardorum* which is extant in a single sixteenth-century manuscript.[78]

The inclusion of the epitaph in the Paris copy of the *Liber Pontificalis* and in an appendix to Paul the Deacon's *Historia Langobardorum* shows that by the twelfth

---

[77] MGH, PLAC I, 101, 165–6. For the epitaph within the verse collection in the Saint-Bertin manuscript, see the edition by André Duchesne [Andreas Quercetanus], *B. Flacci Albini sive Alchuuini Abbatis Karoli Magni Regis ac Imperatoris, magistri* (Paris, 1617), cols 1673–1760, at 1729–30, no. 217–18 and ICUR II.i, 285–6, XXVII.C. The Regensburg manuscript was edited by Frobenius Forster, *Beati Flacci Alcuini seu Alcuini abbatis Caroli Magni Regis ac Imperatoris, magistri. Opera*, 2 vols (Regensburg, 1777) i, 550–1 (Epitaph) and 614 (the Hormisdas 'continuation').

[78] *Pauli continuatio tertia*, ch. 61: ed. G. Waitz, MGH, SS rer. Lang., 203–16 at 214, also 32 and 203 for reference to C5, the sixteenth-century paper manuscript, Saint-Omer, Bibliothèque d'agglomération, MS 736, fols 114v–115r (now fully digitised).

century at least the poem was recognised as an important text for the history of eighth-century Italy. The text of the epitaph in the continuation to the *Historia Langobardorum* is almost identical to that given by Peter Mallius in his later twelfth-century *Opusculum Historiae Sacrae*, and both cite the text only as far as the end of line 14. This led the Bollandist scholar Papebroek to assume that the remainder of the text (concerning Charlemagne) had been cut on a second stone.[79] The copy of the *Liber Pontificalis* in BnF, MS Lat. 16897, which is broadly contemporary with Mallius' text, is essentially in agreement with his readings although, unlike Mallius' transcription, it quotes the complete poem including the closing prose lines, which are not otherwise found in any of the known early manuscript copies; this version may thus ultimately derive from the inscription itself.

Of all these copies, the oldest extant is that in the Reims manuscript, BnF, Lat. 9347 (s. ix[1]). The codex that was in Regensburg in the late eighteenth century was similarly dated but, since we have only the eighteenth-century editor's description of it, it is difficult to say much about the book and its contents. The Paris manuscript, however, is a very handsome, large book of high quality. Measuring $c.365 \times 250$ mm, it was copied by two or three scribes using a good, bold minuscule script with excellent uncial capitals for the headings of many of the poems. It includes Fortunatus' three diagrammatic *carmina figurata*, where the shape of the cross is picked out in red from a grid of black letters. The quality of the book indicates the value placed on the texts by the scholars at Saint-Remigius, and is important evidence for the centrality of Reims in the collection and transmission of late antique and Carolingian-era poetry, not least that of Alcuin.[80] Indeed, it was Reims that was wholly responsible for the transmission of his *York Poem* into the later Middle Ages.[81]

The lost manuscripts from Saint-Bertin and Regensburg were the major vehicles for the transmission of Alcuin's other poems, and both apparently included copies of Hadrian's epitaph as part of Alcuin's corpus of work. The Saint-Bertin book was used by André Duchesne as part of his two-volume edition of Alcuin's works that he published in 1617.[82] This was used as the basis of Frobenius Forster's new edition, published in 1777, which was supplemented by readings from the Salzburg book which he had to hand in Regensburg. Its copy of the epitaph had twelve extra lines appended to the end of it, which Forster printed separately and which de Rossi showed were in fact a separate poem composed for Pope Hormisdas (514–23).[83] It seems that

---

[79] AASS *Maii* vi, 124, cited by de Rossi, 'L'inscription du tombeau', 481.

[80] Godman, *Alcuin*, cxxix and references cited therein.

[81] Godman, *Alcuin*, cxiii–xxix.

[82] A. Duchesne (Quercetanus), *B. Flacci Albini sive Alchvvini…Opera…studio et diligentia Andreas Quercetani Turonensis* (Paris, 1617), 1729–30.

[83] *ICUR* II.i, 130, 286; *ICUR n.s.* ii, no. 4150; de Rossi, 'L'inscription du tombeau', 480. See also Forster, *Beati Flacci Alcuini*, i, 550–1 (Epitaph) and 614 (the Hormisdas 'continuation'). The text of the latter is in MGH, PLAC I, 114 (ll. 39–50), with comments on the manuscript and the ascription of it to Liutpram's

Hadrian's epitaph was included in these two lost manuscripts as part of the corpus of Alcuin poems, although the arrangement of these early editions makes it hard to ascertain whether it would have been considered by the scribes or readers of the manuscripts to have been one of Alcuin's own compositions.

We can add these manuscript copies of Hadrian's epitaph to those known from the descriptions of St Peter's basilica by Mallius and Romanus (s.xii²), by Maffeo Vegio (1455), and Onofrio Panvinio (1560), and from Peter Sabin's imperfect sylloge of Christian inscriptions in Rome made for the French king, Charles VIII, in 1498. All this suggests that Hadrian's epitaph circulated in a variety of textual settings: as an adjunct to the early medieval corpus of poetic 'school texts'; as part of Alcuin's collected poems; an historical document relating to eighth-century Italy or the basilica of St Peter's; and as a text to edify and flatter a French king.

CAROLINGIAN 'SCHOOL TEXTS'

Three of the Carolingian manuscripts discussed above, BnF, Lat. 9347, 2773, and 10307, contain the core of the corpus of classical and late antique verse that was available in England and Francia in the eighth and ninth centuries. They are representative of a number of composite manuscripts of similar date that collectively demonstrate the existence of a coherent 'school canon' of Latin poetry.[84] The scriptorium at Reims was particularly active in the production of such volumes of poetry that set Carolingian compositions alongside the older works of classical poets. Indeed, the earlier of the two Reims volumes containing Hadrian's epitaph cannot be far removed in date from 'one of the most significant collections of Carolingian poetry', also from Reims, which had set the unique copy of the epitaph for Pippin of Italy (d. 810) alongside Alcuin's own epitaph and older verses.[85] In the two Reims books (BnF, Lat. 9347 and MS Lat. 2773), Hadrian's epitaph is part of an anthology, and follows five other short *tituli* concerning saints Andrew, Peter, John the Baptist, Aureus and Justinus, and Martin (discussed below).[86] Neither manuscript names Alcuin as its author, and both entitle the poem *De Adriano papa*.

---

episcopacy at 165–6. On the Forster transcription, see B. Bischoff, *Salzburger Formelbücher und Briefe aus Tassilonischer und Karolingischer Zeit* (Munich, 1973), 7–9, 27–9 and Bullough, *Alcuin*, 406, n. 237.

[84] Godman, ed., *Alcuin*, lxxi, cxxix; J. J. Contreni, 'The Pursuit of Knowledge in Carolingian Europe', in R. E. Sullivan, ed., *"The Gentle Voices of Teachers": Aspects of Learning in the Carolingian Age* (Columbus, OH, 1995), 106–41, esp. 120, n. 66.

[85] BAV, Reg. Lat. 2078 (s. ix¹/⁴/?820s, Reims), with the epitaph of Pippin on fol. 122; ed., Dümmler, MGH, PLAC I, 405; Bischoff, 'The Court Library', 28 and Bullough, *Alcuin*, 122.

[86] *ICUR* II.i, 257–8, no. XXIII. Glauche's lists of the content of both books omits this set of epigrams (including the epitaph); *Schullektüre*, 32–3.

In the later of the two manuscripts, BnF, Lat. 2773, these short *tituli* follow Prosper's *Epigrammata ex sententiis S. Augustini* and some verses falsely attributed to Pope Damasus. After the epitaph, come Sybilline verses,[87] Arator's *Historia apostolica*, the verse *Liber medicinalis* of Quintus Serenus, and a variety of other verses including the *Disticha* of pseudo-Cato and the *Ænigmata* of Aldhelm. In the earlier Reims manuscript, BnF, Lat. 9347, the five short epigrams and Hadrian's epitaph are preceded by the *Carmen paschale* of Caelius Sedulius, the poetic rendering of the Gospels by Juvencus, Alcuin's epitaph for Archbishop Ælberht of York (d. 780) and, again, the *Epigrammata* of Prosper. The medical treatise of Quintus Serenus and Arator's *Historia apostolica* follow Hadrian's epitaph here too, and the volume concludes with the occasional poems of Venatius Fortunatus. There is thus a common core to both these books; Prosper, the five short *tituli* plus Alcuin's epitaph for Hadrian, Quintus Serenus, and Arator.

A third Paris volume, MS Lat. 10307, commonly said to contain Hadrian's epitaph does not in fact contain it. Like the earlier of the two Reims books, however, it opens with the verses of C. Sedulius, Juvencus, and Archbishop Ælberht's epitaph, but whereas the earlier book moves on to Prosper, the five short epigrams, Hadrian's epitaph, Quintus Serenus, and Arator, this volume continues with several works by Vergil (with extensive marginal commentaries). The texts common to both books, however, shows that it is part of the same family of manuscripts.

It is striking that not one, but two poems by Alcuin commemorating late eighth-century churchmen were included within the corpus of early Christian Latin poetry represented by these manuscripts. The coincidence of Alcuin's epitaphs for Pope Hadrian and Ælberht of York within this group of manuscripts is remarkable, not least because of the rarity of both texts; the association of these two 'contemporary' poems by Alcuin among the verses of classical late antique poets imparts to them a special air of canonical authority.[88]

AN ANTHOLOGY FOR ST PETER'S

As indicated already, the copy of Hadrian's epitaph in the two Reims manuscripts is part of a sub-set of texts. In both books, the epitaph is the sixth item and follows five shorter *tituli* about saints Andrew, Peter, John the Baptist, Aureus and Justinus, and Martin.[89] All bar one of these six poems were inscriptions displayed in St Peter's in

---

[87] See Lapidge 'Some Remnants', 366–7; B. Bischoff and M. Lapidge, *Biblical Commentaries from the Canterbury School of Theodore and Hadrian*, CSASE, 10 (Cambridge, 1994), 185–6.
[88] Alcuin, 'Epitaphium Aelberhti'; ed. Dümmler, MGH, PLAC I, 162, 206–7, no. ii.
[89] ICUR II.i, 257–8, no. XXIII; G. Cascioli, *Epigrapfi Cristiane nell'area vaticana III–VI secolo*, Quaderno d'archivio, 7 (Vatican City, 2013), 74–8.

Rome, and there are good grounds for believing that the set of six poems was put together in the form found in these manuscripts in the early ninth century.[90]

De Rossi argued that the first epigram in the set, *De Andrea*, was associated with the dedication by Pope Symmachus (498–514) of the easternmost of the two imperial rotundas on the southern flank of the Vatican hill to St Peter's brother, the Apostle Andrew.[91] The transformation of this structure was the centrepiece of an extensive building campaign by Symmachus who sought to turn St Peter's into a cathedral to rival the Lateran, from where he had been excluded by Lawrence, his rival for the papal throne. Central to this scheme was the creation of a new 'basilica' for St Andrew with its constellation of oratories dedicated to martyrs who represented centres of Lawrence's power, not least the imperial city of Constantinople that was the focus of Andrew's cult.[92] The rotunda of Sant'Andrea itself stood hard up against the obelisk from the circus of Nero that was believed to be the site of Peter's martyrdom (see Figure 1.3). Symmachus' largess towards St Peter's was proclaimed in many inscriptions including this one; it celebrates Andrew's martyrdom by crucifixion and his biological relationship with Peter—a point reinforced by the proximity of the rotunda to the obelisk and the fourth-century basilica containing the relics of his brother.[93]

> *On Andrew*
> Here St Andrew's altar protects the church,
>   Peter's brother, who once joyfully endured
> A terrible death, hung by his holy flesh.
>   When he was hanged as a martyr from the broad tree of the cross,
> He breathed the last breath of this mortal life,
>   Taking on a purple crown in Christ's kingdom.[94]

De Rossi thought that the second inscription in the set, *De Petro*, had probably also been made for a location in the vicinity of Sant'Andrea, and could have referred to the entranceway of Sant'Andrea itself. Alternatively, it could have been placed in the atrium of the main basilica that was also improved by Symmachus. The *De Petro* text

---

[90] Story, 'Aldhelm', 13–15.
[91] *LP* 53.6. *ICUR* II.i, 257; *ICUR* n.s. ii, no. 4126.
[92] Alchermes, 'Petrine Politics', 1–40.
[93] On Symmachus' *tituli* at St Peter's, see *ICUR* n.s. ii, no. 4105–14, all of which name him as donor; Alchermes, 'Petrine Politics', 21–2.
[94] *De Andrea*: Andreas hic sanctus templi tutabitur aram / Petri germanus qui quondam funera loeti / Horrida perpessus sancta quoque carne pependit / Dum crucis in patulo suspensus stipite martyr / Ultima mortalis clausit spiracula vitae / Purpureas sumens Christo regnante coronas; M. Lapidge and J. L. Rosier, tr., *Aldhelm: The Poetic Works* (Woodbridge, 1985), 52. For another translation, see Alchermes, 'Petrine Politics', 23. De Rossi, ed., *ICUR* II.i, 257, no. XXIII.1; *ICUR* n.s. ii, no. 4126; Duchesne, ed., *LP* I, 265–6; Schaller and Könsgen, eds, *Initia*, no. 758.

was evidently intended for a *porticus* or entranceway and plays on the iconography of St Peter as the keeper of the keys and the *ianitor* of Heaven.

> *On Peter*
> Peter crowns this entrance with the blessedness of saints,
>   The celestial key-bearer, who opens the gateway to the heavens
> Doorkeeper who reveals the light of eternal life.
>   To all throughout the world he distributed his two-fold teachings.
> Who God, justly adorned with his heavenly triumphs,
>   Omnipotent Judge, carried to the summits of heaven.[95]

De Rossi and Duchesne thought that this *titulus* was also linked to Symmachus' project at Sant'Andrea not least because of the references to the many saints that lay beyond the *porticus*.[96] Peter alone was revered in his basilica prior to Symmachus' pontificate but, in his efforts to create a cult site at the Vatican to intimidate his political rivals, Symmachus introduced the relics of at least ten other martyrs, many of them into the 'basilica' of Sant'Andrea.[97] He also built a stairway up the sloping ground towards Sant'Andrea to facilitate access to the new church, with a fountain for thirsty pilgrims.[98] These stairs formalised a new entranceway into southern side of the Vatican complex and to St Peter's beyond. The precise site of the steps and fountain are also unknown, though de Blaauw has suggested that they led up to the courtyard between the rotunda and the basilica, and that their construction was also the occasion for the creation of an independent entrance into the basilica through the external wall of the southern aisle (or, alternatively, into the southern exedra or the narthex that joined the western rotunda to the exedra).[99] At some point before 800, perhaps even as early as the pontificate of Symmachus himself, the two rotundas were joined together by a bi-apsidal narthex that must have been linked by an external door to the courtyard and steps in some way. The porticus referred to in the *De Petro* inscription could have been associated with the courtyard created by these steps, or with the

---

[95] *De Petro*: Petrus porticum et hanc sanctorum sorte coronat / Claviger aetherius qui portam pandit in aethram / Ianitor aeternae recludens lumina vitae / Omnibus hic geminum digessit dogma per orbem / Quem Deus aeternis ornatum iure triumphis / Arbiter omnipotens ad caeli culmina vexit; Lapidge and Rosier, tr., *Aldhelm*, 50. ICUR II.i, 257, no. XXIII.2; ICUR n.s. ii, no. 4127; Schaller and Könsgen, eds, *Initia*, no. 11958.

[96] Duchesne, *Le Liber Pontificalis*, I, 267, n. 29; ICUR II.i, 224–5, 257–8. Symmachus also improved the atrium of the main basilica, so it is possible that the inscription was intended for that place.

[97] Alchermes, 'Petrine Politics', 9–10.

[98] *LP* 53.7.

[99] *CD* ii, 467–8. A sixteenth-century plan based on observations of the two rotundas before demolition work began in 1514 shows the narthex that joined the rotundas together, and the narthex that joined the westernmost rotunda to the main basilica. The plan shows no external entrance into the complex by this date (although, given the slope of the hill, it is possible that an entrance was at a higher level); Florence, Uffizi, Arch. 4336; Gem, 'The Vatican Rotunda', 13, fig. 3 and n. 137.

bi-apsidal narthex (if it was Symmachan), or perhaps with the entrance into Sant'Andrea itself, which was by this date in the western side of the rotunda.[100]

Significantly, the *Liber Pontificalis* also records the restoration of a stairway in this area in the early ninth century. The biographer of Leo III notes that he had 'rebuilt anew the steps by which entrance is [gained] to St Peter's from Sant'Andrea which had been worn away by age'.[101] This description of Leo's repairs could refer to the external steps constructed by Symmachus that led up to an external entrance into Sant'Andrea and that also gave access into St Peter's.[102] Leo's repairs are dated *c*.809–10 and, given the Carolingian contexts of other *tituli* in this collection, it is possible that it was these early ninth-century repairs that had attracted someone's attention to the ancient verses to saints Andrew and Peter found close by.

Aldhelm, the West Saxon scholar who died in 709/10, also knew these two epigrams, quoting them in the fourth of his *Carmina Ecclesiastica*, known as, 'On the altars of the twelve apostles'.[103] His use of these sixth-century *tituli* from St Peter's accords with his knowledge of other epigraphic texts from Rome and shows that these too were known in England by the late seventh century. Aldhelm quoted this pair of epigrams almost verbatim, using them as the opening and closing lines of two sets of verses within his poem on the twelve altars. But he altered the location of *De Petro* from a porticus to an apse. This change dilutes the word play of the original with its many allusions to doors, doormen, and keys, and may imply that Aldhelm had modified these verses in order to reflect the decorative programme of an apse in a real West Saxon church.

It has conventionally been thought that Aldhelm's *carmen*, 'On the altars of the twelve apostles', was written as a set of epigraphic-style verses composed for an idealised church where he imagined a set of altars dedicated to twelve apostles. However, the observation that a full twelve lines of this *carmen* are quotations from real *tituli* visible inside St Peter's in Rome should encourage a revision of this view, and suggests that rather more of it may be based on genuine inscriptions for real places than hitherto

---

[100] The direction of the original entrance is disputed; de Blaauw argues that it was always entered from the west, but Rasch and others think that it was originally in the southern side of the rotunda: *CD* ii, 468; J. J. Rasch, 'Zur Rekonstruktion der Andreasrotunde an Alt-St.-Peter', *Römische Quartalschrift für christliche Altertumskunde und Kirchengeschichte*, 85 (1990), 1–18.

[101] *LP* 98.90: 'Gradus vero per quos ingressus est in ecclesia beati Petri apostoli a sancto Andrea apostolo, quem vetustate consumpte erant a novo refecit'; Davis, tr., *Lives of the Eighth-Century Popes*, 222. See also, *LP* 105.84: 'porticus, quae S. Andrea cohaerent ecclesiae' and the *Notitia ecclesiarum urbis Romae*; VZ, ii, 95 and *ICUR* II.i, 224–8: 'Intrante (te) in porticum sancti Andreae …'.

[102] Alternatively, this could be explained by internal steps required by a difference in pavement levels between the rotunda and the basilica; my thanks to Richard Gem for discussion on this point.

[103] Aldhelm, 'In duodecim apostolorum aris', *Carmina Ecclesiastica*, iv; *Aldhelmi Opera Omnia*, ed. P. Ehwald, MGH, AA XV (Berlin 1913), 19–20; (i) *In Sancti Petri*, v. 1–4, 35–36, 22–3; (iii) *In Sancti Andreae*, v. 1–3, 14–16; Lapidge and Rosier, tr., *Aldhelm*, 41–4, 50, 52. Schaller and Könsgen, eds, *Initia*, no. 6094 and no. 6712.

recognised.[104] Indeed, Lapidge has suggested that Aldhelm's *carmen* on the twelve altars might have been intended for a church dedicated to saints Peter and Paul, located perhaps in Malmesbury, for which Aldhelm also composed a long dedicatory epigram.[105] Significantly, that dedicatory epigram borrows from a *titulus* belonging to another Roman church also dedicated to Peter and Paul. Located on the Via Appia, it was known by the eighth century as the *Basilica Apostolorum*. The original inscription at that church is now lost, but the text of it was copied into a sylloge appended to the end of a later ninth-century manuscript from northern Francia, and its opening line is clearly the source for the third line of Aldhelm's *carmen*.[106] This reinforces the claim made by Aldhelm's late eleventh-century biographer, Faricius of Arezzo (d. 1117), who said that Aldhelm had written his verses for Peter and Paul one day in Rome while visiting the 'Apostolorum ecclesiam'.[107] Aldhelm's text reads 'Hic Petrus et Paulus, tenebrosi lumina mundi' ('Here Peter and Paul, lights of a darkened world'), against the opening lines of the Roman *titulus* (as restored by de Rossi), 'Hic Petrus et Paulus mundi [duo] lumina praesunt / Quos caelum similes hos habet aula pares' ('Here Peter and Paul preside, [two] lights of the world / Those who heaven holds together, this hall holds likewise').[108]

---

[104] Lapidge and Rosier, tr., *Aldhelm*, 41–4.

[105] Aldhelm, 'In basilica sanctorum Petri et Pauli', *Carmina Ecclesiastica*, i; ed. Ehwald, *Aldhelmi Opera*, 11–12 (which quotes at line 6 verse 2 of *De Petro*, 'claviger aetherius…', on which, see Story, 'Aldhelm', 18–19); Lapidge, 'Career of Aldhelm', 58.

[106] BnF, Lat. 8071, fol. 61v; Bischoff, *Katalog*, no. 4524, s. ix$^{3/4}$. The *titulus* was attributed to the fourth-century *Basilica Apostolorum* by O. Marucchi, 'Di una iscrizione storica che può attribuirsi alla *Basilica Apostolorum* sulla Via Appia', *Nuovo Bullettino di Archeologia Cristiana*, 27 (1921), 61–9. It is a key source for understanding the basilican building programme in Rome by Constantine and his sons; D. Trout, 'Poetry on Stone: Epigram and Audience in Rome', in S. McGill and J. Pucci, eds, *Classics Renewed: Reception and Innovation in the Latin Poetry of Late Antiquity* (Heidelberg, 2016), 77–95, at 82; Logan, 'Who Built Old St Peter's?', 7–8. On Aldhelm's knowledge of this inscription, see P. Liverani, 'Old St Peter's and the Emperor Constans?', at 501 and, in more detail, 'Pietro e Paolo *Lumina Mundi*: l'iscrizione ICUR 3900 e la fondazione della *Basilia Apostolorum*', *Rendiconti della Pontificia Accademia Romana di Archeologia*, 93 (2021), 217–33, at 224. In the manuscript, the verse for the *Basilica Apostolorum* comes after the text of the large mosaic inscription at Santa Sabina on the Aventine (no. XXI.16) and is followed by Honorius I's verses for the arch and apse at Sant'Agnese on the Via Nomentana. Next follow several inscriptions for St Peter's, mostly in the portico, and measurements for the basilica (*ICUR* II.1, 56–7, no. V.13–20). On the *Basilica Apostolorum* (now San Sebastiano), see Arbeiter, *Alt-St. Peter*, 49–50 and Brandenburg, *Ancient Churches*, 63–9.

[107] Faricius, *Vita S Aldhelmi*, PL 89.63–84 at col. 69, and M. Winterbottom, 'An Edition of Faricius, *Vita S. Aldhelmi*', *The Journal of Medieval Latin*, 15 (2005), 93–147, at 104. Lapidge and Rosier, tr., *Aldhelm*, 38–9, 46, arguing that the source was a church in England, not Rome. But see Orchard, *Poetic Art*, 203–12; Lapidge, 'Career of Aldhelm', 59, and Story, 'Aldhelm', 9, for discussion of Aldhelm's knowledge of an early *titulus* from Santa Maria Maggiore and for his visits to Rome in the late seventh century. On Faricius, see M. Winterbottom, 'Faricius of Arezzo's Life of St Aldhelm', in K. O'Brien O'Keeffe and A. Orchard, eds, *Latin Learning and English Lore*, 2 vols (Toronto, ONT, 2005), i, 109–31.

[108] *ICUR* II.i, 248–9, no. XXI.17; *ICUR* n.s. i, 3900; Aldhelm, 'Carmina Ecclesiastica', i, *Aldhelmi Opera Omnia*, ed. Ehwald, MGH, AA XV, 11, no. 1 at line 3, citing the Paris manuscript but not the location of the inscription. The second line of the Roman inscription implies the presence of corporeal relics in the *aula* (as well as in heaven); for a summary of the early evidence for the cult of Peter and Paul at this site, *ad Catacumbas*, see Brandenburg, *Ancient Churches*, 64–8 and Trout, *Damasus of Rome*, 121–2, no. 20 (*ED*, 139–44, no. 20).

Aldhelm's verses circulated widely in the eighth and ninth centuries and his style of Latin verse greatly influenced later poets. Indeed, one of the Reims manuscripts, BnF, Lat. 2773 contains a copy of his *Epigrammata*. Nevertheless, the tight focus on St Peter's of the six poems in this anthology, as well as Aldhelm's alteration of the site of the *titulus* for Peter from a *porticus* to an apse, suggests that these manuscripts preserve copies of the original *tituli* that had served Aldhelm as one of his sources. Aldhelm's use of these verses provides a definite *terminus ante quem* for the *de Petro* and *de Andrea tituli*, and implies that they were among the corpus of texts derived from inscriptions that circulated in England and Francia from the later seventh century. The compiler of the anthology in the Reims manuscripts could thus have had them from another manuscript source, but the dominant interest shown by the inscriptions from the southern side of St Peter's suggests independent transcription for the purposes of this anthology.

The third epigram in the series relates to the area of the baptistery in St Peter's where Symmachus had dedicated three oratories: to the Holy Cross, St John the Baptist, and St John the Evangelist. These altars were installed in the northern arm of the transept, close to the font in the northern exedra, in direct imitation of the arrangement of altars at the Lateran baptistery.[109] The details are recorded in the same chapter of Symmachus' biography in the *Liber Pontificalis* as his work on the new steps up to Sant'Andrea.[110] The area of the baptistery, and especially the altar of the Holy Cross was also extensively repaired by Leo III in 805–6.[111] The verses in the Reims manuscripts are a conflation of two epigrams: a distich for the baptistery itself followed by the first three lines of a six-line poem to St John the Baptist.[112] The final three lines are recorded in another Carolingian manuscript now in Leiden, after verses to the Holy Cross.[113]

The 'odd-one-out' in the series is the epigram for two fifth-century martyrs, Aureus and Justinus, whose cults were celebrated at Mainz in the early ninth century and who were later translated to Heiligenstadt, near Kassel.[114] This epigram is the only one in the collection with no direct connection to Rome; but it is the first of three with Frankish connections, and its inclusion here should be associated with that for

---

[109] *CD* ii, 489–91, fig. 19. *LP* 48.2; Davis, tr., *Book of Pontiffs*, 40.

[110] *LP* 53.7; Davis, tr., *Book of Pontiffs*, 47.

[111] *LP* 98.66. *CD* ii, 491.

[112] *De Sancto Iohanne baptista*: Qui nos spiritu aquaque lavas a sorde benignus / Conserva in nobis donata chrismata [charismata] Iesu / Ad caeli qui regna vocas aeterna fideles / Te precibus sanctis petimus te poplite flexo / Pro nobis baptista potens dignare precari; *ICUR* II.i, 258, no. XXIII.3–4; *ICUR n.s.* ii, no. 4136–7; Schaller and Könsgen, eds, *Initia*, no. 13321 and no. 153.

[113] Leiden, UB, Voss. Lat. Q. 69, fol. 18v (*CLA* X.1585, *c.* 800). *ICUR n.s.* ii, no. 4136[–38]; Schaller and Könsgen, eds, *Initia*, no. 7135. See also Chapter 7, 296, n. 108.

[114] *ICUR* II.i, 258, no. XXIII.5; Schaller and Könsgen, eds, *Initia*, no. 1479. For details of the cult, see A. Wand, *Heiligenstadt und seine stadpatrone. Die Geschichte der Aureus-und Justinusverehrung* (Heiligenstadt, 2001). There is some confusion over the gender of the second saint: Justina (Aureus' sister) or Justinus (his deacon). On the dedication inscription for the new basilica at Mainz, see Chapter 8, 328.

St Martin and Pope Hadrian's epitaph that follow it. Alcuin's friend, Archbishop Riculf (787–813) is said to have translated the bones of Aureus and Justinus into the monastery of St Alban in Mainz in 805 to celebrate the consecration of the new abbey church. Some of their relics are also said to have gone to Fulda c.819, again for the consecration of a new church, and were thereafter included in Hraban Maur's *Martyrology*, c.845. All this is evidence for active interest in the cults of these martyrs in Francia in the first half of the ninth century.

The inclusion of the epigram for Aureus and Justinus within a collection of epigrams for altars in Rome may have been a means of imparting suitable *romanitas* to the remains of these martyrs at a time when corporeal relics from Rome were highly desired in Francia but were hard to obtain.[115] This was especially true in the late eighth and early ninth centuries, since both Hadrian and Leo III restricted the export of corporeal relics from Rome, and it was not until the later 820s that the translation of such relics from Rome to monasteries in the north was revived. In 826 Abbot Hilduin of Saint-Denis pressured Pope Eugenius (824–7) for relics of St Sebastian from Rome and his agent, Rodoin, a priest of Saint-Médard, Soissons, illicitly acquired corporeal relics of St Gregory the Great.[116] A year later, Einhard sent his own agents to Rome to acquire by stealth the bodies of saints Marcellinus and Peter for his new foundation at Seligenstadt.[117]

The penultimate epigram that precedes Hadrian's epitaph in this collection is dedicated to St Martin, the soldier-saint of Tours.[118] De Rossi noticed that it uses poetic formulae found in Alcuin's poetry and argued that it referred to a gift of precious metal for the ornamentation of an altar to St Martin within St Peter's by Fridugis, Alcuin's pupil and successor as abbot of Saint-Martin at Tours. The poem has been rendered anonymous here with the replacement of the donor's name with the pronoun *ille* in the third line (*ille humilis praesul*). Fridugis' donation, however, is mentioned in the *Liber Pontificalis* referring explicitly to the altar of St Martin in the narthex that joined the rotunda of Sant'Andrea to that of Petronilla.[119] The existence of an altar to St Martin in this place is confirmed by the late eighth-century itinerary

---

[115] J. M. H. Smith, 'Old Saints, New Cults: Roman Relics in Carolingian Francia', in Smith, ed., *Early Medieval Rome*, 317–39.

[116] *ARF* s.a. 826; M. Andrieu, 'La chapelle de St. Grégoire dans l'ancienne basilique vaticane', *Rivista di archeologia cristiana*, 13 (1936), 61–99, at 74. The source for Rodoin's activity is a tenth-century account of the translation of St Sebastian by Odilo, who claimed to have used a memoir written by Rodoin himself; *Ex translatione S. Sebastiani auctore Odilone*, MGH, SS XV.1 (Hanover, 1887), 382–4. Also, *LP* 103.6, and Davis, tr., *Lives of the Ninth-Century Popes*, 51, n. 14.

[117] *ARF* s.a. 827. Einhard, 'Translatio et miracula sanctorum Marcellini et Petri', MGH, SS XV.1 (Hanover 1887), 238–64; Dutton, tr., Charlemagne's *Courtier*, 69–130. See also P. J. Geary, *Furta Sacra: Thefts of Relics in the Central Middle Aged* (Princeton, NJ, 1990), 45–9, 118–21.

[118] 'Ductus amore dei martini et praesulis almi / Iusserat hanc aram sacris ornare metallis / Ille humilis praesul pietate tonantis / Illius esto memor celebrans pia voto sacerdos'; *ICUR* II.i, 258, no. XXIII.6; Schaller and Könsgen, eds, *Initia*, no. 3938; Cascioli, *Epigrapfi Cristiane nell'area vaticana VI–X secolo*, 109–10.

[119] *LP* 98.110, 'ante sanctum Andream'; Davis, tr., *Lives of the Eighth-Century Popes*, 229–30, n. 199.

of the basilica that begins at Sant'Andrea and progresses through Santa Petronilla and the south transept to the high altar.[120] The exact date of Fridugis' gift to St Martin's altar at St Peter's is not known, but should certainly be considered a gift made during his abbacy of Saint-Martin's at Tours, 804–33. The *Liber Pontificalis* narrows the date range, since it records that Leo himself 'coated St Martin's altar with fine silver gilt out of what Abbot Fridugis had formerly sent, weighing overall 17½ lbs'. This description of Leo's embellishment of the altar comes at the end of his biography that treats his patronage in broadly chronological order: arguably, therefore, Leo's work on the altar is unlikely to have occurred much before 815, although Fridugis' gift could have arrived some time before that, perhaps not long after he assumed the abbacy at Tours.

The *titulus* for the altar of St Martin, therefore, provides a *terminus post quem* for the collection of this group of poems. The accession of Fridugis to Tours in 804 marks the earliest possible date for the anthology as it stands in these manuscripts. The revival of interest in the cults of Aureus and Justinus in 805 at Mainz also points to a compilation date around this time. The date of Leo's repairs to the entrance to Sant'Andrea may push this forward by five years or so, to *c*.810, if we regard that as the context for a renewed interest in Symmachus' *tituli*. Leo's embellishment of St Martin's altar using the gold and silver sent by Fridugis could stretch the date of compilation to *c*.815. Either way, the earlier of the two manuscripts, Paris Lat. 9347 (perhaps s. ix$^2_4$) provides the latest possible date for the collection.

These five *tituli* plus Hadrian's epitaph, therefore, should be regarded as a short sylloge of inscriptions that was put together in the form found here not before 804 but probably before *c*.815. It is striking that the anthology concentrates on St Peter's with verses concerning doorways, oratories, and altars on the south side of the basilica that were restored or embellished in the late eighth or early ninth century. This complements other evidence for activity in this part of the complex in the years around 800, not the least of which was Leo III's construction *c*.798–800 of 'a great *triclinium* close to St Peter's at the Needle', that is, just to the south-east of the rotunda of Sant'Andrea.[121] This was the papal audience chamber, and so the entranceway into Sant'Andrea accessed by the steps repaired by Leo would have provided privileged access for important visitors entering the basilica from the pope's palace.

The anthology of inscriptions preserved in the pair of Paris manuscripts thus provides a witness to Alcuin's epitaph for Hadrian that was very probably made during the latter part of the pontificate of Leo III, within Charlemagne's lifetime. These manuscripts show that the epitaph was preserved in this anthology for its association with St Peter's basilica, not because it was known to be a poem by Alcuin. Five of the six texts in the anthology are very likely to have been taken from verses inscribed at

---

[120] *Notitia ecclesiarum urbis Romae*; VZ, ii, 95–9, and *ICUR* II.i, 225, ch. 2; *CD* ii, fig. 25.
[121] *LP* 98.27; Davis, tr., *Lives of the Eighth-Century Popes*, 193. The *triclinium* was later known as the *Domus Aguliae* because of its proximity to the obelisk.

St Peter's, four of them from the south transept and its adjacent chapels. This implies that the text of the epitaph as found here derives ultimately from the inscription displayed in St Peter's, not via independent manuscript transmission from Alcuin's archive. We do not know who was responsible for the collection of the anthology, but the unambiguous Frankish interest in the second part of the group, as well as the origin of the manuscripts, suggests that its intended audience was Frankish and that its compiler may also have had Frankish sympathies. It is unlikely to be a coincidence that Alcuin's epitaph for Hadrian follows the *titulus* recording Abbot Fridugis' gift for the altar of St Martin at St Peter's.

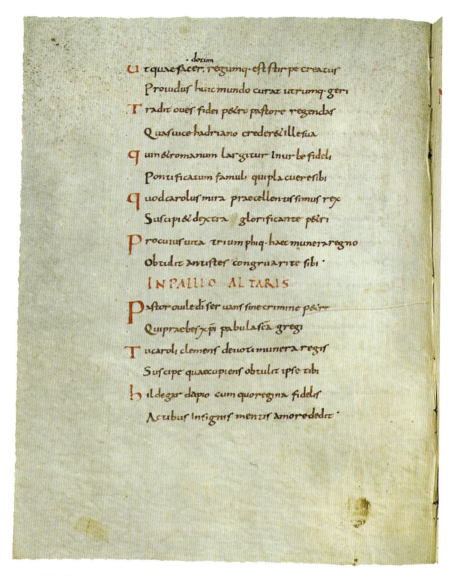

Figure 4.1 The final ten lines of Hadrian's epigram and the full text of the verses for Hildegard's altar cloth; BAV, Pal. Lat. 833, fol. 29v. Photo: Courtesy of the Biblioteca Apostolica Vaticana, Rome.

4

Recalling Rome

Epigraphic *Syllogae* and Itineraries

Many Anglo-Saxons and Franks in the later seventh, eighth, and ninth centuries learned about Rome and its Christian heritage by studying the texts of inscriptions from the city. Especially important were inscriptions that publicly commemorated local martyrs who had been buried in extramural catacombs and whose relics had been objects of popular and papal patronage since the fourth century.[1] The pontificate of Pope Damasus (366–84) was especially important. He promoted the shrines of the martyrs and early popes for two reasons: as a means of securing his own fragile political position and promoting concord within the divided Christian communities of Rome following a contested and bloody election, and to demonstrate that the glory of Rome lay in its Christian heritage not its pagan past.[2] He did this by composing over sixty verse epigrams or *tituli* that were inscribed on large marble slabs and placed in the relevant churches and catacombs.[3] These inscriptions extolled the faith of the Roman saints and, at the same time, proclaimed Damasus as the author of the verses and the patron of the shrines. The Christians of late fourth-century Rome were his primary audience, but the monumentality of the stone-cut inscriptions demonstrates that Damasus also had an eye for posterity.

Some lucky pilgrims doubtless observed inscriptions such as these first-hand on visits to the city's extramural cemeteries. But for others the verses of late antique

---

[1] C. Pietri, *Roma christiana. Recherches sur l'Église de Rome, son organisation, sa politique et son ideéologie de Militade à Sixte III (311–440)* (Rome, 1976), 514–51; Pani Ermini, ed., *Christiana loca*, i, 99–106; ii, 29–60, 99–129; M. Lapidge, *The Roman Martyrs: Introduction, Translations and Commentary* (Oxford, 2018).

[2] Morison, *Politics and Script*, 92–5; M. Sághy, 'Scinditur in partes populus: Pope Damasus and the martyrs of Rome', *Early Medieval Europe*, 9 (2000), 273–87; D. Trout, 'Damasus and the Invention of Early Christian Rome', *Journal of Medieval and Early Modern Studies*, 33 (2003), 517–36; Westall, 'Constantius II and the Basilica of St Peter', 214.

[3] The standard edition is that of A. Ferrua, *Epigrammata Damasiana* (Vatican City, 1942), supplemented and enhanced now by D. Trout, ed., *Damasus of Rome: The Epigraphic Poetry. Introduction, Texts, Translations and Commentary* (Oxford, 2015). See also J. R. Curran, *Pagan City and Christian Capital. Rome in the Fourth Century* (Oxford, 2000), 148–55, and fig. 26; A. Thacker, 'Rome of the Martyrs: Saints Cults and Relics, Fourth To Seventh Centuries', in Ó Carragáin and Neuman de Vegvar, eds, *Roma Felix*, 13–49; E. Thunø, *The Apse Mosaic in Early Medieval Rome: Time, Network, and Repetition* (Cambridge, 2015), 172–87; Lapidge, *Roman Martyrs*, 637–48.

Rome were made known exclusively through manuscript compilations—*syllogae*—of verse epigrams, that circulated in the Anglo-Saxon kingdoms and Francia from the later seventh century. These collections provided English and Frankish readers with authoritative 'Roman' exemplars for Latin verse composition, whether short epigrams recording good deeds of patronage to adorn the walls of buildings, or longer epitaphs to stand over the sepulchres of great men. The poems also provided factual information and could be used as contemplative texts to reflect on the virtuous lives of individual Christians, popes, and martyrs among them.

The epigrams recorded in the *syllogae* also provided topographical information about the locations of the inscribed verses since the poems were often grouped according to the basilica or cemetery in which they were located and were often arranged in a logical sequence, in the order in which they were seen on entering that place. Thus, readers could infer information about the location of particular liturgical fixtures and fittings of major churches of Rome—the altars, oratories, and ornaments—and something of the physical relationship between churches. This way of structuring the collections may also have been an aid to memorisation of the verses since it provides the scaffolding, in a very literal way, for a mnemonic technique common in antiquity of placing a series of 'objects' within a sequence of rooms as a means of prompting recall of a complex text, section by section.[4] By associating text with an object, placed in a room—or, as here, at a significant locus within a church—and by moving mentally between each place in turn and 'collecting the object' placed there, the reader could prompt recollection of each text in turn. This mnemonic technique was particularly well suited for the appreciation of epigraphic verses, since an inscription was both object and text, and often referred implicitly or overtly to the place where it was sited, gaining meaning and authority from the significance of that location.[5] An attentive reader of the *syllogae* could be led thereby on a virtual tour of a particular building via the epigraphy on its walls. Occasionally a rubric recorded the exact location of an inscription within a church: 'at the altar', 'at the font', or 'in the atrium', for example. Someone who had visited the basilica in question would have the memory of the real place to draw down recollection of the text, but the ubiquity of the labels meant that anyone familiar with the common layout and liturgical fittings of a church could apply the verses to any 'memory building', real or imagined.

The topographical information provided by the *syllogae* was complemented and contextualised by another type of text—*itineraria*—that guided pilgrim-readers to the resting places of the saints via the radial network of roads that led out from the

---

[4] F. A. Yates, *The Art of Memory* (Chicago, IL, 1966), 18–19, and 66 for doubts about Alcuin's knowledge of classical methods of training the 'artificial memory', and M. Carruthers, *The Book of Memory* (Cambridge, 1990), 144–8 for modifications to Yates' view, showing that Alcuin knew Quintillian's *Institutio* (XI.2), which described the 'architectural' method, but preferred other techniques.

[5] H. Lefebvre, *The Production of Space*, tr. D. Nicholson-Smith (Oxford, 1991).

heart of the city to the catacombs that lay beyond its ancient walls.[6] These provide direct instructions for visiting the shrines that were based on real-life experience of the journey to these sites: 'From there you go south on the Via Salaria until you come to S. Hermes; pause there in the basilica of Sta. Basilla, virgin and martyr, and next is the martyr Maximus and the martyr S. Hermes, deep underground. And in another catacomb, there is the martyr Protus, and Hyacinthus, and then the martyr Victor. Along the same road you come to S. Panfilus, the martyr, 24 steps underground'.[7]

The earliest surviving pilgrim itineraries of Roman cemeteries and the earliest extant *syllogae* of inscriptions of the city were probably compiled in the second quarter of seventh century. The pontificate of Pope Honorius I (625–38) seems to have been a particularly important period for the development of both types of text; attributable to his pontificate, or shortly afterwards, are two itineraries called the *Notitia ecclesiarum urbis Romae* and *De locis sanctis martyrum quae sunt foris civitatis Romae*, as well as the core of a *sylloge* known as the *Sylloge Centulensis* (i.e. Saint-Riquier).[8] The earliest extant copies of all three were made in Francia in the later eighth century, and the *Notitia ecclesiarum urbis Romae* acquired an important appendix concerning St Peter's basilica around the same time, showing that these texts remained useful and relevant to readers north of the Alps in the Carolingian age. The production of texts of this type in the earlier seventh century, however, suggests that they were being compiled in response to demand from pilgrims wishing to visit the shrines of the saints that lay in the catacombs outside the walls. This corresponds to a boom in the construction of churches in Rome, firstly at the shrines outside the walls and then within city centre where old imperial structures were converted for Christian use.[9] For example, Boniface IV (608–15) consecrated the Pantheon in either 609 or 613 to the Virgin and All Martyrs, and the Senate House in the Forum was remodelled and dedicated to Sant'Adriano by Honorius (625–38), considered 'one of the great building popes'.[10] The altars of intramural churches such as these were supplied either with contact relics or with the corporeal remains of saints who had been martyred and buried far away from Rome; this left intact the treasury of local relics in the extramural

---

[6] Pani Ermini, ed., *Christiana loca*, i, 221–30.

[7] VZ, ii, 74–5. For extant fragments of inscriptions cut for Pope Damasus to Saints Protus, Hyacinthus and Hermetus, see *ED*, 190–7, no. 47–8; Trout, ed. *Damasus of Rome*, 170–3, nos 47–8. See also Lapidge, *Roman Martyrs*, 228–49, 660.

[8] The itineraries are edited by G. B. de Rossi, *La Roma sotteranea cristiana*, 3 vols (Rome, 1864–77), i, 38–43, reprinted in VZ, ii, 72–131, and in Geyer and Cuntz, ed., *Itineraria et alia Geographica*, 303–22; Lapidge, *Roman Martyrs*, 659–64. See also Geertman, *More Veterum*, 198–202. Both of these itineraries are found in ÖNB, Cod. 795, fols 184r–91v (on which, including the important mid-eighth-century appendix, see below, 169–79). On the *Sylloge Centulensis*, see ICUR II.1, 72–94, no. VII. The manuscript was made for Saint-Riquier (s. viii^ex) and is now split between BnF, Lat. 7701, fols 129–34 and St Petersburg, Russian National Library, MS F.v.XIV.1 where the *sylloge* is found on fols 123r–133v; *CLA* V.570 and XI**. Ganz, *Corbie*, 50, dates it to 793.

[9] Thacker, 'Rome of the Martyrs', 18–19.

[10] Krautheimer, *Profile of a City*, 72, 83–7. For the alternative date, see Thunø, 'The Pantheon', at 234.

cemeteries of Rome while permitting the development of the ecclesiastical topography of the city.[11] The increase in pilgrim traffic around this time was also reflected in the development of several new foundations within the city, known as *diaconiae*, that were built and maintained (perhaps initially by non-clerical patrons) to manage the welfare of needy inhabitants of the city, foreign pilgrims among them.[12]

The core of another substantial collection of Christian inscriptions from Rome, the so-called *Sylloge Turonensis* ('Sylloge of Tours') may also date to Honorius' pontificate.[13] This collection was later amplified by verses from Tours composed in the 670s and by a few other texts, including that of the epitaph of the West Saxon king Ceadwalla (who died in Rome in 689) and which was known to Bede in Northumbria in the early 730s.[14] These additions exemplify one of the most important features of this genre of texts: Christian inscriptions of Rome were read avidly outside Italy, especially in the Anglo-Saxon kingdoms and in Francia, inspiring not only the collection of more inscriptions from Rome and other Italian cities but also the composition of brand new verses in the style of these older exemplars. Through collections such as these, the sacred topography of Christian Rome past and present became accessible to educated Anglo-Saxons and Franks, even to those who would never visit the city.

To place an inscription, such as that for Pope Hadrian, in a basilica, such as St Peter's, was to erect a monument not only for the clergy, pilgrims, and mourners who saw it in situ but also to etch it onto the mental topography of all who could encounter that imagined world through manuscript collections of epigrams or itineraries of the shrines. As already seen, scribes in ninth-century Reims included Pope Hadrian's epitaph within a short anthology of epigrams from St Peter's, and readers of these manuscripts would have had no doubt about the cultural context of the poem. In these manuscripts, Hadrian's epitaph was copied alongside the verses of important late antique Christian poets such as Sedulius, Juvencus, Prosper, and Fortunatus, thereby absorbing some of their canonical authority. Here was a text that belonged with the verses of the Christian poets of old, and which was firmly embedded in

---

[11] A. Thacker, 'Martyr Cult within the Walls: Saints and Relics in the Roman *Tituli* of the Fourth to Seventh Centuries', in A. Minnis and J. Roberts, eds, *Text, Image, Interpretation: Studies in Anglo-Saxon Literature and Its Insular Context in honour of Éamonn Ó Carragáin* (Turnhout, 2007), 31–70.

[12] Krautheimer, *Profile of a City*, 77–8; H. Dey, *The Making of Medieval Rome: A New Profile of the City, 400–1420* (Cambridge, 2021), 81–3, 91–4.

[13] The *Sylloge Turonensis* is in two late medieval manuscripts: Klosterneuburg, Stiftsbibliothek, MS 723 (s. xii), fols 264v–269r and Göttweig, Stiftsbibliothek, MS 64 (s. xiii), fols 163v–169v. See de Rossi, ed., *ICUR* II.i, 58–71.

[14] The latest item in the core of the *Sylloge Turonesis* (comprising the first 37 poems) is Honorius' epigram for the rededication of the basilica of Sant'Agnese; de Rossi, ed., *ICUR*, II.i, 58–71 (no. VI.5–6). The items from Tours are no. VI.38–9, Ceadwalla's epitaph is no. VI.40. A helpful summary is provide by R. Sharpe, 'King Ceadwalla's Roman Epitaph', in K. O'Brien O'Keeffe and A. Orchard, eds, *Latin Learning and English Lore: Studies in Anglo-Saxon Literature for Michael Lapidge* (Toronto, ON, 2005), 171–93, at 173. Alfarano's neat copy of the text of Ceadwalla's epitaph is in BAV, Arch. Cap. S. Pietro, G.5, p. 275.

subject matter, verse style, and location in the epigraphic traditions of Rome, and of St Peter's in particular.

The inscribed version of Hadrian's epitaph as fixed in the basilica made this link with Rome and its epigraphic past even more explicit through the particular choice of script with which it was cut. The details of the script, alongside features of the ornamental border and layout, suggest that the designer and letter-cutter of the epitaph drew inspiration from papal inscriptions of the mid-fourth to early seventh centuries as well classical inscriptions, and more recent ones that had been made in Lombard Italy (see Chapter 5). Thus, in both its monumental as well as its manuscript forms, Alcuin's epitaph for Hadrian made multiple connections with the Roman past. However, it was no mere pastiche of past styles but was symptomatic of artistic developments in Francia that were associated with the king's court and which were imbued thereby with contemporary political significance as well as cultural resonance.

EPIGRAPHIC *SYLLOGAE*

Christian inscriptions from Rome have been a topic of antiquarian enquiry for centuries; their greatest modern scholar was Giovanni Battista de Rossi whose seminal investigation of the numerous manuscript collections, published as *Inscriptiones Christianae Urbis Romae* in 1888, still shapes our understanding of the origin and reception of these texts. De Rossi's argument about the transmission of the *syllogae* was predicated on the notion that several collections of epigraphic texts were compiled in Rome during the seventh century, and that these collections were subsequently augmented in northern monasteries such as Tours and Saint-Riquier where they were kept and recopied. De Rossi noticed that several *syllogae* were apparently compiled during the pontificate of Honorius I (625–38) since the latest identifiable inscription referred to restoration or construction work that he had initiated, and important work undertaken by his immediate successors was ignored. De Rossi thus believed the core elements of several *syllogae* had been compiled before about 640; the *Syllogae Centulensis* and *Turonensis*, for example. The compilation of some other groups he thought happened later, noticing that they contained texts—especially epitaphs—that could be dated confidently to the closing years of the seventh century or early years of the eighth. Two *syllogae* containing papal epitaphs fall into this category, the second 'Lorsch' sylloge (on which, see below) and the set that was interpolated into an early twelfth-century copy of the *Liber Pontificalis*, now in Cambridge.[15] All of these,

---

[15] BAV, Pal. Lat. 833 fols 36r–40v (L$_2$), on which see further, below 152–3; Cambridge, University Library, MS Kk.4.6 (Worcester, s. xii[1]) fols 224–80 where the latest epitaph commemorates Pope John VII (705–7) on which, see especially W. Levison, 'Aus Englischen Bibliotheken II', *Neues Archiv*, 35 (1910), 331–431 at 350–66; A. Silvagni, 'La silloge epigrafica di Cambridge', *Rivista di archeologia cristiana*, 20 (1943), 49–112.

he thought, were independent responses to the demand for topographic and devotional texts stimulated in part by an increase in pilgrim traffic from north of the Alps.

The chronological basis of de Rossi's thesis was challenged in 1921 by Antonio Silvagni who argued that all the extant *syllogae* are fragmentary reflections of one, perhaps two, mid-seventh-century collections compiled by a scholar with Anglo-Saxon connections who had travelled to Rome.[16] Silvagni's thesis has not been widely accepted on textual grounds, although his notion that English visitors to Rome were responsible for collecting and transmitting some of the epigrams has proved attractive, not least in the light of what we now know about the visit of Aldhelm to Rome, and his quotation of inscriptions from St Peter's as well as Santa Maria Maggiore in his own compositions.[17]

It is certain that inscriptions from Rome were hugely influential in eighth-century England where they were 'read voraciously and imitated closely' by leading scholars.[18] Bede included verses from epitaphs in Rome in his *Historia Ecclesiastica* and, following Aldhelm's example, composed *tituli* for churches in the English kingdoms of Northumbria and Lindsey as well as epigrammatic verses to preface some of his exegetical works.[19] The epitaphs of Gregory the Great and Ceadwalla of Wessex both circulated in early *syllogae*, and Bede could have acquired these poems from one of them; alternatively, these epitaphs could have reached him independently, perhaps by the monks from Wearmouth and Jarrow who observed the words on the candles in Santa Maria Maggiore in 701, the courier who brought him a copy of the *Liber Pontificalis* in the early 720s, or by Nothhelm, the London priest who searched the papal archive in 728 for copies of letters concerning the mission to the English.[20]

The epitaphs set over the tombs of the metropolitan bishops of Canterbury also owe much to the Roman tradition exemplified by the *syllogae*. Bede recorded the epitaph of Theodore, the last to be sent from Rome, who had died in 690. Those of Archbishop Berhtwald (d. 731) and Archbishop Tatwine (d. 734) are preserved in a *sylloge* that belonged to Bishop Milred of Worcester (743×5–774×5). Milred wrote verses inspired by Roman examples and exchanged precious books with Archbishop Cuthbert of Canterbury (740–60), which may explain how he acquired copies of epitaphs of Cuthbert's forebears. Part of Milred's *sylloge* survives in a partial transcript made by the sixteenth-century antiquary John Leland and also in a fragment of the

---

[16] *ICUR* n.s. i, xxvii–viii.

[17] Orchard, *Poetic Art*, 203; Lapidge, 'The Career of Aldhelm', 52–64; Story, 'Aldhelm and Old St. Peter's, Rome'.

[18] P. Sims-Williams, *Religion and Literature in Western England, 600–800* (Cambridge, 1990), 348.

[19] Bede, *Historia ecclesiastica*, II.1 (the epitaph of Gregory I), V.7 (epitaph of Ceadwalla); Lapidge, 'Some Remnants', 798–820.

[20] Bede's version of Ceadwalla's epitaph is different to that preserved in the extant *syllogae*; Sharpe, 'King Ceadwalla's Roman Epitaph', 179. On the date of the Jarrow monks to Rome, see F. Wallis, trans., *Bede: The Reckoning of Time*, Translated Texts for Historians, 29 (Liverpool, 1995), 128.

tenth-century manuscript that Leland used.[21] This fragmentary text reveals that verses from Rome were circulating alongside Latin epigrams newly composed in eighth-century England, and is hard evidence of the dynamism and popularity of the genre among the higher Anglo-Saxon clergy at that time. Archbishop Cuthbert himself composed verses inspired by Roman example.[22] He also radically altered the burial arrangements for archbishops in Canterbury, planning that his own burial would be within the walls of the city inside the cathedral that was dedicated (like the Lateran in Rome) to the Saviour, rather than in the monastery of saints Peter and Paul that lay outside the walls, as had been the case for previous bishops of the city. This could be seen as a response to developments in contemporary Rome where a change of policy during the pontificate of Paul I (757–67) permitted corporeal relics to be moved from the catacombs into churches within the city walls.[23]

Alcuin was also influenced by the *tituli* of Rome. It is possible that he knew a *sylloge* similar to the collection compiled for Milred while he was still at York.[24] He adapted a line from Sergius' new epitaph for Pope Leo I (whose remains were translated in 688 into a new tomb in the south transept near the high altar) for his *York Poem* and later, when in Francia, he used a line from John VII's epitaph (705–7) for a *titulus* to grace the tomb of St Amandus. Both of these epitaphs are in the *Sylloge Cantabrigensis*, which probably derives from Milred's collection.[25] In Francia, Alcuin composed many *tituli* for the altars and walls of churches and other monastic buildings. None of these survive outside manuscripts, and could have been painted or cut, or indeed intended only for circulation on the page. Most of these are ecclesiastical, but some are distinctly profane:

> *In the latrine*
> Recognise the extravagance of your devouring belly, O reader,
>   You who smell the putrid turds with your nose,
> Shun the greed of your belly with your mouth,
>   May your life be sober for a time.[26]

---

[21] Lapidge, 'Remnants'; Sims-Williams, 'Mildred of Worcester's Collection'; Sims-Williams, *Religion and Literature*, 328–59.

[22] See, for example, his verses for the cross-cloths, inspired by the *titulus* composed for the completion of the church of saints Philip and James by Pope John III (561–74); Sims-Williams, *Religion and Literature*, 340; *LP* 63:1.

[23] Smith, 'Old Saints, New Cults', 320.

[24] Levison, *England and the Continent*, 162; Bullough, *Alcuin*, 277–8; Sims-Williams, 'Milred of Worcester', 37–8.

[25] Sergius' epitaph for Leo I: *ICUR* n.s. ii, no. 4148; it is no. 3 in the Cambridge *sylloge*. The epitaph of John VII is no 41 in the same collection. *ICUR* n.s. ii, xxiii–iv; Sims-Williams, *Religion and Literature*, 346.

[26] Alcuin, *Carmina*, 96.2, MGH, PLAC I, 321, 'In Latrinio: Luxuriam ventris, lector, cognosce vorantis / Putrida qui sentis stercora nare tuo / Ingluviem fugito ventris quapropter in ore / Tempore sit certo sobria vita tibi'. M. Bayless, *Sin and Filth in Medieval Culture: The Devil in the Latrine* (Abingdon, 2012). This verse, and many other similar *tituli* by Alcuin were added to an early collection of Alcuin's letters copied for Arn, now

Alcuin's Frankish contemporaries also indulged in this form of poetic display, Theodulf, bishop of Orléans, and Angilbert, abbot of Saint-Riquier among them.[27] Rome was never far from their minds. As Theodulf wrote:

> *Over the entrance to a house*
> You who wish to see the crowds come and go to and from Rome and Tours,
>   Go and see Rome and Tours.
> Here you will see seeds, vines, and enclosures for animals,
>   Rivers, meadows, roads, and orchards full of fruit.
> When you see these, and find many pleasant things,
>   Be mindful of the author of these, God Himself.[28]

De Rossi noticed that the first couplet of this epigram borrowed from another that probably came from St Peter's in Rome, which is included within the fourth of the Lorsch *syllogae* (L₄) and also in the collection compiled at Saint-Riquier (*Centulensis*).[29] The extant manuscripts of the *syllogae* of Roman inscriptions are graphic testimony of the popularity of this genre of writing in Francia in the late eighth and ninth centuries. Many of the major collections survive first in manuscripts made in Francia during the Carolingian age.[30] These Carolingian manuscripts and the texts they contain fit comfortably with the cultural and spiritual concerns of their age; above all else they demonstrate the intense interest of the Frankish intellectual elite in the early Christian legacy of Rome.

ÖNB, Cod. 808, on which, see Bischoff, *Katalog*, no. 7163; D. Mairhofer, ed., *Handschriften und Papyri: Wege des Wissens* (Vienna, 2017), 119, cat. no. 22.

[27] Theodulf, *Carmina*, nos 57–65, MGH, PLAC I, 554–6. Angilbert, *Carmina*; MGH, PLAC I, 364–5, including the epitaph adorning the sides of the tomb of St Richarius.

[28] Theodulf, *Carmina*, no. 61, MGH, PLAC I, 555. Andersson, tr., *Theodulf of Orléans*, 158; N. Alexandrenko, 'The Poetry of Theodulf of Orléans: A Critical Study', unpublished PhD thesis, Tulane University, New Orleans (1970), 282; P. E. Dutton, *Carolingian Civilization: A Reader* (Peterborough, ON, 1993), 92.

[29] ICUR II.i, 80, no. VII.10–12, 114, no. VIII.80[13–18]–82, and 254, no. XXII.5, the *Anthologia Isidoriana* which excerpts two lines and attributes them *in icona sanci petri*.

[30] *Sylloge Centulensis*, St Petersburg, Russian National Library, MS F.v.XIV.1, fols 123r–133v, Corbie, *s.* viii ex.; Bischoff, *Katalog*, no. 2317; Ganz, *Corbie*, 50. *Syllogae Laureshamensis* I–IV, BAV, Pal. Lat. 833, fols 27–82, from north-east Francia and Lorsch, *c.*820–35; Bischoff, *Katalog*, no. 6559. *Sylloge Einsidlensis*, Einsiedeln, Stiftsbibliothek, Cod. 326 (1076), fols 67r–79v, Fulda-trained scribe, *c.*830–60; Bischoff, *Katalog*, no. 1133. *Codex Thuaneus*, BnF, Lat. 8071, fols 60–1, Loire, ?Fleury, *s.* ix³/⁴; Bischoff, *Katalog*, no. 4524. *Sylloge* Wirceburgensis, Würzburg, Universitätsbibliothek, M.p.misc.f.2, fols 75v–76r, Würzburg, *s.* ix²/³; Bischoff, *Katalog*, no. 7450. *Sylloge Virdunensis*, Verdun, Bibliothèque Municipale, MS 45, fols 212–14, *s.* xi. *Sylloge Passau/Tergensee*, Munich, Bayerische Staatsbibliothek, Clm 19410, pp. 54–7, *s.* ix^med; Bischoff, *Katalog*, no. 3319 (846 at the earliest). Leiden, UB, MS Voss. Lat. Q 69, fols 18–19, Sankt Gallen, *s.* viii/ix; *CLA* X.1585; Bischoff, *Katalog*, no. 2222; Sankt Gallen, Stiftsbibliothek, Cod. Sang. 271, fols 231–4, ?Sankt Gallen, *s.* ix²/⁴; Bischoff, *Katalog*, no. 5713.

THE 'LORSCH' *SYLLOGAE*

One of the most important collections of late antique inscriptions from Rome is preserved in a composite ninth-century Carolingian manuscript now BAV, Pal. Lat. 833.[31] It is part of the collection that came to the Vatican Library in 1623 from Heidelberg that included many books from the nearby monastery at Lorsch, which had been founded in 764 and passed into royal control in 772 when Charlemagne became its protector.[32] Because of its Lorsch provenance, the four *syllogae* contained in this manuscript are commonly called the *Syllogae Laureshamesis I–IV* (hereafter L_{1-4}). The manuscript has two parts that are similarly dated but which were brought together only late in their history. The first part contains Bede's *Martyrology* and was copied in the mid-ninth century, perhaps at Worms. The second part contains the four epigraphic *syllogae* and was copied in Francia probably in the 820s or early 830s; it therefore stands as another key witness to Carolingian interest in the epigraphic heritage of Rome.[33]

The manuscript is dated by palaeographic analysis and internal historical references. The first 'Lorsch' *sylloge* (L_1) includes the verses from the apse mosaic at Santa Cecilia in Trastevere, Rome, erected by Paschal I in 821.[34] It also has two epigrams from the doors at the entrance to St Peter's that were commissioned by Pope Honorius I (625–38) but looted in the Saracen raid on the basilica in 846.[35] De Rossi believed, therefore, that L_1 represented the eyewitness observations of a Carolingian visitor who came to Rome between 821 when Paschal's mosaic was set up and 846 when Honorius' doors were stolen. He argued that it and the two *syllogae* that follow (L_{2-3}) were compiled from existing collections that were amplified by records of near contemporary inscriptions derived from direct observation of monuments in Rome. Bischoff complemented and refined de Rossi's dating, arguing on palaeographic grounds that the fourth and last sylloge in the volume (L_4) had been copied in a 'thick calligraphic Lorsch hand' that he dated *c.*830–5. He too thought that it amplified an

---

[31] BAV, Pal. Lat. 833. Bischoff, *Katalog* III, no. 6559; J. B. Pitra and H. M. Stevenson, *Codices palatini latini Bibliothecae Vaticanae*, i: *1–920* (Rome, 1886), 292. See also C. Vircillo Franklin, 'The Epigraphic Sylloge of BAV Palatinus Latinus 833', in J. Hamesse, ed., *Roma, magistra mundi: Itineraria culturae medievalis. Mélange offerts au Père L.E. Boyle à l'occasion de son 75e anniversaire*, 3 vols (Louvain-la-Neuve, 1998), ii, 975–90. The texts in this manuscript were printed by J. Gruterus, *Inscriptiones antiquae totius orbis Romani in corpus absolutissimum redactae…ingenio ac cura Jani Gruteri, auspiciis Jos. Scaligeri ac M. Velseri* (Heidelberg, 1602), 1163–77, and were cited thence by Grimaldi.

[32] Nelson, *King and Emperor*, 111.

[33] BAV, Pal. Lat. 833, fols 1–25 (Martyrology), fols 27–82 (Syllogae); Vircillo Franklin, 'The Epigraphic Syllogae', 978; Bischoff, *Katalog*, no. 6559.

[34] *ICUR*, II.i, no. XIII.26. C. La Bella et al., eds, *Santa Cecilia in Trastevere* (Rome, 2007), 74–6.

[35] *ICUR n.s.* ii, no. 4119–20.

existing collection that had been made elsewhere.[36] The first three *syllogae* (L[1–3]) were not, in his opinion, copied at Lorsch, but by a single scribe whose work was typical of scriptoria in north-eastern Francia. Bischoff's assessment of the relationship between the work of the two scribes implies that L[1–3] were copied before L[4], that is, before c.835. The presence in L[1] of Paschal's verses for Santa Cecilia means that the work of the Frankish scribe of L[1–3] can be dated between 821 and c.835. Each of the four *syllogae* in the Lorsch manuscript was separately compiled and each has a distinct focus. The final one (L[4]) contains 104 inscriptions from basilicas and cemeteries mostly in Rome (as well as some from Ravenna and Spoleto) and was originally put together in the later seventh century.[37] De Rossi and Bischoff's textual and palaeographic analyses, now widely accepted, propose that this collection was added to the manuscript at Lorsch in the 830s to augment the three other *syllogae* that precede it.[38] L[4] is much discussed by scholars of Anglo-Latin poetry since a *sylloge* like this one was known in the Anglo-Saxon kingdoms by the mid-eighth century when Milred of Worcester made extensive use of many of its verses.[39] It includes two epitaphs from St Peter's: that for Pope Gregory I (d. 604) and another for Ceadwalla, the West Saxon king who died in Rome on 20 April 689 during the pontificate of Sergius I (687–701).[40] Ceadwalla's epitaph is the latest datable item in L[4] and provides a *terminus post quem* for its compilation.

The second sylloge (L[2]) was probably originally compiled around the same time as L[4], that is, in the later seventh century. In the manuscript (fol. 36r) it is entitled *epytaphia apostolicorum in ecclesia beati petri*, and includes thirteen papal epitaphs from St Peter's, the earliest of which is that of Anastasius II (d. 498) and the latest for John V (d. 686). The final epitaph in this set is for a Sicilian woman called Helpis (often thought to have been the wife of Boethius and who died in the late fifth century) who, the manuscript says, was buried *in porticus sancti Petri*; the poem itself refers to her resting within the *porticibus sacris*.[41] The last three papal epitaphs were added in

---

[36] B. Bischoff, *Lorsch im Spiegel seiner Handschriften* (Munich, 1974), 42, 114–15; Bischoff, *Die Abtei Lorsch*, 51, 126–7. See Vircillo Franklin, 'The Epigraphic Syllogae', 987–8 for observations on the codicology of the manuscript, showing that the quires containing the bulk of L[4] were made to match the earlier quires containing L[1–3].

[37] BAV, Pal. Lat. 833, fols 55v–82r: *Sylloge Laureshamensis Quarta*; ICUR II.i, 95–118, no. VIII.

[38] Silvagni favoured the opposite scenario, arguing that L[1–3] were compiled to compliment the 'original' collection that was L[4]; *ICUR n.s.* i: xix, xxvii.

[39] Sims-Williams, 'Milred of Worcester's Collection', 21–38. On Aldhelm's knowledge of a version of L[4], see Orchard, *Poetic Art*, 203–4, countered by Lapidge who argues that Aldhelm's knowledge of some of the Damascan *tituli* it contains may rather have come from personal observation; 'Career of Aldhelm', 55–60.

[40] ICUR II.i, no. VIII.72; Bede, *HE* V.7. On Ceadwalla in Rome, see Aldhelm, 'Hoc templum Bugge'; R. Ehwald, ed., *Aldhelmi Opera*, MGH, AA, XV (Berlin, 1913–19), 14–19; Lapidge and Rosier, tr., *Aldhelm: Poetic Works*, 47–9; Sharpe, 'King Ceadwalla's Roman Epitaph'; Lapidge, 'Career of Aldhelm', 59–60.

[41] Grimaldi, *Descrizione*, ed. Niggl, 416; *PL* 63, col. 558; Cascioli, *Epigrapfi Cristiane nell'area vaticana III–VI secolo*, 30; Vircillo Franklin, 'The Epigraphic Syllogae', 982–3. Troncarelli argues against the association with Boethius; F. Troncarelli, 'L'epitafio di Helpis', in C. Carbonetti, S. Lucà and M. Signorini, eds, *Roma e il*

their proper chronological sequence: Agatho (d. 682); Benedict II (d. 685); John V (d. 686).[42] L₂ does not include either the epitaph of Sergius I (687–702) or the grand new *titulus* made by Sergius for the tomb of Leo I, whose remains he translated in 688 from their original location at the front of the church to a new oratory at the end of the south transept closest to the crossing, or that of Ceadwalla who died in 689; L₂ could well have been compiled, therefore, *c*.687.[43] Alternatively this *sylloge* could reflect texts chosen because they were located close to the atrium of St Peter's; this interpretation would free the *sylloge* from the confines of Sergius' pontificate—although that dating is plausible on other grounds—and could mean that it was compiled at a distance from Rome from a variety of early sources.[44] Some of the *tituli* in L₂ were also known to Bishop Milred at Worcester, so it is possible that a version of this *sylloge* had also made its way to England at least by the mid-eighth century, and perhaps even by the late seventh century.[45]

The third Lorsch *sylloge* (L₃) (fol. 41–54) is rather different in character to the two Rome-centred ones that precede it. It contains thirty-six inscriptions from the heartlands of the Lombard kingdom at Milan, Pavia, Piacenza, Vercelli, and also from Ivrea in the foothills of the Alps. It seems to have been compiled in the mid-eighth century, since none of those that are datable can be later than 778.[46] It includes a group of inscriptions that are associated with Bishop Damian of Pavia (d. 711) and two dedicatory inscriptions erected by the Lombard king Liutprand in 729 for the nearby monastery of Saint Anastasius at Corteolona.[47] The inclusion of texts from Ivrea, which lay at the head of the Great St Bernard Pass through the Alps may indicate that this group of inscriptions was collected by a traveller journeying between Francia and the kingdom of the Lombards. The arrangement of the manuscript suggests that this set of Lombard inscriptions was intended to be read as a complement to the Roman focus of L₁₋₂, but we do not know whether the initiative for juxtaposing the three *syllogae* L₁₋₃ belonged to the northern Frankish scribe of this part of the extant manuscript or to the compiler of his exemplar.

The first *sylloge* in this manuscript (L₁) is, for present purposes, the most intriguing since it focuses squarely on inscriptions from Roman basilicas, primarily St Peter's.[48]

---

suo territorio nel medioevo: Le fonti scritte fra tradizione e innovazione (Spoleto, 2015), 541–52. On the hymn 'Beati pastor Petre clemens accipe' attributed to Helpis, see *PL* 63, col. 538, and below, 177, n. 132.

[42] BAV, Pal. Lat. 833, fols 36r–40v; *Sylloge Lauresheimensis Secunda*, *ICUR* II.i, no. XI. It omits the epitaphs of Leo II (682–3) and Conon (686–7).

[43] *LP* 86:12; Davis, tr., *Book of the Pontiffs*, 88. Duchesne, ed., *LP* i, 379, n. 35. The location of the new tomb of Leo is in a letter by Pope Hadrian to Abbot Fulrad of Saint-Denis; Stoclet, 'Les établissements francs', 245–6.

[44] Vircillo Franklin, 'The Epigraphic Syllogae', 981.

[45] Orchard, *Poetic Art*, 209; Story, 'Aldhelm and Old St. Peter's', 19 on Aldhelm's visit to Rome in 688/9.

[46] *ICUR* II, 159–73, no. XVI; the latest possible date for no. 11 is 778 (the death of Bishop Theodore of Pavia).

[47] N. Everett, *Literacy in Lombard Italy, c.568–714* (Cambridge, 2003), 245–50.

[48] BAV, Pal. Lat. 833, fols 27r–35v; *Sylloge Lauresheimensis Prima*, *ICUR* II.i, no. XIII.

The *sylloge* starts with thirteen epigrams from St Peter's before moving on to report a further twenty-one inscriptions from ten other Roman basilicas.[49] It finishes with an inscription located, according to the rubric, *in prima porta Romae*; this is the name traditionally applied to the 'first' gateway into Rome from the north but here may apply to the arch at the bridge crossing the Tiber at the Via Cornelia, east of St Peter's.[50] Each of the epigrams at St Peter's was given a title by the text scribe to indicate the location of the verses within the basilica. It begins with an inscription *in paradisio beati Petri*, that is, in the atrium of the basilica. Two more *tituli* are recorded, from 'the front of that same church' and 'at the threshold of the entrance to the church', followed by two attributable to Pope Honorius I (625–38) that were inscribed on the doors to the right (*Lumine sed magno*) and left (*Lux arcana*) of the main entrance.[51] The next epigram in the sequence was one that could be found 'at the throne', that is, at the apse, where it could be read at the base of the mosaic in the semi-dome. Its final line makes reference to the *auctor* of the basilica.[52] Hadrian himself quoted its opening line—*Iustitia sedes, fidei domus, aula pudoris* ('Seat of justice, house of faith, hall of modesty')—in a letter-treatise sent to Charlemagne in the autumn of 793. This long document contained the papal response to the capitulary that had been brought to Rome by Angilbert the previous year summarising Frankish objections to the Latin translation of the acts of iconodule synod of Nicaea in 787 (which were subsequently

---

[49] The Lateran Baptistery; Sant'Anastasia, Santi Giovanni e Paulo; Santa Maria Trastevere; San Lorenzo in Damaso; Santa Cecilia; San Chrisogoni; San Stephano Rotondo; San Lorenzo e fuori le Mura; *ICUR* II.i, no. XIII.11. The last four inscriptions from the atrium of St Peter's are misplaced under the heading for the Lateran: *ICUR* II.i, no. XIII.13–116.

[50] Printed separately by *ICUR* II.i, 38, no. III.1–2, noting that the same inscription is in the *Sylloge Einsidlensis*, where it has the rubric *in arcu proximo pont(i) s. petri*; G. Walser, *Die Einsiedler Inschriftensammlung und der Pilgerführer durch Rom (Codex Einsidlensis 326)* (Stuttgart, 1987), 23, 75–6.

[51] *ICUR* II.i, 144–5, no. XIII.4–5; *ICUR* n.s. ii, no. 4119–20; D. Trout, 'Poets and Readers in Seventh-Century Rome: Pope Honorius, Lucretius, and the Doors of St Peter's', *Traditio*, 75 (2020), 39–85, at 57–8.

[52] 'Iustitiae sedes fidei domus aula pudoris / haec est quam cernis pietas quam possidet omnis / quae patris et filii virtutibus inclyta gaudet / auctorumque suum genitoris laudibus aequat' ('Throne of justice, house of faith, hall of modesty / Such is this which you behold, which all piety possesses / Renowned, it rejoices in the virtues of father and son / And renders equal its author with praises of his begetter'): *ICUR* II.i, 145, no. XIII.6, also 21, no. II.10 ('in absidia S[an]c[ti]i Petri'); *ICUR* n.s. ii, no. 4094; Schaller and Könsgen, eds, *Initia*, no. 8587; G. Cascioli, *Epigrapfi Cristiane nell'area vaticana III–VI secolo* (Vatican City, 2013), 19–20. The inscription is early, but its date and patron are contested; Gem, 'From Constantine to Constans', 40 and Thunø, *Apse Mosaic*, 31–2. R. Krautheimer, 'A Note on the Inscription in the Apse of Old St. Peter's', *Dumbarton Oaks Papers*, 41 (1987), 317–20 argued that it refers to the replacement of the original apse mosaic by one of Constantine's sons; Liverani, 'Saint Peter's, Leo the Great', 160–1, thought that the father and son referred to Constantius I (d. 306) and Constantine I (d. 337); Logan, 'Who Built St Peter's?', 4, 10–13, 25, argues that it is the principle dedicatory inscription for the building, and attributable to Constans (d. 350), preceding the apse mosaic, which he attributes to Constantius II (d. 361). The earliest figural mosaic at the apse probably depicted the *traditio legis*, where Christ, standing or enthroned, hands a scroll containing the law to Peter and Paul; *CBCR*, v: 272; M. Andaloro, *La pittura medievale a Roma, 312–1431. Corpus e Atlante,* 9 vols (Milan, 2006), *Corpus*, i: *L'orizzonte tardoantico e le nuove immagini, 312–468*, 87–90 and *Atlante*, i: 24–5 (F2) and 35–6.

explored at greater length by Theodulf in the *Opus Caroli*).[53] Hadrian emphasised the inscribed form of this quotation (*scriptum est*) and he used it to underpin his argument about the antiquity and divine origin of the judicial role ascribed to the Roman Church, as well as its singular Petrine authority, which had been challenged by the Franks' position. The apse inscription used three nouns—*sedes, domus, aula*—as synonyms for both the 'holy catholic and apostolic Church in Rome' and the basilica of St Peter itself, 'which you [the reader] behold', as the *locus* of justice, faith, and modesty. Carolingian readers of the verse—whether seeing it in situ in St Peter's, hearing it when Hadrian's treatise was read out at court, or finding it in the manuscript *sylloge*—would very likely have reflected on its literal and figurative meanings. Those who knew the palace buildings at Aachen as they were being constructed in the 790s may also have heard echoes in the text that was chosen to dedicate the new chapel there, which also referenced *Karolus*, as its *auctor*.[54]

TWO CAROLINGIAN EPIGRAMS AT ST PETER'S

The *sylloge* continues with a series of epigrams at St Peter's, two of which were located at an altar, and another on an altar cloth. These are followed by the text of Damasus' well-known inscription at the font in the north exedra. The scribe paired the epigram for the Vatican font with one for the baptistery at the Lateran, before completing the sequence with four located *in paradisio* (i.e. in the atrium) at St Peter's although mistakenly included under the rubric for the Lateran Baptistery.[55] The sequence suggests that the two texts described as being 'at the altar' and the verses on the altar cloth were to be found somewhere between the apse and north exedra at St Peter's. It may be that the high altar or *confessio* were meant, although a more likely candidate is the altar of *Petrus pastor*, 'Peter the Shepherd', which stood at the base of the northern pier of the triumphal arch that articulated the transept with the nave.[56]

---

[53] This very long letter was not included in the *Codex Carolinus*. It was edited by E. Dümmler, ed., MGH, Epp. V (Berlin, 1899), 5–57, cited here at p. 29 (line 29). On its date and context, see A. Freeman with P. Meyvaert, ed., *Opus Caroli regis contra synodum (Libri Carolini) [Theodulf von Orléans]*, MGH, Conc. II, Supplementum I, Leges IV (Hanover, 1998), 8, with an English version in A. Freeman, *Theodulf of Orléans: Charlemagne's Spokesman against the Second Council of Nicaea* (Aldershot, 2003), ch. 1, at p. 11. There is a useful summary of the debate between Hadrian and the Franks in Price, tr., *Acts of the Second Council*, i, 65–73, noting that the Franks' major objection rested on a mistranslation of a key point from the Greek to the Latin (Hartmann, *Hadrian I*, 278–91).

[54] See Chapter 7, 296–306.

[55] *ED*, 93–4, no. 4; Trout, ed., *Damasus of Rome*, 86–7, no. 4. ICUR II.i, 148–9, no. XIII.13–16. For the inscription at the font, see Chapter 5, Figure 5.13.

[56] Luchterhandt, 'Famulus Petri', 64; Story, 'Carolingians and the Oratory', 265–6 which makes the case for the Oratory of the Shepherd/*Oratorium Pastoris*.

Two of these epigrams name Charlemagne and it is clear that both had been composed during Hadrian's pontificate. The originals are now lost, and the texts are known only through this unique copy (Figure 4.1). Both record gifts: one 'at the altar', from Hadrian, honoured *Carolus praecellentissimus rex*; the other, on an altar cloth (*in pallio altaris*), documents a gift from the king and his queen, Hildegard, to St Peter.[57] The historical contexts, locations, and meanings of these inscriptions has generated much discussion, not least because the text of the longer of the two, recording Hadrian's gift, is evidently corrupt in the Lorsch copy and several variant readings have been proposed, some of which have far-reaching political conclusions. These two epigrams follow one from another in the manuscript, and it is probable, though not explicit, that they were also meant to be read in tandem in their original settings since both refer to *Petrus pastor*, which is a Petrine dedication that can be tied to a particular oratory in the basilica.[58] Together they provide rich material for exploring papal and Frankish perspectives on the bond between this king and pope as well as the way that inscribed texts were used in St Peter's to display and memorialise encounters that were simultaneously spiritual and political. The architectural setting supplied contextual meaning and ample scope for intertextual cross-referencing to other inscriptions displayed in that place.[59]

The insertion of two Carolingian inscriptions within this selective epigraphic tour of St Peter's is clearly of very great interest since they demonstrate that Charlemagne was being remembered in verses inscribed at the liturgical heart of the basilica during Hadrian's lifetime, prefiguring the production of the epitaph. We should not be troubled that the L_1 sylloge does not include the text of Hadrian's epitaph; the inscriptions quoted in L_1 are from two discrete zones of the basilica—the atrium/narthex, the crossing and northern arm of the transept—and those quoted were but a few of those know to have existed in those locations. None from the southern side of the complex are cited, and none in this *sylloge* is an epitaph.[60] Also, the scribe of the manuscript left a full page and a half blank between the final epigram in L_1 on fol. 35r and the opening of L_2 at the head of fol. 36r. It may have been the scribe's wish simply to start the second *sylloge* at the head of a new page; alternatively, the empty pages might imply that the scribe hoped to add more to L_1 at a later stage and had left some space to do so.

---

[57] *ICUR* II.i, 146–7, no. XIII.8–9.

[58] Beumann, 'Paderborner Epos', 373; Story, 'Carolingians and the Oratory', fig. 13.1.

[59] Grimaldi grouped them with the text of Hadrian's epitaph in his description of the basilica: Niggl, ed., *Descrizione*, 395–6; BAV, Barb. Lat. 2733, fols 355r–356v.

[60] Many of the inscriptions from St Peter's are supplied in *ICUR n.s.* ii, nos 4092–4240.

HADRIAN'S VERSES FOR CHARLEMAGNE

The text of Hadrian's twelve-line poem is found on fol. 29 r/v of the Lorsch manuscript, as follows.[61] Grammatical corrections are noted in square brackets, and contested words are underlined:

In eodem

1 Caelorum dominus qui cum patre condidit orbem
       Disponit terras uirgine natus homo
   Utquae sacerdotum regumque est stirpe creatus
       Prouidus huic mundo curat utrumque geri
5 Tradit oues fidei Petro pastore regendas
       Quas uice hadriano crederet ille sua
   Quin et romanum largitur in urbe fideli
       <u>Pontificatum</u> famuli[s] qui placuere sibi
   Quod carolus mira pracellentissimus rex
10   Suscipiet dextra glorificante Petri
   Pro cuius uita triumphi[s]que haec munera <u>regno</u>
       Obtulit antistes congrua rite sibi.

At the same [altar]

1 Lord of the heavens, who created the world with the father,
       Orders the earth, born of the Virgin as man.
   Begotten from the stock of priests and kings,
       With forethought he arranges for the world to be guided by both.
5 He hands over the sheep of faith to the shepherd Peter for ruling,
       Who entrusts them in turn to his deputy, Hadrian.
   Moreover, in the faithful city He lavishes the Roman
       <u>Pontificate</u> on those servants who are pleasing to Him.
   Which Charles, the most exalted king, wonderfully
10   Will receive from the glorious right hand of Peter.
   For whose life, triumphs and <u>kingdom</u>, these gifts
       The bishop bestowed, according to proper rites.

Hadrian is named in line 6 as the heir to the apostolic commission, receiving from Peter the flock of the faithful for ruling. The scriptural allusion is to John 21: 15–17 when Christ called Peter three times to 'feed my sheep' (*pasce oues meas*), before foretelling the manner of Peter's martyrdom. The imagery of *Petrus pastor*, Peter the

---

[61] See Figure 4.1. German translations are provided by: M. Luchterhandt, 'Famulus Petri. Karl der Grosse in den romischen Mosaikbildern Leos III', in SW, *799*, iii, 55–70, at 64; Bauer, *Das Bild der Stadt Rom im Frümittelalter*, 105; Scholz, *Politik*, 91.

Shepherd, therefore, is especially appropriate for the basilica of St Peter's in Rome, erected at the site of Peter's crucifixion.[62] Charles, *praecellentissimus rex*, is named in line 9 as recipient of some form of authority from Christ that he will receive from St Peter. The hierarchy of power envisaged by the opening lines is based on the doctrine articulated in the late fifth century by Pope Gelasius I (492–6) concerning the separation of the two powers that rule the earth—the sacred authority of priests and the power of kings. In this instance, both powers are received from St Peter, who entrusts the Christ-given authority over Christians to Hadrian 'for ruling', and the power to act as protector of the city to Charles.

However, the wording of line 8 causes considerable trouble, since the manuscript reading, *pontificatum* ('pontificate'), makes no sense and disturbs the metrical structure of the line. Various alternatives have been suggested, including *praesidium*, *patriciatum*, *principatum*, *vexillum*, and *imperium*. The Bollandist scholar Papebroek wanted to replace *pontificatum* with *imperium*, 'empire', and he was followed in this interpretation by Dümmler and Beumann, among others who have read into it a prefiguration of the events of 800.[63] Others have favoured *vexillum* ('banner') as the preferred reading, mindful of the reference to the gifts sent to Francia by Leo III announcing his election in 796, and the famous apse mosaic from his triclinium at the Lateran made in 797–8 that depicts Charlemagne receiving the banner of the city of Rome from Peter's left (not right) hand.[64] *Vexillum* is a neuter noun, and this fits the grammar of the following line as recorded in the manuscript, but is metrically too short. Despite the manuscript's use of the future tense for Charlemagne's receipt of the gift, both *imperium* and *vexillum* are anachronistic suggestions made with the benefit of hindsight from the perspective of the turbulent early years of Leo's pontificate. Choosing either of these words is, thus, methodologically problematic and also implies an imperial political vocabulary in papal circles from the earliest days of Hadrian's pontificate which is hard to justify from other evidence.

De Rossi and Duchesne thought that the original version of these lines probably read *romanum largitur... patriciatum famulis* ('he grants the Roman patriciate to his servants'), which does less damage to the rhythm of the verse although it requires grammatical changes and modifications to the next line.[65] This reading fits the historical context of the early 770s since Charlemagne was by then already the *patricius Romanorum*—'patrician of the Romans'. A better option, which respects the prosody,

---

[62] E. Kirschbaum, ed., *Lexikon der Christlichen Ikonographie*, 8 vols (Freiburg, 1968–76), ii, 296. See also Story, 'Carolingians and the Oratory', 265.

[63] 'Tituli codicis palatini', XIII, Dümmler, ed., MGH, PLAC I, 106; H. Beumann, 'Das Paderborner Epos und die Kaiseridee Karls des Grossen', in G. Wolf, ed., *Zum Kaisertum Karls des Grossen. Beiträge und Aufsätze* (Darmstadt, 1972), 309–83, at 371.

[64] M. Luchterhandt, 'Famulus Petri', 55–70, at 64–7; Bauer, *Das Bild der Stadt Rom im Frümittelalter*, 105; C. Goodson and J. L. Nelson, 'The Roman Contexts of the "Donation of Constantine". Review Article', *Early Medieval Europe*, 18.4 (2010), 446–67.

[65] *ICUR*, II.i, 146–7, n. 8.

metrical structure and the historical context is the word *praesidium*, 'protection/ garrison' reflecting the king's obligation to defend the city, its people and the pope as *patricius Romanorum*.[66] Scholz's suggestion fits well in the context of the king's first visit to Rome at Easter 774. Both he and Luchterhandt have followed De Rossi's lead in reading these verses alongside the account in the *Liber Pontificalis* of the rituals around Charlemagne's reaffirmation of Pippin's 'Donation' at St Peter's *confessio* that year, and regard these verses as a papal response to the king's promise and Hadrian's prayers of support for 'his life and victory'.[67] On that occasion, the pope's biographer said, Hadrian offered masses in the principal basilicas of the city, with the singing of *laudes* for the Frankish king and prayers for his eventual victory over the Lombards. Similar emphasis on papal prayer and St Peter's intercessory role in Charles' victories are found in the dedicatory verses of the *Dionysio-Hadriana* canon law collection, which the pope had made for the king at the same time. The epigram in the Lorsch collection likewise shows St Peter as the mediator for Charles' authority, and the final couplet echoes the acclamations of the *laudes* for the king's life and triumphs.

The reference in the penultimate line to the *munera* ('gifts') also reflects the historical context of the masses said by Hadrian for the king since the expression (*munera offere pro*) is commonly used for the Eucharist oblation, and invites a return gift or reward (*remuneratio*) from the dedicatee.[68] That liturgical context is reinforced by the location of the inscription, 'at the altar'. The rubric says that Hadrian's epigram could be read 'at the same' place as the preceding text in the collection which was located, according to its rubric, *ad altare*.[69] That text also named its patron, Pope Pelagius II (579–90) and begins, *Vox arcana patris caelis quibus aequa potestas / Descendit terras luce replere sua / Hanc Deus humanam sumens de virgine formam / Discipulos mundo praecipienda docet* ('Hidden voice of the father, two who share equal power in heaven / Descended to fill the earth with his light. / God taking this human form from a virgin / Taught his disciples the things they were to teach the world').[70] Pelagius' text was referenced by opening words of the much longer inscription set up by Pope Honorius I (625–38) on the left side of the silvered doors at the

---

[66] Scholz, *Politik*, 91–2.

[67] De Rossi (following Baronius and Grimaldi), *ICUR*, II.i, 146; Duchesne, *Le Liber Pontificalis*, i, 516–17;Scholz, *Politik*, 90–2, and Luchterhandt, 'Famulus Petri', 64. Bauer, *Das Bild der Stadt Rom im Frühmittelater*, 104–6, argued that this poem should be linked to Charlemagne's visit in 786/7, followed by G. Curzi, 'Mutual Identities. The Construction of the Figure of the Pope and the Emperor in the Carolingian Age: Historical Perspectives', in C. D'Alberto, ed., *Imago Papae: Le pape en image du Moyen Âge à l'époque contemporaine* (Rome, 2020), 61–8.

[68] M. de Jong, *In Samuel's Image: Child Oblation in the Early Medieval West* (Leiden, 1996), 176, n. 66; Scholz, *Politik*, 92.

[69] *ICUR* II.i, 146, no. XIII.8. Scholz, *Politik*, 90–2. For the inscriptions in this area, see O. Bucarelli, 'Epigraphy and Liturgical Furnishings in St. Peter's Basilica in the Vatican between Late Antiquity and the Middle Ages', *Archiv für Diplomatik*, 60 (2018), 293–322, at 289–302.

[70] *ICUR* II.i, 145–6, no. XIII.7; *ICUR n.s.* ii, no. 4117; Cascioli, *Epigrapfi Cristiane nell'area vaticana III–VI secolo*, 137–8; Schaller, *Initia*, no. 17526.

entrance to the basilica, which began, *Lux arcana Dei verbum sapientia lucis* ('Hidden light of God, the word, light's wisdom'), and which was also copied by the Lorsch scribe, immediately before the text of the apse inscription.[71]

As well as a shared location, the verses of Pelagius and Hadrian have structural and verbal parallels, suggesting that Pelagius' verses were studied and imitated during Hadrian's time. Both texts are twelve lines long, and the first few lines reference the duality of divine authority and Christ's commission to the apostles. Both poems open with verses on the descent of the Son of God from the heavens to the Earth, and his incarnation in human form through a virgin. The Pelagian poem does not honour an individual by name, but line 10 refers to certain 'princes'. Duchesne argued that these 'princes' must be the emperor Maurice and his sons, rather than (as Baronius and de Rossi had argued) the emperor Justinian who had been sole ruler during the pontificate of Pelagius I (556–61). If correct, and if this reading of the epigram was understood in the mid-770s when Hadrian commissioned his verses, the parallel reference to Charlemagne in Hadrian's epigram is extraordinarily precocious.

De Rossi thought that both of the epigrams 'at the altar' referred to large, ornamental, votive crowns (*regna*), designed to hang, perhaps with lights, over the altar.[72] This suggestion arises from his interpretation of the word *regnum* in the penultimate line of Hadrian's verses which he thought referred to the object on which the inscription was set and which was given by Hadrian to celebrate Charlemagne's life and victories. This interpretation was based in part on knowledge of several other votive crowns at the basilica. After mass on Christmas Day 800 Charlemagne gave, among other precious vessels, a fabulous 'gold crown with large jewels...weighing 55lbs' to hang over the altar in St Peter's *confessio*.[73] Leo III also gave similar *regna* for altars in the rotundas of Sant'Andrea and Santa Petronilla, and to many other Roman churches.[74] The *Liber Pontificalis* says that Leo's *regna* for the rotundas were made of purest gold and precious gems, weighing 4lb 8oz in total, adding that they were made for 'hanging over the altar'. The *Liber Pontificalis* records another precedent for a jewelled Frankish crown at St Peter's; during the pontificate of Hormsidas (514–23) 'a crown with precious gems came from Clovis, Christian king of the Franks, as a gift to St Peter, the apostle'.[75] The name of Clovis was added to the second edition of the

---

[71] See *LP* I, 309–10 for the argument that the inscription belongs to the pontificate of Pelagius II, rather than his namesake, Pelagius I (556–61), as de Rossi (following Grimaldi, *Descrizione*, ed. Niggl, 416) had supposed. On the parallel between the two poems, 'Vox arcana' and 'Lux arcana', see both Duchesne, *LP* I, 235 and the insightful analysis by D. Trout, 'Poets and Readers in Seventh-Century Rome: Pope Honorius, Lucretius, and the doors of St Peter's', *Traditio*, 75 (2020), 39–85, at 57–61.

[72] De Rossi, *ICUR* II.1, 146, no. XIII.8, followed by M. Luchterhandt, 'Famulus Petri', in *SW*, *799*, iii, 55–70, at 64 and Story, 'Carolingians and the Oratory', 266–8. See also Cascioli, *Epigrapfi Cristiane nell'area vaticana VI–X secolo*, 99–101.

[73] *LP* 98:24.

[74] *LP* 98:55; Geertman, *More Veterum*, 83–90; Du Cange, *Glossarium*, VII, 96.

[75] *LP* 54:10, 'Eodem tempore venit regnus cum gemmis praetiosis a rege Francorum Cloduveum christianum, donum beato Petri apostolo'.

Liber Pontificalis later in the sixth century—and may have been recalled precisely because it had been inscribed on the crown.[76] As the first orthodox Christian king of the Franks, the reputation of Clovis (481–511) held strong in Carolingian Francia, demonstrated not least through the name of Charlemagne's second son and eventual successor, Louis.

However, Scholz's interpretation of Hadrian's *munera* as the prayers said for the king at mass, as well as his observation that inscriptions themselves do not often refer to the object on which they were displayed, has led him and others to argue that Hadrian's *titulus* was placed not on a votive crown, as de Rossi had thought, but somewhere on the altar itself, perhaps as an altar frontal or precious metal cladding.[77] If so, the *regnum* of the last couplet may refer instead to the kingdom of the Franks, or that of the Lombards which fell to the Frankish army soon after Charles' visit to Rome. Hadrian's inscription at the altar could thus have been intended to imply that the Lombard *regnum* too was in some way a gift from St Peter and his papal representative.[78]

HILDEGARD'S ALTAR CLOTH: FUNCTION AND FORM

The title given to the second Carolingian epigram in L₁, *in pallio altaris*, implies that the text was woven or embroidered on an altar covering (see Figure 4.1).[79] The decorated *pallium* was also a highly symbolic gift. The *pallium altaris* was one of the names given to the *corporale*, or linen cloth, that was placed on the altar by the deacons at the beginning of the offertory before the liturgy of the mass.[80] It was the most important of the altar vestments, since it came into direct contact with the eucharistic offerings of wine and bread (i.e. the *corpus* of Christ, hence *corporale*) and thus symbolised the linen shroud in which Christ's body had been wrapped. As such, the ritual purity of the *pallium altaris* was paramount and on no account could the

---

[76] *LP*, I, 274, n. 23; Davis, tr., *Book of Pontiffs*, xiii, xlvi–xlviii, 111–13. McKitterick, *Rome and the Invention*, 111.

[77] Beumann, 'Das Paderborn Epos', 373; Scholz, *Politik*, 90. The argument put forward by Bauer, *Das Bild der Stadt Rom im Frühmittelater*, 105, that the inscription accompanied the 'oldest verified public representation' of the king in the city is based largely on the assumption that the contested word in line 9 was *vexillum* and on the parallel that this inferred reading draws with the later mosaic at the Lateran; it is unsustainable on grounds of method as well as evidence.

[78] For a closely contemporary parallel, see Cathwulf's letter to Charlemagne where he suggests that the gift of the Lombard kingdom came about as a result of Charlemagne's visit to Rome at Easter 774; Dümmler, ed., MGH, Epp. IV, 501–4, at 502, lines 33–4. J. Story, 'Cathwulf, Kingship and the Royal Abbey of St.-Denis', *Speculum*, 74 (1999), 1–21, at 4.

[79] ICUR II.i, 147, XIII.9; MGH, PLAC I, 106–7; Cascioli, *Epigrapfi Cristiane nell'area vaticana VI–X secolo*, 97–8.

[80] J. Braun, *Ein handbuch der Paramentik* (Freiburg, 1912), 211, 233–9; M. Righetti, ed., *Manuale di storia liturgica*, 4 vols (Milan, 1950), ii, 443–4.

laity touch it.[81] By donating this liturgically special object, the donor was thus involved—but at one remove—in the regular act of offering, sacrament, and remembrance at the altar.[82] The incorporation of a text that named the donor (and her husband) made their participation in this act explicit.

> *In pallio altaris*
> Pastor ouile d[e]i seruans sine crimine Petre
>   Qui praebes xpi pabula s[an]c[t]a gregi
> Tu caroli clemens deuoti munera regis
>   Suscipe quae cupiens obtulit ipse tibi
> Hildegarda pio cum quo regina fidelis
>   Actibus insignis mentis amore dedit.
>
> *On the altar cloth*
> Shepherd serving the sheepfold of God without sin, O Peter,
>   Who offers the holy fodder of Christ to the flock.
> You, merciful one, the gifts of Charles, devoted king,
>   Receive, which he himself eagerly presented to you.
> With whom Hildegard, devoted queen, with pious love,
>   Gave this with the actions of noble judgment.

This epigram comprises three couplets. The first concerns St Peter who—just as in the preceding poem—is referred to as *Pastor*, the shepherd of Christ's flock. This strongly suggests that the inscribed *pallium* was intended for the same altar in the basilica as Hadrian's *titulus* which precedes it in the manuscript (see Figure 4.1). Here, St Peter offers the nourishment of Christ to his flock, recalling the function of the *pallium* as the cloth that bore the Eucharist offerings. The second couplet entreats Peter to accept the gifts (*munera*) that Charles, 'devoted king', has given to him, and again recalls the act of the offertory in the liturgy of the Mass. The name of the donor of the *pallium*, Hildegard, *fidelis regina*, is kept back to the beginning of the third couplet, and her gift of the *pallium* is subordinate to those of her husband.[83]

Hildegard was Charlemagne's third consort and bore him nine children during their eleven-year marriage—*fideliter* indeed. She died, aged about 25, on 30 April 783

---

[81] De Jong, *In Samuel's Image*, 26–9, 179 (on the particularly polluting quality of women).

[82] Compare Alcuin's verses for Saint-Amand, *Carmina*, no. 88.11, Dümmler, ed., MGH, PLAC I, 307, and Theodulf's 'Verses on an altar', *Carmina*, no. 58; ed., MGH, PLAC I, 554, Andersson, tr., *Theodulf of Orléans*, 157, esp. line 5 which uses the same allusion to John 21: 16–17.

[83] Einhard *VK*, ch. 18. Nelson, 'Women at the Court of Charlemagne', 234; also McKitterick, *Charlemagne*, 89–90 where the structure of the MGH edition (which extracted and reordered epigrams from this sylloge) has caused confusion, wrongly attributing Hildegard's poem to a church in northern Italy; *Tituli codicis palatini*, XIV, Dümmler, ed., MGH, PLAC I, 106–7. It is clear from the manuscript context that the poem refers to an inscription in St Peter's in Rome.

at Thionville and was buried in the abbey church of St Arnulf at Metz.[84] She had accompanied the king to the siege of Pavia in 774, but there is no clear evidence that she went with him to Rome that year. She did, however, make that journey in 781, when she accompanied Charlemagne on his second visit to Rome. The event is also recorded in the margins of the Easter table at the end of the Godesscalc Evangelistary that was made in conjunction with this visit.[85] In Rome, at Easter 781, Hildegard's second son, Carloman, was baptised by Pope Hadrian and given the name Pippin. He and his younger brother Louis were crowned as kings: Pippin as king of Italy; Louis as king of Aquitaine. The choice of Pippin as the baptismal name for the new boy-king of Italy may have been intended in part as a reminder of Carolingian promises for the return of lands to the papacy that had been promised by his grandfather and namesake in 754 and reiterated under solemn oath by his father on his earlier visit to Rome in 774.[86] Hildegard's donation of this cloth to St Peter's altar could well have occurred in the context of this visit in 781 and its king-making ceremonies. It is possible, but less likely, that she had accompanied Charles from the siege of Pavia to Rome in 774, though the evidence of her pregnancy at the time, and the reported speed of his journey south, argues against it. The text on the *pallium* speaks directly to Charlemagne's devotion to St Peter, and, by naming Charles and Hildegard, reinforced the perpetual presence of the Carolingian dynasty at the heart of the basilica.[87] The gift of a sacred *pallium altaris* for use in the liturgy of the offertory engaged the donors in a perpetual dialogue of offering and supplication with the prince of the apostles every time that Mass was performed. And, as a sacred vestment, it gave Hildegard as well as her husband the king, a place at the altar.

---

[84] *Annales Mettenses Priores*, s.a. 783; B. de Simson, ed., MGH, SS rer. Germ. (Hannover and Leipzig, 1905), 70. See also the *Epitaphium Hildegardis reginae*; Schaller and Könsgen, eds, *Initia*, no. 1456; Dümmler, ed., MGH, PLAC I, 58–9; D. Kempf, *Paul the Deacon. Liber de episcopis Mettensibus. Edition, Translation, and Introduction*, Dallas Medieval Texts and Translations, 19 (Paris, 2013), 80–3. Paul's text includes the epitaphs of two of Hildegard's daughters: Adelaid, who was 'born near the high walls of Pavia' in 774, and Hildegard, who outlived her mother by less than a year.

[85] BnF, NAL 1203, fol. 125r and fol. 126v where Hildegard is named within the verse dedication. Godesscalc is named at the top of fol. 127r (his name is spelled there with a double ss). The marginal note on fol. 125r, marked adjacent to the date for Easter in 781, reads, 'In isto anno fuit domnus rex karolus ad s[an]c[tu]m Petrum et baptizatus est filius eivs Pippinus a domno apostolico'. The closing lines of the poem record the baptism in greater detail, including the change of the boy's name from Carloman (with uncomfortable resonance of his uncle) to that of Charles' father, Pippin. See Chapter 7, 270.

[86] On Pippin's name change, see C. M. Booker, 'By Any Other Name? Charlemagne, Nomenclature and Performativity', in R. Grosse and M. Sot, eds, *Charlemagne: les temps, les espaces, les hommes. Construction et Déconstruction d'un règne*, Collection Haut Moyen Âge, 34 (Turnhout, 2018), 409–26.

[87] Hildegard's altar cloth for St Peter's was augmented by one from Irmingard, queen of the Emperor Lothar (821–51). This too was commemorated by a poem of thirty-six lines, composed by Sedulius Scottus: *Hoc insigne decus, hoc textile munus amoris / Ermingarda Petro felix regina dicavit*; 'Blessed Queen Irmingard dedicated to Peter this distinguished emblem, this embroidered gift of love', ed. L. Traube, MGH, PLAC III, 187–8, no. 21; I. Meyers, ed., *Sedulii Scotti Carmina*, CCCM 117 (Turnhout, 1991), 41–2, no. 21a; E. G. Doyle, tr., *Sedulius Scottus, On Christian Rulers and The Poems* (Binghamton, NY, 1983), 121–2.

The epigram recording Hildegard's gift runs to thirty-six words, and a poem of this length could easily have been embroidered onto or even woven into a cloth in such a way that rendered it legible from a short distance.[88] But we know for certain neither the shape of the *pallium altaris* nor how the text might have been laid out on it. Were the verses displayed on one side only, as on an altar frontal, or set out around the edges of a cloth that covered the top and sides of the altar like a tablecloth? The three-couplet structure of the poem, each containing a proper name, may provide some clues to help reconstruct both the shape of the textile and the manner in which it vested the altar, pointing to a highly symbolic function for the positioning of the names.

If the cloth covered a square or rectangular altar, the writing could have been positioned to ensure that first couplet, naming *Pastor Petrus* was written on the part of the cloth that hung down the left-hand side of the altar (as viewed by the congregation). The couplet concerning Charlemagne's gifts could have been written on the front, with the final couplet concerning Hildegard on the part of the covering that draped down on the right-hand side of the altar. This arrangement would have made the second couplet the most prominent, naming King Charles and his gifts to St Peter. This reconstruction works best if the inscription had been embroidered directly onto the cloth so that the text was visible when the cloth was draped over the altar. Alternatively, a tablet-woven braid could have been sewn in place, or (less likely) the text woven into a composite cloth made up of more than one piece. A 'tablecloth' style altar-covering is shown in a late Carolingian ivory panel depicting the Presentation of Christ at the Temple, made perhaps in Metz, *c.*900.[89] Similar cloths can also be seen in the Utrecht Psalter (Reims *c.*820–40) and in the Harley Psalter (Canterbury, *c.*1000) that was derived from it, where the draped altar is often paired with a *regnum* suspended above it (Figure 4.2).[90]

---

[88] A twenty-two-word epigram commemorating a gift to St Peter's of a veil (*velum*) by the Visigothic king Chintila (636–40) may have been written on the textile; it was widely copied in the *Anthologia Isidoriana* appended to copies of Isidore's *Etymologiae* (Isidore died during Chintila's reign), which was probably its route of transmission rather than from an inscription seen in Rome; *ICUR* II.i, 254, no. XXII.7; *ICUR* n.s. ii, no. 4121; Cascioli, *Epigrafi Cristiane*, 44–5; Lapidge, 'Some Remnants', 367. For small ink inscriptions written in uncial or Caroline minuscule on textiles as relic labels, see H. Giersiepen, ed., *Die Inschriften des Aachener Doms*, Die deutschen Inschriften, 31 (Wiesbaden, 1992), nos 2–3 and 12.

[89] London, Victoria and Albert Museum, No. 150–1866; R. Deshman, *The Benedictional of Æthelwold* (Princeton, NJ, 1995), figs 13 and 24.

[90] Utrecht, Rijksuniversiteitsbibliothek, MS 32, fol. 25r and BL, MS Harley 603, fol. 25r; see K. van der Horst and J. H. A. Engelbregt, *Utrecht-Psalter. Vollständige Faksimile-Ausgabe im originalformat der Handschrift 32 aus dem besitz der Bibliotheek der Rijksuniversiteit te Utrecht*, Codices Selecti Phototypice Impressi, 69 (Graz, 1982–4), fol. 73, for example; K. van der Horst, W. Noel, and W. C. M. Wüstefeld, eds, *The Utrecht Psalter in Medieval Art: Picturing the Psalms of David* (London, 1996), 27 (fig. 3), 54 (fig. 26), and 18 (fig. 22); T. H. Ohlgren, ed., *Anglo-Saxon Textual Illustration: Photographs of Sixteen Manuscripts with Description and Index* (Kalamazoo, MI, 1992), 189, fig. 2.43.

FIGURE 4.2 Illustration showing the interior of a church with a 'hanging crown' over a draped altar. The Utrecht Psalter, Ps. 42: *Iudica me*; Utrecht, Rijksuniversiteitsbibliotheek MS 32, fol. 25r (detail). Photo: Courtesy of Utrecht University Library.

A simpler reconstruction envisages the *pallium altaris* as a rectangle of cloth that covered the top and sides of the altar only with woven bands bearing the inscription parallel with the narrow edge of the cloth.[91] The three couplets could have been spaced out in such a way that the first one, naming St Peter, hung down one side, the second couplet recording Charlemagne's name and gifts lay atop the altar, and the third bearing Hildegard's name hung down on the other side. This arrangement would have placed Charlemagne's name and the remembrance of his *munera* on the 'working surface' of the altar, in direct contact with the holy vessels and the act of the sacrament.

A near-contemporary textile that may offer a useful comparison was recovered in 1949 from an anonymous bishop's tomb in Sant'Apollinare in Classe, Ravenna.[92]

---

[91] As, for example, in the presentation miniature of the New Minster *Liber Vitae* made in 1031 which shows King Cnut (1016–35) placing a cross on an altar that is covered by two cloths; a large one that reaches to the floor with another smaller one hanging half way down the sides and a little way down the front; BL, MS Stowe 944, fol. 6r. On the mid-eighth-century verses in Mildred's *sylloge* describing cloths for covering an altar cross, see Sims-Williams, *Religion and Literature*, 339–41.

[92] M. Mazzotti, 'Antiche stoffe liturgiche ravennati', *Felix Ravenna*, 3rd ser., 53.ii (1950), 40–5 (with a plate of the *mappa*, though not clear enough to read the text); M. Mazzotti, *La basilica di Sant'Apollinare in Classe* (Vatican City, 1954), fig. 76; H. Granger-Taylor, 'The Weft-Patterned Silks and their Braid: The Remains of an Anglo-Saxon Dalmatic of c. 800', in G. Bonner, C. Stancliffe, and D. Rollason, eds, *St Cuthbert, His Cult and His Community to A.D. 1200* (Woodbridge, 1989), 303–27, at 307–8 and 319, n. 66. In the same tomb was a

The sarcophagus itself is sixth century in date, but seems to have been reused for this burial, perhaps in the later eighth or earlier ninth century.[93] The rectangular cloth recovered from this tomb, known as the Ravenna *mappa*, measures 95cm × *c*.50cm and was made in Italy at around the same time as the reuse of the tomb; it includes four bands of text which appear to have been woven into it, running parallel with the short sides of the cloth (Figure 4.3). Each band of text is about 50cm long, and the bands are spaced about 10cm and 20cm from either end. Two of the text-bands bear a fifteen-word dedication inscription and the others have verses from the Psalms, giving thirty-three words in total. The texts are spaced out so that the number of characters is roughly equal in every line.[94] This is also true of Hildegard's epigram, each and every line of which is, in fact, shorter than the lines of the *mappa* dedication. The six lines of Hildegard's altar *pallium* would easily be accommodated on a rectangular cloth of this type, made long enough to cover two sides and the top of the altar.

The careful placement of personal names is shown again on another near-contemporary textile: the tablet-woven girdle that Emma, wife of the Louis the German, gave to Bishop Witgar of Augsburg sometime between 858 and 887.[95] Witgar's name starts the eleven-word text and Emma's name completes it; this meant that, when worn around the waist and tied at the front, the loose ends displayed the name of the donor and of the recipient for all to see; Emma's on the viewers' left and Witgar's on the right. In Reims, an exotic, red silk cloth imported from the east, was embroidered with the name of a royal Carolingian donor. Made into a *sudarium*, or pillow, it was placed by Bishop Hincmar within the shrine of St Remigius in 852 when the relics were moved to the new church built in his honour. The silk was embroidered with a forty-nine-word inscription that reveals it was made by Alpheide, half-sister of Charles the Bald, at Hincmar's request. She stitched a golden border on both

---

silk braid or girdle (perhaps English in origin) with an inscription based on Psalm 127: 5–6; Granger-Taylor, 'The Weft-patterned silks', 319–20, pl. 56 and L. Webster and J. Backhouse, eds, *The Making of England: Anglo-Saxon Art and Culture AD 600–900* (London, 1991), 136.

[93] Granger-Taylor, 'Weft-Patterned Silks', 308–9.

[94] The dedication text reads: + SUSCIPE DME HANC OBLATIONEM QUE TIBI OFFERT JOHAN / NES ET MARIA PER MAN[*um s*]ACERDOTIS UT INPINGUATA: 'Receive Lord this oblation which is offered to you by John and Mary through the hands of the priests when anointed'. The Psalm texts read: + BEATI OMNES QUI TIMENT DNM QUI AMBULANT IN VIIS EIUS, ' + blessed are all those who fear the lord who walk along his pathway' (Psalm 127: 1) and + EXAUDIAT TE DMS IN DIE TRIBULATIONIS PROTEGAT TE [nomen dei Jacob], 'The Lord hears you in your day of trouble, the name of the God of Jacob protects you' (Psalm 19: 2); Mazzotti, 'Antiche stoffe', 41; Granger-Taylor, 'Weft-Patterned Silks', 307, 319.

[95] P. E. Schramm and F. Mütherich, *Denkmale der deutschen Könige und Kaiser* (Munich 1962), 126, 238 (no. 32); E. J. Goldberg, '"Regina nitens sanctissima Hemma": Queen Emma (827–876), Bishop Witgar of Augsburg, and the Witgar-belt', in B. Weiller and S. MacLean, eds, *Representations of Power in Medieval Germany, 800–1500* (Turnhout, 2006), 57–95. The girdle is 138cm long by 3.8cm wide.

FIGURE 4.3 The Ravenna *mappa*, showing woven bands of text. Reproduced from M. Mazzotti, 'Antiche stoffe liturgiche ravennati', *Felix Ravenna*, 3rd ser., 53.ii (1950), 43. Photo: Courtesy of the Istituzione Biblioteca Classense, Ravenna.

sides of the square pillow, picking out the text against the red silk of the fabric.[96] Alpheide's gift is a good example of the way in which a donor could appropriate the cachet of an expensive, imported object through the application of a secondary, dedicatory inscription.

More directly relevant are the ornate altar vestments (*vestes*) that Pope Leo III gave to St Peter's bearing images and, in at least one instance, some text that was associated with particular feasts of the Church calendar.[97] One of these cloths was made for the high altar; it was decorated with 'three gold panels and an image of the Lord's Passion, reading, "This body shall be given up for you, etc"'.[98] The text is from the antiphon sung on the fifth Sunday in Lent. The full text of the chant runs to twenty-three words, which is shorter than the text on the Ravenna *mappa* or Hildegard's epigram

---

[96] W. F. Volbach, *Early Decorative Textiles* (London, 1969), 106, 112, fig. 68; E. Coatsworth, 'Stitches in Time: Establishing a History of Anglo-Saxon Embroidery', in R. Netherton and G. R. Owen-Crocker, eds, *Medieval Clothing and Textiles* I (Woodbridge, 2006), 1–28 at 8; E. Coatsworth, 'Text and Textile', in Minnis and Roberts, eds, *Text, Image, Interpretation*, 187–208, at 189–190, with the text and a translation.

[97] *CD* ii, 546.

[98] *LP* 98:33, see also chs 27, 48, 53, and 67.

for her *pallium altaris*.⁹⁹ This antiphon quotes part of the canon of the Mass; but perhaps because it is shorter than the canon, and because the rhythm of the chant makes the text memorable, the antiphon rather than the canon seems to have been used for the inscription on this textile.¹⁰⁰ The text is, of course, the dramatic crux of the ceremony of the Mass; juxtaposed with an image of the crucifixion, it connects Christ's sacrifice on the Cross with the regular sacrifice of Mass at the high altar. This vestment was probably an altar frontal, made to dress the high altar and to be displayed to the congregation. Leo's gifts and the Ravenna *mappa* show that contemporary liturgical textiles could accommodate quite lengthy texts as well as images, precious metal, and jewels. The account of Leo's textiles shows that some cloths were reserved for special liturgical functions and that the high altar was dressed according to the calendar. In fact, the exact location of the altar which probably bore Hildegard's inscribed altar cloth and Hadrian's inscription is revealed by another later eighth-century text, which records a pilgrim's itinerary of St Peter's (see below).

CAROLINGIAN ITINERARIES OF ST PETER'S AND ROME

The first Lorsch *sylloge* (L₁) can be read as a kind of itinerary of the basilica. The text scribe provided rubrics that identified the churches and the location of epigrams within them. These are given in a logical order so that the reader could 'progress' through a building reading each inscription in turn; the sequence for St Peter's, which is the longest in the collection, takes the reader from the atrium, to the threshold of the basilica, the high altar, the font, and then back to the atrium. After St Peter's, the reader of the L₁ *sylloge* is presented with epigrams from other major Roman churches, and rubrics state where in these churches they were placed. Thus, the reader moves from St Peter's to the Lateran, to Santa Anastasia, Santi Giovanni e Paolo, Santa Maria Trastevere, San Lorenzo in Damaso, Santa Cecilia, San Crisogono, Santi Cosma e Damiano, San Stephano Rotondo. The sequence finishes with another poem for San Lorenzo and an inscription *in prima porta Romae* that may have been located on the arch next to the bridge that crossed the Tiber at St Peter's. Just as at St Peter's the inscriptions in these other churches—where specified—were located at the font, apse, or entrance. The list of churches in the *sylloge* does not, however, follow a logical

---

⁹⁹ The antiphon for the fifth Sunday in Lent is, 'Hoc corpus quod pro vobis tradetur. Hic calix novi testamenti est in meo sanguine, dicit dominus. Hoc facite quotiescumque sumitis in meam commemorationem' ('This body will be given up for you. This cup is the new testament in my blood, said the Lord. Do this every time that you take it up in remembrance of me'); R. J. Hesbert, ed., *Antiphonale Missarum sextuplex* (Brussels, 1935), 80–3, no. 67b. The Psalm is no. 42: 'Iudica me'.

¹⁰⁰ 1 Corinthians 11.24: 'et gratias agens fregit et dixit hoc est corpus meum pro vobis hoc facite in meam commemorationem [25] similiter et calicem postquam cenavit dicens hic calix novum testamentum est in meo sanguine hoc facite quotienscumque bibetis in meam commemorationem'.

topographical sequence or that of the stational liturgies; the list zigzags back and forwards, crossing the Tiber twice.[101] All of the churches occur south and west of a line drawn between St Peter's and the Lateran. This may explain why the scribe left a page and a half blank between L₁ and L₂, realising perhaps that his exemplar was incomplete. The sylloge says that the penultimate poem was located in *ecclesia beati Laurentii martyris* but does not specify which of the several churches dedicated to Lawrence is meant and it may be that this epigram did not in fact belong to a Roman church. These verses are by Venantius Fortunatus. In his book on the *Glory of the Martyrs*, Gregory of Tours applied them to a church in Brione in the Tyrol. The verses appear there in a run of chapters that mention the martyrs of Rome, and it is plausible to imagine that the context was misunderstood by a reader interested in Rome, its martyrs, and shrines. The version in L₁ could thus have been derived from a manuscript copy of the poems of Fortunatus or Gregory's text rather than from a *titulus* in situ.[102]

A different itinerary of St Peter's is incorporated within another Carolingian manuscript from Salzburg, now ÖNB, Cod. 795, fol. 187r/v.[103] The book was made for Arn, the abbot of Saint-Amand who was made archbishop of Salzburg during a visit to Rome in 798. It includes twenty letters by Alcuin, the latest of which is dated January 799.[104] The palaeography of the whole manuscript fits comfortably with this date, and the analysis of the hands suggests that the book was begun in Saint-Amand but completed at Salzburg. Towards the end of the codex a new scribe started a quire (labelled 'z' by a contemporary hand) with the first of two texts on the topography of Rome (that were probably compiled originally in the mid-seventh century). This scribe's work was finished by two others who had worked in the earlier part of the book, and the two texts on Roman topography were annotated by the prolific Salzburg-based scribe, Baldo.[105] This quire was followed by another with a group of

---

[101] For the sequence of the stational liturgy, see *CD*, II 805–7. See also the list of churches that completes *de locis sanctis*; Geyer and Cuntz, eds, *Itineraria*, 321–2; VZ, ii, 118–31; Lapidge, *Roman Martyrs*, 662–4.

[102] *Laurenti, merito flammis uitalibus uste*: Venatius Fortunatus, *Carmina* IX.14; F. Leo, ed., MGH, AA IV.1 (Berlin, 1881), 218 (IX.14); *ICUR* II.i, 153, no. XIII.34. Ten lines were cited by Gregory of Tours in relation to a miracle at Brione in the Tyrol; Gregory of Tours, *In gloria martyrum*, I.41, ed. B. Krusch, MGH, SS rer. Merov. I.ii (Hannover, 1885), 516; R. Van Dam, *Gregory of Tours: Glory of the Martyrs*, Translated Texts for Historians, 4 (Liverpool, 2004), 41.

[103] CLA X:1490; F. Unterkircher, ed., *Alkuin-Briefe und andere traktate im auftrage des Salzburger Erzbischofs Arn um 799 zu einem Sammelband vereinigt Codex Vindobonensis 795 der Österreichischen Nationalbibliothek*, Codices selecti phototypice impressi, 20 (Graz, 1969).

[104] Alcuin, *Ep.* no. 165; Bullough, *Alcuin*, 44–51; Bischoff, *Südostdeutsche schreibschulen*, ii, 115–19. It also includes Alcuin's *De Orthographia*, important copies of Greek, Runic, and Gothic alphabets, and various exegetical commentaries; Unterkircher, ed., *Alkuin-Briefe*, 20–2. For discussions of the contents and function of this book, see McKitterick, *Perceptions of the Past*, 44–6, and M. Diesenberger and H. Wolfram, 'Arn und Alkuin 790 bis 804: zwei Freund und ihre Schriften', in Niederkorn-Bruck and Scharer, eds, *Erzbischof Arn von Salzburg* (Munich, 2004), 81–106. See also Mairhofer, ed., *Handschriften und Papyri*, 118, cat. no. 21.

[105] ÖNB, Cod. 795, fols 184r–191v; Bullough, *Alcuin*, 45, n. 100.

six letters written by Alcuin to Arn between June 798 and January 799, three letters that Anglibert sent to Arn in 797, and a poem by Alcuin to his student Candidus urging him to visit the sights of Rome.[106] A final quire contains a copy of a letter from Charlemagne to Alcuin written in March 798, and the remaining four folios are blank. The Rome texts were thus understood as an integral part of the manuscript by the team that compiled it. Baldo's editorial contributions to the Rome texts could be read as evidence that he had personal experience of the sites they describe, and felt able to annotate the texts accordingly.[107] Perhaps he had accompanied Arn to Rome in 798, and on returning to Salzburg oversaw the augmentation of the existing portion of the book with copies of recent letters to Arn and the Rome material.[108] Candidus is another plausible candidate for such eye-witness additions, since he too was in Rome at this time, also acting as envoy between Salzburg and Tours.[109] Analysis of this codex suggests that it was created as a handbook for Arn to aid his efforts to evangelize the Avars whose territory, recently annexed by Frankish armies, fell within his new metropolitan see.[110] Its Rome-centred contents underscore the ideological angle of this initiative, and the comparatively low-quality parchment employed for the book reinforces its utilitarian character.[111]

The first of the two Rome texts in this part of the book is known as the *Notitia ecclesiarum urbis Romae*.[112] Using verbs in the second person and future tense (just as in the opening words of this book), it describes the sanctuaries, cemeteries, and churches that 'you will see' along the roads that enter Rome. It begins with an instruction to visit the large and beautiful basilica of Santi Giovanni e Paolo on the Caelian

---

[106] Unterkircher, ed., *Alkuin-Briefe*, 27–8; Bischoff, *Südostdeutsche schreibschulen*, ii, 115. Alcuin, *Carmina*, no. 44; Dümmler, ed., MGH, PLAC I, 255–7: only the first thirty-five lines of the fifty-two-line poem are extant in the manuscript, though since it is at the end of a quire, it is possible that a page has been lost.

[107] Baldo added nothing to the St Peter's appendix, but to the *Notitia* he added notes for the section *ad aquilonem* on the great size of the catacomb of Bishop Urbanus and on the small church of the beheaded St Xystus and his deacons (fol. 185v) and on fol. 186r, a note to say that the church of saints Aristius, Christina, and Victoria lay to the north of the church of St Paul on the western bank of the Tiber; Geyer and Cuntz, eds, *Itineraria*, 308–9. Baldo's annotations to the second itinerary, *De locis sanctis martyrum*, on fols 187v–191v, are more extensive (VZ, ii, 106–31 and Geyer and Cuntz, eds, *Itineraria*, 315–22, annotations noted with an asterisk). The appendix to that text on fol. 191v, *istae vero ecclesiase intus Romae habentur*, is entirely in his hand; Geertman, *More Veterum*, 158–63, 202. McKitterick suggests that this appendix could reflect Arn's record of the churches of Rome, made in 787; R. McKitterick, 'The Constantinian Basilica in the *Liber Pontificalis*', in L. Bosman, I. P. Haynes, and P. Liverani, eds, *The Basilica of St John Lateran to 1600* (Cambridge, 2020), 197–220, at 219 (transposing the *Notitia* for *De locis*). Another ninth-century manuscript from Salzburg, now ÖNB, Cod. 1008, fols 189v–191, also contains *De locis*, on which, see Bischoff, *Südostdeutsche schreibschulen* II, 94, no. 23 and Bischoff, *Katalog*, no. 7198.

[108] Bischoff, *Südostdeutsche schreibschulen*, ii, 119.

[109] Diesenberger and Wolfram, 'Arn und Alkuin', 101.

[110] Diesenberger and Wolfram, 'Arn und Alkuin', 99.

[111] M. Costambeys, 'Alcuin, Rome, and Charlemagne's imperial coronation', in F. Tinti, ed., *England and Rome in the Early Middle Ages: Pilgrimage, Art and Politics* (Turnhout, 2014), 255–90, at 261.

[112] De Rossi, *Roma sotterranea cristiana*, i, 138–40; VZ, ii, 72–99, reprinted (with minimal commentary) by Geyer and Cuntz, eds, *Itineraria*, 305–11. A translation is provided by Lapidge, *Roman Martyrs*, 660–2.

Hill, and then describes the resting places of saints and martyrs in the churches and cemeteries that are on the roads leading out of the city, journeying clockwise around the perimeter of the city walls starting at the Via Flaminia in the north. In this way, the sequence ends up at the Via Vaticana that led west from the city to St Peter's: 'And if you reach the Via Vaticana, you will come to the basilica of blessed Peter—which Constantine, emperor of the whole world (*imperator totius orbis*), built—eminent over all churches and beautiful, in whose western part lies his blessed body'.[113] A ten-line text on Milan follows the *Notitia* without a break; after this is an appendix, that also functions as an itinerary, and describes the sequence of oratories that a pilgrim could see in St Peter's, beginning at Sant'Andrea and finishing at the main entrance to the atrium (Figure 4.4).[114]

The *Notitia ecclesiarum* itself could have been compiled as early as the second quarter of the seventh century, during or shortly after the pontificate of Pope Honorius I (625–38); it does not mention the renovation of the basilica of San Valentino by Theodore I (642–9) or his translation in 648 of saints Primus and Felicianus from the Via Nomentana to the church of San Stephano Rotondo on the Caelian Hill. Missing too is any reference to the relics of Sant'Anastasio that were brought to Rome sometime between 628 and 641, and venerated *ad Aquas Saluias* on the Via Ostiense.[115] The appendix containing the itinerary of St Peter's, however, seems to have been composed rather later than the *Notitia*, during the later eighth century since it mentions the shrine of Petronilla which was dedicated in 757.[116] This appendix conveys a vivid sense of the contemporary experience of a pilgrim to the shrine of the apostle. That both these texts were selected for a late eighth-century Carolingian manuscript shows their continued relevance to Frankish readers *c.*800; their presence there alongside very recent letters from Alcuin suggests that the Rome texts were also considered current reading for Archbishop Arn and his community.[117]

The pilgrim-reader starts the itinerary of St Peter's by 'entering at the *porticus* of St Andrew'. This recalls the context of the two epigrams *Andreas hic sanctus* and *Petrus porticum* recorded in the short anthology of inscriptions associated with St Peter's in the two ninth-century Reims manuscripts discussed earlier (see Chapter 3). There is a striking focus in both on the rotunda of Sant'Andrea and on the southern side of the complex, surely reflecting contemporary interest in that part of the basilica. The correspondence between the two epigrams and the *porticus* of the itinerary is not entirely straightforward, however, since we do not know if the *Andreas* epigram was

---

[113] *Notitia ecclesiarum*, ch. 35; VZ, ii, 94; Geyer and Cuntz, eds, *Itineraria*, 310.
[114] ÖNB, Cod. 795, fol. 187r, line 2–187v, line 16. The whole text, including the Milan section, is printed only by de Rossi, ed., *Roma sotteranea*, 138–40.
[115] VZ, ii, 69–70.
[116] ICUR II.i, 224–8; VZ, ii, 69.
[117] C. Leyser, 'The Temptations of Cult: Roman Martyr Piety in the Age of Gregory the Great', *Early Medieval Europe*, 9 (2000), 289–308, at 298.

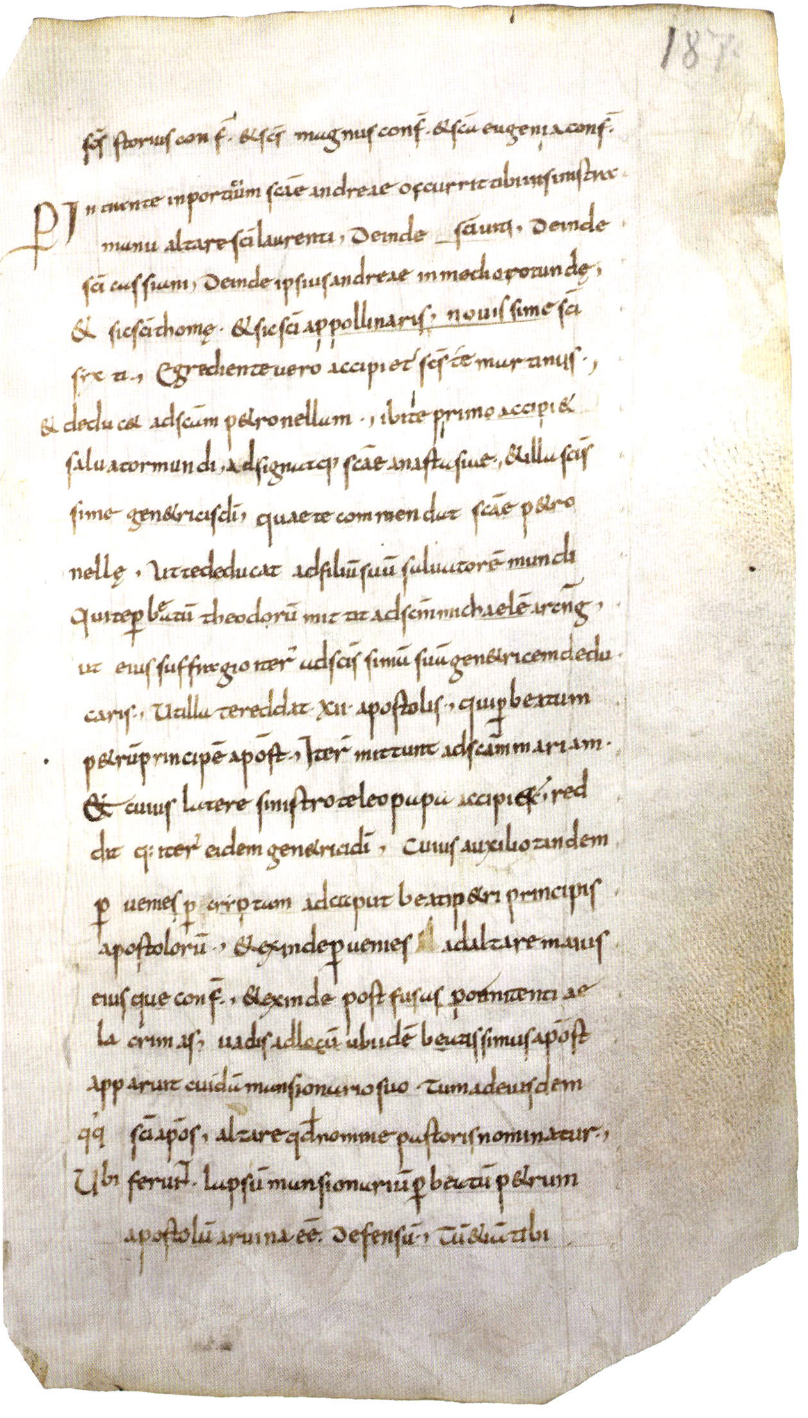

FIGURE 4.4 The opening of the appendix to the *Notitia ecclesiarum urbis Romae* with the pilgrim's itinerary of St Peter's basilica. The first line on the page is the last of the account of cult sites in Milan; Vienna, ÖNB, Cod. 795, fol. 187r. Photo: Courtesy of the Österreichische Nationalbibliothek, Vienna.

mounted over the apostle's altar within the church or over the entrance into the rotunda. It is possible that the *Petrus porticum* epigram was placed at the doorway or else was associated with the entranceway created by the steps that Pope Symmachus built *c*.500 between the basilica and the rotunda. Alternatively, it may have referred to an entrance at the front of the basilica or to the covered walkway that led there from the Tiber. The terminology of the itinerary, however, is repeated later in the ninth century when Leo IV restored the '*porticus* that adjoined the church of St Andrew' (Figure 4.5).[118]

The pilgrim's itinerary in the Vienna manuscript begins with a list of the altars set into the niches within Sant'Andrea. Seven oratories are listed, starting with the altar to St Lawrence on the left of the entrance.[119] On leaving the rotunda, the reader is told, that, 'St Martin will receive you and will lead you out to St Petronilla'. This is the earliest reference to the altar to St Martin located in the narthex that joined the rotunda of Sant'Andrea to that of Petronilla. Leo III's biographer mentions the same altar, saying that it was positioned 'in front' of the church of Sant'Andrea, and it is also the subject of the fifth epigram in the Reims collection.[120] The visitor progresses around the altars of the adjacent rotunda dedicated to Petronilla, whose altar was probably in the niche that faced the entrance to the rotunda from the narthex that joined the rotunda on its northern side to the south exedra of the basilica. This reference to the oratory of Santa Petronilla (and its attendant oratories to the Saviour, Sant'Anastasia, Santa Maria, and San Theodore, and that to St Michael in the narthex between the rotunda and the exedra) means that this itinerary must postdate Stephen II's dedication of the rotunda to Petronilla and the translation of her body there by Paul I on 8 October 757.[121] Paul I also built his own tomb-chapel in the south-west corner of the southern exedra that he dedicated to the Virgin, and this is the next target for the reader of the itinerary.[122]

The pilgrim-reader following the *Notitia*'s itinerary is taken from Paul's oratory 'to the twelve apostles' and thence to another Marian shrine. The exact form and location of these latter two altars is unknown—they are not apparently recorded elsewhere.[123] Either of them could have been placed in the south-east corner of the exedra in the space later occupied by Paschal I's oratory to Saints Processus and Martinianus,[124] or they may have been placed in the south transept proper. The main oratory in the body of the transept noted by the itinerary is that of Pope Leo I, 'on the left-hand side'

---

[118] *LP* 105:85, 'porticum quae sancti Andreae cohaeret ecclesiae'.
[119] Alchermes, 'Petrine Politics', 19–21.
[120] See Chapter 3, 138–9.
[121] Alfarano, *DBV*, 135–7; *LP* 94:52 and 95:3; Davis, tr., *Lives of the Eighth-Century Popes*, 76 and 81, n. 6; *CD* ii, 576–7.
[122] *LP* 95:6. *Notitia* c. 37; *VZ*, ii, 96–7; Geyer and Cuntz, eds, *Itineraria*, 310; Alfarano, *DBV*, no. 17; *CD* ii, 569. Paul's chapel was later known as Santa Maria in Cancellis from the bronze grille that surrounded it.
[123] *CD* ii, 571, n. 336.
[124] *LP* 100:5.

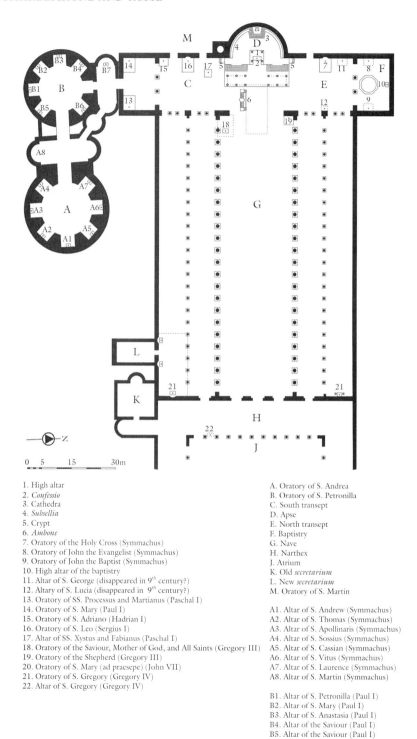

1. High altar
2. *Confessio*
3. Cathedra
4. *Subsellia*
5. Crypt
6. *Ambone*
7. Oratory of the Holy Cross (Symmachus)
8. Oratory of John the Evangelist (Symmachus)
9. Oratory of John the Baptist (Symmachus)
10. High altar of the baptistry
11. Altar of S. George (disappeared in 9th century?)
12. Altary of S. Lucia (disappeared in 9th century?)
13. Oratory of SS. Processus and Martianus (Paschal I)
14. Oratory of S. Mary (Paul I)
15. Oratory of S. Adriano (Hadrian I)
16. Oratory of S. Leo (Sergius I)
17. Altar of SS. Xystus and Fabianus (Paschal I)
18. Oratory of the Saviour, Mother of God, and All Saints (Gregory III)
19. Oratory of the Shepherd (Gregory III)
20. Oratory of S. Mary (ad praesepe) (John VII)
21. Oratory of S. Gregory (Gregory IV)
22. Altar of S. Gregory (Gregory IV)

A. Oratory of S. Andrea
B. Oratory of S. Petronilla
C. South transept
D. Apse
E. North transept
F. Baptistry
G. Nave
H. Narthex
J. Atrium
K. Old *secretarium*
L. New *secretarium*
M. Oratory of S. Martin

A1. Altar of S. Andrew (Symmachus)
A2. Altar of S. Thomas (Symmachus)
A3. Altar of S. Apollinaris (Symmachus)
A4. Altar of S. Sossius (Symmachus)
A5. Altar of S. Cassian (Symmachus)
A6. Altar of S. Vitus (Symmachus)
A7. Altar of S. Laurence (Symmachus)
A8. Altar of S. Martin (Symmachus)

B1. Altar of S. Petronilla (Paul I)
B2. Altar of S. Mary (Paul I)
B3. Altar of S. Anastasia (Paul I)
B4. Altar of the Saviour (Paul I)
B5. Altar of the Saviour (Paul I)
B6. Altar of S. Theodore (Paul I)
B6. Altar of S. Michael (Paul I)

FIGURE 4.5 Plan of St Peter's and its oratories, *s.* viii/ix. © Lacey Wallace.

against the west wall. Pope Sergius I had translated Leo's remains to this spot in 688, and this new tomb was the first major shrine in the south transept. There is no reference to the oratory of Sant'Adriano (later to be the tomb-chapel of Pope Hadrian) that we know stood later between Paul's chapel in the exedra and the oratory of Leo in the transept. It may be that either the altar to the twelve apostles or that to 'Holy Mary', which cannot otherwise be located, had once stood in the place later occupied by Hadrian's oratory. Either way, the absence of Hadrian's oratory from the itinerary dates it to the period between the pontificate of Paul I (757–68) and the early years of Pope Hadrian's reign before the oratory to Sant'Adriano was established.

The itinerary takes the pilgrim-reader next across the south transept to the oratory of Mary, Mother of God, established by Gregory III (731–41) that stood on 'the men's side' (i.e. the south side of the basilica) against the southern pier of the triumphal arch that terminated the nave.[125] Here 'Pope Leo hands over' the pilgrim-reader to Mary, the Mother of God, 'with whose help at last you will come through the crypt to the head of blessed Peter, prince of the apostles'. On leaving the crypt the pilgrim-reader comes to the high altar and the *confessio*, and 'after shedding tears of contrition' is shown the place where St Peter appeared to a sacristan (*mansionarius*). The pilgrim-reader is taken thence to 'that same apostle's altar that is called by the name Shepherd where they say a sacristan who fell was saved from ruin by the blessed Peter'.[126]

The dedication of this altar to St Peter the Shepherd is unusual, and this is the first time that this oratory is specifically mentioned. By the mid-ninth century the dedication had mutated to that of a martyr, St Pastor; it is named as such in the biography of Pope Leo IV (847–54).[127] Gregory the Great, however, had earlier recorded two stories in his *Dialogues* (III. 24–5) that can be linked to this oratory and its patron. The first story corresponds to the itinerary's reference to the sacristan who had a vision of St Peter.[128] Gregory says that the sacristan was called Theodore and that there 'may yet be some alive' who remembered him, implying (according to the traditional dating of this text) that he had been the *mansionarius* at the basilica in the mid-sixth century. St Peter appeared to Theodore as he was up a ladder repairing some lamps and asked him why he had got up so early. Theodore was so panicked by the vision that he was unable to get out of bed for several days. Gregory explains that Peter had appeared to reassure all who serve him that he saw everything that they did

---

[125] *LP* 92:6–7.

[126] *Notitia*, ch. 39: 'Tum ad eiusdem quoque sancti apostolic altare, quod nominee pastoris nominatur; ubi ferunt lapsum mansionarium per beatum Petrum apostolum a ruina esse defensum'; VZ, ii, 97; Geyer and Cuntz, eds, *Itineraria*, 311. Davis, tr., *Lives of the Ninth-Century Popes*, 129, n. 72. For the *mansionarii* in Rome in a later period, see Wickham, *Medieval Rome*, 415.

[127] *LP* 105:43; *ICUR* II.i, 227, ch. 14.

[128] Gregory, *Dialogorum*, II.34, 'De Theodoro mansionario ecclesiae beati Petri apostoli urbis Romae'; *PL* 77, col. 277.

in his honour. The respondent in the *Dialogues* does not understand why Theodore was made so ill by the vision, and Gregory reassures him by recounting biblical precedents of others who were frightened by such an experience. The respondent's confusion is perhaps echoed in the story as told to the mid-eighth-century author of the itinerary (who thought that the sacristan had fallen into error) and may explain why Gregory had needed to provide clarification of the meaning of the vision and the sacristan's response to it.

Furthermore, in the next chapter of the *Dialogues*, Gregory tells of a woman crippled by illness who had prayed to St Peter for a cure. She too had a vision of the apostle, who told her to go to the basilica to seek out a different sacristan by the name of Abundius. When she found him she reported her vision, saying that 'Our shepherd and guardian (*Pastor et nutritor noster*), blessed St Peter the Apostle, has sent me, that you should cure me of this my disease'. Abundius raised her up and she found herself cured. Gregory said nothing about a physical oratory within the basilica dedicated to Peter the Shepherd but his retelling of these miracles that had happened within a generation of his own time may reflect an early stage in the development of this aspect of Peter's cult. The lame woman's reference to Peter as *pastor noster* and the conjunction between Gregory's account of the sacristan's vision with version retold in the itinerary makes it very likely that, by the eighth century at least, the two miracle stories were associated with the *Oratorium Pastoris*.

The name of this oratory and its association with St Peter (rather than Christ) recalls the two Carolingian epigrams both of which refer to Peter as a shepherd. The 'Life' of Stephen II (752–57) also refers to 'the good shepherd our Lord, St Peter'.[129] As noted above, the scriptural context of this dedication is one that is particularly relevant for the basilica of St Peter's. Christ's commission to Peter to 'feed my sheep' presaged his prediction of Peter's crucifixion. The episode was 'evidence' not just for papal authority over Christendom but of the primacy of the basilica that commanded the sites of his martyrdom and burial on the Vatican hill. The repetition of the name of *Petrus pastor* in the two epigrams strongly suggests that the Carolingian gifts were intended to adorn this altar, which was secondary to the main shrine but which nevertheless embodied the legacy of Christ's commission to Peter to guide the flock of the faithful.

The *Oratorium Pastoris* stood on the opposite side of the nave to Gregory III's oratory for Mary, Christ, and All Saints, at the foot of the northern pier of the triumphal arch (see Figure 4.5).[130] The symbolism of the two oratories was complementary: the *Oratorium Pastoris* symbolised the apostolic commission, and the command to Peter to go out into the world (*urbis et orbis*) to evangelise and convert; the altar for 'All Saints', in contrast, gathered the saints of the world back into the basilica where

---

[129] *LP* 94:19, Davis, tr., *Lives of the Eighth-Century Popes*, 60.
[130] *CD* ii, 571; Alfarano, *DBV*, no. 40.

Peter's relics were venerated.[131] Through these two oratories, therefore, Peter sent Christ's message out into the world, returning to his basilica in the form of relics of Christ's favoured servants. Peter's missionary role became increasingly important to Charlemagne and his advisors, especially as his armies moved into Saxony and Pannonia, making Frankish patronage of this particular oratory all the more powerful. In addition, since Gregory III's oratory had been placed on the southern, or 'men's side' of the basilica, so the northern side with the *Oratorium Pastoris*, which gave access to the baptistery in the north exedra, was—in liturgical terms—deemed 'the women's side', making Hildegard's gift doubly appropriate.[132] Gregory's story of the miraculous cure of the crippled woman is also relevant in this gendered context. The proposed reconstruction of Hildegard's inscribed altar cloth, if applied to an altar in this location, would render its inscription easily visible to an attentive pilgrim. The couplet concerning Peter would thus have faced outwards into the nave, with the couplet on Charlemagne at the front facing out towards the faithful ranged in front of it, or on the top, visible to the celebrant. Hildegard's name would then have been on the northern flank of the altar cloth, facing into the aisle that led to the baptistery.

The pilgrim-reader next moves to the oratory (here termed a *porticus*) of the Holy Cross in the north transept and into the north exedra which housed the altar of St George 'in the wall' and the twin oratories of St John the Baptist and St John the Evangelist.[133] After this the pilgrim 'rapidly' (*curre*) goes to the altar of Mary *ad praesepe* ('at the manger'). This is the first occasion that this name is used of the oratory that John VII (705–7) dedicated in the north-east corner of the north aisle.[134] Having kissed the altar, the pilgrim-reader proceeds 'to the entrance of Petronilla' (*ad porticum Petronellae*) and 'rejoicing, ascend to the bed (*lectum*) of the holy father Gregory, on which he gave up his spirit, a worthy gift to God who gave it; and there you have eleven altars'. This section poses problems since there is no other reference to the *porticus* of Petronilla (which might otherwise reasonably be associated with the rotunda beyond the south transept); the location of the chapel containing Pope Gregory's bed is also uncertain, especially if it was large enough to contain eleven altars, as the text suggests. The bed-relic is mentioned again, later in the ninth century, in the biography of Pope Stephen V (885–91).[135] De Rossi and others suggested that a building to the north of the main narthex of the basilica, which was

---

[131] Story, 'Carolingians and the Oratory', 266 and fig. 13.1.

[132] *CD* ii, 504–5. Of early references to Peter the Shepherd, it is particularly interesting to note that the hymn *Beate Pastor Petre, clemens accipe* was set in the early breviaries for the feast of the *Cathedra* of St Peter (18 January in Rome), and is said to have been composed by Helpis, perhaps the same woman whose epitaph is recorded in L$_2$ in the *porticus* of the basilica; Grimaldi, *Descrizione*, ed. Niggl, 416; *PL* 63, col. 537 and col. 558. See above, 152–3, n. 41.

[133] *Notitia*, chs 40–1; VZ, ii, 97–8, and Geyer and Cuntz, eds, *Itineraria*, 311. See also *CD* ii, 568.

[134] *LP* 88:1. The decoration of the chapel was recorded by Grimaldi, *Descrizioni*, ed. Niggl, 106, 126–7. *CD* ii, 573, 713; Andaloro, *Pittura medievale. Atlante* I, 21–5 (G1) and 40–1.

[135] *LP* 112:20. See also Davis, tr., *Lives of the Ninth-Century Popes*, 307, n. 53.

attached to the old papal palace and dedicated before the twelfth century to San Vincenzo, may have been this chapel; it is labelled by Alfarano as *Ecclesia S. Gregorii, olim*.[136]

Finally, the reader of the itinerary it taken to 'the oratory of holy Mary, which is called *Antiqua*', where purple stones are set in the floor in the shape of a cross; thence to the body of the holy father Gregory, and 'from there to the place of Holy Mary which is called *Nova*'.[137] The route given here is also difficult to interpret: Gregory's body lay in a tomb 'in front of the sacristy', between the first and second columns at the southern end of the main narthex of the basilica.[138] De Rossi thought that the 'ancient' oratory of Mary alluded to an oratory to the Virgin near this spot (rather than to the basilica of that name at the foot of the Palatine in the Forum), and indeed an image of the Virgin and Child was venerated here in the later Middle Ages.[139] Whatever its precise location, this 'ancient' oratory of Mary is evidently to be contrasted with the 'new' oratory to the Virgin that is the final destination of our pilgrim-reader. This chapel was more often called Santa Maria 'ad Grada' ('at the steps'), 'Mediana' ('in the middle' of the atrium façade) or, later, 'in Turri' ('in the tower'), and refers to the chapel built by Paul I above the arched gateway at the eastern entrance to the atrium of St Peter's.[140] The newness of this chapel points to a date of composition not long after the chapel was consecrated late in the pontificate of Paul I (757–67).

This text conveys a vivid sense of the experience of a pilgrim to St Peter's in the mid eighth century. The date of the manuscript means that the itinerary of the basilica must have been composed before *c*.800 and the reference to two oratories dedicated to the Virgin by Paul I (Santa Maria in Cancellis and Santa Maria Mediana) dates the itinerary in this form to his pontificate at the earliest. The absence of any reference to the oratory of Sant'Adriano in the south transept makes it likely that the itinerary was written before Pope Hadrian constructed the shrine to his patronymic saint that would eventually house his own tomb. There are other pointers to an early Carolingian

---

[136] *ICUR* II.i, 227–8, n. 20; *VZ*, ii, 98, n. 5. On the new oratory to Gregory the Great placed in the southeast corner of the basilica by Gregory IV in 828–9 after relics had been illicitly removed by a Frankish priest, see *LP* 103.6; Andrieu, 'La chapelle', 74; *CD* ii, 574–5.

[137] *Notitia*, cc. 42–3; *VZ*, ii, 98–9 and Geyer and Cuntz, eds, *Itineraria*, 311. For the church on the Via Sacra of 'the Mother of God which was called Antiqua but is now called Nova' built by Leo IV (847–55) and later embellished by Benedict III (855–8) and Nicholas I (858–67), see *LP* 106.22 and 107.37, and Davis, tr., *Lives of the Ninth-Century Popes*, 178, nn. 50–1. This church was probably founded after Santa Maria Antiqua in the Forum was rendered unusable by the earthquake of 847; it is now known as Santa Francesca Romana.

[138] Andrieu, 'La chapelle', 62, based on the descriptions of the location of Gregory's epitaph as seen by Peter Mallius (*s*.xii²).

[139] *ICUR* II.i, 228, n. 21–3. Perhaps the early fourteenth-century fresco, known as the *Madonna della Bocciata*, replaced an older one in the same place; Alfarano, *DBV*, 117, no. 136; *BSPV* II.i (Essays) 866–7, n. 1671.

[140] *CD* ii, 526–7. Krautheimer, *CBCR* v, 175 and 268–70; Andaloro, ed., *La pittura medievale. Atlante* i, 22–4 (A1).

date of composition, not least the inscription on Hildegard's altar cloth (781) and on Hadrian's votive crown (774) recorded by the first 'Lorsch' *sylloge* (L$_1$) that match the dedication of the *Oratorium Pastoris* to St Peter at the north-west of the nave and which is described in the itinerary. Also, like the short and slightly later *sylloge* in the Reims manuscripts, the itinerary begins in the south at Sant'Andrea and focuses on the oratories that could be seen in the two rotundas and in the transept of the basilica. This reflects the pattern of patronage in St Peter's in the eighth century; after the translation of Leo's remains to the south transept in 688, this zone became a major focus for papal and royal patronage within the basilica.[141] The rotundas and south transept, of course, linked the site of St Peter's martyrdom at the obelisk with the site of his burial at the *confessio*; the space between the two was thus especially sacred. The location of the inscriptions from St Peter's recorded in L$_1$ does not match this focus; rather, its interest on inscriptions in the atrium/narthex and around the high altar and font sets the pattern for the inscriptions from the other Roman churches that follow in the same *sylloge*.

THE EINSIEDELN ITINERARY

The best-known set of Carolingian itineraries of Rome is found in a manuscript now in Einsiedeln, Switzerland.[142] The manuscript comprises five parts put together in the thirteenth century. A single scribe working after 840 copied the fourth of these, writing out five texts: a *sylloge* of inscriptions mostly from Rome (the last five are from Pavia) (fols 67–79r); itineraries of Rome (fols 79v–85r); an account of the walls of Rome (fols 85v–86r); a liturgy for Holy Week (fols 86v–88); and an anthology of Latin verses (fols 89–97), including the anonymous *Conflictus veris et hiemis*, sometimes attributed to Alcuin.[143] The last two poems are funerary epitaphs that can be linked to the monastery of Reichenau, sited on an island in Lake Constanz. One was for Gerold of Bavaria, brother of Queen Hildegard, who was killed in Pannonia on the Avar campaign on 1 September 799 and subsequently buried at Reichenau.[144]

---

[141] *CD* ii, 569–70.

[142] Einsiedeln, Stiftsbibliothek, Cod. 326 (1076) (s. ix^2$_3$, ?Fulda, prov. Pfäfers, then Einsiedeln); Bischoff, *Katalog*, no. 1133. Walser, *Die Einsiedler Inschriftensammlung* has a facsimile and edition of the texts of the *sylloge*, itineraries, and description of the walls (fols 67r–85r). See also the edition and commentary (suggesting the collection of texts was made in the late eighth century), S. del Lungo, *Roma in età Carolingia e gli scritti dell'anonimo Augiense*, Società Romana di Storia Patria, 48 (Rome, 2004), 18.

[143] Einsiedeln, Stiftsbibliothek, Cod. 326, fols 89v–91r; P. Godman, tr., *Poetry of the Carolingian Renaissance* (London, 1985), 144–9, no. 14. The attribution to Alcuin is, in part, because of the repeated reference in the poem to the cuckoo; *Cuculus* was the nickname Alcuin gave to a favoured student (perhaps Dodo); Bullough, *Alcuin*, 93–4. On the anthology of verses in this manuscript, see Maskarinec, *City of Saints*, 141–3.

[144] Einsiedeln, Stiftsbibliothek, Cod. 326, fol. 87v; Dümmler, ed., MGH, PLAC I, 114; J. B. Ross, 'Two Neglected Paladins of Charlemagne: Erich of Friuli and Gerold of Bavaria', *Speculum*, 20 (1945), 212–35;

The final poem, which is incomplete, is an epitaph for Bernald, *praesul*, perhaps the bishop of Strasbourg, who had been trained at Reichenau and who seems to have died in 844.[145] For this reason, it was argued that the core of the collection had been put together at Reichenau in the earlier part of the century, and was augmented there by Bernald's epitaph.[146] Bischoff's palaeographic analysis of the ninth-century elements of the book, however, concluded that the scribe of the extant book was Fulda-trained, and this is the view taken by the most recent editor of the itineraries and *sylloge*.[147] Bischoff conceded the Rome materials could have been collected together, perhaps around the year 800, and brought to Fulda some time before the date at which the manuscript was copied. De Rossi had favoured a pre-eighth-century date for the gathering of the inscriptions in the *sylloge*, but the most recent analysis of the itineraries that follow it favours a compilation date for that text late in the pontificate of Hadrian or in that of Leo III, not least because so many of the sites on the routes are places patronised by these two popes.[148] If correct, the texts in this manuscript provide a further Frankish 'view' of Rome during Charlemagne's reign.

The itineraries in this book are unlike any of the others known from Carolingian era collections. Other itineraries, such as those in ÖNB, Cod. 795, provide routes to shrines that lay in the cemeteries outside the walls of the city; the Einsiedeln itineraries, by contrast, describe routes between monuments and churches within the city's walls. Twelve routes are described that traverse the city, listing structures that can be seen to the left or right of the viewer (in the manner of old-style military route maps). The text is carefully laid out so that things that could be seen *in sinistra* ('on the left') are on the verso of a folio and monuments *in dextra* ('on the right') are on the facing recto. The names of key landmarks such as the Arch of Septimus Severus, the Forum, or the *Forma Virginis* (a 'statue of the virgin' on the *Aqua Virgo* aqueduct) are set out in capitals that span the centre of the book. The titles of each route are similarly picked out in rustic capitals, written in red ink (Figure 4.6).

Nelson, *King and Emperor*, 335, 373 arguing that news of Gerold's death might have been a reason for delaying the king's journey to Rome.

[145] MGH, PLAC II, 420, no. 87 (attributed there, doubtfully, to Walafrid Strabo, and dated 840). See del Lungo, *Roma in età carolingia*, 20. On this epitaph, see Maskarinec, *City of Saints*, 143.

[146] R. Santangeli Valenzani, 'L'Itinerario di Einsiedeln', in M. S. Arena et al., eds, *Roma dall'antichità al medioevo*, 2 vols (Milan, 2001), i, 154–9 (with a plan of the routes of the itineraries).

[147] Bischoff, *Katalog*, nos 1132–33, i.e. section 4 (*Gesta* Salvatoris, fols 11–34) and section 5 (the five Rome/Richenau texts, fols 67–97), dated there s. ix$^{2/4}$; Walser, *Einsiedler Inschriftensammlung*, 9. Also SW, *799*, ii, 607–9, IX.1, where the manuscript is dated *c*.800. It is possible that a Fulda-trained scribe could have worked in another centre such as Reichenau.

[148] ICUR II.i, 9; F. A. Bauer, 'Das Bild der Stadt Rom in karolingischer Zeit: der Anonymus Einsidlensis', *Römische Quartalschrift*, 92 (1992), 190–228, at 209. Santa Prassede is missing, perhaps suggesting that the routes predate the pontificate of Paschal I (817–824). See also Del Lungo, *Roma in età carolingia*, 20 for the argument that the collection of the texts in this section was made in the wake of Charlemagne's imperial coronation.

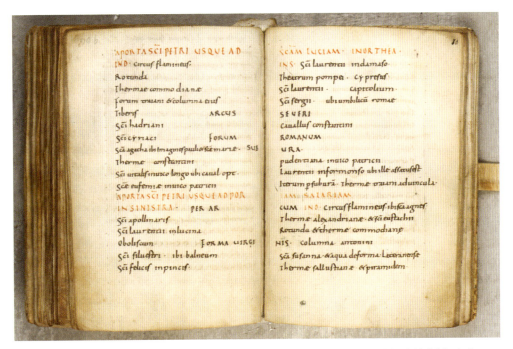

Figure 4.6 *Descriptio Urbis Romae*. The Einsiedeln Itineraries, No. 1; Einsiedeln, Stiftsbibliothek, Cod. 326 (1076), fols 79v–80r. Photo: Courtesy of the Stiftsbibliothek, Einsiedeln.

Doubt has been expressed about the usability of the texts as they exist in the manuscript, and it has been suggested that the version of the itineraries found there are redactions of more complete, coherent routes.[149] The Einsiedeln copy is clearly at some remove from the 'original', as indicated not least by Route 12, which the scribe misplaced and interpolated within the sylloge of inscriptions.[150] The text of this route is, however, rather more detailed and descriptive than the pared-down list of names in the other itineraries, and may preserve an indication of a fuller, more user-friendly text that once existed for all of the itineraries. Nevertheless, the scribe of this book went to considerable pains to lay out the text in a way that reflected the topographical character of his material and the experience of walking the routes through a real urban environment.

These itineraries cannot be divorced from the texts that are found on either side of it in the manuscript, that is, from the *sylloge* that precedes it and the account of the city walls that follows. Clearly, the three texts complement each other, and together constitute a particular vision of the city of Rome. The *sylloge* is unusual among

---

[149] C. Hülsen, 'La pianta di Roma dell'Anonimo Einsidlense', *Dissertazioni della Pontificia Accademia Romana di Archeologia*, ser. 2, 9 (1907), 379–424, at 382; Bauer, 'Das Bild der Stadt Rom in karolingischer Zeit', 204.

[150] Route 12 is on fols 77v–78r; Walser, *Einsiedler Inschriftensammlung*, 54–9 (no. 72 with nos 69–70), 127, 129, and 205–11.

Carolingian collections of inscriptional texts in that it comprises mainly texts taken from pre-Christian monuments, such as bridges, theatres, baths, gates, and arches, as well as Trajan's Column. The last five inscriptions recorded in the *sylloge* were from Pavia, and it may be that these were added to the exemplar of the collection as it was taken north. Of the seventy-five individual inscriptions cited, forty-nine (65.3 per cent) are pre-Christian.[151] Of the remainder, only sixteen (21.3 per cent) are Christian in context or content and, importantly, include the inscriptions at the apse and on the triumphal arch at St Peter's.[152] Four are epigrams by Pope Damasus (366–84) and the latest records Pope Honorius' patronage of the church of St Pancras *c*.630. The Christian inscriptions are interspersed among the earlier ones, often grouped by monument type. Nevertheless, the heavy concentration on imperial rather than papal inscriptions suggests that the compiler deliberately sought out inscriptions that named emperors, lauded their virtues, and described their patronage. The interest in imperial monuments and their inscriptions is also embedded in the itineraries. The primary focus of the itineraries is the churches of the city, but these are located by reference to imperial landmarks nearby that are given names that could have been taken from original inscriptions set upon them. For example, in Route 1 the church of Sant'Adriano (*S[an]c[t]i hadriani*) is identified by reference to the Arch of Severus, as well as the *Forum Romanum* and the equestrian statue of 'Constantine' (*cauallus constantini*).

De Rossi argued that the account of the Aurelian walls of Rome that follows the itineraries in the manuscript was compiled in response to Pope Hadrian's order that the walls should be repaired (as recalled in line 13 of his epitaph); no mention is made of the walls constructed around St Peter's by Leo IV after the Saracen raid of 847.[153] It provides information about the city gates, towers, battlements, postern gates, and latrines. Bauer has argued that this section makes best sense if read as a complement to the itineraries and *sylloge* that precede it; the city walls provide a literal and metaphorical frame for the other texts, determining the topographical extent of the features they describe and providing a means of linking the city's gateways that are also the entry points of the itineraries. The walls literally define the 'intramural' character of the itineraries and inscriptions that are recorded in the *sylloge* and contrast them with the extramural cemeteries that are excluded.

The image of Rome as seen through the lens of these three texts is intriguing, especially if the compilation of the individual sections can be dated to the eighth or earlier ninth century as most commentators suspect. Despite the fact that the texts as we have them are redactions of what might once have existed, the overall vision of Rome

---

[151] Walser lists eighty items (two are Greek), but some are duplicates or belong to the collection of itineraries; Walser, *Einsiedler Inschriftensammlung*, 64–141; Bauer, 'Das Bild der Stadt Rom in karolingischer Zeit', 221, fig. 3.

[152] *ICUR* II.i, no. II.6, II.10–11. See Figure 8.1, below.

[153] See Chapter 3. Earlier opinions concerning hypothetical late antique exemplars are discussed by Bauer, 'Das Bild der Stadt Rom in karolingischer Zeit', 223–4.

that they present is important. Firstly, these texts emphasise the urban space within the walls. This contrasts with other contemporary topographical texts that focus on the cult sites that lay outside the walls, St Peter's among them. This focus on the intramural areas of the city mirrors the trend towards the translation of relics to churches within the city limits that had accelerated in the mid-eighth century.[154] The Einsiedeln texts, however, enmesh Christian cult sites within an imperial city that was entered via monumental gateways and ringed by the huge (if run-down) Aurelian walls that must have so impressed Frankish visitors from the north. The Einsiedeln texts—abbreviated as they are—preserve a powerful impression of a Christianised imperial city as it was envisaged by a compiler around the year 800 and recalled by the Frankish scribe who copied the text a few decades later.

The abbreviated version of the texts preserved in the manuscript records the reception of this vision in northern Francia in the mid-ninth century; the scribe laid out his text in an effort to reflect the topographical character of his material, although a Frankish reader would have had difficulty mapping the imagined city of the book to the real urban spaces of Rome. But to expect a close correspondence between the real city and that of the book is to miss the point. The Einsiedeln texts, as much as the other itineraries and *syllogae* that were read by higher clergy in Francia and England in the eighth and ninth centuries, were a mirror to an idealised place, a 'Rome of the mind' that was the 'threshold of the Apostles'. Texts such as these provided readers from afar with a means of making a virtual pilgrimage to the holy places of the city; their homage to the place was reflected in part by the epigrams for their own churches in Francia and England composed in the style of the inscriptions in their *syllogae*. The writing on their walls was a visual, literal, and metaphorical link with the city of the Apostles.

---

[154] A. Thacker, 'In Search of Saints: The English Church and the Cult of Roman Apostles and Martyrs in the Seventh and Eighth Centuries', in Smith, ed., *Early Medieval Rome*, 247–77, at 250.

FIGURE 5.1 Detail of Hadrian's epitaph showing coral fossils on the edges of the letter *E*. Photo: Author.

5

Writing on the Walls

Epigraphy in Italy and Francia

Classical and late antique epigraphy in its original, monumental form influenced the design of scripts and the layout of inscriptions made in Italy and in Francia in the eighth century. Epigraphic models also influenced the design and use of display scripts in manuscripts from the Carolingian age. The physical location of an inscription—whether experienced in situ at first hand, or indirectly via a rubric in a *sylloge*—provided readers with clues about the value placed on a text by its contemporary custodians. Its location also said much about the significance that its subject once had, and about the power of its original patron to influence its position within a building complex. An inscription was much more than text publicly displayed; the literal meaning of its words was enhanced by qualitative judgements about the composition of the text in verse or prose, the type and quality script used to cut or paint it, its layout, the materials chosen for the ground, its primary location within a structure and its placement there in relationship to other meaningful texts or objects. All these features reflected the wealth, influence, and cultural referents of the patron of the inscription, as well as the significance of the subject matter to its intended audience.

HADRIAN'S EPITAPH: A PHYSICAL DESCRIPTION

The superb quality of the monumental epitaph for Pope Hadrian is displayed in every aspect of its production: its script, text, and decoration, as well as the materials of its manufacture. The form of the poem and the form of the script owe much to classical and late antique exemplars, and it is evident that the epigrapher and the poet of Hadrian's memorial were learned in the epigraphic legacy of late antiquity as transmitted through the pages of books as well as extant inscriptions cut or painted onto walls. Its classical aspect, combined with a distinctive Carolingian aesthetic, signified a renewal of epigraphic standards that had not been seen, in Rome at least, for quite some time. Papal inscriptions made over the decades that follow are noticeably more regular and precise in letterform and layout than their seventh- and eighth-century predecessors, showing the influence that this inscription had on local production.[1] It signified to audiences in Rome a renewed mastery of the art of inscriptional lettering and that the Franks understood the visual and political power of text in monumental form. The superior epigraphic quality of Hadrian's epitaph, and the sources that inspired it, bear close scrutiny, given the overtly political circumstances in which it was commissioned as well as the prestigious location for which it was made.

The epitaph is located now within the portico of the new basilica of St Peter's on the exterior of the nave façade, south of the Porta del Bene e del Male (the 'Door of Good and Evil'). The inscription is complete and the stone, which measures 223cm × 116cm, is substantially intact (see Frontispiece and Figure 1.1). It is set flush to the wall, and surrounded by an elaborate frame made when the inscription was installed there in 1619.[2] Its seventeenth-century setting means that it is not possible to see if the edge of the stone was moulded nor to establish its depth, although given the dimensions of the upper surface and the physical characteristics of the rock, it is likely to be at least 10–20cm thick, maybe more. The colour of the stone is uniform across the exposed upper surface, and its homogeneity is an important diagnostic feature. It is usually described as a black stone although close up it can be seen to be slightly mottled and dark greenish grey in colour rather than jet black. Numerous fossils that are mostly the same colour as the background matrix are also visible to the naked eye. The presence of these fossils indicates that the stone is a carboniferous limestone rather than a true marble (which is a metamorphosed limestone). The fossil assemblage and density, along with other geological characteristics, enable the origin of the limestone to be established with some degree of certainty (see Chapter 6). Superficial cracking along minor fault lines has damaged some of the lettering where the surface of the stone has begun to exfoliate; this is particularly prominent in lines 2–10, from the top right to the centre of the inscription, and lines 23–9, in the centre and left-hand side. There is also some surface pitting where tiny fossils known as ooids on the surface have eroded away, and there are many scratches and chips to the surface (Figure 5.1).

There are two areas of more substantial damage in the middle of the inscription at lines 19–21, on the right-hand side (with maximum dimensions 85mm × 110mm) and on the left edge (with maximum dimensions 155mm × 115mm). Here letters

---

[1] *MEC* I, II.6; H. LeClercq, 'Hadrien I (Épitaph de)', in F. Cabrol, ed., *Dictionnaire d'archéologie chrétienne et de liturgie*, 15 vols (Paris, 1924–53), vi.2, cols 1964–7; F. Schneider and W. Holtzmann, *Die Epitaphien der Päpste und anderer Stadtrömische Inschriften des Mittelalters*. Texte zur Kulturgeschichte des Mittelalters, 6 (Rome, 1932), no. 30; Gray, 'Palaeography of Latin Inscriptions' (1948), no. 76; A. Petrucci, *Writers and Readers in Medieval Italy: Studies in the History of Written Culture*, tr. C. M. Radding (New Haven, CT, and London, 1995), 56–7; Krautheimer, *Profile of a City*, 140–1, fig. 115; C. Treffort, ed., *Épitaphes carolingiennes du Centre-Ouest (milieu VIIIe-fin du Xe siècle)*, Corpus des Inscriptions de la France Médiévale, hors série (Paris, 2020), 9.

[2] See Chapter 1, 82.

have been obliterated, and the damaged areas have been filled in recent times. The fact that both areas of damage are at the same level and at the outer edges of the inscription suggests that they occurred simultaneously, perhaps when scaffolding was rested carelessly against the inscription. This could have happened at any point during the protracted demolition of the south transept before the epitaph was moved to the narthex of the old basilica in 1574, or between 1605 when the order for the demolition of the remaining part of the old nave and narthex was issued and 1619 when the inscription was erected in the new portico, or maybe even during routine cleaning since then (although this is less likely).

Close inspection reveals that white lead has been painted thickly into the letters to enhance the contrast of the letters against the dark background. Often this has been done carelessly, and the white pigment was smeared over the edges of the individual letters and has coagulated in the cut (Figures 5.1–5.6). This has the effect of making the letters seem thicker than originally intended, and much of the subtlety of the letters' form is lost when seen from afar. The careless application of white lead smeared across the surface of the stone also complicates the analysis of the geochemistry of the rock as the signal generated by the lead dominates the readings. The vine scroll border also shows traces of a yellow/orange pigment (Figures 5.2 and 5.3). Analysis of the chemistry of these residues showed no sign of gold, but high levels of arsenic, which is the key element of the yellow pigment orpiment.[3] These white and yellow pigments could have been painted onto the inscription at any point in its history to enhance the visibility of the script and its decoration, although the contemporary description of the epitaph in the Lorsch Annals does refers to its 'golden letters', and the yellow pigment may thus be original. Another possibility is that the arsenic detected in these analyses could be associated with the production of bronze and brass as has been detected in analyses of the contemporary Carolingian metalwork in the Aachen chapel.[4]

The ornamental border

One of the most striking features of the epitaph is the border that frames the text (Figures 5.2 and 5.3). It was mentioned in 1590 in de Winghe's description of the inscription, where he said that it was *cincto opere pampinaceo* ('girded around by vine tendrils').[5] It is a simple, slim rinceau that springs from the centre of the lower border,

---

[3] Orpiment is an arsenical sulfide (AS_2S_3).

[4] For the comparatively high arsenic levels in the Carolingian metalwork from the chapel, see S. Ristow and D. Steiniger, 'Forschungen an den Bronzen des Aachener Domes', *Kölner und Bonner Archaeologica*, 6 (2016), 143–68, at 150–2, and tab. 2.

[5] De Rossi, 'L'inscription du tombeau', 482–3.

and each scroll contains either a bunch of grapes or a vine leaf.[6] In every corner is a five-lobed serrated leaf, and pairs of small leaves grow from the main stem; a longer drop-leaf springs from the node where the main stem branches off for each scroll. Each leaf and grape bunch are different; some are set straight, but others point up or down, left or right, and the sequence is the same in both vertical borders. Only in one place does the pattern break down: in the top border, the serrated leaf in the top left-hand corner should have been followed by a bunch of grapes (as on the other corners), but is instead followed by a leaf, forcing an interruption further along the upper border, where two leaf scrolls occur in sequence. The regularity of the scroll implies that it was mapped out with a compass, but the variability of leaf/grape shapes

FIGURE 5.2 Detail of Hadrian's epitaph showing the ornamental border with golden coloured pigment overlain by white lead in and around the vine scroll. Photo: Author.

---

[6] R. Cramp, *Grammar of Anglo-Saxon Ornament: A General Introduction to the Corpus of Anglo-Saxon Stone Sculpture* (Oxford, 1984), xxiv–viii. A Carolingian parallel, which could date from Charlemagne's time, is the slim rinceau ornament on the broad sides of the 'capsella' of the Hildesheim foundation reliquary. The capsella, which is hemi-ellipsoid in shape, also carries a short inscription, now very rubbed from handling, on the outer edge of the circumference, reading: COR[PO]RAS[AN]C[T]OR[VMINPACE]SEPVLTASV[NT]. The script is a square capital of Carolingian type that would fit comfortably in the early decades of the ninth century (the open bowl to P, the short, raised diagonal on R and the 'insular' z-shaped S are notable). See L. Nees, 'The "Foundation Reliquary" of Hildesheim and Ornamental Art at the Court of Charlemagne', in G. Davies and E. Townsend, eds, *A Reservoir of Ideas: Essays in Honour of Paul Williamson* (London, 2017), 56–66, fig. 1, and M. Brandt, ed., *Kirchenkunst des Mittelalters: Erhalten und erforschen. Katalog zur Ausstellung des Diözesan Museums* (Hildesheim, 1989), 12, figs 3–4a–b.

Figure 5.3 Detail of the central motif in the lower ornamental border of Hadrian's epitaph. Photo: Author.

implies that the motifs at the centre of each scroll were sketched and cut by eye rather than by a fixed template or stencil. It fits well with Pawelec's characterisation of early Carolingian ornamentation as 'lively, spontaneous and improvisatory'.[7] The vine scroll is itself bounded by straight lines, and the whole border is 7cm wide between these parallel lines. As noted, the vine-scroll border shows many traces of a yellow pigment, probably orpiment, as well as the white lead that was also painted into the letters.

Layout

The text and its decorative border fill the available surface of the stone completely, leaving a margin of a couple of centimetres around the outside. This indicates that the layout of the text (i.e. the proportions of the script, line length, and interlinear spacing, as well as the scale of the border relative to the text) was very carefully planned to fit the chosen stone. The dimension of the available writing space within the ornamental border is approximately 205cm × 99cm (i.e. its height is slightly more than

---

[7] K. Pawelec, *Aachener Bronzegitter: Studien zur Karolingischen Ornamentik um 800*, Bonner Beiträge zur Kunstwissenschaft, 12 (Cologne, 1990), 176.

Figure 5.4 Detail of Hadrian's epitaph showing engraved ruling lines. Photo: Author.

double its width). Guidelines are faintly visible in places, engraved into the surface of the stone, creating a writing grid approximately 202cm × 96cm. The ruling comprises a single bounding line on the left and right, with parallel horizontal lines marking the top and bottom of each line of verse, giving a space for each line of lettering 3.3cm high, and an interlinear gap of 1.8cm.

The inscription is made up of forty lines of text, comprising nineteen verse distichs and a two-line prose clause that gives the length of Hadrian's pontificate and the calendar date of his death. A cross with wedge-shaped terminals marks the start of the prose dating clause at the beginning of line 39, and a medial *punctus* is used after each of the three numerals in the last line that give the length of Hadrian's reign in years, months, and days, but not after the numerals of the date of his death.

There are no other punctuation marks within the inscription, no word splitting across lines, and no spacing between the words (*scriptura continua*). Yet the text is easy to read. This is partly a function of the distinctive layout of the text: it is impaginated on the left-hand side so that every second line is indented and is ragged on the right-hand side, rather than being justified across the width of the writing space. This style of layout is a deliberate aid for the viewer who must read forty lines of text

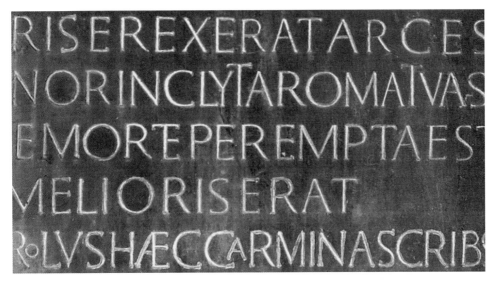

FIGURE 5.5 Detail of Hadrian's epitaph, showing part of lines 14–16. Photo: Author.

FIGURE 5.6 Hadrian's epitaph: detail of letter T, showing traces of chisel marks. Photo: Author.

without accidentally skipping a line or two; the indentation of the beginning of alternate lines and the ragged line endings act as subconscious visual pointers, enabling the reader to move from line to line with relative ease, despite the lack of word division. A similar layout can be seen, for example, in the dedicatory verses of the Dagulf

Psalter, copied in 794–5 for presentation to Hadrian.[8] Earlier examples can be seen in the first part of the epitaph in Bobbio for Bishop Cumian (d. 736) or in the early seventh-century epitaph from the church of Santa Eufemia d'Isola in Como for Bishop Agrippinus (d. 616).[9]

Legibility is also aided by line length—none of the forty lines of text uses more than forty full-size letters—and by the length of the line relative to the height of the script and the interlinear leading. Several space-saving devices were used:

- *Litterae contiguae* (ligatured or linked letters): TE; VP; ME; NE; TR; Æ; AN; AR
- *Tall letters*: the head of the letter T is sometimes raised above the upper ruling line so that the horizontal bar covers adjacent letters (see Frontispiece, lines 4, 17, 33)
- *Litterae insertae* (inserted or 'embraced' letters): a small letter nestles within the area of a regular one, or between two regular-sized letters: LI; CV; PI; QV; CA; ARO; RI. Embraced letters always occur in the middle of a line
- *Abbreviations*: other than the medial *punctus* suspension Q• for QVE in lines 24 and 25, the only other abbreviations are for *nomina sacra*: D̄S, D̄O, D̄I, D̄M (*Deus, Deo, Dei, Deum*), D̄N̄I (*Domini*) SC̄E, SC̄O, SC̄IS (*sancte, sancto, sanctis*), XP̄I, XP̄O (*Christi, Christo*); IĀN for IANUARIAS.

Script

The letter-cutter used a monumental, square *capitalis* script that self-consciously recalls the lettering of ancient Roman inscriptions. As Gray observed, 'the lettering is beautifully formed, regular and skilful; only occasional ligatures and inserted letters differentiate it from a classical inscription' (see Frontispiece and Figure 5.5).[10] The connotations of this choice are important and will be dealt with below since the script encapsulates an array of cultural cross-references and is much more than the medium for the graphic representation of the text. What follows is a discussion of the quality and technical aspects of the lettering.

The essential module of the letters is square (i.e. the O is as wide as it is tall, and other letters such as Q or M, fit within a space of similar proportions). In practice, the

---

[8] See Figure 7.3 below for fol. 4r, and Morison, *Politics and Script*, 139, fig. 90, for fol. 4v. See also the full facsimile, Holter, *Der goldene Psalter*.

[9] For Cumian's epitaph, see Gray, 'Palaeography', no. 33 and MGH, PLAC IV, 723. For an edition, translation, and commentary, see Howlett, 'Two Latin Epitaphs', 235–9, and also Everett, *Literacy in Lombard Italy*, 251–3 and pl. V. For that of Aggripinus in Como, see A. Silvagni, ed., *Monumenta epigraphica christiana saeculo XIII antiquiora*, ii.2: *Comum* (Vatican City, 1943), tav. VIII.1 and P. Rugo, *Le Inscrizioni de sec. VI–VII–VIII esistenti in Italia*, 5 vols (Cittadella, 1974–80), v, 89–90, no. 97. See also M. Richter, *Bobbio in the Early Middle Ages* (Dublin, 2008), 89–94, pl. II, with the Latin text and English translation, and discussion.

[10] Gray, 'Palaeography', 97.

lettering shows some variability and letters are often compressed, tending to be proportionally taller than they are wide (e.g. A B E L S T). The letters are accentuated by substantial, unadorned, triangular serifs: A M N have flattened serif tops (rather than finishing in points), and the serifs of T point slightly outwards and down (see Frontispiece: the high-T in the word AVCTOR in line 1 with its angled serifs rising above the bar is an exception). G does not have a cross bar to the up stroke. The upper bow on B and R generally meets the main stem slightly above the half-way mark, as does the middle bar on E; by contrast, the upper bow on P and the crossbar on A are lower (although note the variability of this rule in line 12). The coda of R starts at the base of the curve of the bow rather than at the stem and curves out to an elegant point. The coda of Q exits from the centre of the base of the letter: it is short, but calligraphic, and is the only element of the script that descends beneath the base line. There is often a backward lean on S.

The letters are incised with an open v-cut, although the crude, white lead over-painting masks much of the subtlety of the craftsmanship. This has misled some to think that the lettering of the epitaph is monoline, that is, it has a constant thickness of stroke. In fact, the letters are built up with both thick lines for the main strokes and thin ones for the secondary strokes. This contrast, in conjunction with the use of a v-cut, creates rhythm and shading in the manner of classical capitals. The 'weight' of the script, however, is heavier than classical exemplars—an impression that is exacerbated by the over-painting. The ratio of the width of the main letter strokes to the height of the letters is about 1:8, which contrasts with the 'Trajanic' order of 1:10, or 3:10 for the late fourth-century 'Filocalian' letter.[11] Occasionally, the incision marks of the chisel can be seen (Figure 5.6). There is no visible sign of gilding within the letters, and no trace of gold was found, although the copious white lead pigment that has been applied to the surface masks traces of other heavy metals that might once have been present.

The ability to maintain the regularity and rhythm of the script across forty lines of text, so that each line contains no more than forty full-sized letters, is the sign of a talented and confident letter-cutter; the fluidity of the inscription as a whole derives from the artistic judgement of an expert craftsman rather than mechanical calculations of a novice (or the aesthetic preferences of a later age). The modulation of the spacing within each line is sensitive, and adjustments are made mid-way across the slab with letters becoming slightly more widely spaced towards the end of the line as the letterer reappraised the remaining space and adjusted the lettering accordingly. This can be seen, for example, in line 11 or 33. Elsewhere, the lettering is more tightly spaced, for example in lines 19, 25, or 27, where the spacing contrasts with the openness of the next one. At first sight, these might be taken as signs of an unpractised hand, and that

---

[11] Morison, *Politics and Script*, 32–7; N. Gray, *A History of Lettering: Creative Experiment and Letter Identity* (Oxford, 1986), 25 and 32.

the epigrapher was careless with the layout in advance of cutting the letters. However, the modulation of the spacing within each lines in fact makes the visual impact of the whole inscription much more comfortable to the viewer's eye than it would be if laid out according to fixed principles of space and proportion: the viewer follows the hand and eye of a human artist rather than letters set down according to a regular grid. The calligraphic flourishes to the diagonal strokes of Q and R, and the occasional tilt to O (e.g. line 40 where the broadest part of the stroke is off-centre), or outward flick of the serifs on T, further support the suggestion that the whole inscription was laid out by someone working quite rapidly, perhaps with paint and a broad, flat brush before being fixed by cutting. This serves as a reminder of the closeness of the association between stone-cut letters and those made with a pen or brush, and of the likelihood that artisans skilled in one medium of graphic display might also be masters of another, regardless of the scale of the work. Though it is impossible to be sure, the eloquent and confident execution of the inscription suggests that the letterer (*ordinator*) responsible for the layout of the inscription may also have been the *sculptor* who cut it, working within the parameters of a careful design rather than mechanically following a scheme prepared by someone else.[12]

What is perhaps most striking about the quality of the lettering of this inscription is the sharp contrast that it provides with inscriptions that had been produced in Rome in the preceding decades, condemned by Gray as 'miserable and ill executed'.[13] Pope Hadrian's epitaph, by contrast, proved to be a turning point for epigraphy in Rome and ninth-century papal inscriptions were noticeably more regular and precise in letterform and layout.[14]

'ROMAN' CAPITALS

It is important to consider the sources of inspiration for the script used for Hadrian's epitaph, in order to understand both the impact that it made on contemporary viewers in Rome, as well as the message inherent in the use of this script and Frankish mastery of it. The choice of square *capitalis* for Hadrian's epitaph was a significant one that was associated with classical antiquity in general as well as the city of Rome itself; by the eighth century its use specifically recalled both the papal authority of the

---

[12] For these terms, see Morison, *Politics and Script*, 29, 38–9; R. Friggeri, *The Epigraphic Collection of the Museo Nazionale Romano at the Baths of Diocletian* (Milan, 2001), 189–91. On the relationship between *ordinator* and letter cutter, see Gray, *History of Lettering*, 25–6.

[13] Gray, 'Palaeography', 45; E. Diehl, ed., *Inscriptiones Latinae*, Tabula in usum scholarum, 4 (Bonn, 1912), pl. 39 (especially 39b made in 783 for Hadrian).

[14] Gray, 'Palaeography', 97.

Christian city as well as its past imperial grandeur.[15] The ideological significance of the use of writing in conscious imitation of Roman authority has been much discussed in the Carolingian context. The special status of *capitalis* and its primacy within the hierarchy of script was clearly understood in Carolingian circles as illustrated by its use as a display script in the finest manuscripts produced in the environs of the court and in painted and stone-cut inscriptions in Carolingian palaces and royal monasteries. Furthermore, its use here, for display, in Rome, and, later, in Milan for inscriptions associated with the Carolingian royal dynasty, suggests that a script of this type was also considered the proper mode of graphic display for texts associated with Carolingian power and patronage in Italy. The church of Sant'Ambrogio contains short epitaphs set on the long edge of white marble sarcophagus lids commemorating Charlemagne's son, Pippin, king of Italy, who died in 810 (Figure 5.7), and his son Bernard, who died in 817 (Figure 5.8). Found in 1875 and 1498, respectively, Gray thought that they had been cut in the same workshop and were 'entirely convincing' as Carolingian inscriptions.[16] Treffort and Caldelli, however, are less convinced that this pair of inscriptions are contemporary, raising questions about the layout and form of the text, all the while acknowledging that the form of the lettering aligns with an earlier ninth-century date.[17]

Capitalis had also been used in a few fourth- and fifth-century deluxe manuscripts that might also have acted as models for Carolingian letterers. Square capitals were sometimes used in antiquity as a book hand for the most prestigious and expensive volumes, and it was the preferred script for the earliest extant copies of the works of Vergil, used perhaps in imitation of the volumes of Homer's work produced in Greek majuscule.[18] Fragments of two Vergil codices written in a time-consuming, majestic square *capitalis* survive, the fourth-century codices known as *Codex Augusteus* and the *Codex Sangallensis* that contain parts of the Aeneid and Georgics.[19] It was used as well for *tituli* in the sixth-century uncial *Codex Agrimensores veterum Romanorum*.[20]

---

[15] For a useful recent overview, see L. Cardin, *Epigrafia a Roma nel Primo Medioevo (secoli IV–X). Modelli grafici e tipologie d'uso* (Rome, 2008).

[16] Gray, 'Palaeography', 86–90, no. 59–60.

[17] C. Treffort, *Mémoires carolingiennes. L'épitaphe entre célébration mémorielle, genre littéraire et manifeste politique (milieu VIIIe–debut XIe siècle)* (Rennes, 2007), 258–9; Caldelli, 'Sull'iscrizione', 62.

[18] Morison, *Politics and Script*, 14–15, 19, 48–51 and pl. 12, 16, 38–9.

[19] *Codex Augusteus*: BAV, Vat. Lat. 3256 and Tübingen, Universitätsbibliothek, Codex Augusteus; *CLA* I.13 and VIII.**13; R. Sabbadini, ed., *Codicis Vergiliani qui Augusteus appellatur reliquiae*, Codices Vaticanus selecti quam simillime expressi, 15 (Turin, 1926), and C. Nordenfalk, *Vergilius Augusteus. Vollständige Faksimile-Ausgabe, Codex Vaticanus latinus 3256 der Biblioteca Apostolica Vaticana und Codex latinus fol. 416 der Staatsbibliothek Preussischer Kulturbesitz*, Codices selecti phototypice impressi, 56 (Graz, 1976). *Codex Sangallensis*: Sankt Gallen, Stiftsbibliothek, Cod. Sang. 1394; *CLA* VII.977.

[20] *Codex Agrimensores veterum Romanorum*, Wolfenbüttel, HAB, Cod. Guelf. 36.23 Aug. 2°, fol. 40v (for example); *CLA* IX:1374a/b; H. Butzmann, ed., *Corpus Agrimensorum Romanorum. Codex Arcerianus A der Herzog-August-Bibliothek zu Wolfenbüttel (cod. Guelf. 36.23 A)*, Codici graeci et latini photographice depicti, 22 (Leiden, 1970).

FIGURE 5.7 The epitaph of Pippin of Italy, d. 810, in Sant'Ambrogio, Milan (detail and complete text). Photo: Author.

FIGURE 5.8 The epitaph of Bernard of Italy, d. 817, in Sant'Ambrogio, Milan (detail and complete text). Photo: Author.

Deluxe books such as these may also have served as epigraphic models for Carolingian lettering.[21] Three other early Vergil codices survive, copied in the fifth or sixth centuries using rustic capitals that were faster to produce than square capitals. Two were illustrated and these seem to have been in Francia by the early ninth century. The so-called *Vaticanus* manuscript of Vergil was at Tours *c*.838 where the text was corrected in Caroline minuscule, missing text replaced, and one of its illustrations

---

[21] A. Petrucci, 'Aspetti simbolici delle testimonianze scritte', in *Simoli e simbologie nell'alto medioevo*, SSCI 23.ii (Spoleto, 1976), 813–44, pl. I–VIII where he argues for the priority of manuscript models for the Hadrian inscription; A. Petrucci, *Writing the Dead: Death and Writing Strategies in the Western Tradition* (Stanford, CA, 1998), 40–1. J. A. Harmon, *Codicology of the Court School of Charlemagne: Gospel Book Production, Illumination and Emphasized Script* (Frankfurt am Main and New York, NY, 1984), 68–9; Bullough, 'Roman Books and Carolingian *renovatio*', 13–15; Ganz, '"Roman Books" Reconsidered', 302–3.

served as a model for an image in one of the great bibles produced there.[22] The other illustrated Vergil, known as the *Romanus*, was certainly at Saint-Denis in the twelfth century, and there is some evidence to suggest that it may have arrived there before the end of the eighth.[23] It was no coincidence that contemporary Carolingian terminology defined *capitalis* scripts as *Virgiliaca manus qua nunc Romanis utuntur* ('the Vergilian hand which is now used by the Romans').[24]

But the 'Roman capitals' of the first few Christian centuries were not homogeneous or static in form, and the evolution of *capitalis* lettering over time means that inscriptions can be dated by script type as well as by historical references embedded in the texts. As Morison argued, changes to the shape of these capitals reflected political or social transitions, and the use or avoidance of those graphic innovations was a means of expressing allegiance or dissent.[25] He suggested, for example, that some changes visible in Latin script in the third and fourth centuries may have occurred because of increased contact between Greek- and Latin-speaking patrons and artisans; but the avoidance of graphic Hellenisms in a Latin text in fifth-century Rome, for example, may have indicated a desire by the patron to distance him/herself from political or religious affiliation with Constantinople. Conversely and more fundamentally, Morison argued that square 'Roman' capitals per se were specifically avoided in the East in late antiquity because they were so closely associated with the pagan traditions of old Rome.[26]

In this respect, the revival and development of *capitalis* for Latin inscriptions in Rome under papal patronage, especially by Pope Damasus in the later fourth century, can be read as an aspect of the papal policy that sought to enforce the primacy of the Roman see over and above the other patriarchates, including Constantinople. Lettering choice might thus express political perspectives, acting as a subliminal messenger to signify the ideological preferences of the author or patron. The script of Hadrian's epitaph deliberately echoes aspects of inscriptions from classical and late antique Rome, many of which were visible to and noted by eighth- and ninth-century visitors to the city in the itineraries of the sights and the *syllogae* of inscriptions that they collected and took back to their homelands.[27] It is clear that the specific historical

---

[22] BAV, Vat. Lat. 3225; *CLA* I.11; D. H. Wright, *The Vatican Vergil: A Masterpiece of Late Antique Art* (Berkeley, CA, 1993), 46, 106–9.

[23] BAV, Vat. Lat. 3867; *CLA* I.9; D. H. Wright, *The Roman Vergil and the Origins of Medieval Book Design* (London, 2001); L. Nees, 'Godescalc's Career and the Problems of Influence', in J. Lowden and A. Bovey, eds, *Under the Influence: The Concept of Influence and the Study of Illuminated Manuscripts* (Turnhout, 2007), 21–44, at 28–9.

[24] The glossary is in Berlin, Staatsbibliothek, MS Diez. B. Sant. 66, and is discussed by B. Bischoff, *Sammelhandschrift Diez. B. Sant 66: Grammatici Latini et Catalogus Librorum*; Codices Selecti, 42 (Graz, 1973), 346, and by Ganz, '"Roman Books" Reconsidered', 298.

[25] Morison, *Politics and Script*, 92–108.

[26] Morison, *Politics and Script*, 102.

[27] See Chapter 4, 147–51.

contexts of these inscriptions were also understood, and, it might be argued, so too were the ideological connotations of particular features of the script used to make them.

Capitalis had been perfected as a monumental display script by the second century AD, and was canonized as the imperial script for major dedications, graphically embodying notions of order, strength, and control.[28] The epitome of such sculpted, monumental capitals is the dedicatory inscription on the base of Trajan's Column (AD 112–13), which was certainly known to Carolingian visitors to the city who labelled it accordingly in manuscript copies and understood that the column stood adjacent to the forum that bore Trajan's name (see Figure 4.6, *Forum traiani et columna eius*).[29] This inscription was of course far from unique, and many other official imperial inscriptions were visible not only in Rome but also in the provinces north of the Alps where the script served to emphasise the imperial authority of the message and its Roman origin.

Capitals were used for titles on one particular imperial inscription in Rome that bears close comparison with Hadrian's epitaph both in terms of its scale and visual impact, as well as its place in later medieval imagination. Part of the text of the Law of the Emperor Vespasian (*Lex de imperio Vespasiani*) survives on a large bronze tablet, measuring 164cm × 113cm. It is about 60 cm shorter than the epitaph slab but of similar width, and with its dark bronze ground, shining surface, and gilded lettering offers a striking parallel to Hadrian's epitaph (Figure 5.9).[30] The bronze tablet is part of a decree that transferred the imperial power bestowed on Augustus to Vespasian (AD 69–79) and is a remarkable survival given the quantity and value of the metal used to make it.[31] The use of bronze for the support of this inscription is an unambiguous statement of imperial wealth, power, and access to scarce resources.

The main text script used on the *Lex* tablet is an expert rustic capital—an anachronistic label that belies the sophistication of the script. Here, the calligraphic coda to Q produces a syncopated effect, linking letters and drawing the reader's eye along the line. Square capitals are reserved for a large, centrally placed, heading near the foot of the tablet, and there would undoubtedly have been others on adjacent panels of the inscription that are now lost. The word picked out in these larger, square capitals, SANCTIO (meaning 'law' or 'sanction') would have caught the eye of many a medieval pilgrim who saw it on display at the Lateran. A pilgrim with limited Latin may have

---

[28] Morison, *Politics and Script*, 31 and 36.

[29] Morison, *Politics and Script*, 32–3, pl. 29; S. Knight, *Historical Scripts from Classical Times to the Renaissance* (New Castle, DE, 2003), 16–17; Gray, *History of Lettering*, 21–25, and fig. 5.

[30] N. Gramaccini, 'Die karolingischen Großbronzen. Brüche und Kontinuitäten in der Werkstoffikonographie', *Anzeiger des Germanischen Nationalmuseums*, 70 (1995), 130–40. This point is also made by I. Weinryb, *The Bronze Object in the Middle Ages* (Cambridge, 2016), 77–9.

[31] *CIL* VI.930; H. Dessau, ed., *Inscriptiones Latinae Selectae*, 3 vols (Berlin, 1892–1916), i, no. 244; V. Ehrenberg and A. H. M. Jones, eds, *Documents Illustrating the Reign of Augustus and Tiberius*, 2nd edn (Oxford, 1976), no. 364; tr. D. Braund, *Augustus to Nero* (London, 1985), no. 293.

WRITING ON THE WALLS: EPIGRAPHY IN ITALY AND FRANCIA 199

FIGURE 5.9 The *Lex de imperio Vespasiani*, Musei Capitolini, Rome. Photo: Courtesy of Archivio Fotografico dei Musei Capitolini, Rome.

seen the similarity of the word to the commonplace *sanctus*, 'saint', and thought it an appropriate statement for the pope's cathedral.

The bronze *Lex* tablet comprises thirty-eight lines of text that are more closely set than the forty lines of Hadrian's epitaph, and it lacks a border. As a prose document, it is set out in paragraphs, but the lines are justified on the left and ragged on the right so that no word is split onto the next line. Here also the text is written with *litterae continua* although medial points (that may not have been original) mark word division. The first letter of each paragraph projects into the left-hand margin and lines are left unfilled at the end of paragraphs, as aids to guide the eye of the reader. Much of this bears comparison with the layout of Hadrian's epitaph, and certainly the scale and visual impact of the two inscriptions is similar.

Gramaccini suggested that the tablet of the *Lex de imperio Vespasiani* was a direct exemplar for the epitaph and that the black marble of the Carolingian inscription was used as a 'surrogate' or lesser material in place of bronze.[32] This seems most improbable given the quality and quantity of bronze being produced in Aachen in conjunction with the building of the chapel at the same time as the production of the epitaph.[33] Certainly the bronze tablet in Rome embodies notions of imperial power and legal authority that would have been attractive to the Carolingian intelligentsia in the closing years of the eighth century. But despite parallels of scale and colour, to see the black marble as a second-rate material deployed instead of burnished bronze is to overlook the rarity of the stone and its value as a large slab of coloured marble, as well as the skill of the stonemasons and artisans who cut it, and the logistical enterprise in transporting it intact long distance to Rome.

As with Hadrian's epitaph, the bronze tablet is mentioned in medieval guides to the city.[34] An English pilgrim known as Master Gregorius, writing probably in the early thirteenth century, described it among the antiquities that that he saw at the Lateran palace in his book, *De mirabilibus urbis Romae*.[35] Gregorius was uncertain of its meaning, saying, 'On this tablet, I read much, but understood little'.[36] Gregorius also described other bronze objects at the Lateran that were thought to be ancient such as the Capitoline She-Wolf, fragments of a colossal statue of Constantine, the Thorn-Picker, and the equestrian statue of Marcus Aurelius that had stood outside the

---

[32] Gramaccini, 'Karolingischen Großbronzen', 134.

[33] See especially Pawelec, *Aachener Bronzegitter* and Weinryb, *The Bronze Object*, 16–20, 39–43.

[34] The tablet is said to have been removed from display by Boniface VIII *c*.1300 'in odium imperii'. It was 'rediscovered' by Cola di Rienzo (1314–1354) and used by him as a prop for his political oratory, though there are indications that others had used it before; M. Greenhalgh, *The Survival of Roman Antiquities in the Middle Ages* (London, 1989), 175–7 and L. Calvelli, 'Un testimone della lex de imperio Vespasiani del tardo Trecento: Francesco Zabarella', *Athenaeum*, 91.2 (2011), 515–24.

[35] VZ, iii, 137–67.

[36] Osborne, *Rome in the Eighth Century*, 153; Master Gregorius, *The Marvels of Rome*, tr. Osborne, 36, 43–8, 53–4, 97–9, cc. 4, 7, 33.

FIGURE 5.10 Maerteen van Heemskerck (c.1536), details of two drawings of the Lateran (conjoined here) showing the equestrian statue of Marcus Aurelius in front of the loggia of Boniface VIII (c.1300) that projects from the southern end of the polyconch triclinium (the *Sala del concilio*) built by Leo III (795–814); Berlin, Kupferstichkabinett, 79 D 2a, fol. 12r and fol. 71r. Photo: Reproduced with permission of the Bildarchiv Preußischer Kulturbesitz, Berlin.

Lateran since at least the mid-tenth century (Figure 5.10).[37] If this equestrian statue is the same as that which the Einsiedeln Itinerary says could be seen in the Forum c.800 (and thought there to be a statue of Constantine) then the date of its transfer to the Lateran can be more confidently assigned to the ninth or earlier tenth centuries (see Figure 4.6: *cavallus constantini*). The She-Wolf is first mentioned at the Lateran in a Carolingian context, albeit retrospectively: two late tenth-century sources from the abbey of Sant'Andrea at Monte Soracte refer to a place of judgement at the Lateran known as *Ad Lupam*, 'the Mother of the Romans', and to a visit there by Louis the Pious in 827/9.[38] It is possible that the tablet of the *Lex de imperio Vespasiani* was also at the Lateran in the ninth century, exhibiting, like the She-Wolf, the papal inheritance of imperial *auctoritas*.

---

[37] Krautheimer, *Profile of a City*, 189–95; Osborne, *Rome in the Eighth Century*, 148–50.

[38] Benedict of Monte Soracte, *Chronicon* and *De Imperatoria Potestate in Urbe Roma Libellus*, ed., G. H. Pertz, MGH, SS III (Hannover 1839), 695–719, at 712, line 7, and 719–22, at 720, line 61, Master Gregorius, *The Marvels of Rome*, tr. Osborne, 96–7. See also the work of A. M. Carruba, *La Lupa capitolina. Un bronzo medievale* (Rome, 2006), who has argued that the lost-wax method of production argues for an early medieval (perhaps Carolingian) rather than Etruscan date for the wolf. It should also be compared with the bronze bear from Aachen, which XRF analysis has demonstrated is clearly of Roman manufacture and of quite different metallurgical composition to the Carolingian metalwork in the chapel where it is now located; Ristow and Steiniger, 'Forschungen an den Bronzen', 158–9.

PAPAL INSCRIPTIONS

Pope Damasus (366–84)

Aspects of the lettering of the Hadrian epitaph recall early papal inscriptions in Rome. Especially important is the work of Furius Dionisius Filocalus. He designed and cut a distinctive, innovative capital script that was used for many monumental inscriptions whose verses, composed by Pope Damasus, extol the virtues of early popes and martyrs whose remains were being uncovered in catacombs outside the city walls.[39] About thirty examples of his work exist, complete or fragmentary, plus many others of lesser quality produced by contemporary imitators.[40] In an act of overt self-promotion, Damasus' name often appears prominently on the inscriptions, either as part of the verses or in the margin, written vertically down the side of the slab to record the fact of his patronage. On two extant examples, Filocalus' name also appears with the statement that he 'wrote' the inscription, which may suggest that the inscriptions were laid out or cut by him.[41] Unusually in the history of lettering design, we can name the innovator and date his work closely.

Damasus' epigrams were a part of his campaign to exemplify the unique Christian heritage of Rome in contradistinction to the claims of the newly imperial city of Constantinople. His inscriptions helped to foster pilgrimage to these sites, and the distinctive and original form of script used to cut them could act as an instantly recognisable 'brand' for pilgrims touring the catacombs that ringed the city. Certainly Damasus' epigrams commonly feature in the early *syllogae* of inscriptions; this is largely because the shrines at which they were located were, by the mid-seventh century, among the oldest and best known on the pilgrims' itineraries. But it is at least possible that his stone-cut epigrams were easily recognised because they had been cut with Filocalus' characteristic script. It was certainly known and mimicked in manuscripts made in Francia in the late eighth century, often in contexts that had a connection with papal Rome, such as the Dagulf Psalter, made for Hadrian in the early 790s.[42]

The script that Filocalus developed for Damasus is essentially that of the imperial monumental capital. But it had important innovations that signified difference as well as descent from the authoritative lettering of imperial, pagan Rome. In contrast to the classical form of the script, the Filocalian lettering is proportionally wider and far more mannered in its execution, and its distinctive ductus is formed by exaggerating

---

[39] N. Gray, 'The Filocalian Letter', *PBSR*, 24 (1956), 5–13, at 6; Trout, ed., *Damasus of Rome*, 2–16. See also H. Stern, *Le Calendrier de 354. Étude sur son texte et ses illustrations*, Bibliothèque archéologique et historique, 4 (Paris, 1953), 122–3.

[40] *ED*, 81–215; Gray, 'Filocalian Letter', 6.

[41] FURIUS DIONYSIUS FILOCALUS SCRIBSIT: *ED*, 134–6 (no. 18.2), 157–9 (no. 27), and 129–134 (no. 18) where his name is inferred opposite that of Damasus; *MEC* I, VI.2. See also Gray, 'Filocalian Letter', 6.

[42] See Chapter 7, 269–75.

the contrast between the very thick vertical strokes and the very thin ones (10:2½ for the height: width-of-thick-stroke: width-of-thin-stroke).[43] Particularly characteristic are the curled finials that spring from rounded terminations to the vertical or diagonal strokes, and the use of hairline, trailing serifs on C E P S T, for example. Other prominent features include: the bow of P that stops short of the stem; the straight coda of R that begins on the 'hip' of the bow; the very long bar on T; the absence of a crossbar on the vertical stem of G; the bulging character of rounded letters such as B D P R where the top of the bow rises upwards and out from the stem (Figure 5.11). Also commonplace—and most significant for comparison with Hadrian's epitaph—is the judicious use of *litterae insertae* or 'embraced' letters, *litterae contiguae* (ligatures), and tall, space-saving letters, especially T.[44] These often cluster towards the end of a line in order to avoid splitting a word across two lines and to enable the text to be justified on both sides; these features are seen most notably on the eulogy for Eutychius (Figure 5.12) and on another, for some unnamed saints, in the cemetery of Callixtus.[45]

These epigraphic features create a script that is clearly recognisable as a form of *capitalis* but which would have been considered wholly unorthodox in earlier centuries; it would never have been mistaken by contemporary (or later) observers as either imperial or pagan (Figure 5.13). Nevertheless, its impact is regular, precise and triumphal.[46] The fact that inscriptions cut for members of Damasus' own family use a more conventional, unadorned form of capital suggests that the script designed by

FIGURE 5.11 Pope Damasus' eulogy at Sant'Agnese fuori le Mura. The text is not in any extant *sylloge*. Photo: Author.

---

[43] *ED*, 22–27; Gray, 'Filocalian Letter', 7; Trout, ed., *Damasus of Rome*, 47–52.

[44] Gray, 'Filocalian Letter', 12.

[45] *ED*, 119–23, no. 16 (from the catacomb of Callistus) and 144–8 (no. 21 for Eutychius) both of which were copied into the fourth Lorsch *sylloge* (L₄); *MEC* I, VIII.2 and V.2. Also, Trout, ed., *Damasus of Rome*, 113–15, no. 16, and 122–5, no. 21.

[46] Gray, 'Filocalian Letter', 9.

Filocalus was reserved principally for texts at martyrial shrines.[47] Morison argued that the innovation and impact of this script was such that it acted as a symbol of the independence of the bishop of Rome and a statement of the special character of Rome in the later fourth century as a Christian city.[48]

Damasus' epigrams feature commonly in the *syllogae*, but it is not known whether this was because of their dramatic graphic impact or because of their explicit papal credentials, several prominently bearing Damasus' name. Certainly, Damasus was better known to later readers than most early popes because it was he who had instructed

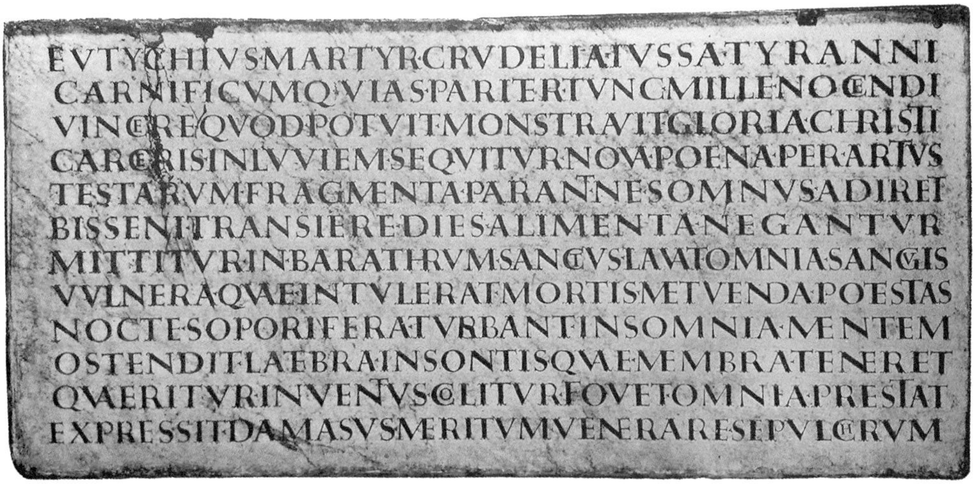

FIGURE 5.12 Pope Damasus' eulogy for S. Eutychius, at S. Sebastiano. This text was copied into the fourth Lorsch *sylloge* (L₄). *MEC* I, V.2. Photo: Reproduced by kind permission of the Pontificio Istituto de Archeologia Cristiana, Rome.

FIGURE 5.13 Pope Damasus' verses for the font at St Peter's. Photo: By kind permission of the Reverenda Fabbrica di San Pietro in Vaticano, Rome.

---

[47] *ED*, 105–11, nos 10–11 (to his mother and sister); Trout, ed., *Damasus of Rome*, 101–5, no. 10–11; Gray, 'Filocalian Letter', 6.

[48] Gray, *History of Lettering*, 32.

Jerome to prepare the new Latin translation of the Bible known as the Vulgate. This scene is shown, for example, on the ivory covers made for the Dagulf Psalter.[49] Complete manuscripts of the Vulgate Bible, New Testament or Gospels often opened with Jerome's preface and his 'Novum opus' letter, addressed to his patron, *Beato pape Damaso Hieronimus* ('Jerome to Blessed Pope Damasus'). The *Liber Pontificalis* also is prefaced by a pair of apocryphal letters between Jerome and Damasus, which credit the pope with the distribution if not the actual composition of the early part of the text.[50] This clustering of texts promoting Damasus and his actions undoubtedly influenced the way he was remembered.

Echoes of the proportions, spacing, and decorative embellishments of the Filocalian letter influenced inscriptions cut in the generations after Damasus' death, often in circumstances that highlighted the triumph of Catholic orthodoxy and papal supremacy. The stateliness of his style of capitals is seen in the large inscription that adorns a panel at Santa Pudenziana naming Pope Siricius (384–99) although the proportions are narrower (Figure 5.14), and in a fragmentary inscription from the cemetery of Commodilla which owes much to the pace, shape, and spacing of the Filocalian inscriptions.[51] The largest and most accomplished extant inscription echoing the Filocalian style is the dedication inscription at Santa Sabina, which spreads across the inner, counter-façade over the main entrance (Figure 5.15). This huge mosaic inscription is set with golden letters on a dark blue ground. Two female figures, personifying the Churches of the Jews and of the Gentiles, are set one at each end, and a golden double-wave border surrounds the whole image.[52] Central to the inscription is the name of Peter, an Illyrian priest, who set up the inscription to commemorate Pope Celestine's pontificate (422–32) and the foundation of the basilica.[53] The text implies that Celestine's pontificate had ended by the time the inscription was made, and this is confirmed by the *Liber Pontificalis*' account of the reign of his successor Sixtus III (432–40).[54] Despite the different medium, the monumental *capitalis* as well as the

---

[49] See Chapter 2, 99–100, and Chapter 7, 272, 278.

[50] Davis, tr., *Book of Pontiffs*, xiii and 1.

[51] *MEC* I, X.1 and X.2 (*ICUR n.s.* II, 6017). See also *CIL* XIV.1941 from Portus, and the modified column, reset in the modern portico at the northern end of the transept at S. Paolo fuori le Mura, carrying an inscription recording Siricius' dedication of that basilica in 391; Camerlenghi, *St Paul's Outside the Walls*, 260, 263, fig. E.18.

[52] These figures were once matched by images of St Paul as the apostle to the Gentiles, and St Peter as the apostle of the Jews; H. Brandenburg, *Ancient Churches of Rome from the Fourth to the Seventh Century* (Turnhout, 2005), 174–5; Maskarinec, *City of Saints*, pl. 10.

[53] *MEC* I, XXX.I. Culmen apostolicum cum Caelestinus haberet / primus et in toto fulgeret episcopus orbe / haec quae miraris fundavit presbyter urbis / Illirica de gente Petrus vir nomine tanto / dignus ab exortu Christi nutritus in aula / pauperibus locuples sibi pauper qui bona vitae / praesentis fugiens meruit sperare futurum. On this inscription and its interaction with the figural images and original decorative schema of the whole church, see especially E. Thunø, 'Looking at Letters: "Living Writing" in S Sabina in Rome', *Marburger Jahrbuch für Kunstwissenschaft* 34 (2007), 19–41.

[54] *LP* 46.8; Davis, tr., *Book of the Pontiffs*, 38.

FIGURE 5.14 Part of an inscription from a pluteus at S. Pudenziana, naming Pope Siricius (385–98). Photo: Author.

FIGURE 5.15 Mosaic dedication inscription at Sta. Sabina (442–32). Pope Celestine's name is in the top line, with the donor's name, Peter, centrally placed in the middle of the text. Photo: Paolo Romiti, Alamy Stock Photo.

curled serifs on A, B, G, R, and T clearly recall the Filocalian lettering of the previous century, combining both imperial and papal *auctoritas*.

These connotations of script were continued in other inscriptions in the city set up by Pope Sixtus. Although it is no longer extant, he was responsible for another donative text that once adorned the counter-façade of Santa Maria Maggiore recording his patronage of that *nova templa* in honour of the Mother of God.[55] As at Santa Sabina, the symbolism and content of the inscription on the counter-façade responded to and interacted with decorative schema elsewhere in that basilica, much of which survives. At the summit of the triumphal arch at the east end of the nave, the figures of Peter and Paul turn towards a roundel containing the empty throne, as described in the

---

[55] The text was recorded in three *syllogae*; De Rossi, ed., *ICUR* II.i, 71, no. VI.42; 98, no. VIII.6; 139, no. XII.28. See also, Thunø, 'Looking at Letters', 29, and Brandenburg, *Ancient Churches*, 178–89.

Book of Revelation, on which Christ will sit in judgement over the living and the dead. The roundel rests on a framed panel containing a short text, 'Xystvs episcopus plebi dei' ('Sixtus, bishop to the people of God'), which proclaims the pope's leadership of God's people, who are, thus, among the saved.[56] This inscription, in mosaic like the figural images above and around it, again uses unadorned golden *capitalis* set on a blue ground. The classical form of the script belies its radical proclamation, that the people of Rome are now the people of God, and, with Sixtus as their bishop, are led by the Apostles Peter and Paul to the safety of Christ's eternal judgement. Once again, the form of the lettering as well as the words themselves work with the figural images of the two 'Roman' apostles to project the authority and primacy of the *Ecclesia Romana* and the bishop who leads it.

Sixtus III had another inscription cut on the entablature that surmounts the inner ring of columns inside the octagonal baptistery at the Lateran that was constructed during his pontificate (Figure 5.16).[57] The *Liber Pontificalis* records the collection and erection of eight porphyry columns, their capitals, and marble entablature, which Sixtus 'adorned with verses'.[58] The entablature that supports the inscription is spolia reused from an earlier imperial building, reversed and modified for its new context. The metrical text is written on the flat, reverse side of the entablature so that it can be read from the floor of the outer ambulatory; it comprises eight couplets. The number eight is symbolically linked to the rite of baptism through Christ's resurrection and 'rebirth' on the eighth day, and Sixtus' verses extol the doctrines of baptism and divine grace (thereby emphasising the recent rejection of the heresy of Pelagius).[59] The poetic structure of Sixtus' poem was thus determined by the eight available surfaces, and the graphic design of the inscription was constrained by the dimensions of

FIGURE 5.16 Inscription by Sixtus III for the Lateran Baptistery (the fifth of eight distiches). Photo: Author.

[56] *MEC* I, XXX.2.
[57] *MEC* I, X.4; Brandenburg, *Ancient Churches*, 37–54, especially 42, 47–8, figs 14 and 15b.
[58] *LP* 46.7; Davis, tr., *Book of the Pontiffs*, 38.
[59] Brandenburg, *Ancient Churches*, 47, citing the eight distichs composed by Ambrose for the octagonal baptistery in Milan, and n. 31 which provides a transcription and translation of Sixtus' verses. See also this volume, Chapter 7, 296–306, for a discussion of the verses inside the octagonal chapel at Aachen.

the writing surfaces and the height of the entablature above floor level. While the lettering of this inscription lacks the subtlety and embellishments of the Filocalian lettering, the earlier script is recalled by exaggerated bifurcated serifs, the long bar on T, and the assertive weight and generous spacing of the *capitalis* script.[60] This type of lettering was also employed for an verse inscription recording substantial repairs to the roof of S. Paolo by Leo I (440–61), Sixtus III's immediate successor. Great care has been taken with the layout of the text and to contrast the main text with the size and spacing of the lettering that completes it and, once again, it was set up on the counter-façade of the nave, in a prominent position (Figure 5.17).[61]

Filocalus' lettering was recalled again in a mid-sixth-century inscription cut for Pope Vigilius (537–55).[62] This text celebrates the destruction of Gothic encampments that had encircled Rome during the Ostrogothic siege led by King Vitigis in 537/8 and, explicitly recalling Damasus' patronage of the martyrs' shrines, it records Virgilius' renewal of those sacred places in the aftermath of the Goths' expulsion from the environs of the city (Figure 5.18). The text of this inscription was recorded in Carolingian era *syllogae*, including the fourth Lorsch collection. Although technically much less competent than its Filocalian exemplars, this inscription retains the broad spacing, bulging D's, and curled filials of the originals (though here they were placed also on the terminals of S), and uses tall, space-saving letters. These tall letters, as well as ligatures and *litterae insertae*, are also found on another inscription from the 530s written for Pope John II (533–5) now in San Pietro in Vincoli (Figure 5.19).[63] Here also the bow of P stops short of the upright and G has a bifurcated serif and short tail on the upright, strongly reminiscent of the Filocalian treatments of those letters. But the compressed and unadorned lettering in this case, shows how far from Filocalus' aesthetic some Roman epigraphy had moved by the middle years of the sixth century.

Pope Gregory the Great (580–604)

One of the best-known inscriptions from early medieval Rome was the epitaph of Pope Gregory I who died in 604. Two small fragments of the original inscription survive in the grotto at St Peter's in the Vatican (Figure 5.20).[64] Bede included the

---

[60] Thunø, *Apse Mosaic*, 186.

[61] *MEC* I, X.5; *ICUR* n.s. ii, no. 4783; Schaller and Könsgen, eds, *Initia*, no. 4861. G. Filippi, *Indice della raccolta epigrafica di San Paolo fuori le Mura*. Inscriptiones Sanctae Sedis, 6 vols (Vatican City, 1998–2011), iii, fig. 154 (SP 673); Camberlenghi, *St. Paul's Outside the Walls*, 84–5, fig. 3.1; A. M. Yasin, 'Shaping the Memory of Early Christian Cult Sites: Conspicuous Antiquity and the Rhetoric of Renovation at Rome, Cimitile-Nola and Poreč', in K. Galinsky and K. Lapatin, eds, *Cultural Memories in the Roman Empire* (Los Angeles, CA, 2015), 116–33 at 118–19.

[62] *ED*, 182–3, no. 41; Silvagni, ed., *MEC* I, XI.7–8; Trout, ed. *Damasus of Rome*, 161–2, no. 41.

[63] *MEC* I, XI.5 (also XI.2–3) the latter of which, from San Clemente, is shown in Brandenburg, *Ancient Churches*, 145 and fig. 71b.

[64] *MEC* I, II.3.

```
EXSVLTATEPIILACRIMISINGAVDIAVERSIS
 ETPROTECTORI ✠ REDDITEVOTADEO
CVIVSSICTENVITRESOLVTVMDEXTERATECTVM
 INVACVVMVTCADERET ✠ TANTARVINASOLVM
SOLVSETINVIDIAEPRINCEPSTORMENTASVBIRET
 QVINVLLVMEXAMPLA ✠ STRAGETVLITSPOLIVM
NAMPOTIORANITENTREPARATICVLMINATEMPLI
 ETSVMPSITVIRES ✠ FIRMIORAVLANOVAS
DVMXPIANTISTESCVNCTISLEOPARTIBVSAEDES
 CONSVLITETCELERI ✠ TECTAREFORMATOPE
DOCTOREMVTMVNDIPAVLVMPLEBSSANCTABEATVM
 INTREPIDESOLITIS ✠ EXCOLATOFFICIIS
LAVSISTAFELIXRESPICITTEPRAESBITER
NECTELEVITESADEODATEPRAETERIT
QVORVMFIDELISATQVEPERVIGILLABOR
DECVSOMNETECTISVTREDIRETINSTITIT
```

FIGURE 5.17 Verse inscription by Pope Leo I commemorating the restoration of the roof at S. Paolo fuori le Mura. *MEC* I, X.5. Photo: Reproduced by kind permission of the Pontificio Istituto de Archeologia Cristiana, Rome.

FIGURE 5.18 Inscription for Pope Vigilius after the Goths' siege of Rome in 537/8. *MEC* I, XI. 7/8. Photo: Reproduced by kind permission of the Pontificio Istituto de Archeologia Cristiana, Rome.

text of the epitaph in his *Historia Ecclesiastica gentis Anglorum*, and it was often copied in eighth- and ninth-century *syllogae* (e.g. L₄ where it was copied twice).[65] Its medieval fame was due partly to the reputation of Gregory (especially in the English kingdoms) and partly to the prominence of his tomb to pilgrim visitors to St Peter's.

[65] Bede, *HE* II.1. The fragments consist of an opening crismon and the first three letters of the first word [+ sus*cipe*] and all or part of fifteen letters from lines 8–12, 'Atque animas monitis texit AB hoste sacris / Implebatque actu quicquid seRMone docebat / Esset ut exemplum mystica uerba loquens / Ad Christum Anglos conueRTIT pietate magistra / Adquirens fidei agMINA gente noua'. In the eighth century, the opening of the text inspired the epitaph of another man named Gregory, which is extant in the Lateran, cut in much rougher script; Gray, 'Palaeography', no. 57; *MEC* I, XXVI.8.

FIGURE 5.19 Inscription for Pope John II (533–5) in S. Pietro in Vincoli. John's name before his election (Mercurius) and his ties to S. Clemente are recorded in lines 2–3. Photo: Author.

Gregory was buried outside the *secretarium* at St Peter's, at the southern end of the narthex at the front of the basilica. His tomb and epitaph were thus easily accessible to visitors to the atrium who could see it without entering the main body of the church. The epitaph may also have been prized because of the quality and legibility of its script as well as the sentiment of its verses.

The legacy of Filocalus' lettering is clear to see in its monumentality, confidence and regularity of execution. Once again, the lettering is wide and well-spaced, the *ductus* contrasts between thick and very thin, the coda of R begins on the 'hip' of the bow, and the serifs of T point downwards and slightly outwards with a hairline trail, just as before. The graphic cross-reference was appropriate since, like Damasus, Gregory vigorously asserted the priority of the Roman see, especially over Constantinople and actively promoted the cults of the Roman martyrs. But there is a major difference in the absence of the curled, ornamental serifs, and in this respect the epitaph of Gregory is more overtly 'classical' than the papal script of Filocalus had been. Morison thought that this change was deliberate, and that the 'Gregorian capitals' used in this epitaph and in the large inscription at San Paolo fuori le Mura, recording a gift of lights to that basilica, were 'as Roman as [Gregory] could make them'.[66] By reverting to a purer form of capitals 'that would have been considered "pagan" in Constantinople' the Gregorian capitals, he argued, helped to consolidate the authority of Gregory and his church in Rome against the claims of the eastern patriarch in Constantinople.[67] Similarly graceful capitals, incised with a deep v-cut,

---

[66] *MEC* I, XII.1; Filippi, *Indice*, iii, fig. 153 (SP 665); Story, 'Lands and Lights', fig. 22.1.
[67] Morison, *Politics and Script*, 104.

FIGURE 5.20 Fragments from the epitaph of Pope Gregory I (d. 604). Photo: Author, with kind permission of the Reverenda Fabbrica di San Pietro in Vaticano, Rome.

survive from a small fragment from the epitaph of Gregory's successor, Sabinian (604–6).[68] Like Gregory's diploma, this inscription employs a flat cap to the tip of A, and the diagonal on N has a distinct curve to it.

These graphic features can be seen in another early seventh-century inscription cut into the base of the Column of Phocas, set up not far from the Senate building in the Forum (Figure 5.21).[69] This dedicatory text names Smaragdus, the exarch of Ravenna, as patron of the monument that was dedicated on 1 August 608 and which, for a short time afterwards, carried a gilded statue of the Emperor Phocas (602–10). The base of the column bearing the inscription was uncovered in 1813, and, although it is ostensibly secular, the style of lettering (note especially the shape of R) is like that of Gregory's epitaph, and, as such, suggests papal interests in the enterprise. Phocas had been fêted by Gregory I on his accession to the imperial throne in 602, and Gregory promptly sent a nuncio to Constantinople to further the interests of the papacy with

---

[68] *MEC* I, II.4, all or part of eight letters, the flat top to A recalls the script of Gregory's diploma.

[69] *CIL* VI.1200; Phocas's turbulent reign in the East culminated in execution by his successor Heraclius in 610. The subsequent *damnatio memoriae* is reflected in the excision of his name on this inscription in Rome, which originally followed the words *principi domino n[ostro]* in line 2.

FIGURE 5.21 The Column of Phocas, dedicatory inscription, 1 August 608. Photo: Gregor Kalas.

the new emperor.[70] That nuncio was elected as pope Boniface III in 607, and he quickly secured from Phocas an imperial proclamation conceding that the see of St Peter 'should be the head of all the churches', quashing the claims of the patriarch of Constantinople to that status.[71] Soon afterwards Phocas granted Boniface IV (608–15) the right to convert the Pantheon from a pagan temple into a church, paving the way for significant changes in the urban fabric of the city.

The shallow-cut, compressed *capitalis* of the epitaph of a Greek man named Theodore, who died in 619 and which is now at Santa Cecilia, shows that the patronage of good quality inscriptions was not restricted to the papal elites in the early decades of the seventh century (Figure 5.22).[72] The first line of this inscription is larger than the text that follows and uses abbreviations and a lone *littera inserta*.

Few other papal inscriptions survive from seventh-century Rome, however. This is particularly frustrating since texts of numerous seventh-century papal epitaphs survive in the *syllogae*, and the *Liber Pontificalis* reports extensive building activity, much of which is likely to have been commemorated in inscriptions celebrating the work of patrons or the translation of relics. Some survive as mosaic inscriptions, such as the dedicatory text at the base of the apse at S. Agnese fuori le Mura, dating from the pontificate of Honorius I (625–38), or that in the oratory of S. Venantius in the

---

[70] Ekonomou, *Byzantine Rome*, 45–50.

[71] 'Ut sedis apostolica beati Petri apostoli caput esset omnium ecclesiarum, quia ecclesias Constantinopolitana prima se omnium ecclesiarum scribebat'; *LP* 68.1; Davis, tr., *Book of Pontiffs*, 64.

[72] Theodore, d. 619, *MEC* I, XII.2.

Figure 5.22 The epitaph of Theodore, d. 619, at Sta. Cecilia (detail). Photo: Author.

Lateran baptistery from the pontificate of John IV (640–2).[73] But nothing is known, for example, of epigrams related to Boniface IV's transformation of the Pantheon into the church of Santa Maria ad Martyres nor of the physical form of any stone-cut inscriptions erected by Honorius I whose pontificate was notable for an energetic construction programme at churches throughout the city.[74] The absence of Honorius' inscriptions is a particular lacuna since so much other evidence points to his pontificate as the period when many of our extant *syllogae* and itineraries of the city may have been collected, suggesting that there was a real, contemporary interest in the graphic culture of the papal city. Also missing are physical traces of the inscriptions known to have been made for Sergius I (687–701), such as that which recorded the translation in 688 of the body of Pope Leo I to a new oratory in the south transept of St Peter's, or the epitaph for the West Saxon king Ceadwalla, who died in Rome in 689.[75] A fragment of a bull issued by Sergius recording a donation to Santa Susanna, now in the Lateran, gives a clue to the form of the monumental lettering used during his pontificate, and whose epitaph was also recorded by Bede and in the *syllogae*.[76] The script

---

[73] *MEC* I, XXX.1; *LP* 74.2; Davis, tr., *Book of Pontiffs*, 68. For Honorius' text, see Schaller and Könsgen, eds, *Initia*, no. 1428; Brandenburg, *Ancient Churches*, 244–7; and Lansford, *Latin Inscriptions*, 286–7 (no. 8.8B).

[74] *LP* 69.2 and 72.2–6; Davis, tr., *Book of Pontiffs*, 64, 66–7.

[75] Sharpe, 'King Ceadwalla's Roman epitaph', 171–93. On Leo I and Ceadwalla, see Cascioli, *Epigrapfi Cristiane nell'area vaticana VI–X secolo*, 55–69.

[76] *MEC* I, XII.3; Gray, 'Palaeography', no. 1.

is an angular capital, competent but mechanical, which becomes cramped towards the end of the lines forcing the use of abbreviations and *litterae insertae*.

EIGHTH-CENTURY EPIGRAPHY IN ROME BEFORE 795

The fragment of Sergius' inscription for Santa Susanna can be grouped with the extant inscriptions from eighth-century Rome, in both content and epigraphic style. Many of the inscribed texts from this period are very long and few of them are epitaphs. Most are in prose, and record details of donations to churches (including lists of relics) or ordinances for prayers and masses, and several were set up in the name of noblemen, showing that they too had the means to memorialise their largess.

Two stone inscriptions survive from the short but artistically influential pontificate of John VII (705–7), and their scale, style, and brevity are not typical of the period. One is from Santa Maria Antiqua and the other from St Peter's, and both record John's devotion to the cult of Mary.[77] The inscription from Santa Maria Antiqua is bilingual (in Greek and Latin, befitting John's Greek origins), and is cut onto the base of an ambo. At St Peter's the Latin inscription was cut on the reverse of a carved screen. Grimaldi recovered it from the ciborium in the Oratory of the Holy Mother of God (where the altar of the Veronica was later established) at the end of the north aisle. John had dedicated this oratory to Mary on 21 March 706 and, not long after, was buried there beneath an epitaph that affirmed his 'pious passion for the mother of God'.[78] Grimaldi also records the recovery of a fragment of a third inscription, in Greek, that, like the Latin one, was set in a *tabula ansata* and invoked the name of the Virgin.[79] This third inscription is now lost, but it was evidently the twin of the extant Latin one. The shape of the lettering used here is monumental but heavy, and epigrapher used ligatures (MA, AE, TH), abbreviations and inserted letters (I, O) to save space. The lettering of both inscriptions is large (16cm at Santa Maria, *c*.8cm at St Peter's) and is cut in relief; they are thus quite unlike anything else surviving from the city at this time (Figure 5.23).[80] The simple monumentality and the overt self-promotion of these bold inscriptions stands in contrast to the complex iconography of the very fine series of mosaics that John commissioned from Constantinopolitan artists in both basilicas, and seems to have been repeated in the dedicatory inscriptions recorded in Grimaldi's drawings of John's oratory at St Peter's (see Figure 1.19).[81]

---

[77] *MEC* I, XII.4–6; Gray, 'Palaeography', nos 2–3.

[78] The epitaph of John VII is in the Cambridge Sylloge; Levison, 'Aus Englischen Bibliotheken II', 363–4.

[79] Ballardini and Pogliani, 'A Reconstruction of the Oratory', 200.

[80] The parallel is with metalwork, where the background is filled in with black niello to enhance the gold of the raised script.

[81] *LP* 88.1–2; Davis, *Book of Pontiffs*, 90. P. J. Nordhagen, 'The Mosaic of John VII: The Mosaic Fragments and their Technique', *Acta ad archeologiam et atrium historiam pertinentia*, 2 (1965), 121–66; A. Monciatti, 'Fragments of Mosaic from the Oratory of John VII', in *BSPV* I.ii, (Atlas), 884–7, no. 1736–8 and 1740.

Figure 5.23 Inscription on a screen from the Oratory of Mary at St Peter's dedicated by John VII (705–7). Photo: By kind permission of the Reverenda Fabbrica di San Pietro in Vaticano, Rome.

The next major inscription at St Peter's belongs to the pontificate of Gregory II (715–31).[82] It now comprises two large slabs inscribed with twenty-six lines of a diploma granting olive groves for the lighting of the basilicas of St Peter and St Paul (Figure 5.24). The inscription is now set in the exterior wall of the portico and was one of the three 'ancient inscriptions' preserved and redisplayed there in the early seventeenth century, alongside Hadrian's epitaph and the bull of Boniface VIII. The existence of a third slab was reported by Romanus in the later twelfth century; the text of this section stated that it had been made during the reign of the Emperor Leo III (717–41). The epigraphy of the inscription as well as its preservation are noteworthy, explained by its original location at the southern end of the portico, close to the tomb of Gregory the Great.[83] Its script, scale, and content deliberately echo the diploma of the first Gregory, extant at San Paulo fuori le Mura. Both texts record donations for the supply of oil for lights from estates in the *Patrimonium Appiae*, and the layout and script of the second Gregory's inscription is evidently intended to recall that of his namesake. In both, the lettering of the first two lines is significantly larger than the text that follows, and the form of the capitals used is similar. There are obvious differences too—in execution and in the use of many space-saving devices in the later inscription (tall and inserted letters, and ligatures). But the overall parallel is striking, and intentionally so, suggesting that Gregory, *indignus servus*, wished to borrow more from his illustrious forebear than just his name.

The epigraphy of mid eighth-century Rome is dominated by a group of long inscriptions that are alike in script, scale, and layout. Three date from the pontificate of Gregory III (731–41) and a similar style was employed for several more up to the 760s. In all these, the capitals are quite regular in form but lack finesse and are shallowly cut, and the spacing between letters and across lines is often uneven. The lines of text are usually closely set, and the lettering usually fills the space available, with few

---

[82] Franzoni, 'Diploma of Gregory II', 493–4; Story, 'Lands and Lights', 324–8, fig. 22.4.

[83] *ICUR* II.i, 223, n. 134—for a reconstruction of its exact position. It was seen in the ninth century by John the Deacon *in tabulis marmoreis prae foribus eiusdem basilicae*; that is, on the façade of the church.

FIGURE 5.24 A diploma of Pope Gregory II (715–31), recording a gift of lights to St Peter's, as displayed in the portico in its seventeenth-century frame. Photo: Author, with kind permission of the Reverenda Fabbrica di San Pietro, Rome.

WRITING ON THE WALLS: EPIGRAPHY IN ITALY AND FRANCIA 217

Figure 5.25 Pope Gregory III, record of the Council of 732 regarding the enactment of the offices to be said in his new oratory. Photo: By kind permission of the Reverenda Fabbrica di San Pietro in Vaticano, Rome.

concessions to aid legibility other than an offset initial letter or a medial *punctus* between clauses.

The most important of Gregory III's inscriptions is the text recording the offices that were to be said in the new oratory dedicated by him to All Saints (i.e. the Virgin, Christ, Apostles, all Martyrs and Confessors), at the foot of the southern pier of the triumphal arch in the nave of St Peter's in 732 (Figure 5.25).[84] The names of the prelates listed here correspond to that in the *Liber Pontificalis*. Two parts of this long prose text survive and a third one, now lost, linked the two extant portions and was recorded by Peter Sabin in 1494. In the same oratory was another inscription, this time recording three prayers to be said for Gregory, who had died in November 741 (Figure 5.26).[85] The lettering of this inscription is more compressed than the earlier one, and makes greater use of inserted letters and ligatures; unlike any other contemporary inscription it is in liturgical Latin. A third fragmentary inscription dating from

---

[84] *MEC* I, XIII.1 (a+b); Gray, 'Palaeography', no. 6 (a+b). The full text is given in *ICUR* II.i, 412–17.
[85] *MEC* I, XIII.2; Gray, 'Palaeography', no. 7.

FIGURE 5.26 Prayers for Pope Gregory III, from the oratory of All Saints: Photo: By kind permission of the Reverenda Fabbrica di San Pietro in Vaticano, Rome.

Gregory's pontificate is at San Paulo fuori le Mura, again recording masses to be said daily in that basilica.[86]

At San Clemente is a substantial inscription recording the donation to that church by a certain Gregory who was its cardinal priest during the pontificate of Zacharias (741–52), *sanctissimus praesul*.[87] The inscription, which is metrical, records a gift of several books, namely copies of: the Old and New Testaments; the Octateuch; Kings; the Book of Psalms and the Prophets; The Song of Songs; the book of Esdras (Figure 5.27).[88] The epigraphic quality of this inscription is rather better than those made in the previous decade for Gregory III. It too uses offset letters to mark out alternate lines, and simple leaf line-fillers on the right-hand side. At least the first part of the text is presented as lines of verse with the caesura in each line denoted by a space (in the upper part of the text) and a medial punctus. Within each line the spacing is well controlled, and the lettering is regular.

Of similar quality is the calendrical list of the feast days of saints 'here lying' at San Silvestro; two inscriptions survive, one listing male saints and another listing female saints (Figure 5.28).[89] On these two stones the text is laid out with text indented where an entry runs over into the next line, and simple decorative leaf-shaped line fillers are used to guide the eye of the reader. The capitals used here are compressed, but the script is regular and easily legible. Palaeographic characteristics include: a flat

[86] *MEC* I, XIII.3(a–e); Gray, 'Palaeography', no. 5.
[87] *MEC* I, XIV.2; Gray, 'Palaeography', no. 8.
[88] See *LP* 93:19 for Zacharias' gift of all the codices in his house (for reading at Matins throughout the year) to a basilica dedicated to St Peter (which one is unclear); see also Duchesne, ed., *LP*, iii, 102.
[89] *MEC* I, XXXVII.1–2; Gray, 'Palaeography', no. 10.

FIGURE 5.27 Verses by Gregory, cardinal priest of S. Clemente, describing a gift of books during the pontificate of Zacharias (741–52). Photo: Reproduced by kind permission of the Pontificio Istituto de Archeologia Cristiana, Rome.

top to A, the cross-bar of which is often slanted downwards to the left; the point of M stops before the base line; the coda of Q is vertical and inserted within the body of the letter; uncial E occurs (penultimate line). Abbreviations are common and marked with a simple macron, and numerals are picked out with a medial punctus on either side. In the lower part of the stone inserted letters are used and the diagonal of R is crossed to save space. The lists at San Silvestro are dated by comparison with another one partially extant in St Peter's dated to the pontificate of Paul I (757–67) (Figure 5.29); both are associated with his campaign to transfer large numbers of relics from the extra mural cemeteries into the city. The *Liber Pontificalis* records that Paul took care, 'to have some of the buried with fitting honour around the *tituli*, deaconries, monasteries and other churches'.[90] He also constructed a monastery in his own house dedicated to St Stephen and St Sylvester, and 'with great respect and reverence he deposited the bodies of the uncounted saints he removed from the demolished cemeteries', and it is this act which is recorded in the inscription.

---

[90] *LP* 95:4–5; Davis, tr., *Lives of the Eighth-Century Popes*, 82–3.

FIGURE 5.28 List of the feast days of male saints buried at S. Silvestro by Pope Paul I (757–67). Photo: Author.

WRITING ON THE WALLS: EPIGRAPHY IN ITALY AND FRANCIA 221

FIGURE 5.29 A list of saints, from the pontificate of Paul I (757–67), at St Peter's. Photo: By kind permission of the Reverenda Fabbrica di San Pietro in Vaticano, Rome.

At Sant'Angelo in Pescheria is a similar list of relics that preface a record of the foundation of a church dedicated to St Paul by Theodotus 'holim dux nunc primicerius sanctae sedis apostolicae'. The text contains a date, 755, noted by indiction, *annus mundi* (AM 6263), and the pontificate of *Stephanus Iunior* (752–7).[91] The lettering of this list is very like those of Paul I, and closely comparable with the two long

---

[91] *MEC* I, XIV.3; Gray, 'Palaeography', no. 9; Davis, tr., *Lives of the Eighth-Century Popes*, 52.

Figure 5.30 Record of gifts of land by Eustathius and George, Sta. Maria in Cosmedin (s. viii med.) (detail). Photo: Author.

inscriptions now in the portico of Santa Maria in Cosmedin which record gifts of land by Eustathius, *dux* and *dispensator*, and George, *gloriosissimus* (Figure 5.30).[92] Here, the crossbar of A slants upwards from the base of the first diagonal stroke, and the script is, at least initially, regular and well-spaced. In all of these inscriptions, ligatures (especially TH) and small inserted letters (especially I) are used to conserve space, frequently in those from Santa Maria in Cosmedin and Sant'Angelo in Pescheria.

Another inscription recording the translation of relics survives from the early part of the pontificate of Hadrian (Figure 5.31). It includes a date, 22 November 783, and refers to the concealment of a relic of the 'holiest of holies', 'twice enclosed' within the altar. This reference probably accounts for the careful preservation of this inscription, since it was later read as proof of the existence of the veil of Veronica at St Peter's in Hadrian's time (see Figure 1.19). There is, however, no direct evidence of the Veronica before *c*.1000, so the identity of the relic recorded here is uncertain. Gray condemned this inscription as the very worst of the period, saying that, 'some of the letters are so shapeless that they seem a reversion to senseless marks, as if the mason

---

[92] *MEC* I, XXXVII.4–5; Gray, 'Palaeography', no. 15.

WRITING ON THE WALLS: EPIGRAPHY IN ITALY AND FRANCIA 223

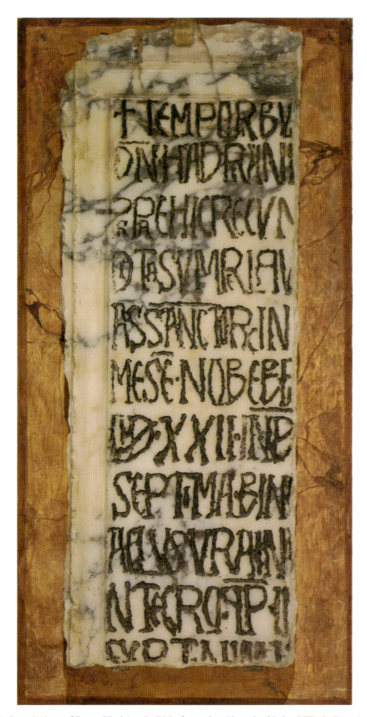

Figure 5.31 Inscription of Pope Hadrian I, 783, from the Chapel of John VII, St Peter's. Photo: By kind permission of the Reverenda Fabbrica di San Pietro in Vaticano, Rome.

were illiterate'.[93] In her view, the contrast with Hadrian's epitaph made a decade or so later could not be more stark. Here the text is written in compressed capitals, and the mason used numerous abbreviations and inserted letters to squeeze the text onto the piece of marble, which is framed on two sides by a moulded border. As elsewhere, numerals are marked with a medial punctus, and the inscription begins with a chrismon. The cutting of the letters is crude, but it is legible and regular in letter size and interlinear spacing.

This relic inscription has recently been rescued from epigraphic ignominy by Ballardini who has reconstructed its place and function within John VII's Oratory of the Holy Mother of God.[94] Ballardini's thesis stems from her observations about the piece of marble onto which the text is cut. The inscription has evidently been forced to fit this particular piece of stone; its text is complete, truncated only on the last line. What is striking is that the slab is a piece of *pavonazzetto* marble of the very highest quality; it is directly comparable to the *pavonazzetto* used first for the fourth-century altar of St Peter, and each time thereafter that the high altar over the *confessio* was remodelled. Ballardini suggests that this piece of marble was part of the casing for the altar in the Oratory of the Holy Mother of God, and that the inscription was cut onto it in situ during a rededication of the altar in 783. She suggests that the reference to the precious relic being *bina clusura* ('twice encased') implies that the altar had a second cover with an opening or *fenestella confessionis* to view the relic inside. This would account, in part, both for the compression of the text onto this slab and for the quality of the cutting, rendered more difficult on the vertical plane of the altar. Thus, she has argued, what this inscription lacks in epigraphic quality, it gains in its physical context and content. It is testimony from the middle years of Hadrian's pontificate of papal patronage at the basilica of relics of great sanctity with materials of the highest quality.

Despite the difference in the quality of the letter cutting, the 783 inscription shares more with Hadrian's epitaph than his name. Their intended locations deployed the potency of sacred space for the memorialisation of historical events and, in both instances, the inscription was redeployed and reinterpreted to fit with later medieval and Renaissance concerns. More prosaically, the epigraphic medium and size of the stone placed constraints on the text, but the quality and rarity of the marble used in both cases added value and status to the text and the people associated with it. Much of the meaning of these inscriptions, therefore, lay in that intersection between medium and text within an architectural space that facilitated and encouraged recall and cross referencing to inscriptional texts elsewhere in the basilica, city and beyond.

---

[93] *MEC* I, XIV.4; Gray, 'Palaeography', no. 12; Cascioli, *Epigrapfi Cristiane nell'area vaticana VI–X secolo*, 102–3. See Hartmann, *Hadrian I*, 263 for a similar condemnation of the Latinity of Hadrian's writing office.

[94] Ballardini and Pogliani, 'A Reconstruction of the Oratory', 200–4.

Figure 6.1 The black marble inscription of Verus, *moritex*, from Cologne (dimensions: 104cm × 82cm × 8cm; CIL XIII.8164a = ILS 7522). Photo: Courtesy of the Romisch-Germanisches Museum, Köln.

6

Black Stone

Materials, Methods, and Motives

The exceptional quality of the stone used for the 783 inscription at St Peter's provides another clue to evaluating the epitaph that was sent to Rome after Hadrian's death in 795. One of the most notable features of Hadrian's epitaph is the black stone on which it was cut; fine-grained and monochrome, the dark stone appears unremarkable to modern eyes as an entirely appropriate medium for a funerary inscription.[1] However, the choice of a coloured stone was highly unusual; prior to 800 the norm for monumental stone inscriptions in the western Roman provinces was a light coloured or white ground and it was very rare for inscriptions to be cut on coloured stone. The colour of the stone used for Hadrian's epitaph, would, therefore, have been striking to contemporary viewers, carrying resonances that are different from modern perceptions. In his study of the monuments of Rome, de Rossi knew of none other, pagan or Christian, carved on black stone.[2] Where these are found outside Rome, they come from areas close to sources of black or dark grey stone, such as the Pyrenees or northern Germany.[3] Among the rare northern examples is a votive inscription from Cologne, which names Gaius Aurelius Verus as *negotiator Britannicianus*.[4] This inscription is best known for its use of a Celtic word, *moritex* (attested elsewhere in only one other place), to describe the trading credentials of Verus; but striking also

---

[1] This chapter is based on an article published in *PBSR* in 2005, amplified by additional evidence collected in 2014; J. Story, J. Bunbury, A. C. Felici, G. Fronterotta, M. Piacentini, C. Nicolais, D. Scacciatelli, S. Sciuti, and M. Vendittelli, 'Charlemagne's Black Marble: The Origins of the Epitaph of Pope Hadrian I', *PBSR*, 73 (2005), 157–90. I am grateful to the BSR for permission to re-use the material from the earlier study, and to Ulrike Heckner and Christoph Schaab for sharing data from Aachen, and Francis Tourneur for his assistance with the petrology of the cathedral at Tournai.

[2] De Rossi, 'L'inscription du tombeau', 484.

[3] At Ampurias/Empuries (Girona, Spain) twelve inscriptions cut on local black limestone have been recovered, including a commemorative inscription of Lucius Caecilius Macer, *aedil* and *duumvir* (1st century BC–1st century AD): see G. Fabre, M. Mayer, and I. Rodà, eds, *Inscriptions Romaines de Catalogne*, iii: Gérone (Paris, 1991), 4–5, 70–1, no. 35, pl. XX.

[4] *CIL* XIII.8164a = *ILS* 7522; *Römische Inscriften Datenbank*, no. 4. The dimensions of the inscription are 104.5cm × 82cm × 8.2cm. R. S. O. Tomlin, *Britannia Romana: Roman Inscriptions and Roman Britain* (Oxford and Philadelphia, PA, 2018), 302–5, no. 11.31 (also nos 11.33–5).

was the choice of a black limestone for his inscription, sourced from strata near Namur in Belgium (Figure 6.1).[5]

It is hard to find large-scale, monumental inscriptions with a coloured background in Rome, and where these do occur the material is usually not stone, such as the *Lex de imperio Vespasiani* (*c*. AD 70) (see Figure 5.9) incised in rustic capitals onto a large bronze tablet, or mosaic inscriptions such as that of Pope Celestine at Santa Sabina, Rome (422–32).[6] At Santa Maria Antiqua there are many painted inscriptions, including a large and very competent Greek text from the time of John VII (705–7) which deployed a white uncial lettering set off against a red ground.[7] Other painted texts in the same church have black letters on a yellow ground, and white lettering on black, including the now-fragmentary inscription identifying the donor portrait of Pope Hadrian.[8] It may be that Hadrian's epitaph was intended to recall these other non-lapidary types of inscriptions. Certainly it is of a similar scale and visual impact to the bronze *leges*, which may still have been displayed in Rome at this time, but it is possible also that the black stone was chosen because it had other connotations for the patron who commissioned it and the audience that viewed it.

In the Roman period the geographical origin of marbles was remembered in their names, and so, in pragmatic as well as symbolic ways, the selection of particular marbles resonated with the power of empire to control scarce resources in far-away lands. Thus red porphyry, such as was used for the *rotae* in the pavement of St Peter's, was so called because it came from *Mons Porphyrites* in Egypt; yellow *Lapis Numidicum* came from the land of the Numidians in North Africa; purple-streaked *Phrygium* came from the province of Phrygia in western central Turkey; a white marble

---

[5] On the Celtic word *moritex*, see J. N. Adams, *The Regional Diversification of Latin 200 BC to AD 600* (Cambridge, 2007), 311–12, with reference to the inscription recovered from London in 2007 which contains the phrase *moritex Londiniensium* (RIB: 3014). See also J. Bogaers, 'Foreign Affairs', in B. Hartley and J. Wacher, eds, *Rome and her Northern Provinces: Papers Presented to Sheppard Frere in Honour of his Retirement from the Chair of the Archaeology of the Roman Empire. University of Oxford, 1983* (Gloucester, 1983), 3–32, at 18–21 and pl. IV for discussion of another altar dedicated by Verus to the local goddess Nehalennia, recovered from the Sheldt near Colijnsplaat, dated AD 150–250.

[6] On the medieval history of the *Lex de imperio Vespasiani*, see Krautheimer, *Profile of a City*, 192–3; for the mosaic inscription at Santa Sabina, see Diehl, ed., *Inscriptiones Latinae*, 36 and this volume, Chapter 5, 206, Figure 5.15.

[7] The surviving inscription comprises a text-*catena* of extracts from Canticles and the Books of Amos and Baruch; P. O. Folgerø, 'Expressions of Dogma: Text and Imagery in the Apsidal Arch Decoration of Santa Maria Antiqua', in Rubery, Brodi and Osborne, eds, *Santa Maria Antiqua*, 319–33, figs 1, 8–9.

[8] See above, Fig. 2.1. Grüneisen, *Sainte-Marie-Antique*, 415 and 439, no. 172 (XIII.1, John VII), 421 and 436, no. 126 (IX.9, Hadrian: [Sanct]ISSIMVS [had]RIANVS [papa romanus]), and Federici, ed., *Album Epigraphique*, Pl. IX.9, 10, 13 (Hadrian) and Pl. XIII (John VII). Plates of the latter are in F. de Rubeis, 'Epigrafi a Roma dall'età classica all'alto medioevo', in M. S. Arena, P. Delogu, L. Paroli, M. Ricci, L. Saguì, and L. Venditelli, eds, *Roma dall'antichità al Medioevo: archeologia e storia nel Museo nationale romana, Crypta Balbi*, 2 vols (Rome, 2001), i, 104–21, at 109, fig. 76. See also G. Bordi, 'The Apse Wall of Santa Maria Antiqua' and R. Price, 'The Frescos in Santa Maria Antiqua, the Lateran Synod of 649 and Pope Vitalian', in Rubery, Brodi and Osborne, eds, *Santa Maria Antiqua*, 387–422 and 449–59, figs 1–2.

dramatically veined with black and known as *Aquitanicum* came from the Pyrenees.[9] Coloured marbles such as these were valued not simply for their aesthetic impact but because they provided a material map of empire and, when used in Rome and its provincial capitals, were a bold and physical statement of the mastery of distant lands and peoples. The ability to extract and transport monolithic blocks of marbles great distances across sea and land thus symbolised the dominion of empire over the resources of the natural world in lands far from Rome itself.[10] A Late Antique *opus sectile* floor or wall, made from shaped pieces of these coloured marbles, made manifest this geography of power, and to walk across an *opus sectile* floor was to traverse a map of empire.

Black marble was scarce in Rome. Prominent in the classical sources is the so-called *Lapis Niger* which is an area of paving in the Forum within the *Comitium* opposite the *Curia*, made from black limestone streaked with white veins, that is thought to have come from the Tolfa district north of Rome.[11] The *Lapis Niger* was linked in early imperial texts with the place of the death of Romulus, the legendary founder of Rome; the place (and thus the coloured stone) acquired inauspicious connotations as a *locus funestus*, a place associated with death. However, it is unlikely that the *Lapis Niger* was known by the late eighth century; the area of paving would not have been visible by that date, and it could only have been known indirectly through literary sources that described the antiquities of Rome, namely Sextus Pompeius Festus' epitome of the late first-century BC work of M. Verrius Flaccus.[12] The Lombard scholar Paul the Deacon abridged Festus' work in the 780s, and sent the text to Charlemagne, but he did not select this entry for his epitome.[13] It thus seems unlikely that the *Lapis Niger* was known even as a literary *topos* in Carolingian court circles, in spite of the fact that Pope Hadrian carried out extensive restoration works in that part of the Forum, restoring the *Curia* which was by then a church dedicated to his patronymic saint, the martyr Adrianus.[14]

---

[9] H. Dodge and B. Ward-Perkins, eds, *Marble in Antiquity: The Collected Papers of J. B. Ward Perkins*, Archaeological Monographs of the British School at Rome, 6 (London, 1992), 153–9; Greenhalgh, *Survival of Roman Antiquities*, 126–34; D. P. S. Peacock, *Rome in the Desert: A Symbol of Power* (Southampton, 1993).

[10] For an introduction to the growing literature on this subject, see R. M. Schneider, 'Coloured Marble: The Splendour and Power of imperial Rome', *Apollo* 154 (July 2001), 3–10.

[11] M. Fornaseri, L. Lazzarini, P. Pensabene, M. P. Martinez, and B. Turi, '"Lapis Niger" and Other Black Limestones Used in Antiquity', in Y. Maniatis, N. Herz, and Y. Basiakos, eds, *The Study of Marble and Other Stones Used in Antiquity*, ASMOSIA III, Athens (London, 1995), 235–40.

[12] Festus, *De verborum significatu*, sub n. 'Niger lapis'; W. M. Lindsay, ed., *Glossaria Latina*, 5 vols (Paris, 1926–31), iv, 293; L. D. Reynolds, ed., *Texts and Transmission: A Survey of the Latin Classics* (Oxford, 1983), 162–4; F. Coarelli, 'Sepulchrum Romuli', in E. M. Steinby, ed., *Lexicon Topographicum Urbis Romae* (Roma, 1999), 295–6; T. N. Gantz, 'Lapis Niger: The Tomb of Romulus', *La Parola del Passato. Rivista di Studi Antichi*, 29 (1974), 350–61.

[13] Paul the Deacon, 'Letter to Charlemagne'; Dümmler, ed., MGH, Epp. IV, 508.

[14] *Vita Honori*, ch. 72.6, Davis, tr., *Book of the Pontiffs*, 67; *Vita Hadriani*, LP 97:51, 97:73, 97:81; Davis, tr., *Lives of the Eighth-Century Popes*, 145–6 (n. 83), 160 and 165.

More significant was the marble known later as *nero antico*. The ancient name of this fine-grained black marble is unknown but it was valued as a source for small columns and veneer in the first to third centuries AD, and was sourced in Tunisia.[15] Pliny had known of another 'generally black' marble that was remarkable not just for its colour, but also because it had been named after the consul, Lucullus, who had particularly favoured it, rather than the place where it was quarried.[16] Pliny's discussion of this 'generally black' marble followed immediately after his account of the importation and use in Rome of another variety of coloured stone called *Lapis Numidicum*. This chapter of his *Natural History* seems to have been the source of information for later commentators, such as Vegio, Alfarano, and Grimaldi, who remarked on the unusual character of the stone used for Hadrian's epitaph.[17] Maffeo Vegio, a canon of St Peter's, saw the epitaph in the mid-fifteenth century (*c.*1455) in situ in its original location; he quoted all forty lines of the text, which he said was engraved on a 'remarkable rectangular block of marble' that was 'fixed to the flank of the basilica'.[18] 'The marble', Vegio said, 'is certainly Numidian and black, and is a great rarity'.

Vegio's account of the old basilica, *De rebus antiquis memorabilibus basilicae S. Petri Romae*, is highly regarded by modern scholarship for its historical and archaeological accuracy. A leading humanist and accomplished Latin poet, he sought to pinpoint the location of St Peter's tomb, and used topographical, archaeological, and textual evidence (including inscriptions) to explain the circumstances of the foundation of the basilica over the circus of Nero and to trace its development as the central sanctuary of all Christendom.[19] In this context, he observed and described Hadrian's epitaph, noting the location of the inscription and the state of the oratory following the architectural interventions of Nicholas V (1447–55), and also that the verses revealed that Hadrian had been buried there under Charlemagne's attentive care. In describing the stone of the epitaph as both black and Numidian, Vegio conflated Pliny's comments on two varieties of stone, ascribing the blackness of the marble of Lucullus to the

---

[15] Pliny, *NH* 36.29. R. Gnoli, *Marmora Romana*, rev. edn (Rome, 1988), 193–5; Dodge and Ward-Perkins, eds, *Marble in Antiquity*, 158; G. Borghini and R. Gnoli, eds, *Marmi Antichi*, Materiali della cultura artistica, 1 (Rome, 1998), 254–5.

[16] Pliny, *NH*, 36.8, the reading of the name of the island is uncertain. This marble is now thought probably to be the dark brecchia from Teos in western Turkey (known later as *africano* in ignorance of its origin); M. H. Ballance, 'The Origin of *africano*', *PBSR*, 34 (1966), 79–81; Gnoli, *Marmora Romana*, 174–8, pl. 132–4, 197; Dodge and Ward-Perkins, eds, *Marble in Antiquity*, 157; M. De Nuccio and L. Ungaro, eds, *I Marmi colorati della Roma imperiali* (Venice, 2002), 244, 250–1, 262–5 (for the black marble of Chios, long thought to be that of Lucullus).

[17] De Rossi, 'L'Inscription', 285.

[18] 'Insigne marmor quadratum cum insculptis ei versibus, qui ostendunt ipsum ibi curante Carolo Magno sepultim esse. Est sane marmor Numidicum et atrum ac quale rarum habeatur'; Maffeo Vegio, 'De rebus antiquis memorabilibus basilicae S. Petri Romae'; VZ, iv, 375–98.

[19] C. L. Stinger, *The Renaissance in Rome* (Bloomington, IN, 1998), 179–80; Smith and O'Connor, *Eyewitness to Old St. Peter's*, 201–4 (IV.122–4).

stone imported from Numidia.[20] Pliny had not mentioned the colour of *Lapis Numidicum*, which is in fact bright yellow (it is later called *giallo antico*). In the absence of an adjective, and drawing on the wider connotations of its African origin, Vegio assumed that *Lapis Numidicum* was black like the marble of Lucullus. Deploying the same allusions of colour and exotic origin, Alfarano (*c*.1570) twice referred to the epitaph as *magnus lapis numidicus* and Philippe de Winghe (*c*.1590) agreed, saying that the elegant lettering 'girded with vines' was set *in marmore numidico*.[21] This etymology was confirmed by Grimaldi (1619), who wrote that, 'the epitaph of blessed Hadrian I, *pontifex maximus*, on a great, unbroken, Numidian marble slab of the black stone of Lucullus, from the ruins of the temple, had been fixed to the wall of the old portico'.[22]

Of all the later commentators who mention the material of the epitaph, only Peter Sabin departs from this explanation of provenance. Writing for Charles VIII of France in 1494, he concurred with Vegio's assessment of the rarity and prestige of the stone and of the quality of the lettering but provided an alternative adjective for the stone, describing the verses as having been *incisum in tabula porphyretica litteris elegantissimis*.[23] The stone of Hadrian's epitaph is neither purple (as most porphyry) nor speckled and so, as de Rossi observed, Sabin 'l'avait faussement jugé'. Indeed, Sabin's error in his description of the substance of the stone is in line with the many mistakes made in the transcript of his *sylloge*, condemned by de Rossi to be 'full of errors and the scrappy notes of an inexperienced antiquary'.[24]

'IN FRANCIA': SOURCING THE BLACK STONE

The contemporary *Annales Laureshamenses* (Lorsch Annals) state that the epitaph was made *in Francia* and that it was sent to Rome as a finished object to grace the tomb of the pope.[25] Following the lead of the annals, two main arguments have been proposed for the origin of the black stone, and the location of the workshop where the epitaph was made. In 1888, believing that Alcuin was the author of the epitaph,

---

[20] Vegio discussed Pliny's attribution of black marble to Lucullus, and invented an alternative association with Pescennius Niger, the late second-century challenger to Severus.

[21] Alfarano describes the stone as *magnus lapis numidicus*, *DBV*, III.15 and IX.132, ed., Cerrati, 41–2 and 116. For de Winghe's comment, see de Rossi, 'L'inscription', 482–3.

[22] 'Epitaphium Beati Hadriani primi pontificis maximi in magna integra tabula marmorea Numidica Lucullei lapidis nigri ex temple ruinis in vetere portico muro affixa', Grimaldi, *Descrizione*, 396.

[23] *ICUR* II.i, 411, no. 6.

[24] 'Apographum syllogae Sabinianae...mendosum est exaratumque ab antiquario imperito'; *ICUR* II.i, 409 and 411, n. 6; De Rossi, 'L'inscription d'Hadrien I', 484.

[25] '...ebitaffium aureis litteris in marmore conscriptum iussit in Francia fieri, ut eum partibus Romae transmitteret ad sepultura summi pontificis Adriani ornandam', *Annales Laureshamenses*, s.a. 795, ed., Pertz, MGH, SS I, 36. See also Chapter 2, 102–3.

de Rossi argued that the stone for the inscription had been quarried in western Francia in the vicinity of Alcuin's own monastery at Tours, which had a famous scriptorium and maintained a late-antique tradition of metrical inscriptions.[26] High-quality inscriptions survive from Tours and the surrounding region and although some used slate, none was on the local black limestone. Those that date from the earlier ninth century often used Roman-style capitals, and some of the best had lettering inlaid with lead.[27] De Rossi acquired a sample of a black marble (*noir de Sablé*) from a quarry on the river Sarthe, at Port Étroit, very close to the Benedictine abbey of Solesmes, about 100km north-west of Tours. Noticing that it had broadly similar morphological characteristics to the stone of Hadrian's epitaph, he concluded that the same quarry had been the source for the stone of the epitaph over a thousand years before.[28]

Koehler, however, argued for an east Frankish origin for the stone. His opinion was later developed by Ramackers, who argued that the stone had been sourced much closer to Aachen, in the region around Dinant in modern Belgium.[29] Koehler's and Ramacker's conclusions were based in part on their knowledge of the exploitation of fine black marble from that region in modern times, but more specifically on comparisons of the epigraphy of the inscription with display scripts used in contemporary manuscripts made in the vicinity of Charlemagne's court then based at Aachen.

Underpinning all these arguments was a comparison of the epigraphy of the monument with the palaeography of deluxe Carolingian manuscripts made in the Tours scriptorium and at the court, centred on Aachen. Geological considerations were of secondary significance and were made on the basis of broad probabilities rather than direct comparative petrological analysis of the inscription with possible quarry sources. The imprecision on the petrology of the inscription is largely a result of its inaccessible location. Its current site, more than thirty feet above the ground in the portico of St Peter's, does not lend itself easily to close palaeontological or petrological inspection.

An opportunity to investigate the monument arose in 2002 when the Reverenda Fabbrica di San Pietro gave permission to examine the epitaph and agreed to the use of a scaffolding tower to allow close-up petrological and palaeontological observation, and geochemical analysis of the black marble. The results were compared in the first instance with samples taken from eight modern quarries from the east and west of Charlemagne's Frankish kingdom, and subsequently with samples from the construction phases of Charlemagne's chapel in Aachen. Restoration work on the

---

[26] De Rossi, 'L'inscription', 487–9; E. K. Rand, *A Survey of the Manuscripts of Tours* (Cambridge, MA, 1929), 41–2; Wallach, *Alcuin and Charlemagne*, 178–9; F. de Rubeis, 'Epigrafi a Roma dall'età classica all'alto medioevo', in Arena et al., *Roma dall'antichità al Medioevo*, i, 104–21, at 112–13, fig. 83.

[27] Treffort, *Mémoires carolingiennes*, 345–7 and Treffort, ed., *Épitaphes carolingiennes*, esp. nos 1, 5, 6, 9, 12, 14–16, 20–1, 30, 32, 41, 50, 52, 69.

[28] De Rossi, 'L'inscription', 485.

[29] W. Koehler, *Die karolingischen Miniaturen*, i: *Die Schule von Tours*, 2 vols (Berlin, 1930), i, 87; J. Ramackers, 'Die Werstattheimat der Grabplatte papst Hadrians I', *Romische Quartalschrift*, 59 (1964), 36–78.

chapel, completed in 2014 for the 1,200th anniversary of Charlemagne's death, shows that Charlemagne's architects made copious use of locally sourced black stone (*Blaustein*) in both the masonry and decorative elements of that structure (see below).[30] The Aachen samples provided for comparative analysis derive from the ashlar blocks of the exterior walls of the chapel and the remains of the original Carolingian floor surviving between the south-west piers of the central octagon where floor tiles set on the original Carolingian mortar survived the redecoration programmes and excavations of the early twentieth century. This comparative geological analysis not only enables the identification of the likely source of the stone used for Hadrian's epitaph but also demonstrates conclusively that local sources of black marble were being selectively exploited in the vicinity of Aachen in Charlemagne's reign.

Some basic observations of the stone of the epitaph help quickly to narrow down possible sources. Firstly, it is not a true marble in the technical geological sense of a recrystallised metamorphosed limestone; the word 'marble' is commonly used today, just as it was in antiquity (*marmor*), to describe any hard stone that can take a polish and that was suitable for sculpture or high-quality architecture.[31] Secondly, the stone contains several identifiable fossils, some visible by eye and others with a handheld magnifying glass. The presence of these fossils within a black-coloured matrix confirms that it is a carboniferous limestone. The size, structure, and colour of the epitaph are also important indicators of its petrological qualities; it is a substantial slab measuring 223cm × 116cm. The depth of the inscription is unknown since it is set tightly in a seventeenth-century frame, but is likely to be (at least) 10–20cm in depth. The colour is uniform across the surface of the slab and is now a very dark greenish grey rather than jet black; the matrix is fine-grained, showing no lighter-coloured inclusions and no mineral veins, and the fossils are a similar colour to the rest of the stone. These observations of fossil content, size of the slab, and consistency of colour and texture help to characterize the petrology of the stone and to narrow down possible geological sources.

Black limestones were created across what is now northern Europe during the later Devonian and Carboniferous periods under different marine environments; of these the Belgian sequences are the most substantial and historically the most significant (Figure 6.2). Fluctuations in sea level and changes in the sources of sediment mean that limestones vary palaeontologically and chemically, and strata laid down under different environmental conditions are distinct from each other. Thus, it is possible to distinguish between limestones of different geological stages by comparing the

---

[30] U. Heckner and C. Schaab, 'Baumaterial, Bautechnik und Bauausführung der Aachener Pfalzkapelle', in U. Heckner and E.-M. Beckmann, eds, *Die karolingische Pfalzkaplle in Aachen. Material, Bautechnick, Restaurierung*, Arbeitsheft der rheinischen Denkmalpflege, 78 (Karlsruhe, 2012), 117–228, esp. 137–8.

[31] J. B. Ward-Perkins, 'Materials, Quarries and Transportation', in Dodge and Ward-Perkins, eds, *Marble in Antiquity*, 13–22, at 13–14.

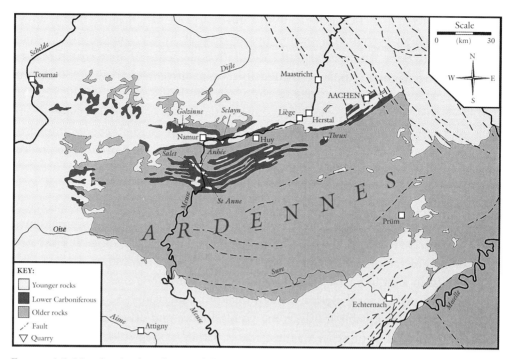

Figure 6.2 Map showing key places and the underlying geology of eastern Francia. © Tom Knott.

geochemistry and fossil content of samples derived from different strata.[32] Comparative analysis of the geochemistry shows that the stone used for the epitaph was most likely to have been sourced from strata of the middle Viséan stage, laid down in the later phases of the Dinantian series within the Carboniferous period. The palaeontology narrows this further, producing a very close analogue with a sample from a quarry at Sclayn, on the south bank of the Meuse, 14km from its confluence with the Sambre at Namur. The 'Mosan marble' produced here (from the strata known as the *Calcaire des Lives*) displays a similar range of fossils in similar density to the stone of the epitaph, with the matrix comprising about 5–10 per cent of the make-up of the rock by volume. The 'Mosan marble' from Sclayn produces a much better parallel to the epitaph than any of the other samples from middle Viséan quarries in Belgium (Anhée) or France (Port Étroit), or from older geological sequences at Salet, St Anne, and Theux (lower Viséan stage), Tournai (Tournaisian stage, Dinantian series), and Golzinne (Frasnian stage, Devonian period).[33]

---

[32] Gnoli, *Marmora Romana*, 194, n. 3; Borghini and Gnoli, eds, *Marmi Antichi*, 256; F. Boulvain, G. Poulain, F. Tourneur, and J. Yans, 'Potential Discrimination of Belgian Black Marbles Using Petrography, Magnetic Susceptibility and Geochemistry', *Archaeometry*, 62 (2020), 469–92, esp. fig. 7.

[33] For details, see Story et al., 'Charlemagne's Black Marble', 169–81. See also Boulvain et al., 'Potential Discrimination', 478–80, 482–3.

There is a considerable history of exploitation of the black limestones in Belgium.[34] Marble known as 'Belgian Black' was very highly valued during the seventeenth and eighteenth centuries because of its homogeneous, intense black colour, and its very fine grain which enabled the creation of complex three-dimensional sculptures. The best source of this 'Belgian Black' comes from Golzinne (Mazy) to the north of Namur, where it is quarried underground. Geologically, however, the black marble from Golzinne significantly predates the Dinantian series of rocks, belonging to the last stage of the Devonian period (middle Frasnian). This is important since, although the Golzinne quarry is close to Namur, to the river Meuse and to the younger marbles of the middle Viséan stage found along the banks of that river, the palaeontology and geochemical properties of marble from Golzinne are quite different from the geologically much younger rocks that outcrop close to the river.[35] The first quarry exploiting marble from the Golzinne area was opened in 1645, and there is no evidence that it was used before that time.

The modern term 'Belgian Black' is also applied to marbles quarried from these lower Viséan strata, near Dinant. The stone from this region was also prized in the seventeenth and eighteenth centuries but could only be quarried in blocks of relatively small size; it was used therefore for floor tiles and tomb slabs (and is now quarried at Salet) (Figure 6.3).[36] There is some textual evidence for the use of the stone in the later Middle Ages, and surviving tomb monuments such as the tomb of John the Fearless (1371–1419) in Dijon and other royal tombs at Saint-Denis in Paris show that it was used for high-status commissions.[37] Marble from thicker middle Viséan layers was preferred for Romanesque sculpture, especially fonts, in the twelfth and thirteenth centuries.[38] Many survive within the diocese of Liège, some very finely carved, others with less sophistication. The colour of the stone is often quite grey from atmospheric exposure and weathering, but where features and figures have been polished a smooth, shiny black patina is created.

The famous black stone of Tournai in western Belgium is representative of the lower Carboniferous period and so is geologically older than the Viséan series; thus it has different lithological and palaeontological properties, and ages differently from

---

[34] Boulvain et al., 'Potential Discrimination', 470–2; F. Tourneur, 'Global Heritage Stone: Belgian Black 'Marbles', in T. J. Hannibal, S. Kramar, and B. J. Cooper, eds, *Global Heritage Stones: Worldwide Examples of Heritage Stones*, Geological Society Special Publications, 486 (London, 2020), 129–47.

[35] E. Groessens, 'L'industrie du marbre en Belgique', *Mémoires de l'Institut Géologique de l'Université de Louvain*, 31 (1981), 219–53, at 222; Boulvain et al., 'Potential Discrimination', 475, 487.

[36] Boulvain et al., 'Potential Discrimination', 476–8.

[37] E. Groessens, 'L'exploitation et l'emploi du marbre noir de Dinant sous "Ancien Régime"', in J. Lorenz, ed., *Carrières et constructions en France et dans les pays limitrophes,* III (119ᵉ Congrès national des sociétés historiques scientifiques, 1994 Amiens) (Paris, 1996), 73–87; B. Delcambre and J. L. Pingot, *Hastiere–Dinant: Carte géologique de Wallonie, Notice Explicative* (Namur, n.d.), 49.

[38] L. Tollenaere, *La sculpture sur pierre de l'ancien diocèse de Liège a l'époque romane* (Gembloux, 1957), 157–65.

Figure 6.3 The modern quarry at Salet, Belgium (lower Viséan). Photo: Author.

the Viséan rocks, developing a yellowish tinge as the surface layers oxidise.[39] The black stone from Tournai is well known to scholars of medieval sculpture, especially through the fonts and low-relief tomb monuments that were exported up the river Schelde into southern and eastern England in the twelfth and thirteenth centuries.[40] It is also

---

[39] F. Anderson and E. Groessens, 'The Black Altars of Nehalennia', *Oufheidkundige mededelingen uit het Rijksmuseum van oudheden te Leiden, Nieuwe Reeks*, 76 (1996), 129–38, at 133.

[40] Boulvain et al., 'Potential Discrimination', 470–2; F. Tourneur and E. Groessens, 'Le matériau, d'ici et d'ailleurs', in L. Nys and L. D. Caterman, eds, *La sculpture gothique à Tournai. Splendeur, ruines, vestiges* (Brussels, 2018), 46–55.

the primary building stone of the Gothic cathedral at Tournai, constructed *c*.1220–40. It was exploited also in the Roman period. Tournai was an active quarrying centre and stones from that region were transported along the Schelde for use in the construction of the third-century coastal fort at Aardenburg. Black Tournai stone was used in the construction of its walls, the *principia*, and two towers, and it has been suggested that an internal temple at the site may have been made of polished black marble. Black stone was also used at the nearby Saxon shore fort at Oudenburg, from where it was quarried for reuse in the walls of Bruges in the late eleventh century.[41] It has also been argued that the stone of the eastern Belgian site at Theux (where a window of lower Viséan rock outcrops) was used in the Roman period, but the argument has been confused by a misplaced nineteenth-century attempt to associate this source with Pliny's Lucullan marble.[42]

Roman quarries were also worked along the banks of the river Meuse between Namur and Liège, producing middle Viséan 'Mosan marble'. Fragments of black stone from this phase are known from the Roman villa at Echternach, Luxembourg, and from several funerary slabs dating from the late first to mid-third century from the citadel at Namur (*Civitas Tungrorum*), such as that bearing the name of Cassio, discovered in 1999.[43] A third-century altar and the octagonal itinerary column from Tongeren, Belgium, now in the Musées Royaux du Cinquantenaire in Brussels, are also made from black Mosan marble (Figure 6.4).[44] A fragmentary late fifth or early sixth-century funerary inscription from the Abbey of St Servatius in Maastricht was made from a piece of the same stone, possibly spolia.[45] Black Mosan marble is also the

---

[41] Anderson and Groessens, 'Black Altars', 132.

[42] P. den Dooven, 'Histoire de la Marbrerie antique de Theux et les tombeaux des la Marck dans l'Eifel', *Bulletin Société Verviétoise d'Archéologie et d'Histoire*, 53 (1966), 115–55; E. M. Wightman, *Gallia Belgica* (London, 1985), 136; Boulvain et al., 'Potential Discrimination', 478. A small building with wall mosaics of glass *tesserae* of Merovingian date has recently been excavated there; F. Theuws, 'Maastricht as a Centre of Power', in M. de Jong, F. Theuws, and C. van Rhijn, eds, *Topographies of Power in the Early Middle Ages* (Leiden, 2001), 155–216, at 208, n. 172.

[43] A. Deman and M.-T. Raepsaet-Charlier, *Nouvelle recueil des Inscriptions latines de Belgique* (Brussels, 2002), 262–4, no. 166; R. Frei-Stolba, 'Belgique', *Année Épigraphique*, 2002 (2005), 357–65, no. 1012 ('Mosan marble', discovered in excavation in 1999). See also the late first-century inscription honouring Sicinius Flauinus, discovered in 1991; M.-T. Raepsaet-Charlier, 'Belgique', *Année Épigraphique* 1998 (2001), 354–6, no. 0951 ('calcaire de Meuse').

[44] Groessens, 'L'industrie', 228; Anderson and Groessens, 'Black Altars', 133. For the Tongeren itinerary column (Inv. No. B000189-001), see: *CIL* XIII 9158 = XVII/2 675; F. Cumont, *Catalogue des sculptures et inscriptions antiques (Monuments Lapidaires) des Musées Royaux du cinquantenaire* (Brussels, 1913), 235–8, no. 196; B. Salway, 'Putting the World in Order: Mapping in Roman Texts', in R. J. A. Talbert, ed., *Ancient Perspectives: Maps and their Place in Mesopotamia, Egypt, Greece and Rome* (Chicago, IL, 2012), 193–234, at 205–6, fig. 7.6.

[45] T. Panhuysen, 'Maastricht, centre de production de sculptures gallo-romaines et d'inscriptions paléo-chrétiennes', *Studien zur Sachsenforschung* 8 (Hildesheim, 1993), 83–96, no. 4; W. Boppert, 'Die frühchristlichen Grabinschriften aus der Servatiuskirche in Maastricht', in C. G. De Dijn, ed., *Sint-Servatius, bisschop van Tongeren-Maastricht (Actes du Colloque à Alden biesen (Bilzen), Tongres et Maastricht 1984)* (Borgloon-Rijkel, 1986), 64–96, at 80–3.

Figure 6.4 Octagonal itinerary column from Tongeren, Belgium, made of black Mosan marble (36cm × 38cm). Brussels, Musées Royaux d'Art et d'Histoire, Inv. No. B000189-001. Photo: CC BY–MRAH/KMKG.

material of several of the remarkable group of altars dedicated to the goddess Nehalennia recovered from a temple site off the Dutch coast at Colijnsplaat, transported there via the Meuse to the mouth of the Rhine. Seventeen whole or fragmentary altars made from this type of black stone are among a large group of monuments dredged from the site, bearing votive inscriptions to Nehalennia (Figure 6.5).[46] Among these three hundred altars is another dedicated by G. Aurelius Verus, the *negotiator Britannicianus moritex* who had sponsored the black stone inscription to Apollo found in Cologne.[47] This group of inscriptions, along with one from London that names another *moritex*, are almost unparalleled in the Roman world for their focus on the activities of sea-faring traders.

---

[46] About three hundred complete or fragmentary altars dated *c*. AD 150–250 were dredged from the site (most made of 'white' limestone); P. Stuart and J. E. Bogaers, *Nehalennia. Römische Steindenkmäler aus der Oosterschelde bei Colijnsplaat* (*Corpus signorum Imperii Romani, Nederland 2, Collections of the National Museum of Antiquities at Leiden*, IX), 2 vols (Leiden, 2001), i: 18, 132–7, 147–8, 156–7, 184, tav. 91–2, 101.

[47] Bogaers, 'Foreign Affairs', 18–21 and pl. IV.

Figure 6.5 Altar to the goddess Nehalennia, from Colijnsplaat, Netherlands, made of black Mosan marble. Photo: Courtesy of the Rijksmuseum van Oudheden, Leiden.

The use of black Mosan marble for votive inscriptions not least by traders who had links to Britain and the wider world, and the regional movement of these artefacts in the Roman period, finds echoes in two Carolingian texts that stress the desirability of the black stones of this region and their use in a religious context. Hincmar of Reims wrote to his diocesan priests *c.*856, instructing them to make altars *de marmore vel nigra petra*, suggesting that in the mid-ninth century black stone was both attainable and prestigious, and was as suitable as marble as a material for altars.[48] The value and desirability of black stone is emphasised also in a letter sent some sixty years earlier, from Charlemagne to Offa, king of the Mercians. This letter was written in the first half of 796 when Charlemagne was at Aachen, following the death of Hadrian the previous Christmas and before news of the assassination in mid-April of the Northumbrian king, Æthelred, had reached Francia. It covers a variety of topics of concern to the two rulers, including the fate of political exiles, the reciprocal treatment of traders and pilgrims, and Charlemagne's gift of alms to the episcopal sees of Mercia and Northumbria for intercessions for the soul of Hadrian.[49] Among the important issues discussed, Charlemagne's letter also dwells on the topic of *petrae nigrae* ('black stones') that Offa had asked to be sent to him:

> As for the black stones which your Reverence demands urgently to be sent to you, let a messenger come, who may consider what sort you have in mind, and wherever they are to be found we will willingly order them to be given and to help with their transport. But just as you have intimated your wishes concerning the length of the stones [*de longitudine petrarum*], so our people make a demand about the size of the cloaks, that you may order them to be such as used to come to us in times past.[50]

It is striking that this dialogue about *petrae nigrae* is exactly contemporaneous with the creation of the epitaph. The form and function of the black stones that Offa wanted from Francia is not specified in Charlemagne's letter but they were evidently worthy of extended negotiation between the two kings. Levison thought that the reference in Charlemagne's letter might have been for building stones, but others have favoured a more prosaic interpretation arguing that these *petrae nigrae* were quern stones made of dark Mayen lava, commonly imported into Britain in earlier

---

[48] Hincmar, *Capitula synodica*, III.3, PL 125, col. 794C; M. McCormick, *Origins of the European Economy: Community and Commerce, AD 300–900* (Cambridge, 2001), 700.

[49] See Chapter 2, 104 and Chapter 7, 313. *Alc. Ep.*, no. 100; Dümmler, ed., MGH, Epp. IV, 144–6; Whitelock, tr., *EHD* I, no. 197 and Allott, tr., *Alcuin*, no. 40. The letter was written after Hadrian's death but before news of the assassination of Æthelred of Northumbria on 18 April 796 had reached Francia.

[50] 'Petras vero nigras, quas vestra flagitabat reverentia vobis diregi, veniat missus qui considerat, quales animus vester desideret. Et ubicumque inventi fuerint, dari et in vehendo adiuari libenter mandabimus. Sed dicut vos de longitudine petrarum desiderium vestrum intimastis, ita et nostri de prolixitate sagorum depuscunt: ut tales iubeatis fieri, quales antiquis temporibus ad nos venire solebant', Alcuin, *Ep.* no. 100, lines 36–41.

centuries.[51] However, the letter clearly specifies that it is the length of the stones that is important to Offa and this, along with the rather quotidian character of quern stones, makes them an unlikely candidate for the kings' attention.[52] It is notable too that, although Charlemagne readily agreed to supply Offa with black stones and to help with their transport in the future, he did not in fact hand over any on this occasion and instead imposed two prior conditions: first, another messenger must come from England with more information about exactly what sort of stone was required; second, Offa must intercede to ensure that textiles exported from England conformed to the demands of the Frankish export market. The wording here implies direct royal control of a scarce, desirable resource both via the supply of the raw material and through its onward transportation. Offa's persistent demands for this material and Charlemagne's apparent ability to control its supply evidently gave the Frankish ruler some diplomatic leverage in his dealings with the Mercian king.

The letter also says that the Charlemagne would source the black stones, 'wherever (*ubicumque*) they are to be found'. This, in combination with the request for more specificity about the type of stone required, may imply local knowledge of sources of stone with different properties, and also that acquisition of those materials required the cognisance and permission of the king. There are two possible types of source: firstly, local quarries that produced black stones of different dimensions and properties; secondly, that black stones were acquired through the spoliation of Roman sites—either locally in the region where the king was based, or from much more distant sites. Peacock argued that the reference to the length of the 'black stones' that Offa required meant that he was after columns rather than querns, the length of which would be crucial. Furthermore, he argued that such columns must have been spolia from Roman sites in Italy rather than ones quarried *de novo* in Francia in the later eighth century. Charlemagne's comment in his letter to Offa that he would arrange collection of the black stones from 'wherever they are to be found' could refer to local supplies from open quarries or Roman buildings within his own family estates and need not refer to spolia collected in Italy as Peacock suggests. Peacock rejected on chronological grounds the notion that the black marbles of Belgium were the topic of Charlemagne's deliberations with Offa, arguing that Tournai marble was not imported into Britain before the twelfth century, and that the other zones of black marble around the Meuse valley were not exploited before the nineteenth century.[53] But, as we have seen, the evidence of the Nehalennia altars and other objects proves that

---

[51] Levison, *England and the Continent*, 111; P. Rahtz, 'Medieval Milling', in D. W. Crossley, ed., *Medieval Industry, Council for British Archaeology Research Reports*, 40 (London, 1981), 1–15; R. Hodges, *Dark Age Economics: The Origin of Towns and Trade, AD 600–1000* (London, 1982), 124, and R. Hodges, *The Anglo-Saxon Achievement* (London, 1989), 136. Examples of these quern stones are in SW, 799, i, VI.80 a–d.

[52] D. P. S. Peacock, 'Charlemagne's Black Stones: The Re-Use of Roman Columns in Early Medieval Europe', *Antiquity*, 71 (1997), 709–15, at 709.

[53] Peacock, 'Charlemagne's Black Stones', 709–10.

Mosan marble was exploited in the Roman period and was transported away from its source, downstream to the Rhine delta. The same is true of black stones from Tournai.

BLACK STONES AND THE MEUSE VALLEY IN THE AGE OF CHARLEMAGNE

The Meuse is one of the major rivers of Francia, central to the eastern kingdom of Austrasia, providing a communication link northwards and, through its proximity in its upper reaches to the Rhône-Saône axis, to the southern provinces and the Mediterranean.[54] It rises in the plateau of Langres and flows north through the forested lands of the Ardennes, cutting and exposing the carboniferous limestone geology between Dinant and Namur. At Namur it joins the course of the Sambre and turns eastwards, following the line of the geology (exposing the coal and dolomite), before turning north again at Liège, through Maastricht, to Frisia, the Rhine delta and the North Sea.

From the mid-seventh to early eighth centuries this region formed a discrete political unit—the kingdom of Austrasia—which was one of the three major units of Merovingian Francia and often in political opposition to Neustria and Burgundy. It was here that the Carolingian (Pippinid) dynasty rose to prominence from the ranks of the Austrasian aristocracy, acquiring political influence and control of the region through marriage into families that had well-established claims to lands and monastic foundations around the central Meuse valley.[55] The charter evidence suggests that the core of the family lands lay to the west of Namur, focused around the monastery of Nivelles that had been founded *c.*640 on lands owned by Itta, the wife of Pippin I and Charlemagne's great-great-great grandmother. Pippin II (d. 714) extended the family's influence further south by marrying Plectrude, whose family had founded the monastery at Echternach and controlled great tracts of land in the Ardennes and the middle Moselle region. He consolidated his influence further east by marrying again into another family based in Maastricht, which possessed lands around Liège. The lower Meuse came under his control through the conquest of Frisia in the 690s and the consequent division of land, churches, and monasteries among men loyal to him and to Plectrude and her sons. This policy was disliked by the aristocracy of Liège-Maastricht, who resented the intrusion of Plectrude's southerners into a region which

---

[54] F. Rousseau, *La Meuse et le pays Mosan. Leur importance historique avant le XIIIe siècle* (Namur, 1930); A. Dierkens, ed., *Mosa Nostra. La Meuse mérovingienne de Verdun à Maastricht Ve–VIIIe siècles* (Namur, 1999).

[55] The most important studies of the aristocratic families of the early medieval Meuse region are: M. Werner, *Der Lütticher Raum in frükarolingischerzeit: Untersuchungen zur Geschichte einer karolingischen Stammlandschaft*, Veröffentlichungen des Max-Planck-Instituts für Geschichte, 62 (Göttingen, 1980); R. A. Gerberding, *The Rise of the Carolingians and the 'Liber Historiae Francorum'* (Oxford 1987), 116–45 and map 2; Theuws, 'Maastricht', 186–93 and fig. 8.

they felt should have come within the diocese of Tongeren/Maastricht/Liège.[56] Charles Martel, Pippin's son by his second wife, was eventually able to overturn the influence of Plectrude and to succeed his father as mayor of the palace in Austrasia by marshalling this unrest among the local aristocracy of Liège-Maastricht, where his own maternal family was based, against the considerable forces of his step-mother, culminating in his victory at Amblève in April 716. It was from here that Charles was able to gather sufficient strength to take on the Neustrian forces and to become de facto ruler of all Francia, as his father had been before him.[57]

The central Meuse valley was thus a crucial powerbase for the nascent Carolingian dynasty in the late seventh and early eighth centuries, articulated by a network of aristocratic centres that either belonged to the immediate family of Charles Martel or identified with his cause. The creation of a new cult centre at Liège in the early eighth century focused on the remains of the martyred bishop Lambert was a demonstration of Pippinid power within the extensive diocese of Tongeren/Maastrich/Liège, and served to marginalise the claims of other regional aristocratic families to control of the bishopric and its dispersed estates, and to act as an alternative focus to the royal demesne focused on Maastricht.[58] Namur had been a stronghold of the Pippinid family since the time of Pippin I in the earlier seventh century, and his wife Itta seems also to have owned lands through her family further downstream around Andenne.[59] Their daughter Begga founded a monastery at Andenne, which probably lay within a bigger estate that straddled the river and included Seilles, Landenne, and Vezin on the north bank and Andenne, Sclayn, Bonneville, and Coutisse to the south.[60]

Begga's monastery at Andenne never rivalled that of her sister Geretrude at Nivelles, which over time became one of the most influential royal nunneries in Francia, but the location of Andenne on the banks of the Meuse was an important marker of Pippinid presence which complemented the family's other centres of power along the central Meuse, such as Namur, Huy, Chèvremont/Liège, and the *palatia publica* at Jupille and Herstal.[61] Werner and Theuws have shown how the social landscape of the central Meuse became Carolingianised during the eighth century as the properties possessed

---

[56] Gerberding, *Rise of the Carolingians*, 125–8.

[57] P. Fouracre, *The Age of Charles Martel* (Harlow, 2000), 61–4; Gerberding, *Rise of the Carolingians*, 180; Theuws, 'Maastricht', 180.

[58] Theuws, 'Maastricht', 174–91.

[59] Gerberding, *Rise of the Carolingians*, 99, 125; Theuws, 'Maastricht', 188–90, n. 100; Y. Fox, *Power and Religion in Merovingian Gaul: Columbanian Monasticism and the Frankish Elites*, Cambridge Studies in Medieval Life and Thought, 4th ser. (Cambridge, 2014), 182–3, 271.

[60] For the possible boundaries of the estate, see G. Despy, 'Henri IV et la fondation du chapitre de Sclayn', in *Mélanges Félix Rousseau: Études sur l'histoire du pays mosan au moyen age* (Brussels, 1958), 221–36. Seilles is later mentioned as Carolingian property; the *ARF s.a.* 806 report that Charlemagne met his eldest son and the army there; F. Kurze, ed., MGH, SRG (Berlin 1895), 122; Theuws, 'Maastricht', 209.

[61] Theuws, 'Maastricht', 192–3, 209. See, for example, the high-status settlement site at Thier d'Olne, near Amay, in F. Pohle, ed., *Karl der Grosse/Charlemagne. Orte der Macht: Katalog* (Aachen, 2014), 114–19.

by Pippin's family along the Meuse and its hinterland were amplified by additional estates to the east of the river, including that which later became Charlemagne's favoured residence at Aachen 40km to the east of Herstal.[62] Theuws has shown how the middle Meuse valley became the heartland of the Carolingian dynastic powerbase, with a dense network of royal palaces and estates, and riverine trading sites that had access to the coast.[63] These family Carolingian estates included the areas that produce the black Mosan marbles, and Charlemagne's comments in his letter to Offa would fit the notion of royal control over the supply of high-status raw materials. The modern quarry at Sclayn even lies within the suggested boundaries of the estate on which the monastery of Andenne was founded, and an earlier quarry (possibly Roman in origin) lies between it and Namur. Local white limestone from this area was certainly used in the early Middle Ages, especially for sarcophagi and monumental sculpture.[64] Located on the banks of the Meuse, stone quarried from Sclayn or nearby sites could be transported long distances by water with comparative ease.

BLACK STONES AT AACHEN

Recent excavation and restoration work at Aachen has revealed important new information about the materials, technology, and dating of the construction of Charlemagne's palace complex. Dendrochronological analysis of wooden piles from the foundations of the chapel and anchor-ties at the top of the cupola provide dates of 798 (± 5) and 803 (± 10), respectively, giving parameters of *c*.793–813 for the construction of the chapel. A solitary coin, minted at the West Frankish mint at Melles following Charlemagne's 794 coinage reform, was recovered at ground-floor level, and is thought to have been deposited during construction phases.[65] The recent restoration work has also examined the types and sources of the stone used in the construction of the chapel (and subsequent restorations), and shows that the Carolingian builders used a variety of types of local stones. The dominant building

---

[62] Werner, *Der Lütticher Raum*, map 14; Theuws, 'Maastricht', 208–13; M. Untermann, '*Opere mirabile constructa*: Die Aachener 'Residenz' Karl des Grossen', in SW, *799*, iii, 152–64; J. L. Nelson, 'Aachen as a Place of Power', in De Jong, Theuws, and van Rijn, eds, *Topographies of Power*, 217–41.

[63] F. Theuws, 'Das mittlere Maastal und wie es zu einem Kerngebeit des Karolingerreichs wurde', in Pohle, ed., *Karl der Grosse/Charlemagne*, 200–9.

[64] See especially the sarcophagus of St Chrodoara at Amay; F. Tourneur, 'Le travail de la pierre', in Dierkens, ed., *Mosa Nostra*, 40, 56–57; J. Stiennon, 'Le sarcopharge de Sancta Chrodoara à St.-Georges d'Amay. Essai d'interprétation d'une découverte exceptionnelle', *Comptes rendus des seeances de l'Académie des Inscriptions et Belles-Lettres*, 123 (1979), 10–31.

[65] T. Kohlberger-Schaub and A. Schaub, 'Neues zu Bau und Bauplatz der Marienkirche. Die Domgrabung 2007 bis 2011', in Pohle, ed., *Karl der Grosse: Essays* (Aachen, 2014), 364–9, at 366; U. Heckner 'Der Tempel Salomos in Aachen – Datierung und geometrischer Entwurf der karolingischen Pfalzkapelle', in U. Heckner and E.-M. Beckmann, eds, *Die karolingische Pfalzkapelle in Aachen. Material, Bautechnik, Restaurierung* (Worms, 2012), 25–62, at 25 and Abb. 4.

stone is a variety of sandstone known as greywacke, which was used to make up the main body of the walls. For the loadbearing parts of the building, that is, the lower levels of the foundations, the corners and angles of the exterior walls of the chapel and western portico, and the stringcourse between the lower and upper floors, the Carolingian architects made use of larger ashlar blocks, made mostly of locally sourced limestone of various types, with some local sandstones.[66] Among these are blocks of a very dark grey limestone, given the generic label *Blaustein* in German. This broad term includes the black/dark grey limestones of the lower Carboniferous, including the Dinantian series that are found further west. Indeed, the Viséan stages of that formation which outcrop along the banks of the Meuse (producing 'Mosan marble') continue eastwards below ground, emerging at Theux in eastern Belgium and around Kornelimünster and Hastenrath (Stolenberg) to the south and east of Aachen, respectively, where they are currently quarried. The term *Blaustein* is also applied to the thicker bands of dark grey [shelly] limestone that derive from the Frasnian stages of the Devonian period and which emerge a short way from Kornelimünster at Hahn (Walheim).[67] Excavations within Aachen itself, close to the location of the Roman bath complex, revealed a source of 'jet black' *Blaustein* only a few metres below the ground surface, suggesting that small lenses of the stone could be sourced in the immediate vicinity of the palace.[68]

Blaustein was used throughout the external masonry of the chapel, usually in the form of squared, ashlar blocks, shaped where necessary to function in the angles of the superstructure (Figure 6.6). In some places smaller pieces were used within the make-up of the wall, revealing perhaps the delivery of a cartload of small pieces of *Blaustein* to the masons at work on the construction of the chapel.[69] The blocks made of this material have been recognised only recently, since they had weathered over time so that the surface of them had become almost white, disguising the extensive use of the distinctively coloured *Blaustein* in the fabric of the chapel.[70] Following restoration, the stone now appears grey/blue, and some blocks have distinctive white veins running through them. Some of the larger blocks are clearly reused from Roman structures (Figure 6.6) displaying clamp holes in the sides and centrally placed lewis holes, made to lift and fix the stone into place in its original location. It is likely that most of

---

[66] Heckner and Schaab, 'Baumaterial', at 117–228, esp. 137–8 and fig. 17. Currently quarried at Blees/Kornelimünster and Meyer/Hastenrath.

[67] An der Kier quarry; S. Siegesmund, W-D. Grimm, H. Dürrast, and J. Ruedrich, 'Limestones in Germany used as Building Stones: An Overview', in B. J. Smith, M. Gomez-Heras, H. A. Viles, and J. Cassar, eds, *Limestone in the Built Environment: Present-Day Challenges for the Preservation of the Past*, Geological Society, Special Publication, 331 (London, 2010), 37–60, at 43, tab. 1.

[68] Heckner and Schaab, 'Baumaterial', 138.

[69] See especially the lower parts of the south wall of the chapel; Heckner and Schaab, 'Baumaterial', fig. 98 and 101. For a verse invocation of wagons and masons at the palace, see *Karolus Magnus et Leo Papa*, lines 111–22; Dümmler, ed., *PLAC* I, 366–79, at 368–9; Godman, *Poetry*, 202–5.

[70] Heckner and Schaab, 'Baumaterial', 138, 165 (fig. 90) and 174 (fig. 98).

FIGURE 6.6 *Blaustein* blocks in the masonry of the NNW exterior wall of the Carolingian chapel at Aachen. Note the large block with clamp and lewis holes showing likely reuse from a Roman structure. Photo: Author.

the large dressed stones were recycled from Roman buildings in the vicinity, and that Carolingian architects selected squared blocks of *Blaustein* and other varieties of local limestone and sandstone for their structural as well as aesthetic properties.[71]

Inside the chapel, black stone was employed both in the fabric of the structure and for decorative elements. Again, the recent restoration work has produced evidence of

[71] Heckner and Schaab, 'Baumaterial', 128–9.

the materials and methods employed by the Carolingian architects.[72] Marking out lines are clearly visible cut into the surface of a set of substantial *Blaustein* blocks close to one of the northern piers of the octagon.[73] Also, part of the original floor surface has survived on the ground floor, around Piers 3 and 4 in the south-west section of the central octagon, revealing sections of the Carolingian tiles and mortar that survived the extensive remodelling of the early twentieth century when a new Cosmatesque pavement was laid and the interior walls clad with coloured marble veneers and new mosaics. The Carolingian floor slabs are made from long black limestone slabs $c.8$–10cm thick, some with clear horizontal layering and others with white veins. Crucially, these slabs are set in mortar of the type that was used throughout the building by the Carolingian masons thereby demonstrating contemporaneity with the construction of the building.[74] The excavators think that these long black stone slabs framed rectangular mosaics of *opus sectile* and *opus regulatum* that were set between the columns. Evidence of mosaics of this sort, in eight different designs, has been preserved in the upper level of the chapel where the mosaics were framed by light coloured marble (in contrast to the black frames on the ground floor); early modern sources suggest that a similar decorative scheme was originally on the ground floor as well.[75] The *opus regulatum* mosaics built of small square tesserae are probably of Carolingian manufacture, imitating late antique designs. The *opus sectile* pavements, made of larger shaped pieces of coloured marble, however, are more certainly spolia, taken from Roman structures. The evidence for this is partly textual and partly archaeological; the *opus sectile* fragments found in situ on the upper floor were in-filled around the edges with *opus tessellatum* made of irregular tesserae suggesting that the panels of *opus sectile* were not designed to fit the polygonal area between the columns and the outer wall of the chapel, and had to be adapted to fit those areas (Figure 6.7).[76] This situation is paralleled by the variety of column capitals used at Aachen; some are clearly antique, but others were probably made in Carolingian times using local stone and reflecting knowledge of the form of late antique exemplars.[77]

---

[72] Heckner and Schaab, 'Baumaterial', 138. On the floor, see especially U. Heckner, 'Wie sah der karolingische Fußboden in der Aachener Pfalzkapelle aus?', *Jahrbuch der Rheinischen denkmalpflege*, 42 (2011), 29–39.

[73] Kohlberger-Schaub and Schaub, 'Neues zu Bau und Bauplatz der Marienkirche', 368, and fig. 4.

[74] The presence of the distinctive Carolingian mortar is important because regular square *Blaustein* tiles were laid on both floors of the chapel by the mid-sixteenth century. On the analysis of the Carolingian pink mortar, see Heckner and Schaab, 'Baumaterial', 138–43, and C. Goedicke, 'Datierung von Ziegelfragmenten und Mörtel aus der Pfalzkapelle Aachen mittels optisch stimulierter Lumineszenz', in Heckner and Beckmann, eds, *Die karolingische Pfalzkaplle in Aachen*, 297–302.

[75] L. Konnegen, 'Stiftmosaikboden (Frament)', in *Karl der Grosse. Orte der Macht. Katalog*, 178, no. 205 (*opus regulatum*), also nos 209 and 210; SW, 799, i, 107–10, II.67 (*opus regulatum*) and II.68 (*opus sectile*).

[76] Heckner, 'Wie sah der karolingische Fußboden', 31 and figs 4–5.

[77] F. Kreusch, 'Im Louvre wiedergefundene kapitele und bronzbasen aus der Pflazkirche Karls des Grossen zu Aachen', *Cahiers archéologiques fin de l'antiquité et moyen âge* 18 (1968), 71–98, at 75–7; Heckner and Schaab, 'Baumaterial', 192–9.

Figure 6.7 Opus sectile from the upper floor at Aachen. Photo: Courtesy of Ulrike Heckner.

Black stone of more exotic origin and certain antiquity was on prominent display elsewhere in the chapel. Nineteen antique columns survive in the building and, of these, two are made of very rare black porphyry, although they are no longer in situ (Figure 6.8).[78] Of the rest, there is a marked preference for grey marbles and granites, which had come originally from the imperial quarries in Eastern Turkey and Egypt.[79] The black porphyry columns in Charlemagne's chapel are too slim and too short to have been used in the structure of the central octagon, and are thought to have come from a structure such as a chancel barrier sited on the east side of the gallery, opposite the king's throne and over the altar on the ground floor below. They are topped by antique Corinthian capitals and stand on bronze bases that were probably made for them in the late eighth century.[80] The columns are significant; black porphyry is exceedingly scarce, and it would have been of immense value and prestige in the

---

[78] SW, 799 i, II.69.

[79] Dodge and Ward Perkins, eds, *Marble in Antiquity* 152–9; J. C. Fant, 'Ideology, Gift, and Trade: A Distribution Model for the Roman Imperial Marbles', in W. V. Harris, ed., *The Inscribed Economy: Production and Distribution in the Roman Empire in the Light of 'instrumentum domesticum'*, JRA Supplementary Series, 6 (Ann Arbor, MI, 1993), 145–70, at 164–5.

[80] Kreusch, 'Im Louvre wiedergefundene kapitelle und bronzbasen', 89 (for a comparative analysis of the metal of the bases).

BLACK STONE: MATERIALS, METHODS, AND MOTIVES 249

FIGURE 6.8 Black porphyry columns in Aachen. Reproduced by permission of the Domkapitel Aachen. Photo: Ann Münchow/Pit Siebigs.

Roman world. Porphyry was the stone of Imperial Rome *par excellence*. It comes only from the quarries at *Mons Porphyrites* in Egypt and was normally purple in colour. Its exotic origin, the difficulty of extraction and transport, as well as its intense purple colour meant that it more than any other stone came to symbolise imperial power, and efforts were made to limit its use to imperial projects. Black porphyry could be extracted from only a few places on the mountain, and was thus even rarer than the purple variety; Peacock argued that it may have had 'a value almost beyond comprehension'.[81] Objects made from black porphyry are few and far between, which makes it difficult to generalise about their primary use; Gnoli knew only of two other columns which are said to have come from an altar commemorating the decapitation of St Paul in the church of San Paolo alle Tre Fontane ('Ad Aquas Salvias') south of Rome on the Via Laurentina where the saint was said to have been martyred.[82] Two more stand at the entrance to the *capella* of San Zeno in Santa Prassede, Rome (Figure 6.9). Another black porphyry column is to be found—with four regular porphyry columns—in the apse of the thirteenth-century cathedral in Magdeburg, perhaps reused from the tenth-century palace of Otto I nearby.[83]

SPOLIA—NEAR AND FAR

The fabric of Charlemagne's chapel shows that worked stone from Roman buildings was used both for structural and decorative elements of the building. The structural material—ashlar blocks made of *Blaustein* as well as other local varieties of limestone and sandstone—was doubtless acquired from old buildings in the region or quarried afresh. Decorative elements could have been sourced locally too, from imperial structures that survived north of the Alps, although textual evidence suggests that worked stone was also bought from Italy. A letter from Hadrian survives in the *Codex Carolinus* in which he gave Charlemagne's agents permission to collect 'mosaic and marbles and other specimens from the pavements and walls' of a palace in Ravenna.[84] This could

---

[81] Peacock, 'Charlemagne's Black Stones', 712.

[82] The church was reconstructed by Sergius I in 689; R. Coates-Stephens, 'Dark Age Architecture in Rome', *PBSR* 65 (1997), 177–232, at 180. The columns were moved to the stairs of the Vatican Museum in the eighteenth century. Fragments of black porphyry are known from the pavement of the *Domus Flavia* in Rome and other pieces were reused in twelfth-century panels in Santa Saba, Rome, and the cathedral at Salerno; Gnoli, *Marmora Romana*, 77 and 138, and Borghini, ed., *Marmi Antichi*, 272–3.

[83] Peacock, 'Charlemagne's Black Stones', 713; C. Meckseper, 'Antike Spolien in der ottonischen Architektur', in J. Poeschke, ed., *Antike Spolien in der Architektur des Mittelalters und der Renaissance*, 179–204.

[84] *CC* 81/*CeC* 67, 'In quibus referebatur, quod palatii Ravennate civitatis mosivo atque marmores ceterisque exemplis tam in strato quamque in parietibus sitis vobis tribuissemus. Nos quippe libenti animo et puro corde cum nimio amore vestre excellentiae tribuimus effectum et tam marmores quamque mosivo certisque exemplis de eodem palatio vobis concedimus abstollendum,...', referring perhaps to the building known as the 'Palace of Theoderic'; *Codex Carolinus*, ed. Gundlach, MGH, Epp. I, 614; C. Ricci, 'Marmi ravennati erratici', *Ausonia*, 4 (1909), 247–89, at 247–8; W. Jacobsen, 'Spolien in der karolingischen Architektur', in J. Poeschke, ed.,

Figure 6.9 Black porphyry column from the chapel of S. Zeno, Sta Prassede, Rome. Photo: Author.

refer to objects of varying size and function, such as small coloured tiles, large pieces of marble veneer, or squared blocks, as well as columns, capitals, or other architectural

Antike Spolien in der Architektur des Mittelalters und der Renaissance (Munich, 1996), 155–77; C. M. M. Bayer, M. Kerner, and H. Müller, 'Schriftquellen zur Geschichte der Marienkirche bis ca. 1000', in H. Müller, C. M. M. Bayer, and M. Kerner, eds, *Die Aachener Marienkirche. Aspekte ihrer Archäologie und frühen Geschichte. Der Aachener Dom in seiner Geschichte.* Quellen und Forschungen 1 (Regensburg 2014), 113–189, at 115–16 (no. 1). On the tense diplomacy of this letter, see J. L. Nelson, 'The Settings of the Gift in the Reign of Charlemagne', in W. Davies and P. Fouracre, eds, *The Languages of Gift in the Early Middle Ages* (Cambridge, 2010), 116–48, at 134–40.

elements. The letter is undated but was probably written in mid-787 in connection with Charlemagne's visit to Ravenna after spending Easter in Rome. The reference to *mosiva* in Hadrian's letter could be to *opus regulatum* or—more likely—to the larger, coloured pieces of *opus sectile*, the fashion for which had been revived in Rome during Hadrian's pontificate.[85] Such spolia could also have come from Roman buildings closer to home than Ravenna, such as Trier, which had also been an imperial capital. But, whatever its origin, the reuse of coloured, worked stone in prestige buildings in Francia, at Aachen, and elsewhere mirrored the latest fashion in Rome, which was itself derived from Late Antique interior design.[86] Hadrian's letter shows that Carolingian agents were actively seeking and collecting worked stone from Italy for building projects in Francia, with considerable logistical implications. Einhard agrees, saying in his account of the building of the chapel in Aachen, that when Charlemagne, 'could not obtain the columns and marble from somewhere else, he took the trouble to have them brought from Rome and Ravenna'.[87] Einhard's words are often cited to show the reliance of the Carolingian builders on spolia from Italy, but in fact he says that Charlemagne turned to Italy for supplies of worked marble only when such material could not be found 'from somewhere else', implying that other sources existed closer to home.

In this context, the reuse of antique columns in Charlemagne's chapel is particularly important. Many were deployed in a structural setting which implies that they were integral to the original design concept and architectural planning of the chapel; the architect must have acquired or have known he could acquire enough columns of the right dimensions at the outset of the building project. In October 1520, Albrecht Dürer, who was in Aachen for the coronation of the Emperor Charles V as Holy Roman Emperor, was particularly struck by the 'well-proportioned pillars with their good capitals of porphyry, green and red, and "Gassenstein" which Charles [the Great] had brought from Rome thither and set up there'.[88] Roman columns were essentially modular and tended to be prepared for trimming into lengths that were

---

[85] C. B. McClendon, 'The Revival of *opus sectile* Pavements in Rome and the Vicinity in the Carolingian Period', *PBSR*, 48 (1980), 157–65; L. Paroli, 'La scultura a Roma tra il VI e il IX secolo', in Arena et al., eds, *Roma dall'antichità al medioevo*, i, 132–43, at 132; L. Paroli, 'La scultura in marmo a Roma tra l'VIII e il IX secolo', in P. Delogu, ed., *Roma Medievale: aggiornamenti* (Florence, 1998), 93–122.

[86] McClendon, 'The Revival of *opus sectile* Pavements', 162–5, with reference to *opus sectile* floors at Centula (Saint-Riquier), St Germain (Auxerre), Lorsch, and Germigny-des-Prés. For spolia at the palace sites, see SW, 799, ii.59–63, 65 (Ingelheim); II.67–70 (Aachen). For the spiritual symbolism of 'spolia' columns in manuscripts associated with the court, especially columns in canon tables, see I. Mestemacher, *Marmor, Gold und Edelsteine. Materialimitation in der karolingischen Buchmalerei* (Berlin, 2021), 103–49.

[87] Einhard, *VK*, ch. 26; Dutton, tr., *Charlemagne's Courtier*, 32.

[88] J.-A. Goris and G. Marlier, *Albrecht Dürer. Diary of his Journey to the Netherlands, 1520–1521* (London, 1971), 69–70. The meaning of 'Gassenstein' is uncertain but may refer to granite rather than cast-stone or concrete. While in Aachen, Dürer twice spent money on going to the baths, and made silverpoint sketches of the chapel and Rathaus (Pl. 2–3), as well as witnessing the pageantry surrounding the coronation of Charles V on 23 October 1520.

multiples of four or five Roman feet.[89] Dürer noted that the Aachen columns were, 'correctly made according to Vitruvius' writings'. Thirty-two columns were used in the central octagon at Aachen, creating two levels within the tall arches of the gallery. Each of the eight arches was divided by a lintel (or architrave), capping two columns below it and supporting two slightly shorter ones above (Figure 6.10). Used like this the columns are not structural in the sense of being load bearing, but the lintels must have been inserted when the arch was constructed. Thus, the columns were integral to the design of the proportions of the octagon and their length ultimately determined the height of the gallery arches. Columns could of course be modified by trimming them to make them shorter or by adjusting the height of the capitals and bases, but both the number and the fundamental dimensions of the columns required for the gallery arches must have been part of the original design of the chapel. This is important because it is the gallery arches that give the central octagon its exceptional height.[90] Elsewhere in the chapel, more columns were used; for example, in the articulation of the *westwerk* with the gallery and in the altar screen at that level which may well have included the two extant black porphyry columns that are now kept in the cloister.

These two black columns and perhaps as many as thirty-eight in total were taken from Aachen to Paris in 1794 by French Revolutionary troops; inventories survive at the Louvre describing the columns, capitals, bases, and sculpture that were delivered there, including the 'Proserpine' sarcophagus thought to have been used for the tomb of Charlemagne himself.[91] Twenty-eight columns and other artefacts were brought back to Aachen in 1815 and some were later reset in the chapel. The spoliation of Charlemagne's chapel in the late eighteenth century makes it difficult to be sure which of the columns now in the octagon were part of the original Carolingian scheme and which are modern replacements. It is clear, however, that antique columns were a key part of the original architectural programme of the chapel, and the length of the columns available to (or required by) Charlemagne's architect must have been one of the fundamental modules of its design—certainly of the height of the central octagon and dome.

Spolia from Roman structures was probably used in the building and decoration of Charlemagne's chapel for reasons of pragmatism and speed, as well as symbolism. Roman buildings were convenient stockpiles of worked stone, and the use of Roman

---

[89] Bosman, *Power of Tradition*, 41.

[90] On the proportions of the chapel, see especially Heckner, 'Der Tempel Salomos in Aachen', 46; J. Ley, 'Warum ist die Aachener Pfalzkirche ein Zentralbau? Der Neue Salomonische Tempel als Vorbild herrschaftlicher Kirchenstiftung', in Bayer et al., eds, *Die Aachener Marienkirche*, 95–110.

[91] E. G. Grimme, *Der Dom zu Aachen: Architektur und Ausstattung* (Aachen, 1994), 56–7 and 338; Kreusch, 'Kapitelle und Bronzebasen aus Aachen', 93–8; Mestemacher, *Marmor, Gold und Edelsteine*, 348–9, listing two 'very rare' porphyry columns. These inventories record the height and diameter of the columns when catalogued in Paris, which is important because when returned to Aachen some were re-polished and thus reduced in width. My thanks to Richard Gem for very helpful discussions on the Aachen columns.

FIGURE 6.10 Upper-level columns and arcading in the interior of the Aachen chapel. Photo: Author.

ashlar blocks made from regional limestone in the fabric of the chapel walls shows that building stones were acquired locally, from Roman-period buildings that lay in Carolingian lands. The regional character of the supply of such stone is demonstrated by the excavation of a Carolingian-era boat, recovered from a gravel pit at Kalkar on the west bank of the lower Rhine near Xanten and dated 802 ± five years. It had sunk carrying a load of worked stone, including tufa blocks that were probably of Roman manufacture.[92] Later medieval traditions also claim that marble came to Aachen from imperial buildings in Trier and Cologne.[93] The dates derived from the timbers in the foundations and roof show that the chapel was topped out, at most, twenty years after the foundations were laid, and a letter written by Alcuin to Charlemagne on 23 July 798 which refers to the columns which have been set up in 'the most beautiful and marvellous church' suggests that rapid progress had been made by that date.[94] The speed of construction is another reason why spolia would have been a valuable resource for the master mason and architect.

Most of all, the use of spolia was an overt and unmistakable symbol of imperial pretensions and made manifest the Carolingian capacity to borrow from and rework not just the aesthetic schema of antique decoration but also the idioms of late imperial architecture. Hadrian's grant to carry away 'marble, mosaics and other specimens' from an Ostrogothic or imperial palace in Ravenna was not a neutral donation. It might rightly be regarded as one of the most politically sensitive acts of his pontificate since it gave papal sanction to the acquisition of materials that were resonant with connotations of wealth, power, and ultimately of empire, from places that had belonged until recently to the Roman Empire based in Constantinople. In the context of late eighth-century Aachen, the use of Roman spolia in the fabric of the building, whether gathered regionally or from afar, was a self-conscious statement of authority, ability, and ambition.

All this has implications for the study of the marble selected for Hadrian's epitaph. Firstly, it raises the question of whether the inscription was also made from a piece of spolia, taken from an imperial building in the vicinity of Aachen or a stockpile of stone cut during the Roman period. Secondly, is the choice of a black-coloured stone for the epitaph reflected in other contemporary settings and media, and did the colour, as well as the nature of the material, carry with it particular cultural connotations that added to the significance of the gift when it arrived in Rome? The structural and decorative evidence from Aachen makes it clear that black stone was locally available

---

[92] J. Opladen-Kauder and A. Peiss, 'Ein Flusskhan aus der Zeit Karls des Froßen', in H. G. Horn, ed., *Fundort Nordrhein-Westfalen. Millionen Jahre Geschichte* (Cologne, 2000), 378–80; J. Opladen-Kauder, 'Flusskahn aus der Zeit Karls des Großen', in Pohle, ed., *Karl der Grosse. Katalog*, 28–9, no. 004.

[93] Heckner and Schaab, 'Baumaterial', 128.

[94] 'Fuit quoque nobis sermo de columnis, quae in opere pulcherrimo et mirabili ecclesiae, quam vestra dictavit sapientia, statutae sunt'; Alcuin, *Ep.* no. 149; Dümmler, ed., *Epp.* IV, 241–5; quoted in Bayer et al., 'Schriftquellen', 118–20, no. 3.

to Charlemagne in the later eighth century and that these local resources were used for Hadrian's epitaph; what remains ambiguous is whether such stones were necessarily spolia because the Carolingians lacked the ability to extract the marble on this scale from a quarry, or whether they were indeed freshly quarried, 'wherever they are to be found'. In either case, the use of a rare, coloured stone for the pope's epitaph derived from the heartlands of Charlemagne's own lands was surely a deliberate and careful choice that complemented the echoes of empire embedded in the poetry and epigraphy of the monument.

7
Aachen and the Art of the Court

Archaeological and historical evidence shows that the decades around 800 were a period of intense construction work at the palace complex in Aachen. The use of *Blaustein* in the masonry of the chapel and for its fine internal decoration demonstrates that the stonemasons and artisans employed at the site used supplies of local black limestone alongside other sources of stone, including spolia. The selection of black limestone for the epitaph for Hadrian, commissioned early in 796 and sourced from the regional hinterland of the palace, must be associated with the building project at Aachen, which concentrated resources and could have supplied both the skilled manpower and raw materials for the manufacture of a prestige, large-scale inscription of this type. Aachen and other Carolingian royal palace sites provide rich comparative evidence to compare with Hadrian's epitaph—from extant inscriptions and architectural decoration, to deluxe manuscripts that were commissioned by the elite of Carolingian society.

Aachen features frequently in the contemporary sources, especially for the latter part of Charlemagne's reign, and the annals suggest that he spent a substantial part of the last decade of his life there.[1] Described as a *villa* in Pippinid charters, it is termed a *palatium* in documents from Charlemagne's reign as early as 769.[2] Building work was probably underway by the mid-780s, when, as noted above, Hadrian granted permission for Charlemagne's agents to take marbles and mosaics from palaces in Ravenna for construction projects in Francia. Writing some decades later, Einhard claimed that columns and marble used in the palace chapel at Aachen had been procured from Rome as well.[3] Following the major assembly held *in Aquis palatio publico* in 789, when the *Admonitio generalis* was promulgated, Charlemagne started to favour Aachen as a place of muster for the army in springtime as well as a winter

---

[1] McKitterick, *Charlemagne*, 161 (estimating 64 per cent from 804 to 814); J. L. Nelson, 'Why Are There So Many Different Accounts of Charlemagne's Imperial Coronation?', in her *Courts, Elites and Gendered Power in the Early Middle Ages: Charlemagne and Others* (Aldershot, 2007), no. XII, 1–27, at 20–1.

[2] MGH, DD. Kar. 1, nos 55–6.

[3] *CC* 81/*CeC* 67; Einhard, *VK*, ch. 26. See also the *Chronicon Moissacense (Anianense)*, s.a. 796 (BnF, Lat. 5941, fol. 19r); G. H. Pertz, ed., MGH, SS I (Hannover, 1826), 303; Müller et al., eds, *Die Aachener Marienkirche*, 115–16, 126–7, 129.

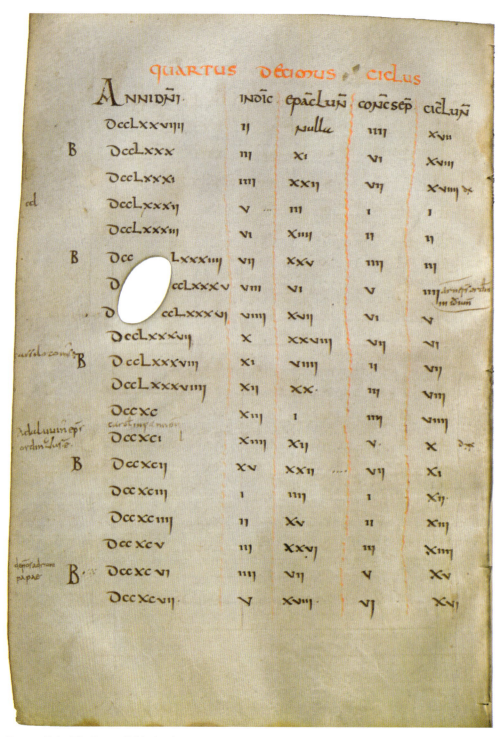

FIGURE 7.1 The Easter Table for the years 779–97 with marginal annotations recording the death of Pope Hadrian against the entry for 796 in the left-hand margin, and in the right-hand margin the places where Charlemagne celebrated Easter in the years 787–97. Würzburg, Universitätsbibliothek, M.p.th.f.46, fols 14v–15r. Photo: Reproduced with permission of Würzburg Universitätsbibliothek.

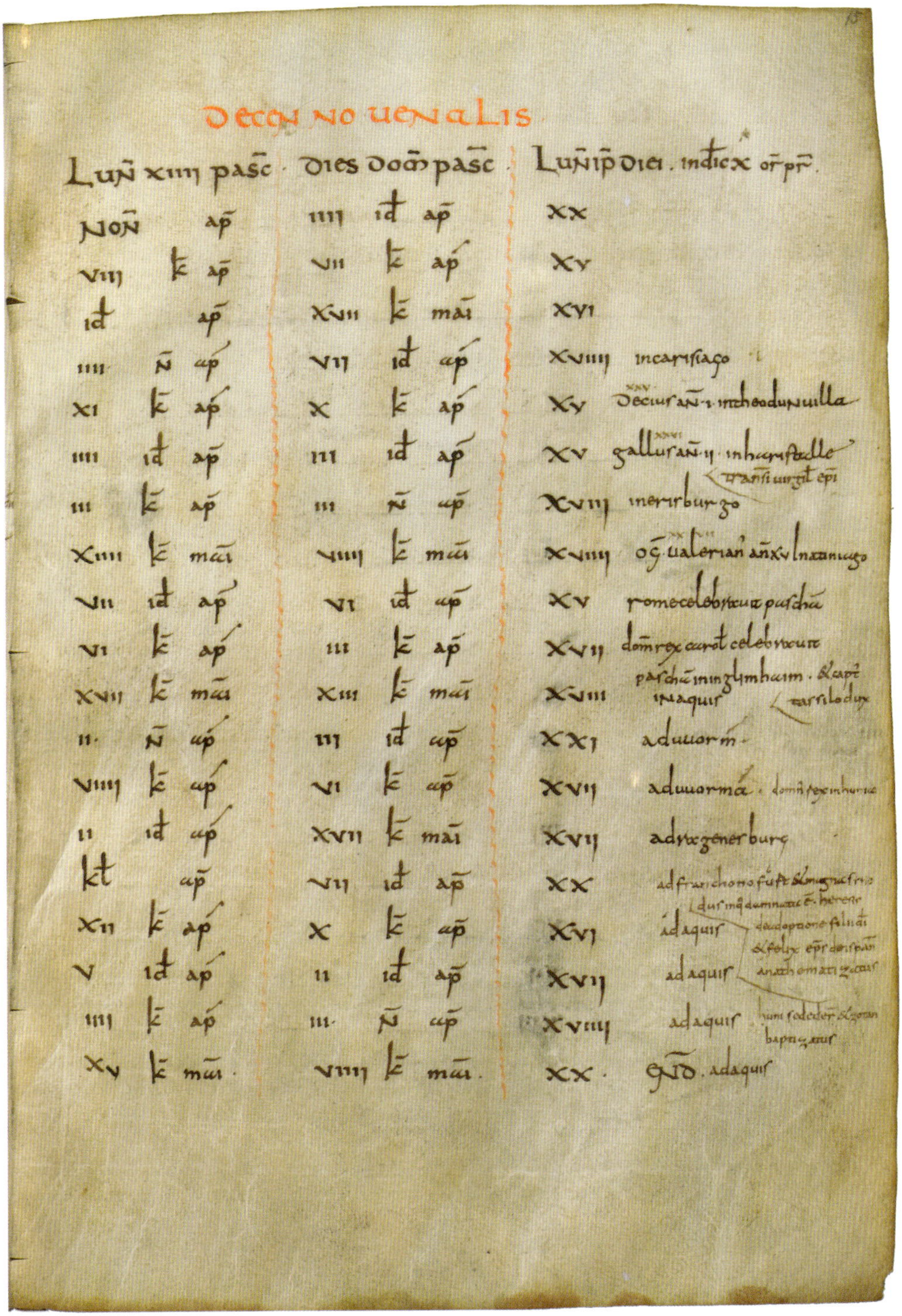

DECENNOUENALIS

Luñ XIIII pasc	dies dom pasc	Luñ ip̃ diei. índex oř p̃r.
Noñ ap̃	IIII id ap̃	XX
VIII k̄ ap̃	VII k̄ ap̃	XV
id ap̃	XVIII k̄ mai	XVI
IIII ñ ap̃	VII id ap̃	XVIIII incarisiaco
XI k̄ ap̃	X k̄ ap̃	XV decuran̄ ĩ theodunuilla
IIII id ap̃	III id ap̃	XV galluran̄ ij in hacriftellø trañ siurgit ep̃i
III k̄ ap̃	III ñ ap̃	XVII in erirburgo
XIIII k̄ mai	VIII k̄ mai	XVIIII oḡ ualerian añ xv in zanuego
VII id ap̃	VI id ap̃	XV rome celebr̄ cur pasc̄hā
VI k̄ ap̃	III k̄ ap̃	XVII dom̃ rex carol celebr̄ cur pasc̄ha in zulpihaim. & cap̃ in aquir tarsilo dux
XVII k̄ mai	XIII k̄ mai	XVIII
II ñ ap̃	III id ap̃	XXI ad uuorm
VIII k̄ ap̃	VI k̄ ap̃	XVII ad uuorma. dom̃ rex in huria
II id ap̃	XVII k̄ mai	XVII ad regenerburg
kt ap̃	VII id ap̃	XX ad francnono furt & maṇ̄ gnat’ris durī̄g̃ damnat̃ ë ĥetenē
XII k̄ ap̃	X k̄ ap̃	XVI ad aquir. dauid pono filii di & felix ep̃r deir̄ spn̄
V id ap̃	II id ap̃	XVII ad aquir anathomatizat’
IIII k̄ ap̃	III ñ ap̃	XVIII ad aquir uuit̃ sodedertz & gotan baptizat’
XV k̄ mai	VIII k̄ mai	XX end. ad aquir

Figure 7.1 Continued

residence.[4] The major sets of annals record that the king celebrated the feasts of Christmas and Easter at Aachen in 794/5, 795/6, 796/7, and 798/9, which suggests that he remained in the vicinity of that palace for the period between December and April in those years. These annals are corroborated by other closely contemporary sources; a copy of Bede's *De temporum ratione* seemingly copied in 800 by a scribe working in either Saint-Amand or Salzburg contains a set of Easter Tables that are extensively annotated with marginal notes, including a record of the burial of *domnus adrianus papa* (Figures 7.1a and 7.1b).[5] In the right hand margin of the same table is a list of places where the king spent Easter, including Aachen in 796 when the feast day fell on 3 April, confirming the report of the major annals. It would thus have been to Aachen that messengers came from Rome bearing news of the death of Hadrian at Christmas and of the election of Leo immediately afterwards. It was likely at Aachen too that Charlemagne mourned the passing of the old pope, where he issued orders for litanies to be sung 'throughout his realm', for alms to be sent to Rome, and where—according to the Annals of Lorsch—he commissioned the epitaph 'written in gold letters on marble, to be made in Francia so that he might send it to Rome to adorn the sepulchre of the supreme pontiff Hadrian'.[6]

THE COURT

Before looking in more detail at the evidence which points to the production of the epitaph in the vicinity of Aachen, it is important to remember that 'the court' was a diffuse concept in Charlemagne's day and was static in terms of neither place nor personnel.[7] With a kingdom as large and a reign as long as his, this is to be expected; the influence of different individuals waxed and waned over time, groups of courtiers came and went, and the dynamics of government adjusted as the kingdom expanded and the king's domestic household changed as the king grew older, new queens arrived, and his sons matured. It has long been assumed that Carolingian government relied in large measure on the itinerancy of the king. This model—derived largely

---

[4] Kraus, ed., *Aachen*, 54–60, 66–72. The Double Edict of Commission, enacted on 23 March 789; Boretius, ed., MGH, Capit. no. 23. On the *Admonitio generalis* thought to have been promulgated at the same time, see Mordek et al., eds, *Admonitio generalis*, MGH, Fontes XVI, 238–9.

[5] Würzburg, Universitätsbibliothek, M.p.th.f.46, fols 14v–15r with the Easter Table for 779–97, plus marginal annotations. Hadrian's burial is recorded against the year 796, reflecting the start of the year at Christmas time. The *annus praesens* is given as 800 in chapter 49 of Bede's *De temporum ratione* on fol. 89r. *CLA* IX.1413; Bischoff, *Katalog*, no. 7484; J. Story, 'Frankish Annals of Lindisfarne and Kent', *Anglo-Saxon England*, 34 (2005), 59–109, at 68–71.

[6] *Annales Laureshamenses*, s.a. 795; Pertz, ed., MGH, SS I, 36.

[7] D. A. Bullough, '*Aula Renovata*: The Court before the Aachen Palace', *Proceedings of the British Academy*, 71 (1985), 267–301, reprinted and updated in *Carolingian Renewal: Sources and Heritage* (Manchester, 1991), 123–60.

from analysis of later Ottonian evidence—assumes that the king and his entourage moved almost continuously between royal sites and noble residences. Itinerancy was pragmatic; it ensured continuous provisioning and was an instrument of government. The king's presence ensured the application of royal justice and the maintenance of royal authority across the realm in the absence of more sophisticated methods of communication and judicial enforcement. Evidence of such a practice can be traced through the descriptions in the annals of the king's travels, and in charters and capitularies that were dated and witnessed at specified locations in the name of the king.

Under such a system as this, the growth of a dominant central place at Aachen, where the king and his court 'settled' and which developed some of the characteristics of an administrative as well as a symbolic capital, is anomalous. Thus scholars have tended to regard Charlemagne's Aachen years following 794 as a watershed in his reign, and as something of an experiment in a different type of rulership where the king was essentially sedentary, sending his agents (*missi*) and armies out from this central place, which consequently became a courtly hub and a destination for courtiers, scholars, and foreign dignitaries. This paradigm has sometimes been questioned, probing both the historiographical reliance on models derived from later periods, as well as the assumption that Aachen operated as a quasi-capital city throughout Charlemagne's reign. McKitterick, for example, points out that most of the explicit evidence for Aachen as Charlemagne's principal residence derives from the very last years of his rule, and from the reign of his son, Louis the Pious (814–40), who certainly favoured that palace over others and whose travels concentrated on the heartlands of the empire between the Meuse and the Rhine.[8]

Modern models of economic growth can also be helpful for thinking about the role of the court in Charlemagne's kingdom. Endogenous growth theory focuses attention on investment in human capital as well as place, and on the longer term impact of that investment in the creation of sustainable and productive knowledge networks.[9] Charlemagne's reforms and concern for education, as articulated in the *Admonitio generalis* (789) and *Epistola de litteris colendis* (790s), prioritised the allocation of human and material resources for learning, literacy, and knowledge exchange. Done at scale, through the widespread creation of schools in bishoprics and monasteries, and via the educational capacity of local priests, these reforms created a critical mass of *literati* (those educated in Latin), who were able to generate a quantitative and qualitative increase in knowledge through centrally driven investment priorities. Absolute numbers were important in order to create the numbers of *literati* whose human capital value could be realised through the potential mobility of both people

---

[8] McKitterick, *Charlemagne*, 157–8; M. Costambeys, M. Innes, and S. MacLean, *The Carolingian World* (Cambridge, 2011), 174; Kraus, ed., *Aachen*, 286–90, 344–8.

[9] For an introduction, see P. Howitt, 'Endogenous Growth Theory', in S. N. Durlauf and L. E. Blume, eds, *Economic Growth* (London, 2010), 68–73.

and the books they made in order to share and build on knowledge gained. One measure of the success of this sustained investment is the very large number of surviving Frankish manuscripts that can be dated to the ninth century.[10] Increased literacy was fundamental—so that ideas could move even if the mobility of individual scholars or scribes was sometimes constrained. The movement of people and wealth, ideas and objects, was actively encouraged by the centripetal pull of royal patronage that drew scholars, artisans, and resources into the king's orbit, as well as the opposite, centrifugal effects of the same royal favour that sent courtiers and treasures back out into the bishoprics, monasteries, and grand estates of the kingdom. All this, it can be argued, facilitated a dynamic 'knowledge economy' that generated creativity and innovation, catalysed by the injection of bullion and treasure from external sources such as the vanquished Avars.

It is important also not to underestimate the substantial archaeological and textual evidence for major investment in other palaces during Charlemagne's reign and to understand the role that these places played in the mechanics of government and the consolidation of Carolingian power, especially in areas that lay beyond the dynasty's traditional heartlands in central Austrasia. Charlemagne and Pippin before him had used and renewed palace sites in Neustria—Samoussy, Quierzy, Attigny, Compiègne, and Saint-Denis (where Pippin was buried)—all of which had been important centres for the Merovingian kings. Carolingian patronage of these palaces demonstrated continuity of kingship as well as control of lands that had been part of the Merovingian royal domain. Archaeological evidence in all these places indicates building activity in the early Carolingian period before 800.[11] Similarly, palaces were also constructed at Nijmegen in northern Frisia, near the confluence of the Maal and Rhine, and at Paderborn in Saxony. Those palaces functioned both as central places for concentrating resources and as physical statements of Carolingian lordship in regions newly annexed by the Frankish armies. Einhard says that Charlemagne began another palace 'of beautiful workmanship . . . in his villa called Ingelheim, not far from Mainz'.[12] Ingelheim, like Frankfurt and Worms, facilitated control of the central Rhineland. The building complexes erected in all these places functioned as administrative centres, as well as places of military muster and annual assembly. They were also monumental expressions of Carolingian prestige and power in strategically important regions, drawing the Rhineland, Frisia, and Saxony more tightly under Carolingian governance.

---

[10] Bischoff's *Katalog* lists 7,656 extant ninth-century Frankish manuscripts. This is a striking number in comparison with the few extant manuscripts from the Anglo-Saxon kingdoms in the same period; Story, 'Insular Manuscripts', 66–8.

[11] A. Renoux, 'Karolingische Pfalzen in Nordfrankreich (751–987), in SW, *799*, iii, 130–7; U. Lobbedey, 'Carolingian Royal Palaces: The State of Research from an Architectural Historian's Viewpoint', in C. Cubitt, ed., *Court Cultures in the Early Middle Ages: The Proceedings of the First Alcuin Conference*, Studies in the Early Middle Ages, 3 (Turnhout, 2003), 131–54.

[12] Einhard, *VK*, ch. 17; Dutton, tr., *Charlemagne's Courtier*, 26–7.

Regensburg in Bavaria and Pavia in Lombard Italy were similarly patronised when annexed to the Carolingian domain. The chronology of building work at these palaces is hard to define precisely but archaeological evidence demonstrates construction activity in the second half of the eighth century, complementing historical evidence showing that places such as Frankfurt (794) and Paderborn (777, 785, 799) supported major assemblies before 800.

Contemporary texts, surviving architecture, and later tradition all serve to shine a bright light on Aachen as the key central place in Charlemagne's kingdom. But the brightness of that light puts into comparative shadow other places—palaces, bishoprics, and monasteries—that are less well served than Aachen by surviving physical and textual evidence. But what does exist shows that these places were also enriched and sustained by royal patronage and were very important nodes in the network of places through which the kingdom functioned.[13] These were places of power that consolidated regional resources and local patronage and were networked with other centres through bonds of lordship, literate communication, and liturgical commemoration. In an era when communication was neither instant nor certain, 'virtual' connections could be sustained across time and space through prayer confraternities, synchronised liturgical practices, and the exchange of letters and gifts: 'Run now, little letter, through the sacred palaces (*per sacra palatia*) of David', reminisced Angilbert in verses for his friends in Aachen, 'then hurry back swiftly to the sacred chapel (*ad sacram capellam*)'.[14] Aachen is thus a luminous star in a constellation of places that concentrated the resources and refracted the power of Charlemagne's regime. And, although it is not the only place where a complex inscription such as this could have been produced, the local supply of black stone as well as the concentration of talent in and around Aachen in the mid- to late 790s during the construction of the palace and chapel complex, points strongly to this place as the probable location of the stone cutters, the *ordinator*, and the *sculptor* of the inscription, as well as Alcuin who was the *auctor* of these verses for the dead pope.

POETRY AT THE COURT

The character of Charlemagne's court at this time is illuminated by the poetry that was written by three of his closest courtiers. Alcuin, Angilbert, and Theodulf each wrote a long poem recalling life at the court when they themselves were distant from

---

[13] L. Nees, 'Networks or Schools? Production of Illuminated Manuscripts and Ivories during the Reign of Charlemagne', in R. Grosse and M. Sot, eds, *Charlemagne: les temps, les espaces, les hommes. Construction et Déconstruction d'un règne*, Collection Haut Moyen Âge, 34 (Turnhout, 2018), 385–407.

[14] Angilbert, 'To Charlemagne and his entourage', *Cartula, curre modo per sacra palatia David…Et sic ad sacram citius tunc curre capellam*; Dümmler, ed., MGH, PLAC I, 360–3; Godman, tr., *Poetry*, no. 6, 112–19, at lines 72 and 83; *CSLMA* I, 152–79 (ANGCE 5.34).

it. All use the word *aula* as an architectural term and as a synonym for 'the court', embracing both the physical place and the people who were there. Theodulf's invocation for prayers in the *aula*, 'which rises up, a noble building, with marvellous domes (*miris...tholis*)', and as 'a lofty palace' with a 'long atrium', sounds very like a reference to the Aachen complex.[15] Angilbert describes the foundation of a 'celebrated temple' (*inclita templa*) using diction similar to the dedication inscription for the chapel.[16]

The three poems are best understood as dated to a period between late 794 and late 796 when other sources show that the king was resident in Aachen for several months at a time. Bullough proposed a tighter chronology than this, arguing that the poems were composed in 796: the first, he argued, was written by Angilbert after he had left for Rome in early spring; the second by Theodulf when Alcuin was still at court; the third by Alcuin himself before the end of the year, after he had left Aachen for Tours but before Angilbert had returned from Rome *ad sacram aulam*.[17] The poems are high art, literary confections to be read as an evocation rather than literal description of life at the court. Even so, and notwithstanding the conventions of genre or the personal rivalries that simmer not far from the surface of the verses, these poem-epistles reveal much about the character and composition of the king's court at a time when its centre of gravity was at Aachen. The verses concentrate on the people who were there; the reader encounters the king's immediate *familia* (particularly the women) and important office holders, such as Magenfrith the chamberlain, Audulf the seneschal, and the arch-chaplain Hildebald who 'holds in his hands the key to the doors of the chapel', as well as the 'wise teachers [who] lend distinction and fame to every discipline at the court'. Alcuin added the clergy of the chapel—'a sacred hierarchy' (*ordinibus sacris*)—and the doctors who tended the sick, as well as vignettes of others such as Eberhard, the cupbearer, and the *lector* and the choir master who taught the boys sacred chant. Both Alcuin and Theodulf pick out Einhard, carrying books, dashing 'back and forth like an ant', and Ercambald, the head of the chancery, who had a double tablet hanging from his belt and sat perched high at a desk 'to

---

[15] Theodulf, *Ad Carolum regem*; Dümmler, ed., MGH, PLAC I, 483–9, no. 25, lines 61–4; Godman, tr., *Poetry*, no. 15, 150–63; Andersson, tr., *Theodulf of Orléans*, 65–73, no. 25. See below for discussion of the dedication inscription. For line 61, see also D. Schaller, 'Frühkarolingische Corippus-Rezeption', *Wiener Studien* 105 (1992) 178–84, at 179, reprinted in his *Studien zur lateinischen Dichtung des Frühmittelalters* (Stuttgart 1995), 346–60. On Theodulf's use of *tholos*, see F. Stella, 'Autore e attribuzioni del "Karolus Magnus et Leo Papa"', in P. Godman, J. Jarnut, and P. Johanna, eds, *Am Vorabend der Kaiserkrönung: das Epos "Karolus magnus et Leo papa" und der papstbesuch in Paderborn 799* (Berlin, 2002), 19–34, at 29, n. 72.

[16] Angilbert, 'To Charlemagne and his entourage', lines 23–6, *Fundamenta super petram quoque ponit in altum / Ut domus alma deo maneat firmissima Christo / Felix sic lapides posuit [sua] dextera primum / Inclita celiarono fierent ut templa tonant*. Dümmler, ed., MGH, PLAC I, 360–3; Godman, tr., *Poetry*, 114–15, no. 6. For the dedication inscription at the chapel, see below.

[17] Bullough, *Alcuin*, 437–41. Others have argued that Anglibert wrote the poem from Frankfurt in 794 or Saint-Riquier in 795; D. Schaller, 'Vortrags- und Zirkulardichtung am Hof Karls des Grossen', *Mittellateinisches Jahrbuch*, 6 (1970), 14–36; Godman, tr., *Poetry*, 10–12, 118.

watch the crowd of scribes running about'.[18] The overall impression is one of industry, where each person has a role, and everyone is busy about their task.

The poems reflect both ubiquity of the written word at the court and the mobility of people and texts. Some people were visitors to the court and travelled back and forwards on local, regional or more distant business for the king. Some, such as the Irishman whose accent was mocked mercilessly by Theodulf, represents both mobility and scholarship. The epistle-poems are themselves also evidence of the absence of their authors who had penned their verses when distant from courtly company. A good example of the mobility of texts, and their interaction with the king's inner circle, is contained in one of Alcuin's slightly later letters, written late in March 798, when he was in Tours and the king was in Saxony. Alcuin wrote in response to two letters from the king; he said that he would come as the king requested, but asked if he might have permission to make the journey after Charles had returned from campaign in Saxony. The letter explains that he was sending a new piece on the cycles of the moon and was also working on another essay addressing the Adoptionist Controversy. Alcuin thought that this matter had been resolved at the Frankfurt assembly in 794, when statements largely drafted by him had been sent to the Spanish clergy who were involved in the dispute. But the issue resurfaced and, after he had moved to Tours, he wrote again to the main antagonists, Felix of Urgel and Elipand of Toledo.[19] Those letters provided him with the basis of a longer *libellus* 'against the heresy of Felix' and it is this to which Alcuin refers in his letter to the king. The *libellus* was a work-in-progress. He says:

> I have sent another work to your benevolent sweetness against the champions of the Adoption of Christ; it is not yet polished nor presented in a named booklet, but is still in unbound leaves [*in scedulis dispersum*] awaiting your kind authority [to identify] that which may be pleasing, or what could be put in another way and sent back to me, if that seems appropriate, so that the title of the booklet can be decided and it may be circulated for reading.

He went on to request that the draft text

> ...might be read within the hearing of your household (*inter familiares legatur aures*) and decisions made if anything is to be taken out from this trifling work (*opusculum*), guiding me for a second time. Following your advice, I will understand, and either compose the title or use the one that is assigned to it.[20]

---

[18] See also Theodulf's four-line poem, 'De Tabella', on a two-leaf tablet, decorated on the outside; Dümmler, ed., MGH, PLAC I, 553, no. 56; Andersson, tr., *Theodulf of Orléans*, 155.

[19] Dümmler, ed., MGH, Epp. IV, 60–5, no. 23 (to Felix), on which, see Bullough, *Alcuin*, 49 who dates it to late 797, On Alcuin's role in the Adoptionist debate, see especially Cavadini, *Last Christology*, 71–102.

[20] Dümmler, ed., MGH, Epp. IV, 231–5, no. 145; *ARF s.a.* 798. The key manuscript for this letter is London, Lambeth Palace Library, MS 218 (s. x^{in}, S. England), on which, see Breay and Story, eds, *Anglo-Saxon Kingdoms*, no. 48.

This extract reveals a lot about Alcuin's working methods, and that (though he was by then distant from the court) he understood that a work of this sort would be received and read aloud for comment and correction in the presence of the king's *familiares*. An extant copy of conciliar decrees, which dates to the second half of the eighth century and was probably made at Tours, may even preserve preparatory notes in Alcuin's own hand; marginal annotations in Insular minuscule script mark out portions of the text that Alcuin quoted in his *libellus*.[21] His comments in the letter to Charlemagne are also rare textual evidence of the sharing of drafts in an unbound, loose-leaf format (*in scedulis dispersum*), and of the function of the title in the publication and circulation of the finished product.[22] Alcuin craved the king's approval, knowing doubtless that the royal imprimatur (what he called 'the shimmer of purple') would give the treatise an official status and speed its circulation.[23]

Manuscripts and the 'Court School'

Assumptions about the centrality of Aachen in Charlemagne's later years also feed into the analysis of a group of deluxe manuscripts that are traditionally associated with the patronage of his court. Art historical, palaeographic, and textual connections that link nine richly decorated books (plus one fragment) suggest that they were made by about ten highly skilled scribes and artists who were familiar with each other's work, over a period of about three decades from the early 780s.[24] Some of the scribes who

---

[21] BnF, Lat. 1572, fols 8v–10v (decrees from the Council of Ephesus, 431). On this manuscript and its possible connections with Alcuin, see Bullough, *Alcuin*, 103 (n. 258) and 223 (n. 281). Three quotations from Cyril of Alexandria are marked out in this manuscript ('s' at the beginning and 'd' at the end of each extract) and these are also quoted in successive chapters (chs 14–16) of Alcuin's *libellus contra heresim felicis* (*PL* 101, cols. 87–120).

[22] On *scedulae* see, Diesenberger and Wolfram, 'Arn und Alkuin', 90–1.

[23] Here Alcuin quoted a pseudo-Vergilian text ('*Carmina si fuerint te iudice [digna] coturno / Reddetur titulus purpuriusque nitor*) which he may have known via Aldhelm's *De metris*, c. 9; J. Ziolkowski and M. Putnam, *The Virgilian Tradition: The First Fifteen Hundred Years* (New Haven, CT, 2008), 92–3.

[24] The gospel manuscripts in this group are: the two parts of the so-called Ada Gospels, in Trier, Stadtbibliothek, Cod. 22 (Part 1: fols 17–38v; Part 2: fols 39–172v, *CLA* IX: 1366; Bischoff, *Katalog*, no. 6166); the Arsenal Gospels: Paris, Bibliothèque de l'Arsenal, MS 599 (*CLA* IV: 517); the Harley Golden Gospels: BL, Harley MS 2788 (*CLA* II. 198); Abbeville Gospels: Abbeville, Bibliothèque municipale, MS 4 (*CLA* VI: 704); Soissons Gospels: BnF, Lat. 8850 (Bischoff, *Katalog*, no. 4568); Lorsch Gospels: BAV, Pal. Lat. 50 and Bukarest, Biblioteca Naţionalǎ a României (Alba Julia, Biblioteca Documentarǎ Batthyáneum), MS R.II.1. A fragment containing a framed miniature of the Annunciation to Zacharias and one line of text, which may once have been part of an evangelistary and is now BL, Cotton MS Claudius B V, fol. 134v (olim 132v), is also attributed to this group (*CLA* S: 1702; Bischoff, *Katalog*, no. 2419). Also included are the Godesscalc Evangelistary, now Paris, BnF, NAL 1203 (*CLA* V: 681), which is the earliest of the group, and the Dagulf Psalter, now Vienna, ÖNB Cod. 1861 (*CLA* X: 1504). On these MSS, see especially W. Koehler, *Die karolingischen Miniaturen*, ii: *Die Hofschule Karls des Grossen* (Berlin, 1958) and B. Bischoff, 'Die Hofbibliothek Karls des Großen', in *KdG* ii, 42–62, reprinted with revisions in *MS* 3, 149–69 and tr. M. Gorman, 'Manuscripts in the Age of Charlemagne', in B. Bischoff, *Manuscripts and Libraries in the Age of Charlemagne*, Cambridge Studies in Palaeography and Codicology, 1 (Cambridge, 1995), 56–75, at 65. See also McKitterick, *Charlemagne*, 354–6; C. Winterer, 'Die

worked on manuscripts in this core group can be traced in other books that contain copies of library rather than liturgical texts, several of which, consequently, have also been localised to court circles.[25]

The core group of ornate liturgical manuscripts are often described as products of a 'Court School' largely because of the ostentatious display of the sacred texts, and the material and intellectual resources invested in them, especially gold. The pull of the king's wealth and power, and the textual evidence for Charlemagne's presence at Aachen in his later years, encouraged Koehler and others to assume that Aachen, after 794, may also have been the location for the king's library as well as a 'Court School' which functioned both as a place of learning and as a centralised atelier for manuscript production.[26] So, this group of manuscripts, previously known as the 'Ada-Group' after the patron of one of them, was relabelled accordingly.[27] The term has stuck, and with it a set of often unspoken assumptions about the location and chronology of the scribes and artists who made these manuscripts as well as the reference collection of exemplars that lies behind them.[28]

The concept of a school of this sort emerges from analyses of the methods of some monastic writing centres whose output was sufficiently large and long-lived to provide evidence of the training of numerous scribes over time in a common and distinctive style of writing.[29] Indeed, the principal objection to the existence of a 'Court School' during Charlemagne's time derives from Bischoff's observation that the ten or so scribes responsible for the extant group of deluxe books associated with the court do not seem routinely to have trained others, and that the type of script visible in these codices did not evolve beyond this generation of scribes.[30] A school such as this did develop at Tours, starting under Alcuin's abbacy (796–804) with his project to edit the text of the Bible. A series of manuscripts, linked by script, decoration, and book

Miniatur im (karolingischen) Zeitalter ihrer technischen Reproduzierbarkeit? Beobachtungen und Überlegungen zu den Handschriften der Hofschule Karls des Grossen', in M. Embach, C. Moulin, and H. Wolter-von dem Knesebeck, eds, *Die Handschriften der Hofschule Kaiser Karls des Grossen. Individuelle Gestalt und europäisches Kulturerbe* (Trier, 2019), 267–93, at 270–2; Mestemacher, *Marmor, Gold und Edelsteine*, 319–32.

[25] Summarised by D. Ganz, 'The Scripts of the Court Group Manuscripts', in Embach, Moulin and Wolter-von dem Knesebeck, eds, *Die Handschriften der Hofschule*, 297–314.

[26] Koehler, *Die karolingischen Miniaturen*, ii, 11–13; Bischoff, 'The Court Library under Louis the Pious', 76–7.

[27] M. Embach, 'Das Ada-Evangeliar. Kodex und Einband (Stadtbibliothek Trier, HS 22)', in Embach, Moulin, and Wolter-von dem Knesebeck, eds, *Die Handschriften der Hofschule*, 69–95, at 69.

[28] For concerns about the limitations of the term 'Hofschule' and the uncertainty around the place(s) of production, see Winterer, 'Die Miniatur im (karolingischen) Zeitalter', 268–9 and Mestemacher, *Marmor, Gold und Edelsteine*, 316–18.

[29] B. Bischoff, 'Die Hofbibliothek under Ludwig dem Frommen', in J. J. G. Alexander and M. T. Gibson, eds, *Medieval Learning and Literature: Essays Presented to Richard William Hunt* (Oxford, 1976), 3–22; English tr. M. Gorman, 'The Court Library Under Louis the Pious', in Bischoff, *Manuscripts and Libraries*, 76–92, at 83.

[30] Bischoff, *Die Abtei Lorsch*, 31, 36 and Bischoff, *Manuscripts and Libraries*, 21 (for the similarity of the script of the Godesscalc Evangelistary and the Arsenal Gospels with those that developed in Metz and Lorsch), see Ganz, 'The Scripts', 302.

design can be confidently linked to this 'Tours School' in the ninth century, and some may be as early as Alcuin's abbacy.[31] Standing behind the Tours School lies textual evidence (but regrettably no certain manuscripts) for the archbishop's cathedral school and library at York where Alcuin was made *magister* in 767. At York, we are told, the 'exceptional treasures' that Archbishop Ælberht had collected were 'stored under one roof'.[32] But despite Alcuin's many comments in his *York Poem* and later letters, there is no unequivocal surviving manuscript evidence for an active writing centre at York at this time (in contrast to that which can be confidently attributed, for example, to the Northumbrian monastery at Wearmouth Jarrow earlier in the century) and this despite the fact that there were evidently many people there who could both read and write.[33] Observing the extant manuscripts associated with Cologne during Hildebald's tenure as bishop and archbishop (788–818), Bullough thought that an in-house scriptorium at that bishopric probably concentrated primarily on the production of books required for the celebration of the liturgy, and that other scholarly works of exegesis were brought in from elsewhere.[34] This was probably a function of scale, he argued, adding that cathedral chapters, such as York and Cologne, were 'generally small-scale bodies compared with major monasteries'. Counting as many as twenty hands in two computistical manuscripts that were certainly produced at Cologne during Hildebald's rule, Bullough thought these might represent the entirety of that cathedral's community in this period.

In similar vein, it is possible that the recruitment, training, and perhaps the retention of scribes within a secular community, such as the cathedrals at York, Cologne, and perhaps also the palace chapel at Aachen, differed in significant ways from what is often assumed to have been the 'closed scriptorium' of a monastery. The development of a 'school style' over time depends to a large degree on continuity of personnel and uniformity of training over a long period. Stability was inherent in the enclosed environment of a monastery, even though the movement of experienced scribes can sometimes be inferred from the transition in an established scriptorium to a new style of writing.[35] If scribal stability could be considered commonplace in a monastic writing centre, the mobility of scribes and especially artists may have been much more

---

[31] W. Koehler, *Die karolingischen Miniaturen* i: *Die Schule von Tours*, 2 vols (Berlin, 1930); R. McKitterick, 'Carolingian Bible Production: The Tours Anomaly', in R. Gameson, ed., *The Early Medieval Bible: Its Production, Decoration and Use* (Cambridge, 1994), 53–62.

[32] *YP* 1534–5 and Alcuin, *Ep.* 121 (on Alcuin's teaching at Tours and the library at York) 'exquisitiores eruditionis scolasticae libelli' (Allott, tr., *Alcuin*, no. 8). See also Godman, ed., *Alcuin*, lxii–lxiii and Garrison, 'The Library of Alcuin's York', 635–9.

[33] R. Gameson, 'Script at Wearmouth and Jarrow', in C. Breay and J. Story, eds, *Manuscripts in the Anglo-Saxon Kingdoms: Cultures and Connections* (Dublin, 2020), 28–44.

[34] See, for example, Cologne, Dombibliothek, Cod. 63, 65, 67, a copy of Augustine's *Ennarationes in Psalmos* made probably in Chelles; D. A. Bullough, 'Charlemagne's "Men of God": Alcuin, Hildebald and Arn', in J. Story, ed., *Charlemagne: Empire and Society* (Manchester, 2005), 136–50, at 144–5.

[35] Bischoff, 'Court Library under Louis the Pious', 83.

frequent among secular church communities. Yet, even without factoring in the mobility of people, scribal communication through the exchange of books, exemplars, letters, and messages was clearly routine.[36]

The court group manuscripts are deluxe liturgical books, characterised by extensive use of golden lettering with rich and plentiful polychrome illumination that is often figural, as well as architectural and decorative frameworks for text and image.[37] These paintings often show imitative marbles and cut gemstones that served to ornament the Word of God, and reflect a contemporary aesthetic delighting in richly coloured stone.[38] Most of the manuscripts are large format gospel books that are not closely datable. But there is also an evangelistary and a small psalter that can be dated by internal textual references.[39] The evangelistary includes full-page, painted miniatures and the psalter has pages of decorated text, some laid out in capitals reminiscent of epigraphic lettering. Both books have purpled pages and texts that were copied in gold, or gold and silver, with illuminated initials. Each one contains verses that address Charlemagne and Hadrian by name and identify the principal scribe: Godesscalc for the evangelistary and Dagulf for the psalter. Both men refer to themselves in their verses as the king's *famulus* ('servant').[40] This label suggests that they had positions at court, probably within the chapel. If so, they would have had access to the chapel's resources, including manuscripts. The evidence of the verses ties these two small, sumptuous volumes securely to the king's patronage and immediate circle, in contrast to the gospel books where the connections to the king's inner circle are rather more circumspect, such as the later medieval tradition that Ada, the *ancilla Dei* who is named as patron of the Trier Gospels, was Charlemagne's sister.[41]

Little is known about these two named scribes: Godesscalc may have been the deacon of that name at the cathedral in Liège (which was the diocese in which Aachen lay) at the time of Bishop Agilfrid (d. 787), who was said by a later author to have

---

[36] L. Nees, 'On Carolingian Book Painters: The Ottoboni Gospels and its Transfiguration Master', *The Art Bulletin* 83 (2001), 209–39, at 210–13 which makes a case for scribe-artist mobility. See also Winterer, 'Die Miniatur im (karolingischen) Zeitalter', 288–9 for the heterogeneous origins of the group of scribe-artists who made the court group manuscripts.

[37] Ganz, 'The Scripts', 303–5.

[38] I. Mestemacher, 'Images of Architecture and Materials: The Miniatures in the Soissons Gospels (Bibliothèque nationale de France MS. Lat. 8850)', in Embach, Moulin, and Wolter-von dem Knesebeck, eds, *Die Handschriften der Hofschule*, 39–67, at 45.

[39] Paris, BnF, NAL 1203 and Vienna, ÖNB Cod. 1861.

[40] Godesscalc: 'Ultimus hoc famulus studuit complere Godesscalc'; Dümmler, ed., MGH, PLAC I, 94–5, line 16. Dagulf: 'Exigui famuli Dagulfi sume laborem / Dignanter, docto mitis et ore lege'; Dümmler, ed., MGH, PLAC I, 91–2, lines 15–16. See also the verses presented to Charlemagne by Adam, abbot of Masmünster, 'tuus famulus', in a copy of the *ars grammatica* of Diomedes when the king was in the city of Worms (probably in 780/1 en route to Rome); Dümmler, ed., MGH, PLAC I, 93, ll. 5–7 (preserved in a later copy, now BnF, Lat. 7494, s. ix 2/4 (Bischoff, *Katalog*, no. 4447)), and Bullough, '*Aula Renovata*', 138. Ganz, 'The Scripts', 300.

[41] Trier, *Stadtbibliothek*, Cod. 22, fol. 172r; M. Embach, *Das Ada-Evangeliar (StB Trier, Hs 22). Ein Hauptwerk der Hofschule Karls des Großen*, Kostbarkeiten der Stadtbibliothek Trier, 2 (Trier 2018), 18–28 and Embach, 'Das Ada-Evangeliar', 71–3.

been expert in writing lettering in gold.[42] A letter from Alcuin to a 'beloved friend' called Dogwulfus may have been meant for the man responsible for the psalter.[43] Alcuin calls him a *scrinarius*, which is a title also used in the context of the papal writing office, suggesting perhaps that he had a role in the court chancery as notary.[44] A poem, apparently composed by a pupil of *sacer magister* Dagulf, named Deodatus, who wrote and ornamented another copy of the psalter, implies that Dagulf held a senior role as an overseer and master.[45]

Internal evidence supplies dates for both these manuscripts. Godesscalc's Evangelistary must have been completed sometime between mid-781 and early 783. It includes two references to the baptism of Charlemagne's son, Pippin, by Hadrian in Rome at Easter 781, as well as a full page illumination (fol. 3v) of the baptismal *fons vitae*, shown as an octagonal structure surrounded by eight columns that support an ornamental architrave with a pointed roof surmounted by a cross. This image of the 'Fountain of Life' is juxtaposed by the title of the first pericope for the vigil of Christmas, *statio ad Sanctam Mariam*, that begins on the facing page (fol. 4r). The Marian reference in the context of the Roman liturgy refers to Sta Maria Maggiore, with its relic of the crib; the octagonal font echoes the form of the Lateran Baptistery. On fol. 125r, space was left next to one of the two Easter Tables for a note alongside the year 781 recording that, 'in this year, lord king Charles came to St Peter's and Pippin his son was baptised by the apostolic lord'.[46] The closing lines of Godesscalc's verses, on fol. 127r, recall Hadrian receiving Pippin in his white baptismal robes from the font as his sacred 'conpater'. Godesscalc's poem also says that 'Charles, pious king of the Franks, with Hildegard his eminent wife', had ordered the book to be written.[47]

---

[42] Sigibert of Gembloux (d. 1112), *Vita Landiberti*, ch. 28; ed. B. Krusch and W. Levison, *Passiones vitaeque sanctorum aevi Merovingici* IV, MGH, SS rer. Merov. VI (Hanover and Leipzig, 1913), 106; Bischoff, 'Court Library of Charlemagne', 65; F. Crivello, C. Denoël, and P. Orth, eds, *Das Godesscalc-Evangelistar*, 12, no. 25. Nees, 'Godesscalc's Career', 28 preferring a link with the royal abbey at Saint-Denis.

[43] Alcuin, *Letter to Dogvulf*; Dümmler, ed., MGH, Epp. IV, 115, no. 73. The title of the letter in London, BL Cotton MS Tiberius A XV, fol. 15r refers to Alcuin as *magister*.

[44] Toubert, '"Scrinium" et "Palatium"', 101–4.

[45] The names are not found in the earliest copy of the poem, which is given the title *versus de laude psalterii* in the prefatory matter of a psalter, s. ix$^{2/3}$, now Angers, Bibliothèque Municipale 18 (14), fol. 9v (Bischoff, *Katalog*, no. 48); Deodatus, 'Ad Moulinum de Dagulf Scriptore', Dümmler, ed., MGH, PLAC I, 92–3 no. 5; CSLMA I, 292–3 (DEO 1). L. Délisle, 'Notice sur un manuscript de l'église de lyon au temps de Charlemagne', *Tiré de notice et extraits des manuscrits de la bibliothèque nationale et autres bibliothèques*, 35 (Paris, 1898), 838–42, at 841.

[46] BnF, NAL 1203, fol. 125r; 'in isto anno fuit domnus rex Karolus ad sanctum Petrum et baptizatus est filius Pippinus a domno apostolico'.

[47] Dümmler, ed., MGH, PLAC I, 91–2, lines 12–13 and 23–8, and (with German translation) in H. Wolter-von dem Knesebeck, 'Godesscalc, Dagulf und Demetrius. Überlegungen zu den Buchkünstlern am Hof Karls des Grossen und ihrem Selbstveständnis', in P. van den Brink and S. Ayooghi, *Karl der Grosse. Charlemagne. Karls Kunst* (Aachen, 2014), 31–45, at 44–5 and by Mestemacher, *Marmor, Gold und Edelsteine*, 344–6.

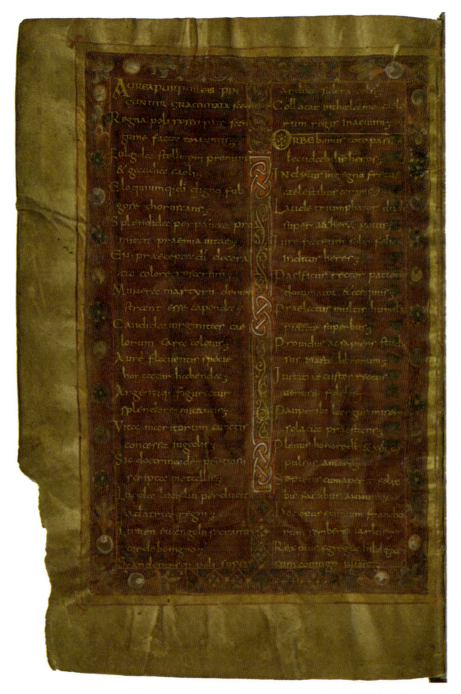

FIGURE 7.2 Dedicatory verses in Godesscalc's Evangelistary. Charlemagne and Hildegard are named at the foot of the second column; Paris, BnF, NAL 1203, fol. 126v. Photo: Courtesy of the Bibliothèque nationale de France, Paris.

The queen's death in April 783 thus provides the latest possible date for the commission (Figure 7.2).[48]

'Dagulf's Psalter' was also made during Hadrian's lifetime, probably in the years just before his death.[49] The manuscript opens with a twenty-line poem dedicating the volume to the pope in the king's name (fol. 4r), showing that it must have been written before Hadrian's death in December 795 (Figure 7.3).[50] On the verso of the same leaf is a second poem, which honours the king as patron of the work, describes the ivory panels that had been 'sculpted by ingenious hand' for its cover (which still survive), and names Dagulf as scribe.[51] The leaf carrying the poems is a singleton that was added to the front of the book, and was copied by the same hand as the first three quires (fols 5–24). These quires form a coherent codicological unit containing a set of credal and other prefatory texts as well as the decorated *incipit* page on fol. 24v that introduces the psalter proper (see Figure 7.4).[52] The choice of creeds and other texts in this prefatory section point clearly to the interests and activities of court scholars such as Alcuin and Theodulf in the early 790s, including the production of the *Opus Caroli* against image worship, and thence to the widely accepted argument that this first part of the book was made at that time, most likely *c*.793–5.[53]

It is universally accepted that the scribe of the first part of the book, named as Dagulf, also copied the psalter (fols 25r–145v), and that he worked contemporaneously with a second scribe who took over part way through a quire to write the canticles and remaining texts at the end of the volume (fols 146r–158v).[54] Holter, wanting to align the codicology with late medieval and early modern traditions that

---

[48] On the date of the death of Hildegard, see *Pauli Gesta Episcopum Mettensium*, MGH, SS II, 267. For Godesscalc's verses (BnF, NAL 1203, fols 126v–127r), see Crivello et al., eds, *Das Godescalc-Evangelistar*, 10, 38–9. It is striking that the metrical parallels are predominantly papal epitaphs and Anglo-Latin verse (especially Aldhelm and Bede), on which, see also Bullough, 'Roman Books', 11.

[49] D. A. Bullough, '"Imagines Regum" and Their Significance in the Early Medieval West', in G. Robertson and G. Henderson, eds, *Studies in Memory of David Talbot Rice* (Edinburgh, 1975), 223–76, reprinted in his *Carolingian Renewal*, 39–96, at 56; L. Nees, 'Review of K. Holter, ed., *Der goldene Psalter, "Dagulf-Psalter": Vollständige Faksimile-Ausgabe im Originalformat von Codex 1861 Der Österreichischen Nationalbibliothek*', Codices Selecti Phototypice Impressi, 2 vols, 69 (Facsimile) and 69* (Commentarium) (Graz, 1980), in *The Art Bulletin*, 67 (1985), 681–90; F. Mütherich, 'Die Erneuerung der Buchmalerei am Hof Karls des Grossen', in SW, *799*, iii, 560–609, at 563; Nees, *Frankish Manuscripts*, no. 35.

[50] ÖNB, Cod. 1861, fol. 4r. *CSLMA* I, 287–9 (DAGU 1 and DAGU 2).

[51] Dümmler, ed., MGH, PLAC I, 92, and partially (with German translation), Mestemacher, *Marmor, Gold und Edelsteine*, 347. For discussion of the ivory panels, see this volume, Chapter 2, 99–100. On the word 'labour' (line 15) to describe the toil of the scribe, see F. Newton, 'Leo Marsicanus and the Dedicatory Text and Drawing in Monte Cassino 99', *Scriptorium*, 33 (1979), 181–205, at 191–3.

[52] Holter, ed., *Der goldene Psalter*, Commentarium, 15; Nees, 'Review of K. Holter, ed., *Der goldene Psalter*', 683.

[53] Linking the prefatory material to Alcuin, see D. A. Bullough, 'Alcuin and the Kingdom of Heaven: Liturgy, Theology, and the Carolingian Age', in his *Carolingian Renewal*, 161–240, at 192. For the rare credal text shared with the *Opus Caroli*, see Bullough, '"Imagines Regum"', 58–9.

[54] Koehler, *Die karolingischen Miniaturen*, ii, 42–6.

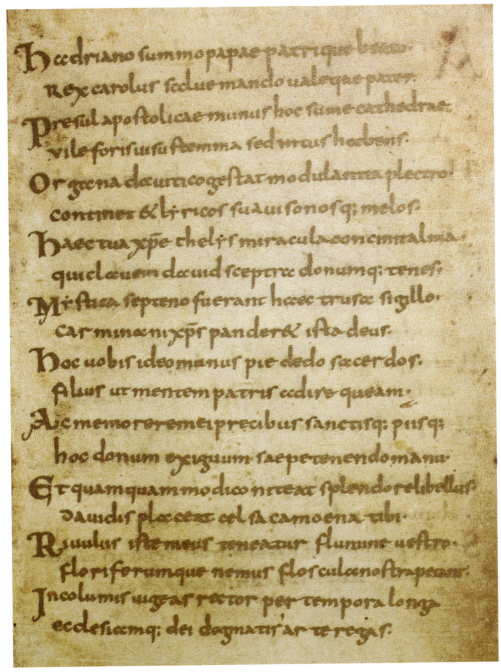

Figure 7.3 Dedicatory verses from Charlemagne to Pope Hadrian in the Dagulf Psalter; Vienna, ÖNB, Cod. 1861, fol. 4r (detail). Photo: Courtesy of the Österreichische Nationalbibliothek, Vienna.

link the manuscript with Hildegard, concluded that the manuscript was produced in two stages. He argued that the quires containing the psalter were produced in the mid-780s, akin to the date of Godesscalc's Evangelistary, and that a decade later Dagulf modified the psalter by adding prefatory material and the poems, including the dedication to Hadrian.[55]

Others, however, consider the whole book (ivory panels, poems, prefatory texts, psalter, canticles, and other closing texts), as a unitary product, commissioned as a gift for Hadrian but not delivered before his death in December 795.[56] The textual evidence is crucial for this argument (alongside art historical, codicological, and palaeographic considerations), in light of Charlemagne's demands for correct texts and their dissemination for proper use across the Frankish Church. Godesscalc's Evangelistary dates to the period before those centralised views had been clearly articulated in the *Admonitio generalis* (789), and before the text of the Roman sacramentary known as the *Hadrianum* had reached Francia (*c*.790).[57] The Evangelistary contains the extracts from the gospel texts that were to be read aloud during the annual cycle of feasts, beginning with the vigil for Christmas, and follows an admixture of two mid-eighth-century versions of what it calls the *ordinem Romanam*.[58] Bullough thought it likely that it was made for use in the palace chapel.[59] Dagulf's work, however, used the *Gallicanum* version of the psalter, laid out and punctuated in novel style, in accordance with the strictures of the *Admonitio generalis* that priests must sing the psalms properly, 'according to the division of the verses'.[60] As Rankin demonstrates, this manuscript laid out (perhaps for the first time) a very Frankish view of the correct way to sing the psalms in the daily office that was different from and contrasted with the version of the psalter known as the *Romanum* that was used in Rome.[61] Since this was a book intended for Pope Hadrian himself, its distinctively Frankish formulation rendered it a gift that was not entirely neutral.

---

[55] Holter, ed., *Der goldene Psalter*, Commentarium, 91–2. The wide date range is reflected for example in the 2014 exhibition catalogue, which dates the psalter 'after 783 and before 795'; Van den Brink and Ayooghi, eds, *Karls Kunst*, 220–3, cat. no. 15, and also by Mestemacher, *Marmor, Gold und Edelsteine*, 323.

[56] Bullough, '"Imagines Regum"', 56; Nees, 'Review of K. Holter, ed., *Der goldene Psalter*', 689–90; Ganz, 'The Scripts', 302; S. Rankin, 'Singing from the Dagulf Psalter', in Embach, Moulin, and Wolter-von dem Knesebeck, eds, *Die Handschriften*, 473–84.

[57] Vogel, *Medieval Liturgy*, 79–85; Y. Hen, *The Royal Patronage of Liturgy in Frankish Gaul to the Death of Charles the Bald* (London, 2011), 68–78.

[58] BnF, NAL 1203, fol. 106r. See Crivello et al., eds, *Das Godescalc-Evangelistar*, 13–14; T. Klauser, *Das römische Capitulare Evangeliorum. Texte und untersuchungen zu seiner ältesten gesichte*, i: *Typen*, Liturgiegeschichtekuche quellen und Forschungen, 28 (Münster, 1935), 47–92 and 131–72; Godesscalc's manuscript combines readings from Klauser's types L (Rome, *c*.740) and D (Francia-Rome, *c*.750).

[59] Bullough, 'Roman Books', 11.

[60] *Admonitio generalis*, ch. 68; Mordek et al., eds, MGH, Fontes XVI, 220–1.

[61] Rankin, 'Singing from the Dagulf Psalter', 478–81 and S. Rankin, *Sounding the Word of God. Carolingian Books for Singers* (Notre Dame, IN, 2022), 148–76. The *Romanum* was also used at this date in England.

The Psalter echoes Alcuin's comments in his court poem on the insistence of proper performance of the liturgy in the palace chapel; 'Sulpicius' the *lector* guides and teaches his charges that they 'may not err on the correct intonation' of the texts recited during the liturgy, and 'Idithun' the *cantor* taught singing and the proper 'metres, numbers and rhythms' of sacred chant.[62] Whereas Godesscalc's Evangelistary was made a decade before Charlemagne started to use Aachen regularly, the psalter made by Dagulf must represent the ideal usage of the palace chapel itself in the early to mid-790s, after the promulgation of the *Admonitio generalis* in 789. Perhaps (as Bullough thought) it was Hildebald himself, as archchaplain of the palace chapel, who was responsible for its liturgical innovations, novel structure, and lavish decoration.[63] Putting this evidence alongside that which links the choice of prefatory texts with the chronology of both Alcuin's and Theodulf's writing, as well as the palaeographic and codicological coherence of the opening quires with the psalter text itself, makes it probable that Dagulf's Psalter in its entirety dates a year or two before Hadrian's death and was perhaps intended as a counter gift to those brought by papal legates to Francia in 793.[64] As such, it would be very close in date to the composition, design, and perhaps also the place of production of Hadrian's epitaph.

Display script and painted letters

The deluxe group of manuscripts associated with the court is defined by shared features of script and decoration.[65] The text pages often have elaborate borders and there are carefully marbled columns in the canon tables, as well as opulent materials, including the widespread use of gold both for writing and ornament, and purple parchment. Fine display script is common, often outlined in red and picked out with gold. The display scripts vary in form, and several types may be found within the same book. Elongated letters, often interlocking, are also found, as are capitals deploying *litterae insertae*, ligatures, and tall letters as space-saving devices. The classical resonance of these scripts is obvious, and their use here was 'one conscious aspect of the antique revival' at Charlemagne's court.[66]

Important also are the papal connotations. Some manuscripts in this group contain capitals that have curlicues on the ends of the serifs, recalling and experimenting with the script of late fourth-century inscriptions in Rome that had been designed by Filocalus for Pope Damasus I (d. 384). Filocalian capitals may have been available in manuscript form at or close to the Carolingian court since there is good evidence that

---

[62] Alcuin, *Ad Carolum Regem*; Dümmler, ed., MGH, PLAC I, 245–6, no. 26, lines 36–40.
[63] Bullough, 'Alcuin and the Kingdom of Heaven', 229, n. 112 and 'Charlemagne's "Men of God"', 145.
[64] *ARF* s.a. 793; Nees, *Frankish Manuscripts*, no. 35.
[65] G. Denzinger, *Die Handschriften der Hofschule Karls des Großen*, Studien zu ihrer Ornamentik (Langwarden, 2001).
[66] Bullough, 'Roman Books', 15; Ganz, '"Roman Book" Reconsidered', 302.

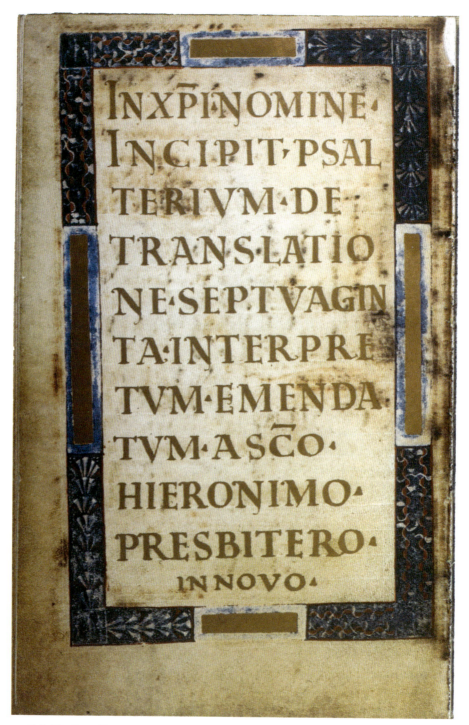

FIGURE 7.4 The Dagulf Psalter showing the Incipit facing the Beatus; Vienna, ÖNB, Cod. 1861, fols 24v–25r. Photo: Courtesy of the Österreichische Nationalbibliothek, Vienna.

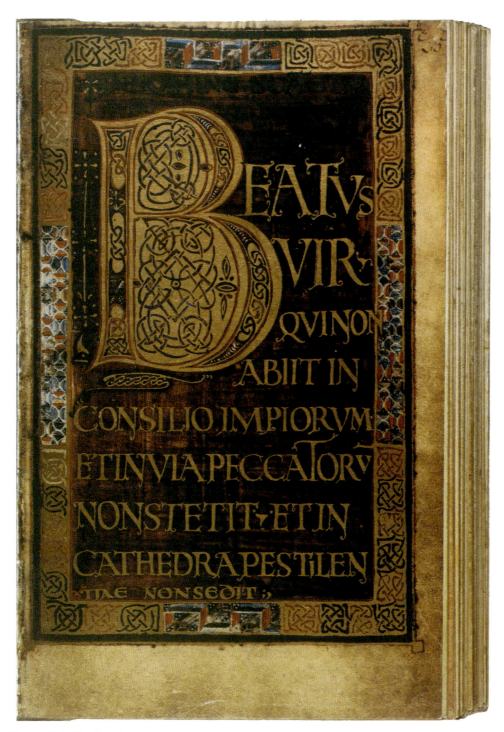

FIGURE 7.4 Continued

Theodulf of Orléans knew an illustrated manuscript of the 'Calendar of 354' by the time that he was preparing the *Opus Caroli* in 792–3. The early modern copies of the (now lost) Carolingian copy of that text include the dedication text naming Filocalus, set within an ansate slab held by a pair of winged putti, although none deploy the distinctive ornamented display script associated with him.[67]

This graphic experimentation is contextually pertinent in Dagulf's Psalter, which was a book intended for Hadrian in Rome and bore an ivory panel on the front cover showing Jerome as translator of the psalms receiving instructions from his master, Pope Damasus, and contained copies of apocryphal correspondence between the two among its prefatory texts.[68] The three major openings in the Psalter (fols 25r, 67v, 108v) have lettering in gold, or alternating lines of gold and silver, on a rich purple or dark blue ground, accompanying a large opening initial ornamented with interlace, all set within a wide frame with decorated panels. The terminals of most letters are bifurcated and extended by curled finials in the manner (but not identical to) the lettering of the fourth-century monumental inscriptions in Rome. The *incipit* page (fol. 24v) deploys a largely unornamented form of the script, sharing with the script of the major openings only the exaggerated descender on the second vertical of N as well as an ornamental frame. This page announces the authenticity of the version of the psalter text 'translated and emended by St Jerome, the priest', and is epigraphic in layout as well as script. The differences between the script of this page and the facing *Beatus* page reflect a hierarchy of script common in contemporary manuscripts and register the change between the introductory text on one side, and the words of the psalter on the other (Figure 7.4).[69]

Another clear example of Carolingian experimentation with Filocalian-style lettering can be seen on the title page of a very fine copy of the *Collectio Canonum Quesnelliana*, similarly dated to the end of the eighth century (the list of popes on fol. 1v names Hadrian but not the length of his pontificate) that Bischoff considered 'a book worthy of a king'.[70] This was an influential collection of canon law that made extensive use of letters of Pope Leo I (440–61), and the title page proclaims its origin in the *sedis apostolica*. Again, the papal connection is explicit. Bischoff thought that the scribe who added a set of notes on fol. 8v of this volume concerning the chronology of six major synods had also worked on the text of another manuscript in the court group. Only a fragment of that manuscript now survives in the collections of the

[67] The illustrations are known only through early modern copies of a Carolingian copy of the fourth-century original; Stern, *Le Calendrier de 354*, pl. I; Freeman and Meyvaert, eds, *Opus Caroli regis*, 442, 581; J. Divjak and W. Wischmeyer, eds, *Das Kalenderhandbuch von 354*: i, *Der Bildteil des Chronographen*, ii, *Der Texteil, Listen der Verwaltung* (Vienna, 2014), i, 6, 75–80. See also this volume, Chapter 8, 324, n. 64.

[68] Paris, Louvre, Département des Objets d'art, MR370 and MR371. See also Chapter 2, 99–100.

[69] Contra Holter, ed., *Der goldene Psalter*, Commentarium, 19–20. See also Nees, 'Review of K. Holter, ed., *Der goldene Psalter*', 686.

[70] Einsiedeln, Stiftsbibliothek, Cod. 191, fol. 3r; *CLA* VII.874; Bischoff, *Katalog*, no. 1116 (s. viii/ix, probably north-east France), and 'Court Library of Charlemagne', 66.

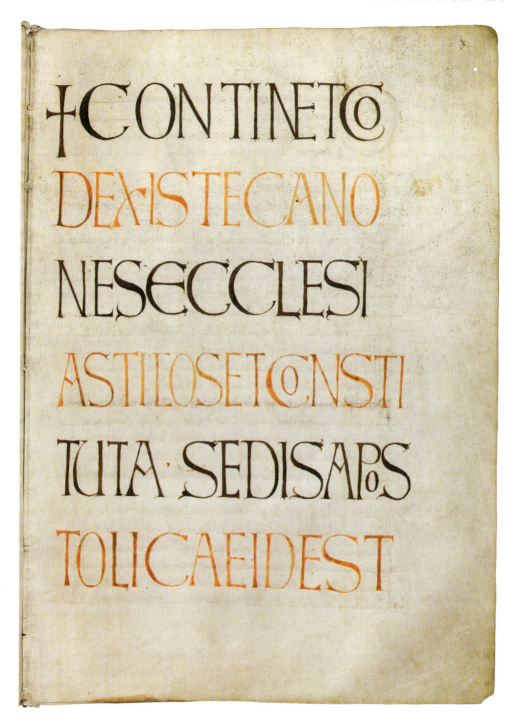

FIGURE 7.5 The title page of a copy of the *Collectio Canonum Quesnelliana*; Einsiedeln, Stiftsbibliothek, Cod. 191, fol. 3r. Photo: Courtesy of the Stiftsbibliothek, Einsiedeln.

British Library but it may originally have been an evangelistary rather than a gospel book and was illustrated with classicising panel miniatures.[71] The title page of the canon law book is written in red and black capitals, with curlicues on the terminals of many of the black letters springing from exaggerated, rounded terminations like many of Filocalus's inscriptions in Rome. However, the Carolingian scribe applied these terminals to the ends of rounded letters such as c and s, whereas Filocalus had avoided them on c, s, and g, preferring simple serifs on those letters (Figure 7.5).

Within the group of deluxe manuscripts associated with the patronage of Charlemagne's inner circle, the very best *capitalis quadrata* is found in the Abbeville Gospels which, with the exception of a few minor headings, is written entirely in gold. Monumental capitals were used for major titles especially at the opening of each gospel; the main text was written in uncial, and the gospel pericopes at the end of the volume in caroline minuscule. The quality of the display capitals in this book is exemplified by the lettering on the page that opens the gospel of John.[72] Koehler thought that this page was the work of a new scribe, using a different model for the script, but Denoël has shown that this folio and the distinctive evangelist portrait opposite are integral to the quire, and must have been part of the original schema for the book (Figure 7.6).[73] Here, the large initial letter 'I' is ornamented with three decorative panels and interlace finials, much like the opening letters of the other three gospel texts. But the rest of the page is strikingly plain, relying on the lettering for its impact. It lacks an ornamental border to constrain the text, and the visual power of the page derives from the shape, spacing and sheer quality of the *capitalis quadrata* used for the opening two verses. Script as image in this pared-down design relies on the lettering alone to capture and illuminate the meaning of the text. The near absence of ornament and the clean gold lines highlights the iconicity of the lettering and focuses

---

[71] Einsiedeln, Stiftsbibliothek, Cod. 191, fol. 8v which Bischoff rightly compares with a fragment of a manuscript now pasted into BL, Cotton MS Claudius B V, fol. 134v (olim fol. 132v) (*CLA* S: 1702; Bischoff, *Katalog*, no. 2419). Only one side of the fragment is visible and shows an image of the Annunciation to Zacharias (Luke 1:11) and one line of text reading 'angelus d[omi]ni stans a dextris altaris incensi'. Bischoff ('Court Library of Charlemagne', 66) observed that the scribe was familiar with Insular minuscule (using long s on the first and last line of the list in the Einsiedeln manuscript). See also W. Koehler, 'An Illustrated Evangelistary of the Ada School and its Model', *Journal of the Warburg and Courtauld Institutes*, 15 (1952), 48–66, and P. McGurk, *Latin Gospel Books from A.D. 400 to A.D. 800* (Amsterdam, 1961), 33, no. 21. The main portion of London, BL Cotton MS Claudius B V is a copy of the canons of the Council of Constantinople in 680, which dates to the second if not the first quarter of the ninth century (Bischoff, *Katalog*, no. 2418); its dramatic opening titles on fols 4v–5r use grand square capitals in alternating lines of red and black, diminishing in size on fol. 5r, with the text completed in rustic capitals. At the foot of that folio is an inscription recording the gifting of the book by King Æthelstan (924–39) to the community at Bath; S. Keynes, 'King Æthelstan's books', in M. Lapidge and H. Gneuss, eds, *Learning and Literature in Anglo-Saxon England: Studies Presented to Peter Clemoes on the Occasion of his Sixty-Fifth Birthday* (Cambridge, 1985), 143–201, at 159–65.

[72] Abbeville, Bibliothèque municipale, MS 4, fol. 154r. *CLA* VI: 704; Koehler, *Die karolingischen Miniaturen*, ii, 49–55, pl. 33–41; McGurk, *Latin Gospel Books*, 49–50, no. 45; Bischoff, *Katalog*, no. 8; C. Denoël, *Les Évangiles de St.-Riquier. Un manuscript pour Charlemagne*, Art de l'enluminure, 46 (Dijon, 2013).

[73] Koehler, *Die karolingischen Miniaturen*, iii.1, 29; Denoël, *Les Évangiles de St.-Riquier*, 25–6.

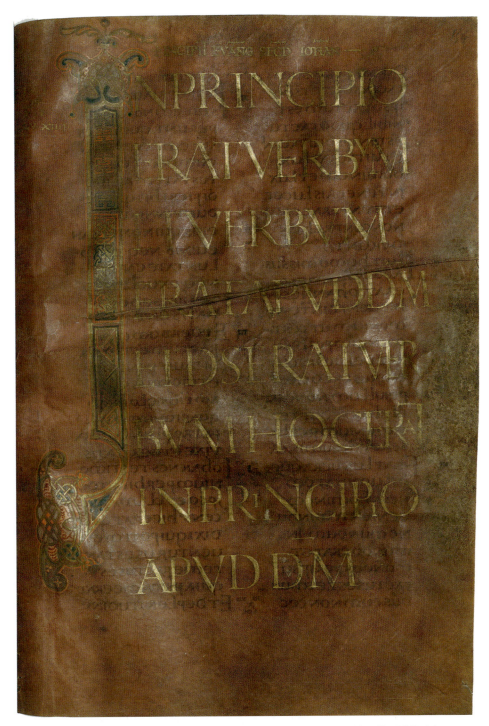

Figure 7.6 Opening to the gospel of St John in the Abbeville Gospels; Abbeville, Bibliothèque municipale, MS 4, fol. 154r. Photo: Courtesy of the Archives e Bibliothèque patrimoniale, Abbeville.

attention on John's profound opening statement that unites *Verbum* with *Deus* and invests script with divinity.[74]

The *capitalis quadrata* used on this page is profoundly epigraphic in its proportions, pace, and regularity. It exemplifies Augustine's comment that John's opening words 'should be inscribed in letters of gold and displayed in the most prominent place in every church'.[75] The scribe used abbreviations for the *nomina sacra*, smaller letters, and a tall letter T on line 6, ensuring that all except line 5 finishes with a complete word. There is no word spacing (*scriptio continua*) and no punctuation, even at the hiatus between verses in line 6. All this bears close comparison with the layout and lettering of Hadrian's epitaph. There are differences; in the Abbeville Gospels, the letter A has a head stroke, the M and N are generally square, and the cauda of R joins the bowl closer to the stem than the same letter on the epitaph. But overall, there is a strong resemblance between the two in the treatment both of groups of letters and individual graphs. This impression is greatly reinforced by the use of gold on a dark coloured ground. With the exception of the final 10 folios (fols 189–98, one quire and a bifolium) that carry the pericopes, the Abbeville Gospels are written on parchment entirely stained with purple. In a gospel book the colour purple evokes the blood and passion of Christ more so than any classical associations of imperial status; it is an ostentatious statement of the ability of a wealthy patron to deploy scarce raw materials and rare skills in the service of God and, as such, need not only be associated with royal patronage.

The version of the gospel text used for the Abbeville manuscript is much closer to that in the Coronation Gospels (so-called from its role in later coronation ceremonies for Holy Roman Emperors) than it is to the others in the 'Court School' group.[76] The Coronation Gospels is also the only other extant manuscript from Francia in the period made entirely of purple-dyed parchment. Several other deluxe manuscripts

---

[74] John 1:1–2, 'In principio erat verbum, et verbum erat apud Deum, et Deus erat verbum. Hoc erat in principio apud Deum'. Ganz, '"Roman Books" Reconsidered', 314, n. 79; E. Thunø, 'Inscription and Divine Presence: Golden Letters in the Early Medieval Apse Mosaic', *Word and Image*, 27 (2011), 279–91; Thunø, *Apse Mosaic*, 47–52, 112–14. More generally, the singularity and special treatment of John's gospel is explored by J. F. Hamburger, *St John the Divine: The Deified Evangelist in Medieval Art and Theology* (Berkeley, CA, 2003), especially 21–42.

[75] 'Aureis litteris conscribendum et per omnes ecclesias in locis eminentissimis proponendum esse dicebat'; Augustine, *De Civitate Dei*, X.29; tr. D. S. Wiesen, *The City of God Against the Pagans. Volume III: Books 8–11*, Loeb Classical Library 413 (Cambridge, MA, 1968), 392–3. Ganz, 'The Scripts', 298.

[76] Vienna, Kunsthistorisches Museum, Schatzkammer, Inv. XIII.18; *CLA* X:1469; Bischoff, *Katalog*, no. 7100 where it is assigned to the 'Hof Karls des Großen'. W. Koehler, *Die karolingischen Miniaturen*, iii.1. *Die Gruppe des wiener Krönungsevangeliars* (Berlin, 1960), 38 considered the text type of the Coronation and Abbeville Gospels to be 'as good as identical'. See also S. Haag and F. Kirchweger, eds, *Das Krönungsevangeliar des Heiligen Römischen Reiches* (Vienna, 2014), containing, especially, F. Crivello, 'Die Handschriften und ihr Schmuck', 45–8, who prefers an early ninth-century date for the Coronation Gospels, and notes that the type of text used for the pericopes in that manuscript is that which was revised in Rome in 755, *pace* Denoël, *Les Évangiles de St.-Riquier*, 12–14.

from Charlemagne's reign contain pages where the background of the text block was painted purple (such as Godesscalc's Evangelistary), but only the Abbeville and Coronation Gospels are made from pages that seem to have been completely dipped in purple dye, which was a far more expensive process than painting the surface with purple tint. Because many of the extant parallels are Greek, Bischoff suggested that purple parchment such as this could have been imported, pre-prepared from Constantinople.[77] The dating of the Coronation Gospels remains contentious, however, and, although it is clear that it and three other related books are quite different artistically to the 'Court School' group, it is uncertain whether the Coronation Gospels also belongs to the reign of Charlemagne (as Koehler thought on art historical grounds, and others have agreed on the basis of textual filiations) or during the reign of his son, Louis the Pious, as Bischoff argued for the three other manuscripts in that group.[78] Nevertheless, it is striking that these two purple-dyed codices belong to the same text family, and that each one displays a hierarchy of classicising scripts deployed to great effect by a master scribe.

The Abbeville Gospels can be tied to the heart of Charlemagne's *familia*. The book is included in the inventory of the abbey of Saint-Riquier, and it was almost certainly among many given to that monastery by Angilbert, who was made abbot in about 789 and during his tenure oversaw the construction of a spectacular monastic complex with three new churches.[79] He died, soon after his king, in 814.[80] Angilbert had been one of Charlemagne's closest courtiers, and his epistle-poem reveals his central place in the court. This poem was probably written in early 796 following Pope Leo's request that Charlemagne send 'one of his *optimates*' to Rome to receive

[77] B. Bischoff, *Latin Palaeography: Antiquity and the Middle Ages*, tr. D. Ó Cróinín and D. Ganz (Cambridge, 1991), 10–11.

[78] Aachen, Domschatzkammer, Inv.-Nr. 4 (Bischoff, *Katalog*, no. 1, 'before 830'); Brescia, Biblioteca Civica Queriniana E.II.9 (Bischoff, *Katalog*, no. 682, '814–40'); Brussels, Bibliothèque royale 18723 (Bischoff, *Katalog*, no. 745, 'first quarter of the ninth century'). Koehler placed all of these manuscripts during the lifetime of Charlemagne (Koehler, *Die karolingischen Miniaturen*, iii.1, 13), but Bischoff preferred to date them to the reign of Louis the Pious; Bischoff, 'The Court Library under Louis the Pious', 85. The textual arguments are based on Fischer's analysis which suggests that the text type represented by Abbeville and the Coronation Gospels contributed to the revision of the gospels text known as the 'Lothar-text' (after its best exemplar), which he argued was made in Aachen in the early ninth century; B. Fischer, 'Der Text des Quedlinburger Evangeliars', in P. McGurk and F. Mütherich, eds, *Das Quedlinburger Evangeliar. Das Samuhel-Evangeliar aus dem Quedlinburger Dom* (Munich, 1991), 35–41.

[79] For a summary, see S. A. Rabe, *Faith, Art, and Politics at Saint-Riquier. The Symbolic Vision of Angilbert* (Philadelphia, PA, 1995).

[80] The Abbeville Gospels seems to be the volume with a treasure binding described in a text believed to have been written by Angilbert himself, and in an inventory of the library dated to 831, both preserved by Hariulf, in his late eleventh-century history, *Gesta ecclesiae Centulensis*, II.10 (Angilbert's text), 'Evangelium auro scriptum cum tabulis argenteis auro et lapidibus preciosis mirifice paratum 1', and III.3 (831 inventory), 'Evangelium auro scriptum unum cum capsa argentea, gemmis, et lapidibus fabricata', and as 'Textus Evangelii IV, aureis litteris scriptis totus, 1'; F. Lot, ed., *Hariulf. Chronique de l'abbaye du St. Riquier, Ve siècle –1104* (Paris, 1894), xxvii, 63 (and n. 1), 88, and 93.

the oaths of fidelity of the Roman people. Charlemagne chose Angilbert for this task and, in his letter to Leo lamenting Hadrian's death, the king referred to Angilbert as 'the secret counsellor and secretary of our intimacy'.[81] 'Brought up almost from the beginnings of infancy' in Charlemagne's palace, Angilbert was a lifelong confidante of the king, witness to his will, *primicerius palatii* for the young King Pippin in Italy, envoy to the papal court in matters of theology and politics, poet, lover of Charlemagne's daughter Bertha, and father to her children.[82] Bischoff calls Angilbert 'the luxury-loving favourite of Charlemagne', which is a description that fits well with the splendour of the Abbeville Gospels.[83] His profile makes him a plausible patron of the purple gospel book that he subsequently gave to his abbey rather than having to assume it was necessarily a royal commission.[84] Angilbert's connections to the king's family and his own love of learning would have given him access to the financial, material, and human resources needed to create a manuscript of this quality. Based on its place in the sequence of witnesses to the revision of the gospels text as well as art historical parallels, it was almost certainly made in the last decade of the eighth century and could well have been a gift to Saint-Riquier on the occasion of the dedication of the new church there in 800.[85] If so, the person responsible for its display capitals was working close in time, if not also in place, with the *ordinator* responsible for the layout of the text on Hadrian's epitaph.

The volume known as the Lorsch Gospels probably dates to the first quarter of the ninth century, perhaps even a little later, and thus responds rather than contributes to the graphic innovations that lie behind Hadrian's epitaph.[86] Here the opening words of the text face the incipits to the gospels of Matthew, Luke, and John rather than evangelist portraits, which in this book are deployed at the front of the summary *capitula* for each gospel. A portrait of Christ in Majesty faces the opening words of the gospel of Matthew and uses two lines of unornamented square capitals with inserted and elongated letters, above and below the central roundel. Both pages in this opening use gold, or gold and silver lettering, on a purple background. The opening letters of the *Liber generationis* follow an Insular-style layout, as in other books in this group, and serifed capitals decorated with Filocalian-type curls are also

---

[81] Charlemagne, 'Letter to Angilbert' and 'Letter to Leo III'; Dümmler, ed., MGH, Epp. IV, 135–8, nos 92–3.

[82] Rabe, *Faith, Art, and Politics*, 52–4, 71–5.

[83] Bischoff, 'Manuscripts and Libraries', 63.

[84] Koehler, *Die karolingischen Miniaturen*, ii, 16; Winterer, 'Die Miniatur im (karolingischen) Zeitalter', 273; Mestemacher, *Marmor, Gold und Edelsteine*, 326–7.

[85] Ganz, '"Roman Books" Reconsidered', 307.

[86] Lorsch Gospels: Bukarest, Biblioteca Natională a României (Alba Julia, Biblioteca Documentară Batthyáneum), MS R.II.1 (prefatory matter, canon tables, Matthew, Mark) and BAV, Pal. Lat. 50 (Luke, John). For printed facsimiles, see W. Braunfels, ed., *The Lorsch Gospels* (New York, 1967) and H. Schefers, ed., *Das Lorscher Evangeliar. Biblioteca Documentara Batthyaneum, Alba Iulia, Ms R II 1, Biblioteca Apostolica Vaticana, Codex Vaticanus Palatinus Latinus 50* (Luzern, 2000).

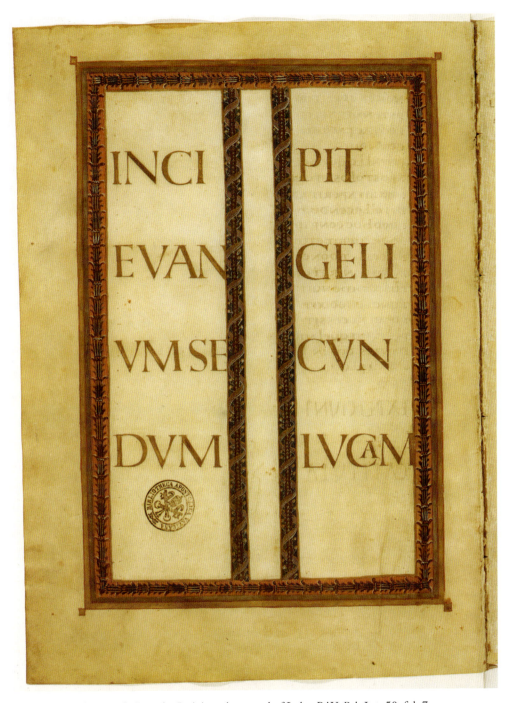

FIGURE 7.7 The Lorsch Gospels, *Incipit* to the gospel of Luke. BAV, Pal. Lat. 50, fol. 7v. Photo: Reproduced by kind permission of the Biblioteca Apostolica Vaticana, Rome.

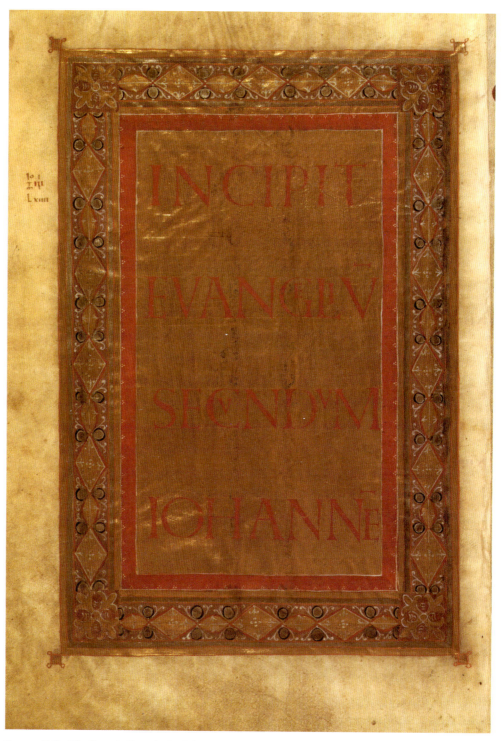

FIGURE 7.8 The Lorsch Gospels, *Incipit* to the gospel of John. BAV, Pal. Lat. 50, fol. 70v. Photo: Reproduced by kind permission of the Biblioteca Apostolica Vaticana, Rome.

used.[87] The incipits to the other three gospels are all unornamented square capitals of classical type. The capitals used for the incipit and opening words of Mark are in black ink, laid out in bands with alternating gold or silver ground.[88] The capitals on this opening are epigraphic in proportion and layout; the scribe used smaller letters, nested to modulate the spacing, but avoided the use of elongated letters in all but the initial I. For the opening of Luke the text is laid out in two columns with gold ink on the plain parchment ground, surrounded by an ornamental border (Figure 7.7). The large lettering of the incipit is juxtaposed by the page opposite where the *capitalis* diminishes in size five times, and inserted letters and ligatures are used to save space, especially towards the end of each line.

The incipit to John in this manuscript is, once again, the most striking of the gospel openings in the Lorsch Gospels. A much wider border is used here than elsewhere, framing the text with gold lozenges and silver circles on a purple ground, and bold red lettering is set centrally within a red border on a shining golden ground. Again, the use of colour enhances the meaning of the text; gold represents the splendour of holy wisdom and red the blood of Christ.[89] The large expanse of gold leaf glitters with reflected light, recalling Jerome's comment that 'all we read in sacred books shines and sparkles', as well as the association with holy wisdom and the flesh of Christ that lies within and beneath the written Word (Figure 7.8).[90]

The incipits to the gospel texts in another deluxe manuscript in this group also make creative use of *capitalis* and decorative ornamentation, with extensive gold leaf laid on coloured grounds. The title page that follows the canon tables in the book now known as the Harley Golden Gospels, uses gold and silver in alternate bands of lettering that fills a central purple disc, recalling the massive porphyry roundels set into the floor of St Peter's basilica (Figure 7.9).[91] Here, the gold and silver letters appear inlaid in the surface of the purple setting. The capitals sport curls on the serifs and the space between the lines is filled with a motif of four short lines, diminishing in size, with a hook centrally placed below. This motif is widely used across the court group of manuscripts and is a decorative 'tick' that links the makers of these illuminated pages. The incipit to the gospel of John on fol. 162r lays out the opening verses in four zones beneath an arch that is supported by marble columns with Corinthian-style capitals. The *capitalis* varies in scale in each zone, with the uppermost and lowest zones using red letters, reserving the middle two bands for just three words, '[*I*]*n*

---

[87] Bukarest, Biblioteca Națională a României (Alba Julia, Biblioteca Documentară Batthyáneum), MS R.II.1, 36–7 (fols 18v–19r).

[88] Bukarest, Biblioteca Națională a României (Alba Julia, Biblioteca Documentară Batthyáneum), MS R.II.1, 154–5 (fols 77v–78r).

[89] This is explicitly stated in Godesscalc's opening verses; Dümmler, ed., MGH, PLAC I, 94, lines 1–3.

[90] Jerome, *Ad Paulinum Presbyterum*; J. Labourt, ed. and tr., St. Jérôme, Lettres, 8 vols (Paris, 1949–63), iii, 93, Ep. 58.9; L. Kendrick, *Animating the Letter: The Figurative Embodiment of Writing from Late Antiquity to the Renaissance* (Columbus, OH, 1999), 45–8, 67, 81–2; Thunø, *Apse Mosaic*, 114.

[91] BL, Harley, MS 2788, fol. 12v.

Figure 7.9 The title page to the four gospels; London, British Library, Harley MS 2788, fol. 12v. Photo: Reproduced with permission of The British Library Board.

principio erat', picked out in gold leaf within orange painted outlines on a contrasting purple ground. The four zones within the arch are linked by a large letter 'I', ornamented with interlace, lozenges and roundels containing depictions of the Agnus Dei, St John (pointing upwards), and his eagle with its wings supporting roundels containing busts of two men. The space between the left-hand column and this large initial is filled with three lattice panels that are remarkably like the patterns of the closely contemporary Carolingian bronze grilles that still stand around the upper level of the Aachen chapel (Figures 7.10 and 7.11).[92]

The prestige of capital lettering, and the skill needed to create it, was mentioned by Lupus of Ferrières. In a long letter to Einhard, written in May 836, Lupus explained why he had to delay his next visit, and confirmed that he would arrive at Einhard's monastery in Seligenstadt the week beginning 5 June.[93] In the meantime, he requested more help from Einhard in understanding some problems of geometry outlined in Boethius' *De Arithmetica*, as well as guidance on how to study the calculus of Victorius of Aquitaine and clarification of some finer points of metrics. He also promised to return the books that Einhard had loaned to him, including a rare work by Aulus Gellius. Lupus explained that Hraban Maur, abbot of Fulda, had borrowed this book from him and had not yet returned it.[94] His letter continued with another request:

> …the royal scribe, Bertcaud, is said to have a measured drawing (*mensuram descriptam*) of antique lettering, at any rate of those letters that are the biggest and are considered by some to be called 'uncials'. Therefore, if this is in your hands, I beg, send it to me now through this painter when he returns, on a parchment leaf (*scedula*) protected most carefully with a seal.[95]

Here Lupus reveals the existence of a court official known as the *scriptor regius*, who was, at the time of writing, a man named Bertcaud. He seems to have possessed something akin to a technical drawing of antique display script. Lupus, and other Carolingian writers, followed Jerome who defined *unciales* as 'the large letters which are found at

---

[92] Pawelec, *Aachener Bronzegitter*, 53, 141–2, Abb. 101, 189, 192–3. There is a striking parallel also with the grid pattern contained by the bowl of the large initial Q[oniam] which opens Psalm 51 in a surviving fragment of the Faddan More Psalter (Dublin, National Museum of Ireland, 06E0786:13), and which is also dated *c*.800; A. Read, *The Faddan More Psalter. Discovery, Conservation and Investigation* (Dublin, 2011), 67, 73.

[93] L. Levillain, ed. and tr., *Loup de Ferrières. Correspondance*, 2 vols (Paris, 1927–35), i, 40–51.

[94] This is apparently the first post-classical reference to Gellius' *Noctes Atticae* ('Attic Nights'); Reynolds, *Texts and Transmission*, 176–80. The manuscript made for Hraban at Fulda in 836 survives as Leeuwarden, Provincale Bibliotheek van Friesland, 55 Hs (B. A. Fr. 55), copied in a combination of Insular and Caroline minuscule (Bischoff, *Katalog*, no. 2133).

[95] 'Praeterea scriptor regius Bertcaudus dicitur antiquarum litterarum, dumtaxat earum quae maximae sunt et unciales a quibusdam vocari existimantur, habere mensuram descriptam. Itaque, si poenes vos est, mittite mihi iam per hunc, quaeso, pictorem, cum redierit, scedula tamen diligentissime sigillo munita'; Levillain, ed. and tr., *Loup de Ferrières*, 50–1.

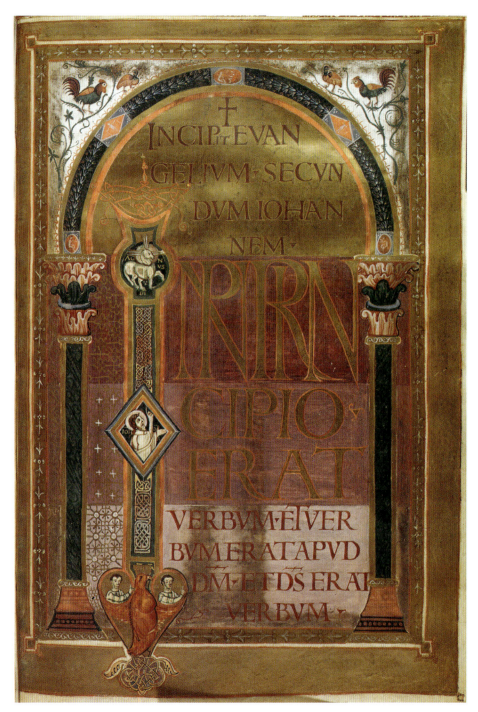

Figure 7.10 *Incipit* to the Gospel of John; London, British Library, Harley MS 2788, fol. 162r. Photo: Reproduced with permission of The British Library Board.

FIGURE 7.11 The second set of bronze railings in the Aachen Chapel. Reproduced by permission of the Domkapitel Aachen. Photo: Ann Münchow/Pit Siebigs.

the beginning of books'; these are thus highly likely to have been classical, monumental capitals rather than rounded uncials, as favoured later for gospel books.[96] Bischoff argued that Bertcaud, acting in his capacity as *scriptor regius*, may have been responsible for designing a monumental alphabet rather than just copying antique letter forms. He made this claim on the basis of a page of fine *capitalis* found in a copy of Victorius' texts *On Calculus* and *On Weights and Measures* which he linked to Einhard, and which he thought were of a later type than those found within the 'Court School' group. This manuscript, he argued, could have been made at Seligenstadt for Lupus, in direct response to his request as recorded in this letter.[97] The alphabet in that manuscript includes a *capitalis* K, which takes the form of R with the upper portion of the bow removed, resolving into a horizontal line and serif. Clearly this graph would not have been found in any classical inscription and must have been devised by a later designer, plausibly Bertcaud or another like him. But, tempting though it is to link this manuscript directly with Lupus' letter and Einhard, the connections between them are more circumstantial than certain (Figure 7.12).

The precision of Lupus' request is significant. He asked for a copy of the antique letters to be drawn out on a loose-leaf parchment sheet (*scedula*) and for it to be delivered to him, securely sealed, by 'this painter' (*hunc pictor*) on his return. This implies that Lupus was sending a painter to Seligenstadt who was skilled in the art of

---

[96] E. T. Merrill, 'The "Uncial" in Jerome and Lupus', *Classical Philology*, 11.4 (1916), 452–7; B. Bischoff, 'Die alten Namen der lateinischen Schriftarten', *Mittelalterlichen Studien*, I, 1–6; Ganz, '"Roman Books" Reconsidered', 298–9. See also E. A. Lowe, *English Uncial* (Oxford, 1960), 1–2. The second glossary contained in Cambridge, Corpus Christi College MS 144 (s. ix[1]) refers, on fol. 8v, to a scribe as an *Antiquarius*, 'one who writes big letters' (*qui grandes litteras scribit*).

[97] Berne, Bergerbibliothek, Cod. 250, fol. 11v. Bischoff, *Katalog*, I.562. Bischoff also found the name 'Bertcaud' among those of twenty-six scribes in a copy of Rufinus' translation of Eusebius, *Historia ecclesiastica*, now Angers, Bibliothèque Municipale, MS 675, f. 101v, *s.* IX2/3; Bischoff, *Katalog*, I.72.

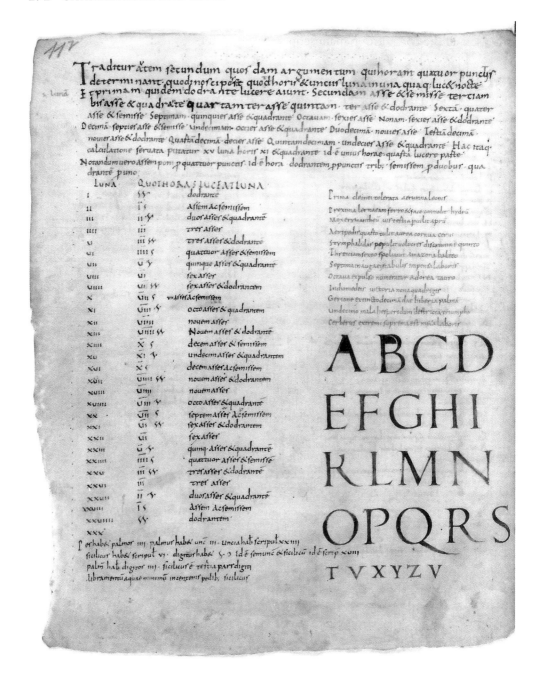

FIGURE 7.12 'Bertcaud's alphabet'; Bern, Burgerbibliothek, Cod. 250, fol. 11v. Photo: Courtesy of the Bergerbibliothek, Bern.

laying out display script to make a copy of Bertcaud's alphabet, authenticated and protected by a seal. Not only is this evidence of the movement of skilled artisans for specific commissions, as well as the circulation of loose-leaf exemplars, but may also suggest that, as *pictor*, this man had a different skillset to that of the *scriptor*, perhaps in the laying out of large-scale lettering. Ganz has suggested that the monumental capitals in all the court group manuscripts were probably painted, as standard practice, citing as an example the red capitals on the gold ground at the opening of John's gospel in the Lorsch Gospels (see Figure 7.8).[98] The opening lines of the dedicatory verses in both Godesscalc's Evangelistary and Dagulf's Psalter lead with an invocation to the painting of golden letters.[99] Dagulf, writing before Hadrian's death in 795, clearly followed the diction and metrical structure of Godesscalc's verse, composed about a decade earlier, that was copied into the Evangelistary which was almost certainly available to Dagulf and others among the volumes belonging to the king's chapel. Subsequently, Theodulf adapted Dagulf's opening line when composing his own verses commemorating Hadrian.

Aurea purpureis **pinguntur grammata** scedis
Golden letters are painted on purple leaves
(Godesscalc's Evangelistary, fol. 127v, lines 1–2)

Aurea Daviticos en **pingit littera** cantus
Golden lettering paints David's chant. Behold!
(Dagulf's Psalter, fol. 4v, line 1)

Aurea funereum complectit **littera** carmen
Golden lettering takes up the funereal song
(Theodulf, *Super sepulcrum Hadriani papae*, line 1)

Godesscalc's verse may also have inspired the poet who wrote the epitaph for Queen Hildegard, who had died on 30 April 783 and was buried in the church of St Arnulf at Metz. Her thirty-six-line epitaph is reported by Paul the Deacon alongside those of four other royal women and girls buried at Metz, and it is possible that he composed it.[100] The first line begins, *Aurea que fulvis rutilant elementa figuris* ('Golden letters

---

[98] Ganz, '"Roman Books" Reconsidered', 303.

[99] Thunø, *Apse Mosaic*, 114. Godesscalc's verse goes back, ultimately, to Vergil's *Aeneid* IV:139, 'Aurea purpuream subnectit fibula uestem' ('a golden clasp fastens the purple robe'), which sets gold alongside purple but lacks the link to lettering. Vergil's *Aeneid* was known to court scholars, but the line could also have been mediated through Corippus' four-book Vergilian panegyric on Justin II and Sophia written in 567/8, where Book III.111 reads, 'Aurea purpureis adponunt fercula mensis' ('they placed golden platters on purple tables'). This text also circulated at the Carolingian court, and was used especially by Theodulf (see Chapter 8, 321–5). See A. Cameron, ed. and tr., *Flavius Cresconius Corippus. In laudem Iustini Augusti minoris* (London, 1976), 64, 104 and Schaller, 'Frühkarolingische Corippus-Rezeption', 183. Another parallel in structure and diction is the opening line to the dedication inscription in mosaic at the apse at S. Agnese fuori le Mura by Honorius I (625–38), which begins, 'Aurea concisis surgit pictura metallis' ('The golden picture emerges from clipped metal'), on which, see Schaller and Könsgen, eds, *Initia*, no. 1428; Brandenburg, *Ancient Churches*, 244–7 and Lansford, *Latin Inscriptions*, 286–7 (no. 8.8B).

[100] Kempf, *Paul the Deacon*, 80–1. Paul was in Francia when Hildegard died, and was commissioned by Angilram, who became bishop of Metz in 784, to write the *Liber de episcopis Mettensibus*, which was completed

gleam in their yellow lines'), reusing the tight metrical format found in Godesscalc's verse as well as his reference to golden lettering. Paul says that the epitaph for the queen (and those for two of her daughters) were 'composed at the order of the glorious king Charles', but it is not certain if it was ever displayed over Hildegard's tomb in monumental form, either in stone or as a painted text. Nevertheless, it adds to the evidence that the topos of golden lettering (laid out in a metrical 'golden line') was favoured by court poets seeking to praise the king and those close to him, including Hadrian.

Painted lettering survives from the walls of a number of Carolingian buildings, including the palace at Paderborn.[101] There, the material composition of plaster varied by period, enabling archaeologists to group the fragments into decorative schema that can be dated via the construction and destruction phases of the buildings in which the plaster fragments were found. About two hundred of the ten thousand fragments recovered reveal traces of painted lettering, most in a red pigment on a pale background but with some larger letters in black.[102] All these fragmentary inscriptions were found in the interior of rooms to the east of the *aula*, on the northern side of the church, and can be dated by their archaeological stratification to sequences before 800. Some, including the only clear sequence of letters (spelling DRACO), are from contexts that can be dated with some confidence to the early construction phases of the building, probably in 776/7.[103] Other fragments of painted lettering survive from a structure slightly to the north which is thought to have been demolished in 794. Yet more fragments of painted plaster survive from the period of the construction of the new church in 799, but none of those elements preserve lettering.

The surviving lettering at Paderborn was laid out between pairs of parallel bounding lines that had been incised into the surface of the fresh plaster, about 5cm apart, soon after it had been applied to the wall.[104] This suggests that the lettering was part of the original decorative programme of these rooms, not added subsequently as an afterthought (unless the surface had subsequently been re-skimmed with a thin layer of plaster specifically for this purpose). Tall, stemmed crosses and simple ornamental plant scrolls were also used (both horizontally and vertically) to demarcate areas of lettering. The script is a classicising *capitalis quadrata*, with substantial serifs and

---

probably before 786. The epitaphs of the royal women buried at Metz are found in only one copy of Paul's *Liber*, namely, BnF, Lat. 5294, fols 11v–13v. On Paul, Angilram, and the texts of these epitaphs, see Kempf, *Paul the Deacon*, 14, 16, 35, 80–3.

[101] M. Preissler, 'Fragmente einer verlorenen Kunst. Die Paderborner Wandmalerei', in SW, *799*, iii, 197–206. M. Preissler, *Die karolingischen Malereifragmente aus Paderborn. Zu den Putzfunden aus der Pfalzanlage Karls des Großen, Archäologie und Wandmalerei*, Denkmalpflege und Forschung in Westfalen, 40.1 (Mainz, 2003).

[102] Preissler, 'Die Wandmalerei', in SW, *799*, i, 133–43, III.17–20. The red letters are *c.*5cm, the black letters are *c.*7cm.

[103] Preissler, *Die karolingischen Malereifragmente*, 13, 19–20, 39–41 (Plans 11 and 12), 49–50 and Tafel 1.

[104] See especially Preissler, *Die karolingischen Malereifragmente*, 76–8, abb. 32–3.

differentiation between thick and think lines; however, the letter A always has both a flat top and a broken crossbar which is quite different from the script of the epitaph. Nor is there evidence of space-saving devices, such as inserted or tall letters. It is especially helpful that these fragmentary inscriptions are archaeological dateable, independent of art historical or epigraphic comparanda. The painted lettering at Paderborn can be placed firmly, on archaeological grounds, into the last quarter of the eighth century, and as such provide a valuable reference point for analysis of script in manuscripts and on stone. Similar painted plasterwork has also been recovered from the palace site at Ingelheim, dating to the final third of the eighth century, and from the Torhalle at Lorsch, but these assemblages do not preserve plaster fragments with lettering.[105]

The preservation of painted inscriptions from the walls of secular buildings such as these is a reminder that verse epigrams and prose texts were just as, if not more likely, to have been painted as inscribed in stone, and that painted display scripts were not reserved for the pages of books. Indeed, painted inscriptions such as these are a missing link between 'epigraphic' lettering in books and inscriptions cut on stone, since the latter would have been laid out with a broad brush before being cut with a chisel; the difference is a matter of medium and scale rather than the principles of technique. The permanence of stone favours preservation of inscribed texts over painted ones, but the speed and cost differential between the two media may well have meant that both formal and informal painted texts were far more commonplace than current visibility suggests in both ecclesiastical and elite secular structures. This is supported by the *syllogae*, which preserve many epigrams that seem to have been intended for display but of which no physical trace remains, and by the frequency of painted inscriptions in early medieval churches, especially in Italy but also in Francia, in those places where wall painting survives. Among important early Carolingian examples, dating *c.*800, are the Southern Alpine churches at Mals (South Tyrol, Italy) and Müstair (Braubünden, Switzerland).[106] Further south, from the same period, substantial painted texts are found at San Vincenzo al Volturno (Isernia, Italy), Santa Tecla and Sant'Ambrogio in Milan and at Santa Maria Antiqua and Sant'Adriano in Rome, to name but a few of the most important examples.[107]

---

[105] SW, *799*, i, 106–7, II.66.

[106] Mid-ninth-century fresco cycles are preserved at St Germain, Auxerre, and St Maximin, Trier, although neither preserves texts alongside the fragmentary images. On the painted scenes and texts at Mals, see E. Robert, *Sankt Benedikt in Mals* (Bozen, 1992), fig. 6, abb. 52, 60, 63, 67.

[107] Preissler, *Die Malerei*, 79–86. J. Mitchell, 'Literacy Displayed: The Use of Inscriptions at the Monastery of San Vincezo al Volturno in the Early Ninth Century', in R. McKitterick, ed., *The Uses of Literacy in early Medieval Europe* (Cambridge, 1990), 186–225, and J. Mitchell, 'The Display of Script and the Uses of Painting in Longobard Italy', in *Testo e imagine nell'alto medioevo*, SSCI, 41 (1994), 887–954; Maskarinec, *City of Saints*, pl. 9.

The dedication inscription at Aachen

No painted inscriptions survive from the Carolingian buildings at Aachen. However, the text of an eight-line dedicatory epigram for the chapel survives uniquely in a manuscript that was compiled at Sankt Gallen, shortly after 800,[108] where it is the last item in an anthology of twenty-two poems, many of which were inscriptions associated with St Peter's basilica in Rome.[109] The manuscript supplies a title that leaves no doubt about the original location of these four elegiac couplets (Figure 7.13):

VERSUS IN AULA ECCLESIAE IN AQUIS PALATIO

1   Cum lapides vivi pacis conpage ligantur,
      Inque pares numeros omnia conveniunt,
3   Claret opus domini, totam qui construit aulam,
      Effectusque piis dat studiis hominum,
5   Quorum perpetui decoris structura manebit,
      Si perfecta auctor protegat atque regat.
7   Sic deus hoc tutum stabili fundamine templum,
      Quod Karolus princeps condidit, esse velit.[110]

VERSES IN THE HALL OF THE CHURCH IN AACHEN PALACE
    When the living stones are joined by a bond of peace,
And by equal numbers all things are harmonised,
    Let shine the work of the lord who built the entire hall,
And bring about the pious efforts of the people,
    Whose structure of perpetual beauty will endure
If the founder protects and rules has been completed.
    Thus, may God will that this temple be secure on a stable foundation
Which Charles the prince built.[111]

---

[108] Leiden, UB, Voss. Lat. Q. 69, fols 7–47, at fol. 19r/v; Bischoff, *Katalog*, no. 2222; *CLA* X.1585. On this manuscript, see R. H. Bremmer, 'Leiden, Vossianus Lat. Q. 69 (Part 2): Schoolbook or Proto-Encyclopaedic Miscellany?', in R. H. Bremmer and K. Dekker, eds, *Practice in Learning: The Transfer of Encyclopaedic Knowledge in the Early Middle Ages*, Mediaevalia Groningana, NS 16 (Paris, 2010), 19–54. For commentary on the inscription, see Giersiepen, ed., *Die Inscriften des Aachener Doms*, 6, no. 6 and C. Bayer, 'Die karolingische Bauinschrift des Aachener Dom', in M. Kerner, ed., *Der verschleierte Karl. Karl der Grosse zwischen Mythos und Wirklichkeit* (Aachen, 1999), 445–52.

[109] This *sylloge* uses texts familiar from other anthologies, including the verses in praise of the Apostle Paul by Damasus (*ED*, 81–7, no. 1; Trout, *Damasus of Rome*, 75–8, no. 1), the eight verses of the *Anthologia Isidoriana* which often circulated with copies of Isidore's *Etymologiae*, *ICUR*, II.i, no. XXII, and which includes the thirty-two-line *Carmen Eucheriae* (*ICUR*, II.i, 58) and the epitaph of Gregory the Great as well as two epigrams that are included in a short anthology for St Peter's basilica, extant in two Paris MSS, *ICUR* II.1, no. XXIII.3–4. See also Chapter 3, 137, n. 112.

[110] *ICUR* II.1, no. XXVI.22; Dümmler, ed., PLAC I, 432.

[111] Translation (adapted from), C. Kendall, *The Allegory of the Church: Romanesque Portals and their Verse Inscriptions* (Toronto, ON, 1996), 43.

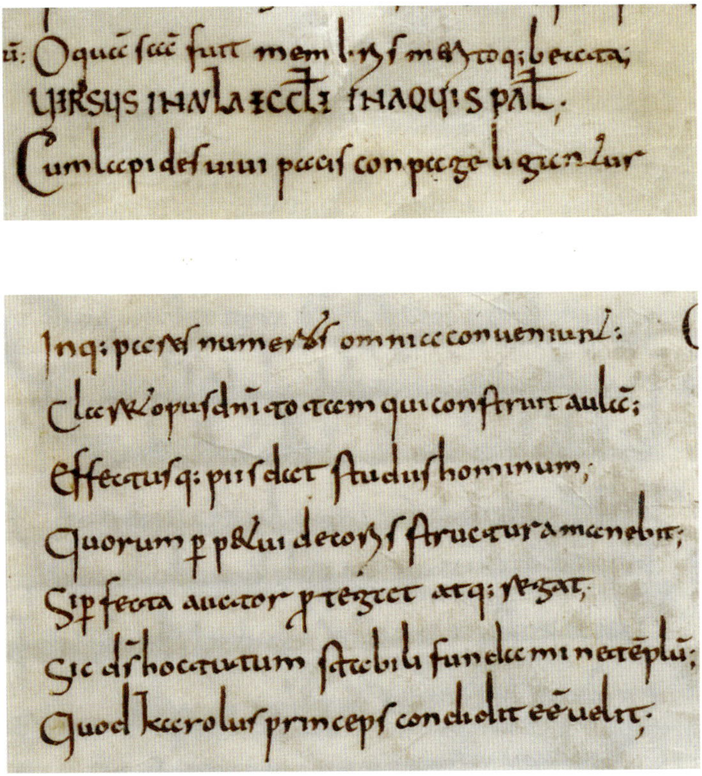

FIGURE 7.13 The dedication verses for the palace chapel, Aachen. The first two lines are at the foot of fol. 19r and the text continues with six lines at the top of the first column of fol. 19v; Leiden, Universiteitsbibliotheek, Voss. Lat. 69, fol. 19 r/v. Photo: Courtesy of Leiden University Libraries.

Einhard mentioned this inscription in his account of Charlemagne's last days. He makes it clear that the verses were painted, not inscribed.

> Erat in eadem basilicae in margine coronae quae inter superiores et inferiores arcus interiorem aedis partem ambiebat, epigramma sinopide scriptum, continens quis auctor eiusdem templi, cuius in extremo versu legebantur, KAROLUS PRINCEPS. Notatum est a quibusdam eodem, quo decessit, anno paucis ante mortem mensibus eas, quae PRINCEPS exprimebant, litteras ita esse deletas, ut penitus non apparerent.

> In that same church, on the crowning band that encircles part of the interior of the building between the upper and lower arches, was an epigram written in red, preserving the name of the founder of that same temple, in which, in the very last verse, *Karolus princeps* could be read. But it was observed by some people that in the very year that he died, a few months before his death, the letters that formed *princeps* became so faint that they were almost invisible.[112]

---

[112] Einhard, *VK*, ch. 32; Dutton, tr., *Charlemagne's Courtier*, 36–7.

This anecdote recalls the disturbing biblical story of Belshazzar's feast (Daniel 5:1–26) but borrows overtly from Suetonius' description of the portents that preceded the death of the first Roman emperor, Augustus.[113] Then, Suetonius says, a flash of lightning had melted the first letter of the word, *caesar*, causing viewers to conclude that Augustus had barely a hundred (= C(entum)) days left to live. Suetonius also said that this event predicted Augustus' deification, since the remaining letters (*aesar*) spelled the word for 'god' in the Etruscan language. Einhard's wide-ranging debt to Suetonius' account of the first emperor is well known and in this episode he followed Suetonius closely; Charlemagne had but 'a few months' to Augustus' hundred days, and the portents of impending death focused on the titles of the men (*caesar/princeps*) as well as the physical form of the lettering that spelled out the word. The inscription bearing Augustus's name and title was made of metal, and individual bronze letters inlaid in marble are doubtless implied. In contrast, Einhard describes verses written in red (*epigramma sinopide scriptum*). This detail sounds authentic, especially alongside his use of a precise architectural term to describe the location of the inscription, which he says was laid out within the 'crowning band' (*in margine coronae*) that encircled the central octagon, above the head of the arches on the ground floor and below the level of the gallery.[114]

Einhard's anecdote about the fading of both the title and the life of *Karolus princeps* works on its own terms as a story to explain the imminence of the death of the king. But for the cognoscenti who knew the building as well as Einhard did there were additional layers of meaning in his account of this episode that could transport the reader of the *Vita Karoli* into the three-dimensional space of Charlemagne's palace chapel. Writing probably a decade or so after Charlemagne's death, Einhard described the king's last days, his death, and his burial, as well as the words of a short epitaph that was inscribed alongside an image (*imago*) on a golden arch over the king's tomb.[115] The widespread and rapid circulation of the *Vita Karoli* ensured the

---

[113] Suetonius, *Life of the Caesars*, Book II: *The Deified Augustus*, ch. 97; tr. J. C. Rolfe, *Lives of the Caesars*, i: *Julius. Augustus. Tiberius. Gaius. Caligula*, Loeb Classical Library, 31 (Cambridge, MA, 1914), 296–7.

[114] The phrase *in margine coronae* ('crowning band') is an architectural term for a decorated strip that runs horizontally above the head of an arch. See, for example, J.-P. Adam, *Roman Building: Materials and Techniques* (Abingdon, 2007), 170, pl. 407. The Aachen inscription was replaced in this position in mosaic when the interior of the chapel was clad in marble in 1913.

[115] Einhard, *VK* chs 31–2; 'Sub hoc conditorio situm est corpus Karoli magni atque orthodoxi imperatoris, qui regnum Francorum nobiliter ampliait et per annos XLVII feliciter rexit. Decessit septuagenarius, anno Domini DCCCXIIII, indictione VII, V. Kal Febr' ('Under this tomb lies the body of Charles, the great and orthodox emperor, who gloriously increased the kingdom of the Franks and reigned with great success for forty-seven years. He died in his seventies, in the year of our Lord 814, in the 7th indiction, on the 5th kalends of February (28 January)'). For another slightly different version, perhaps independent of the VK, see Figure 3.4 in this volume. On the dating of the *VK*, which is disputed, see M. M. Tischler, *Einharts Vita Karoli: Studien zur Entstehung, Überlieferung und Rezeption* (Hanover, 2001), (late 820s); K. H. Krüger, 'Neue Beobachtungen zur Datierung von Einhards Karlsvita', *Frühmittelalterliche Studien*, 32 (1998), 124–45 (*c*.823); M. Innes and R. McKitterick, 'The Writing of History', in McKitterick, ed., *Carolingian Culture*, 193–202; McKitterick,

transmission of these stories as well as those that reinforced the intimate connection between the palace at Aachen and the king in his dying days. Einhard says that portents of the end were made manifest in the very fabric of the palace complex: part of the portico joining the *aula* and chapel collapsed; the ceiling panels of the buildings where the king was living creaked constantly; frequent tremors were felt; the chapel was struck by lightning (echoing Suetonius) causing the gilded pole on the pinnacle of the roof to fall off and strike the cornice of the bishop's house next door. Most tellingly, Einhard says, the epigram that was painted in red letters around the inside of the chapel, which recorded Charlemagne's role as *auctor eiusdem templi*, began to fade. Like the palace itself, this verse inscription actively altered, prefiguring the demise of the king. In Einhard's hands, the palace itself becomes the agent of change, portending the death of its founder. The structure groans and moves: its floors collapse, its ceilings creak, it is shaken by earthquakes, and is struck by lightning. The movement and instability of the physical structures of the building complex inverts and challenges the meaning of verses displayed in the chapel that commemorated its dedication and which stress the solidity of its foundations.

Einhard does not quote the dedicatory epigram in the *Vita Karoli* but his text shows that he knew it very well and expected his readers to do likewise. The diction of the inscription is quoted, with reference to Charlemagne as the *auctor* of the *templum* (lines 6–7). The last distich of the epigram enjoins God to watch over the *templum* that *Karolus princeps* had 'constructed on stable foundations'. It is this verse that Einhard interjects as an intertext within his account of the pre-mortem portents. There is a striking contrast between the God-protected temple with its steady foundations, and the structural groans of the same building in the months before Charlemagne's death that Einhard describes, and this juxtaposition was surely intentional. The activity of the building (tremors, groans, collapsing, fading) also invokes the 'living stones' of the opening verse and plainly contradicts the claim that they are 'joined in bonds of harmony'. The straightforward reading of Einhard's account is that anxiety about Charlemagne's advancing age was being projected onto and through the building that he had founded. But an exegetical interpretation of these lines may also suggest that the distress of the building was an allegory of disharmony in the wider Frankish Church and realm, brought on by the anticipation of the regime change that would surely follow the old king's death. This section of Einhard's text may thus have been directed specifically to contemporary readers at Aachen or to those who had been there, who knew the text of the epigram in the octagon, and who could draw out the allusions to it that are embedded in his account of the portents of the king's death.

Charlemagne, 11–14 (*c*.817). Note that the epitaph says Charlemagne was 'in his seventies' when he died, whereas Einhard offered a more precise figure, saying that he was 72 at his death.

These allusions can be explored further through the literary sources of the Aachen verses. The Aachen dedication epigram modifies an earlier poem, *De aedificatione domus Dei*, composed by the mid-fifth-century theologian and poet Prosper of Aquitaine.[116] It formed part of Prosper's *Epigrammata ex sententiis S Augustini*, which were very well known and formed part of the canon of early Christian poetry that circulated widely in Francia and the Anglo-Saxon kingdoms. Alcuin certainly knew the *Epigrammata*, saying that they could be read at the archbishop's library in York, and they are commonplace in Carolingian manuscripts of classical and contemporary poetry.[117] There is every reason to think, therefore, that any learned visitor to the Aachen chapel would have recognised and could remember the text of Prosper's original epigram, and could have reflected on its re-use and applied meaning in this specific, new, architectural context. Alcuin himself could have been responsible for the modifications to Prosper's verses as used in the chapel, but evidence for this is circumstantial.[118] 'Eloquent' (*facundus*) Angilbert is another possible author, since the title *princeps* was also used for Charlemagne in the dedicatory epigram for the *templum* at Saint-Riquier, which was dedicated at Easter 800.[119] It is doubtless significant that Angilbert's court poem, written probably in early 796, draws on similar vocabulary and scriptural references to the Aachen epigram in the sections describing Charlemagne's building projects in Aachen.[120]

Whether it was Alcuin, Angilbert, or another, the Aachen poet adapted Prosper's original six-line epigram, *De aedificatione domus Dei*, in significant ways. A fourth distich was added to Prosper's three, thereby appropriating the whole poem for *Karolus princeps*, named in the penultimate line as the founder of the *templum*. This final couplet transforms Prosper's generic epigram 'On the building of the house of God' into a dedication inscription for a real, earthly building—Charlemagne's

---

[116] Prosper, *Epigrammata ex sententiis S Augustini*, no. 36, 'De aedificatione domus Dei'; *PL* 51, col. 509r; Schaller and Könsgen, eds, *Initia*, no. 3044.

[117] *YP*, 1552. Prosper's *Epigrammata* are found, for example, in Paris, BnF, Lat. 2773 and BnF, Lat. 9347 discussed above, Chapter 3, 127–32.

[118] In his own poetry, Alcuin was particularly fond of the phrase 'protegat atque regat', found here in line 6 as noted by Bayer ('Die karolingische Bauinschrift', 446–7). But this phrase comes from Prosper and so is not of Alcuin's invention, and was also used by other Carolingian scholars such as Paul the Deacon and Hraban Maur, who could also have acquired it from schoolbook knowledge of Prosper's verses. Alcuin's authorship is claimed by Bremmer, 'Leiden, Voss. Lat. Q. 69', 26, 53.

[119] Hariulf, *Gesta ecclesiae Centulensis*, II.11, ed. Lot, *Chronique de l'abbaye*, 74; Huic Karolus princeps condignum mente benigna / Perficiens templum, condidit et tumulum / Post sexagenos et centum circiter annos / Cum Domini servus integer extat adhuc. The epithet 'facundus' is used in line 74 of the panegyric verses, *Karolus Magnus et Leo Papa*.

[120] Angilbert: 'To Charlemagne and his entourage', 'Fundamenta super petram quoque ponit in altum / Ut domus alma deo manebat firmissa Christo / Felix sic lapides posuit sua dextera primum / Inclita celsitrono fierent ut templa tonanti'; MGH, PLAC I, 361, lines 23–6; Godman, tr., *Poetry*, no. 6; the scriptural allusion is to Luke 6:48. For a discussion of the date of Angilbert's court poem, see Bullough, *Alcuin*, 438–9 and D. Lohrmann, 'Das geistige Leben in Aachen our Karolingerzeit', in T. R. Kraus, ed., *Aachen von den anfängen bis our gegenwart*, ii: *Karolinger—Ottonen—Salier, 767 bis 1137* (Neustadt, 2013), 409–70, at 429.

chapel—lengthening it so that it fitted around the eight sides of the octagon, one line for each side.[121] The verses are rich with architectural language and symbolism that is applicable to the Aachen chapel: the eight lines of verses match the eight sides of the central octagon; the measurements are in harmony; the work of the *dominus* who built the *aula* is famous; the *auctor* protects it and rules over it; it is a 'structure of perpetual beauty'. Displayed like this inside Charlemagne's chapel, the epigram must be read as an immersive four-fold eulogy to the mathematical perfection of the surrounding building—*lapides*, *aula*, *structura*, *templum*—and to the honour of the prince who had made it—*dominus*, *auctor*, *princeps*, *fundator*.[122]

The Aachen poet also modified the last words of the second line in a way that casts light on the allegorical symbolism of the chapel itself as well as its pragmatic function at the heart of Charlemagne's religious reform programme. The second line of Prosper's original epigram reads, *Inque pares numeros convenit una domus* ('And by equal numbers one house is constructed'). The Aachen version exchanges Prosper's *una domus* for *omnia*, and so 'one house' becomes 'all things'. The reason for altering the *una domus* of Prosper's original is puzzling and not immediately obvious, but the decision to change the diction of such a familiar verse would have invariably drawn attention to it, inviting reflection by a knowing audience. This is especially true in a case like this where the revision deviates not just from the original epigram but also from its scriptural context, and when *una domus* would have fitted the architectural context of the chapel very well, both literally and figuratively.

The scriptural context of the epigram is clear. Broadly, it recalls Luke 6:48 and Matthew 16:18, referring to the stability of the house built on rock, equating the house with the Church and the rock with Peter, on whom the Church was built.[123] More exactly, the opening couplet of Prosper's epigram quotes the First Letter of Peter: 'You also, like living stones (*lapides vivi*), are being built into a spiritual house (*domus spiritalis*) to be a holy priesthood'.[124] The *lapides vivi* are the true believers in

---

[121] This arrangement is reminiscent of the verses cut for Sixtus III on the entablature of the Lateran baptistery, on which, see Chapter 5, 207.

[122] Heckner, 'Der Tempel Salomos in Aachen', 25–62; C. Heitz, 'L'architettura dell'età Carolingia in relazione alla liturgica sacra', in *Culto cristiano politica imperiale carolingia*, Convegni del centro di studi sulla spiritualità medievale XVIII (Todi, 1979), 339–62, at 349–50; C. Heitz, 'Vitruve et l'architecture du haut Moyen Âge', in *La cultura antica nell'Occidente Latino dal VII all'XI secolo*, SSCI, 22 (1974), 725–57, at 741–4; A. Hausmann, '"...Inque pares numeros omnia convenient...": Der Bauplan der Aachener Palastkapelle', in *Karl der Grosse und sein Nachwirken*, ed. P. L. Butzer, M. Kerner, and W. Oberschelp (Turnhout, 1997), 321–36.

[123] Luke 6:48: 'He is like a man which built an house, and digged deep, and laid the foundation on a rock: and when the flood arose, the stream beat vehemently upon that house, and could not shake it: for it was founded upon a rock'; Matthew 16:18: 'And I say also unto thee, That thou art Peter, and upon this rock I will build my church; and the gates of hell shall not prevail against it'.

[124] 1 Peter 2:5: *tamquam lapides vivi aedificamini domus spiritalis in sacerdotium sanctum*. On the exegesis of the *Lapides vivi*, see especially J. O'Reilly, 'Introduction', in *Bede: On the Temple*, ed. S. Connolly, Translated Texts for Historians 21 (Liverpool, 1995), xvii–lv, esp. xxii–xxviii and xlvi–li, reprinted in J. O'Reilly, *History, Hagiography and Biblical Exegesis: Essays on Bede, Adomnán and Thomas Becket*, ed. M. MacCarron and D. Scully

Christ who collectively, through faith, are shaped to form the spiritual house of God. Here, the metaphor of a building is used figuratively to describe the community of Christians who comprise the living Church; without believers, a church building would be an empty shell. The patristic and exegetical commentaries on this passage and its ramifications are plentiful; Ambrose, Augustine, Leo, Gregory, Bede, and Alcuin all drew on the architectural allegory of the living stones as the living Church, with Christ as its cornerstone or capstone that holds the structure together. Consequently, this was a text that featured in homilies and hymns for the dedication of churches, and its use here doubtless also reflects that specific liturgical context.[125] In Prosper's verse rendering of Augustine's commentary on 1 Peter 2:5, the Christians who are the 'living stones' have come together to form the single, spiritual unit: a house (*domus*) that is God's holy Church. From this, his epigram unfolds as a commentary on the perfection of the temporal Church in God's care. For Prosper it was God who is *Dominus* and *Auctor*, and the *domus—aula—structura—*is his Universal Church. Contemporary exegesis also elaborated the motif of the *domus* as the body of the individual Christian, holy to God, which is exchanged at death for 'a house not made with hands, eternal in heaven'.[126] This use of the *domus spiritalis* to represent both the community of believers and the individual Christian is reinforced by scripture which compares the Temple of Solomon with the incarnate body of Christ himself.[127]

A key to the alteration at Aachen of the second line from *una domus* to *omnia* may be a verse from Paul's First Letter to the Corinthians that was often cited by early exegetes as the principle behind the method of exegesis itself, which sought to parallel meaning in the Old Testament with the insights of the New.

> haec autem **omnia in figura** contingebant illis scripta sunt autem ad correptionem nostram in quos fines saeculorum devenerunt.
>
> But **all these things** happened to them **in figure**, but were written down for the correction of us, upon whom the end of ages have come.
>
> (1 Corinthians 10:11)

(London, 2019), 3–35. On this metaphor, in the context of Aachen and the architectural iconography of court group manuscripts, see Mestemacher, *Marmor, Gold und Edelsteine*, 140–6.

[125] Prosper's epigram is in itself a commentary on Augustine's extensive exegesis on these verses. On the use of this text in the dedication of churches, see Bede, *Hom.* II.24 and *In Vivis ex lapidis*, a seventh- or eighth-century hymn for the dedication of a church: 'Urbs beata Jerusalem, dicta pacis visio, | Quae construitur in coelo [caelis], vivis ex lapidibus | Et angelis coronata | ut sponsata comite'; Schaller and Köngsen, eds, *Initia*, no. 16818.

[126] 2 Corinthians 5:1: scimus enim quoniam si terrestris domus nostra huius habitationis dissolvatur quod aedificationem ex Deo habeamus domum non manufactam aeternam in caelis. Also 1 Corinthians 3:16–17.

[127] 1 Corinthians 3:16–17, 2 Corinthians 6:16; John 2:19–21. For the exegesis on these themes, see, for example, Bede, *De schematibus et tropis*, CCSL 123A, 147 and *De templo Salomonis*, CCSL, 119A, 147–8, Connolly, tr., *Bede: On the Temple*, 5–6. I am indebted to Jennifer O'Reilly for her insights into these passages.

Thus, it was argued, the Old Testament could be analysed figuratively in order to illuminate the texts concerning the life of Christ, and thereby act as an example for Christians in life seeking 'correction' (*correctio*) before Judgement Day. In this way, exegesis linked time past with the contemporary world, and also looked forwards to future time, and especially the Last Judgement. Bede (for example) had dwelt on this text many times, especially in his commentaries on *De templo* and *De tabernaculo* that discussed the inner meanings of the biblical accounts the building of the Temple in Jerusalem and the fitting out of the Tabernacle, exploring the exemplars that they offered to contemporary Christians. For Bede and other early medieval exegetes, the Temple was the Old Testament prefiguration of the Church of Christ (and of the incarnate body of Christ himself), and so analysis of the minutiae of its construction held figurative lessons that could be transferred to Christians in contemporary times.[128] Bede was not interested in the building as a real, physical structure, rather in how biblical descriptions of the Old Testament Temple and its measurements could be used metaphorically to guide believers who were the 'living stones' of the New Testament Church. In his opening words to *De tabernaculo*, Bede quoted Paul to explain why it is necessary to examine all aspects of the making of the shrine:

> 'For all these things', as the Apostle [Paul] says, 'happened to them in figure, but were written down for us'. **'All these things'** (*omnia*) includes not only the deeds or words that are contained in the Sacred Writings, but also the descriptions of the locations, and hours and times, and the things themselves, as well as the circumstances under which they were done or said.
>
> (Bede, *De tabernaculo*, prologue)[129]

For Bede, Paul's words clearly meant that *omnia*, 'all things', held figurative meanings that could provide examples for his readers. The whole context mattered: not just what people had said or had done, but also where and when they did it, and how. The divine presence in 'all things' recalls also the familiar opening to the Gospel of John, *omnia per ipsum facta sunt* ('by Whom all things were made'). Bede had used Paul's words to gloss John 1:17, that *gratia et veritas per Iesum Christum facta est*/'grace and truth came through Jesus Christ', and these words were copied verbatim by Alcuin in his commentary on the Gospel of John which he sent to Gisela and Rotrude, the sister and daughter of Charlemagne, respectively.[130]

---

[128] For example, Bede, *Homilies*, II.24; *CCSL* 122, 358–67, L. T. Martin, tr., *Bede the Venerable. Homilies on the Gospels*, ii: *Lent to the Dedication of the Church* (Kalamazoo, MI, 1991), 249.

[129] 'Omnia autem, sicut apostolus ait, *in figura contingebant illis: scripta sunt autem propter nos*, omnia uidelicet, non solum facta uel uerba, quae sacris litteris continentur, uerum etiam locorum, et horarum, et temporum situs, et ipsarum quoque in quibus gesta, siue dicta sunt circumstantia rerum', Bede, *De tabernaculo*, CCSL, 119A, 1; Holder, tr., *Bede: On the Tabernacle*, 1.

[130] Bede, *Homily*, 1.2; Hurst, ed., CCSL 122, 7–13, at 10; Martin and Hurst, tr., *Bede the Venerable. Homilies*, I, 9–17 at 13; Alcuin, 'Commentariorum in Joannem liber primus', *PL* 100, cols 743–72, at 751. Alcuin's letter

Bede had elaborated the concept of seeking exemplars for *correctio* specifically in the context of the construction of the Temple in Jerusalem by arguing that understanding the materiality of the building helped Christians in their spiritual journey:

> Therefore, as we, with the Lord's help, set about treating of the building of the temple and **seeking the spiritual mansion of God in the material structure** (*in structura materiali spiritalem dei mansionem*) it seems opportune to say something first about its builders, who they were, and where they were from, and at the same time something about the material structure itself and what it was made of. For these matters too are pregnant with spiritual mysteries according to the testimony of the Apostle [Paul], who says, '**all these things** happened to them by way of example, and they were recorded in writing to be a lesson for us'.
>
> (Bede, *De templo*, prologue)[131]

So, for Bede and his readers, all aspects of the physical structure of the building could be analysed to deduce lessons for Christians seeking salvation. In the context of the Aachen inscription, Bede's explanation of why 'all things' mattered would have encouraged readers there to consider *omnia* about the construction of that building, and to seek figural meaning in them—especially *inque pares numeros*. We don't know for sure if Bede's commentaries and homilies on these themes were known at the Frankish court itself in the 790s although his commentary on *De Templo* was certainly available in Francia before 800, and Paul the Deacon used Bede's homiletic collection when compiling his own, at Charlemagne's behest, *c*.797–8.[132] Alcuin's presence in the king's company, intermittently between 786 and 796, and his affection for the writings of *domnus Beda, magister noster*, provides a plausible context for knowledge of such texts that would have been especially pertinent during the period of the planning and construction of the palace and chapel. Alcuin's pupil, Hraban Maur,

---

to Gisela and Rotrude concerning his Commentary on John, in which he explains his debt to Bede's homilies, is *Ep.* no. 213; Dümmler, ed., MGH, Epp. IV, 354–7.

[131] 'Tractaturi igitur iuuante domino de aedificatione templi et in structura materiali spiritalem dei mansionem quaesituri oportunum uidetur ut primo de operariis eius qui uel unde fuerint simul et de ipsa materia unde factum est aliqua dicamus. Nam et haec spiritalibus grauida esse sacramentis testatur apostolus qui ait: omnia in figura contingebant illis, scripta sunt autem propter nos'; *CCSL* 119A, 148; Connolly, tr., *Bede: On the Temple*, 7.

[132] *De templo Salomonis* was among the earliest exports of Bede's works to Francia; a copy was sent by Abbot Cuthbert to Bishop Lul in Mainz before 767; J. Westgard, 'Bede and the Continent in the Carolingian Age and Beyond', in S. DeGregorio, ed., *The Cambridge Companion to Bede* (Cambridge, 2010), 201–15, at 206. Many manuscripts of Bede's homilies, dating from the ninth century and later, some of which are Frankish, retain characteristic Insular abbreviations demonstrating the existence of eighth-century Insular exemplars (now lost); *CCSL* 122, xvii–xxi. On Paul the Deacon's knowledge of Bede's homilies, see M. L. W. Laistner and H. H. King, *A Hand-List of Bede Manuscripts* (Ithaca, NY, 1943), 114 (with reference to *PL* XCV, cols 1574, 1577). On Paul's knowledge of Bede, the dating of his own homiliary, and the argument that Paul was peripatetic while writing gathering sources from several locations, see Z. Guiliano, *The Homiliary of Paul the Deacon: Religious and Cultural Reform in Carolingian Europe*, Sermo 16 (Turnhout, 2021), 107–113, 121.

writing at Fulda probably in the 820s about the training of clergy, recalled both the exegetical and practical value of a knowledge of geometry, saying that it had been used in the construction of the Tabernacle and the Temple, and that 'the knowledge of these things helps the exegete not a little in spiritual understanding'.[133]

There is also an eschatological dimension to the Aachen verses, linked to the change from 'one' to 'all' in the first couplet. The Aachen poet encouraged observers to find figural meaning in all aspects of the building, especially in the 'equal numbers' of the structure. Scholars have long recognised that the architectural mathematics of the building and its centralised construction reflect symbolic as well as structural affiliations. Heckner and others have shown that the dimensions of the building both in plan and elevation correspond not only to the measurements of the Temple of Solomon as described in the Old Testament but also to the construction of the Heavenly Jerusalem, as described in the New Testament Book of Revelation. Using a measurement of 32.24cm (the so-called 'Carolingian foot'), Heckner has shown how the plan of the chapel is based on the exegetically 'perfect number' 6 (as the sum of its factors, 1 + 2 + 3) and builds up in a duodecimal pattern on the ratios 6 : 12 : 24 : 48 : 96 : 144, where the diameter of the central octagon is 48ft, the diameter of the outer rotunda is 96ft, which nests within a circle that envelops the two exedra and measures 144ft across.[134] These dimensions are matched in elevation, with the height of the central octagon double that of its plan (i.e. equal to two circles each of 48ft). The number 144 is also the figure given in the Book of Revelation to express the dimensions of the Heavenly Jerusalem, and for exegetes this number symbolised 'stable perfection'.[135] The idea of the foundation of a New Jerusalem is embedded also in the shape of the central octagon, whose eight sides evoke the Eighth Age when Christ would come again.[136] In these ways, the physical structure of the Aachen chapel embodies the principles of exegesis, that the Old Testament prefigures the events of the New and contains lessons for contemporary Christians who seek salvation at Judgement Day and admittance into the Heavenly Jerusalem. Worshippers at the Aachen chapel and readers of the dedicatory inscription could reflect on all aspects of

---

[133] Hraban Maur, *De Institutione Clericorum* III.23, *PL* 107, col. 401; cited by Heckner, 'Der Tempel Salomos', 55. On the use of this metaphor for the Hraban's buildings at Fulda, see Mestemacher, *Marmor, Gold und Edelsteine*, 142.

[134] On the number six as the perfect number, see F. Wallis, tr., *Bede: Commentary on Revelation*, Translated Texts for Historians, 58 (Liverpool, 2013), 135, n. 184. On the measurements of the chapel, see Heckner, 'Der Tempel Salomos', 43–55.

[135] *Ipsa stabilem ciuitatis sanctae perfectionem*, i.e. 12 × 12 = 144; see Wallis, tr., *Commentary on Revelation*, 226 who also notes that the Church was made perfect in the product of four virtues and faith shown through the Trinity (i.e. 4 × 3 = 12).

[136] N. Hiscock, 'The Aachen Chapel: A Model of Salvation', in P. L. Butzer and D. Lohrmann, ed., *Science in Western and Eastern Civilization in Carolingian Times* (Basel, 1993), 115–26. See also Story, 'Cathwulf, Kingship', 8–9.

its construction and form and find meaning in its material structure which would guide them in their journey to the 'spiritual mansion of God'.

Texts such as these help to contextualise the exegetical meaning of Prosper's verses as adapted for the Aachen chapel: *Inque pares numeros omnia conveniunt*. In the architectural context of the painted verses at Aachen, the allusion in Prosper's original to the spiritual mansion of God could be easily transferred to the physical structure of the palace chapel, and the metaphor of the *domus spiritalis* and *aula domini* could be read as fitting synonyms for Charlemagne's *sacrum palatium*.[137] This literal interpretation was readily accessible for the educated Carolingian who had learned Prosper's poetry at school. It was also obvious to any who had been to Rome and seen the verses in the apse at St Peter's that praised the *Iustitiae sedes, fidei domus, aula pudoris* ('Throne of justice, house of faith, court of modesty'), including the Carolingian court poets—Alcuin, Anglibert, and Theodulf.[138] But the alteration of the second line from 'one house' to 'all things' stretched Prosper's metaphor to encompass the universality of harmony that will occur when Christians everywhere are bound by bonds of peace and proper devotion. In this sense, the Aachen verses manifest both the symbolic and the practical role of the palace chapel itself as the 'principal engine room' of liturgical reform for the kingdom, as well as the broader policy of the *renovatio* and *correctio* of Christian people that underpinned policy throughout Charlemagne's reign and had been articulated most clearly in the *Admonitio generalis* delivered at Aachen in 789.[139] The modified epigram was thus both a dedicatory inscription for the physical structure of the *templum* in Aachen as well as an invocation to God for the eternal protection of the *opus domini* that was the Frankish Church writ large, 'which Charles the prince has built, secure on a stable foundation'. The existential warning embedded in Einhard's reportage of the portents was crystal clear.

The major sets of Frankish Annals record that in November 804, Pope Leo III sent word that he wished to celebrate Christmas with the emperor. His eldest son, Charles, was dispatched to meet the pope at St-Maurice d'Agaune (Valais, Switzerland) which overlooked one of the major mountain passes into northern Italy. Leo met Charlemagne in Reims, and they spent Christmas at Quierzy before travelling on to Aachen.[140] The Salzburg Easter Table annals include an entry saying that Leo was at Aachen for Epiphany, and an entry in the Tiel Annals, which survive in a manuscript of the mid-fourteenth century, says that Leo consecrated the chapel during this visit, most likely at the feast of the Epiphany, on Sunday 6 January 805:

---

[137] M. de Jong, 'Sacrum palatium et ecclesia: L'authorité religieuse royale sous les Carolingiens (790–840)', *Annales*, 58 (2003), 1234–69, and 'Charlemagne's Church', in J. Story, ed., *Charlemagne: Empire and Society* (Manchester, 2005), 103–35, at 129–31.

[138] Quoted also by Hadrian in a letter to Charlemagne: see E. Dümmler, ed., MGH, Epp. V (Berlin, 1899), 29, on which, see Chapter 4, 154–5, n. 53.

[139] McKitterick, *Charlemagne*, 306–11, 340–5.

[140] *ARF s.a.* 804.

In this year, Pope Leo was in Francia; Christmas in Quierzy; epiphany in Aachen.

(*Annales Iuvavenses Maiores*, s.a. 805)[141]

Pope Leo overwintered in Aachen, and there he consecrated with great solemnity the church which Charles had constructed in honour of the Blessed Virgin Mary.

(*Annales Tielenses*, s.a. 804)[142]

This date for the consecration accords with the archaeological evidence that the roof of the chapel was topped out using timber felled in 803.[143] Evidently, by this date the chapel was sufficiently advanced for it to be put into full commission as a functioning place of worship, although undoubtedly construction work would have continued on and around the whole of the palace complex well after the formal consecration of the chapel.[144] The poet of the now-fragmentary epic, *Karolus magnus et Leo papa*, written not long after 800, evokes a busy building site. Sixteen lines describe masons at work; 'some hew stones in readiness for the straight columns... others roll up the blocks of stone with their hands, some keenly place the stones far up on the top of the towers, joining the marble in solid slabs, others stand on the steps receiving in turn the loads of the bearers bring and pass on the heavy rocks with eager hands, while others approach from below and roll blocks of stone up to the walls'.[145] The poet depicts the king in command of the project, recalling his role as *fundator* in the chapel's dedicatory verses. Famously also, the poet called Charlemagne *rex pater Europae* ('king and father of Europe') and that the palace being built under his command was a *Roma secunda*.[146] Falkstein, Schaller, and others read this section of the poem, with its

---

[141] *Annales Iuvavenses Maiores* s.a. 805, 'Hoc anno Leo papa in Francia. Natalis Domini in Carisiaco; epiphania in Aquis'; G. H. Pertz, ed., MGH, SS I (Hannover, 1826), 87–8. For the manuscript, Würzburg, Universitätsbibliothek, M.p.th.f.46, see Figure 7.1; the scribe who added this entry to fol. 16r was not the same as the scribe who entered the information about where Charlemagne spent Easter in the 790s. Many different, broadly contemporary, hands annotate the margins of this Easter Table.

[142] *Annales Tielenses*, s.a. 804, 'Leo papa hyemavit in Aquisgrani et ibidem ecclesia a Karoli constructam in honore beate Marie virginia cum magna solempnitate consecravit'; G. H. Waitz, ed., MGH, SS XXIV (Hannover, 1879), 21–7, at 22.

[143] See Chapter 6, 244.

[144] Labour services were demanded from Reims for work at Aachen in the first and second decades of the ninth century; McKitterick, *Charlemagne*, 167, n. 112.

[145] *Karolus Magnus et Leo Papa*, lines 111–26; Dümmler, ed., MGH, PLAC I, 368–9, with a newer edition in H. Neumann, F. Brunhölzl, and W. Winkelmann, eds, *Karolus Magnus et Leo Papa: Ein Paderborner Epos vol Jahre 799* (Paderborn, 1966). Arguments have been made in favour of Einhard as the poet and for Aachen as the place being described (D. Schaller, 'Das Aachener Epos für Karl den Kaiser', *Frühmittelalterlich Studien*, 10 (1976), 134–68, reprinted in his *Studien zur lateinischen Dichtung des Frühmittelalters* (Stuttgart, 1995), 129–63) or Modoin, whose 'Eclogue' (written 804–14) quotes the verses (F. Stella, 'Autore e attribuzioni', 19–34). See also A. T. Hack, 'Das Zeremoniell des Papstempfangs 799 in Paderborn', in SW, *799*, iii, 19–33, at 22–8, and Lohrmann, 'Das geistige Leben', in Kraus, ed., *Aachen von den anfängen*, 409–70, at 433.

[146] *Karolus Magnus et Leo Papa*, lines 94 and 504; Dümmler, ed., MGH, PLAC I, 368 and 379.

references to the building of baths at the hot springs as well as the *templum* and atrium with lofty rotunda, as an imaginative evocation of the construction of the palace complex at Aachen,[147] reading the post-coronation connotations of imperial Rome retrospectively back into the 790s when the Solomonic design and architectural plans of the chapel had already been determined and building work was in full flow.

The decade or so around 795 was thus a period of extraordinary cultural vigour in Francia, drawing strength from a virtuous cycle of military power, dynastic consolidation, and political focus.[148] The person of the king was at the centre of this dynamic, and surrounding his household was a court comprising clerics, scholars, and fighting men who sought patronage and preferment through short-term proximity to the king and his family. Among these courtiers were scholars who vied for the king's attention, not least through the production of works of high art that reflected and flattered the wealth and power of the ruler as well as the growing confidence, ambition and reflexivity of the Carolingian 'project'.[149] Surviving texts, manuscripts, architecture, and applied arts (in paint, metal, stone, and ivory) attest to the concentration of talent and technology as well as human and material resources in Charlemagne's kingdom in the late eighth and early ninth centuries. Scholars came from far beyond Francia— Visigothic Spain, Lombard Italy, the Anglo-Saxon kingdoms, Ireland—and knowledge of classical texts, and mastery of the metrical forms and lexical references of Latin poetry in particular was a marker of belonging to this elite. Carolingian art was deeply influenced by the aesthetic habits of the contemporary world, absorbing elements of Insular, Lombard, Visigothic, and imperial art into the culture inherited from Merovingian Francia. Of course, Rome's imperial past and papal present were profound influences, a source of inspiration and authority. But Carolingian creativity was more than a sum of these parts and, from the 780s onwards, the cultural output from Francia was distinctive and transformative, complementing and reflecting centripetal forces of social and religious renewal through the development of an increasingly distinctive Carolingian aesthetic that was expressed in multiple media, including script and graphic art. Hadrian's epitaph in its monumental form is a product of that same creative and intellectually inquisitive environment; it is a mirror to the moment. With virtuoso flair the epitaph reveals Carolingian ownership of composite influences from

---

[147] L. Falkenstein, *Der "Lateran" der karolingischen Pfalz zu Aachen*, Kölner Historische Abhandlungen, 13 (Cologne, 1966), 95–139 and 112–28 for the *Chronicon Moissiacense*, s.a. 796, with its reference to Aachen as the 'palatium, quod nominavit Laternanis' (Pertz, ed., MGH, SS I, 303). For a revised view, which emphasises symbolic rather than physical traces, see R. Kramer and C. Gantner, '"Lateran Thinking": Building on the Idea of Rome in the Carolingian Empire', *Viator*, 47.3 (2016), 1–26.

[148] Nelson, *King and Emperor*, 364.

[149] A good example is Alcuin's gift of a copy of the gospels to Charlemagne at Christmas time (*Ep.* 261; Dümmler, ed., MGH, Epp. IV, 418–19; Allott, tr., *Alcuin*, no. 72). A good case can be made for this book being the manuscript that is now Trier, Stadtbibliothek, MS 23, containing a verse dedication to the king in Alcuin's name before his (rare) commentary on Hebrew Names, although Bischoff thought it was a copy made after 814. See Bischoff, *Katalog*, no. 6167 and Nees, 'Networks or Schools?', 404.

the classical past and the contemporary world; at the same time it looks forward, suggesting through the text and as well as the embedded cultural associations of its script, ornament, and materials that Charlemagne was destined not just for a place in the heavenly kingdom but that he was also the heir to empire on Earth. As Ganz has rightly observed of its script, 'such classicising capitals assumed the symbolic function of expressing specific values, and the political and intellectual theory of the *renovatio imperii* in particular'.[150]

[150] See Hadrian's epitaph, Frontispiece, lines 33–6, and Ganz ' "Roman Books" Reconsidered', 302.

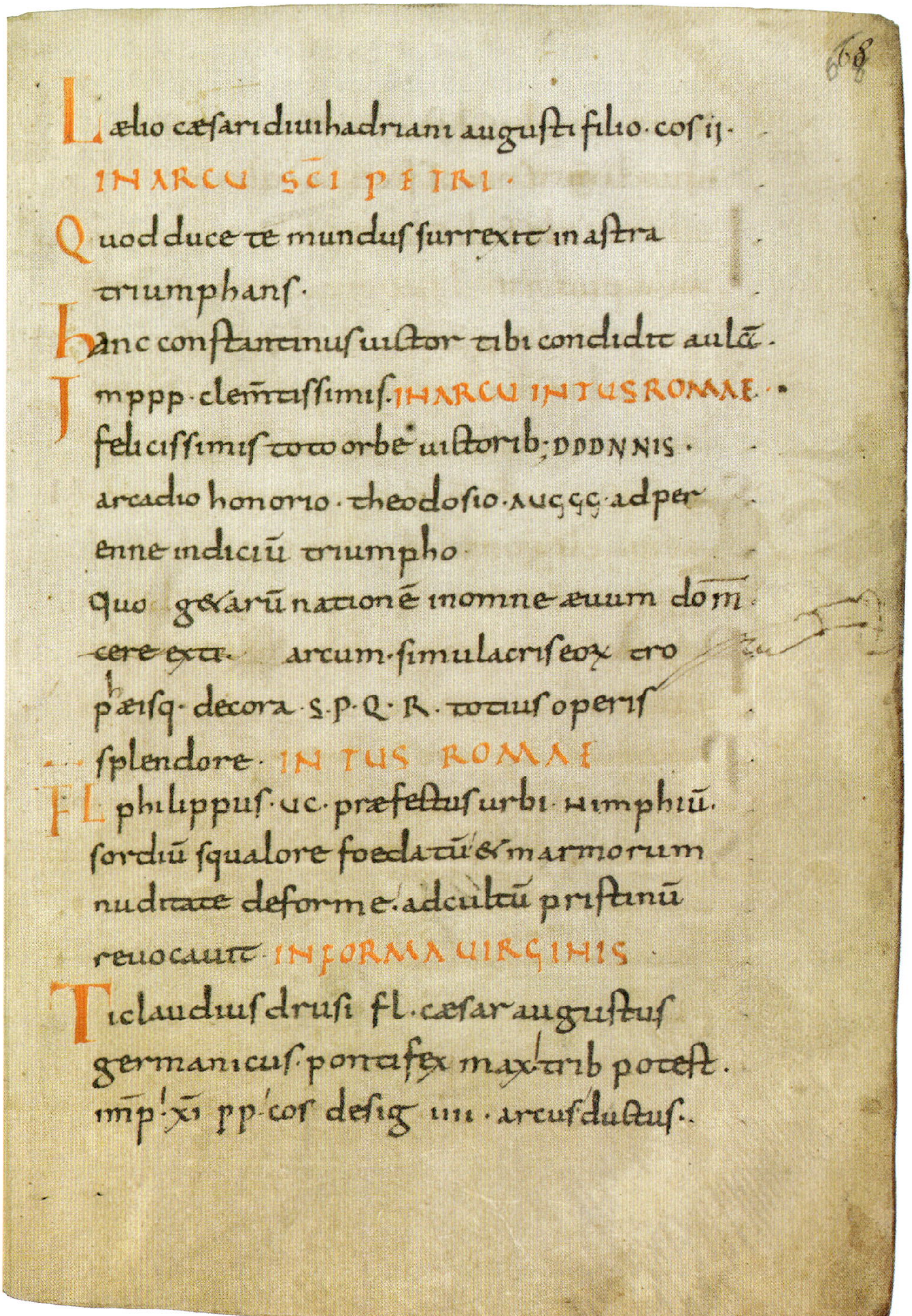

Laelio caesari diui hadriani augusti filio. cos ij.
IN ARCU SCI PETRI.
Quod duce te mundus surrexit in astra
triumphans.
hanc constantinus uictor tibi condidit aulam.
Imppp. clementissimis. IN ARCU IN TUS ROMAE.
felicissimis toto orbe uictorib; DDD NNIS.
arcadio honorio. theodosio. auggg. ad per
enne indicium tripho
quo g&arum nationem in omne aeuum dom
ere ex... arcum simulacris eoq; tro
paeisq; decora. S. P. Q. R. totius operis
splendore. IN TUS ROMAE
FL philippus. uc. praefectus urbi. numphiū.
sordium squalore foedatum & marmorum
nuditate deforme. ad cultum pristinum
reuocauit. IN FORMA UIRGINIS.
Ti claudius drusi fl. caesar augustus
germanicus pontifex max. trib potest.
imp. xi. pp. cos desig iiii. arcus ductus.

FIGURE 8.1 Einsiedeln, Stiftsbibliothek, Cod. 326 (1076), fol. 68r, detail showing the correction of the first word in line 5, from *hinc* to *hanc*. Photo: Courtesy of the Stiftsbibliothek, Einsiedeln.

8

Charlemagne, St Peter's, and the Imperial Coronation

> He [Charlemagne] cherished the church of St Peter the Apostle at Rome, above all other holy and sacred places. He gave its treasury a vast wealth of gold, silver and precious stones. He sent great and countless gifts to the popes; and throughout his whole reign he considered nothing more important than to re-establish the ancient authority of the city of Rome by his care and by his influence, and not only to defend and protect the church of St Peter, but to beautify and enrich it out of his own store above all other churches. Although he held it in such veneration, he only went to Rome to pay his vows and to pray four times during the whole forty-seven years that he reigned.[1]

Einhard's statement about Charlemagne's devotion to the church of St Peter in Rome prefigures his brief account of the king's fourth visit to the city in the winter of 800 which culminated in the imperial coronation in the basilica on Christmas Day. The king went to Rome, Einhard said, because of the need to renew the state of the church which was 'exceedingly disturbed' following the attack on Pope Leo the previous year, which had compelled the pontiff to appeal to 'the king's loyalty'. Einhard stated the outcome in simple terms; 'It was at this time that [Charles] accepted the name of emperor and augustus'. But had he been forewarned of the pope's intention, Einhard famously claimed, the king 'would not have entered the church' that he so cherished, even though it was a feast day.

When Pope Hadrian died at Christmas 795, no one in Rome or in Francia can have predicted how events would unfold over the next few years nor that only five years later St Peter's basilica would host an imperial coronation for the Frankish king. Nevertheless, the commission and production of an epitaph for Hadrian shows that Charlemagne and those around him had thought about and intended to influence the way that the old pope would be remembered, and that *Karolus rex ego* would be central to that commemoration in Rome. The epitaph augmented earlier Carolingian gifts to St Peter's basilica and enriched the symbolic presence of the dynasty within its architectural space. What is more, it was clear evidence of Frankish mastery of the

---

[1] Einhard, *VK*, ch. 27; Ganz, tr., *Einhard and Notker*, 37.

medium and aesthetic vocabulary of monumental inscriptions, ostentatiously recalling the motifs, materials, and methods of ancient Rome, drawing inspiration from both papal verse inscriptions and imperial epigraphy. The confidence and connotations of the inscription and its patron were clear for all to see. The making of the monument in Francia, its transportation to Rome and positioning over Hadrian's tomb ensured this message was disseminated and displayed in the heart of St Peter's basilica itself, and its prominent setting in the south transept between the shrines of Peter and Petronilla was a guarantee of enduring prayerfulness for the royal petitioner as well as the old pope, set amid the *familia* of St Peter.

When did the inscription reach Rome? Angilbert's high-profile mission in 796 is a plausible context for its transport, but had he left Francia in the spring of that year (as is generally assumed) there may not have been enough time for Alcuin's verses to have been composed, the stone sourced, and the inscription cut. This embassy had been planned for some time, and preparations were evidently at an advanced stage when papal messengers arrived bearing news of Hadrian's death and Leo's election, forcing a delay. Travelling in winter, they cannot have arrived in Aachen very much before the end of February, perhaps later. The Frankish sources make it clear that Angilbert's departure for Rome was set back by the news of the pope's death as well as the king's period of mourning that followed.[2] That unexpected delay, however, created time to rethink the objectives of the mission under the changed political circumstances. A letter from the king to the new pope confirms that Charles had already promised Hadrian that Angilbert would come to Rome. This message had been relayed by two 'devout men', named Campulus and Anastasius, and gifts had been prepared in readiness for Angilbert's mission.[3] Some of the issues slated for discussion with Hadrian were laid out in a contemporaneous letter from the king to Angilbert, instructing him to pursue these topics with Leo instead; but doubtless there were now also other issues on the agenda.[4] Both of these letters had been drafted by Alcuin, and that sent to the pope mirrors the lachrymose sentiment of the epitaph verses, suggesting closely contemporary composition.[5] The rhetorical climax of the letter and the crux of the poem are

---

[2] Charlemagne, 'Letter to Leo III', Alcuin, *Ep.* no. 93; Dümmler, ed., MGH, Epp. IV, 136–8. See also Chapter 2, 98–9.

[3] Charlemagne, 'Letter to Leo III', Alcuin, *Ep.* no. 93; Dümmler, ed., MGH, Epp. IV, 137, lines 18–19, 'per religiosos viros'. The letter is translated by King, *Charlemagne*, 311–12 and H. R. Loyn and J. Percival, tr., *The Reign of Charlemagne: Documents on Carolingian Government and Administration* (London, 1975), 117–19. If this Campulus was the same man as the *sacellarius* who conspired against Leo in 799 (*LP* 98: 11–13) this letter is evidence that he had acted as a papal emissary to Francia and was known to the king (and probably to Alcuin too). A *notarius* of the same name was recorded in a letter from Hadrian to Charles written in May/June 781 (*CC* 67/*CeC* 72) as party to the resolution of a dispute at San Vincenzo al Volturno. Duchesne thought that the *notarius* and the *sacellarius* were one and the same person. Both offices are high ranking and influential (Hadrian had been a regional notary and Gregory II had been *sacellarius* before promotion to the pontificate).

[4] Charlemagne, 'Letter to Angilbert'; Alcuin, *Ep.* no. 92; Dümmler, ed., MGH, Epp. IV, 135–6.

[5] Alcuin sent a third letter, addressed to Leo, in his own name; Alcuin, *Ep.* no. 94; Dümmler, ed., MGH, Epp. IV, 138–9. On Alcuin's authorship of all three (and their survival in Alcuin's letter collection), see Bullough, *Alcuin*, 448, 455.

also linked. Famously, the letter delineates the responsibilities of king and pope, as seen from Aachen.[6] This clear division of labour finds a parallel in line 24 of the epitaph which defines the roles of both men, and positions the words *Hadrianus pater* around *Karolus rex*, supporting and embracing his central place.

HADRIANVS KAROLVS REX EGO TVQVE PATER

(Hadrian's epitaph, line 24)

It is our function—to the extent that Divine goodness aids us—externally to defend Christ's holy church on every side by force against the incursion of pagans and the ravaging of infidels, inwardly to strengthen it in knowledge of the catholic faith. It is yours, most holy father (*sanctissime pater*), to aid our struggle with hands raised to God…

(Alcuin, *Ep.* no. 93)

Another royal letter, almost certainly also drafted by Alcuin, was written at around the same time and confirms the court's activity. It was evidently composed after the king had finished mourning and had issued his order for alms but before news reached Aachen of the assassination on 18 April of the Northumbrian king.[7] This letter, addressed to Offa of Mercia, discussed the dispatch to England of precious objects from the Avar treasure hoard and alms to facilitate prayers for Hadrian's soul. It also discussed the size of the black stones that Offa had asked Charles to seek out and have sent to him. It is striking that the timing of this last request corresponds so closely to the period of the production of the epitaph, when the slab of black limestone used to make it was being sourced in Francia.[8]

It is probable that Angilbert departed for Rome as quickly as he could. The mission had already been delayed, and the new pope's request for a high-ranking Frankish witness to the oath of loyalty and submission by the *populus Romanus* was pressing and probably time-sensitive.[9] The annals add that a 'large part' of the Avar treasure hoard was sent to enrich Leo's coffers, and a substantial baggage train doubtless accompanied the Frankish delegation. If Hadrian's epitaph was not on board, then perhaps it travelled south later that same year. 'It is a reasonable assumption', Bullough argued, that the inscription had been completed and dispatched by the time that Theodulf composed his long court poem, *Ad Carolum regem*, eulogising Alcuin as the 'glory of our poets'. On various grounds he argued that Theodulf wrote that poem at a point in 796 when both Angilbert and Theodulf himself were absent from court but when Alcuin was still present, that is, before Alcuin had left to take up the

---

[6] Bullough, *Alcuin*, 456–8 (with notes on the extensive commentary on this letter); Hartmann, *Hadrian I*, 258.

[7] Alcuin, *Ep.* 100; Dümmler, ed., MGH, Epp. IV, 144–6; Allott, tr., *Alcuin*, no. 40 and Whitelock, *EHD* 1, no. 197. The *terminus ante quem* is the death of Offa on 29 July 796. Alcuin's hand is highly likely; Keynes, 'The Canterbury Letter-Book', 126–7.

[8] See Chapter 6, 231–42.

[9] *Rev. s.a.* 796, 'qui populum Romanum ad suam fidem atque subiectionem per sacramenta firmaret'.

abbacy at Tours in the late summer or autumn. Alcuin's own court poem was sent in response, after he had arrived in Tours but before the end of the year, and before Angilbert had come back from Rome. Bullough also made the perceptive observation that Theodulf's own memorial verses for Hadrian suggest direct knowledge of the form and function of the finished inscription: 'Golden lettering embraces the funeral song'. With two lines addressing Leo directly, it might thus have accompanied the presentation of the marble slab in Rome, raising the possibility that Theodulf may even have taken it himself.[10]

Speaking in the king's voice, both sets of memorial verses—Alcuin's inscribed text and Theodulf's accompanying presentation poem (if that was indeed its role)—stress the strength of the relationship between the two men that had existed while Hadrian lived. Alcuin's verses pitch this bond forward in time, using the king's voice to talk in the first person and present tense (*scribsi, plango, iungo, scio, posco*) about the strength and persistence of the relationship. Notwithstanding its rhetorical and poetic context, any such statement of Charles' devotion to the late pope must have resonated with the Roman audience that had to swear a public oath of allegiance in Angilbert's presence. This group is likely to have included the 'devout men' Campulus and Anastasius, who had acted as Hadrian's envoys to Francia the previous year. If, as seems likely, this Campulus was the high-ranking cleric of the same name who, less than three years later, emerged as one of the leaders of the revolt against Leo, he and his co-conspirators might have regarded the sentiment of the memorial verses sent from Francia as grounds for encouragement, and of Frankish king's continued respect for Hadrian and his cause.[11] Much of the power of the epitaph was vested in its intended setting over the pope's tomb, and its impact there was all the greater for an audience that had lived and flourished under Hadrian's regime and whose vested interests in the city were likely to be challenged by the new man set up in his place.

There is comparatively little information about the early phase of Leo's rule between the arrival of envoys announcing his election to Charlemagne in early spring 796 and the assassination attempt in April 799. Extant letters and annalistic notes show sustained Frankish interest at this time in the acquisition of relics from Rome and in a scheme to build a monastery at San Paolo fuori le Mura.[12] Alcuin's letters, however, make it clear that that troubling rumours about the pope's behaviour were also reaching Francia.[13] Alcuin's voice on these matters is loud because his move to the abbey of

---

[10] Bullough, *Alcuin*, 439, n. 24, 460–1. For Theodulf's journey to Rome in 800/1, see Freeman and Meyvaert, 'The Meaning of Theodulf's Apse Mosaic', 125–6.

[11] *CC* 61/*CeC* 73 reveals that the leader of the rebels, Primicerius, was Hadrian's nephew. Davis, *Lives of the Eighth-Century Popes*, 184–5, nn. 27 and 29.

[12] Ferrari, *Early Roman Monasteries*, 255–6, 261–4 and pl. V; Leyser, 'Temptations of Cult', 297; Costambeys, 'Alcuin, Rome', 256–61. The *Annales sancti Amandi, s.a.* 797, refer to a council meeting held at Aachen to debate how the monastery at San Paolo should be established; Pertz, ed., MGH, SS 1 (Hanover, 1826), 14.

[13] Alcuin, *Ep.* nos 146 and 159; Dümmler, ed., MGH, Epp. IV, 235–6, 257–9; Allott, tr., *Alcuin*, nos 138 and 100; M. Becher, 'Die Reise Papst Leos III. Zu Karl dem Großen. Überlegungen zu Chronologie, Verlauf

Saint-Martin in the late summer of 796 obliged him to resort to letter-writing to maintain his connections with the court, and his role as abbot meant that copies of his letters were systematically preserved at source and occasionally by their recipients.[14] Ironically, therefore, it was Alcuin's distance from the centre of power that gave rise to the creation and preservation of such a rich set of letters; yet his absence from court meant that his contact with the king was less direct than it had been and his letters may overstate his influence at the expense of other actors.

Alcuin had several points of contact. Angilbert delivered a letter from him to Leo III when he went to Rome in early 796 and reported on his return that it had been well received in the papal court. Alcuin followed this up a year later, in early 797, with a letter to Leo introducing some Northumbrian envoys who were travelling to Rome to obtain the pallium for his friend, Archbishop Eanbald II of York.[15] Candidus too was in Rome around this time, as is shown by Alcuin's letter-poem which encouraged him to see the sights of the city and to observe and report back on Leo's condition.[16] That visit could have taken place in 798 or, alternatively, it may refer to Candidus' journey to Rome with Theodulf and the king's retinue in 800/1.[17] The letter-poem was among the elements added to the manuscript containing the itineraries of Rome in the handbook that was compiled for Arn in 798, and could have been incorporated there following one of Candidus' visits to Salzburg.[18]

Arn of Salzburg was Alcuin's most important source of information, however, and many letters show Alcuin's eagerness—sometimes frustrated—to acquire news of Rome from him. Arn led a delegation to Rome in late 797 and was there until April 798 when he received the pallium from Leo elevating him to archiepiscopal rank. It is possible that he was also in Rome a year later when Leo was attacked.[19] One letter sent probably in August 799 may even refer to this moment and highlights the sensitivity of their correspondence. Alcuin thanked Arn for the letter that Baldric the priest had delivered, and for the gift of a cloak sewn in Roman style. Arn's letter had contained 'complaints about the behaviour of the pope', however, and revealed that Arn himself had been in serious danger in Rome. 'I did not want your letter to get into other

---

und Inhalt der Paderborner Verhandlungen des Jahres 799', in P. Godman, J. Jarnut, and P. Johanek, *Am vorabend der Kaiser Krönung. Das Epos "Karolus Magnus et Leo papa" und der Papstbesuch in Paderborn 799* (Berlin, 2002), 87–112, at 100.

[14] On the recipient Salzburg collection, see Bullough, *Alcuin*, 52–7 and Diesenberger and Wolfram, 'Arn und Alkuin', 89–90; Nelson, *King and Emperor*, 415.

[15] Alcuin, *Epp.* nos 94 and 125; Dümmler, ed., MGH, Epp. IV, 138–9, 184; Allott, tr., *Alcuin*, nos 99 and 18. Eanbald II was confirmed in office on 8 September 797, 'having received the pallium from the apostolic see'; *Historia Regum*, s.a. 797, Arnold, ed., *Symeonis Monachis*, ii, 58.

[16] Alcuin, *Carmina*, no. 44; Dümmler, ed., MGH, PLAC I, 255–6, esp. lines 29–32.

[17] Freeman and Meyvaert, 'The Meaning of Theodulf's Apse Mosaic', 126.

[18] ÖNB, Cod. 795, on which, see Diesenberger and Wolfram, 'Arn und Alkuin', 92–3, 101. On Candidus' presence in Rome in 800, see Alcuin, *Ep.* no. 216; Dümmler, ed., MGH, Epp. IV, 359–60; Allott, tr., *Alcuin*, no. 90.

[19] Becher, 'Die Reise Papst Leo III', 97; Diesenberger and Wolfram, 'Arn und Alkuin', 84.

hands', Alcuin continued, 'so Candidus was the only one to read it with me, and it was then put into the fire, lest any scandal should arise through the carelessness of the man who keeps my correspondence'.[20]

Frankish and papal sources describing the events of the late 790s have been picked over by generations of historians keen to understand the context of the crisis of 799 which catalysed Charlemagne's imperial coronation in Rome the following year.[21] The story that is built up from diverse sources is very well known, and St Peter's basilica features prominently in all of them.[22] On 25 April 799, while following the processional route of the *Letania maior*, Leo was attacked in front of the monastery of St Stephen and St Sylvester close to the Via Lata and there, before the altar, he was beaten again, and renewed efforts were made to blind and silence him. He was incarcerated at the monastery of St Erasmus, where he remained (probably for a couple of months) until, with the help of his chamberlain, Albinus, he escaped to the *aula* of St Peter's where he was met by the duke of Spoleto and the abbot of Stavelot, a Frankish abbey about forty miles south of Aachen.[23] With their help, Leo fled north to Francia. Received by Charlemagne at Paderborn in Saxony in late summer, he remained with the king for perhaps only a couple of weeks before returning south, escorted by an influential and high-ranking group of Frankish clerics and nobles.[24] On 29 November, Leo arrived at the Milvian Bridge to the north of the city, and was greeted by the leading clerics, city militia, and 'entire Roman people' who took him straight to St Peter's where he celebrated Mass. Entering into the city the next day, Leo went to the Lateran. There, the ten Frankish envoys who had accompanied Leo to Rome, including archbishops Arn and Hildebald, assembled in the triclinium to interrogate the pope's accusers, deciding to send them into exile in Francia, pending trial.[25]

Almost exactly a year later, having made a tour of his kingdom that took in many of the places where his key advisors were based—Angilbert at Saint-Riquier, Alcuin at Tours, Theodulf at Orléans, Fardulf in Paris, and Riculf at Mainz—Charles made the journey to Rome accompanied by his sons and daughters. The pope met him at Mentana, twelve miles outside the city walls, and, on 24 November, received him 'with great honour' on the steps of St Peter's and led him into the church with prayers

---

[20] Alcuin, *Ep.* no. 184; Dümmler, ed., MGH, Epp. IV, 308–10; Allott, tr., *Alcuin*, no. 65. See also Becher, 'De Reise Papst Leo III', 91.

[21] For recent summaries, see R. Schieffer, *Neues von der Kaiserkrönung Karls des Großen* (Munich, 2004) and Nelson, 'Why Are There So Many Different Accounts', 8–16.

[22] Osborne, *Rome in the Eighth Century*, 226.

[23] The presence of Abbot Wirund of Stavelot at St Peter's and his status as a *legatus* of the king is mentioned only by the *ARF s.a.* 799; Becher, 'Die Reise', 93–6.

[24] Becher's close reading of the sources and his re-evaluation of the chronology of the events of 799–800 has been widely accepted; M. Becher, 'Die Reise', 111 and Nelson, *King and Emperor*, 372–3.

[25] So says the *Liber Pontificalis*. The Lorsch Annals agrees saying (note the tense) that 'they are now in exile as they deserve' (contra Collins who thought that this referred to their fate after the trial in early 801, and thus that the Lorsch Annals could not be strictly contemporary).

and the chanting of psalms. It was the king, however, who gave the orders for a great assembly to be held in St Peter's basilica the following week, to be attended by the clerical elite, the Roman senate, and the Frankish nobles who had come south with the king in order to clear up the charges of perjury and adultery levelled against the pontiff.[26] On 23 December, standing in the ambo of St Peter's, Leo absolved himself by oath of all charges, and, on Christmas Day, crowned Charlemagne as he rose from prayer in front of the *confessio* before Mass. The assembled company acclaimed him as emperor and augustus, forsaking the title *patricius Romanorum* that was now superseded. Immediately afterwards, the pope anointed his son, the younger Charles, as king.[27] The *Liber Pontificalis* concluded its account of this day with a list of gifts made to Rome's basilicas by the new emperor and his children. To St Peter's, he gave a silver table intended for use at the *confessio* of the apostle as well as liturgical vessels for its service, including a votive crown, a paten, and two chalices. Another large, gold-rimmed chalice was supplied for use at the principal altar. This table joined another which had been donated by his father, Pippin, and had been placed in the *confessio* by Pope Paul I amid litanies of praise and prayer. Charles' gifts in 800 served to reinforce the liturgical presence of the Carolingian dynasty in the most potent parts of the basilica.[28]

Most accounts of these events, whether Frankish or papal, are partisan and retrospective having been composed or edited after the coup against Leo had failed and the imperial title had been conferred on the Frankish king. The exception is the account in the Lorsch Annals that is preserved in the Vienna manuscript, which may be strictly contemporary at this point.[29] Its entry for 800 is in two parts, copied by a scribe working in separate stints. For the first part, the scribe used a dark brown ink to recount the events of the first half of the year including the assembly held at Mainz in early August when the king decided to go to Rome, wrapping up this section with the words, 'And this he did'.[30] The scribe left the rest of the line blank and, using a lighter brown ink, started a new line for the second section which described events in Rome at the end of the year including the 'great assembly' (*conuentum maximum*) at St Peter's and Leo's oath that followed it, quoting the opening words of the *Te Deum* that was sung in celebration. An erasure at the start of this section shows that the scribe had

---

[26] *LP* 98:21, the text is clear that the synod took place at St Peter's, contra Osborne, *Rome in the Eighth Century*, 221 and P. Lauer, *Le Palais du Latran: étude historique et archéologique* (Paris, 1911), 105 who both state that it took place at the Lateran. Freeman and Meyvaert thought that this synod (at St Peter's) ran for three weeks, 1–23 December 800; Freeman and Meyvaert, 'The Meaning of Theodulf's Apse Mosaic', 126.

[27] C. I. Hammer, 'Christmas Day 800: Charles the Younger, Alcuin and the Frankish Royal Succession', *EHR* 127 (2012), 1–23; Nelson, *King and Emperor*, 376–9, 385–6. For Alcuin's letter to Charles the Younger written early in 801, see Alcuin, *Ep.* 217; Dümmler, ed., MGH, Epp. IV, 360–1.

[28] *CC* 21/*CeC* 14. B. Mauskopf Deliyannis, 'Charlemagne's Silver Tables: The Ideology of an Imperial Capital', *EME*, 12 (2003), 159–78, at 174–7.

[29] ÖNB, Cod. 515; Bischoff, *Katalog*, no. 7132. See Chapter 2, 101–3.

[30] The August date is recorded by the *ARF s.a.* 800.

originally written the numeral for 801 and had allocated this second paragraph to that year. But, having started the text, the scribe scratched out the numeral, leaving a gap. Instead, the year's number was added before the account of the imperial coronation on Christmas Day (which was indeed the first day of the new year) and the trial of the conspirators that followed. The change of ink and layout within the annal for 800 could well reflect contemporaneous record keeping, with the first part copied after the August assembly at Mainz and the second part added when details emerged the following spring of the momentous events that had taken place in Rome.

Another manuscript takes us close to the action in 800. A liturgical psalter, likely copied in the Rhine–Meuse area of the Austrasian heartland in the closing years of the eighth century, concludes with a series of liturgical texts, including the *Te Deum*, the Anthanasian Creed, a set of royal acclamations or *laudes regiae*, three litanies, part of a gradual marked with tones for singing, and a fragmentary hymnal.[31] The first of the litanies invokes saints with a strongly Roman focus, but the others call upon Francocentric lists of saints, including Quentin and Firmin (Amiens), Crispin and Crispinian (Soissons), Richarius (Centula/Saint-Riquier), Vedast (Saint-Omer), Landebert (Maastricht), Geretrude (Nivelles) and Aldegund (Maubeuge) in the second litany, and Eligius (Noyon), Martin (Tours), Audoen (Rouen), Arnulf (Metz), Amandus (Saint-Amand), and Bavo (Gent) in the third, closing with a list of six female saints, including Petronilla, and a plea for 'all saints' to intercede *pro nobis*.[32] The gradual was added by a different but contemporary hand and seems to have been made for Saint-Riquier, which remained the manuscript's medieval home.[33] Its connection with Saint-Riquier, controlled at this time by Angilbert, as well as the invocation of saints close to the Carolingian family and heartlands, provides a strong steer to the elite patronage of this book—long since (but not necessarily) associated with Charlemagne himself. Indeed, it is often called the 'Psalter of Charlemagne'.[34]

---

[31] BnF, Lat. 13159, fols 160v–168v; *CLA* V.652; Bischoff, *Katalog*, no. 4873; *CLLA*, ii, no. 1619; SW, *799*, ii, IX.19; M.-P. Laffitte and C. Denoël, *Trésors carolingiens. Livres manuscrits de Charlemagne à Charles le Chauve* (Paris, 2007), 136–8, no. 26; Nees, *Frankish Manuscripts*, no. 15; Rankin, 'Singing from the Dagulf Psalter', 475.

[32] The three litanies are on fols 164v–165v. The first two are titled, *laetania gallica*, and the third, *laetania italica*, on which, see E. H. Kantorowicz, *Laudes Regiae: A Study in Liturgical Acclamations Aand Mediaeval Ruler Worship*, University of California publications in history, 33 (Berkeley and Los Angeles, CA, 1958), 41. For the suggestion that the celebration of All Saints in Francia was catalysed by these *laudes*, see G. Knopp, 'Sanctorum Nomina seriatim. Die Anfänge der Allerheiligenlitanei und ihre Verbindung mid den "Laudes regiae"', *Römische Quartalschrift*, 65 (1970), 185–321. For Alcuin's influence on the introduction of this tradition, see Diesenberger and Wolfram, 'Arn und Alkuin', 88.

[33] M. Huglo, 'Un tonaire du Graduel de la fin du VIIIe Siecle (Paris B. N. Lat. 13159)', *Revue Gregorienne* 31 (1952), 176–86, 224–33.

[34] F. Masai, 'Observations sur le Psautier dit de Charlemagne (Paris, Lat. 13159)', *Scriptorium* 6 (1952), 299–303. The high quality, confident initials in the psalter are Insular in style, and some have a strong Irish feel (fols 28v, 70r) and are likely the work of an artist from the islands at work in an Austrasian scriptorium. For the mermaid in the initial on fol. 13v (and other mermaids *c.*800), see L. Nees, 'The European Context of Manuscript

The *laudes regiae* and two of the three litanies that follow it in this book include acclamations to Pope Leo and the king. In the text of the *laudes*, his title was given in full:

Carolo, excellentissimo et a Deo coronato atque magno et pacifico regi Francorum et Longobardorum ac patricio Romanorum.

Vita et victoria!³⁵

This implies that the texts were composed for use, and probably copied into this manuscript between early 796 and late 800, that is, after Leo's accession but before the imperial coronation; any later and the king's titles would doubtless have been updated.³⁶ These *laudes*, with their acclamations for the pope, king, his children, the justices of the kingdom, and the Frankish army could have been intended for use at special occasions throughout the realm.³⁷ If a specific moment is sought for their composition, then the meeting of king and pope at Paderborn in the late summer of 799 is one possibility.³⁸ Another context may be suggested by the absence in these *laudes* (and in the litanies that follow) of any reference to the queen. Liutgard died in June 800 and was buried at Tours. Although not explicitly called a queen in the narrative sources, Theodulf's verse epitaph for Liutgard did acknowledge her royal status, *O regina potens, o magni gloria regis*.³⁹ An earlier set of *laudes regiae* made during Hadrian's pontificate, which might have been used during Charlemagne's visit to Rome in 786/7, did incorporate acclamations for Fastrada (d. 794) following the *laudes* for the king and his sons, suggesting that salutations for the king's wife were an integral part of these grand public ceremonies.⁴⁰ If so, the absence of any reference to Liutgard in the later set of *laudes* could suggest that, in the form recorded in this manuscript, the text should be dated to the second half of 800 and perhaps to one of the set-piece events held at the end of that year after Charlemagne had arrived in Rome. The *Liber Pontificalis* recalled how the king, pope, and clerical elite met in St Peter's with 'the leading men of the Franks and Romans in attendance' to resolve the charges that had been levelled against Leo. At the end of the synod, Leo mounted the steps of the ambo, just to the west of the great arch in St Peter's, and swore an oath of innocence while clutching a copy of the gospels. This done, 'all the archbishops,

Illumination in the Anglo-Saxon Kingdoms, 600–900', in Breay and Story, eds, *Manuscripts in the Anglo-Saxon Kingdoms*, 45–65, at 49–51.

³⁵ BnF, Lat. 13159, fol. 163 r/v; Duchesne, *Le Liber Pontificalis*, ii, 37.
³⁶ Duchesne, ed., *Le Liber Pontificalis*, ii, 37–8, n. 33.
³⁷ Hen, *Royal Patronage of Liturgy*, 92–3.
³⁸ Duchesne, ed., *Le Liber Pontificalis*, ii, 37–8.
³⁹ Dümmler, ed., MGH, PLAC I, 522–3. On her status, see Nelson, *King and Emperor*, 377–80.
⁴⁰ Montpellier, Bibliothèque Interuniversitaire de Montpellier, section Médecine, MS 409, fol. 344r/v; *CLA* VI.795; Bischoff, *Katalog*, no. 2871a; SW, *799*, ii, IX.18. For the suggestion that these *laudes* could have been formulated for use during visit of 786/7, see Kantorowicz, *Laudes Regiae*, 21, n. 19, and 38. On the manuscript, see Nees, *Frankish Manuscripts*, no. 29.

bishops and abbots, and the whole clergy performed a litany and gave praise to God, to his mother our lady the ever-virgin Mary, St Peter, prince of the apostles, and all God's saints'.[41]

Both the *Liber Pontificalis* and the *Annales regni Francorum* agree that the acclamation of *laudes* was an essential element of the emperor-making ceremony that took place in St Peter's on Christmas Day 800. Both quote the words that the Roman crowd called out in unison after the pope had performed the coronation:

> Carolo [piissimo] augusto, a Deo coronato, magno et pacifico imperatore [Romanorum].
> Vita et victoria![42]

The *Liber Pontificalis* says that this imperial form of acclamation was made three times as Charles stood in front of the *confessio*, and that it was followed by the invocation of many saints. The annals add that once the *laudes* were complete, Charlemagne 'was honoured by the pope in the manner of the ancient emperors' (*ab apostolico more antiquorum principum adoratus est*). In that context, it may be important that the imperial *laudes* used on this occasion echo not only the recent Franco-papal *laudes regiae* discussed above but also, and more specifically, revive the formulae which the emperor Justinian I had insisted was to be used on documents issued in his name after 537, and which was used thereafter in letters emanating from the papacy until the mid-eighth century:

> Imperante domino piisimo augusto, N., a Deo coronato, magno imperatore.[43]

Imperial *auctoritas* was familiar through other media such as architecture, wall paintings, mosaics, and coins. Charlemagne's retinue had passed through Ravenna on the way south, and its imperial buildings and decoration had long been admired by the Franks.[44] Figural depictions of rulers, such as the mosaics showing Justinian and Theodora in their imperial finery on the walls of San Vitale, are likely to have been known to the architects and scholars who encountered that octagonal building in previous visits, perhaps informing discussion about the structure and plan of palace chapel in Aachen alongside the imagined biblical Temple. On his return north in 801, Charlemagne is alleged (in later sources) to have seen in Ravenna a gilded equestrian statue and is said to have arranged for it to be carried back to Aachen and installed there. Agnellus of Ravenna, who is a notoriously unreliable narrator, however, tells the story and claims that the statue was thought to represent the Ostrogothic king

---

[41] *LP* 98:21–22. See also *ARF s.a.* 800.
[42] *LP* 98: 23 (adds 'piissimo'); *ARF s.a.* 801 (adds 'Romanorum').
[43] Noble, 'Topography, Celebration, and Power', 75; see also Chapter 2, 94.
[44] *CC* 81/*CeC* 67; see also Chapter 6, 250.

Theoderic (d. 526) but had originally depicted the Emperor Zeno (d. 491), neither of whom was an especially edifying exemplar.[45]

Textual accounts of imperial ceremonial may also have mattered. Theodulf's funerary lament for Hadrian suggests that he knew the poetry of Corippus, a mid-sixth-century poet from north Africa who went to Constantinople in the 550s. Corippus' panegyric, *In laudem Iustini*, includes rich visual descriptions of the circumstances and ceremonies surrounding the accession of Justin II to the imperial title in Constantinople on 14 November 565 and his inauguration as consul on 1 January 566.[46] This four-book epic was written in Latin rather than Greek, and seems to have been transmitted quite quickly to Visigothic Spain, where it circulated and was preserved.[47] Theodulf's Visigothic origin is likely to account for his knowledge of it and may also explain one route of transmission for (or reintroduction of) the poem to Francia where it influenced not only Theodulf's own verse composition but also that of others writing for Charlemagne in the closing years of the eighth century.[48] It seems to have been an especially significant model for the structure and metrical style of the (now fragmentary) Paderborn epic, *Karolus Magnus et Leo Papa*, composed shortly after 800, suggesting that the whole poem, rather than excerpts, was accessible to some in Francia around the turn of the century.[49] Thick with ekphrastic accounts of figural mosaics, textiles,

---

[45] Agnelli Ravennatis, *Liber Pontificalis Ecclesiae Ravennatis*, c. 94; D. Mauskopf Deliyannis, ed., CCCM 199 (Turnhout, 2006), 259–60; D. Mauskopf Deliyannis, tr., *Agnellus of Ravenna: The Book of Pontiffs of the Church of Ravenna* (Washington, DC, 2004), 205–7. In another, subsequent, poetic ekphrasis, Walafrid Strabo claimed that the equestrian statue was in Aachen, although it is unmentioned by any other writer. See M. W. Herren, 'The *De Imagine Tetrici* of Walahfrid Strabo: Edition and Translation', *Journal of Medieval Latin*, 1 (1991), 118–39.

[46] A. Cameron, ed. and tr., *Flavius Cresconius Corippus: In Laudem Iustini Augusti minoris, Libri IV* (London, 1976).

[47] Schaller, 'Frühkarolingische Corippus-Rezeption', 177–9. On the manuscript, see M. C. Díaz y Díaz, *Manuscritos visigóticos del sur de la Península*. Ensayo de distribución regional, Universidad de Sevilla, Historia y Geografía, 11 (Seville, 1995), 130–4. Orchard has shown several links with Aldhelm's verse and, more recently, with Ædiluulf's; Orchard, *Poetic Art*, 188–91, 237 and A. Orchard, 'Alcuin and Cynewulf: The Art and Craft of Anglo-Saxon Verse', *Journal of the British Academy*, 8 (2020), 295–399. See also Lapidge, *Anglo-Saxon Library*, 116–19. My thanks to Andy Orchard for his help with this section.

[48] It is probable that Corippus' text was also known to Venantius Fortunatus, who became bishop of Poitiers *c*.600, raising the possibility that the text was available in that part of Francia when Theodulf became bishop of Orléans *c*.798: Andersson, tr., *Theodulf of Orléans*, 3; Schaller, 'Frühkarolingische Corippus-Rezeption', 179; J. Gregory, tr., *Venantius Fortunatus: Personal and Political Poems*, Translated Texts for Historians, 23 (Liverpool, 1995), 113, 128. See also Bullough, 'Empire and Emperordom', 385.

[49] A strong case is made for the importance of Corippus (alongside the Æneid and Fortunatus' *Vita S. Martini*) as a source for the Paderborn epic by C. Ratkowitsch, *Karolus Magnus—alter Aeneas, alter Martinus, alter Iustinus. Zu Intention und Datierung des 'Aachener Karlsepos'*, Wiener Studien, Beiheft 24, Arbeiten zur mittel- und neulateinischen Philologie, 4 (Vienna, 1997). Her argument that Theodulf's close friend Modoin was the author of the Paderborn epic is supported by Stella, 'Autore e attribuzioni', 19–34. For use of Corippus' text by the author of a Carolingian grammatical text (perhaps Clemens Scottus, *fl.* 825–50), see P. F. Alberto, 'Corippus' Panegyric of Justin II in Carolingian Grammatical Texts', in D. Paniagua and M. A. Andrés Sanz, eds, *Formas de acceso al saber en la Antigüedad Tardía y en la Alta Edad Media: La transmision del conocimiento dentro y fuera de la escuela*, Textes et Études du Moyen Âge, 84 (Turnhout, 2016), 198–209.

and imperial regalia, Corippus' description of Justin's imperial coronation sparkles with resonance for a Carolingian audience, detailing (for example) the golden jewelled clothing of the emperor, the three-fold offering of the diadem, crowning by the leading bishop, and the sudden shouts of acclamation from the crowd.[50] Had the Paderborn epic survived intact, its fourth book would likely have described Charlemagne's imperial coronation at St Peter's and may have drawn other parallels with this sixth-century eulogy to an earlier, imperial inauguration ceremony.[51]

Theodulf's use of Corippus in his verses for Hadrian go beyond lexical borrowing, reflecting appreciation of the context as well as the structure and diction of selected lines. In the first part of Theodulf's poem, Charlemagne speaks directly to Hadrian, as if he were still alive, saying: 'You are the glory of the Church, resplendent beacon of the city and the world / More precious, beloved father, to me than light'.[52]

> **Tu decus** ecclesiae **fax** splendens **urbis et orbis**
> Carior, egregie, tu mihi **luce**, **pater.**
>
> (Theodulf, lines 9–10)

These lines correspond closely to Corippus' dramatisation in Book 1 of reactions to the death of Justinian (d. 565). In Corippus' text Justinian's leading courtier addressed his chosen successor directly, saying to Justin, 'You are the glory of the Latin empire, its torch and its strength'.

> **Tu decus** imperii **lumen** virtusque Latini
>
> (Corippus, 1.149)

Theodulf's use of the *Tu decus* construction at the start of the line followed by the metaphor of the beacon or torch argues in favour of a direct borrowing from Corippus, rather than his source or an intermediary writer such as Eugenius II of Toledo (d. 657).[53] Appropriately for the context, however, Theodulf switched the noun from empire to church. This version had also been used by Eugenius of Toledo, and was a favourite of Alcuin's too.[54] He deployed it numerous times, twice, as here, in the initial position in poems that postdate Theodulf's verses for Hadrian and which address Charlemagne, 'Tu decus ecclesiae, rector, defendor, amator', and Pope Leo,

---

[50] Corippus, *In Laudem Iustini*, II.100–74; Ratkowitsch, *Karolus Magnus*, 38–9 for the parallel descriptions of the robing ceremony.

[51] Schaller, 'Aachener Epos', argued against the previous views that the poem as it now exists is complete; Godman, tr., *Poetry*, 22; Ratkowitsch, *Karolus Magnus*, 9–10, 61–3.

[52] Theodulf, *Carmina*, no. XXVI; Dümmler, ed., MGH, PLAC I, 489–90; Andersson, tr., *Theodulf of Orléans*, 73–5.

[53] The phrase is first found in Vergil (*Ecl.* 5.34), 'Tu decus omne tuis', and was taken up by Sedulius (*Hymn.* 1.47, 1.48).

[54] Eugenius, *Carmina*, Appendix, no. XXI, line 1 (*De sacerdotibus*) and no. XXIII, line 9 (*De presbyteris*); F. Vollmer, ed., MGH, AA XIV (Berlin, 1905), 276–7.

'Tu decus ecclesiae, mundi laus, glora cleri'.[55] It was clearly a phrase current in courtly circles in the late 790s.

Theodulf's debt to Corippus is more secure with the correspondence between the second part of this line and a subsequent passage in the panegyric where Justin, standing in front of the dead emperor, cries out: 'Light of the city and the world, Justinian, father, are you leaving your beloved palace?'.

> Cum lacrimis Iustinus ait: <u>lux</u> urbis et orbis,
> Iustiniane **pater**, dilectam deseris aulam?
> (Corippus, 1.250–1)

From here, Theodulf seems to have taken both the potent *urbis et orbis* phrase and its association with light, as well as the speaker's tears for the dead father-figure.[56] The correspondence is much closer to Corippus than it is to Alcuin's line in his epitaph for Hadrian which had used the phrase *urbs caput orbis*, as derived from Ovid.[57] So, although both parts of Theodulf's line can be paralleled in other classical, post-classical, and contemporary metrical sources that were likely known to him (not least Alcuin's own poetry), it is only Corippus who linked these phrases with the metaphor of light, just as Theodulf did with the 'resplendent beacon' that functions as the fulcrum of his line. For Corippus, the new emperor was like the sun, the light of *Roma nova*.[58] Striking, in both contexts, is the parallel with Christ's command to his disciples in the Sermon on the Mount that linked light–city–world; 'You are the light of the world (*lux mundi*) / a city (*civitas*) on a hill which cannot be hidden'.[59] This Christological context was relevant for both emperor and pope as servants of Christ,

---

[55] Alcuin, *Carmina*, no. XXIV, line 6, and no. XLIII, line 7; Dümmler, ed., MGH, PLAC I, 245, 254. The poem to Leo is dated, probably to the period between August 796 and September 797, by its reference in line 40 to *praesul* Eanbald II of York. There are thirteen other uses of 'decus ecclesiae' without the initial 'Tu' in Alcuin's extant poetry.

[56] The phrase originates with Ovid, *Fasti*, 2.684, *Romanae spatium est urbis et orbis idem* ('The area of the city of Rome and the world is the same'). It was a particular favourite of Corippus who used it three times *In laudem Iustini* (1.181, 1.250, 3.79). Corippus' use of the word *aula* to mean both people and palace also resonates with Carolingian usage. The prominent usage of the phrase in an eighteenth-century cartouche on the façade of San Giovanni in Laterano arises from the title assigned to the basilica in a bull of 1372, 'Omnium urbis et orbis ecclesiarum mater et caput'; C. Jäggi, 'MATER ET CAPUT OMNIUM ECCLESIARUM: Visual Strategies in the Rivalry between San Giovanni in Laterano and San Pietro in Vaticano', in L. Bosman, I. P. Haynes, and P. Liverani, eds, *The Basilica of St John Lateran to 1600* (Cambridge, 2020), 294–317, at 294–5, and fig. 15.1.

[57] Note that the MGH edition of Alcuin's verse for Hadrian has 'urbis et orbis' in line 14, which is an error, and is not the text of the inscription (see above, frontispiece and xxii); Dümmler, ed., MGH, PLAC I, 113.

[58] For example, Corippus, *In Laudem Iustini*, II.91–7, 149–51, IV.90–101. On this metaphor, see U. J. Stache, *Flavius Cresconius Corippus, In Laudem Iustini Augusti Minoris. Ein Kommentar* (Berlin 1976), 206–10. For the borrowing of it in *Karolus Magnus et Leo Papa*, see Stella, 'Autore e attribuzioni', 26 and 31.

[59] Matthew 5:13–14, 'Vos estis sal terrae…Vos estis lux mundi non potest civitas abscondi supra montem posita'.

as recognised by Alcuin in a subsequent poem to Leo, 'Aurea lux mundi, terrae sal, porta salutis / Et decus ecclesiae gemmisque corona refulgens'.[60]

Metrical correspondences such as these would have been understood and enjoyed by a select few among the Frankish court elite. On a broader level, however, this type of poetic cross-referencing reveals those same scholars engaging with an older language of power, appropriating it for their own times. The very proximity of these scholars to the king and their roles as his confidants and advisors makes this type of material important as historical as well as literary evidence of imperial prototypes. In that respect, *In laudem Iustini* is especially intriguing, given both its rich descriptions of courtly ceremony and its historical subject matter. The panegyric for Justin incorporates set piece accounts of public mourning for the old emperor, the piety of his chosen successor, his crowning, and public acclamations. It describes the arrival at court of an Avar embassy, buildings and construction work, the orthodoxy of the Creed, and the emperor's inauguration as consul. All of these topics would have resonated loudly with the Carolingian court poets, and, whether Theodulf held the panegyric in his head or in his hands, in the closing years of the eighth century the parallels between the events of the poem and his own times must have seemed compelling. Corippus' description of the Avar delegation at Justin's court was easily paralleled by the arrival and submission of the Avar envoys in Francia in 795, the submission of the *tudun*, and the delivery of the Avar war booty in 796.[61] Corippus' reflection of Justin's statement on the orthodoxy of the Creed would have engaged the interest of both Theodulf and Alcuin in their work on the *Opus Caroli* and countering the heresy of Adoptionism.[62] Theodulf's analysis of the nature of image and *imago* in the *Opus Caroli*, as well as his sensitivity to ornament and art as displayed throughout his surviving compositions, would surely have been piqued by Corippus' ekphrastic descriptions of textiles, figural imagery, and architecture.[63] Theodulf seems to have known, for example, an antique codex of the *Calendar of 354*, with its full page figural personifications of the months as well as seated ruler portraits of the emperor Constantius II (d. 361) and his co-ruler Gallus (d. 354).[64] At a meta level, the overarching theme in Corippus' text is one of *translatio imperii* and

---

[60] Alcuin, *Carmina*, no. 28, lines 27–8; Dümmler, ed., MGH, PLAC I, 247; 'Golden light of the world, salt of the earth, gateway to prosperity / And glory of the Church, glistening with gems and garlands'.

[61] See Schaller, 'Frühkarolingische Corippus-Rezeption', 178 for the correspondence between Corippus' and Theodulf's descriptions of the Avars, especially their striking hairstyles; Dümmler, ed., MGH, PLAC I, no. 25, at 37–40 and n. 8. For Frankish involvement in the Avar mission from 796 and Alcuin's correspondence on the topic, see Diesenberger and Wolfram, 'Arn und Alkuin', 87.

[62] Corippus, *In Laudem Iustini*, IV.294–310; Cameron, ed. *Corippus*, 82, 116, 206–7. Corippus' paraphrase stops before the line in which the controversial *Filioque* clause had been inserted. Bullough, 'Alcuin, Arn and the Creed', 132–4; A. E. Siecenski, *The Filioque: History of a Doctrinal Controversy* (Oxford, 2010), 91–6.

[63] Theodulf, *Carmina*, 28, lines 179–204; Dümmler, ed., MGH, PLAC I, 498–9; Andersson, tr., *Theodulf of Orléans*, 88.

[64] Stern, *Le Calendrier de 354*, pl. XIV–XV; Freeman and Meyvaert, eds, *Opus Caroli regis*, 442 (line 10) and 581.

the *renovatio* of rulership under a new leader. In the late 790s, as the compositions of Alcuin, Theodulf, and others show, the vocabulary of empire was current even if the concept had not crystalised, and the form and foundations of the king's power were being discussed by his closest advisors.[65] Theodulf's reflections of *In Laudem Iustini* in his funerary verses for Hadrian, as well as its influence on the Paderborn epic, shows that it was circulating in courtly circles in Francia before 800 as well as afterwards. The emperor Justin II as described by the panegyric may therefore be added to the list of imperial exemplars familiar to Charles and his scholarly advisors in the 790s.

Justin's name and apparent piety may also have been known to the Carolingian elite through a large *crux gemmata* preserved today at St Peter's.[66] It is a reliquary containing a fragment of the True Cross, and bears an inscription on its front as well as stylised portraits of the emperor and his wife, Sophia, on the reverse, set either side of an Agnus Dei clipeus in the centre. The inscription is carried on the four arms of the cross. Starting at the top, charter-like with a small inscribed cross, the first line, written in *scriptura continua*, reads vertically downwards. The second line naming the donors runs across the arm and, thus, a reader's eyes make the sign of the cross.[67] Justin's name is prominent at the beginning of the line, but his wife, as donor of the jewels, is not named.

> + Ligno quo Christus humanum / subdidit hostem dat Romae
>   Iustinus opem / et socia decorem
>
> + With the wood that Christ subdued the enemy of man
>   Justin [gives] this work to Rome and his consort [gives] its adornment.

Justin II's jewelled cross is the earliest surviving reliquary of the True Cross and may also have had a processional as well as a votive function.[68] The inscription places the names of the donors in close proximity to the precious relic, ensuring that the donors were repeatedly included in the liturgical activity. As such it bears comparison to the

---

[65] Alcuin, *Ep.* 174 written after the attack on Leo, about the three powers; Allott, tr., *Alcuin*, no. 103. Nelson, 'Why Are There So Many Different Accounts', 17–18; Bullough, 'Empire and Emperordom', 386–7.

[66] V. H. Elbern, 'Zum Justinuskreuz im Schatz von Sankt Peter zu Rom', *Jahrbuch der Berliner Museen*, 6 (1964), 24–38. The cross was restored in 2009: see V. Pace, S. Guido, and P. Radiciotti, *La Crux Vaticana o Croce di Giustino II*, Bolletino d'archivio, 4–5 (Padua, 2013), 34–7; Bucarelli, 'Epigraphy and Liturgical Furnishings', 306–7. Justin also sent a relic of the True Cross to Radegonde at Poitiers, which would probably also have been known to Theodulf, not least through Venantius Fortunatus' verses in praise of Justin and Sophia which mention this gift of the relic to Radegonde; Venantius Fortunatus, 'Ad Iustinum et Sophiam Augustos', ed. Leo, MGH, AA IV.1 (Hannover, 1888), 275–8; C. Hahn, 'Collector and Saint: Queen Radegund and Her Devotion to the Relic of the True Cross', *Word and Image*, 22 (2006), 268–74.

[67] Cascioli, *Epigrapfi Cristiane nell'area vaticana III–VI secolo*, 95–6. The vertical arrangement of the letters on the shaft is an important parallel to the layout of the runic inscription on the Ruthwell Cross; É. Ó Carragáin, *Ritual and the Rood* (Toronto, ON, 2005), 236–7.

[68] For relics of the Cross in Rome and the development of the liturgy of the Cross in the city, see especially S. de Blaauw, 'Jerusalem in Rome and the Cult of the Cross', in R. Colella, M. Gill, L. Jenkins, and P. Lamers, eds, *In Pratum Romanum: Richard Krautheimer zum 100. Geburtstag* (Wiesbaden, 1997), 55–73.

treasures that Charles brought to Rome in 800. Those for St Peter's included 'a large gold paten, with various jewels, inscribed *KAROLVS*, weighing 30lb'.[69] The king's name on the surface of the paten—echoing its central position on the epitaph—ensured that he was involved each time the paten was used in the Mass. On the same occasion Charles also gave a *crux gemmata* to the Constantinian basilica at the Lateran, 'which the bountiful pontiff [Leo] assigned for the litany procession as the pious emperor suggested'.[70]

This jewelled cross was a fitting gift with clear imperial precedents. Inspired not just by the sixth-century reliquary cross of Justin and Sophia preserved at St Peter's, it also recalled the heavy gold cross that was said to have been set above the tomb of the Apostle by the first Christian emperor, Constantine, and his mother Helena. The 'Life' of Pope Sylvester in the *Liber Pontificalis* recorded and made much of the inscription that it carried which named the imperial donors.[71]

> Constantinus augustus et Helena augusta
> Hanc domum regale simili fulgore coruscans aula circumdat.
>
> Constantine augustus and Helena augusta
> This regal house is surround by an *aula*, glittering with like splendour.

It is not known how long Constantine and Helena's cross survived.[72] Nevertheless, from at least the mid-sixth century, when the first iterations of the *Liber Pontificalis* began to circulate, readers of Sylvester's 'Life' in that text would have known about this cross, its form, its location in St Peter's, and its donors, as well as the wording of the donative inscription. Some elements of the 'Life' relating to Constantine's donations were modified at this time, and it may be that the special emphasis given to Constantine and Helena's cross in that text reveals in part a contemporary interest in the symbolism of the Cross reflected also in Justin and Sophia's gift.[73] Early readers of

---

[69] Cascioli, *Epigrapfi Cristiane nell'area vaticana VI–X secolo*, 111.

[70] *LP* 98:24–5; Davis, *Lives of the Eighth-Century Popes*, 191–2. The cross was set with jacinths which are clear red gemstones, visually similar to garnet. Charlemagne's cross didn't survive long and was stolen during Paschal's pontificate, *LP* 105:17. On crosses donated by Leo III, see K. C. Schüppel, 'The stucco crucifix of St Peter's reconsidered: textual sources and visual evidence for the Renaissance copy of a medieval silver crucifix', in *OSPR* (2013), 306–23, at 311–13.

[71] *LP* 34:17; Cascioli, *Epigrapfi Cristiane nell'area vaticana III–VI secolo*, 48–9; Brandenburg, Ballardini, and Theones, *Saint Peter's*, 20.

[72] Toynbee and Ward Perkins, *Shrine of St. Peter*, 203–4 suggested that the cross shown at the back of the niche on the fifth-century Pola casket might have been that described in the 'Life of Sylvester'. See also Liverani, 'Old St Peter's', 490 and Bucarelli, 'Epigraphy and Liturgical Furnishings', 294–5; Brandenburg, Ballardini, and Theones, *Saint Peter's*, 16, fig. 11.

[73] For the argument that the list of donations is essentially Constantinian in date and based on archival records, with a few later modifications, see P. Liverani, 'Osservazioni sul libellus delle donazioni costantine nel Liber Pontificalis', *Athenaeum* 107 (2019), 169–217. For discussion of later modifications made in the sixth and seventh centuries, see F. Montinaro, 'Les fausses donations de Constantin dans le *Liber Pontificalis*', *Millennium*, 12 (2015), 203–29.

the *Liber Pontificalis* may, furthermore, have noticed that the description of this cross was central to the claim in that text that Constantine had built a basilica to honour St Peter. The biographer said that Constantine encased the saint's tomb in bronze and decorated it with porphyry columns and others, twisted like vines (*alias columnas vitineas*), that he had brought from Greece. The apse above the shrine was decorated with gold and above the tomb was placed the gold cross which, the papal biographer stressed (in case anyone should doubt), had been 'made to measure' (*in mensurae locus*).[74] The author of the 'Life' made no mention of any other Constantinian inscription at St Peter's, neither at the apse nor on the triumphal arch, and it is only the nielloed words on the cross that are presented to readers of the *Liber Pontificalis* as textual evidence of Constantine's patronage of St Peter's shrine.[75]

The tall arch that spanned the nave of the basilica connected that great hall with the transept that housed the high altar, the *confessio*, and the oratories to the north and south. This 'triumphal' arch marked the transition from the public space of the nave to the more restricted, liturgical, and pilgrim spaces around the shrine.[76] On the archway high above was another inscription, probably in mosaic but unmentioned in the *Liber Pontificalis*. Yet, this inscription identified Constantine as *victor* and founder of 'this basilica' (*hanc... condidit aulam*) and was certainly known to Carolingian visitors to the basilica.[77]

> Quod duce te mundus surrexit in astra triumphans
>   Hanc Constantinus victor tibi condidit aulam.
>
> Because You [Christ] are leader, the world has risen triumphant to the stars
>   Constantine, the victor, built this hall for You.

[74] But see R. Krautheimer, 'The Building Inscriptions and Dates of Construction of Old St. Peter's: A Reconsideration', *Römisches Jahrbuch für Kunstgeschichte*, 25 (1989), 3–23, at 4.

[75] For the arguments in favour of St Peter's as the primary place of display of Constantine and Helena's cross, see Liverani, 'Old St Peter's', 489–90. For the suggestion that the cross described here was originally made for Santa Croce in Gerusalemme (*LP* 34:22) and that the *aula* of the text referred to the Sessorian palace rather than St Peter's, and was transferred later to St Peter's, see Bowersock 'Peter and Constantine', 9–11; J. W. Drijvers, 'Helena Augusta and the City of Rome', in M. Verhoeven, L. Bosman, and H. van Asperen, eds, *Monuments and Memory: Christian Cult Buildings and Constructions of the Past: Essays in Honour of Sible de Blaauw* (Turnhout, 2016), 147–55 at 149–50; Westall, 'Constantius II', 224; contra Gem, 'From Constantine', in *OSPR*, 38–9.

[76] The contemporary term was *arcus maior*. Krautheimer notes that it is in the papal biographies of Paschal I and Gregory IV that the term *arcus triumphalis* is first used for ecclesiastical architecture; R. Krautheimer, 'The Carolingian Revival of Early Christian Architecture', *The Art Bulletin*, 24 (1942), 1–38 in his *Studies in Early Christian, Medieval and Renaissance Art* (New York, 1969), 203–56, at 233; Arbeiter, *Alt-St. Peter*, 200–6.

[77] *ICUR* n.s. ii: 4092; Schaller and Könsgen, eds, *Initia*, no. 13892; Cascioli, *Epigrapfi Cristiane nell'area vaticana III–VI secolo*, 52. It is a central text for attributing the construction of the basilica to Constantine; Krautheimer, 'The Building Inscriptions', 7–9, 14–15 arguing that the placing of the dedication inscription on the triumphal arch implies that the spaces around the apse which normally carried such texts were already full. P. Liverani, 'Old St Peter's', 492–3, notes a parallel use of the opening words 'Quod duce' in a verse inscription for Felicissimus and Agapitus by Pope Damasus, which survives in its original Filocalian form (on which, see *ED*, 152–6, no. 25; Trout, ed., *Damasus of Rome*, 126–7, no. 25). See also, Arbeiter, *Alt-St. Peter*, 55–9 and Thunø, *Apse Mosaic*, 32.

These are weighty words. The distich encapsulates the theology of universal salvation through Christ's resurrection as well as the historically specific claim that, following victory over his rivals, Constantine had initiated construction of the basilica. Two types of evidence—manuscripts and intertextual quotations—demonstrate that these lines of verse were visible in situ to Frankish observers *c*.800. Some contemporary Carolingian inscriptions echo both its diction and context. The clearest example is the opening line of the dedicatory inscription for the new church of St Alban at Mainz, consecrated on 1 December 805, recording the role of Archbishop Riculf in its creation: *Antistes humilis Riculf hanc condidit aulam*.[78] The quotation here contrasts Riculf's humility with the triumphalism of the original in Rome. Riculf had been to Rome on the king's business. He was part of the king's entourage in 781 for the baptism of Louis and Pippin at St Peter's (very probably the context of the donation of Hildegard's pallium to the altar of the Shepherd at the foot of the northern pier of the arch), and was sent thence with legates of the pope as the king's envoy to Tassilo in Bavaria.[79] Elevated to the see of Mainz in 787, Riculf remained close to the court, and was among the Frankish magnates who went to Rome with the king in 800, having hosted the preliminary assembly at Mainz in August.[80] He would surely have seen the original inscription in situ in St Peter's, and appreciated the flattering quotation in the subsequent dedicatory verses at Mainz. The verses that were adapted for use in the palace chapel at Aachen provide another echo. Dedicated by Leo III himself in January 805, verses painted around the interior of the octagon praised the *aula...quod Karolus princeps condidit*.[81] Less directly, but also resonant, Alcuin's commemorative verses for Hadrian deploy the classical motif of astral immortality, proclaiming that 'for all', Hadrian 'opens the way to the stars' (*...cunctis pandit ad astra viam*).[82]

Despite the importance of the inscription on the triumphal arch as a statement of the Constantinian origins of the basilica, it is not mentioned in the *Liber Pontificalis* and there is no record of it before the ninth century. Two Carolingian manuscripts include it within *syllogae* of inscriptions from Rome, showing that it was known to Frankish readers.[83] The earlier of the two manuscripts was made *c*.820–30 probably at Sankt Gallen, and here the arch inscription is entitled, *Versus de ecl sci Petri ad corbus*

---

[78] 'De conditore ecclesiae Sancti Albani', ed., Dümmler, MGH, PLAC I, 431; Schaller and Könsgen, eds, *Initia*, no. 912.

[79] *Rev. s.a.* 781. Alcuin says Riculf accompanied the king into Saxony in 794; Alcuin, *Ep.* no. 24; Dümmler, ed., MGH, Epp. IV, 65. He remained close to the king, witnessing his will in 811; Einhard, *VK*, ch. 33.

[80] Fastrada was buried in St Albans, Mainz on 12 August 794; Nelson, *King and Emperor*, 304. On Riculf's journey in 800, see Alcuin, *Ep.* no. 212; Dümmler, ed., MGH, Epp. IV, 352–3.

[81] See Chapter 7, 296.

[82] On the astral motif in Christian verse and iconography, see, for example, Marucchi, 'Di una iscrizione storica', 67.

[83] St Gallen, Stiftsbibliothek, Cod. 271, at 231 (Bischoff, *Katalog*, no. 5713); Einsiedeln, Stiftsbibliothek, Cod. 326 (1076), fols 67–97, at 68r (Bischoff, *Katalog*, no. 1133).

('Verses from the church of St Peter, at the body [i.e. the shrine]'). It is first in a short *sylloge* of four inscriptions from Rome copied at the end of a substantial set Alcuin's letters, and is followed by the text of two inscriptions on the doors at the entrance to St Peter's, on the right (*Lumine sed magno*) and left (*Lux arcana*).[84] The fourth text is an eight-line epigram recording the reconstruction by Justinian's general, Narses (d. 573), of a bridge over the River Anio, on the Via Salaria, not far to the north of the city.[85] The manuscript is distinctly utilitarian, made in haste by two scribes using low-grade parchment. The epigrams were copied at more or less the same time as the letters, although the ink change reveals a break between the writing episodes. The Alcuin letters are a copy of the 'basic collection' brought together at Tours during Alcuin's lifetime or very soon afterwards. A copy of Charlemagne's letter to the emperor Nicephorus, dated 811, is interpolated into the middle of the set revealing the earliest possible date for the collection as found here, although the script of the collection suggests a slightly later date. It has been proposed that this copy of the letter collection was made in the context of a confraternity agreement brokered by Fridugis, Alcuin's successor as abbot at Saint-Martin's, with the Sankt Gallen community.[86] It remains an open question whether the texts of the inscriptions travelled with the exemplar of the letters from Tours, or were added to fill empty leaves at the end of the hastily made book from exemplars found locally. The only other early medieval copy of the inscription on the arch at St Peter's is in the 'imperial' *sylloge* that was copied by a Fulda-trained scribe after 840, now Einsiedeln, Stiftsbibliothek, Cod. 326 (1076). It is found there on an opening that also includes the epigram for the bridge over the Anio.[87] The texts from the bridge and the doors of the basilica were copied into other Carolingian manuscripts, but the verses on the principal arch at St Peter's were not.[88]

The collocation in the St Gallen manuscript of letters from Alcuin alongside copies of texts about Rome is reminiscent of the handbook made for Archbishop Arn not long after his return from Rome in 798, now ÖNB, Cod. 795, the final stages of which were overseen by the Salzburg-based scribe Baldo.[89] The itinerary of Rome in

---

[84] *ICUR* II.i, no. X:1–4; Schaller and Könsgen, eds., *Initia*, no. 9087 and no. 9109; Cascioli, *Epigrapfi Cristiane nell'area vaticana VI–X secolo*, 37–41. On the Alcuin letter book, see Bullough, *Alcuin*, 61–2.

[85] Composed probably in 565, these verses were set on the left side of the bridge and begin: *quam bene curati directa est semita pontis*. On the villa and bridge at *Ponte Salario*, see L. Quilici and S. Quilici Gigli, *Fidenae*, Latium Vetus, 5 (Rome, 1986), 258–60.

[86] Bullough, *Alcuin*, 62, n. 146.

[87] Einsiedeln, Stiftsbibliothek, Cod. 326 (1076), fols 67r–68r, *In ipso ponte in occidente* (*ICUR* II.i, 18, no. II.2) and *in arcu sci Petri* (*ICUR* II.i, 20, no. II.6).

[88] The sylloge from Saint-Riquier (now, St Petersburg, Russian National Library, MS F. v. XIV.1) includes the inscriptions on the bronze doors (*ICUR* II.i, 78, no. VII:1–2) and the bridge over the Anio (*ICUR* II.i, 89, no. VII.41). The first Lorsch sylloge (L₁) has the pair of verses for the doors (*ICUR* II.i, 144–5, no. XIII 4–5) and the fourth Lorsch sylloge (L₄) has the bridge text (*ICUR* II.i, 115, no. VIII.87); BAV, Pal. Lat. 833, fols 27v–28v and 77v.

[89] Diesenberger and Wolfram, 'Alkuin und Arn', 100–3; see also Chapter 4, 169–70.

Arn's handbook begins its section on St Peter's with a statement about the beauty and pre-eminence over other churches of 'the basilica of blessed Peter', *quam Constantinus imperator totius orbis condidit...in cuius occidentali plaga beatum corpus eius quiescit.*[90] This recalls the title of the verses on the arch as recorded by the Sankt Gallen manuscript as well as the wording of the inscription itself, and reflects what must have been a view widely held by the early ninth century, at least to Frankish readers of the *Liber Pontificalis*, itineraries, and *syllogae*, that Constantine had indeed built the *aula* at St Peter's shrine.

The two Carolingian manuscripts agree on the wording of the arch inscription, with one small exception. The first word of the second line in the older manuscript, at Sankt Gallen, is *hinc* ('thereafter/hence'). The scribe of the later copy embedded in the Einsiedeln *sylloge* used the same word, showing that *hinc* was the accepted reading in the exemplars of both. However, subsequently, another hand changed this word, using a lighter, brown ink to overwrite, altering *hinc* to *hanc* (Figure 8.1).[91] The scribe who made this change may also have been responsible for amending punctuation and making changes elsewhere in the early pages of this section of the Einsiedeln *sylloge*, leading de Rossi to suppose the existence of another manuscript with variant readings, although it is not certain when these corrections were added or if they were made in a single campaign.[92] Nevertheless, ever since the fifteenth century when scholars rediscovered the manuscripts recording the St Peter's arch inscription, the secondary, amended reading is the one that has been universally accepted. This small change, of one letter from *-i* to *-a*, is small but significant, since it changes the emphasis of the verse from a generic hall in an unspecified location to 'this hall', that is, St Peter's basilica itself. If the primary reading diluted the connection between patron and place, the amended reading aligns the inscription unambiguously with the traditional story of Constantine's foundational role at St Peter's as found in the *Liber Pontificalis*.

The transmission history of this key inscription is important but complex, since it is tangled in the internal struggles of the medieval Church. Fifteenth-century interest in it was initiated by Poggio Bracciolino (1380–1459), a renowned scholar of classical Latin, an accomplished humanist scribe, and a seeker of early manuscripts. He spent time in Germany and Switzerland while on official duties as a member of the papal chancery at the Council of Constance (1414–18), which sought to resolve the schism

---

[90] 'That Constantine, emperor of the whole world, founded...at the western end of which rests the blessed body of [Peter]'; ÖNB, Cod. 795, fol. 186v, lines 11–14; VZ, ii, 94. This *titulus* also shows understanding of the unusual alignment of the basilica, with the sacral focus at the western end of the basilica.

[91] The alteration is not noted in Del Lungo's edition, *Roma in età carolingia*, 31. The digital facsimile of the manuscript available via eCodices shows the alteration very clearly.

[92] De Rossi argued that the work of the corrector implied access to another codex containing these variant readings (*ICUR* II.i, 11–13, 20, 345). De Rossi is clear that Poggio's exemplars read *hinc* but he, nevertheless, preferred *hanc*. De Rossi thought that the Poggio's exemplar, now lost, might have been part of Sankt Gallen, Stiftsbibliothek, Cod. Sang. 899 (Bischoff, *Katalog*, no. 5865), which still includes the epitaph to Gerold on page 57. See Del Lungo, *Roma in età carolingia*, 25 for the stemma.

caused by the Avignon papacy. Poggio eventually became apostolic secretary and was thus close to the project to re-establish the person of the pope and the office of the papacy in Rome. Poggio made his own *sylloge* of early inscriptions, published in 1429, revealing his scholarly interest in this type of material. He seems to have known the Einsiedeln manuscript or a copy of it, encountered perhaps at Sankt Gallen where he spent time in between meetings of the Council.[93] The sources available to him for this particular text seem to have used *hinc* but Poggio proposed what de Rossi considered to be 'the very easy and obvious correction' to *hanc*, aligning the inscription with received wisdom and sidestepping any possible ambiguity over the Constantinian origins of the basilica.[94] As amended, the second line of the arch inscription matches the second line of the inscription on the silver cross donated by Constantine and Helena, presented by the *Liber Pontificalis* as proof of Constantine's largess to St Peter's. Constantine's patronage had been an important factor in the very long-standing rivalry between the 'Basilica Constantiniana' at the Lateran and St Peter's at the Vatican, with the former's claim to primacy within Rome pivoting on its foundation by the first Christian emperor. That position had, of course, been reinforced by the document which became known as the *Constitutum Constantini* or 'Donation of Constantine' which made much of the gift of emperor's possessions at the Lateran to Pope Sylvester. In the 1430s, when Poggio was investigating these early inscriptions, the 'Donation of Constantine' was under renewed scrutiny. In 1440 Poggio's great rival, Lorenzo Valla, demonstrated definitively that it was a medieval forgery, with significant consequences for age-old arguments that underpinned the temporal authority of the papacy writ large.[95] Poggio's preference for *hanc...aula*, connecting Constantine firmly to the foundation of St Peter's, in preference to the primary reading he had found in his manuscript exemplars, fits with his local loyalties and to the febrile papal politics of Rome in the 1430s. Indeed, his abilities as a humanist scribe and as a scholar leave him open to the charge that the amendment to the Carolingian manuscript could have been by his hand.[96]

The inscription on the triumphal arch at St Peter's was recorded again in the later 1450s by Maffeo Vegio, perhaps supplemented by direct observation of the building rather than relying solely on manuscript transmission. Vegio began his account of the

---

[93] *ICUR* II.i, 12–13, 341 and no. XLII (de Rossi's edition of Poggio's *sylloge* was planned but not published, *ICUR* II.i, 532). The manuscript containing Poggio Bracciolini's notes derived from manuscript sources and extant inscriptions, is now BAV, Vat. Lat. 9152; the text from the arch at St Peter's is given at the foot of fol. 26v (available on DigiVatLib). On Poggio's sylloge, see E. Walser, *Poggius Florentinus. Leben unde Werke*, Beiträge zur kulturgeschichte des Mittelalters und der Renaissance, 14 (Berlin, 1914), 145–8. See also Stenhouse, *Reading Inscriptions*, 21–3, 163.

[94] *ICUR* II.i, 12, 345.

[95] C. Coleman, *The Treatise of Lorenzo Valla on the Donation of Constantine* (New Haven, CT, 1922).

[96] See de Rossi's comments on the work of the corrector, *ICUR* II.i, 11–13, 20, 123, 345 leaving open the possibility that this correction to the manuscript could have been made by Poggio himself ('sive emendavit sive antiquam emendationem recepit, scripsit *Hanc*').

'abundant remains of antiquity' in St Peter's basilica by compiling evidence which underpinned and supported claims of its foundation by Constantine.[97] Writing a few years after Valla had exposed the Donation as a forgery, Vegio, who was a canon of St Peter's, sought to re-establish the Constantinian credentials of the basilica on secure historical grounds by quoting ancient inscriptions that he said were still visible on the walls of the church alongside stories from Rufinus' Latin translation of Eusebius's *Ecclesiastical History*. In explaining Constantine's motives for the foundation of St Peter's, Vegio debunked as apocryphal the traditional tale of Constantine's cure from leprosy—as told in the late fifth-century *Actus beati Sylvestri papae* and repeated by the *Liber Pontificalis*—and replaced it with the Eusebian story of Constantine's vision of the cross (*in hoc signo vinces*) before the decisive battle with Maxentius. The principal proof presented by Vegio was the text of an inscription which he quoted and said was written 'on the main and triumphal arch in letters that are very old and, I would say, almost decrepit with age, which shows that they were written there in Constantine's time, not later'.[98] By comparison, he said that another inscription on the arch of the apse that he thought was also from Constantine's time was, 'for the greater part destroyed and scarcely legible'.[99]

Like Poggio, Vegio said nothing about any image associated with the inscription on the triumphal arch although he did mention important decorative schema elsewhere in the basilica. The solitary reference to a pictorial image at the arch is very late, made by Domenico Giacobacci who was cardinal bishop of Nocera dei Pagani from 1524 to 1528. It is found on the final page of his long work defending papal authority over Church councils, *De concilio tractatus*, which was published posthumously in 1538.[100] Giacobacci described a mosaic showing a donation scene with golden lettering: 'Until our own times in the church of St Peter, above the great arch in front of the high altar, the Emperor Constantine was depicted in mosaic, with golden letters, holding out to the Saviour and blessed Peter the Apostle this very church that he had built, that is, the church of St Peter'.[101] Despite its very late date, great weight has been attached to

---

[97] Smith and O'Connor, tr., *Eyewitness to Old St Peter's*, 14–15, 127 (c. 1.1.4).

[98] 'Versus in arcu maiore ac triumphali, quorum characteres longe vetusti paeneque dixerim decrepiti nullum aliud quam Constantini tempus, quo ibi conscripti sunt, manifeste arguere videntur'; *ICUR* II.i, 345, no. XLIV.1; BAV, Arch. Cap. S. Pietro, G.12, fol. 2v.

[99] *ICUR* II.i, 345, no. XLIV.2, 'quod negligentius habitae maiore ex parte corruerunt, sed ex paucis earum, quae vix adhuc legi possunt, deprehenduntur licet non integra verba'. Alfarano misread Vegio and conflated the triumphal arch inscription with the mosaic at the apse; *DVB*, 29. An autograph note, interpolated between fols 17 and 18 of his draft of *DBV* (BAV, Arch. Cap. S. Pietro, G.4), shows that he initially thought that the inscription naming Constantine ('Quod duce te') had been located on the arch over the apse. For the debate around the date of the fragmentary inscription on the arch of the apse ('Constantini...expiata...hostile incursione') see Gem, 'The Chronology', 41–2 and Liverani, 'Old St Peter's', 494.

[100] D. Giacobacci, *De consilio tractatus* (Rome, 1538), 783; Brandenburg, Ballardini, and Theones, *Saint Peter's*, 19–20.

[101] A. L. Frothingham, 'Une mosaïque Constantinienne inconnue a Saint-Pierre de Rome', *Revue Archéologique*, 3rd ser., 1 (1883), 68–72.

Giacobacci's description because it seems to depict a figural scene that matched the inscription, and because it implies that the inscription was also of mosaic and of one piece with the image.

Giacobacci had a personal connection with the basilica, having been made a canon there in 1504. However, almost immediately after his appointment to that role, Bramante began work on the south-east pier of the new church, precipitating the demolition of parts of the nave close to the southern pier of the triumphal arch; the arch itself did not survive for long thereafter. The primary description of the mosaic depicting Constantine as donor of the basilica was, thus, published decades after that part of the basilica had disappeared and this fact as well as the context of the reference should give pause for thought. Giacobacci's book is in essence a history of conciliarism, presented from a firmly papal perspective. It concluded with a justification of papal authority over councils of the Church and cites the Donation of Constantine as a central piece of supporting evidence, which he treated as genuine despite Valla's arguments that were well known by the early years of the sixteenth century. It is in this precise context, as evidence in support of the veracity of Constantine's imagined donation, that a mosaic—long since destroyed—said to show Constantine's presenting the church to Christ and St Peter was described for the first time.

Scholarly opinion of Giacobacci's account is divided. Some have accepted it as a description of an original fourth-century mosaic, but others have been more sceptical.[102] Krautheimer, followed by de Blaauw, thought that the inscription was contemporary with the foundation of the basilica but that the date of the mosaic scene was 'questionable', suggesting in passing that it might have been a product of the Carolingian era.[103] Others have argued that both elements, inscription and figural mosaic, were made later than the mid-fourth century and put it alongside the architectural evidence which, they argue, points to a foundational date for the basilica after Constantine, and that the tradition linking its origin to his reign was a later, papal fabrication linked perhaps to the Symmachan debate at the turn of the sixth century on the primacy of St Peter's over the Lateran, or later in the sixth century, when donor images start to be found elsewhere and the early iterations of the *Liber Pontificalis*, with its claims about Constantine's largess, were formalised as the preferred papal narrative.[104] No one has suggested that Giacobacci's account may be the product of wishful thinking by a Vatican loyalist but that is a possibility that should be

---

[102] P. Liverani, 'Costatino offie il model della basilica sull'arco tronfale', in Andarolo, ed., *La pittura medievale a Roma, 312–1431, i: L'orizzonte tardo antico e le nuove immagini, 312–468, Corpus* (Rome, 2006), 90–1, and Liverani, 'Old St Peter's', 492–3. E. Klinkenberg, *Compressed Meanings: The Donor's Model in Medieval Art to around 1300* (Turnhout, 2009) considers it contemporary with the foundation of the building.

[103] *CBCR* v, 172, modified in R. Krautheimer, 'The Building Inscriptions of Old St. Peter's: A Reconsideration', *Römische Jahrbuch der Bibliotheca Hertziana*, 25 (1989), 1–23 at 7–9; *CD* ii, 461–2.

[104] Bowersock, 'Constantine and Peter', 8; Westall, 'Constantius II and the Basilica of St Peter', 224–5, referring to the inscription as 'pious fraud'; Logan 'Who Built Old St Peter's', 6.

allowed given the context of his comment and its timing so long after the destruction of the arch.

Another famous mosaic and inscription that is intimately connected with the historiography of both the Donation of Constantine and of Charlemagne's relationship with Rome is known through a similar combination of early medieval and early modern evidence, much of which is of dubious authenticity. The *Liber Pontificalis* provides the primary account, recording the construction during the year 797/8 of a large triconch hall, or triclinium, at the Lateran.[105] Both this structure and the larger, polyconch reception hall commissioned by Leo at the Lateran after 801 had imperial models, recalling especially the building known as the 'triclinium of nineteen couches' in Constantinople.[106] The papal biographer says that the walls and floor of the Leo's triclinium were inlaid with marble slabs, and its many porphyry and marble columns were set with sculpted bases and imposts shaped as lilies.[107] What is more, the author of the 'Life' continues, Pope Leo 'decorated the apse-vault with mosaics while the other two apses depicting various scenes above the marble cladding, and the surrounding area, he decorated likewise'.[108] This grand and richly decorated hall was fit for use by the time the Frankish legates arrived in late 799 to hear the case against the anti-Leonine conspirators.[109]

Details of its decoration, however, were not described until Onofrio Panvinio's account was published in 1570, and he makes it clear that by then the building was derelict. 'Still surviving from the old mosaics', he said, 'is a device (*emblema*) around the main apse by an entrance to the hall, in which St Peter is shown seated, holding out a banner to the emperor Charles the Great on the left and a pallium to Pope Leo III on the right, kneeling before him'.[110] Panvinio quoted the surviving portions of

---

[105] *LP* 98:10. The date of the first triclinium is established by the internal structure of the 'Life': see Geertman, *More Veterum*, 40. See also Scholz, *Politik*, 115–16.

[106] *LP* 98:39; Geertman, *More Veterum*, 43; Lauer, *Le Palais du Latran*, 104–5. This larger hall, later known as the *Sala del concilio*, joined the triclinium via a vestibule at their southern ends; see Bauer, *Das Bild der Stadt Rom im Frühmittelater*, 64–7, pl. 19–20 and 70–1; M. D'Onofrio, 'Leone III (795–816)', in M. D'Onofrio, ed., *La committenza artistica dei papi a Roma nel Medioevo* (Rome, 2016), 213–18, at 215. On Leo's apse mosaics, see Thunø, *Apse Mosaic*, 52–8.

[107] *LP* 98:10. Column capitals shaped as lilies are associated with Solomon's Temple, as described in 1 Kings 7:19–22.

[108] *LP* 98:10, 'Et camera cum absida de musibo seu alias II absidas diversas storias pingens super marmorum constructione pariter in circuitu decoravit'. The verb *pingere* implies the use of colour, but not necessarily paint. On the revival of monumental mosaics at this time, see C. Davis-Weyer, 'Die Mosaiken Leos III und die Anfänge der karolingischen Renaissance in Rom', *Zeitschrift für Kunstgeschichte*, 29 (1966), 111–32.

[109] *LP* 98:20; Davis-Weyer, 'Die Mosaiken Leos III', 115.

[110] 'Superest adhuc vetustum e musivo emblema circum absidam tribunae in portico aulae, in quo Sanctus Petrus sedens pictus est, qui Carolo Magno imperatori leva vexillum, Leoni vero III Papae dextera pallium, ante se genuflexis porrigit'; O. Panvinio, *De praecipuis urbis Romae sanctioribusque basilicis, quas septem ecclesias vulgo vocant liber* (Rome, 1570), 180; Lauer, *Le Palais du Latran*, 480–1; C. Davis-Weyer, tr., *Early Medieval Art, 300–1150: Sources and Documents* (Toronto, ON, 1986), 89–90. There was a doorway in the eastern wall of the building close to its junction with the south wall from which the principal apse projected. For a plan and

the inscriptions that labelled the figures and which referred to Charles as *rex* rather than *imperator*, confirming a pre-800 date for the design of this part of the mosaic as well as the building.[111] A series of inter-related manuscript drawings made before *c*.1600 show the location and composition of this figural scene on the right-hand side of the south wall of the triclinium. They also reveal clearly that the apse mosaic was fragmentary and that none of the decoration remained visible on the left-hand side. Panvinio's attention was focused on the historical figures of Leo and Charlemagne, and his description of that tableau and the drawings of it collated by his Spanish contemporary, Alfonso Chacón (d. 1599), were widely distributed before the end of the century.[112] The intense scholarly interest in this particular mosaic scene at the Lateran is contemporary with efforts at St Peter's in the early 1570s to move the epitaph of Hadrian into the narthex of St Peter's in readiness for the Jubilee celebrations of 1575, discussed above. The Lateran mosaic and Hadrian's inscription at St Peter's exemplified and idealised the spiritual and political relationship between king and pope at the end of the eighth century from two perspectives, one papal, the other Frankish. The actions taken in the later sixteenth century to identify these early medieval records and to preserve and share them with contemporary audiences invited those modern viewers to contemplate the nature of the relationship between the secular and spiritual powers in ancient times, and to draw lessons from them for their own.[113]

Similar motivations lie behind the preservation and restoration of the triclinium mosaic. The medieval palace at the Lateran was demolished after 1585, but the remains of the south wall of the triclinium including the surviving parts of the mosaic

---

diagram, see Luchterhandt, '*Famulus Petri*', 67, pl. 9 and Bauer, *Das Bild der Stadt Rom im Frühmittelater*, 64, pl. 19, and 69, pl. 23. Note that the basilica faces east, with its high altar at the west end.

[111] Panvinio noted three texts including the lacunae in the third of them which was located under the feet of the image of St Peter: SANCTISSIMVS.D.N.LEOIII.PAPA.; D.N.CARVLOREGI.; BEATE PETRE ...... LEONI PAPAE ET BITORIA CARVLO REGI DONA. On the significance of the betacism (b for v) as evidence of the accurate transmission of an eighth-century spelling, see Osborne, *Rome in the Eighth Century*, 225. On this linguistic phenomenon more generally and its frequency on inscriptions from Rome itself (perhaps under the influence of Greek speakers of Latin), see Adams, *Regional Diversification*, 633, 657, 663–5 and J. N. Adams, *Social Variation and the Latin Language* (Cambridge, 2013), 183–90.

[112] Herklotz, 'Francesco Barberini', 177–8; Herklotz, 'Historia sacra und mittelalterliche Kunst', 34–6, n. 26 on Chacón's role. Alfonso Chacón was involved in the compilation of the manuscript which contains probably the earliest image of this scene, BAV, Barb. Lat. 2738, fol. 104r (see, Herklotz, 'Francesco Barberini', fig. 7). Panvinio's reading was quoted at the foot of another Chacon drawing, made in the 1590s, now BAV, Barb. Lat. 5407, fol. 97r/v. 186 (a full digital facsimile is available on DigiVatLib). On fols 95v–96r Chacón explicitly compared the images of king and pope at the Lateran with those at Santa Susanna although the drawings are not independent witnesses (see Osborne, *Rome in the Eighth Century*, 228). A sketch plan made by Pompeo Ugonio before the triclinium was demolished in 1585 shows the basic arrangement of the scene in the apse, Leo's monogram and the fragment of the inscription on the outer rim on the right-hand side of the apse, and three figures adjacent to it on the same side. The left-hand side of the wall is blank; Lauer, *Le Palais de Latran*, 104, fig. 40 (from BAV, Barb. Lat. 2160, fol. 55). On Chacón, see Stenhouse, *Reading Inscriptions*, 59–61, 163.

[113] See Chapter 1, 69–78.

were left standing, and were comprehensively repaired under the patronage of Cardinal Francesco Barberini in readiness for the Jubilee of 1625.[114] Open to the air, the south wall was converted into a free-standing, aedicule, crowned with a baroque pediment, flanking pilasters, and a raised terrace from which viewers might inspect the mosaic images and inscriptions. The mosaics in the apse and to its right were thoroughly restored, with missing elements replaced. Another was created, *de novo*, for the blank space on the left. Writing in 1619, Grimaldi had said that the central apse mosaic had depicted Christ's commission to the apostles; its subject was deemed a fitting one for a new age of mission to the newly conquered Saxons and Avars. For the right-hand scene, he argued (against the evidence of the inscription) that the insignia of crown and standard held by Charlemagne signified his imperial rather than royal status, and Grimaldi followed some earlier commentators by interpreting this part of the scene as a commemoration of Charlemagne's investiture as emperor in 800.[115]

Grimaldi was also the first to speculate about the possible iconography of the image that may once have filled the space on the other, left-hand side of the apse but which had been lost since at least 1570 when the earliest surviving record of the mosaics on this wall was made. He suggested that the figure of St Peter on the right-hand side would originally have been balanced on the left by a scene focused on the figure of St Paul.[116] Instead, the Barberini restoration programme installed in that empty space an image of Christ, centrally placed, handing keys to an unnamed pope (logically St Peter, but arguably Sylvester) and a banner to Constantine kneeling before him.[117] This provided a pleasing typological counterpart to the composition of the group on the viewers' right that encouraged contemplation of the divine source of temporal power and the balance of that power between secular and spiritual leaders across the centuries.[118] The arguments underpinning the iconography of the new scene were summarised in a treatise funded by Barberini and published in 1625 by the Vatican Librarian, Nicolò Alemanni. Claiming sight of earlier evidence (which has not survived), Alemanni argued for an integrated reading of the decorative programme of the entire south wall that he regarded as pendant tableaux showing the *translatio imperii* on either side of the central apse mosaic which he read as an allegory of the restoration of peace to the city of Rome after the disruption of 799/800.[119] His interpretation and promotion of the heavily restored and reimagined version of the late eighth-century composition did not go unchallenged, not least because of the anachronistic

---

[114] Herklotz, 'Francesco Barberini', 176–80.

[115] Osborne, *Rome in the Eighth Century*, 221; Herklotz, 'Francesco Barberini', 178.

[116] Herklotz, 'Francesco Barberini', 178.

[117] The ambiguity was addressed directly by Niccolo Alemanni, *De lateranensibus parietinis ab Illustriss. et Reverendiss. Domino D. Francisco Cardinale Barberino restitutis dissertatio historica* (Rome, 1625), 59–63.

[118] Herklotz, 'Francesco Barberini', 179.

[119] Alemanni, *De lateranensibus parietinis*, 55, 58–9; Herklotz, 'Francesco Barberini', 180; H. W. Goetz, *Translatio imperii: Ein Beitrag zur Geschichte des Geschichtsdenkens und der politischen Theorien im Mittelater und in der frühen Neuzeit* (Tübingen, 1958), 62–76, 88–9; Scholz, *Politik*, 118–19.

projection of the late twelfth-century doctrine that papal approval had been granted for the *translatio* of empire from Constantinople to the Franks and the highly controversial implications of this doctrine for papal primacy over the empire.[120] Nevertheless, despite extensive objections to Alemanni's interpretation and the scant evidence he offered for the source of the reconstructed scene on the left, the three-part composition itself was not seriously challenged. Indeed, it was recreated wholesale in 1743 when the original aedicule was dismantled and a facsimile rebuilt a short distance away, adjacent to the chapel of the *Sancta Sanctorum*, where it remains (Figure 8.2).

Despite the circularity of the argument and the complete absence of early evidence for the tripartite scene, the attraction of the 1625 composition to subsequent scholarship on Charlemagne lies partly in the straightforward symmetry of its symbolism and partly in its resonance with traces of genuine interests in papal circles in the mid-eighth-century in Constantine and his legacy.[121] The notorious document known as the *Constitutum Constantini*, or 'Donation of Constantine' seems likely to have been composed in Rome around this time.[122] There are lexical echoes of it in letters sent by Pope Paul I (757–67).[123] Paul was also responsible for the decoration of the oratory dedicated to Petronilla in the rotunda adjacent to the south transept at St Peter's, which was said in 1458 to contain 'ancient' paintings showing scenes from the life of Constantine; given what else is known about his patronage of art within the basilica, these may also be attributable to Paul's pontificate.[124]

---

[120] Herklotz, 'Francesco Barberini', 183–9.

[121] That is, using an early modern reconstruction that relied on contested medieval political theory as evidence of early medieval art that itself (supposedly) referenced an earlier forgery which underpinned the early modern reconstruction. Those who regard the composition as a likely reflection of the original schema include, for example; A. Iacobini, 'Il mosaico del triclinio Lateranense', in M. Andaloro, ed., *Fragmenta picta: affreschi e mosaici staccati del Medioevo romano* (Roma, Castel Sant'Angelo, 15 dicembre 1989–18 febbraio 1990) (Rome, 1989), 189–96; D'Onofrio, 'Leone III (795–816)', 214; C. Goodson and J. L. Nelson, 'The Roman Contexts of the "Donation of Constantine". Review Article', *Early Medieval Europe*, 18.4 (2010), 446–67; Osborne, *Rome in the Eighth Century*, 225. Those who are sceptical include Herklotz, 'Francesco Barberini', 184–5; M. Luchterhand, 'Rom und Aachen: Die Karolinger und der päpstliche Hof um 800', in F. Pohle, ed., *Karl der Große/Charlemagne: Orte der Macht* (Aachen, 2014), 104–13, and 'Famulus Petri', 66–7; Bauer, *Das Bild der Stadt Rom im Frühmittelalter*, 109–19.

[122] For a summary of the evidence, see H. Fuhrmann, 'Das frühmittelalterliche Papsttum und die Konstantinische Schenkung', in *I problemi dell'Occidente nel secolo VIII*, SSCI, 20 (Spoleto, 1973), 257–92, who stresses the point that the document was widely known before the later ninth century and evidence for its use before then is very limited. Fried has argued for Frankish composition in the late ninth century, pointing to the earliest manuscript copy in BnF, Lat. 2777 within the letter-book of the abbots of Saint-Denis (Bischoff, *Katalog*, no. 4229); J. Fried, *Donation of Constantine and Constitutum Constantini: The Misinterpretation of a Fiction and Its Original Meaning* (Berlin, 2007).

[123] For the literary resonance with the letters composed in Pope Paul's secretariat, see Fuhrmann, 'Das frühmittelalterliche Papsttum', 273 and R. M. Pollard, 'The Language and Style of the Codex Epistolaris Carolinus and their Affinities with Other Papal Documents', in McKitterick et al., tr., *Codex Epistolaris Carolinus*, 80–4.

[124] *LP* 95.3; Davis, tr., *Lives of the Eighth-Century Popes*, 81, n. 6. The ancient fresco was described by Niccolò della Tuccia in 1458; see Blaauw, *CD* ii, 639 n. 127.

FIGURE 8.2 The Lateran Triclinium mosaic, as recreated in 1743. Photo: Author.

Awareness of the pseudo-historical context that lay behind the Donation of Constantine is also revealed in a letter that Hadrian sent to Charlemagne in May 778, and which is the first in the sequence of Hadrian-letters in the *Codex Carolinus*, although not the earliest by date. Its reference to Constantine's large-scale donations to the Western Church could reflect either familiarity with the Donation document itself, or the stories that lay behind it, or with the account of Constantine's largess preserved in the 'Life' of Pope Sylvester in the *Liber Pontificalis*. Hadrian acknowledged the reality of Charles' sovereignty in Italy, addressing him as *rex Langobardorum et patricius Romanorum*, and expressed frustration that the king had not come to Rome at Easter, as suggested he might, to have his new-born son baptised.[125] But he

---

[125] Carloman, later baptised with the name of Pippin by Hadrian in Rome in 781, as recorded in Godesscalc's Evangelistary: see Chapter 4, 163 and Chapter 7, 270. Pippin was king of Italy until his death in 810; see M. Stofella, 'Staying Lombard While Becoming Carolingian? Italy under King Pippin', in C. Gantner and W. Pohl, eds, *After Charlemagne: Carolingian Italy and Its Rulers* (Cambridge, 2021), 135–47.

went on to praise Charles as 'a new Constantine, God's most Christian emperor' (*novus christianissimus Dei Constantinus imperator*) and compared the present day to the pontificate of Pope Sylvester, under whom the Church had received extensive lands and powers from the first Christian emperor.[126]

> And just as during the time of blessed pontiff Sylvester by the generosity of that great emperor, the most pious Constantine of holy memory, the catholic and apostolic Roman church was raised up and exalted, and invested with authority in these western regions, so in your most blessed time and ours may God's holy church, that is of blessed Peter the apostle, flourish and rejoice and be exalted more and more, so that everyone who hears these things may loudly proclaim, 'Lord, save the king, and hear us in the day when we call to you' [Psalm 19:10]. Indeed, here this day, a new Constantine, God's most Christian emperor, has arisen, through whom God has thought worthy to bestow everything on the holy Church of Peter, prince of the apostles.[127]

Hadrian's letter continued the analogy with a list of the specific places now under Lombard control that he wanted restored to papal authority, stressing that, 'We have documentation for the many deeds of gift in our sacred archives of the Lateran' (*in sacro nostro scrinio Lateranensae*). Proofs had been sent to Francia, he said, and he pressed the king for restitution of these territories to the patrimony of St Peter.

Hadrian's May 778 letter should be read as a counterpart to the near contemporary account in the *Liber Pontificalis* of Charles' reaffirmation and augmentation in 774 during his first visit to Rome of the so-called 'Donation of Quierzy' that had been agreed between Pippin and Stephen II in 756.[128] The first part of the 'Life' of Hadrian, which concentrates on the events of the first two years of his pontificate, concludes with this episode, emphasising the documentary record that had been made and archived in Rome in support of pope's claim. The biographer carefully described the ritual sanctification and legal safeguards attached to Charles' donation. Having been ratified by the *christianissimus Francorum rex* 'in his own hand', the charter of donation was placed first on the high altar and then into the *confessio*, before being handed over to Hadrian in the presence of his judges, with a promise taken under oath that all would be fulfilled. The king then ordered his chaplain and notary, Itherius

---

[126] Fuhrmann, 'Das frühmittelalterliche Papsttum', 281–5; Nelson, *King and Emperor*, 353–7.

[127] *CC* 60/*CeC* 49; 'Et sicut temporibus beati Silvestri Romani pontificis a sanctae recordationis piissimo Constantino, magno imperatore, per eius largitatem sancta Dei catholica et apostolica Romana ecclesia elevata atque exaltata est et potestatem in his Hesperiae partibus largiri dignatus, ita et in his vestris felicissimis temporibus atque nostris sancta Dei ecclesia, id est beati Petri apostoli, germinet atque exultet et amplius quam amplius exaltata permaneat, ut omnes gentes, quae hec audierint, edicere valeant: "Domine, salvum fac regem, et exaudi nos in die, in qua invocaverimus te"; quia ecce novus christianissimus Dei Constantinus imperator his temporibus surrexit, per quem omnia Deus sanctae suae ecclesiae beati apostolorum principis Petri largiri dignatus est', ed. Gundlach, MGH, Epp. III, 585–6.

[128] *LP* 97:41–3. On the connection with this letter, see Davis, tr., *Lives of the Eighth-Century Popes*, 113–14. See also this volume, Introduction, 13.

(later abbot of Saint-Martin at Tours), to make a copy which he placed inside the *confessio* beneath the gospels that were kept there, as 'firm security and an eternal reminder of his name and the kingdom of the Franks' in that place. The 'Life' completes this account of the authentication of Charles' 774 donation by saying that the king took away with him another copy that had been made in the papal *scrinium*.[129] There was, therefore, a 'Frankish'-made copy of the text in Rome, and a Rome-made copy of it in Francia. The triple-lock on the agreement—a charter and two authenticated copies—as well as the ritual sanctification of the documents, was intended by Hadrian to enforce the highest levels of legal and sacred security on the deal.

The comparison of Charlemagne to the first Constantine in May 778 was doubtless intended to flatter the Frankish king but the analogy served mostly to remind him of the oath that he had taken to transfer control of lands in Italy to Hadrian and his obligations to fulfil his duty to the city as *patricius Romanorum*. What is more, it seems to have had no effect, since the lands pledged in 774 were not transferred, despite many more letters from Rome pressing the case. Any references to Constantine in Hadrian's subsequent letters to the Franks referred only to his role as convenor of the synod of Nicaea in 325, rather than as the progenitor of St Peter's patrimony in the west; the parallel drawn in 778 between Constantine and Charlemagne was thus an isolated one.[130] Indeed, the next time that Hadrian quoted Psalm 19:10, in a renewed effort to persuade Charles to part with the promised lands, it was the Old Testament king David, not the fourth-century emperor, who was invoked as an exemplar and model of rulership, perhaps reflecting what was by then the preferred referent for Charles by those around him.[131]

Charlemagne's early promise to Hadrian was not forgotten at St Peter's; the fact of the donative act, and the record of it in both documentary and literary sources, had value even though it remained unfulfilled in practice. Writing in the mid-twelfth century, Peter Mallius reported that a list of the cities in Charlemagne's charter of donation was set in letters of silver, next to the ancient bronze doors that had been taken from Perugia and installed by Hadrian at the top of the steps at the entrance to the atrium; 'We have seen it, and often read it with our brothers', Mallius said, before listing the cities one by one.[132]

---

[129] *LP* 97:43. On this episode, see Scholz, *Politik*, 81–2.

[130] *CC* 95, 96/*CeC* 96, 97, both quoting the first capitulum of the Council of Antioch. Fuhrmann, 'Das frühmittelalterliche Papsttum', 286–7. Bullough, 'The Dating of Codex Carolinus No. 95, 96, 97', dates these letters to c.785. In October 785, in a letter urging the restoration of images, Hadrian compared the present emperor, Constantine VI and his mother Irene to Constantine I and his mother Helena; Scholz, *Politik*, 97.

[131] *CC* 68/*CeC* 69, quoting Psalm 67:29–30 and Psalm 19:10; written after Easter 781, not long after the royal visit which saw Pippin and Louis baptised and crowned as kings. On the priority of David over Constantine, see especially Emerick, 'Charlemagne: A New Constantine?', 133–61, at 138–40; Scholz, *Politik*, 107; Bullough, 'Empire and Emperordom', 386.

[132] Mallius, *Descriptio Basilicae Vaticanae*, ch. 53; *VZ*, iii, 432–3. On the 'great bronze decorated doors of wondrous size' from Perugia installed at St Peter's in 791–2, see *LP* 97:96; Davis, *Lives of the Eighth-Century*

Mallius' report of the afterlife of the 'Donation of Charlemagne' makes a crucial point about the function of inscriptions within the built environment early medieval Rome. Documents kept in the *scrinium*, or manuscript copies of the *Liber Pontificalis*, were inaccessible to almost everyone. Inscriptions, however, especially in the public areas of a basilica, could be read by the literate or observed and admired by viewers who had little or no ability to read the Latin words but understood the significance of writing so displayed. Inscriptions were accessible in a way that books and documents were not. Mallius' observations highlight another important aspect of inscriptional texts, that of the aspiration to permanence and awareness of an imagined posterity as well as present-day audiences. In this instance a documentary text, inscribed to widen its contemporary audience, served also to remind future viewers, Mallius and his brothers among them as well as the readers of his treatise beyond that, of a particular event, donor, or gift. Mallius and others like him could read, discuss, and give new impetus to an old text, using contextual information as well as privileged knowledge to absorb its meaning for their own times.

The visual power of an inscription was vested in its location and materiality as much as in its text; whether set high up or low down, large or small in scale, in a public area or a liturgically restricted space, such choices defined access to the text and its meaning, and filtered audiences by status, rank, and gender, as well as education. The material of which an inscription was made, whether painted, cut into marble, or made up of golden tesserae or bronze or silver letters, encoded messages about the patron of the text, their access to precious raw materials, as well as the skilled workers to make and transport it. The choice of script too made visual cross-references that could be understood by viewers brought up with the 'epigraphic habit', accustomed or trained to notice display script on walls or on the page. The viewers of texts set onto fixtures and fittings or on objects used in liturgy or ceremonies were more rarefied still, although secular patrons of such objects could continue to 'witness' sacred moments through words that recorded gifts used in the performance of the liturgy, even if they themselves were not present in person. A manuscript, chalice, paten, table, altar cloth, jewelled cross, or hanging crown could function in this way, by placing the donor's text and those named within it in close physical proximity to the action at the altar. The visual context of an inscription—its location, materials, size, colour, and script—augmented the meaning of the words; for those with limited literacy, its pictorial status might be the primary medium of the message that the inscriptional text was intended to convey.

Inscriptions on or within buildings thus engender a kind of spatial intertextuality, where a text acquires auxiliary power from its architectural location and juxtaposition with other meaningful things, as well as the activities that take place there. The power

---

Popes, 171–2; Geertman, *More Veterum*, 20; Brandenburg, Ballardini, and Theones, *Saint Peter's*, 46. For group reading of inscriptions, see also Thunø, *Apse Mosaic*, 185.

of place can be sufficient to carry its specific context into a manuscript copy of the text or a quotation from it into another inscribed building in a distant location, and for this to remain meaningful over time to different audiences. A building such as St Peter's in Rome inevitably conditioned the behaviour and expectations of individuals and groups who entered or encountered it, partly because of its scale and partly because of all that it represented in terms of its accumulated history, wealth, and the repeated performances of faith, both personal and institutional. When the last major elements of the fourth-century basilica were finally removed in the early seventeenth century, the architects settled on a design that enveloped the footprint of the old building, and which encompassed the active spaces of the ancient structure as well as its institutional memory within the new. Hadrian's epitaph, composed in the name of the first Frankish emperor who had been crowned within that ancient structure, was reset high up in the new portico. By then, its meaning and significance had transcended the words of Alcuin's verses, and Charlemagne's message to his own and future audiences was conveyed primarily by its location and the visual power of an inscription that had been made in Francia but which laid claim unambiguously to the legacy of empire.

LIST OF MANUSCRIPT SOURCES

Abbeville, Bibliothèque municipale, MS 4 (Abbeville Gospels) 266n.24, 280–4
Angers,
    Bibliothèque Municipale, MS 18 (14) 270n.45
    Bibliothèque Municipale, MS 675 291n.97
Berlin,
    Kupferstichkabinett, 79 D 2a 52–3, 201
    Staatsbibliothek, MS Diez. B. Sant. 66 197n.24
Brussels, Bibliothèque Royale de Belgique, MS II 2572 122–4
Bukarest, Biblioteca Națională a României (Alba Julia, Biblioteca Documentară Batthyáneum),
    MS R.II.1 (Lorsch Gospels, Mt, Mk) 266n.24, 284–7nn.86–88
Cambridge,
    Corpus Christi College, MS 139 106n.85
    Corpus Christi College, MS 144 291n.96
    University Library, MS Kk. 4.6 147n.15
Cologne, Dombibliothek, Cod. 63, 65, 67 268n.34
Dublin, National Museum of Ireland, 06E0786:13 (Faddan More Psalter) 289n.92
Einsiedeln,
    Stiftsbibliothek, Cod. 191 (277) 278–80nn.70–71, 279
    Stiftsbibliothek, Cod. 326 (1076) 150n.30, 179–83, 310, 328–9
Florence,
    Uffizi, Arch. 4336 134n.99
    Uffizi, Gabinetto dei Sidegni e della Stampe, Inv. GDSU n. 20 A 47
    Uffizi, Gabinetto dei Sidegni e della Stampe, Inv. GDSU n. 91 A 56
Göttweig, Stiftsbibliothek, MS 64 146n.13
Hamburg, Kunsthalle, Inv. Nr 21311 57
Klosterneuburg, Stiftsbibliothek, MS 723 146n.13
Laon, Bibliothèque Municipale, MS 324 89n.18
Leiden,
    Universiteitsbibliotheek, MS Voss. Lat. Q. 41 89n.17
    Universiteitsbibliotheek, MS Voss. Lat. Q. 69 137n.113, 150n.30, 296n.108, 297,
        300n.118
Leeuwarden, Provinciale Bibliotheek van Friesland 55 Hs (B. A. Fr. 55) 289n.94
London,
    British Library, Cotton MS Claudius B V 266n.24, 280n.71
    British Library, Cotton MS Tiberius A XV 270n.43
    British Library, Cotton MS Vespasian A XIV 117n.35
    British Library, Harley MS 603 (Harley Psalter) 164n.90
    British Library, Harley MS 2788 (Harley Golden Gospels) 266n.24, 287n.91, 288, 290
    British Library, Stowe MS 944 165n.91
    Lambeth Palace Library, MS 218 117n.35, 265n.20
Montpellier, Bibliothèque Interuniversitaire de Montpellier, section Médecine, MS 409
    126n.71, 319n.40

Munich,
    Bayerische Staatsbibliothek, Clm 6355 96n.51
    Bayerische Staatsbibliothek, Clm 6424 96n.51
    Bayerische Staatsbibliothek, Clm 14641 125n.69, 126
    Bayerische Staatsbibliothek, Clm 19410 150n.30
Paris,
    Archives Nationales, K.7 No. 9[1] 93n.37
    Archives Nationales, K.7 No. 9[2] 93n.37
    Bibliothèque de l'Arsenal, MS 599 (Arsenal Gospels) 266n.24
    BnF, Fr. 6465 xxiv, 1–2
    BnF, Lat. 1452 96n.51
    BnF, Lat. 1572 266n.21
    BnF, Lat. 2773 127–8, 131–2, 137, 300n.117
    BnF, Lat. 3182 96n.51
    BnF, Lat. 3844 96n.51
    BnF, Lat. 4278 96n.51
    BnF, Lat. 5294 293n.100
    BnF, Lat. 5941 257–60
    BnF, Lat. 7701 145n.8
    BnF, Lat. 8071 136n.106, 150n.30
    BnF, Lat. 8850 266n.24, 269n.38
    BnF, Lat. 9347 127, 130–2, 139, 300n.117
    BnF, Lat. 10307 127, 131–2
    BnF, Lat. 11710 96n.51
    BnF, Lat. 13159 (Psalter of Charlemagne) 318
    BnF, Lat. 13729 89n.18
    BnF, Lat. 16897 127n.76, 129–30
    BnF, NAL 1203 (Godesscalc's Evangelistary) 163n.85, 266n.24, 269n.39, 270n.46, 271, 272n.48, 274n.58
    Louvre, Département des Objets d'art, MR370 and MR371 100n.63, 278n.68
Sankt Gallen,
    Stiftsbibliothek, Cod. Sang. 899 330n.92
    Stiftsbibliothek, Cod. Sang. 1394 (*Codex Sangallensis*) 195n.19
    Stiftsbibliothek, Cod. Sang. 271 150n.30, 328n.83
Sankt Paul in Kärnten, Stiftsbibliothek St. Paul im Lavanttal, Cod. 8/1 (25.4.9a) 101n.71
Saint-Omer, Bibliothèque d'agglomération, MS 736 129n.78
St Petersburg, Russian National Library, MS F.v.XIV.1 145n.8, 150n.30, 329n.88
Stockholm, National Museum, coll. Anckarsvärd 637 54
Trier, Stadtbibliothek, Cod. 22 (Part 1: fols. 17–38v; Part 2: fols. 39–172v) (Ada Gospels) 266n.24, 269
Tübingen, Universitätsbibliothek, Codex Augusteus (*Codex Augusteus*) 195–7
Utrecht, Rijksuniversiteitsbibliotheek, MS 32 (Utrecht Psalter) 164n.90, 165
Vatican City,
    AFSP, Arm. 24. F. 1 38n.31
    AFSP, Arm. 26 C. 227 (Spesi 1619) 82n.168

AFSP, Arm. 26 C. 229 82n.168
BAV, Arch. Cap. S. Pietro, A.64.ter 59
BAV, Arch. Cap. S. Pietro, G.4 64n.104, 73n.131, 332n.99
BAV, Arch. Cap. S. Pietro, G.5 70nn.122, 123, 72n.126, 75n.137, 81n.160, 146n.14
BAV, Arch. Cap. S. Pietro, G.10 64n.101
BAV, Arch. Cap. S. Pietro, G.12 332n.98
BAV, Arch. Cap. S. Pietro, H.87 64n.101
BAV, Barb. Lat. 2160 335n.112
BAV, Barb. Lat. 2733 29n.2, 44nn.45–46, 46n.56, 80, 156n.59
BAV, Barb. Lat. 2738 335n.112
BAV, Barb. Lat. 5407 335n.112
BAV, Collezione Ashby no. 329 50n.70, 51
BAV, Pal. Lat. 50 (Lorsch Gospels, Lk, Jn) 266n.24, 284n.86, 285–6
BAV, Pal. Lat. 833 (Lorsch Sylloge) 142, 147n.15, 150n.30, 151–5, 329n.88
BAV, Reg. Lat. 2078 131n.85
BAV, Reg. Lat. 2100 78n.154
BAV, Vat. Lat. 3225 197n.22
BAV, Vat. Lat. 3256 (*Codex Augusteus*) 195n.19
BAV, Vat. Lat. 3867 197n.23
BAV, Vat. Lat. 6438 81n.159
BAV, Vat. Lat, 9152 331n.93
Verdun, Bibliothèque Municipale, MS 45 150n.30
Vienna,
    ÖNB, Cod. 449 (*Codex Carolinus*) 20n.85, 91n.28
    ÖNB, Cod. 515 (Lorsch Annals) 101n.71, 103, 317n.29
    ÖNB, Cod. 795 145n.8, 169–70, 171n.114, 172, 180, 148n.18, 329–30, 330n.90
    ÖNB, Cod. 1861 (Dagulf's Psalter) 266n.24, 269, 272–6
Wolfenbüttel,
    HAB, Cod. Guelf. 254 Helmst. 93n.39
    HAB, Cod. Guelf. 36.23 Aug. 2° (*Codex Agrimensores*) 195n.20
    HAB, Cod. Guelf. 454 95n.48
Würzburg,
    Universitätsbibliothek, M.p.f.th.46 258, 260n.5, 307n.141
    Universitätsbibliothek, M.p.misc.f.2 150n.30

BIBLIOGRAPHY

PRINTED PRIMARY SOURCES

Agnellus of Ravenna: *Agnelli Ravennatis, Liber Pontificalis ecclesiae Ravennatis*, ed. D. Mauskopf Deliyannis, CCCM 199 (Turnhout, 2006).

Alcuin [see also *Vita Alcuini*]; A. Duchesne (Andreas Quercetanus), *B. Flacci Albini, sive Alchvvini abbatis, Karoli Magni regis, ac imperatoris, magistri opera quæ hactenus reperiri potuerunt, nonnvlla avctivs et emendativs, pleráque nunc primùm ex Codd. MSS. Edita accessere B. Pavlini Aqvileiensis Patriarchæ contra Felicem Vrgel. Episc. Libri III qui etiam nunc prodeunt. Omnia studio & diligentia Andreæ Qvercetani Turonensis* (Paris, 1617); F. Forster, *Beati Flacci Albini seu Alcuini abbatis, Caroli Magni regis ac imperatoris, magistri opera*, 2 vols (Regensburg, 1777).

Alcuin, *Carmina*: ed. E. Dümmler, MGH, Poetae, I, PLAC 1 (Berlin, 1881), 160–351.

Alcuin, *Commentaria in S. Iohannis evangelium*: ed. J.-P. Migne, *PL* 100 (Paris, 1863), cols 737–1008.

Alcuin, *Epistolae*: ed. E. Dümmler, MGH Epp. IV, *Epistolae Karolini Aevi*, 2 (Berlin, 1895); partial tr., S. Allott, *Alcuin of York: His Life and Letters* (York, 1974).

Alcuin, *Epitaphium Hadriani Papae*: ed. E. Dümmler, MGH, Poetae, I, PLAC 1 (Berlin 1881), 113–14.

Alcuin, *Versus de Patribus, Regibus et Sanctis Euboricensis Eccelsiae* (York Poem): ed. E. Dümmler, MGH, Poetae, I, PLAC 1 (Berlin, 1881), 169–206; ed. and tr., P. Godman, *Alcuin: The Bishops, Kings, and Saints of York* (Oxford, 1982).

Alcuin, *Vita Willibrordi*: ed. W. Levison, MGH, SS rer. Merov. VII, *Passiones vitaeque sanctorum aevi Merovingici*, 5 (Hannover and Leipzig), 81–144.

Admonitio Generalis. Die Admonitio generalis Karls des Grossen, ed. H. Mordek, K. Zechiel-Eckes and M. Glatthaar, ed. and (German) tr. MGH, Fontes XVI (Wiesbaden, 2013), 180–239; tr., P. D. King, *Charlemagne. Translated Sources* (Kendal, 1987), 209–20.

Aldhelm, *Carmina ecclesiastica*: *Aldhelmi Opera Omnia*, ed. P. Ehwald, MGH, AA XV (Berlin 1913), 11–32; M. Lapidge and J. L. Rosier, tr., *Aldhelm: The Poetic Works* (Woodbridge, 1985), 46–58.

Alemanni, Niccolo, *De lateranensibus parietinis ab Illustriss. et Reverendiss. Domino D. Francisco Cardinale Barberino restitutis dissertatio historica* (Rome, 1625).

Alfarano, Tiberio: *Tiberii Alpharani: De Basilicae Vaticanae Antiquissima et Nova Structura*, ed. C. M. Cerrati, Studi e Testi, 26, Documenti e Ricerche per la storia dell'antica basilica Vaticana, 1 (Vatican City, 1914).

Alpharanus, Tiberius, *see* Alfarano, Tiberio.

Angilbert, *Carmina*: ed. E. Dümmler, MGH, MGH, Poetae, I, PLAC 1 (Berlin, 1881), 355–81.

Anglo-Saxon Chronicle: ed. G. P. Cubbin, *The Anglo-Saxon Chronicle: A Collaborative Edition*, vi: *MS D* (Cambridge, 1996), 16; S. Irvine, ed., *The Anglo-Saxon Chronicle: A Collaborative Edition*, vii: *MS E* (Cambridge, 2004); tr. D. Whitelock, *English Historical Documents*, Vol. 1, *c.500–1042* (London, 1955), 136–235, no. 1.

Annales Iuvavenses breves: ed. G. H. Pertz, MGH, SS III, 123.

Annales Iuvavenses maiores: ed. G. H. Pertz, MGH, SS I (Hannover, 1826), 87–8.

Annales Laureshamenses: ed. G. H. Pertz, MGH, SS I (Hannover, 1826), 22–39; tr. P. D. King, *Charlemagne: Translated Sources* (Kendal, 1987), 137–45; facs., F. Unterkircher, ed., *Das Wiener Fragment der Lorscher Annalen [Annales Laureshamenses], Christus und die Samariterin, Katechese des Niceta von Remesiana: Codex Vindobonensis 515 der Österreichischen Nationalbibliothek*, Codices selecti phototypice impressi, 15 (Graz, 1967).

Annales Mettenses Priores: ed. B. de Simson, MGH, SS rer. Germ. X (Hannover and Leipzig, 1905).

Annales Regni Francorum: *Annales regni francorum unde ab a. 741 usque ad a. 829, qui dicuntur Annales laurissenses maiores et Einhardi*, ed. F. Kurze, MGH, SS rer. Germ. 6 (Hannover, 1895); tr. B. W. Scholz, *Carolingian Chronicles: Royal Frankish Annals and Nithard's Histories* (Ann Arbor, MI, 1972), 37–125; tr. P. D. King, *Charlemagne: Translated Sources* (Kendal, 1987), 74–107.

Annales Sancti Amandi: ed. G. H. Pertz, MGH, SS I (Hannover, 1826), 6–14.

Annales Tielenses, ed. G. H. Waitz, MGH, SS XXIV (Hannover, 1879), 21–7.

Arator, *Historia Apostolica*: *Aratoris subdiaconi Historia apostolica*, ed. A.P. Orbán, CCSL 130, 130A (Turnhout, 2006); tr. R. Hillier, *Arator, Historia Apostolica*, Translated Texts for Historians, 73 (Liverpool, 2020).

Augustine, *De Civitate Dei*: ed. and tr. D. S. Wiesen, *Augustine: The City of God Against the Pagans. Books VIII–XI*, Loeb Classical Library 413 (Cambridge, MA, 1968).

Bede, *De schematibus et tropis*: ed. C. B. Kendall, *Opera didascalica*, CCSL 123A, 142–71.

Bede, *De tabernaculo*: ed. D. Hurst, *Opera exegetica*, CCSL 119A, 1–139; A. Holder, tr., *Bede: On the Tabernacle*, Translated Texts for Historians 18 (Liverpool, 1994).

Bede, *De templo Salomonis*: ed. D. Hurst, *Opera exegetica*, CCSL 119A, 143–234; S. Connolly, tr., *Bede: On the Temple*, Translated Texts for Historians, 21 (Liverpool, 1995).

Bede, *Historia Ecclesiastica gentis Anglorum*: ed. B. Colgrave (trans.) and R. Mynors (ed.), *Bede's Ecclesiastical History of the English People*, Oxford Medieval Texts (Oxford, 1969, rev. edn 1991); M. Lapidge (ed.) and P. Chiesa (trans.), *Beda: Storia degli Inglesi*, 2 vols (Milan, 2008–10).

Bede, *Homeliarum euangelii libri ii*: ed. D. Hurst, CCSL 122; tr. L. Martin and D. Hurst, *Bede the Venerable: Homilies on the Gospels*, 2 vols, Cistercian Studies, 110–11 (Kalamazoo, MI, 1991).

Benedict of Monte Soracte, *Chronicon* and *De Imperatoria Potestate in Urbe Roma Libellus*: ed. G. H. Pertz, MGH, SS III (Hannover, 1839), 695–719.

Boniface, *Epistolae*: ed. M. Tangl, *Die Briefe des heiligen Bonifatius und Lullus*, MGH, Epp. sel. 1 (Berlin, 1916); tr. E. Emerton, *The Letters of Saint Boniface*, Records of Civilization. Sources and Studies, 31 (New York, NY, 1940).

Capitulare de Villis: ed. A. Boretius, MGH, Capit. I (Hannover, 1883), 82–91, no. 32; facs. and comm., ed., C. Brühl, ed., *Capitulare de villis. Cod. Guelf. 254 Helmst. der Herzog August Bibliothek Wolfenbüttel*, 2 vols (Stuttgart, 1971).

Cathwulf, *Epistola ad Carolum*: ed. E. Dümmler, MGH, Epp. IV, *Epistolae Karolini Aevi*, 2 (Berlin, 1895), 501–4.

Charlemagne, *Epistolae*: 'To Leo III': Alcuin, 'Epistolae', no. 93, ed. E. Dümmler, MGH Epp. IV, *Epistolae Karolini Aevi*, 136–8; tr. P. D. King, *Charlemagne: Translated Sources* (Kendal,

1987), 311–12 and H. R. Loyn and J. Percival, *The Reign of Charlemagne: Documents on Carolingian Government and Administration* (London, 1975), 117–19. 'To Offa': ed. E. Dümmler, MGH, Epp. IV, *Epistolae Karolini Aevi*, 2 (Berlin, 1895), 144–6, no. 100; tr. S. Allott, *Alcuin of York: His Life and Letters* (York, 1974), 51–3, no. 40. 'To Angilbert': ed. E. Dümmler, MGH, Epp. IV, *Epistolae Karolini Aevi*, 2 (Berlin, 1895), 135–8, no. 92.

Chartae Latini Antiquiores: Facsimile Edition of the Latin Charters prior to the Ninth Century, 49 vols, ed. A. Brucker and R. Marichal (Olten and Lausanne, 1954–).

Chronicon Moissiacense: ed. G. H. Pertz, MGH, SS I, 282–313.

Codex Carolinus/Codex epistolaris Carolinus: ed. W. Gundlach, MGH, Epp. III, *Epistolae Merowingici et Karolini Aevi*, 1 (Berlin, 1892), 469–653; ed. and German tr. F. Hartmann and T. B. Orth-Müller, *Codex epistolaris Carolinus. Frühmittelatlerliche Papstbriefe an die Karolingerherrscher*, Ausgewählte quellen zur Geschichte des Mittelalters Freiherr-vom Stein-Gedächtnisausgabe, 49 (Darmstadt, 2017); English tr. R. McKitterick, D. van Espelo, R. Pollard, and R. Price, *Codex Epistolaris Carolinus: Letters from the Popes to the Frankish Rulers, 739–791*, Translated Texts for Historians, 77 (Liverpool, 2021).

Concilium Romanum, 769: ed. A. Werminghoff, MGH Conc. II.1 *Concilia aevi Karolini*, I, (Hannover, 1906), 74–92, no. 14.

Constitutum Constantini [Donation of Constantine]: ed. H. Fuhrmann, *Das Constitutum Constantini*, MGH, Fontes Iuris Germanici Antiqui, 10 (Hannover, 1968), 55–98.

Corippus, *In laudem Iustini Augusti minoris*: ed. and tr. A. Cameron, *Flavius Cresconius Corippus. In laudem Iustini Augusti minoris* (London, 1976).

Council of Clovesho, 747: ed. A. W. Haddan and W. Stubbs, *Councils and Ecclesiastical Documents Relating to Great Britain and Ireland*, 3 vols (Oxford, 1869–78), iii, 362–76.

Dagulf, *Carmina*: ed. E. Dümmler, MGH, Poetae, I, PLAC 1 (Berlin, 1881), 91–2.

Damasus, *Epigrammata*: A. Ferrua, *Epigrammata Damasiana* (Vatican City, 1942).

De litteris colendis: ed. A. Boretius, MGH, Capit. I (Hannover, 1883), 78–9; tr. H. R. Loyn and J. Percival, *The Reign of Charlemagne: Documents on Carolingian Government and Administration* (London, 1975), 63–4.

Deodatus, *Carmen*: ed. E. Dümmler, MGH, Poetae, I, PLAC 1 (Berlin, 1881) 92–3.

Dionysio-Hadriana, *Carmen*: ed. E. Dümmler, MGH, MGH, Poetae, I, PLAC 1 (Berlin 1881), 90–1; German tr. S. Scholz, *Politik—Selbstverständnis—Selbstdarstellung. Die Päpste in karolingischer und ottonischer Zeit*, Historische Forschung, 26 (Stuttgart, 2006), 82–5.

Donation of Constantine, *see Constitutum Constantini*.

Einhard, *Vita Karoli*: ed. O. Holder-Egger, MGH, SS rer. Germ. (Hannover and Leipzig, 1911); tr. P. E. Dutton, *Charlemagne's Courtier: The Complete Einhard*, Readings in Medieval Civilizations and Cultures, 2 (Peterborough, ON, 1998); tr. D. Ganz, *Einhard and Notker the Stammerer: Two Lives of Charlemagne* (London, 2008).

Einsiedeln Itinerary: facs., G. Walser, *Die Einsiedler Inschriftensammlung und der Pilgerführer durch Rom (Codex Einsiedlensis 326): Facsimile, Umschrift, Übersetzung und Kommentar* (Stuttgart, 29–87).

Epitaphium Hadriani Papae: ed. E. Dümmler, MGH, MGH, Poetae, I, PLAC 1 (Berlin 1881), 113–14.

Eugenius of Toledo, *Carmina*: ed. F. Vollmer, MGH, AA XIV (Berlin, 1905), 230–82.

Faricius, *Vita S Aldhelmi*: ed. J.-P. Migne, *PL* 89 (Paris, 1963), cols 63–84; ed. M. Winterbottom, 'An Edition of Faricius, *Vita S. Aldhelmi*', *The Journal of Medieval Latin*, 15 (2005), 93–147.

Festus, *De verborum significatu*: ed. W. M. Lindsay, *Glossaria Latina*, 5 vols (Paris, 1926–31).

Fredegar, *Chronicarum quae dicunur Fredegarii Scholasici Libri IV cum Continuationibus*: ed. B. Krusch, MGH SS rer. Merov. II (Hannover, 1888), 1–193; ed. and tr. J. M. Wallace-Hadrill, *The Fourth Book of Fredegar with its Continuations* (London, 1960).

George, bishop of Ostia and Amiens, 'Legates' report to Pope Hadrian': ed. E. Dümmler, MGH, Epp. IV, *Epistolae Karolini Aevi*, 2 (Berlin, 1895), 19–29; partial tr. D. Whitelock, *English Historical Documents*, Vol. 1, *c.500–1042* (London, 1955), 770–74, no. 191.

Giacobacci, Domenico, *De consilio tractatus* (Rome, 1538).

Godesscalc, *Carmen*: ed. E. Dümmler, MGH, Poetae, I, PLAC 1 (Berlin 1881), 94–5.

Gregory the Great: *Dialogorum Libri IV*, ed. J.-P. Migne, *PL* 77 (Paris, 1862), cols 149–427; ed. A. de Vogüé, *Dialogorum libri quattuor seu De miraculis patrum italicorum: Grégoire le Grand, Dialogues*, Sources crétiennes, 3 vols, 251, 260, 265 (Paris, 1978–80).

Gregory of Tours, *In gloria martyrum*: ed. B. Krusch, MGH, SS rer. Merov. I.ii (Hannover, 1885), 34–111; tr. R. Van Dam, *Gregory of Tours: Glory of the Martyrs*, Translated Texts for Historians, 4 (Liverpool, 2004).

Grimaldi, Giacomo, *Descrizione della basilica antica di S. Pietro in Vaticano: codice Barberini latino 2733*, ed. R. Niggl, Codices e Vaticanis Selecti, 32 (Vatican City, 1972).

Guicciardini, Luigi, *The Sack of Rome*, tr. J. H. McGregor (New York, NY, 1993).

Hariulf, *Gesta ecclesiae Centulensis*: ed. F. Lot, *Hariulf. Chronique de l'abbaye du St. Riquier, Ve siècle –1104* (Paris, 1894).

Hincmar, *Capitula synodica*: ed. J.-P. Migne, *PL* 125 (Paris, 1852), cols 773–804.

Historia Regum [*History of the Kings*], ed. T. Arnold, *Symeonis Monachis Opera Omnia*, Rolls Series 75, 2 vols (London, 1885), ii, 2–283; partial tr. D. Whitelock, *English Historical Documents*, Vol. 1, *c.500–1042* (London, 1955), 239–54, no. 3.

Hraban Maur, *De Institutione Clericorum*: ed. J.-P. Migne, *PL* 107 (Paris, 1864), cols 293–419.

Inscriptiones Christianae Urbis Romae: ed. G. B. de Rossi, *Inscriptiones Christianae Urbis Romae septimo saeculo antiquiores*, II.i: *pars prima ab originibus ad saeculum XII* (Rome, 1888); ed. A. Silvagni, *Inscriptiones Christianae Urbis Romae septimo saeculo antiquiores: nova series*, 10 vols (Rome, 1922–92), i: *Inscriptiones incertae originis*; ii: *Coemeteria in viis Cornelia Aurelia, Portuensi et Ostiensi*.

Inscriptiones Latinae, ed. E. Diehl, Tabula in usum scholarum, 4 (Bonn, 1912).

Itineraria: ed. P. Geyer and O. Cuntz, *Itineraria et alia Geographica*, 2 vols, CCSL, 175–6 (Turnhout, 1965).

Jerome, *Ad Paulinum Presbyterum*: ed. and tr. J. Labourt, *St. Jérôme, Lettres*, 8 vols (Paris, 1949–63).

Justinian, *Novellae Constitutiones*: tr. D. J. D. Miller and P. Sarris, *The Novels of Justinian, A Complete Annotated English Translation*, 2 vols (Cambridge, 2018).

Karolus Magnus et Leo Papa: ed. E. Dümmler, MGH, Poetae, I, PLAC 1 (Berlin 1881), 366–79; ed. and German trans. H. Neumann, F. Brunhölzl and W. Winkelmann, *Karolus Magnus et Leo Papa: Ein Paderborner Epos vol Jahre 799* (Paderborn, 1966); partial tr. P. Godman, *Poetry of the Carolingian Renaissance* (London, 1985), 197–206, no. 25.

Laudes Vernonensis Civitatis: ed. E. Dümmler, MGH, Poetae, I, PLAC 1 (Berlin 1881), 122.

Leo the Great, *Sermon* 82.1, 'In natale apostolorum Petri et Pauli': ed. J.-P. Migne, *PL* 54 (Paris, 1846), cols 422–8.

Lex de imperio Vespasiani: ed. H. Dessau, *Inscriptiones Latinae Selectae*, 3 vols (Berlin, 1892–1916), i, no. 244; ed. V. Ehrenberg and A. H. M. Jones, *Documents Illustrating the Reign of Augustus and Tiberius*, 2nd edn (Oxford, 1976), no. 364; tr. D. Braund, *Augustus to Nero* (London, 1985), no. 293.

Liber Pontificalis: ed. L. Duchesne, *Le* Liber pontificalis: *texte, introduction et commentaire*, 2 vols (Paris, 1886–92); tr. R. Davis, *The Book of Pontiffs (*Liber Pontificalis*): The Ancient Biographies of the First Ninety Roman Bishops to AD 715*, Translated Texts for Historians, 6 (Liverpool, 1989); trR. Davis, *The Lives of the Eighth-Century Popes (*Liber Pontificalis*)*, Translated Texts for Historians, 13 (Liverpool, 1992); tr. R. Davis, *The Lives of the Ninth-Century Popes (*Liber Pontificalis*)*, Translated Texts for Historians, 20 (Liverpool, 1995).

Lorsch Annals, *see* Annales Laureshamenses.

Lupus of Ferriers, *Epistolae*: ed. and tr. L. Levillain, *Loup de Ferrières. Correspondance*, 2 vols (Paris, 1927–35).

Mallius, Peter, 'Historia Basilicae antiquae S. Petri Apostoli in Vaticano', *AASS* Iunii vii, cols 34A–52; 'Opusculum Historiae Sacrae ad Beatissimum Patrem Alexandrum III Pont. Max.', VZ, iii, 382–442.

Martin, Gregory, *Roma Sancta (1581)*, ed. and tr. G. Bruner Parks (Rome, 1969).

Masson, Jean-Papire, *Annalium libri quatuor: Quibus res gestae Francorum explicantur. Ad Henricvm Tertium Regem Franciae et Poloniae* (Paris, 1578).

Master Gregorius, *The Marvels of Rome*, tr. J. Osborne, Mediaeval Sources in Translation, 31 (Toronto, ON, 1987).

Monumenta epigraphica christiana saeculo XIII antiquiora quae in Italiae finibus adhuc exstant iussu Pii XII pontificis maximi, ed. A. Silvagni, 4 vols in 7 (Rome, 1943); i: *Roma*; ii.1: *Mediolanum*; ii.2: *Comum*; ii.3: *Papia*; iii.1: *Luca*; iv.1: *Neapolis*; iv.2: *Beneventum*.

Muret, Marc Antoine, *Orationes XXIII* (Venice, 1575).

Notitia ecclesiarum urbis Romae: ed. R. Valentini, and G. Zucchetti, *Codice topografico della città di Roma*, 4 vols, Fonti per la Storia d'Italia 81, 88, 90 (Rome, 1940–53), ii: *Scrittori secoli IV–XI*, 67–99, at 94–9 and P. Geyer and O. Cuntz, eds, *Itineraria et alia Geographica. Itineraria Hierosolymitana. Itineraria Romana. Geographica*, CCSL 175 (Turnhout, 1965), 303–11.

Panvinio, Onofrio, *De praecipuis urbis Romae sanctioribusque basilicis, quas septem ecclesias vulgo vocant liber* (Rome, 1570).

Panvinio, Onofrio, 'De rebus antiquis memoratu dignis basilicae S. Petri Vaticanae libri VII'; ed. A. Mai, *Spicilegium Romanum*, 10 vols (Rome, 1843), ix, 94–328.

Paul the Deacon, *Epistola ad Carolum*: ed. E. Dümmler, MGH Epp. IV, *Epistolae Karolini Aevi*, 2 (Berlin, 1895), 508.

Platina, Bartolomeo, *Historia de vitis pontificum Romanorum: a D.N. Iesv Christo usque ad Paulum Papam II. Cvi Onvphrii Panvinii Veronensisfratris Eremitæ Augustiniani opera, reliquiorum quoque pontificium uitæ usque ad Pium IIII pontifciem maximum adiunctæ sunt* (Venice, 1562).

Pliny, *Naturalis Historia*: ed. H. Rackham, W. H. S. Jones, and D. e. Eichholz, *Natural History*, 10 vols, 220, 352–3, 370–1, 392–3, 394, 418–19 (Cambridge, MA, 1938–62).

Prosper, *Epigrammata ex sententiis S. Augustini*: ed. J.-P. Migne, *PL* 51 (Paris, 1861), cols 497–532.

Revised Royal Frankish Annals: *Annales regni francorum unde ab a. 741 usque ad a. 829, qui dicuntur Annales laurissenses maiores et Einhardi*, ed. F. Kurze, MGH, SS rer. Germ., 6 (Hannover, 1895); tr. B. W. Scholz, *Carolingian Chronicles: Royal Frankish Annals and Nithard's Histories* (Ann Arbor, MI, 1972), 37–125; tr. P. D. King, *Charlemagne: Translated Sources* (Kendal, 1987), 108–31.

Royal Frankish Annals, see *Annales Regni Francorum*.

Second Council of Nicaea, 787: tr. R. Price, *The Acts of the Second Council of Nicaea (787)*, Translated Texts for Historians 68, 2 vols (Liverpool, 2018).

Sedulius Scottus, *Carmina*: ed. I. Meyers, *Sedulii Scotti Carmina*, CCCM 117 (Turnhout, 1991); tr. E. G. Doyle, *Sedulius Scottus, On Christian Rulers and The Poems* (Binghamton, NY, 1983).

Sigibert of Gembloux, *Vita Landiberti episcopi Traiectensis*: ed. B. Krusch and W. Levison, MGH, SS rer. Merov. VI, *Passiones vitaeque sanctorum aevi Merovingici* IV (Hannover and Leipzig, 1913), 353–429.

Suetonius, *De vita Caesarum*: ed. and tr. J. C. Rolfe, *Lives of the Caesars, i: Julius. Augustus. Tiberius. Gaius. Caligula*, Loeb Classical Library, 31 (Cambridge, MA, 1914).

Symeon of Durham, see *Historia Regum*.

Synodus Franconfurtensis, 794: ed. A. Boretius, MGH, Capit. I (Hannover, 1883), 73–8.

Theodulf of Orléans, *Carmina*: ed. E. Dümmler, MGH, Poetae, I, PLAC 1 (Berlin 1881), 445–581; tr. T. Andersson, *Theodulf of Orléans: The Verse* (Tempe, AZ, 2014).

Theodulf of Orléans, 'Super sepulchrum Hadriani papae' ['Over the Tomb of Pope Hadrian']: ed. E. Dümmler, MGH, Poetae, I, PLAC 1 (Berlin 1881), 489–90; tr. T. Andersson, *Theodulf of Orléans. The Verse* (Tempe, AZ, 2014), 73–5.

Theophylact [archdeacon], *Epistola ad Bonifatium*: ed. M. Tangl, MGH, Epp. sel. 1 (Berlin, 1916), 189–91; E. Emerton, tr., *The Letters of Saint Boniface*, Records of Civilization. Sources and Studies, 31 (New York, NY, 1940), 156–7.

Tomassetti, Aloysius, ed., *Bullarum Diplomatum et Privilegiorum Romanorum Pontificum*, 24 vols (Rome, 1857–1972).

Vegio, Maffeo, 'De antiqua S. Petri apostoli Basilica in Vaticano, c.1455', *AASS* Junii vii (Paris and Rome 1867), cols 57A–85D or 'De rebus antiquis memorabilibus basilicae S. Petri Romae', ed. R. Valentini, and G. Zucchetti, *Codice topografico della città di Roma*, 4 vols, Fonti per la Storia d'Italia 81, 88, 90 (Rome, 1940–53), iv: *Scrittori XV*, 375–98; tr. C. Smith and J. F. O'Connor, *Eyewitness to Old St. Peter's: A Study of Maffeo Vegio's 'Remembering the ancient history of St. Peter's basilica in Rome'* (Cambridge, 2019).

Venatius Fortunatus, *Opera poetica*: ed. F. Leo, MGH, AA IV.1 (Berlin, 1881); tr. J. Gregory, *Venantius Fortunatus: Personal and Political Poems*, Translated Texts for Historians, 23 (Liverpool, 1995).

Vita Alcuini (Anon.): ed. W. Arndt, MGH, SS XV.1 (Hannover, 1887), 182–97.

PRINTED SECONDARY SOURCES

AA.VV., ed., *Culto cristiano politica imperiale carolingia*, Convegni del centro di Studi sulla AA.VV. *Culto cristiano politica imperiale carolingia*, Convegni del centro di studi sulla spiritualità medievale XVIII (Todi, 1979).

Adam, J.-P., *Roman Building: Materials and Techniques* (Abingdon, 2007).
Adams, J. N., *The Regional Diversification of Latin 200 BC to AD 600* (Cambridge, 2007).
Adams, J. N., *Social Variation and the Latin Language* (Cambridge, 2013).
Alberto, P. F., 'Corippus' Panegyric of Justin II in Carolingian Grammatical Texts', in D. Paniagua and M. A. Andrés Sanz, eds, *Formas de acceso al saber en la Antigüedad Tardía y en la Alta Edad Media: La transmision del conocimiento dentro y fuera de la escuela*, Textes et Études du Moyen Âge, 84 (Turnhout, 2016), 198–209.
Alchermes, J. D., 'Petrine Politics: Pope Symmachus and the Rotunda of St. Andrew at Old St. Peter's', *The Catholic Historical Review*, 81 (1995), 1–40.
Alexander, J. J. G. and M. T. Gibson, eds, *Medieval Learning and Literature: Essays Presented to Richard William Hunt* (Oxford, 1976), 3–22.
Alexandrenko, N., 'The Poetry of Theodulf of Orléans: A Translation and Critical Study', PhD thesis, Tulane University, New Orleans, 1970.
Anastos, M. V., 'The Transfer of Illyricum, Calabria and Sicily to the Jurisdiction of the Patriarchate of Constantinople in 732–733', *Studi bizantini e neoellenico*, 9 (1957), 14–31.
Andaloro, M., *Pittura Medievale a Roma, 312–1431. Corpus e Atlante*, 9 vols (Milan, 2006).
Anderson, F. and E. Groessens, 'The Black Altars of Nehalennia', *Oufheidkundige mededelingen uit het Rijksmuseum van oudheden te Leiden, Nieuwe Reeks*, 76 (1996), 129–38.
Andersson, T. M., tr. with Å. Ommundsen and L. S. B MacCoull, *Theodulf of Orléans: The Verse*, Medieval and Renaissance Texts and Studies, 450 (Tempe, AZ, 2014).
Andrieu, M., 'La chapelle de St. Grégoire dans l'ancienne basilique Vaticane', *Rivista di archeologia Cristiana*, 13 (1936), 61–99.
Andrieu, M., 'La 'Rota porphyretica' de la basilique Vaticane', *Mélange d'Archéologie et d'Histoire*, 66 (1954), 189–218.
Andrieu, M., *Les ordines Roman du Haut Moyen Age*, 5 vols (Louvain, 1931–56).
Angenendt, A., 'Das geistliche Bündnis der Päpste mit den Karolingern (754–796)', *Historisches Jahrbuch*, 100 (1980), 1–94.
Angenendt, A., 'Der römische und gallisch-fränkische Anti-Ikonolasmus', *Frühmittelalterlich Studien*, 35 (2001), 201–25.
Angenendt, A., *Liturgie im Mittelalter: ausgewählte Augsätze zum 70. Geburtstag* (Münster, 2005).
Angenendt, A., '*Mensa Pippini Regis*. Zur liturgischen präsenz der Karolinger in Sankt Peter', in E. Gatz, ed., *Hundert Jahre Deutsches Priesterkolleg beim Campo Santo Teutonico 1876–1976. Beiträge zu seiner Geschichte*, Römische Quartalschrift für christliche Altertumskunde und Kirchengeschichte, 35 (Rome, 1977), 52–68, reprinted in his *Liturgie im Mittelalter: ausgewählte Augsätze zum 70. Geburtstag* (Münster, 2005), 89–110.
Apollonj Ghetti, B. M., A. Ferrua, E. Josi, and E. Kirschbaum, eds, *Esplorazione sotto la confessione di san Pietro in Vaticano, eseguit e negli anni 1940–1949*, 2 vols (Vatican City, 1951).
Arbeiter, A., *Alt-St. Peter in Geschichte und Wissenschaft: Abfolge der Bauten, Rekonstruktion, Architekturprogramm* (Berlin, 1988).
Arena, M. S., P. Delogu, L. Paroli, M. Ricci, L. Saguì, and L. Vendittelli, eds, *Roma dall'antichità al Medioevo: archeologia e storia nel Museo nationale romana, Crypta Balbi*, 2 vols (Milan, 2001–4).
Ballance, M. H., 'The Origin of *africano*', *Papers of the British School at Rome*, 34 (1966), 79–81.

Ballardini, A. and P. Pogliani, 'A Reconstruction of the Oratory of John VII (705–707)', in *OSPR*, 190–213.

Balzaretti, R., J. Barrow, and P. Skinner, eds, *Italy and Early Medieval Europe: Papers for Chris Wickham*, Past and Present Book Series (Oxford, 2018).

Bandini, C., *Gli Anni Santi* (Turin, 1934).

Barral I Altet, X., 'L'VIII secolo: da Giovanni VI (701–705) ad Adriano I (772–795)', in M. D'Onofrio, ed., *La committenza artistica dei papi a Roma nel Medioevo* (Rome, 2016), 181–212.

Bately, J., M. P. Brown, and J. Roberts, eds, *A Palaeographer's View: Selected Writings of Julian Brown* (London, 1993).

Bauer, F. A., *Das Bild der Stadt Rom im Frühmittelalter. Papststiftungen im Spiegel des Liber Pontificalis von Gregor dem Dritten bis zu Leo dem Dritten*, Palilia, 14 (Wiesbaden, 2014).

Bauer, F. A., 'Das Bild der Stadt Rom in karolingischer Zeit: der Anonymus Einsidlensis', *Romische Quartalschrift*, 92 (1992), 190–228.

Bauer, F. A., 'Die Bau- und Stiftungspolitik der Päpste Hadrian I (772–795) und Leo III (795–816)', in SW, *799*, iii, 514–28.

Bauer, F. A., 'Il rinnovamento di Roma sotto Adriano I alla luce del *Liber Pontificalis*. Immagine e realtà', in H. Geertman, ed., *Atti del Colloquio Internazionale Il* Liber Pontificalis *e la storia materiale* (Roma, 21–22 febbraio 2002), Mededelingen van het Nederlands Instituut te Rome, 60–1 (Rome, 2003), 189–203.

Bauer, S., *The Censorship and Fortuna of Platina's* 'Lives of the Popes' *in the Sixteenth Century*, Late Medieval and Early Modern Studies, 9 (Turnhout, 2006).

Bauer, S. *The Invention of Papal History. Onofrio Panvinio between Renaissance and Catholic Reform* (Oxford, 2020).

Bayer, C. M. M., 'Die karolingische Bauinschrift des Aachener Dom', in M. Kerner, ed., *Der verschleierte Karl. Karl der Grosse zwischen Mythos und Wirklichkeit* (Aachen, 1999), 445–52.

Bayer, C. M. M., M. Kerner, and H. Müller, 'Schriftquellen zur Geschichte der Marienkirche bis ca. 1000', in H. Müller, C. M. M. Bayer, and M. Kerner, eds, *Die Aachener Marienkirche. Aspekte ihrer Archäologie und frühen Geschichte*, Der Aachener Dom in seiner Geschichte. Quellen und Forschungen, 1 (Regensburg, 2014), 113–89.

Bayless, M., *Sin and Filth in Medieval Culture: The Devil in the Latrine* (Abingdon, 2012).

Becher, M., *Charlemagne* (New Haven, CT, and London, 2003).

Becher, M. 'Die Reise Papst Leos III. Zu Karl dem Großen. Überlegungen zu Chronologie, Verlauf und Inhalt der Paderborner Verhandlungen des Jahres 799', in P. Godman, J. Jarnut, and P. Johanek, *Am vorabend der Kaiser Krönung. Das Epos "Karolus Magnus et Leo papa" und der Papstbesuch in Paderborn 799* (Berlin, 2002), 87–112.

Bellinger, A. R. and P. Grierson, eds, *Catalogue of the Byzantine Coins in the Dumbarton Oaks Collection and in the Whittemore Collection*, 3.i (Washington, DC, 1993).

Beltramini, M., 'Porta (1433–1445)', in *BSPV* I.i (*Atlas*), 252–71 and II.ii (*Notes*), 483–90.

Benedetti, S., 'The Fabric of St Peter's', in *BSPV*, II.i (*Essays*), 53–128.

Benedetti, S. and G. Zander, eds, *L'arte in Roma nel secolo XVI*, 2 vols (Bologna, 1990).

Berndt, R., *Das Frankfurter Konzil Von 794: Kristallisationspunkt Karolingischer Kultur: Akten Zweier Symposien (vom 23. bis 27. Februar und vom 13. bis 15. Oktober 1994) Anlässlich der 1200-Jahrfeier der Stadt Frankfurt Am Main*, Quellen und Abhandlungen zur Mittelrheinischen Kirchengeschichte, 2 vols (Mainz, 1997).

Bertolini, O., 'Per la storia delle diaconie romane', *Archivio della Società romana di Storia patria*, 70 (1947), 1–145.

Beumann, H., 'Das Paderborner Epos und die Kaiseridee Karls des Grossen' in G. G. Wolf, ed., *Zum Kaisertum Karls des Grossen. Beiträge und Aufsätze* (Darmstadt, 1972), 309–83.

Bischoff, B., *Die Abtei Lorsch im Spiegel ihrer Handschriften* (Lorsch, 1989).

Bischoff, B., 'Die alten Namen der lateinischen Schriftarten', *Philologus. Zeitschrift für antike Literatur und ihre Rezeption*, 89 (1934), 461–5, reprinted in *Mittelalterliche Studien. Ausgewählte Aufsätze zur Schriftkunde und Literaturgeschichte*, 3 vols (Stuttgart, 1966–81), i, 1–6.

Bischoff, B., 'Die Hofbibliothek Karls des Grossen', in W. Braunfels, ed., *Karl Der Grosse: Lebenswerk und Nachleben*, ii: *Das geistige Leben* (Düsseldorf, 1965), 42–62, reprinted with revisions in *Mittelalterliche Studien. Ausgewählte Aufsätze zur Schriftkunde und Literaturgeschichte*, 3 vols (Stuttgart, 1966–81), iii, 149–69, and in English as 'The Court Library of Charlemagne', in B. Bischoff, *Manuscripts and Libraries in the Age of Charlemagne*, tr. M. Gorman (Cambridge, 1994), 56–75.

Bischoff, B., 'Die Hofbibliothek unter Ludwig dem Frommen', in J. J. G. Alexander and M. T. Gibson, eds, *Medieval Learning and Literature: Essays Presented to Richard William Hunt* (Oxford, 1976), 3–22; reprinted in English as 'The Court Library under Louis the Pious', in B. Bischoff, *Manuscripts and Libraries in the Age of Charlemagne*, tr. M. Gorman (Cambridge, 1994), 76–92.

Bischoff, B., *Die Südostdeutschen schreibschulen und bibliotheken in der karolingerzeit*, i: Die Bayrischen Diözesen; ii: Die Vorwiegend Österreichischen Diözesen (Wiesbaden, 1974–80).

Bischoff, B., *Latin Palaeography: Antiquity and the Middle Ages*, tr. D. Ó Cróinín and D. Ganz (Cambridge, 1991).

Bischoff, B., *Lorsch im Spiegel seiner Handschriften* (Munich, 1974).

Bischoff, B., *Manuscripts and Libraries in the Age of Charlemagne*, Cambridge Studies in Palaeography and Codicology, 1, tr. M. Gorman (Cambridge, 1994).

Bischoff, B., *Mittelalterliche Studien. Ausgewählte Aufsätze zur Schriftkunde und Literaturgeschichte*, 3 vols (Stuttgart, 1966–81).

Bischoff, B., *Salzburger Formelbücher und Briefe aus Tassilonischer und Karolingischer Zeit*, Sitzungsberichte der Bayerische Akademie der Wissenschaften, Philosophisch-historische Klasse, Sitzungsberichte 1973.iv (Munich, 1973).

Bischoff, B., *Sammelhandschrift Diez. B. Sant 66: Grammatici Latini et Catalogus Librorum*; Codices Selecti, 42 (Graz, 1973).

Bischoff, B. with B. Epersberger, *Katalog der Festländischen Handschriften des Neunten Jahrhunderts (mit Ausnahme der Wisigotischen)*, 4 vols (Wiesbaden, 2004–17).

Bischoff, B., and M. Lapidge, *Biblical Commentaries from the Canterbury School of Theodore and Hadrian*, Cambridge Studies in Anglo-Saxon England, 10 (Cambridge, 1994).

Blaauw, S. de, *Cultus et Decor: Liturgia e Architettura nella Roma Tardoantica e Medievale. Basilica Salvatoris, Sanctae Mariae, Sancti Petri*. Studie e Testi, 355–6, 2 vols (Vatican City, 1994).

Blaauw, S. de, 'Jerusalem in Rome and the Cult of the Cross', in R. Colella, M. Gill, L. Jenkins, and P. Lamers, eds, *In Pratum Romanum. Richard Krautheimer zum 100. Geburtstag* (Wiesbaden, 1997), 55–73.

Bogaers, J. 'Foreign Affairs', in B. Hartley and J. Wacher, eds, *Rome and her Northern Provinces: Papers Presented to Sheppard Frere in Honour of His Retirement from the Chair of The Archaeology of the Roman Empire. University of Oxford, 1983* (Gloucester, 1983), 13–32.

Bolgia, C., R. McKitterick, and J. Osborne, eds, *Rome across Time and Space, c.500–c.1400: Cultural Translation and the Exchange of Ideas* (Cambridge, 2011).

Bonner, G., C. Stancliffe, and D. Rollason, eds, *St. Cuthbert, His Cult, and His Community to AD 1200* (Woodbridge, 1989).

Booker, C. M., 'By Any Other Name? Charlemagne, Nomenclature and Performativity', in R. Grosse and M. Sot, eds, *Charlemagne: les temps, les espaces, les hommes. Construction et Déconstruction d'un règne*, Collection Haut Moyen Âge, 34 (Turnhout, 2018), 409–26.

Boppert, W., 'Die frühchristlichen Grabinschriften aus der Servatiuskirche in Maastricht', in C. D. De Dijn, ed., *Sint-Servatius, bisschop van -Maastricht (Actes du Colloque à Alden biesen (Bilzen), Tongres et Maastricht 1984)* (Borgloon-Rijkel, 1986), 64–96.

Borghini, G. and R. Gnoli, eds, *Marmi Antichi*, Materiali della cultura artistica, 1 (Rome, 1998).

Borgolte, M., *Petrusnachfolge Und Kaiserimitation: Die Grablegen der Päpste, ihre Genese und Traditionsbildung*, Veröffentlichungen des Max-Planck-Instituts für Geschichte, 95 (Göttingen, 1989).

Bortolozzi, A., 'Two Drawings by Giovan Battista Ricci da Novara for the Decoration of the Portico of New St Peter's', *The Burlington Magazine*, 153 (2011), 163–7.

Bosman, L., *The Power of Tradition: Spolia in the Architecture of St. Peter's in the Vatican* (Hilversum, 2004).

Bosman, L., I. P. Haynes, and P. Liverani, eds, *The Basilica of St John Lateran to 1600* (Cambridge, 2020), 294–317.

Boulvain, F., G. Poulain, F. Tourneur, and J. Yans, 'Potential Discrimination of Belgian Black Marbles Using Petrography, Magnetic Susceptibility and Geochemistry', *Archaeometry*, 62 (2020), 469–92.

Bowersock, G. W., 'Peter and Constantine', in W. Tronzo, ed., *St. Peter's in the Vatican* (Cambridge, 2005), 5–15.

Bozzoni, C., 'L'immagine dell'antico San Pietro nell rappresentazioni figurate e nella architettura costruita', in G. Spagnesi, ed., *L'architettura della Basilica di San Pietro: Storia e Costruzione: Atti del convegno internazionale di studi, Roma, Castel S. Angelo, 7–10 novembre 1995* (Rome, 1997), 63–72.

Brandenburg, H., *Ancient Churches of Rome from the Fourth to the Seventh Century*, The Dawn of Christian Architecture in the West, 8 (Turnhout, 2005).

Brandenburg, H., A. Ballardini, and C. Theones, *Saint Peter's: The Story of a Monument*, Monumenta Vaticana Selecta (Vatican City, 2017).

Brandt, M., ed., *Kirchenkunst des Mittelalters. Erhalten und erforschen. Katalog zur Ausstellung des Diözesan-Museums Hildesheim* (Hildesheim, 1989).

Braun, J., *Ein handbuch der Paramentik* (Freiburg, 1912).

Braund, D., *Augustus to Nero* (London, 1985).

Braunfels, W., ed., *The Lorsch Gospels* (New York, NY, 1967).

Braunfels, W. and P. E. Schramm, eds, *Karl der Grosse. Lebenswerk und Nachleben*, 5 vols (Dusseldorf, 1967).

Breay, C. and J. Story, eds, *Anglo-Saxon Kingdoms: Art, Word, War* (London, 2018).

Breay C., and J. Story, eds., *Manuscripts in the Anglo-Saxon Kingdoms: Cultures and Connections* (Dublin, 2021).

Bremmer, R. H., 'Leiden, Vossianus Lat. Q. 69 (Part 2): Schoolbook or Proto-Encyclopaedic Miscellany?', in R. H. Bremmer and K. Dekker, eds, *Practice in Learning: The Transfer of Encyclopaedic Knowledge in the Early Middle Ages*, Mediaevalia Groningana, NS 16 (Paris, 2010), 19–54.

Brink, P. van den and S. Ayooghi, *Karl der Grosse. Charlemagne. Karls Kunst* (Aachen, 2014).

Brodini, A., 'Michelangelo e la volta della cappella del re di Francia in San Pietro', *Annali di architettura*, 17 (2005), 115–26.

Brown, P., 'Aspects of the Christianization of the Roman Aristocracy', *Journal of Roman Studies*, 51 (1961), 1–11.

Brown, T. J. 'On the Distribution and Significance of Membrane Prepared in the Insular Manner', in J. Glenisson and C. Sirat, eds, *La Paléographie Hébraïque Médiévale*, Colloques Internationaux du CNRS 547 (Paris, 1974), 127–35, reprinted in J. Bately, M. Brown, and J. Roberts, eds, *A Palaeographer's View: Selected Writings of Julian Brown* (London, 1993), 125–40.

Brown, T. S., *Gentlemen and Officers: Imperial Administration and Aristocratic Power in Byzantine Italy, AD 554–800* (London, 1984).

Brown, T. S., 'Byzantine Italy *c*.680–*c*.876', in R. McKitterick, ed., *New Cambridge Medieval History*, ii: *c.700–c.900* (Cambridge, 1995), 320–48.

Brubaker, L. and J. Haldon, *Byzantium in the Iconoclast Era, c.680–850: A History* (Cambridge, 2011).

Brühl, C., ed., *Capitulare de villis. Cod. Guelf. 254 Helmst. der Herzog August Bibliothek, Wolfenbüttel*, 2 vols (Stuttgart, 1971).

Bruschi, A., 'The Drawings of Antonio da Sangallo the Younger at St. Peter's under Leo X', in C. L. Frommel and N. Adams, eds, *The Architectural Drawings of Antonio Da Sangallo the Younger and His Circle*, 2 vols (New York, 2000), ii, 23–32.

Bucarelli, O., 'Epigraphy and Liturgical Furnishings in St. Peter's Basilica in the Vatican between Late Antiquity and the Middle Ages', *Archiv für Diplomatik*, 60 (2018), 293–322.

Buchner, M., 'Zur Überlieferungsgeschichte des *Liber Pontificalis* und zu seiner Verbreitung im Frankenreich im 9. Jh.', *Römische Quartalschrift für christliche Altertumskunde und Kirchengeschichte*, 34 (1926), 141–65.

Bullough, D. A., *Alcuin: Achievement and Reputation*, Education and Society in the Middle Ages and Renaissance, 16 (Leiden, 2004).

Bullough, D. A., 'Alcuin, Arn and the Creed in the Mass', in M. Niederkorn-Bruck and A. Scharer, *Erzbischof Arn von Salzburg*, Veröffentlichungen des Instituts für Österreichische Geschichtsforschung, 40 (Munich, 2004), 128–38.

Bullough, D. A., '*Aula Renovata*: The Court before the Aachen Palace', *Proceedings of the British Academy*, 71 (1985), 267–30, reprinted in *Carolingian Renewal: Sources and Heritage* (Manchester, 1991), 123–60.

Bullough, D. A., *Carolingian Renewal: Sources and Heritage* (Manchester, 1991).
Bullough, D. A., 'Charlemagne's "Men of God": Alcuin, Hildebald and Arn', in J. Story, ed., *Charlemagne: Empire and Society* (Manchester, 2005), 136–50.
Bullough, D. A., 'The Dating of the Codex Carolinus nos. 95, 96, 97, Wilchar and the Beginnings of the Archbishopric of Sens', *Deutsches Archiv für Erforschung des Mittelalters*, 18 (1962), 223–30.
Bullough, D. A., 'Empire and Emperordom from Late Antiquity to 799', *Early Medieval Europe*, 12 (2003), 377–87 (English translation of 'Der Kaiseridee zwischen Antike und Mittelalter', in SW, *799*, iii, 36–46).
Bullough, D. A., '"Imagines Regum" and their Significance in the Early Medieval West', in G. Robertson and G. Henderson, eds, *Studies in Memory of David Talbot Rice* (Edinburgh, 1975), 223–76, reprinted in his *Carolingian Renewal: Sources and Heritage* (Manchester, 1991), 39–96.
Bullough, D. A., 'Reminiscence and Reality: Text, Translation and Testimony of an Alcuin Letter', *Journal of Medieval Latin*, 5 (1995), 174–201.
Bullough, D. A., 'Roman Books and Carolingian *renovatio*', *Studies in Church History*, 14 (1977), 23–50, reprinted in *Carolingian Renewal: Sources and Heritage* (Manchester, 1991), 1–38.
Butzer, P. L. and D. Lohrmann, eds, *Science in Western and Eastern Civilization in Carolingian Times* (Basel, 1993).
Butzmann, A. H., ed., *Corpus Agrimensorum Romanorum. Codex Arcerianus A der Herzog-August-Bibliothek zu Wolfenbüttel (cod. Guelf. 36.23 A)*, Codici graeci et latini photographice depicti, 22 (Leiden, 1970).
Caldelli, E., 'Sull'iscrizione di Adriano I', *Scrineum Rivista*, 13 (2016), 49–91.
Calvelli, L. 'Un testimone della lex de imperio Vespasiani del tardo Trecento: Francesco Zabarella', *Athenaeum*, 91.2 (2011), 515–24.
Camerlenghi, N., *St. Paul's Outside the Walls: A Roman Basilica, from Antiquity to the Modern Era* (Cambridge, 2018).
Cameron, A., ed. and tr., *Flavius Cresconius Corippus. In laudem Iustini Augusti minoris* (London, 1976).
Carbonetti, C., S. Lucà, and M. Signorini, eds, *Roma e il suo territorio nel medioevo. Le fonti scritte fra traditzione e innovazione. Atti del Convegno internazionale di studio dell'Associazione italiana dei paleografi e diplomatisti* (Roma, 25–29 ottobre 2012). Studi e ricerche, 6 (Spoleto, 2015).
Cardin, L., *Epigrafia a Roma nel Primo Medioevo (secoli IV–X). Modelli grafici e tipologie d'uso* (Rome, 2008).
Carey, F. M., 'The Scriptorium of Reims during the Archbishopric of Hincmar (845–882 AD)', in L. Webber Jones, ed., *Classical and Mediaeval Studies in Honour of Edward Kennard Rand* (New York, NY, 1938), 41–60.
Carpiceci, A., 'La basilica Vaticana vista da Martin van Heemskerck', *Bollettino d'arte*, 44 (1987), 67–128.
Carruba, A. M., *La Lupa capitolina. Un bronzo medievale* (Rome, 2006).
Carruthers, M., *The Book of Memory* (Cambridge, 1990).

Cascioli, G., *Epigrapfi Cristiane nell'area vaticana III–VI secolo. Trascrizione delle epigrafi, a cura di Luigi Marsili. Sistemazione redazionale del comment a cura di Dario Rezza. Apparato critico a cura di Fabio Paolucci*, Quaderno d'archivio, 7 (Vatican City, 2013).

Cascioli, G., *Epigrapfi Cristiane nell'area vaticana VI–X secolo. Trascrizione delle epigrafi, sistemazione redazionale e apparato critico a cura di Fabio Paolucci*, Quaderno d'archivio, 9 (Vatican City, 2014).

Cavadini, J. C., *The Last Christology of the West: Adoptionism in Spain and Gaul, 785–820* (Philadelphia, PA, 1993).

Cavallero, D. G., F. D'Amico, and C. Strinati, *L'Arte in Roma nel secolo XVI*, ii: *La pittura e la scultura* (Bologna, 1992).

Cerrati, D. M., ed., *Tiberii Alpharani. De Basilicae Vaticanae antiquissima et nova structura*, Studi e Testi, 26 (Rome, 1914).

Chadwick, N. K., ed., *Celt and Saxon: Studies in the Early British Border* (Cambridge, 1963).

Clarke, C. A. M., *Writing Power in Anglo-Saxon England: Texts, Hierarchies, Economies* (Cambridge, 2012).

Coarelli, F., 'Sepulchrum Romuli', in E. M. Steinby, ed., *Lexicon Topographicum Urbis Romae* (Rome, 1999), 295–6.

Coates-Stephens, R., 'Dark Age Architecture in Rome', *Papers of the British School at Rome* 65 (1997), 177–232.

Coatsworth, E., 'Stitches in Time: Establishing a History of Anglo-Saxon Embroidery', in R. Netherton and G. R. Owen-Crocker, eds, *Medieval Clothing and Textiles* (Woodbridge, 2006), 1–28.

Coatsworth, E., 'Text and Textile', in A. Minnis and J. Roberts, eds, *Text, Image, Interpretation: Studies in Anglo-Saxon Literature and Its Insular Context in Honour of Éamonn Ó Carragáin*, Studies in the Early Middle Ages (Turnhout, 2007), 187–208.

Coffin, D. R. *Pirro Ligorio: The Renaissance Artist, Architect and Antiquarian* (Philadelphia, PA, 2004).

Coleman, C., *The Treatise of Lorenzo Valla on the Donation of Constantine* (New Haven, CT, 1922).

Collins, R., 'Charlemagne's Imperial Coronation and the Annals of Lorsch', in J. Story, ed., *Charlemagne: Empire and Society* (Manchester, 2005), 52–70.

Contreni, J. J., 'The Pursuit of Knowledge in Carolingian Europe', in R. E. Sullivan, ed., *"The Gentle Voices of Teachers": Aspects of Learning in the Carolingian Age* (Columbus, OH, 1995), 106–41.

Coring, H., *Varia scripta ad historiam et ius publicum imperii germanici* (Brunswick, 1730).

Cormack, R., *Byzantine Art* (Oxford, 2000).

Costambeys, M., 'Alcuin, Rome, and Charlemagne's Imperial Coronation', in F. Tinti, ed., *England and Rome in the Early Middle Ages: Pilgrimage, Art and Politics* (Turnhout, 2014), 255–90.

Costambeys, M., 'Pope Hadrian I and Santa Maria Antiqua: Liturgy and Patronage in the Late Eighth Century', in E. Rubery, G. Bordi, and J. Osborne, eds, *Santa Maria Antiqua: The Sistine Chapel of the Early Middle Ages* (London, 2021), 373–83.

Costambeys, M., M. Innes, and S. MacLean, *The Carolingian World* (Cambridge, 2011).

Coupland, S., 'Charlemagne's Coinage: Ideology and Economy', in J. Story, ed. *Charlemagne: Empire and Society* (Manchester, 2005), 211–29.

Coupland, S., 'The Formation of a European Identity: Revisiting Charlemagne's Coinage', in E. Screen and C. West, eds, *Writing the Early Medieval West: Studies in Honour of Rosamond McKitterick* (Cambridge, 2018), 213–29.

Courtright, N., *The Papacy and the Art of Reform in Sixteenth-Century Rome: Gregory XIII's Tower of the Winds in the Vatican*, Monuments of Papal Rome (Cambridge, 2003).

Cramp, R., *Grammar of Anglo-Saxon Ornament: A General Introduction to the Corpus of Anglo-Saxon Stone Sculpture* (Oxford, 1984).

Crivello, F., 'Die Handschriften und ihr Schmuck', in S. Haag and F. Kirchweger, eds, *Das Krönungsevangeliar des Heiligen Römischen Reiches* (Vienna, 2014), 45–8.

Crivello, F., C. Denoël, and P. Orth, *Das Godescalc-Evangelistar: Eine Prachthandschrift für Karl den Großen* (Munich, 2011).

Crivello, F. and C. Segre Montel, *Carlo Magno e le Alpi: Viaggio al centro del Medioevo* (Milan, 2006).

Crosby, S. McKnight, *The Royal Abbey of St.-Denis from its Beginnings to the Death of Suger, 475–1151* (New Haven, CT, and London, 1987).

Cubitt, C., *Anglo-Saxon Church Councils, c.650–c.850*, Studies in the Early History of Britain (London, 1995).

Cumont, F., *Catalogue des sculptures et inscriptions antiques (Monuments Lapidaires) des Musées Royaux du cinquantenaire* (Brussels, 1913).

Curran, B. A., A. Grafton, P. O. Long, and B. Weiss, *Obelisk: A History* (Cambridge, MA, 2009).

Curran, J. R., *Pagan City and Christian Capital: Rome in the Fourth Century* (Oxford, 2000).

Curzi, G., 'Mutual Identities: The Construction of the Figure of the Pope and the Emperor in the Carolingian Age: Historical Perspectives', in C. D'Alberto, ed., *Imago Papae: Le pape en image du Moyen Âge à l'époque contemporaine* (Rome, 2020), 61–8.

Dangelfort, P., *Sainte Pétronille, fille de St. Pierre, patronne et auxiliatrice de la France.* (Avignon, 1911).

Daniel, G., *Histoire de France, depuis l'établissement de la monarchie françoise dans les Gaules*, i: *486–768* (Paris, 1729).

Davies, G. and E. Townsend, eds, *A Reservoir of Ideas: Essays in Honour of Paul Williamson* (London, 2017).

Davies, W. and P. Fouracre, eds, *The Languages of Gift in the Early Middle Ages* (Cambridge, 2010).

Davis, R., tr., *The Book of Pontiffs (Liber Pontificalis): The Ancient Biographies of the First Ninety Roman Bishops to AD 715*, Translated Texts for Historians, 6 (Liverpool, 1989).

Davis, R., tr., *The Lives of the Eighth-Century Popes (Liber Pontificalis)*, Translated Texts for Historians, 13 (Liverpool, 1992).

Davis, R., tr., *The Lives of the Ninth-Century Popes (Liber Pontificalis)*, Translated Texts for Historians, 20 (Liverpool, 1995).

Davis-Weyer, C. 'Die Mosaiken Leos III und die Anfänge der Karolingischen Renaissance in Rom', *Zeitschrift für Kunstgeschichte*, 29 (1966), 111–32.

Davis-Weyer, C., tr., *Early Medieval Art, 300–1150: Sources and Documents* (Toronto, ON, 1986).

De Maio, R., ed., *Baronio e l'arte. Atti del convegno internazionale di studi. Sora 10–13 ottobre 1984*, Fonti e studi Baroniani, 2 (Sora, 1985).

De Nuccio, M. and L. Ungaro, eds, *I Marmi colorati della Roma imperiali* (Venice, 2002).

De Rossi, G. B., *Inscriptiones Christianae Urbis Romae septimo saeculo antiquiores*, 2 vols (Rome, 1861–88).

De Rossi, G. B., *La Roma sotterranea cristiana*, 3 vols (Rome, 1864–77).

De Rossi, G. B., 'L'inscription du tombeau d'Hadrien I', *Mélanges d'archéologie et d'histoire l'École française de Rome*, 8 (1888), 478–501.

De Rubeis, F., 'Epigrafi a Roma dall'età classica all'alto medioevo', in M. S. Arena, P. Delogu, L. Paroli, M. Ricci, L. Saguì, and L. Venditelli, eds, *Roma dall'antichità al Medioevo: archeologia e storia nel Museo nationale romana, Crypta Balbi*, 2 vols (Rome, 2001), i, 104–21.

De Rubeis, F., '*Verba volant, scripta manent*. Epigrafia e fama', in I. Lori Sanfilippo and A. Rigoni, eds, *Fama e* Publica Vox *nel Medioevo*, Atti del convegno di studio svoltosi in occasione della XXI edizione del Premio internazionale Ascoli Piceno, Palzzo dei Capitani, 3–5 dicembre, 2009 (Rome, 2011), 191–210.

Del Lungo, S., *Roma in età carolingia e gli scritti dell'anonimo augiense*, Società Romana di Storia Patria, 48 (Rome, 2004).

Delcambre, B. and J. L. Pingot, *Hastiere–Dinant: Carte géologique de Wallonie, Notice Explicative* (Namur, n.d.).

Della Schiava, F., 'Per la storia della basilica Vaticana nel '500: una nuova silloge di Tiberio Alfarano a Catania', *Italia Medioevale e Umanistica*, 48 (2007), 257–82.

Della Schiava, F., '"Sicuti traditum est a maioribus" Maffeo Vegio antiquario tra fonti classiche e medievali', *Aevum*, 84 (2010), 617–39.

Délisle, L., 'Notice sur un manuscript de l'église de lyon au temps de Charlemagne', *Tiré de notice et extraits des manuscrits de la bibliothèque nationale et autres bibliothèques*, 35 (Paris, 1898), 838–42.

Délisle, L. 'Notice sur un manuscript de l'église de Lyon au temps de Charlemagne', *Tiré de notice et extraits des manuscrits de la bibliothèque nationale et autres bibliothèques*, 35 (Paris, 1898), 422–31.

Delogu, P., 'Lombard and Carolingian Italy', in R. McKitterick, ed., *New Cambridge Medieval History*, ii: *c.700–c.900* (Cambridge, 1995), 290–319.

Deman, A. and M.-T. Raepsaet-Charlier, *Nouvelle recueil des Inscriptions latines de Belgique* (Brussels, 2002).

Denoël, C., *Les Évangiles de St.-Riquier: Un manuscript pour Charlemagne*, Art de l'enluminure, 46 (Dijon 2013).

Denzinger, G., *Die Handschriften der Hofschule Karls des Großen. Studien zu ihrer Ornamentik* (Langwarden, 2001).

Deshman, R., *The Benedictional of Æthelwold*, Studies in Manuscript Illumination (Princeton, NJ, 1995).

Despy, G., 'Henri IV et la fondation du chapitre de Sclayn', in *Mélanges Félix Rousseau: Études sur l'histoire du pays mosan au moyen age* (Brussels, 1958), 221–36.

Dessau, H., *Inscriptiones latinae selectae* (Berlin, 1892–1916).

Dey, H. W., *The Aurelian Wall and the Refashioning of Imperial Rome, AD 271–855* (Cambridge, 2011).

Díaz y Díaz, M. C., *Manuscritos visigóticos del sur de la Península*, Ensayo de distribución regional, Universidad de Sevilla, Historia y Geografía, 11 (Sevilla 1995).

Diehl, E., ed., *Inscriptiones Latinae*, Tabula in usum scholarum, 4 (Bonn, 1912).

Dierkens, A., ed., *Mosa Nostra. La Meuse mérovingienne de Verdun à Maastricht Ve–VIIIe siècles* (Namur, 1999).

Diesenberger, M. and H. Wolfram, 'Arn und Alkuin 790 bis 804: zwei Freund und ihre Schriften', in M. Niederkorn-Bruck and A. Scharer, eds, *Erzbischof Arn von Salzburg*, Veröffentlichungen des Instituts für Österreichische Geschichtsforschung (Munich, 2004), 81–106.

Ditchfield, S., *Liturgy, Sanctity and History in Tridentine Italy: Pietro Maria Campi and the Preservation of the Particular*, Cambridge Studies in Italian History and Culture, (Cambridge, 1995).

Divjak, J. and W. Wischmeyer, eds, *Das Kalenderhandbuch von 354*: i, *Der Bildteil des Chronographen*, ii, Der Texteil, Listen der Verwaltung (Vienna, 2014).

Dodge, H. and B. Ward-Perkins, eds, *Marble in Antiquity: The Collected Papers of J. B. Ward-Perkins*, Archaeological Monographs of the British School at Rome, 6 (London, 1992).

D'Onofrio, M. ed., *La committenza artistica dei papi a Roma nel Medioevo* (Rome, 2016).

D'Onofrio, M. 'Leone III (795–816)', in M. D'Onofrio, ed., *La committenza artistica dei papi a Roma nel Medioevo* (Rome, 2016), 213–18.

Dooven, P. den, 'Histoire de la Marbrerie antique de Theux et les tombeaux des la Marck dans l'Eifel', *Bulletin Société Verviétoise d'Archéologie et d'Histoire*, 53 (1966), 115–55.

Doyle, E. G., ed., *Sedulius Scottus: On Christian Rulers and the Poems*, Medieval and Renaissance Texts and Studies, 17 (Binghamton, NY, 1983).

Drijvers, J. W., 'Helena Augusta and the City of Rome', in M. Verhoeven, L. Bosman, and H. van Asperen, eds, *Monuments and Memory: Christian Cult Buildings and Constructions of the Past: Essays in Honour of Sible de Blaauw* (Turnhout, 2016), 147–55.

Du Cange, C., *Glossarium Mediae et Infimae Latinitatis*, 10 vols (Niort and London, 1883–7).

Du Chesne, A. [Andreas Quercetanus], *B. Flacci Albini sive Alchuuini abbatis, Karoli Magni Regis ac Imperatoris, magistri Opera quae hactenus reperiri potuerunt: nonvlla auctis et emendatius pleràque num primum ex Codd. MSS. edita* (Paris, 1617).

Duchesne, L., *Le Liber Pontificalis. Texte, introduction et commentaire*, 2 vols (Paris, 1886–92).

Duchesne, L., *Scripta minora. Etudes de topographie romaine et d géographie ecclésiastique* (Rome, 1913).

Dufresne, D., *Les Cryptes Vaticanes* (Paris and Rome, 1902).

Dutton, P. E., *Carolingian Civilization: A Reader* (Peterborough, ON, 1993).

Dutton, P. E., *Charlemagne's Courtier: The Complete Einhard*, Readings in Medieval Civilizations and Cultures, 2 (Peterborough, ON, 1998).

Ehrenberg, V. and A. H. M. Jones, *Documents Illustrating the Reign of Augustus and Tiberius*, 2nd edn (Oxford, 1976).

Ehrle, F. and H. Egger, *Piante e vedute di Roma e del Vaticano dal 1300 al 1676*, Studi e documenti per la storia del Palazzo Apostolico Vaticano, i: Tavole (Vatican City, 1956).

Ekonomou, A. J., *Byzantine Rome and the Greek Popes: Eastern Influences on Rome and the Papacy from Gregory the Great to Zacharias, AD 590–752* (Lanham, MD, 2007).

Elbern, V. H., 'Zum Justinuskreuz im Schatz von Sankt Peter zu Rom', *Jahrbuch der Berliner Museen*, 6 (1964), 24–38.

Embach, M., *Das Ada-Evangeliar (StB Trier, Hs 22). Ein Hauptwerk der Hofschule Karls des Großen*, Kostbarkeiten der Stadtbibliothek Trier, 2 (Trier, 2018).

Embach, M., 'Das Ada-Evangeliar. Kodex und Einband (Stadtbibliothek Trier, HS 22)', in M. Embach, C. Moulin, and H. Wolter-von dem Knesebeck, eds, *Die Handschriften der Hofschule Kaiser Karls des Grossen. Individuelle Gestalt und europäisches Kulturerbe* (Trier, 2019), 69–95.

Embach, M., C. Moulin and H. Wolter-von dem Knesebeck, eds, *Die Handschriften der Hofschule Kaiser Karls des Grossen. Individuelle Gestalt und europäisches Kulturerbe* (Trier, 2019).

Emerick, J., 'Charlemagne: A New Constantine?', in M. S. Bjornlie, ed., *The Life and Legacy of Constantine: Traditions through the Ages* (London and New York, NY, 2017), 133–61.

Emerton, E., tr., *The Letters of Saint Boniface*, Records of Civilization. Sources and Studies, 31 (New York, NY, 1940).

Espelo, D. B. van, 'A Testimony of Carolingian Rule? The *Codex epistolaris carolinus*, Its Historical Context and the Meaning of *imperium*', *Early Medieval Europe*, 21 (2013), 254–82.

Espelo, D. B. van, 'Rulers, Popes and Bishops: The Historical Context of the Ninth-Century Cologne *Codex Carolinus* Manuscript (Codex Vindobonensis 449)', in R. Meens et al., eds, *Religious Franks: Religion and Power in the Frankish Kingdoms: Studies in Honour of Mayke de Jong* (Manchester, 2016), 455–71.

Everett, N., *Literacy in Lombard Italy, c.568–714* (Cambridge, 2003).

Ewig, E., 'The Papacy's Alienation from Byzantium and the Rapprochement with the Franks', in H. Jedin and D. Dolan, eds, *The Church in the Age of Feudalism* (New York, NY, 1969), 3–25.

Fabre, G., M. Mayer, and I. Rodà, eds, *Inscriptions Romaines de Catalogne*, iii: *Gérone*, Publications du Centre Pierre Paris, 22 (Paris, 1991).

Falkenstein, L., *Der 'Lateran' der karolingischen Pfalz zu Aachen*, Kölner Historische Abhandlungen, 13 (Cologne, 1966).

Fant, J. C., 'Ideology, Gift, and Trade: A Distribution Model for the Roman Imperial Marbles', in W. V. Harris, ed., *The Inscribed Economy: Production and Distribution in the Roman Empire in the Light of 'instrumentum domesticum'*, Journal of Roman Archaeology Supplementary Series, 6 (Ann Arbor, MI, 1993), 145–70.

Favreau, R., *Épigraphie Médiévale*. L'atelier du médiéviste, 5 (Turnhout, 1997).

Federici, V., *Sainte-Marie Antique. Atlas: Album épigraphique. Supplément au chapitre: Épigraphie de l'Église Sainte-Marie-Antique* (Rome, 1911).

Ferrari, G., *Early Roman Monasteries: Notes for the History of the Monasteries and Convents at Rome from the V through the X Century*, Studi di antichità cristiana, 23 (Vatican City, 1957).

Ferrua, A., *Epigrammata Damasiana*, Sussidi allo studio delle antichità cristiane, 2 (Vatican City, 1942).

Fichtenau, H., 'Abt Richbod und die Annales Laureshamenses', *Beiträge zur Geschichte des Klosters Lorsch*, Geschichtsblätter für den Kreis Berstrasse, Sonderband 4 (Lorsch, 1978), 277–301.

Fichtenau, H., 'Karl der Grosse und des Kaisertum', *Mitteleilungen des Instituts für Österreichische Geschichtsforschung*, 61 (1953), 257–334.

Filippi, G., *Indice della raccolta epigrafica di San Paolo fuori le Mura*. Inscriptiones Sanctae Sedis, 6 vols (Vatican City, 1998–2011).

Firey, A., 'Mutating Monsters: Approaches to "Living Texts" of the Carolingian Era', *Digital Proceedings of the Lawrence J. Schoenberg Symposium on Manuscript Studies in the Digital Age*, 2 (2010), 1–14.

Fischer, B., 'Der Text des Quedlinburger Evangeliars', in P. McGurk and F. Mütherich, eds, *Das Quedlinburger Evangeliar. Das Samuhel-Evangeliar aus dem Quedlinburger Dom* (Munich, 1991), 35–41.

Foffano, T., 'Il *De rebus antiquis memorabilibus Basilice Sancti Petri Rome* di Maffeo Vegio e i primordi dell'archeologia cristiana', in L. Secchi Tarugi, ed., *Il sacro nel Rinascimento*. Atti del XII convegno internazionale (Chianciano-Pienza, 17–20 July 2000) (Florence, 2002), 719–29.

Foot, S., 'Anglo-Saxon "Purgatory"', in P. D. Clarke and T. Claydon, eds, *The Church, The Afterlife and the Fate of the Soul*, Studies in Church History, 45 (Woodbridge, 2009), 87–96.

Fornaseri, M., L. Lazzarini, P. Pensabenee, M. Preite Martinez, and B. Turi. '"Lapis Niger" and Other Black Limestones Used in Antiquity', in Y. Maniatis, N. Hertz, and Y. Basiakos, eds, *The Study of Marble and other Stones used in Antiquity*, Asmosia III Athens: Transactions of the 3rd International Symposium of the Association for the Study of Marble and other Stones used in Antiquity (London, 1995), 235–40.

Forster, F., *Beati Flacci Albini seu Alcuini Abbatis Caroli Magni Regis ac Imperatoris, Magistri. Opera. Post primam editionem a viro clarissimo D. Andrea Quercetano, de novo collecta, multis locis emendata, et opusculis primum repertis plurimum aucta, variisque modis illustrate*, 2 vols (Regensburg, 1777).

Forsyth, G. H., 'The Transept of Old St. Peter's at Rome', in K. Weitzmann, ed., *Late Classical and Mediaeval Studies in Honor of Albert Mathias Friend, Jr* (Princeton, NJ, 1955), 56–70.

Fouracre, P., *The Age of Charles Martel* (Harlow, 2000).

Fouracre, P., *Eternal Light and Earthly Concerns: Belief and the Shaping of Medieval Society* (Manchester, 2021).

Fox, Y., *Power and Religion in Merovingian Gaul: Columbanian Monasticism and the Frankish Elites*, Cambridge Studies in Medieval Life and Thought, 4th ser. (Cambridge, 2014).

Franzoni, C., 'Diploma of Gregory II Referring to the Donation of Olive Trees for the Supply of Oil to the Lamps of the Old Basilica (711–730)', in *BSPV* II.ii: *Notes*, 493–4.

Franzoni, C., 'Epitaph of Hadrian I (795)', in *BSPV*, II.ii: *Notes*, 494–6.

Franzoni, C., 'Inscription with the Bull *Antiquiorum Habet Fida Relatio* Regarding the Jubilee of Boniface VIII (22 February 1300)', in *BSPV*, II.ii: *Notes*, 496–7.

Freeman, A., *Theodulf of Orléans: Charlemagne's Spokesman against the Second Council of Nicaea* (Aldershot, 2003).

Freeman, A. and P. Meyvaert, 'The Meaning of Theodulf's Apse at Germigny-des-Prés', *Gesta*, 40 (2001), 125–39.

Frei-Stolba, R., 'Belgique', *Année Épigraphique*, 2002 (2005), 357–65.

Freiburg, J., 'The Lateran Patronage of Gregory XIII and the Holy Year 1575', *Zeitschrift für Kunstgeschichte*, 57 (1991), 66–87.

Fried, J., *Donation of Constantine and Constitutum Constantini: The Misinterpretation of a Fiction and Its Original Meaning* (Berlin, 2007).

Friggeri, R., *The Epigraphic Collection of the Museo Nazionale Romano at the Baths of Diocletian* (Milan, 2001).

Frommel, C. L., *Baldassare Peruzzi als Maler und Zeichner*, Römischen Jahrbuch für Kunstgeschichte, Beiheft, 9 (Vienna and Munich, 1967–8).

Frommel, C. L., 'Die Peterskirche unter Papst Julius II. im lichter neuer Dokumente', *Römisches Jahrbuch für Kunstgeschichte*, 16 (1976), 57–136.

Frommel, C. L., 'S. Pietro. Storia della sua costruzione', in C. L. Frommel, S. Ray, and M. Tafuri, eds, *Raffaello architetto* (Milan, 1984), 241–310.

Frommel, C. L., 'St. Peter's: The Early History', in H. A. Millon and V. Magnago Lampugnani, eds, *The Renaissance: From Brunelleschi to Michelangelo: The Representation of Architecture* (London, 1994), 398–423.

Frommel, C. L. and N. Adams, eds, *The Architectural Drawings of Antonio da Sangallo the Younger and His Circle*, 2 vols (New York, NY, 2000).

Frommel, C. L. and M. Winner, eds, *'Il se rendit en Italie': Études offertes à André Chastel* (Rome, 1987).

Frothingham, A. L., 'Une mosaïque Constantinienne inconnue a Saint-Pierre de Rome', *Revue Archéologique*, 3rd ser., 1 (1883), 68–72.

Fuhrmann, H., 'Das frühmittelalterliche Papsttum und die konstantinische Schenkung. Meditationen über ein unausgeführtes Thema', in *I problemi dell'Occidente nel secolo VIII*, SSCI, 20 (Spoleto, 1973), 257–92.

Galinsky, K. and K. Lapatin, eds, *Cultural Memories in the Roman Empire* (Los Angeles, CA, 2015).

Gameson, R., ed., *The Cambridge History of the Book in Britain*, i: *c.400–1100* (Cambridge, 2012).

Gameson, R. 'Script at Wearmouth and Jarrow', in C. Breay and J. Story, eds, *Manuscripts in the Anglo-Saxon Kingdoms: Cultures and Connections* (Dublin, 2020), 28–44.

Gani, M., 'Plaque with Inscription of Paul V', in *BSPV*, II.ii: *Notes*, 739.

Gani, M., 'Rota porphiretica', in *BSPV*, II.ii: *Notes*, 741.

Gantner, C. and W. Pohl, eds, *After Charlemagne: Carolingian Italy and Its Rulers* (Cambridge, 2021).

Gantz, T. N., '*Lapis Niger*: The Tomb of Romulus', *La Parola del Passato. Rivista di Studi Antichi*, 29 (1974), 350–61.

Ganz, D., '"Roman Books" Reconsidered: The Theology of Carolingian Display Script', in J. M. H. Smith, ed., *Early Medieval Rome and the Christian West: Essays in Honour of Donald Bullough*, The Medieval Mediterranean, 28 (Leiden, 2000), 297–315.

Ganz, D., 'The Scripts of the Court Group Manuscripts', in M. Embach, C. Moulin, and H. Wolter-von dem Knesebeck, eds, *Die Handschriften der Hofschule Kaiser Karls des Grossen. Individuelle Gestalt und europäisches Kulturerbe* (Trier, 2019), 297–314.

Garipzanov, I. H., 'Metamorphoses of the Early Medieval Signum of a Ruler in the Carolingian World', *Early Medieval Europe*, 14 (2006), 419–64.

Garipzanov, I. H., 'Regensburg, Wandalgarius, and the *novi denarii*: Charlemagne's Monetary Reform Revisited', *Early Medieval Europe*, 24 (2016), 58–73.

Garipzanov, I. H., *The Symbolic Language of Authority in the Carolingian World (c.751–877)* (Leiden, 2008).

Garrison, M., 'The Library of Alcuin's York', in R. Gameson, ed., *The Cambridge History of the Book in Britain*, i: *c.400–1100* (Cambridge, 2012), 633–64.

Garrison, M., 'The Social World of Alcuin: Nicknames at York and the Carolingian Court', in L. Houwen and A. A. MacDonald, eds, *Alcuin of York: Scholar at the Carolingian Court* (Groningen, 1998), 59–79.

Gatz, E. ed., *Hundert Jahre Deutsches Priesterkolleg beim Campo Santo Teutonico 1876–1976. Beiträge zu seiner Geschichte*, Römische Quartalschrift für christliche Altertumskunde und Kirchengeschichte, 35 (Rome, 1977).

Geary, P. J., *Furta Sacra: Thefts of Relics in the Central Middle Ages* (Princeton, NJ, 1990).

Geertman, H., *More Veterum. Il Liber Pontificalis e gli edifici ecclesiastici di Roma nella Tarda Antichita e nell'alto Medioevo*. Archaeologica Traiectina (Groningen, 1975).

Geertman, H., ed., *Atti del Colloquio Internazionale Il* Liber Pontificalis *e la storia materiale* (Roma, 21–22 febbraio 2002), Mededelingen van het Nederlands Instituut te Rome, 60–1 (Rome, 2003).

Geertman, H., 'Gli spostamenti di testo nella vita di Adriano I', in H. Geertman, ed., *Atti del Colloquio Internazionale Il* Liber Pontificalis *e la storia materiale* (Roma, 21–22 febbraio 2002), Mededelingen van het Nederlands Instituut te Rome, 60–1 (Rome, 2003), 155–66.

Gem, R., 'From Constantine to Constans: The Chronology of the Construction of Saint Peter's Basilica', *OSPR*, 35–64.

Gem, R., 'The Vatican Rotunda: A Severan Monument and its Early History, *c*.200 to 500', *Journal of the British Archaeological Association*, 85 (2005), 1–45.

Gerberding, R. A., *The Rise of the Carolingians and the 'Liber Historiae Francorum'*, (Oxford, 1987).

Geyer, P. and O. Cuntz, eds, *Itineraria et alia Geographica*, 2 vols, Corpus Christianorum Series Latina, 175–6 (Turnhout, 1965).

Giersiepen, H., ed., *Die Inschriften des Aachener Doms*, Die Deutschen Inschriften 31, Düsseldorfer Reihe, 1 (Wiesbaden, 1992).

Glass, R., 'Filarete's Renovation of the Porta Argentea at Old St. Peter's', in *OSPR*, 348–70.

Glauche, G., *Schullektüre im Mittelalter. Entstehung und Wandlungen des Lektürkanons bis 1200*, Münchener Beiträge zur Mediävistik und Renaissance-Forschung, 5 (Munich, 1970).

Glenisson, J. and C. Sirat, eds, *La Paléographie Hébraïque Médiévale*, Colloques Internationaux du CNRS, 547 (Paris, 1974).

Gnoli, R., *Marmora Romana*, rev. edn (Rome, 1988).

Godman, P., *Poets and Emperors: Frankish Politics and Carolingian Poetry* (Oxford, 1987).

Godman, P., J. Jarnut, and P. Johanna, eds, *Am Vorabend der Kaiserkrönung: das Epos "Karolus magnus et Leo papa" und der papstbesuch in Paderborn 799* (Berlin, 2002).

Godman, P., tr., *Poetry of the Carolingian Renaissance* (London, 1985).

Goedicke, C., 'Datierung von Ziegelfragmenten und Mörtel aus der Pfalzkapelle Aachen mittels optisch stimulierter Lumineszenz', in U. Heckner and E. M. Beckmann, eds, *Die karolingische Pfalzkapelle in Aachen: Material, Bautechnik, Restauierung* (Worms, 2012), 297–302.

Goetz, H. W., *Translatio imperii: Ein Beitrag zur Geschichte des Geschichtsdenkens und der politischen Theorien im Mittelater und in der frühen Neuzeit* (Tübingen, 1958).

Goldberg, E. J., '"Regina nitens sanctissima Hemma": Queen Emma (827–876), Bishop Witgar of Augsburg, and the Witgar-belt', in B. Weiler and S. MacLean, eds, *Representations of Power in Medieval Germany 800–1500* (Turnhout, 2006), 57–95.

Goodson, C., '"To be the daughter of Saint Peter": S. Petronilla and the Forging of the Franco-Papal Alliance', in V. West-Harling, ed., *Three Empires, Three Cities: Identity, Material Culture and Legitimacy in Venice, Ravenna and Rome, 750–1000* (Turnhout, 2015), 159–82.

Goodson, C. and J. L. Nelson, 'The Roman Contexts of the "Donation of Constantine". Review Article', *Early Medieval Europe*, 18.4 (2010), 446–67.

Goris, J.-A. and G. Marlier, *Albrecht Dürer: Diary of his Journey to the Netherlands, 1520–1521* (London, 1971).

Gramaccini, N., 'Die Karolingischen Großbronzen. Brüche und Kontinuitäten in der Werkstoffikonographie', *Anzeiger des Germanischen Nationalmuseums und Berichte aus dem Forschungsinstitut für Realienkunde*, 70 (1995), 130–40.

Granger-Taylor, H., 'The Weft-Patterned Silks and their Braid: The Remains of an Anglo-Saxon Dalmatic of *c*.800', in G. Bonner, C. Stancliffe, and D. Rollason, eds, *St. Cuthbert: His Cult and His Community to AD 1200* (Woodbridge, 1989), 303–27.

Gray, N., *A History of Lettering: Creative Experiment and Letter Identity* (Oxford, 1986).

Gray, N., 'The Filocalian Letter', *Papers of the British School at Rome*, 24 (1956), 5–13.

Gray, N., 'The Palaeography of Latin Inscriptions in the 8th, 9th and 10th Centuries in Italy', *Papers of the British School at Rome*, 16 (1948), 38–162.

Green, D. H. and F. Siegmund, eds, *The Continental Saxons from the Migration Period to the Tenth Century: An Ethnographic Perspective*, Studies in Historical Archaeoethnology (Rochester, NY, 2003).

Greenhalgh, M., *The Survival of Roman Antiquities in the Middle Ages* (London, 1989).

Gregorovius, F., *The Tombs of the Popes: Landmarks in Papal History*, tr. R. W. Seton-Watson (London, 1903).

Grierson P. and M. A. S. Blackburn, *Medieval European Coinage with a Catalogue of the Coins in the Fitzwilliam Museum, Cambridge*, i: *The Early Middle Ages (5th–10th Centuries)* (Cambridge, 1986).

Grimme, E. G., *Der Dom zu Aachen: Architektur und Ausstattung* (Aachen, 1994).

Groessens, É. 'L'exploitation et l'emploi du marbre noir de Dinant sous "Ancien Régime"', in J. Lorenz, ed., *Carrières et constructions en France et dans les pays limitrophes*, III, 119e Congrès national des sociétés historiques scientifiques, 1994 Amiens (Paris, 1996), 73–87.

Groessens, É., 'L'industrie du marbre en Belgique', *Mémoires de l'Institut Géologique de l'Université de Louvain*, 31 (1981), 219–53.

Grosse, R., 'La Collection de formules de Saint-Denis (Bibl. nat. Fr., lat. 2777): un dossier controversé', *Bibliothèque de l'École des chartes*, 172 (2014), 185–97.

Grosse, R. and M. Sot, eds, *Charlemagne: les temps, les espaces, les hommes: Construction et Déconstruction d'un règne*, Collection Haut Moyen Âge, 34 (Turnhout, 2018).

Grüneisen, W. de, *Sainte Marie Antique avec le concours de Huelsen, Giorgis, Federici, David* (Rome, 1911).

Guarducci, M., *La Cattedra di San Pietro nella scienza e nelle fede* (Rome, 1982).

Guicciardini, L. and J. H. McGregor, *The Sack of Rome* (New York, NY, 1993).

Guiliano, Z., *The Homiliary of Paul the Deacon: Religious and Cultural Reform in Carolingian Europe*, Sermo 16 (Turnhout, 2021).

Guillaume, J., 'François Ier en Charlemagne. Réflexions sur un portrait', in C. L. Frommel and M. Winner, eds, *'Il se rendit en Italie': Études Offertes À André Chastel* (Rome, 1987), 159–62.

Haag, S. and F. Kirchweger, eds, *Das Krönungsevangeliar des Heiligen Römischen Reiches* (Vienna, 2014).

Hack, A. T., *Codex Carolinus: Päpstliche Epistolograpie im 8. Jahrhundert*, Päpste und Papsttum, 35, 2 vols (Stuttgart, 2007).

Hack, A. T., 'Das Zeremoniell des Papstempfangs 799 in Paderborn', in SW, *799*, iii, 19–33.

Hahn, C. 'Collector and Saint: Queen Radegund and Her Devotion to the Relic of the True Cross', *Word and Image*, 22 (2006), 268–74.

Hallenbeck, J. T., 'The Roman-Byzantine Reconciliation of 728: Genesis and Significance', *Byzantinische Zeitschrift*, 74 (1981), 29–41.

Hamburger, J. F., *St John the Divine: The Deified Evangelist in Medieval Art and Theology* (Berkeley, CA, 2003).

Hamesse, J., ed., *Roma, magistra mundi: itineraria culturae medievalis. Mélange offerts au Père L. E. Boyle à l'occasion de son 75e anniversaire*, 3 vols (Louvain-la-Neuve, 1998).

Hammer, C. I., 'Christmas Day 800: Charles the Younger, Alcuin and the Frankish Royal Succession', *English Historical Review*, 127 (2012), 1–23.

Harmon, J. A., *Codicology of the Court School of Charlemagne: Gospel Book Production, Illumination, and Emphasized Script* (Frankfurt am Main and New York, NY, 1984).

Hartley, B. and J. Wacher, eds, *Rome and Her Northern Provinces: Papers Presented to Sheppard Frere in Honour of his Retirement from the Chair of The Archaeology of the Roman Empire. University of Oxford, 1983* (Gloucester, 1983).

Hartmann, F., *Hadrian I (772–795). Frühmittelalterliches Adelspapsttum und die lösung Roms vom Byzantinischen Kaiser*, Päpste und Papsttum, 34 (Stuttgart, 2006).

Hartmann, F. and T. B. Orth-Müller, eds, *Codex Epistolaris Carolinus: Frühmittelalterlich Papstbriefe an die Karolingerherrscher* (Darmstadt, 2017).

Hausmann, A., '"…Inque pares numeros omnia convenient…": Der Bauplan der Aachener Palastkapelle', in P. L. Butzer, M. Kerner, and W. Oberschelp, eds, *Karl der Grosse und sein Nachwirken* (Turnhout, 1997), 321–36.

Heckner, U., 'Wie sah der karolingische Fußboden in der Aachener Pfalzkapelle aus?', *Jahrbuch der Rheinischen denkmalpflege*, 42 (2011), 29–39.

Heckner, U., 'Der Tempel Salomos in Aachen – Datierung und geometrischer Entwurf der karolingischen Pfalzkapelle', in U. Heckner and E.-M. Beckmann, eds, *Die karolingische Pfalzkapelle in Aachen: Material, Bautechnik, Restaurierung* (Worms, 2012), 25–62.

Heckner, U. and E.-M. Beckmann, eds, *Die karolingische Pfalzkaple in Aachen: Material, Bautechnick, Restaurierung*, Arbeitsheft der rheinischen Denkmalpflege, 78 (Karlsruhe, 2012).

Heckner, U. and C. Schaab, 'Baumaterial, Bautechnik und Bauausführung der Aachener Pfalzkapelle', in U. Heckner and E.-M. Beckmann, eds, *Die karolingische Pfalzkaplle in Aachen: Material, Bautechnick, Restaurierung*, Arbeitsheft der rheinischen Denkmalpflege, 78 (Karlsruhe, 2012), 117–228.

Hegener, N., '"VIVIT POST FVUNERA VIRTUS" Albrecht von Brandenburg, seine römischen Prokuratoren und Francesco Salviati in er Markgrafenkappel von S. Maria dell'Anima', in M. Matheus, ed., *S. Maria dell'Anima: Zur Geschichte einer 'deutschen' Stiftung in Rom*, Bibliothek des Deutschen Historischen Instituts in Rom, 121 (Berlin, 2010), 137–214.

Heitz, C., 'L'architettura dell'età Carolingia in relazione alla liturgica sacra', in *Culto Cristiano e politica imperiale carolingia: 9–12 ottobre 1977*, Convegni del centro di studi sulla spiritualità medieval, 18 (Todi, 1979), 339–62.

Heitz, C., 'Vitruve et l'architecture du haut Moyen Age', in *La cultura antica nell'Occidente Latino dal VII all'XI secolo*, SSCI, 22 (1975), 725–57.

Hen, Y., *The Royal Patronage of Liturgy in Frankish Gaul to the Death of Charles the Bald (877)* (London, 2011).

Hendrix, S. H. *Luther and the Papacy: Stages in a Reformation Conflict* (Philadelphia, PA, 1981).

Herbers, K., 'Konkurrenz und Gegnerschaft. "Gegenpäpste" im 8. und 9. Jahrhundert', in H. Müller and B. Hotz, eds, *Gegenpäpste: Eine unerwünschtes mittelalterliches Phänomen* (Vienna, 2012), 55–70.

Herklotz, I., 'Francesco Barberini, Nicolò Alemanni, and the Lateran Triclinium of Leo III: An Episode in Restoration and Seicento Medieval Studies', *Memoires of the American Academy in Rome*, 40 (1995), 175–96.

Herklotz, I., '*Historia Sacra* und mittelalterliche Kunst während der zweiten Hälfte des 16. Jahrhunderts in Rom', in R. De Maio, ed., *Baronio e l'Arte. Atti del convegno internazionale di studi. Sora 10–13 ottobre 1984* (Sora, 1985), 21–72.

Herren, M. W., 'The *De Imagine Tetrici* of Walahfrid Strabo: Edition and Translation', *Journal of Medieval Latin*, 1 (1991), 118–39.

Hesbert, R. J., ed., *Antiphonale Missarum Sextuplex* (Brussels, 1935).

Hibbard, H., *Carlo Maderno and Roman Architecture 1580–1630* (London, 1971).

Hiscock, N., 'The Aachen Chapel: A Model of Salvation', in P. L. Butzer and D. Lohrmann, eds, *Science in Western and Eastern Civilization in Carolingian Times* (Basel, 1993), 115–26.

Hodges, R., *Dark Age Economics: The Origin of Towns and Trade, AD 600–1000* (London, 1982).

Hodges, R., *The Anglo-Saxon Achievement* (London, 1989).

Holter, K., *Der goldene Psalter, 'Dagulf-Psalter': Vollständige Faksimile-Ausgabe im Originalformat von Codex 1861 Der Österreichischen Nationalbibliothek*, Codices Selecti Phototypice Impressi, 69 (Facsimile) and 69* (Commentarium) (Graz, 1980).

Horst, K. van der and J. H. A. Engelbregt, *Utrecht-Psalter. Vollständige Faksimile-Ausgabe im originalformat der Handschrift 32 aus dem besitz der Bibliotheek der Rijksuniversiteit te Utrecht*, Codices Selecti Phototypice Impressi, 75 (Graz, 1984).

Horst, K. van der, W. Noel, and W. C. M. Wüstefeld, eds, *The Utrecht Psalter in Medieval Art: Picturing the Psalms of David* (London, 1996).

Howitt, P., 'Endogenous Growth Theory', in S. N. Durlauf and L. E. Blume, eds, *Economic Growth* (London, 2010), 68–73.

Howlett, D., 'Two Latin Epitaphs', *Archivvm Latinitatis Medii Aevi (ALMA)*, 67 (2009), 235–47.

Huglo, M., 'Un tonaire du Graduel de la fin du VIIIe Siecle (Paris B. N. lat. 13159)', *Revue Gregorienne* 31 (1952), 176–86, 224–33.

Hülsen, C., 'La pianta di Roma dell'Anonimo Einsidlense', *Dissertazioni della Pontificia Accademia Romana di Archeologia*, 2nd ser., 9 (1907), 379–424.

Hunter Blair, P., 'Some Observations on the *Historia Regum* Attributed to Symeon of Durham', in N. K. Chadwick, ed., *Celt and Saxon: Studies in the Early British Border* (Cambridge, 1963), 63–118.

Iacobini, A., 'Il mosaico del triclinio Lateranense', in M. Andaloro, ed., *Fragmenta picta: affreschi e mosaici staccati del Medioevo romano* (Roma, Castel Sant'Angelo, 15 dicembre 1989–18 febbraio 1990) (Rome, 1989), 189–96.

Innes, M. and R. McKitterick, 'The Writing of History', in R. McKitterick, ed., *Carolingian Culture: Emulation and Innovation* (Cambridge, 1994), 193–202.

Jacks, P., 'A Sacred Meta for Pilgrims in the Holy Year 1575', *Architectura*, 19 (1989), 137–65.

Jacobsen, W., 'Spolien in der karolingischen Architektur', in J. Poeschke, ed., *Antike Spolien in der Architektur des Mittelalters und der Renaissance* (Munich, 1996), 155–77.

Jäggi, C., 'MATER ET CAPUT OMNIUM ECCLESIARUM: Visual Strategies in the Rivalry between San Giovanni in Laterano and San Pietro in Vaticano', in L. Bosman, I. P. Haynes, and P. Liverani, eds, *The Basilica of St John Lateran to 1600* (Cambridge, 2020), 294–317.

Johnson, M. J., *The Roman Imperial Mausoleum in Late Antiquity* (Cambridge, 2009).

Jones, I., 'L'archivio della Fabbrica di San Pietro', in *BSPV*, II.i (*Essays*), 399–407.

Jong, M. de, 'Charlemagne's Church', in J. Story, ed., *Charlemagne: Empire and Society* (Manchester, 2005), 103–35.

Jong, M. de, *In Samuel's Image: Child Oblation in the Early Medieval West* (Leiden, 1996).

Jong, M. de, 'Sacrum palatium et ecclesia: l'authorité religieuse royale sous les Carolingiens (790–840)', *Annales*, 58 (2003), 1234–69.

Jong, M. de and F. Theuws, eds, *Topographies of Power in the Early Middle Ages*, Transformation of the Roman World, 6 (Leiden, 2001).

Jongkees, J. H., *Studies on Old St. Peter's*, Archaeologica Traiectina, 8 (Groningen, 1966).

Kantorowicz, E. H., *The King's Two Bodies: A Study in Mediaeval Political Theology* (Princeton, NJ, 1957).

Kantorowicz, E. H., *Laudes regiae: A Study in Liturgical Acclamations and Mediaeval Ruler Worship*, University of California Publications in History, 33 (Berkeley and Los Angeles, CA, 1958).

Kehr, P., 'Die sognenante karolingische Schenkung von 774', *Historische Zeitschrift*, 70 (1893), 335–441.

Kehr, P. F., *Regesta Pontificum Romanorum. Italia Pontificia*, ii: *Latium* (Berlin, 1907).

Kempers, B., 'Diverging Perspectives – New St. Peter's: Artistic Ambitions, Liturgical Requirements, Financial Limitations and Historical Interpretations', *Mededelingen van het Nederlands Instituut te Rome*, 55 (1996), 213–51.

Kempf, D., *Paul the Deacon. Liber de episcopis Mettensibus. Edition, Translation, and Introduction*, Dallas Medieval Texts and Translations, 19 (Paris, 2013).

Kendall, C., *The Allegory of the Church: Romanesque Portals and their Verse Inscriptions* (Toronto, ON, 1996).

Kendrick, L., *Animating the Letter: The Figurative Embodiment of Writing from Late Antiquity to the Renaissance* (Columbus, OH, 1999).

Kerner, M., ed., *Der verschleierte Karl: Karl der Grosse zwischen Mythos und Wirklichkeit* (Aachen, 1999).

Kéry, L., *Canonical Collections of the Early Middle Ages (ca. 400–1140:, A Bibliographical Guide to the Manuscripts and Literature*, History of Medieval Canon Law (Washington, DC, 1999).

Kessler, H. L. and J. Zacharias, *Rome 1300: On the Path of the Pilgrim* (New Haven, CT, and London, 2000).

Keynes, S., 'King Æthelstan's Books', in M. Lapidge and H. Gneuss, eds, *Learning and Literature in Anglo-Saxon England: Studies Presented to Peter Clemoes on the Occasion of his Sixty-Fifth Birthday* (Cambridge, 1985), 143–201.

Keynes, S., 'The Canterbury Letter-Book: Alcuin and After', in C. Breay and J. Story, eds, *Manuscripts in the Anglo-Saxon Kingdoms: Cultures and Connections* (Dublin, 2021), 119–40.

King, P. D., *Charlemagne Translated Sources* (Kendal, 1987).

Kinney, D., 'Spolia', in W. Tronzo, ed., *St. Peter's in the Vatican* (Cambridge, 2005), 16–47.

Kirschbaum, E., ed., *Lexikon der Christlichen Ikonographie*, 8 vols (Freiburg, 1968–76).

Kitzinger, B. E., *The Cross, the Gospels, and the Work of Art* (Cambridge, 2019).

Klauser, T., *Das römische Capitulare Evangeliorum. Texte und untersuchungen zu seiner ältesten gesichte*, i: *Typen*, Liturgiegeschichtekuche quellen und Forschungen, 28 (Münster, 1935).

Klinkenberg, E., *Compressed Meanings: The Donor's Model in Medieval Art to around 1300* (Turnhout, 2009).

Knight, S., *Historical Scripts from Classical Times to the Renaissance* (New Castle, DE, 2003).

Knopp, G., 'Sanctorum Nomina seriatim. Die Anfänge der Allerheiligenlitanei und ihre Verbindung mid den "Laudes regiae"', *Römische Quartalschrift*, 65 (1970), 185–321.

Koch, W., *Inschriftenpaläographie des abenländischen Mittelalters und der früheren Neuzeit. Früh- und Hochmittelalter*. Oldenbourg Historische Hilfswissenschaften (Vienna and Munich, 2007).

Koehler, W., 'An Illustrated Evangelistary of the Ada School and its Model', *Journal of the Warburg and Courtauld Institutes*, 15 (1952), 48–66.

Koehler, W., *Die karolingischen Miniaturen*, i: *Die Schule von Tours*, 2 vols (Berlin, 1930); ii: Die Hofschule Karls des Grossen (Berlin, 1958); iii.1: Die Gruppe der Wiener Krönungs-Evangeliar; iii.2: Metzer Handschriften (Berlin, 1960).

Koethe, H., 'Zum Mausoleum der weströmischen Dynastie bei Alt-Sankt-Peter', *Römische Mitteilunge*, 46 (1931), 9–26.

Kohlberger-Schaub, T. and A. Schaub, 'Neues zu Bau und Bauplatz der Marienkirche. Die Domgrabung 2007 bis 2011', in F. Pohle, ed., *Karl der Grosse/Charlemagne: Orte der Macht: Essays* (Dresden, 2014), 364–9.

Konnegen, L., 'Stiftmosaikboden (Frament)', in F. Pohle, ed., *Karl der Grosse/Charlemagne: Orte der Macht: Katalog* (Dresden, 2014), 178.

Kramer, R. and C. Gantner, '"Lateran Thinking": Building on the Idea of Rome in the Carolingian Empire', *Viator*, 47.3 (2016), 1–26.

Kraus, T. R., ed., *Aachen von den anfängen bis our gegenwart*, II. *Karolinger—Ottonen—Salier, 767 bis 1137* (Neustadt, 2013).

Krautheimer, R., 'The Building Inscriptions and the Dates of Construction of Old St. Peter's: A Reconsideration', *Römisches Jahrbuch der Bibliotheca Hertziana*, 25 (1989), 1–23.

Krautheimer, R., 'The Carolingian Revival of Early Christian Architecture', *The Art Bulletin* 24 (1942), 1–38, reprinted in his *Studies in Early Christian, Medieval and Renaissance Art* (New York, NY, 1969), 203–56.

Krautheimer, R., 'A Note on the Inscription in the Apse of Old St. Peter's', *Dumbarton Oaks Papers*, 41 (1987), 317–20.

Krautheimer, R., *Rome, Profile of a City, 312–1308* (Princeton, NJ, 1980).

Krautheimer, R., 'Some Drawings of Early Christian Basilicas in Rome: St. Peter's and S. Maria Maggiore', *The Art Bulletin*, 31 (1949), 211–15.

Krautheimer, R., W. Frankl, and S. Corbett, eds, *Corpus basilicarum Christianarum Romae: The Early Christian Basilicas of Rome (IV–IX Cent.)*, 5 vols (Vatican City, 1937–77).

Kreusch, F., 'Im Louvre wiedergefundene Kapitelle und Bronzbasen aus der Pfalzkirche Karls des Grossen zu Aachen', *Cahiers archéologiques fin de l'antiquité et moyen âge*, 18 (1968), 71–98.

Krüger, K. H., 'Neue Beobachtungen zur Datierung von Einhards Karlsvita', *Frühmittelalterliche Studien*, 32 (1998), 124–45.

La Bella, C., A. Lo Bianco, P. Marchetti, N. Parmegiani, S. Petrocchi, A. Pronti, D. Radeglia, and M. Righetti, eds, *Santa Cecilia in Trastevere* (Rome, 2007).

La Rocca, C., ed., *Italy in the Early Middle Ages 476–1000*, The Short Oxford History of Italy (Oxford, 2002).

Lafaurie, J., 'Les monnaies impériales de Charlemagne', *Comptes rendus des séances de l'Académie des Inscriptions et Belles-Lettres*, 122.i (1978), 154–76.

Laffitte, M.-P. and C. Denoël, *Trésors carolingiens: Livres manuscrits de Charlemagne à Charles le Chauve* (Paris, 2007).

Laistner M. L. W. and H. H. King, *A Hand-List of Bede Manuscripts* (Ithaca, NY, 1943).

Lanciani, R., 'L'aula e gli uffici del senato Romano', *Atti della Reale Accademia dei Lincei. Memorie della classe di scienze morali, storiche e filologiche*, 3rd ser., 11 (1882–3), 13–14.

Lanciani, R., *Storia degli scavi di Roma e notizie intorno le collezioni romane di antichità*, 4 vols (Rome, 1902).

Lansford, T., *The Latin Inscriptions of Rome: A Walking Guide* (Baltimore, MD, 2009).

Lanzani, V., *The Vatican Grottoes*, Roma Sacra. Guide to the Churches in the Eternal City, Itineraries, 26–7 (Vatican City, 2003).

Lapidge, M., *The Anglo-Saxon Library* (Oxford, 2006).

Lapidge, M., 'Byrhtferth of Ramsey and the Early Sections of the *Historia Regum* Attributed to Symeon of Durham', *Anglo-Saxon England*, 10 (1982), 97–122.

Lapidge, M., 'The Career of Aldhelm', *Anglo-Saxon England*, 36 (2007), 15–69.

Lapidge, M., *The Roman Martyrs: Introduction, Translations, and Commentary* (Oxford, 2018).

Lapidge, M., 'Some Remnants of Bede's Lost *Liber Epigrammatum*', *English Historical Review*, 90 (1975), 798–820, reprinted in his *Anglo-Latin Literature, 600–899* (London and Rio Grande, 1996), 357–81.

Lapidge, M. and J. L. Rosier, tr., *Aldhelm: The Poetic Works* (Woodbridge, 1985).

Lauer, P. *Le Palais du Latran: étude historique et archéologique* (Paris, 1911).

LeClercq, H., 'Hadrien I (Épitaph de)', in F. Cabrol, ed., *Dictionnaire d'archéologie chrétienne et de liturgie*, 15 vols (Paris, 1924–53), vi.2, cols 1964–7.

Lefebvre, H., *The Production of Space*, tr. D. Nicholson-Smith (Oxford, 1991).

Levison, W., 'Aus Englischen Bibliotheken II', *Neues Archiv*, 35 (1910), 331–431.

Levison, W., *England and the Continent in the Eighth Century* (Oxford, 1946).

Ley, J., 'Warum ist die Aachener Pfalzkirche ein Zentralbau? Der neue Salomonische Tempel als vorbild herrschaftlicher Kirchenstiftung', in H. Müller, C. M. M. Bayer, and M. Kerner, eds, *Die Aachener Marienkirche: Aspekte ihrer Archäologie und frühen Geschichte*, Der Aachener Dom in seiner Geschichte. Quellen und Forschungen, 1 (Regensburg, 2014), 95–110.

Leyser, C., 'The Temptations of Cult: Roman Martyr Piety in the Age of Gregory the Great', *Early Medieval Europe*, 9 (2000), 289–308.

Lindsay, W. M., ed., *Glossaria Latina*, 5 vols (Paris, 1926–31).

Liverani, P., *La topografia antica del Vaticano*. Monumenta Sanctae Sedis (Vatican City, 1999).

Liverani, P., 'Costatino offie il model della basilica sull'arco tronfale', in M. Andaloro, ed., *La pittura medievale a Roma, 312–1431, i: L'orizzonte tardo antico e le nuove immagini, 312–468, Corpus* (Rome, 2006), 90–1.

Liverani, P., 'Old St Peter's and the Emperor Constans? A Debate with G. W. Bowersock', *Journal of Roman Archaeology*, 28 (2015), 485–504.

Liverani, P., 'Osservazioni sul libellus delle donazioni costantine nel Liber Pontificalis' *Athenaeum*, 107 (2019), 169–217.

Liverani, P., 'Pietro e Paolo *Lumina Mundi*: l'iscrizione ICUR 3900 e la fondazione della *Basilia Apostolorum*', *Rendiconti della Pontificia Accademia Romana di Archeologia*, 93 (2021), 217–33.

Liverani, P., 'Saint Peter's, Leo the Great and the Leprosy of Constantine', *Papers of the British School at Rome*, 76 (2008), 155–72.

Lobbedey, U., 'Carolingian Royal Palaces: The State of Research from an Architectural Historian's Viewpoint', in C. Cubitt, ed., *Court Cultures in the Early Middle Ages: The Proceedings of the First Alcuin Conference*, Studies in the Early Middle Ages, 3 (Turnhout, 2003), 131–54.

Logan, A., 'Who Built Old St Peter's. The Evidence of the Inscriptions and Mosaics', *Vigiliae Christianae*, 75 (2020), 43–69.

Lohrmann, D., 'Das geistige Leben in Aachen our Karolingerzeit', in T. R. Kraus, ed., *Aachen von den anfängen bis our gegenwart*, ii: *Karolinger—Ottonen—Salier, 767 bis 1137* (Neustadt, 2013), 409–70.

Lowe, E. A., *English Uncial* (Oxford, 1960).

Loyn, H. R. and J. Percival, tr., *The Reign of Charlemagne: Documents on Carolingian Government and Administration* (London, 1975).

Lucey, S. J., 'Art and Socio-Cultural Identity in Early Medieval Rome: The Patrons of Santa Maria Antiqua', in E. Ó Carragáin and C. L. Neuman de Vegvar, eds, *Roma Felix—Formation and Reflections of Early Medieval Rome* (Aldershot, 2007), 139–59.

Luchterhandt, M., 'Famulus Petri. Karl der Grosse in den romischen Mosaikbildern Leos III', in SW, *799*, iii, 55–70.

Luchterhandt, M., 'Rom und Aachen: Die Karolinger und der päpstliche Hof um 800', in F. Pohle, ed., *Karl der Große/Charlemagne: Orte der Macht* (Aachen, 2014), 104–13.

Maccarrone, M. and D. Rezza, *La cattedra lignea di San Pietro*, Archivum Sancti Petri, Bolletino d'archivio (Vatican City, 2010).

Maffei, G. P., *Degli annali di Gregorio XIII pontefice Massimo*, ed. C. Cocquelines, 2 vols (Rome, 1742).

Mai, A., ed., *Spicilegium Romanum*, 10 vols (Rome, 1839–44).

Mairhofer, D., ed., *Handschriften und Papyri: Wege des Wissens* (Vienna, 2017).

Mairhofer, D., *Medieval Manuscripts from Würzburg in the Bodleian Library, Oxford: A Descriptive Catalogue* (Oxford, 2014).

Mancinelli, F., 'L'Incoronazione di Francesco I nella Stanza dell'Incendio di Borgo', in C. L. Frommel and M. Winner, eds, *'Il se rendit en Italie': Études Offertes à André Chastel* (Rome, 1987), 163–72.

Marazzi, F., 'Aristocrazia e società (seculi VI–XI)', in A. Vauchez, ed., *Roma medievale* (Bari, 2001), 41–69.

Marazzi, F., 'Il conflitto fra Leone III Isaurico e il papato fra il 725 e il 733, e il "definitive" inizio del medioevo a Roma: un'ipotesi in discussione', *Papers of the British School at Rome*, 59 (1991), 231–57.

Marazzi, F., 'Il *Liber Pontificalis* e la fondazione delle Domuscultae', in H. Geertman, ed., *Atti del Colloquio Internazionale Il* Liber Pontificalis *e la storia material* (Roma, 21–22 febbraio 2002), Mededelingen van het Nederlands Instituut te Rome, 60–1 (Rome, 2003), 167–88.

Marazzi, F., *I 'Patrimonia Sanctae Romanae Ecclesiae' nel Lazio (secoli IV–X). Struttura amministrativa e prassi gestionali*, Nuovi studi storici, 37 (Rome, 1998).

Marini, G., *I Papiri Diplomatici* (Rome, 1805).

Martin, T., 'Bemerkungen zur "Epistola de litteris colendis"', *Archiv für Diplomatik*, 31 (1985), 227–72.

Marucchi, O., 'Di una iscrizione storica che può attribuirsi alla Basilica Apostolorum sulla Via Appia', *Nuovo Bullettino di Archeologia Cristiana*, 27 (1921), 61–9.

Masai, F., 'Observations sur le Psautier dit de Charlemagne (Paris, Lat. 13159)', *Scriptorium*, 6 (1952), 299–303.

Maskarinec, M., *City of Saints: Rebuilding Rome in the Early Middle Ages* (Philadelphia, PA, 2018).

Masson, J.-P., *Annalium libri quatvor: quibus res gestae Francorum explicantur. Ad Henricum Tertium Regem Franciae et Poloniae* (Paris, 1578).

Matheus, M. ed., *S. Maria dell'Anima: Zur Geschichte einer 'deutschen' Stiftung in Rom*, Bibliothek des Deutschen Historischen Instituts in Rom, 121 (Berlin, 2010).

Mauskopf Deliyannis, B., 'Charlemagne's Silver Tables: The Ideology of an Imperial Capital', *Early Medieval Europe*, 12 (2003), 159–78.

Mazzotti, M., 'Antiche stoffe liturgiche ravennati', *Felix Ravenna*, 3rd ser., 53.ii (1950), 40–5.

Mazzotti, M., *La basilica di Sant'Appollinare in Classe* (Vatican City, 1954).

McClendon, C. B., *The Origins of Medieval Architecture* (New Haven, CT, and London, 2005).

McClendon, C. B., 'The Revival of *opus sectile* Pavements in Rome and the Vicinity in the Carolingian Period', *Papers of the British School at Rome*, 48 (1980), 157–65.

McCormick, M., *Eternal Victory: Triumphal Rulership in Late Antiquity, Byzantium and the Early Medieval West* (Cambridge, 1986).

McCormick, M., 'The Liturgy of War in the Early Middle Ages', *Viator*, 15 (1984), 1–24.

McCormick, M., *Origins of the European Economy: Community and Commerce, AD 300–900* (Cambridge, 2001).

McEvoy, M. 'The Mausoleum of Honorius: Late Roman Imperial Christianity and the City of Rome in the Fifth Century', in *OSPR*, 119–37.

McGurk, P., *Latin Gospel Books from AD 400 to AD 800* (Amsterdam, 1961).

McGurk, P. and F. Mütherich, eds, *Das Quedlinburger Evangeliar: Das Samuhel-Evangeliar aus dem Quedlinburger Dom* (Munich, 1991).

McKitterick, R., 'Carolingian Bible Production: The Tours Anomaly', in R. Gameson, ed., *The Early Medieval Bible: Its Production, Decoration and Use* (Cambridge, 1994), 53–62.

McKitterick, R., ed., *Carolingian Culture: Emulation and Innovation* (Cambridge, 1994).

McKitterick, R., *Charlemagne: The Formation of a European Identity* (Cambridge, 2008).

McKitterick, R., 'The Constantinian Basilica in the *Liber Pontificalis*', in L. Bosman, I. P. Haynes, and P. Liverani, eds, *The Basilica of St John Lateran to 1600* (Cambridge, 2020), 197–220.

McKitterick, R., 'The *Damnatio Memoriae* of Pope Constantine I (767–768)', in R. Balzaretti, J. Barrow, and P. Skinner, eds, *Italy and Early Medieval Europe: Papers for Chris Wickham*, Past and Present Book Series (Oxford, 2018), 231–48.

McKitterick, R., *History and Memory in the Carolingian World* (Cambridge, 2004).

McKitterick, R., *Perceptions of the Past in the Early Middle Ages* (Notre Dame, IN, 2004).

McKitterick, R., 'The Representation of Old St. Peter's Basilica in the *Liber Pontificalis*', in *OSPR*, 95–118.

McKitterick, R., 'Roman Texts and Roman History in the early Middle Ages', in C. Bolgia, R. McKitterick, and J. Osborne, eds, *Rome across Time and Space, c.500–c.1400: Cultural Translation and the Exchange of Ideas* (Cambridge, 2011), 19–34.

McKitterick, R., *Rome and the Invention of the Papacy: The* Liber Pontificalis (Cambridge, 2020).

McKitterick, R., ed., *The Uses of Literacy in Early Medieval Europe* (Cambridge, 1990).

McKitterick, R., J. Osborne, C. M. Richardson, and J. Story, eds, *Old St Peter's, Rome* (Cambridge, 2013).

McKitterick, R., D. van Espelo, R. Pollard, and R. Price, tr., *Codex Epistolaris Carolinus: Letters from the Popes to the Frankish Rulers, 739–791*, Translated Texts for Historians, 77 (Liverpool, 2021).

Meckseper, C., 'Antike Spolien in der ottonischen Architektur', in J. Poeschke, ed., *Antike Spolien in der Architektur des Mittelalters und der Renaissance* (Munich, 1996), 179–204.

Meens, R., D. van Espelo, B. van den Hoven van Genderen, J. Raaijmakers, I. van Renswoude and C. van Rhijn, eds, *Religious Franks: Religion and Power in the Frankish Kingdoms: Studies in Honour of Mayke de Jong* (Manchester, 2016).

Merrill, E. T., 'The "uncial" in Jerome and Lupus', *Classical Philology*, 11.4 (1916), 452–7.

Mersiowsky, M., 'Preserved by Destruction: Carolingian Original Letters and Clm 6333', in G. Declercq, ed., *Early Medieval Palimpsests*, Bibliologia, 26 (Turnhout, 2007), 73–98.

Mestemacher, I., 'Images of Architecture and Materials: The Miniatures in the Soissons Gospels (Bibliothèque nationale de France MS. Lat. 8850)', in M. Embach, C. Moulin, and H. Wolter-von dem Knesebeck, eds, *Die Handschriften der Hofschule Kaiser Karls des Grossen. Individuelle Gestalt und europäisches Kulturerbe* (Trier, 2019), 39–67.

Mestemacher, I., *Marmor, Gold und Edelsteine: Materialimitation in der karolingischen Buchmalerei*, Naturbilder, Images of Nature, 11 (Berlin, 2021).

Miarelli Mariani, G., 'L'antico San Pietro, demoliro o conservarlo?', in G. Spagnesi, ed., *L'architettura della Basilica di San Pietro: Storia e Costruzione: Atti del convegno internazionale di Studi, Roma, Castel S. Angelo, 7–10 novembre 1995* (Rome, 1997), 229–42.

Miller, D. J. D. and P. Sarris, *The Novels of Justinian: A Complete Annotated English Translation*, 2 vols (Cambridge, 2018).

Millon, H. A., 'Michaelangelo to Marchionni, 1546–1784', in W. Tronzo, ed., *St. Peter's in the Vatican* (Cambridge, 2005), 93–110.

Millon, H. A. and V. Magnago Lampugnani, *The Renaissance: From Brunelleschi to Michelangelo. The Representation of Architecture* (London, 1994)/*Rinascimento: Da Brunelleschi a Michelangelo. La Rappresentazione Dell'architettura [Catalogo della mostra al Palazzo Grassi, Venezia, marzo-novembre 1994]* (Milan, 1994).

Minnis, A. and J. Roberts, eds, *Text, Image, Interpretation: Studies in Anglo-Saxon Literature and Its Insular Context in Honour of Éamonn Ó Carragáin*, Studies in the Early Middle Ages, 18 (Turnhout, 2007).

Mitchell, J., 'The Display of Script and the Uses of Painting in Longobard Italy', in *Testo e imagine nell'alto medioevo*, SSCI, 41 (1994), 887–954.

Mitchell, J., 'Literacy Displayed: The Use of Inscriptions at the Monastery of San Vincenzo al Voluturno in the Early Ninth Century', in R. McKitterick, ed., *The Uses of Literacy in Early Medieval Europe* (Cambridge, 1990), 186–225.

Monciatti, A., 'Fragments of Mosaic from the Oratory of John VII', in *BSPV* I.ii (Atlas), no. 1736–8 and 1740, 884–7.

Montinaro, F., 'Les fausses donations de Constantin dans le *Liber Pontificalis*', *Millennium*, 12 (2015), 203–29.

Mordek, H. 'Dionysio-Hadriana', *Lexikon des Mittelalters*, 9 vols (Stuttgart, 1999), iii, 1074–5.

Mordek, H., 'Rom, Byzanz und die Franken im 8. Jahrhundert: Zur Überlieferung und kirchenpolitischen Bedeutung der Synodus Romana papst Gregors III. vom Jahr 732 (mit Edition)', in G. Althoff, ed., *Personen und Gemeinschaft im Mittelalter: Karl Schmid zum fünf und sechsigsten Geburtstag* (Sigmaringen, 1988), 123–56.

Morison, S., *Politics and Script: Aspects of Authority and Freedom in the Development of Graeco-Latin Script from the Sixth Century BC* (Oxford, 1972).

Morrissey, R., *Charlemagne and France: A Thousand Years of Mythology*, tr. C. Tihanyi (Notre Dame, IN, 2003).

Müller, H., C. M. M. Bayer, and M. Kerner, eds, *Die Aachener Marienkirche. Aspekte ihrer Archäologie und frühen Geschichte.* Der Aachener Dom in seiner Geschichte. Quellen und Forschungen, 1 (Regensburg, 2014).

Muret, M. A., *Orationes XXIII* (Venice, 1575).

Mutherich, F., 'Die Erneuerung der Buchmalerei am Hof Karls des Grossen', in SW, *799*, iii, 560–609.

Mütherich, F. and J. E. Gaehde, *Carolingian Painting* (New York, NY, 1976).

Nardella, C., *Il fascino di Roma nel Medioevo. Le 'Meravglie di Roma' di maestro Gregorio* (Rome, 1997).

Nees, L., *Early Medieval Art*, Oxford History of Art (Oxford, 2002).

Nees, L., 'The European Context of Manuscript Illumination in the Anglo-Saxon Kingdoms, 600–900', in C. Breay and J. Story, eds, *Manuscripts in the Anglo-Saxon Kingdoms: Cultures and Connections* (Dublin, 2021), 45–65.

Nees, L., 'The "Foundation Reliquary" of Hildesheim and Ornamental Art at the Court of Charlemagne', in G. Davies and E. Townsend, eds, *A Reservoir of Ideas: Essays in Honour of Paul Williamson* (London, 2017), 56–66.

Nees, L., *Frankish Manuscripts: The Seventh to the Tenth Century*, Survey of Manuscripts Illuminated in France, 1 (London and Turnhout, 2022).

Nees, L., 'Godescalc's Career and the Problems of Influence', in J. Lowden and A. Bovey, eds, *Under the Influence: The Concept of Influence and the Study of Illuminated Manuscripts* (Turnhout, 2007), 21–44.

Nees, L., 'Networks or Schools? Production of Illuminated Manuscripts and Ivories during the Reign of Charlemagne', in R. Grosse and M. Sot, eds, *Charlemagne: les temps, les espaces, les hommes: Construction et Déconstruction d'un règne*, Collection Haut Moyen Âge, 34 (Turnhout, 2018), 385–407.

Nees, L., 'On Carolingian Book Painters: The Ottoboni Gospels and its Transfiguration Master', *The Art Bulletin*, 83 (2001), 209–39.

Nees, L., review of K. Holter, ed., *Der goldene Psalter, 'Dagulf-Psalter': Vollständige Faksimile-Ausgabe im Originalformat von Codex 1861 Der Österreichischen Nationalbibliothek*, Codices Selecti Phototypice Impressi, 69 (facsimile) and 69* (commentarium) (Graz, 1980), in *The Art Bulletin*, 67 (1985), 681–90.

Nees, L., *A Tainted Mantle: Hercules and the Classical Tradition at the Carolingian Court* (Philadelphia, PA, 1991).

Nelson, J. L. 'Aachen as a Place of Power', in M. de Jong and F. Theuws, eds, *Topographies of Power in the Early Middle Ages*, The Transformation of the Roman World, 6 (Leiden, 2001), 217–41.

Nelson, J. L., 'Carolingian Royal Funerals', in F. Theuws and J. L. Nelson, eds, *Rituals of Power from Late Antiquity to the Early Middle Ages*, The Transformation of the Roman World, 8 (Leiden, 2000), 131–84.

Nelson, J. L. *King and Emperor: A New Life of Charlemagne* (London, 2019).

Nelson, J. L., 'The Settings of the Gift in the Reign of Charlemagne', in W. Davies and P. Fouracre, eds, *The Languages of Gift in the Early Middle Ages* (Cambridge, 2010), 116–48.

Nelson, J. L. 'Why Are There So Many Different Accounts of Charlemagne's Imperial Coronation?', in her *Courts, Elites and Gendered Power in the Early Middle Ages: Charlemagne and Others* (Aldershot, 2007), no. XII, 1–27.

Nelson, J. L., 'Women at the Court of Charlemagne: A Case of Monstrous Regiment?', *Studies in Church History*, 27 (1990), 53–78, reprinted in *The Frankish World, 750–900* (London, 1996), 223–42.

Neumann, H., F. Brunhöltl, and W. Winkelmann, *Karolus Magnus et Leo Papa: ein Paderborner Epos vol Jahre 799* (Paderborn, 1966).

Newton, F., 'Leo Marsicanus and the Dedicatory Text and Drawing in Monte Cassino 99', *Scriptorium*, 33 (1979), 181–205.

Niederkorn-Bruck, M. and A. Scharer, eds, *Erzbischof Arn von Salzburg*, Veröffentlichungen des Instituts für Österreichische Geschichtsforschung, 40 (Munich, 2004).

Noble, T. F. X. *Icons, Iconoclasm and the Carolingians* (Philadelphia, PA, 2013).

Noble, T. F. X., 'Paradoxes and Possibilities in the Sources for Roman Society in the Early Middle Ages', in J. M. H. Smith, ed., *Early Medieval Rome and the Christian West: Essays in Honour of Donald Bullough*, The Medieval Mediterranean, 28 (Leiden, 2000), 55–83.

Noble, T. F. X., *The Republic of St. Peter: The Birth of the Papal State, 680–825* (Philadelphia, PA, 1984).

Noble, T. F. X., 'Topography, Celebration, and Power: The Making of a Papal Rome in the Eighth and Ninth Centuries', in M. de Jong and F. Theuws, eds, *Topographies of Power in the Early Middle Ages*, The Transformation of the Roman World, 6 (Leiden, 2001), 45–91.

Nordenfalk, C., *Vergilius Augusteus. Vollständige Faksimile-Ausgabe, Codex Vaticanus latinus 3256 der Biblioteca Apostolica Vaticana und Codex latinus fol. 416 der Staatsbibliothek Preussischer Kulturbesitz*, Codices selecti phototypice impressi, 56 (Graz, 1976).

Nordhagen, P. J., 'The Mosaics of John VII (705–707): The Mosaic Fragments and their Technique', *Acta ad archeologiam et atrium historiam pertinentia*, 2 (1965), 121–66.

Ó Carragaín, É., *Ritual and the Rood* (Toronto, ON, 2005).

Ó Carragain, É. and C. Neuman de Vegvar, eds, *Roma Felix—Formation and Reflections of Medieval Rome*, Church, Faith and Culture in the Medieval West (Aldershot, 2007).

O'Brien O'Keeffe, K. and A. Orchard, eds, *Latin Learning and English Lore: Studies in Anglo-Saxon Literature for Michael Lapidge*, 2 vols (Toronto, ON, 2005).

O'Neill, J. P., ed., *The Art of Medieval Spain, AD 500–1200* (New York, NY, 1994).

O'Reilly, J., 'Introduction', in S. Connolly, tr., *Bede: On the Temple*, Translated Texts for Historians, 21 (Liverpool, 1995), xvii–lv, reprinted in J. O'Reilly, *History, Hagiography and Biblical Exegesis: Essays on Bede, Adomnán and Thomas Becket*, ed. M. MacCarron and D. Scully (London, 2019), 3–35.

Ohlgren, T. H., ed., *Anglo-Saxon Textual Illustration: Photographs of Sixteen Manuscripts with Description and Index* (Kalamazoo, MI, 1992).

Opladen-Kauder, J., 'Flusskahn aus der Zeit Karls des Großen', in F. Pohle, ed., *Karl der Grosse/Charlemagne: Orte der Macht: Katalog* (Dresden, 2014), 8–29.

Opladen-Kauder, J. and A. Peiss, 'Ein Flusskhan aus der zeit Karls des Großen', in H. G. Horn, ed., *Fundort Nordrhein-Westfalen: Millionen Jahre Geschichte* (Cologne, 2000), 378–80.

Orchard, A., 'Alcuin and Cynewulf: The Art and Craft of Anglo-Saxon Verse', *Journal of the British Academy*, 8 (2020), 295–399.

Orchard, A., *The Poetic Art of Aldhelm*, Cambridge Studies in Anglo-Saxon England, 8 (Cambridge, 1994).

Osborne, J., *Rome in the Eighth Century: A History in Art*, British School at Rome Studies (Cambridge, 2020).

Ostrow, S. F., 'The Gregorian Chapel and Its Adjacent Spaces', in *BSPV*, II.ii (*Notes*), 666–8.

Ostrow, S. F., 'Piazza San Pietro: The Obelisk', in *BSPV* II.ii (*Notes*), 445–7.

Pace, V., S. Guido, and P. Radiciotti, *La Crux Vaticana o Croce di Giustino II*, Bolletino d'archivio, 4–5 (Padua, 2013).

Pagi, F., *Breviarum historico-chronologico-criticum, illustriora pontificum romanorum gesta, conciliorum generalium acta* (Antwerp, 1717).

Panhuysen, T., 'Maastricht, centre de production de sculptures gallo-romaines et d'inscriptions paléo-chrétiennes', *Studien zur Sachsenforschung*, 8 (Hildesheim, 1993), 83–9.

Pani Ermini, L., ed., *Christiana loca: lo spazio cristiano nella Roma del primo millennio*, 2 vols (Rome, 2000).

Pani Ermini, L., 'Forma Urbis: lo spazio urbano tra VI e IX secolo', *Roma nell'alto Medioevo*, 48.1 (2001), 255–324.

Paolucci, F., 'La tomba dell'imperatrice Maria e altre sepolture di rango di età tardoantica a San Pietro', *Temporis Signa: archeologia della tarda antichità e del medioevo*, 3 (2008), 225–52.

Paroli, L.,'La scultura a Roma tra il VI e il IX secolo', in M. S. Arena, P. Delogu, L. Paroli, M. Ricci, L. Saguì, and L. Vendittelli, eds, *Roma dall'antichità al Medioevo: archeologia e storia nel Museo nationale romana, Crypta Balbi*, 2 vols (Milan, 2001–4), i, 132–43.

Paroli, L., 'La scultura in marmo a Roma tra l'VIII e il IX secolo', in P. Delogu, ed., *Roma Medievale: aggiornamenti* (Florence, 1998), 93–122.

Pastor, L. von, *The History of the Popes from the Close of the Middle Ages*, tr. R. F. Kerr, 17 vols (London, 1908–33).

Pawelec, K., *Aachener Bronzegitter. Studien zur Karolingischen Ornamentik um 800*, Bonner Beiträge zur Kunstwissenschaft, 12 (Cologne, 1990).

Peacock, D. P. S., 'Charlemagne's Black Stones: The Re-Use of Roman Columns in Early Medieval Europe', *Antiquity*, 71 (1997), 709–15.

Peacock, D. P. S., *Rome in the Desert: A Symbol of Power* (Southampton, 1993).

Petrucci, A., 'Aspetti simbolici delle testimonianze scritte', in *Simboli e simbologia nell'alto medioevo*, SSCI 23, 2 vols (Spoleto, 1976), ii, 813–44.

Petrucci, A., *Le Scritture Ultime: Ideologia della Morte e Strategie dello Scrivere nella Tradizione Occidentale* (Turin, 1995), tr. M. Sullivan, *Writing the Dead: Death and Writing Strategies in the Western Tradition* (Stanford, CA, 1997).

Petrucci, A., *Writers and Readers in Medieval Italy: Studies in the History of Written Culture*, tr. C. M. Radding (New Haven, CT, and London, 1995).

Petrucci A., and C. Romeo, *Scriptores in urbibus: Alfabetisimo e cultura scritta nell'Italia altomedievale* (Bologna, 1992).

Picard, J.-C., 'Étude sur l'emplacement des tombes des papes du III au Xe siècle', *Mélanges d'archeologie et d'histoire*, 81 (1969), 725–82.

Pietri, C., *Roma christiana. Recherches sur l'Église de Rome, son organisation, sa politique et son idéologie de Militade à Sixte III (311–440)* (Rome, 1976).

Pinelli, A., 'The Old Basilica', in *BSPV* II.i (*Essays*), 9–51.

Pinelli, A., M. Beltramini, and A. Angeli, eds, *La Basilica di San Pietro in Vaticano/The Basilica of St Peter in the Vatican*, Mirabilia Italiae 10, 4 vols (Modena, 2000), I.i–ii (*Atlas*), II.i (*Essays*) II.ii (*Notes*).

Pitra, J. B. and H. Stevenson, *Codices palatini latini Bibliothecae Vaticanae descripti Praeside I. B. Cardinali Pitra*, i: *1–920* (Rome, 1886).

Poeschke, J., *Antike Spolien in der Architektur des Mittelalters und der Renaissance* (Munich, 1996).

Pohl, W., 'Why Not to Marry a Foreign Woman', in V. L. Garver and O. M. Phelan, eds, *Rome and Religion in the Medieval World: Studies in Honor of Thomas F. X. Noble*, Church, Faith and Culture in the Medieval West (Farnham, 2014).

Pohle, F., ed., *Karl der Grosse/Charlemagne. Orte der Macht: Essays* (Dresden, 2014).

Pohle, F., ed., *Karl der Grosse/Charlemagne. Orte der Macht: Katalog* (Dresden, 2014).

Pollard, R. M., 'The Language and Style of the Codex Epistolaris Carolinus and their Affinities with Other Papal Documents', in R. McKitterick, D. van Espelo, R. Pollard, and R. Price, tr., *Codex Epistolaris Carolinus: Letters from the Popes to the Frankish Rulers, 739–791*, Translated Texts for Historians, 77 (Liverpool, 2021), 80–4.

Polman, P. L., *Élément historique dans la controverse religieuse du XVIe siècle* (Gembloux, 1932).

Preissler, M. 'Fragmente einer verlorenen Kunst. Die Paderborner Wandmalerei', in SW, *799*, Preißler, 197–206.

Preissler, M., *Die karolingischen Malereifragmente aus Paderborn. Zu den Putzfunden aus der Pfalzanlage Karls des Großen, Archäologie und Wandmalerei*, Denkmalpflege und Forschung in Westfalen, 40.1 (Mainz, 2003).

Preissler, M. 'Die Wandmalerei', in SW, *799*, i, 133–43.

Price, R., tr., *The Acts of the Second Council of Nicaea (787)*, Translated Texts for Historians, 68, 2 vols (Liverpool, 2018).

Prigent, V., 'Les empereurs isauriens et la confiscation des patrimoines pontificaux d'Italie du Sud', *Mélanges de l'école française de Rome: Moyen Âge*, 146 (2004), 557–94.

Quilici, L. and S. Quilici Gigli, *Fidenae*, Latium Vetus 5 (Rome, 1986).

Rabe, S. A., *Faith, Art, and Politics at Saint-Riquier: The Symbolic Vision of Angilbert* (Philadelphia, PA, 1995).

Raepsaet-Charlier, M.-T., 'Belgique', *Année Épigraphique*, 1998 (2001), 354–6.
Rahtz, P., 'Medieval Milling', in D. W. Crossley, ed., *Medieval Industry*, Council for British Archaeology Research Reports, 40 (London, 1981), 1–15.
Ramackers, J., 'Die Werkstattheimat der Grabplatte papst Hadrians I', *Römisches Quartalschrift*, 59 (1964), 36–78.
Rand, E. K., *A Survey of the Manuscripts of Tours*, 2 vols, Studies in the Script of Tours, 1 (Cambridge, MA, 1929).
Rankin, S., 'Singing from the Dagulf Psalter', in M. Embach, C. Moulin, and H. Wolter-von dem Knesebeck, eds, *Die Handschriften der Hofschule Kaiser Karls des Grossen. Individuelle Gestalt und europäisches Kulturerbe* (Trier, 2019), 473–84.
Rankin, S., *Sounding the Word of God. Carolingian Books for Singers* (Notre Dame, IN, 2022).
Rasch, J. J., 'Zur Rekonstruktion der Andreasrotunde an Alt-St.-Peter', *Römische Quartalschrift für christliche Altertumskunde und Kirchengeschichte*, 85 (1990), 1–18.
Ratkowitsch, C., *Karolus Magnus—alter Aeneas, alter Martinus, alter Iustinus. Zu Intention und Datierung des 'Aachener Karlsepos'*, Wiener Studien, Beiheft 24. Arbeiten zur mittel- und neulateinischen Philologie, 4 (Vienna, 1997).
Recchia, V., *Gregorio Magno e la società Agricola*, Verba Seniorum, n.s., 8 (Rome, 1978).
Renoux, A., 'Karolingische Pfalzen in Nordfrankreich (751–987)', in SW, *799*, iii, 30–7.
Reynolds, L. D., ed., *Texts and Transmission: A Survey of the Latin Classics* (Oxford, 1983).
Ricci, C., 'Marmi ravennati erratici', *Ausonia*, 4 (1909), 247–89.
Rice, L., *The Altars and Altarpieces of New St. Peter's: Outfitting the Basilica, 1621–1666* (Cambridge, 1997).
Rice, L., 'La coesistenza delle due basiliche', in G. G. Spagnesi, ed., *L'architettura della basilica di San Pietro: storia e costruzione* (Rome, 1997), 255–60.
Richardson, C. M. 'St. Peter's in the Fifteenth Century: Paul II, the Archpriests and the Case for Continuity', in *OSPR*, 324–47.
Richardson, C. M. and J. Story, 'Letter of the Canons of St. Peter's to Paul V Concerning the Demolition of the Old Basilica, 1605', in *OSPR*, 404–15.
Richter, M., *Bobbio in the Early Middle Ages* (Dublin, 2008).
Righetti, M., ed., *Manuale di storia liturgica*, 4 vols (Milan, 1950).
Ristow, S. and D. Steiniger, 'Forschungen an den Bronzen des Aachener Domes', *Kölner und Bonner Archaeologica*, 6 (2016), 143–68.
Robert, E., *Sankt Benedikt in Mals* (Bozen, 1992).
Roberts, M., 'Rome Personified, Rome Epitomized: Representations of Rome in the Poetry of the Early Fifth Century', *The American Journal of Philology*, 122 (2001), 533–65.
Ross, J. B., 'Two Neglected Paladins of Charlemagne: Erich of Friuli and Gerold of Bavaria', *Speculum*, 20 (1945), 212–35.
Rossi, G. B. de, 'L'Inscription du tombeau d'Hadrien I, composée et gravée par ordre de Charlemagne', *Mélanges d'archéologie et d'histoire*, 8 (1888), 478–501.
Rossi, G. B. de, *Inscriptiones Christianae Urbis Romae septimo saeculo antiquiores*, II.i: *pars prima ab originibus ad saeculum XII* (Rome, 1888).
Rossi, G. B. de, *La Roma sotteranea cristiana*, 3 vols (Rome, 1864–77).
Rousseau, F., *La Meuse et le pays Mosan. Leur importance historique avant le XIIIe siècle* (Namur, 1930).
Rubery, E., G. Bordi, and J. Osborne, eds, *Santa Maria Antiqua: The Sistine Chapel of the Early Middle Ages* (London, 2021).

Rugo, P., *Le inscrizioni de sec. VI–VII–VIII esistenti in Italia*, 5 vols (Cittadella, 1974–80).

Sabbadini, R., *Codicis Vergiliani qui Augusteus appellatur, reliquiae quam simillime expressae ad Vergili natalem MM celebrandvm qvi erit id. oct. a. MDCCCCXXX*, Codices Vaticanus selecti, 15 (Turin, 1926).

Sághy, M., '"*Scinditur in partes populus*": Pope Damasus and the Martyrs of Rome', *Early Medieval Europe*, 9 (2000), 273–87.

Salway, B., 'Putting the World in Order: Mapping in Roman Texts', in R. J. A. Talbert, ed., *Ancient Perspectives: Maps and their Place in Mesopotamia, Egypt, Greece and Rome* (Chicago, IL, 2012), 193–234.

Santangeli Valenzani, R., 'L'Itinerario di Einsiedeln', in M. S. Arena, P. Delogu, L. Paroli, M. Ricci, L. Saguì, and L. Vendittelli, eds, *Roma dall'antichità al Medioevo: archeologia e storia nel Museo nationale romana, Crypta Balbi*, 2 vols (Milan, 2001–4), i, 154–9.

Sauer, H. and J. Story, with G. Waxenberger, eds, *Anglo-Saxon England and the Continent*, Essays in Anglo-Saxon Studies, 3 (Tempe, AZ, 2011).

Savio, G., *Monumenta onomastica romana medii aevi (X–XII sec.)*, 5 vols (Rome, 1999).

Savettieri, C., 'The Atrium', in *BSPV* II.i (Essays), 321–4.

Schaller, D., 'Das Aachener Epos für Karl den Kaiser', *Frühmittelalterlich Studien*, 10 (1976), 134–68, reprinted in his *Studien zur lateinischen Dichtung des Frühmittelalters* (Stuttgart, 1995), 129–63.

Schaller, D., 'Frühkarolingische Corippus-Rezeption', *Wiener Studien*, 105 (1992) 173–84, reprinted in his *Studien zur lateinischen Dichtung des Frühmittelalters* (Stuttgart, 1995), 346–60.

Schaller, D., *Studien zur lateinischen Dichtung des Frühmittelalters*, Quellen und Untersuchungen zur lateinischen Philologie des Mittelalters, 11 (Stuttgart, 1995).

Schaller, D., 'Vortrags- und Zirkulardichtung am Hof Karls des Grossen', *Mittellateinisches Jahrbuch*, 6 (1970), 14–36; reprinted in his *Studien zur lateinischen Dichtung des Frühmittelalters* (Stuttgart, 1995), 87–109.

Schaller, D. and E. Könsgen, with J. Tagliabue, eds, *Initia carminum Latinorum saeculo undecimo antiquiorum: bibliographisches Repertorium für die lateinische Dichtung der Antike und des früheren Mittelalters* (Göttingen, 1977).

Schefers, H., ed., *Das Lorscher Evangeliar: Biblioteca Documentara Batthyaneum, Alba Iulia, Ms R II 1, Biblioteca Apostolica Vaticana, Codex Vaticanus Palatinus Latinus 50* (Luzern, 2000).

Schiaparelli, L., 'Le carte antiche dell'Archivio Capitolare di S. Pietro in Vaticano', *Archivio della Reale Società romana di storia patria*, 24 (1901), 393–496.

Schieffer, R., 'Charlemagne and Rome', in J. M. H. Smith, ed., *Early Medieval Rome and the Christian West: Essays in Honour of Donald A. Bullough*, The Medieval Mediterranean, 28 (Leiden, 2000), 279–96.

Schieffer, R. *Neues von der Kaiserkrönung Karls des Großen* (Munich, 2004).

Schmidlin, J., *Geschichte der deutschen Nationalkirche in Rom. S. Maria dell'Anima* (Freiburg, 1906).

Schneider, F. and W. Holtzmann, *Die Epitaphien der Päpste und anderer Stadtrömische Inschriften des Mittelalters*, Texte zur Kulturgeschichte des Mittelalters, 6 (Rome, 1932).

Schneider, R. M., 'Coloured Marble: The Splendour and Power of Imperial Rome', *Apollo*, 154.473 (2001), 3–10.

Scholz, S., 'Karl der Große und das Epitaphium Hadriani. Ein Beitrag zum Gebetsgedenken der Karolinger', in R. Berndt, ed., *Das Frankfurter Konzil von 794. Kristallisationspunkt karolingischer kultur*, 2 vols (Mainz, 1997), i, 373–94.

Scholz, S., *Politik—Selbstverständnis—Selbstdarstellung: Die Päpste in karolingischer und ottonischer Zeit*, Historische Forschung, 26 (Stuttgart, 2006).

Schramm, P. E., 'Die Anerkennung Karls des Grossen als Kaiser. Ein Kapitel aus der Geschichte der mittelalterlichen "Staatsymbolik"', *Historische Zeitschrift*, 172 (1951), 449–516, reprinted in *Kaiser, Könige, und Päpste. Gesammelte Aufsätze zur Geschichte des Mittelalters*, 4 vols (Stuttgart, 1968–71), i, 215–63.

Schramm, P. E. and F. Mütherich, *Denkmale der deutschen Könige und Kaiser* (Munich, 1962).

Schüppel, K. C., 'The Stucco Crucifix of St. Peter's Reconsidered: Textual Sources and Visual Evidence for the Renaissance Copy of a Medieval Silver Crucifix', in *OSPR* (2013), 306–23.

Screen, E. and C. West, eds, *Writing the Early Medieval West: Studies in Honour of Rosamond McKitterick* (Cambridge, 2018).

Sefton, D. S., 'The Pontificate of Hadrian I (772–795): Papal Theory and Political Reality in the Reign of Charlemagne', PhD thesis, Michigan State University, East Lansing (1975).

Sharpe, R., 'King Ceadwalla's Roman Epitaph', in K. O'Brien O'Keeffe and A. Orchard, eds, *Latin Learning and English Lore: Studies in Anglo-Saxon Literature for Michael Lapidge*, 2 vols (Toronto, ON, 2005), i, 171–93.

Siecenski, A. E., *The Filioque: History of a Doctrinal Controversy* (Oxford, 2010).

Siegesmund, S., W.-D. Grimm, H. Dürrast, and J. Ruedrich, 'Limestones in Germany Used as Building Stones: An Overview', in B. J. Smith, M. Gomez-Heras, H. A. Viles, and J. Cassar, eds, *Limestone in the Built Environment: Present-day Challenges for the Preservation of the Past*, Geological Society, Special Publication, 331 (London, 2010), 37–60.

Silvagni, A. ed., *Inscriptiones Christianae Urbis Romae septimo saeculo antiquiores: nova series*, i: *Inscriptiones incertae originis*; ii: *Coemeteria in viis Cornelia Aurelia, Portuensi et Ostiensi* (Rome, 1922–35).

Silvagni, A., ed., *Monumenta epigraphica christiana saeculo XIII antiquiora quae in Italiae finibus adhuc exstant iussu Pii XII pontificis maximi*, 4 vols in 7 (Rome, 1943); i: *Roma*; ii.1: *Mediolanum*; ii.2: *Comum*; ii.3: *Papia*; iii.1: *Luca*; iv.1: *Neapolis*; iv.2: *Beneventum*.

Silvagni, A., 'La silloge epigrafica di Cambridge', *Rivista di archeologia cristiana*, 20 (1943), 49–112.

Sims-Williams, P., 'Mildred of Worcester's Collection of Latin Epigrams and Its Continental Counterparts', *Anglo-Saxon England*, 10 (1982), 21–38.

Sims-Williams, P., *Religion and Literature in Western England, 600–800*, Cambridge Studies in Anglo-Saxon England, 3 (Cambridge, 1990).

Sinisi, L., 'From York to Paris: Reinterpreting Alcuin's Virtual Tour of the Continent', in H. Sauer and J. Story, with G. Waxenberger, eds, *Anglo-Saxon England and the Continent*, Essays in Anglo-Saxon Studies, 3 (Tempe, AZ, 2011), 275–92.

Smith, C. and J. F. O'Connor, tr., *Eyewitness to Old St. Peter's: Maffeo Vegio's "Remembering the Ancient History of St. Peter's Basilica in Rome"* (Cambridge, 2019).

Smith, J. M. H., 'Old Saints, New Cults: Roman Relics in Carolingian Francia', in J. M. H. Smith, ed., *Early Medieval Rome and the Christian West: Essays in Honour of Donald A. Bullough*, The Medieval Mediterranean, 28 (Leiden, 2000), 317–39.

Smith, J. M. H. ed., *Early Medieval Rome and the Christian West: Essays in Honour of Donald Bullough*, The Medieval Mediterranean, 28 (Leiden, 2000).

Spagnesi, G., *L'Architettura della basilica di San Pietro: storia e costruzione. Atti del convegno internazionale di studi, Roma, Castel S. Angelo, 7–10 novembre 1995*, Quaderni dell'istituto di storia dell'architettura, nuova ser., 25–30 (Rome, 1997).

Spearing, E., *The Patrimony of the Roman Church in the Time of Gregory the Great* (Cambridge, 1918).

Stache, U. J., *Flavius Cresconius Corippus, In Laudem Iustini Augusti Minoris. Ein Kommentar* (Berlin 1976).

Stella, F., 'Autore e attribuzioni del "Karolus Magnus et Leo Papa"', in P. Godman, J. Jarnut, and P. Johanna, eds, *Am Vorabend der Kaiserkrönung: das Epos "Karolus magnus et Leo papa" und der papstbesuch in Paderborn 799* (Berlin, 2002), 19–34.

Stenhouse, W., *Reading Inscriptions and Writing Ancient History: Historical Scholarship in the Late Renaissance* (London, 2005).

Stern, H., *Le Calendrier de 354; étude sur son texte et ses illustrations*, Bibliothèque archéologique et historique, 4 (Paris, 1953).

Stiegemann, C. and M. Wemhoff, eds, *799. Kunst und Kultur der Karolingerzeit. Karl der Große und Papst Leo III in Paderborn*, 3 vols (Mainz, 1999), i–ii: *Katalog der Ausstellung, Paderborn 1999*; iii: *Beiträge*.

Stiennon, J., 'Le sarcopharge de Sancta Chrodoara à St.-Georges d'Amay. Essai d'interprétation d'une découverte exceptionnelle', *Comptes-rendus des séances de l'Académie des Inscriptions et Belles-Lettres*, 123 (1979), 10–31.

Stinger, C. L., *The Renaissance in Rome* (Bloomington, IN, 1998).

Stoclet, A., 'Les établissements francs à Rome au VIIIe siècle: "Hospitale intus basilicam beati Petru, domus Nazarii, schola Francorum" et palais de Charlemagne', in M. Sot, ed., *Haut Moyen Âge. Culture, Éducation et Société: Études offertes à Pierre Riché* (Nanterre, 1990), 231–47.

Stofella, M., 'Staying Lombard While Becoming Carolingian? Italy under King Pippin', in C. Gantner and W. Pohl, eds, *After Charlemagne: Carolingian Italy and Its Rulers* (Cambridge, 2021), 135–47.

Story, J., 'Aldhelm and Old St. Peter's, Rome', *Anglo-Saxon England*, 37 (2009) 7–20.

Story, J., 'Bede, Willibrord and the Letters of Pope Honorius I on the Genesis of the Archbishopric of York', *English Historical Review*, 127 (2012), 783–818.

Story, J., *Carolingian Connections: Anglo-Saxon England and Carolingian Francia, c.750–c.870*, Studies in the Early History of Britain, 2 (Aldershot, 2003).

Story, J., 'The Carolingians and the Oratory of Peter the Shepherd', in *OSPR*, 257–73.

Story, J., 'Cathwulf, Kingship and the Royal Abbey of St.-Denis', *Speculum*, 74 (1999), 1–21.

Story, J., ed., *Charlemagne: Empire and Society* (Manchester, 2005).

Story, J., 'Frankish Annals of Lindisfarne and Kent', *Anglo-Saxon England*, 34 (2005), 59–109.

Story, J., 'Insular Manuscripts in Carolingian Francia', in C. Breay and J. Story, eds, *Manuscripts in the Anglo-Saxon Kingdoms: Cultures and Connections* (Dublin, 2021), 66–85.

Story, J., 'Lands and Lights in Early Medieval Rome', in R. Balzaretti, J. Barrow, and P. Skinner, eds, *Italy and Early Medieval Europe: Papers for Chris Wickham*, Past and Present Book Series (Oxford, 2018), 315–38.

Story, J., J. Bunbury, A. C. Felici, G. Fronterotta, M. Piacentini, C. Nicolais, D. Scacciatelli, S. Sciuti, and M. Vendittelli, 'Charlemagne's Black Marble: The Origins of the Epitaph of Pope Hadrian I', *Papers of the British School at Rome*, 73 (2005), 157–90.

Stuart, P. and J. E. Bogaers, *Nehalennia. Römische Steindenkmäler aus der Oosterschelde bei Colijnsplaat*, Corpus Signorum Imperii Romani, Nederland. Germania inferior, Colinjsplaat, 2, Collections of the National Museum of Antiquities at Leiden, 9, 2 vols (Leiden, 2001).

Sullivan, R. E., ed., *'The Gentle Voices of Teachers': Aspects of Learning in the Carolingian Age* (Columbus, OH, 1995).

Tea, E., *La basilica di S. Maria Antiqua* (Milan, 1937).

Thacker, A., 'Martyr Cult within the Walls: Saints and Relics in the Roman *tituli* of the Fourth to Seventh Centuries', in A. Minnis and J. Roberts, eds, *Text, Image, Interpretation: Studies in Anglo-Saxon Literature and Its Insular Context in Honour of Éamonn Ó Carragáin*, Studies in the Early Middle Ages (Turnhout, 2007), 31–70.

Thacker, A., 'Rome of the Martyrs: Saints, Cults and Relics, Fourth to Seventh Centuries', in É. Ó Carragáin and C. Neuman de Vegvar, eds, *Roma Felix—Formation and Reflections of Medieval Rome*, Church, Faith and Culture in the Medieval West (Aldershot, 2007), 13–49.

Thacker, A., 'In Search of Saints: The English Church and the Cult of Roman Apostles and Martyrs in the Seventh and Eighth Centuries', in J. M. H. Smith, ed., *Early Medieval Rome and the Christian West: Essays in Honour of Donald A. Bullough*, The Medieval Mediterranean, 28 (Leiden, 2000), 247–77.

Theones, C., 'Alt und Neu St. Peter unter einem Dach. Zu Antonio da Sangallo *Muro divisorio*', in M. Jansen and K. Winands, eds, *Architektur und Kunst im Abenland: Festschrift zur vollendung des 65. Lebensjahres von Günter Urban* (Rome, 1992), 51–61.

Theones, C., 'Renaissance St. Peter's', in W. Tronzo, ed., *St. Peter's in the Vatican* (Cambridge, 2005), 64–93.

Theones, C., 'St. Peter's, 1534–1546', in C. L. Frommel and N. Adams, eds, *The Architectural Drawings of Antonio Da Sangallo the Younger and His Circle*, ii: *Churches, Villas, the Pantheon, Tombs and Ancient Inscriptions* (New York, NY, 2000), 33–44.

Theuws, F., 'Maastricht as a Centre of Power', in M. de Jong, F. Theuws, and C. van Rhijn, eds, *Topographies of Power in the Early Middle Ages* (Leiden, 2001), 155–216.

Theuws, F., 'Das mittlere Maastal und wie es zu einem Kerngebeit des Karolingerreichs wurde', in F. Pohle, ed., *Karl der Grosse/Charlemagne. Orte der Macht: Essays* (Dresden, 2014), 200–9.

Thunø, E., *The Apse Mosaic in Early Medieval Rome: Tome, Network, and Repetition* (Cambridge, 2015).

Thunø, E., 'Inscription and Divine Presence: Golden Letters in the Early Medieval Apse Mosaic', *Word and Image*, 27 (2011), 279–91.

Thunø, E., 'Looking at Letters: "Living Writing" in S. Sabina in Rome', *Marburger Jahrbuch für Kunstwissenschaft*, 34 (2007), 19–41.

Thunø, E., 'The Pantheon in the Middle Ages', in T. A. Marder and M. Wilson Jones, eds, *The Pantheon from Antiquity to the Present* (Cambridge, 2015), 231–54.

Tinti, F., ed., *England and Rome in the Early Middle Ages: Pilgrimage, Art and Politics* (Turnhout, 2014).

Tischler, M. M., *Einharts Vita Karoli: Studien zur Entstehung, Überlieferung und Rezeption*, 2 vols (Hannover, 2001).

Tollenaere, L., *La sculpture sur pierre de l'ancien diocèse de Liège a l'époque romane* (Gembloux, 1957).

Tomassetti, A., ed., *Bullarum Diplomatum et Privilegiorum Romanorum Pontificum*, 24 vols (Rome, 1857–72).

Tomlin, R. S. O., *Britannia Romana: Roman Inscriptions and Roman Britain* (Oxford and Philadelphia, PA, 2018).

Toubert, P., '"Scrinium" et "Palatium": la formation de la bureaucratie romano-pontificale aux VIIIᵉ–IXᵉ siècles', in *Roma nell'alto Medioevo*, SSCI, 48.i (Spoleto, 2001), 57–118.

Tourneur, F., 'Global Heritage Stone: Belgian Black 'Marbles', in T. J. Hannibal, S. Kramar, and B. J. Cooper, eds, *Global Heritage Stones: Worldwide Examples of Heritage Stones*, Geological Society Special Publications, 486 (London, 2020), 129–47.

Tourneur, F., 'Le travail de la pierre', in A. Dierkens, ed., *Mosa Nostra. La Meuse mérovingienne de Verdun à Maastricht Vᵉ–VIIIᵉ siècles* (Namur, 1999), 56–7.

Tourneur, F., and E. Groessens, 'Le matériau, d'ici et d'ailleurs', in L. Nys and L. D. Caterman, eds, *La sculpture gothique à Tournai: Splendeur, ruines, vestiges* (Brussels, 2018), 46–55.

Toynbee, J. M. C. and J. B. Ward-Perkins, *The Shrine of St. Peter and the Vatican Excavations* (London, 1956).

Treffort, C., ed., *Épitaphes carolingiennes du Centre-Ouest (milieu VIIIe–fin du Xe siècle)*, Corpus des Inscriptions de la France Médiévale, hors série (Paris, 2020).

Treffort, C., *Mémoires carolingiennes. L'épitaphe entre célébration mémorielle, genre littéraire et manifeste politique (milieu VIIIe–debut XIe siècle)* (Rennes, 2007).

Troncarelli, F., 'L'epitafio di Helpis', in C. Carbonetti, S. Lucà, and M. Signorini, eds, *Roma e il suo territorio nel medioevo. Le fonti scritte fra traditzione e innovazione. Atti del Convegno internazionale di studio dell'Associazione italiana dei paleografi e diplomatisti* (Roma, 25–29 ottobre 2012). Studi e ricerche, 6 (Spoleto, 2015), 541–52.

Tronzo, W., ed., *St. Peter's in the Vatican* (Cambridge, 2005).

Tronzo, W., 'Il Tegurium di Bramante', in G. Spagnesi, ed., *L'architettura della basilica di San Pietro: Storia e Costruzione* (Rome, 1997), 161–6.

Trout, D., 'Damasus and the Invention of Early Christian Rome', *Journal of Medieval and Early Modern* Studies, 33 (2003), 517–36.

Trout, D., ed., *Damasus of Rome: The Epigraphic Poetry. Introduction, Texts, Translations and Commentary* (Oxford, 2015).

Trout, D., 'Poetry on Stone: Epigram and Audience in Rome', in S. McGill and J. Pucci, eds, *Classics Renewed: Reception and Innovation in the Latin Poetry of Late Antiquity* (Heidelberg, 2016), 77–95.

Trout, D., 'Poets and Readers in Seventh-Century Rome: Pope Honorius, Lucretius, and the Doors of St Peter's', *Traditio*, 75 (2020), 39–85.

Unterkircher, F., ed., *Alkuin-Briefe und andere traktate im auftrage des Salzburger Erzbischofs Arn um 799 zu einem Sammelband vereinigt Codex Vindobonensis 795 der Österreichischen Nationalbibliothek*, Codices selecti phototypice impressi, 20 (Graz, 1969).

Unterkircher, F., ed., *Codex Epistolaris Carolinus: Österreichische Nationalbibliothek Codex 449*, Codices selecti phototypice impressi, 3 (Graz, 1962).

Unterkircher, F., ed., *Das Wiener Fragment der Lorscher Annalen [Annales Laureshamenses], Christus und die Samariterin, Katechese des Niceta von Remesiana: Codex Vindobonensis 515 der Österreichischen Nationalbibliothek*, Codices selecti phototypice impressi, 15 (Graz, 1967).

Untermann, M., '"*Opere mirabile constructa*": Die Aachener "Residenz" Karl des Grossen', in SW, *799*, iii, 152–64.

Van Dijk, A., 'The Afterlife of an Early Medieval Chapel: Giovanni Battista Ricci and Perceptions of the Christian Past in Post-Tridentine Rome', *Renaissance Studies*, 19.5 (2005), 686–98.

Vauchez, A., ed., *Roma medievale* (Bari, 2001).

Verweij, M., *Adrianus VI (1459–1523), de tragische paus uit de Nederlanden* (Antwerp, 2011).

Verweij, M., ed., *De Paus uit de lage landen Adrianus VI, 1459–1523: catalogus bij de tentoonstelling ter gelegenheid van het 550ste geboortejaar van Adriaan van Utrecht*, Supplementa humanistica Lovaniensia, 27 (Leuven, 2009).

Vircillo Franklin, C., 'The Epigraphic Syllogae of BAV Palatinus Latinus 833', in J. Hamesse, ed., *Roma, magistra mundi: itineraria culturae medievalis. Mélange offerts au Père L. E. Boyle à l'occasion de son 75e anniversaire*, 3 vols (Louvain-la-Neuve, 1998), ii, 975–90.

Voci, A. M., '"Petronilla auxiliatrix regis Francorum", anno 757: sulla "memoria" del re dei Franchi presso San Pietro', *Bullettino dell'Istituto storico italiano per il Medio Evo e archivio muratoriano*, 99 (1993), 1–28.

Vogel, C., *Medieval Liturgy: An Introduction to the Sources* (Washington, DC, 1986).

Volbach, W. F., *Early Decorative Textiles* (London, 1969).

Wallach, L., *Alcuin and Charlemagne: Studies in Carolingian History and Literature* (Ithaca, NY, 1959).

Wallach, L., 'Alcuin's Epitaph of Hadrian I: A Study in Carolingian Epigraphy', *The American Journal of Philology*, 72 (1951), 128–44.

Wallach, L., 'The Epitaph of Alcuin: A Model of Carolingian Epigraphy', *Speculum*, 30 (1955), 367–73.

Wallach, L., 'The Epitaph of Hadrian I Composed for Charlemagne by Alcuin', in *Alcuin and Charlemagne: Studies in Carolingian History and Literature*, Cornell Studies in Classical Philology, 32 (Ithaca, NY, 1959), 178–97.

Walser, E., *Poggius Florentinus. Leben unde Werke*, Beiträge zur kulturgeschichte des Mittelalters und der Renaissance, 14 (Berlin, 1914).

Walser, G., *Die Einsiedler Inschriftensammlung und der Pilgerführer durch Rom (Codex Einsidlensis 326)*, Historia. Einzelschriften, 53 (Stuttgart, 1987).

Wand, A., *Heiligenstadt und seine Stadtpatrone. Die Geschichte der Aureus-und Justinusverehrung* (Heiligenstadt, 2001).

Ward-Perkins, J. B. 'Materials, Quarries and Transportation', in H. Dodge and B. Ward-Perkins, eds, *Marble in Antiquity: The Collected Papers of J. B. Ward-Perkins*, Archaeological Monographs of the British School at Rome, 6 (London, 1992), 13–22.

Ward-Perkins, J. B., 'The Shrine of St. Peter and its Twelve Spiral Columns', *Journal of Roman Studies*, 42 (1952), 21–33.

Webster, L. and J. Backhouse, eds, *The Making of England: Anglo-Saxon Art and Culture, 600–900* (London, 1991).

Weil-Garris Brandt, K., 'Michelangelo's *Pietà* for the Cappella del Re di Francia', in C. L. Frommel and M. Winner, eds, *"Il se rendit en Italie": études offertes à André Chastel* (Rome, 1987), 77–108.

Weiller, B. and S. MacLean, *Representations of Power in Medieval Germany 800–1500* (Turnhout, 2006).

Weinryb, I., *The Bronze Object in the Middle Ages* (Cambridge, 2016).

Werner, M., *Der Lütticher Raum in Frühkarolingischer Zeit: Untersuchungen zur Geschichte einer karolingischen Stammlandschaft*, Veröffentlichungen des Max-Planck-Instituts für Geschichte, 62 (Göttingen, 1980).

Westall, R., 'Constantius II and the Basilica of St Peter in Vatican', *Historia. Zeitschrift für Alte Geschichte*, 64.2 (2015), 205–42.

Westgard, J., 'Bede and the Continent in the Carolingian Age and Beyond', in S. DeGregorio, ed., *The Cambridge Companion to Bede* (Cambridge, 2010), 201–15.

Wickham, C., *Medieval Rome: Stability and Crisis of a City, 900–1150* (Oxford, 2015).

Wightman, E. M., *Gallia Belgica* (London, 1985).

Winterbottom, M., 'An Edition of Faricius, *Vita S. Aldhelmi*', *The Journal of Medieval Latin*, 15 (2005), 93–147.

Winterbottom, M., 'Faricius of Arezzo's Life of St Aldhelm', in K. O'Brien O'Keeffe and A. Orchard, eds, *Latin Learning and English Lore/Studies in Anglo-Saxon Literature for Michael Lapidge*, 2 vols (Toronto, ON, 2005), i, 109–31.

Winterer, C., 'Die Miniatur im (karolingischen) Zeitalter ihrer technischen Reproduzierbarkeit? Beobachtungen und Überlegungen zu den Handschriften der Hofschule Karls des Grossen', in M. Embach, C. Moulin, and H. Wolter-von dem Knesebeck, eds, *Die Handschriften der Hofschule Kaiser Karls des Grossen. Individuelle Gestalt und europäisches Kulturerbe* (Trier, 2019), 267–93.

Wolfram, H., A. Scharer, and H. Kleinschmidt, eds, *Intitulatio*, 3 vols, Mitteilungen des Instituts für Österreichische Geschichtsforschung, 21, 24, 29 (Vienna, 1967–88).

Wolter-von dem Knesebeck, H., 'Godescalc, Dagulf und Demetrius. Überlegungen zu den Buchkünstlern am Hof Karls des Grossen und ihrem Selbstveständnis', in P. van den Brink and S. Ayooghi, eds, *Karl der Grosse. Charlemagne. Karls Kunst* (Aachen, 2014), 31–45.

Wright, D. H., *The Vatican Vergil: A Masterpiece of Late Antique* Art (Berkeley, CA, 1993).

Wright, D. H., *The Roman Vergil and the Origins of Medieval Book Design* (London, 2001).

Yasin, A. M., 'Shaping the Memory of Early Christian Cult Sites: Conspicuous Antiquity and the Rhetoric of Renovation at Rome, Cimitile-Nola and Porec', in K. Galinsky and K. Lapatin, eds, *Cultural Memories in the Roman Empire* (Los Angeles, CA, 2015), 116–33.

Yates, F. A., *The Art of Memory* (Chicago, IL, 1966).

Zalum, M., 'La Cattedra Ligena di San Pietro (sec. IX)', in *BSPV*, I.1 (Atlas), 616–19.

Ziolkowski, J. and M. Putnam, *The Virgilian Tradition: The First Fifteen Hundred Years* (New Haven, CT, 2008).

INDEX

Note: Figures are indicated by an italic "*f*", following the page number.

For the benefit of digital users, indexed terms that span two pages (e.g., 52–53) may, on occasion, appear on only one of those pages.

Aachen 4–5, 92–3, 99–100, 114–17, 232–3, 234*f*, 240, 243–4, 257–61, 263–7, 269–70, 275, 306–7, 312–13, 316
   archaeology 226*f*, 232, 244–5, 246*f*–249*f*, 253–5
   black stones 232, 244–50, 246*f*–249*f*; see also, Stone, *Blaustein*
   chapel 226*f*, 244–50, 246*f*–248*f*, 253–5, 263, 268–9, 291*f*, 305–6, 320–1
     columns 250–5, 254*f*
     dedication 207n.59, 263–4, 296–309, 297*f*, 328
     metalwork 187, 200, 201n.38, 287–9, 291*f*
   palace 153–5, 257–61, 296, 307–8
Abbeville Gospels 266n.24, 280–4, 281*f*
Abundius, sacristan 176
Ada, possible sister of Charlemagne 266n.24, 267, 269
Adalhard, abbot of Corbie 115–16
Admonitio generalis, 789 95, 114–15, 257–62, 274–5, 306
Adoptionism 87–8, 265, 324–5
Ælberht, archbishop of York (767–78) 112–14, 117–19, 132, 267–8
Æthelred, king of Northumbria (790–96) 105n.82, 119n.42, 240
Afiata, Paul 23
Agnellus of Ravenna 320–1
Aistulf, Lombard king (749–56) 13–14
Albertini, Matteo, *scarpellino* 82
Albinus, chamberlain 315–16
Alcuin
   abbot of St Martin's, Tours 111, 117, 138–9, 231–2, 267–8, 313–14, 316–17

Adoptionism 265–6, 324–5
author of Hadrian's epitaph 2–3, 97–8, 100–1, 111–12, 119–20, 128*f*, 139–40, 231–2, 263, 312–14, 328
Commentary on the Gospel of John 303
death 101–2, 111, 117, 126n.72, 131
in Francia 112–17, 304–5
in Northumbria 2–3, 105, 112–117, 267–8
knowledge of Rome 118–19, 315–16
letters 97–8, 104–5, 117, 119, 127, 169–71, 253–5, 265–6, 269–70, 312–15, 328–30
Life of 113–14
meeting at Parma 111, 113–14
nickname 100–1
poet 74, 111, 121–2, 126n.72, 127–32, 139–40, 149–50, 179–80, 263–5, 275, 300–1, 306, 313–14, 322–4
poetry, *Cartula perge cito* 113, 117, 127, 130n.82, 138–9
poetry, *York Poem* 112–13, 117–19, 121, 130–1, 149, 267–8
possible autograph 266
Aldhelm (d. 709/10) 118, 132, 135–7, 148
Alemanni, Nicolò, Vatican librarian 336–7
Alfarano, Tiberio 30–1, 46, 54–5, 60–7, 69–72, 75, 77, 80–1, 112, 177–8, 230–1
Alpheide, half-sister of Charles the Bald 166–7
Angilbert, courtier and abbot of Saint-Riquier 98–100, 115–16, 119, 150, 153–5, 263–5, 283–4, 300–1, 312–18
Annales Laureshamenses, *see* Annals, Lorsch Annals

Annals, Anglo-Saxon Chronicle 105, 113–14
   Easter tables 116–17, 257–60, 258*f*, 306–7
   Historia Regum (*York Annals*) 105–6, 114n.15, 116, 315n.15
   Lorsch Annals / *Annales Lauresbamenses* 23, 101–5, 103*f*, 111, 125–6, 187, 231–2, 257–60, 316n.25, 317–18; *see also*, Index of Manuscripts
   Revised Royal Frankish Annals 98–9, 313n.9, 328n.79
   Royal Frankish Annals / *Annales regni Francorum* 98–9, 115n.23, 138nn.116–117, 243n.60, 257–60, 265n.20, 275n.64, 306, 306n.140, 316n.23, 317n.30, 320, 320n.41
Anointing 13, 26, 316–17
Anthat, Frankish envoy 11–12
Arator, poet 73n.133, 118, 132
Arianism 9–10, 89–90
Army
   Lombard 6–7, 11–12
   Frankish 27, 116, 161, 243n.60, 257–60, 319–20
   French 35, 44–5
Arn, abbot of Saint-Amand (782–821), archbishop of Salzburg (798–821) 115–16, 149n.26, 169–71, 315–16, 329–30
Arsenic 187
Audulf, seneschal 264–5
Aula (court, palace, basilica) 18–19, 95–7, 135–6, 153–5, 205n.53, 263–4, 294, 296, 298–302, 306, 316, 323, 326, 327n.75, 328–31
Avars 98–100, 104–5, 179–80, 313–14, 324–5

Baldo, scribe at Salzburg 169–70, 329–30
Baldric, priest and envoy 315–16
baptism 17–18, 162–3, 207–8, 270–2, 328
Barberini, Francesco, cardinal 335–7
Baronio, Cesare, cardinal 67–9

Basilica Constantiniana, *see* Rome, churches, Lateran
Bede 76n.144, 89–90, 118, 121, 146, 148–9, 151, 152n.40, 208–10, 212–14, 257–60, 272n.48, 301–5
Belgium, black marble and quarries 226*f*, 227–8, 235–8, 236*f*–238*f*, 241–2, 244–5, 313, 315
Benevento, Lombard duchy 8–9, 23, 92–3
Berhtwald, archbishop of Canterbury (692–731) 148–9
Bernald, bishop of Strasbourg (d. 844) 179–80
Bernard, king of Italy (d. 817) 194–5, 196*f*
Bertcaud, scribe 289–93, 292*f*
Bertha, Charlemagne's daughter 115–16, 283–4
Bertrada, mother of Charlemagne, wife of Pippin III (d. 783) 21–3, 98
Bobbio, Italy 190–2
Boniface, West-Saxon missionary and bishop of Mainz (d. 754) 11–12, 94n.41
Bracciolino, Poggio, humanist scholar (1380–1459) 330–3
Bramante, Donato 42–3, 45–51, 47*f*, 53–5, 54*f*–57*f*, 65, 68, 77–8, 333
Brione, Tyrol 168–9
Britain 95, 104–5, 226*f*, 227–8, 237–42
Bronze 29–30, 74–5, 170n.111, 187, 198–201, 228, 248–50, 287–9, 291*f*, 298, 327, 329n.88, 340–1
Byzantium (see, *Roman Empire*)

Calendar of 354 278n.67, 324–5
Campulus 312–14
Candidus, Alcuin's pupil 169–70, 315–16
Canon law 20–1, 39, 42–3, 120–1, 122n.60, 132, 146–7, 159–60, 167–8, 278–80, 279*f*
Canterbury 104–5, 118, 148–9
Capitoline She-Wolf 200–1
Carloman, king of the Franks, 768–71, brother of Charlemagne 20–3, 26–7
Carloman, son of Charlemagne, *see* Pippin

Carmen paschale, see Sedulius, Caelius
Carolingians, see Ada, Bernard, Bertha, Bertrada, Carloman, Charlemagne, Charles the Bald, Charles Martel, Charles the Younger, Gisela, Fastrada, Hildegard, Liutgard, Louis the Pious, Pippin II, Pippin III, Pippin of Italy, Pippin (son of Carloman), Rotrude
Casalano, Giovanni 82
Ceadwalla, king of the West Saxons (d. 689) 146, 148, 151–3, 212–14
Charlemagne
   comparison to Constantine 338–9
   death and epitaph 125–6, 126f, 297–9
   epithet 95–9
   imperial coronation 311–12, 320
   library 122–3, 124f, 267
   name spelling 121–2, 125–7, 297
   voice 2–3, 74–5, 97–101, 120–1, 126–7, 314
   weeping 74, 97–8, 112, 312–13
Charles IX, king of France (r. 1550–74) 14–15
Charles Martel, mayor of the palace (d. 741) 11–13, 92, 242–3
Charles the Bald, king of the Franks (d. 877) 63n.99, 166–7
Charles the Younger, son of Charlemagne (d. 810) 306, 316–17
Charles V, Holy Roman Emperor (1519–1556) 38–9, 252–3
Charles VIII, king of France (1483–98) 35, 44–5, 131, 231
Christopher, *primicerius* 21, 23, 25n.110
Clovis, king of the Franks (509–511) 160–1
Codex Agrimensores 195–7; see also, List of Manuscripts
Codex Augusteus 195–7; see also, List of Manuscripts
Codex Carolinus (*Codex epistolaris Carolinus*) 11–13, 17–20, 86, 88–97, 250–2, 338–9; see also, List of Manuscripts

Codex Sangallensis 195–7; see also List of Manuscripts
Coinage
   Charlemagne 3–4, 122–6, 123f, 244–5
   Hadrian 87, 88f
Collectio Canonum Quesnelliana 278–80, 279f
Cologne 91, 113, 226f, 227–8, 237–8, 253–5, 267–9
Columns 10–11, 29–33, 40, 41f, 46–8, 47f, 48f, 50–3, 55–61, 65–7, 82–3, 106, 178, 181–2, 198, 207–8, 211–12, 212f, 230, 237–8, 238f, 241–2, 246–55, 249f–254f, 257–60, 270–2, 275, 287–9, 307–8, 326–7, 334
Constantinople, imperial city 3–4, 6–8, 13–14, 17, 86–7, 116–17, 133, 197–8, 202, 210–12, 255, 282–3, 321–2, 334, 336–7; see also Roman Empire, emperors
Corippus, *In laudem Iustini* 293n.99, 321–5
Council
   Constance, 1414–18 330–1
   Constantinople, 381 76–7
   Constantinople, 680 280n.71
   Frankfurt, 794 87–8, 116–17, 119, 123–5, 126n.71, 262–3, 264n.17, 265
   Nicaea, 325 340
   Nicaea, 787 87–8, 92–3, 116, 120–1, 153–5
   Rome, 767 10n.36, 20–1, 88–9, 93–5, 107n.92
   Trent, 1545–63 67–9
   Legates', 786 95, 114
Counter Reformation 34, 67–9, 74–8, 81
Crowns, votive 160–1, 178–9, 316–17
Crux gemmate 325–6
Cumian, bishop (d. 736) 190–2
Cuthbert, archbishop of Canterbury (740–60) 118, 148–9

Dagulf Psalter 197n.24, 202–5, 273f–276f; see also, Index of Manuscripts

Dagulf, scribe 115–16, 190–2, 269–70;
    Psalter 99–101, 202, 204–5,
    266n.24, 272–5, 273f–276f, 278,
    291–3
Damian, bishop of Pavia (d. 711) 153
David, Old Testament king 99–101, 263,
    293, 340
*De locis sanctis martyrum quae sunt foris
    civitatis Romae* 145–6, 170n.107
Dedal, Adrian Florenz (*see* Papacy,
    Hadrian VI)
Dendrochronology 244–5, 301–2
Desiderius, Lombard king (756–74)
    6, 14n.52, 22–3, 26–7, 90–1,
    96n.49, 118–19
Diaconiae 24–6, 87–8, 145–6
Dionysio-Hadriana 95–7, 120–1, 122n.60
Domuscultae 87–8, 90–1
Donation of Charlemagne, 774 158–60,
    339–41
Donation of Constantine / *Constitutum
    Constantini* 75n.141, 330–4,
    337–9
Donation of Pippin, Second Treaty of Pavia,
    756 13–15, 158–9, 339–40
Dosio, Antonio 55, 56f, 63–4, 70, 71f
Dryhthelm, visionary 121
Duchy / duke of Rome 6–11, 14n.52, 20–1,
Durante, Anibale 82
Dürer, Albrecht 252–3

Eanbald I, archbishop of York (780–796)
    113–14, 119
Eanbald II, archbishop of York (796–808)
    315, 323n.55
Ecgberht, archbishop of York (732–66) 112
Ecgfrith, king of Mercia (796) 114
Einhard 23, 97–8, 116–17, 125–6, 138,
    250–2, 257–60, 262–5, 289–91,
    297–9, 306, 307n.145, 311;
    see also, Seligenstadt
Einsiedeln Itinerary 179–83, 181f, 200–1
Emma, queen (827–76) 166–7
Endogenous growth theory 261–2
Epistola de litteris colendis 114–15, 261–2

Equestrian statue
    Constantine 181–2, 200–1
    Marcus Aurelius 200–1, 201f
    Theoderic 320–1
Ercambald 264–5
Eugenius II, bishop of Toledo (647–57)
    322–3
Eustathius, dux 221–2, 222f
Eutychios, exarch of Ravenna 6–8
Exarch, exarchate 6–8, 38–9, 45, 211–12

Fabbrica di San Pietro 63, 65, 82–3,
    232–3
Farfa, abbey 94–5
Faricius of Arezzo (d. 1117) 135–6
Fastrada, queen (d. 794) 126n.71, 319–20,
    328n.80
Festus, Sextus Pompeius 229
Filarete 29–30
Filocalus, Furius Dionysius 193, 202–3,
    203f–204f, 275–8
Flacius Illyricus, Matthias 67
Forster, Frobenius 130–1
Fortunatus, Venantius 118, 130, 132,
    146–7, 168–9, 321n.48, 325n.66
Fouquet, Jean xxivf, 1–2
France, kings
    Charles VIII (1483–1498) 35, 44–5,
        131, 231
    Francis I (1515–47) 35–6, 37f
    Louis XII (1498–1515) 35
Frederick III, Elector of Saxony
    (1468–1525) 38–9
Fridugis, abbot of St Martins, Tours
    116–17, 138–40, 328–9
Fulda, abbey 125–6, 137–8, 150n.30,
    179–80, 289, 304–5, 328–9
Fulrad, abbot of Saint-Denis (d. 784)
    13–14, 31n.8, 101–2, 153n.43
Funerals and mourning 74, 97–8, 102–4,
    106–8, 112, 126–7, 312–14

Garvo, Leone 82–3
George, bishop of Ostia and Amiens 95,
    114–16

Gerold, duke of Bavaria, brother of Hildegard 179–80, 330n.92
Giacobacci, Domenico, bishop of Nocera (1524–8) 332–4
Gifts 17–19, 311–12, 316–17, 325–6, 339–40
Gisela, Charlemagne's sister, abbess of Chelles 17–18
Godesscalc, Evangelistary 269–74, 271*f*, 291–3; *see also*, List of Manuscripts
Godesscalc, scribe 269–70
Golden lettering 269–70, 284–9
Golden line 100n.65, 293–4, 293n.99
Golzinne, Belgium 233–5, 234*f*
Gregory of Tours 168–9
Gregory, cardinal priest at San Clemente 218, 219*f*
Grimaldi, Giacomo, canon at St Peter's 151n.31, 214, 230–1, 335–7
Grimo, abbot of Corbie 12–13

Hadrian's epitaph
  antiquarian descriptions 45–70, 78, 187–9, 230–1; *see also*, Mallius, Romanus, Sabin, Vegio, Panvinio
  arrival in Rome 100–1, 313–14
  description 185–94
  geology 233–5
  layout 189–92
  lettering 189–94, 308–9
  location 105–6, 230–1, 311–12, 314, 341–2
  manuscript copies 127–32, 128*f*, 129*f*, 146–7
  metrical structure 119–20, 313
  ornament 4–5, 78, 187–9, 188*f*–189*f*, 308–9
  thickness 44, 80–1, 186, 233
Hadrianum, sacramentary 120–1, 122n.60, 274
Harley Golden Gospels 266n.24, 287–9, 288*f*–290*f* (*see also*, List of Manuscripts)
Heemskerck, Maerteen van 52–4, 52*f*–4*f*, 201*f*

Heiligenstadt, abbey 137–8
Helpis, wife of Boethius (?) 152–3, 177n.132
Hercolano, Giacomo, canon 70
Heresy, heretic 8, 38–9, 85, 207–8, 265, 324–5; *see also*, Adoptionism
Higbald, bishop of Lindisfarne (780–803) 116
Hildebald, archbishop of Cologne (788–818) 264–5, 267–8, 275, 316
Hildegard, queen (d. 783) 27, 142*f*, 156, 161–8, 176–80, 270–4, 271*f*, 293–5
Hilduin, abbot of Saint-Denis 138
Hincmar, archbishop of Reims (845–82) 127, 166–7, 240
Historia Regum see Annals
Holy Year, *see* Jubilee
Horace 100–1
Hraban Maur 137–8, 289, 300n.118, 304–5

Iconoclasm 7–11, 17, 21, 87–8
Ingelheim 252n.86, 262–3, 294–5
Ireland / Irish 104, 114–15, 265, 308–9, 318n.34
Islam, Arabs, Saracens, Turks 7–8, 11–12, 35–6, 151–2, 182
Itherius, chaplain and notary 339–40
Itineraries 30, 76n.144, 138–9, 168–83, 172*f*, 237–8, 238*f*, 260–1, 329–30; *see also*, Einsiedeln Itinerary; *Notitia ecclesiarum urbis Romae*

Janning, Conrad 112
John, the Deacon 75, 215
Joseph, Alcuin's pupil 115–16
Jubilee (1300, 1450, 1575, 1625) 61–3, 70–5, 334–6
Juvencus 118, 132, 146–7

Karolus Magnus et Leo Papa 245n.69, 307–8, 321–2, 323n.58, 324–5
Knowledge economy 261–2

Laudes 125–7, 318–20
Leland, John 148–9

Lettering 33–4, 76, 85, 100–1, 121–6, 147, 185–6, 189–90, 192–208, 210–18, 228, 230–2, 269, 278–82, 284–95, 313–14, 332–3; *see* also Filocalus; golden
Letters, *see* Alcuin; Codex Carolinus; *Epistola de litteris colendis*; Papacy, popes, Hadrian
Lex de imperio Vespasiani 74–5, 198–201, 199*f*, 228
Liber Pontificalis 11–12, 14–18, 24–7, 31–3, 36, 75–6, 86–97, 106–8, 120–1, 127–30, 129*f*, 135, 137–9, 147–8, 158–62, 212–14, 217–18, 316–17, 319–20, 326–34, 338–41
Lights, lighting 75–6, 87–8, 160–1, 210–11, 215, 216*f*
Lindisfarne 116
Litany / liturgy 18–19, 104, 108, 126–7, 161–3, 169n.101, 179–80, 257–60, 267–8, 270–2, 275, 316–20, 325n.68, 326, 341; see also, *Laudes*
Liudger, bishop of Münster (805–9) 113–14
Liutgard, queen (d. 800) 319–20
Liutprand, Lombard king (712–44) 9, 11–12, 153
Livy 73
Lombard duchy, *see* Spoleto, Benevento
Lombard kingdom 6–9, 11, 20–3, 262–3, 308–9
Lombard kingdom, conquest and rule by Franks 6, 13–14, 23–4, 27, 86, 90–1, 93–9, 113–14, 153, 158–9, 161, 302
Lombard kings, *see* Desiderius, Liutprand, Aistulf
Lombard princess, marriage to Charlemagne 22–3
Lorsch Annals, *see* Annals, Lorsch
Lorsch Gospels 266n.24, 284–7, 285*f*–286*f*, 291–3; *see also*, Index of Manuscripts
Lorsch Sylloge *see* Sylloge, Lorsch; *see also*, Index of Manuscripts

Louis the Pious (814–40) 160–3, 200–1, 261, 282–3, 327, 340n.131
Lul, archbishop of Mainz (754–86) 112–13
Lupus, abbot of Ferrières (d. *c*.862) 289–93
Luther, Martin 38–9, 49–50

Maderno, Carlo, architect 29–30, 81–3
Magenfrith, chamberlain 264–5
Maginar, abbot of St Denis (789–93) 92–3
Mainz 20–1, 113, 137–9, 262–3, 316–18, 328
Mallius, Peter, canon at St Peter's 29–31, 64n.102, 69–70, 75, 80–1, 111–12, 120, 129–31, 340–1
Malmesbury, abbey 135–6
Manuscripts, *see* List of Manuscripts
Martin, Gregory 70–2
Masson, Jean-Papire 14–15
Master Gregorius, pilgrim 74n.135, 200–1
Memory techniques 144
Mercia 104–5, 114, 119, 240–1, 313; *see also*, Offa
Metz, St Arnulf's abbey 162–4, 293–4, 318
Meuse, river and valley 233–4, 234*f*, 237–8, 241–4, 261–2; *see also*, stone, Mosan marble
Michelangelo, Buonarroti 35–6, 42–3, 45–8, 60, 65
Milan 35, 153, 194–5, 295
  itinerary 170–1, 172*f*
  Sant'Ambrogio 196*f*, 205n.50, 211*f*, 295
Milred, bishop of Worcester (d. 774) 118, 148–9, 151–3
Mobility 261–2, 265, 268–9, 308–9
Monastery
  Andenne 243–4
  Ferrières 117, 289–93
  Lorsch 101–2, 150n.30, 151–2, 252n.86, 267n.30, 294–5
  Murbach 112–13
  Saint-Bertin 111, 127–31
  Saint-Josse, Quentavic 117
  Saint-Remigius, Reims 127, 130, 166–7

Saint-Riquier 98–9, 115–16, 145–8, 150, 264n.17, 283–4, 300, 316–18, 329n.88
Sant'Andrea at Monte Soracte 200–1
Troyes 117
see also, Tours, St Martin's
Moritex 226f, 227–8, 237–8
Mosaic 54–5, 79–80, 107–8, 136n.106, 151–5, 158, 161n.77, 205–7, 206f, 212–14, 228, 237n.42, 246–7, 248f, 250–2, 255, 257–60, 293n.99, 298n.114
Muret, Marc Antoine 14–15
Müstair, Switzerland 295

Naldini, Battista 55, 57f
Namur, Belgium 227–8, 233–5, 237–8, 242–4
Naples 6–9, 35, 44–5
Nehalennia, altars 237–8, 239f, 241–2
Nicaea, synods 76–7, 87–8, 92–3, 116, 120–1, 153–5, 340
Northumbria 2–3, 89–90, 104–5, 111–12, 114–16, 118–19, 146, 148, 240, 267–8, 313, 315
Notitia ecclesiarum urbis Romae 17n.71, 31–3, 76n.144, 135n.101, 139n.120, 145–6, 170–5, 172f
Numidia 69–70, 228–31; *see also*, Stone, *Lapis Numidicum*

Offa, king of Mercia (757–96) 98, 104–5, 114–15, 119, 240–2, 313
Oil 75–6, 87–8, 114–15, 215
Opus Caroli 155, 272, 275–8, 324–5
Ordinator 193–4, 263, 283–4
Orpiment 187–9
Ostrogoths 89–90, 208, 209f, 255, 320–1

Paderborn epic, see *Karolus Magnus et Leo Papa*
Paderborn, palace 262–3, 294–5, 316, 319–20

Palaces 194–5, 243–4, 257–60, 262–3, 307–8, 323, 323n.56, 327n.75, 335–6; *see also*, Aachen; Ingelheim; Paderborn; Rome, Lateran Palace; Rome, Vatican Palace, Thionville
Pallium 113–14, 119, 161–8
Panvinio, Onofrio 60, 63–4, 70, 131, 334–5
Papacy
  bullae 31–3, 40, 77, 108, 212–15, 323n.56
  curia 24–6, 38–40, 42–3, 49–50, 58–60
  elections 9–10, 19–21, 24–7, 38–9, 78, 92–4, 97–100, 106–7, 119, 143, 158, 210f, 257–60, 312–15
  exile in Avignon 42–3, 330–1
  Lawrence, rival of Symmachus 133
  patrimonia 5–11, 13, 23–6, 76, 215, 339
  popes
    Agatho (678–81) 152–3
    Alexander III (1159–81) 30
    Alexander VI (1492–1503) 35, 44–5
    Anastasius II (496–8) 152–3
    Benedict II 684–5) 40–2
    Benedict III (855–8) 178n.137
    Benedict XVI (2005–2022) 38
    Boniface III (607) 211–12
    Boniface IV (608–15) 145–6, 211–14
    Boniface VIII (1294–1303) 77, 184f, 200n.34, 215
    Celestine I (422–32) 205–6, 206f
    Clement VII (1523–34) 40, 50, 55–8
    Constantine II (767–8) 19–20, 92–4
    Damasus I (366–84) 99–100, 106, 132, 143, 155, 181–2, 197–8, 202–8, 203f–204f, 210–11, 275–8, 327n.77
    Eugenius II (824–7) 138
    Felix IV (526–30) 89–90
    Formosus I (891–6) 79–80
    Gelasius I (492–6) 157–8
    Gregory I, the Great (590–604) 6n.20, 9–10, 18–19, 75–7, 138, 148, 151–2, 175–8, 208–14, 211f, 296n.109, 301–2

Papacy (*cont.*)
    Gregory II (715–31) 6n.20, 8–11, 75–7, 89–90, 215, 216*f*, 312n.3
    Gregory III (731–41) 9–13, 92, 106–7, 174*f*, 175, 215–18, 217*f*–218*f*
    Gregory IV (827–44) 174*f*, 178n.136, 327n.76
    Gregory V (996–9) 39
    Gregory IX (1227–41) 79–80
    Gregory XIII (1572–85) 32n.9, 69–70, 71*f*, 72–8
    Hadrian I (772–795)
        achievements and virtues 2, 86–8, 90–1, 97, 111–12, 120–1
        building work 86–7, 120–1
        coins 87, 88*f*
        death and burial 2, 43, 85, 90–1, 97, 105–8, 230–1, 257–60, 311–12
        early career 23–7, 86–97
        epitaph, *see* Hadrian's epitaph
        family estates 24–6, 87–8
        inscriptions 222–4, 223*f*
        letters to Charlemagne 26, 86, 91–3, 98–9, 153–5, 250–2, 255, 338–40
        portrait 84*f*, 86–7, 228
    Hadrian IV (1154–9) 53n.74, 80*f*, 81
    Hadrian VI (1522–23) 38–40, 41*f*, 49–50
    Honorius I (625–38) 33n.11, 89–90, 136n.106, 145–8, 151–5, 159–60, 171, 181–2, 212–14, 293n.99
    Hormsidas (514–23) 160–1
    John II (533–5) 208, 210*f*
    John V (685–6) 152–3
    John VII (705–7) 79–81, 80*f*, 147–9, 174*f*, 177–8, 214, 215*f*, 223*f*, 228
    Julius II (1503–13) 14–15, 29–30, 35, 42–3, 45–9, 65
    Leo I, the Great (440–61) 30–3, 31*f*, 60–3, 65–7, 82, 149, 152–3, 173–5, 178–9, 207–8, 209*f*, 212–14, 278–80, 301–2
    Leo III, pope (795–816) 15–16, 36, 51n.71, 74, 98–9, 106–7, 119, 135, 137–40, 158, 160–1, 167–8, 173, 179–80, 184*f*, 283–4, 306–7, 311–20, 322–6, 328, 334–5
    Leo IV (847–55) 14–15, 31–3, 36, 173, 175–6, 178n.137, 182
    Leo X (1513–21) 6–7, 14–15, 36–9, 48–50, 55–8
    Nicholas I (858–67) 178n.137
    Nicholas V (1447–55) 42–3, 49, 63, 230–1
    Paschal I (817–24) 127n.76, 151–2, 173–5, 174*f*, 180n.148, 327n.76
    Paschal II (1099–1118) 32n.9
    Paul I (757–67) 15–17, 19–20, 26, 30–3, 88–9, 92, 94n.41, 106–8, 148–9, 173–5, 174*f*, 178–9, 218–22, 220*f*–221*f*, 316–17, 337
    Paul III (1534–49) 55–8, 67
    Paul V (1605–21) 33–4, 40–2, 78–82
    Pelagius I (556–61) 160
    Pelagius II (579–90) 159–60
    Pius V (1566–72) 14–15
    Sergius I (687–701) 149, 151–3, 173–5, 174*f*, 212, 214, 250n.82
    Siricius (384–99) 205–6, 206*f*
    Sixtus III (432–40) 106, 205–8, 207*f*, 301n.121
    Stephen II (752–7) 13–14, 17–20, 22, 24n.108, 88–9, 92, 94n.41, 127–9, 129*f*, 173, 176, 339–40
    Stephen III (768–72) 19–24, 26, 92–4, 339–40
    Stephen V (885–91) 89–90, 177–8
    Sylvester I (314–35) 81, 326–7, 330–1, 336–9, 338*f*
    Symmachus (498–514) 16–17, 17n.71, 133–5, 137, 139, 171–3, 174*f*
    Theodore I (642–9) 171
    Urban II (1088–99) 30
    Vigilius (537–55) 208, 209*f*
    Zacharias I (741–52) 13, 24–6, 87–8, 92, 94n.41, 218, 219*f*
Papebroek, Daniel 129–30, 158
Papyrus 19–20, 91–3

Parchment, membrane 20n.86, 91–3,
    122n.60, 170–1, 275, 282–7, 289,
    291–3, 328–9, 339–40
Patricius Romanorum 13, 95–9, 158–9,
    316–17, 338–40
Paul the Deacon 122–3, 124*f*, 127–30, 229,
    293–4, 300n.118, 304–5
Paulinus of Aquileia 114–15
Paulinus of Nola 118
Peter of Pisa 116–17, 122n.60
Peter, archdeacon 122–3
Peter, Illyrian priest 205–6
Pictor 291–3
Pilgrims, pilgrimage 18–19, 70–9, 112–13,
    118, 134–5, 143–8, 170–9, 172*f*,
    183, 198–202, 208–10, 240, 327
Pippin II, mayor of the palace
    (d. 714) 242–3
Pippin III, king (751–68) 13, 17–18,
    94n.41
Pippin, king of Italy, son of Charlemagne
    (d. 810) 162–3, 338n.125
Pippin, son of Carloman, nephew of
    Charlemagne 22–3, 27
Platina, Bartolomeo 63–4
Pliny 69–70, 118, 230–1, 235–7
Poetry 95–7, 100–1, 158, 179–80, 312–13
    classical / Late Antique 118, 120, 127,
        130, 132, 143–4, 185–6, 207–8,
        300–1, 306, 308–9, 321–5
    Carolingian court poetry 99–101,
        111–13, 117–29, 131, 263–309,
        312–14
    in Rome 40, 76–7, 95–7, 132–40, 143–9,
        151–5, 157–68
    epigrams and *tituli* 118–19, 121–2,
        132–9, 143, 148–9, 152–5, 161,
        168–9, 179–80, 325–7
    epitaphs 40, 76–7, 117–19, 125–6, 126*f*,
        126n.72, 131–2, 143–4, 146–9,
        147n.15, 150n.27, 151–3,
        163n.84, 164, 177n.132, 179–80,
        190–2, 194–5, 196*f*, 208–14,
        211*f*, 213*f*, 272n.48, 293–4,
    296n.109, 298–9, 319–20; *see also*,
        Hadrian's epitaph
    insular 117–19, 121–3, 151–3, 272n.48
    manuscripts 117, 127–33
    see also, Alcuin; Angilbert; Corippus;
        Dagulf; Fortunatus; Godesscalc;
        Karolus Magnus et Leo Papa;
        Milred, Prosper; Sylloges; Theodulf
Primicerius 5n.15, 21, 24–6, 221–2, 283–4
Probus, Sextus Petronius 44
Prosper of Aquitaine 118, 132, 146–7,
    300–2, 306
Prudentius 118
Psalter of Charlemagne 318; *see also*, List of
    Manuscripts
Purple
    colour and meaning 100–1, 133, 228–9,
        231, 248–50, 266, 269, 275, 278,
        282–9, 293, 293n.99
    parchment 281*f*, 282–3; stone, *see*
        porphyry
Pyttel, Alcuin's assistant 114

Quierzy, palace 13–14, 125n.66, 262–3,
    306–7, 339–40
Quintus Serenus 132

Radegonde, abbess at Poitiers (d. 587)
    325n.66
Raphael 14–15, 35–6, 37*f*, 42–3, 49–50
Ravenna, Sant'Apollinare in Classe 8–9,
    165–6, 167*f*
Reformation 38–9, 42–3, 49–50; *see also*,
    Luther; Counter Reformation
Regensburg 127–31, 262–3
Regnante invocation 91, 93–5
Reichenau, monastery 179–80
Reims 20–1, 117, 127, 130–3, 137, 146–7,
    164, 166–7, 171–3, 178–9, 306–8
Richbod, abbot of Lorsch (784–804),
    archbishop of Trier (791–804)
    101–2, 118
Riculf, archbishop of Mainz (787–813)
    137–8, 316–17, 328

Rodoin, priest at Saint-Médard, Soissons 138
Roman Empire, emperors
    Constantine I (306–37) 3, 17, 29–30, 154n.52, 200–1, 326, 332–3, 338–40; *see also*, 'Donation of Constantine'
    Constantine V (741–75) 7–8
    Constantine VI (306–37) 340n.130
    Constantius II (337–61) 29n.2, 154n.52, 324–5
    Helena (d. *c*.330) 326–7, 330–1, 340n.130
    Honorius I (384–432) 16–17
    Irene, empress (797–802) 3–4, 340n.130
    Justin II (565–78) 293n.99, 321–7
    Justinian (527–65) 6–7, 93–7, 160, 320–3, 328–9
    Leo III, the Isaurian (717–41) 7–8, 75, 215
    Maria, empress (d. 407/8) 16–17, 36n.23
    Maurice (582–602) 160
    Michael I (811–13) 3–4
    Pelagius I (556–61) 160
    Pelagius II (579–90) 159–60
    Phocas (601–10) 211–12, 212*f*
    Sophia, empress (d. *c*.601) 293n.99, 325–7
    Vespasian (69–79) 74–5, 198, 199*f*, 200–1, 228
Romanus, canon at St Peter's 33n.12, 111–12, 120, 131, 215
Rome
    aqueduct 86–7, 180
    Arch of Septimus Severus 180
    aristocracy 19–20, 24–6, 73, 87–8
    bridge 153–5, 168–9, 316, 328–9
    Caelian Hill 170–1
    Campo Marzio 76–7
    Capitoline 74–5, 200–1
    catacombs 143–6, 148–9, 170n.107, 202–3
    churches
        Basilica Apostolorum 106, 122n.57, 135–6
        Lateran 17, 24–6, 74–5, 75n.141, 87–8, 116, 168–9, 184*f*, 198–201, 316, 325–6, 330–1
        archives 21, 339
        baptistery 72n.127, 137, 154n.49, 155, 184*f*, 207–8, 207*f*, 212–14, 270–2, 301n.121
        rivalry with the Vatican 42–3, 120, 133, 323n.56, 330–1, 333–4
        Sancta Sanctorum 336–7
        triclinium and mosaic 158, 161n.77, 334–6, 338*f*
        oratory to S. Venantius 212–14
    San Clemente 208n.63, 210*f*, 218, 219*f*
    San Crisogono 168–9
    San Lorenzo e fuori le mura 106, 154n.49
    San Lorenzo in Damaso 154n.49, 168–9
    San Marco 24n.106
    San Panfilus 144–5
    San Paolo alle Tre Fontane ('Ad Aquas Salvias') 248–50
    San Paolo fuori le Mura 72–3, 76, 106, 154n.49, 205n.51, 209*f*, 210–11, 215, 217–18, 314–15
    San Pietro in Vincoli 208, 210*f*
    San Silvestro 218–19, 220*f*
    San Stephan Rotondo 154n.49, 168–9, 171
    San Valentino 171
    Sant'Adriano in Foro 31–3, 86–8, 108, 145–6, 181–2, 295
    Sant'Agnese fuori le Mura 136n.106, 146n.14, 203*f*, 212–14, 293n.99
    Sant'Anastasia 154n.49, 168–9
    Sant'Angelo in Pescheria 24n.106, 25n.110, 221–2
    Sant'Hermes 144–5
    Santa Basilla 144–5
    Santa Cecilia 151–5, 168–9, 212, 213*f*
    Santa Maria ad Martyres (Pantheon) 145–6, 212–14
    Santa Maria Antiqua 24–6, 84*f*, 86–7, 178n.137, 214, 228, 295
    Santa Maria in Cosmedin 221–2, 222*f*
    Santa Maria Maggiore 72–3, 148, 206–7, 270–2

Santa Maria Trastevere 151–2, 154n.49, 168–9
Santa Prassede 248–50, 251f
Santa Pudenziana 205–6, 206f
Santa Sabina 136n.106, 205–7, 206f, 228
Santa Susanna 212–14
Santi Cosma e Damiano 168–9
Santi Giovanni e Paolo 154n.49, 168–71
St Peter's
  aedicules 53–8
  apse, mosaic and inscription 1–2, 18–19, 30, 31f, 40–4, 46n.56, 49, 55, 56f–57f, 61, 65, 70, 75–8, 153–5, 159–60, 168–9, 174f, 181–2, 306, 326–7, 327n.77, 331–2
  architects 35–6, 45–50, 60n.90; *see also*, Bramante, Maderno, Michelangelo, Raphael, Sangallo
  campanile 51
  canons 1–2, 30, 33n.12, 42–3, 65, 78–80, 82–3, 230, 331–3; *see also*, Giacobacci, Grimaldi, Hercolano, Mallius, Romanus, Sabin, Vegio
  Capella del Re di Francia 15–16, 33, 35–6
  Capella della Bocciata 61, 178n.139
  Capella Gregoriana 76–8
  cathedra / throne 45, 61–3, 69–70, 77, 174f, 177n.132
  ciborium of the Sudarium / Holy Veil of the Veronica 79–81, 87n.7, 214, 222–4
  columns 46–8, 55–8, 82–3
  confessio 10–11, 18–19, 33, 40–2, 44–6, 49, 53–4, 58, 60–1, 72–3, 77–8, 98–9, 108, 155, 158–61, 174f, 175, 179–80, 224, 316–17, 320, 327, 339–40
  cost of new church 35–6, 42–3
  Door of Good and Evil 29–30, 186
  exedra 17, 30–1, 31f–32f, 46–8, 48f, 51–5, 54f, 60–3, 62f, 107–8, 134–5, 137, 155, 173–8, 305–6
  floor level 33–4, 58–60, 59f
  font 137, 144, 155, 168–9, 178–9, 204f
  foundation date 327–30, 332–4
  Frankish gifts 17–19, 311–12, 316–17, 325–6, 339–41
  grotto 33–4, 61, 63, 82, 208–10
  high altar 2, 18–19, 30, 33, 44–5, 46n.54, 65, 72–3, 77, 138–9, 149, 155, 167–9, 174f, 175, 178–9, 224, 327, 332–3, 339–40
  imperial patronage 16–17, 29–30, 35–6, 60n.88, 75–6, 326–33
  lights 75–6, 87–8, 160–1, 215, 216f
  liturgical presence 19, 316–17
  Madonna del Soccorso 76–7
  Madonna of the Column / della Colonna 61n.93, 78
  Mausoleum of the Anicii 44
  monastery of San Martino 31f, 46, 65–7
  muro divisorio 40–2, 55–61, 59f, 64–7, 76–8
  narthex 32f, 70, 76–82, 156, 174f, 177–9, 186–7, 208–10, 334–5
  nave 1–2, 29–30, 32f, 40, 42–3, 46, 47f, 49–53, 55–60, 57f–59f, 64–5, 72–3, 77–9, 81–3, 155, 174f, 175–9, 186–7, 217–18, 327, 333
  Nicholas V rebuilding 42–6, 49, 61–3, 230–1
  obelisk 16–17, 32f, 51, 72–3, 133, 139, 178–9
  oratorium Pastoris 31–3, 155–8, 162, 175–7
  oratory of All Saints 10–11, 174f, 176–8, 217f–218f
  oratory of John the Baptist 137, 174f, 177–8
  oratory of John VII 79–81, 80f, 174, 177–8, 214, 215f, 223f, 224
  oratory of Paul I 30–3, 107–8, 174f, 178–9, 221f
  oratory of Processus and Martinianus 60–1, 173–5, 174f

Rome (*cont.*)
    oratory of Sylvester 81
    oratory of Santa Maria de Praegnantibus 60–1
    oratory of St George 174*f*, 177–8
    oratory of St John the Evangelist 137, 174*f*, 177–8
    oratory of St Martin 31*f*, 46, 65–7, 138–40, 174*f*
    oratory of Sta Maria *in Cancellis* 107–8, 173n.122, 178–9
    oratory of Sta Petronilla 17–19, 33, 44–6, 108, 173, 174*f*
    oratory of the Holy Cross 137, 174*f*, 177–8
    oratory of the Leos 30–3, 31*f*, 60–1, 63–7, 69, 76–7, 82, 174*f*, 175
    oratory of Urban II 30
    oratory to S Adriano / Hadrian 30–3, 43, 69, 108, 174*f*, 175, 178–9
    papal necropolis 17
    Porta Santa 71*f*
    portico 2–3, 28*f*, 29–30, 33–4, 44, 69, 72–3, 75–9, 82–3, 186–7, 215, 216*f*, 230–2, 341–2
    rivalry with the Lateran 42–3, 120, 133, 323n.56, 330–1, 333–4
    rotundas 16–18, 30, 33, 46, 51, 60n.88, 65–7, 129–30, 133–5, 135n.102, 138–9, 171–3, 177–8, 305–8, 337
    sacristy 76–9, 178
    Santa Maria ad Grada / Mediana / in Turri 178–9
    shrine 1–2, 16–19, 27, 29–30, 34–5, 40–2, 44–6, 48–9, 70–3, 77–8, 85, 171, 326–30; see also, *confessio*
    tegurium 49, 53–5, 54*f*, 56*f*–57*f*, 58, 65, 70, 78
    transept 16–17, 30–6, 31*f*–32*f*, 38, 42–61, 48*f*, 53*f*–57*f*, 62*f*, 63–7, 69–70, 73, 76–7, 81–2, 107–8, 107n.90, 137–40, 149, 152–3, 155–6, 173–5, 174*f*, 177–9, 186–7, 212–14, 311–12, 327, 337
    triumphal arch, inscription and mosaic 1–2, 46, 155, 175–7, 181–2, 217–18, 310*f*, 326–9, 331–3
circus of Nero 16–17, 133, 230–1
city walls 86–7, 120–1, 144–6, 148–9, 170–1, 179–83, 202, 316–17
Column of Phocas 211–12, 212*f*
Forum 24–6, 86–7, 145–6, 178, 180, 198, 200–1, 211–12, 228–9
Lateran Palace (Sessorian) 87–8, 158, 184*f*, 200–1, 316, 327n.75, 334–6, 338*f*
Palatine 24–6, 178
Pantheon 145–6, 165, 212–14; *see also* Santa Maria ad Martyres
Porta del Popolo 46–8, 48*f*, 60
roads
  Via Appia 106, 135–6
  Via Cornelia 153–5
  Via Flaminia 46–8, 170–1
  Via Lata 24–6, 316
  Via Laurentina 248–50
  Via Nomentana 136n.106, 171
  Via Ostiense 171
  Via Sacra 178n.137
  Via Salaria 144–5, 328–9
  Via Vaticana 170–1
Sack of Rome (1527) 50, 67
Senate House (later Sant'Adriano) 145–6, 165, 316–17
Trajan's Column and Forum 181–2, 193, 198
Vatican Palace 36, 37*f*, 49–50, 82n.165
  Borgia Tower 14–15
  Stanza del Incendio 14–15, 36, 37*f*
Romulus and Remus 73, 229
Rotrude, Charlemagne's daughter 115–16, 303

Sabin, Peter 44–5, 63–4, 69–70, 75, 81n.159, 131, 217–18, 231
Saints
  Adriano of Nicomedia 31–3
  Aldegund (Maubeuge) 318
  Amandus (Saint-Amand) 149, 318
  Anastasia 173
  Anastasius (Corteolona) 153
  Andrew 16–17, 30, 32f, 33, 51n.71, 65–7, 131–3, 135, 171–3, 174f
  Arnulf (Metz) 171, 293–4, 318
  Audoen (Rouen) 318
  Aureus and Justinus 132–3, 137–9
  Bavo (Ghent) 318
  Crispin and Crispinian (Soissons) 318
  Cuthbert (Lindisfarne) 116
  Denis (Paris) 17–18, 33n.15
  Eligius (Noyon) 318
  Eutychius (Rome) 202–3, 204f
  Geretrude (Nivelles) 243–4, 318
  Gregory Nazianus (Rome) 76–7
  Jerome 99–100, 204–5, 278, 287, 289–91
  John the Baptist 131–3, 137, 174f, 177–8
  Landebert (Maastricht) 318
  Marcellinus and Peter (Seligenstadt) 138
  Martin (Tours) 131–3, 137–9, 173, 174f, 318
  Michael 173, 174f
  Paul 82–3, 205n.52, 215, 221–2, 248–50, 336–7
  Petronilla 15–19, 30, 32f, 33, 35–6, 44–5, 60n.88, 65–7, 88–9, 108, 138–9, 160–1, 171, 173, 174f, 177–8, 311–12, 318
  Primus and Felicianus 171
  Protus and Hyacinthus 144–5
  Quentin and Firmin (Amiens) 318
  Richarius (Centula) 150n.27, 318
  Sebastian 138
  Simon and Jude 58–60
  Stephen and Sylvester 218–19, 316
  Theodore 173
  Vedast (Saint-Omer) 318
  Victor 144–5
Salet, Belgium 233–5, 234f, 236f
Salzburg 111, 169–70, 257–60, 315–16, 329–30
San Vincenzo, Isernia, Italy 295, 312n.3
Sangallo, Antonio da 42–3, 49–51, 55–60
Saxons 38–40, 101–2, 176–7, 262–3, 265, 316, 328n.79, 335–6
Scedulae / loose leafs 265–6, 289, 291–3
Scrinium / writing office 19–20, 224n.93, 269–70, 339–41
Script, *Capitalis* and display 121–3, 185, 192–201, 232, 275–95, 281f
Scriptor 289–93, *see also* Baldo, Bertcaud, Dagulf
Sculptor 65, 193–4, 263
Sedulius Scottus 163n.87
Sedulius, Caelius, poet 118, 132, 146–7, 322n.53
Seligenstadt, abbey 138, 289–93
Sigebert, monk at Saint-Denis 12–13
Slavs 114–15
Smaragdus, exarch of Ravenna (603–11) 211–12
Solomon, *see* Temple
Spoleto, Lombard duchy 8–9, 14–15, 94–5, 151–2, 316
Stone
  africano 40, 41f, 82–3, 230n.16
  black limestone 186, 226f, 227–9, 231–8, 236f–239f, 242, 244–7, 257, 313
  Blaustein 232–3, 244–7, 246f, 250–2, 257
  carboniferous limestone 186, 233–7, 234f, 242, 244–5
  coloured marble 4–5, 41f, 76–7, 200, 228–9, 246–7, 269
  Lapis Niger 229
  Lapis Numidicum 43, 69–70, 73, 101n.69, 228–31, 323–4
  limekiln 63
  Lucullus 69–70, 230–1

Stone (cont.)
  Mosan marble 226f, 234f, 237–8, 238f–239f, 240–1, 243–5
  nero antico 230
  noir de Sablé 231–2
  opus sectile 76–7, 228–9, 246–7, 246f, 250–2
  pavonazzetto 224
  platoma 105–6
  porphyry 1–2, 45, 80f, 81, 106, 178, 207–8, 228–9, 231, 248–50, 249f–251f, 252–3, 287–9, 326–7, 334
  spolia 29–30, 40–2, 193, 207–8, 241–2, 245–6, 250–7
  symbolism 82–3, 228–9, 255–6, 301–2
Suetonius 298–9
Sylloge
  Centulensis 145–8, 150
  Circulation in Francia and England 143–4, 148–9
  Einsiedeln 150n.30, 310f, 328–31
  Lorsch 147–8, 151–5, 168–9, 178–9, 203n.45, 204f, 329n.88
  Turonensis 146–8
Symeon of Durham 105
Synod of Rome, 767 *see*, Council of Rome

Tasselli, Domenico 59f
Tassilo, duke of Bavaria 22, 126n.71, 328
Tatwine, archbishop of Canterbury (731–34) 148–9
Temple of Solomon 58, 301–6
Textiles 17–18, 31–3, 142f–167f, 155–6, 161–8, 176–7, 240–1, 315–16, 321–2, 324–5, 341
Theodore, epitaph at Santa Cecilia 212, 213f
Theodore, sacristan/*mansionarius* at St Peter's 175–6
Theodotus, duke, *primicerius notariorum* 24–6, 221–2
Theodulf, bishop of Orléans (*c*.798–818) 74, 97–8, 100–1, 105, 150, 153–5, 263–5, 272, 275–8, 291–3, 306, 313–17, 319–25; *see also*, Opus Caroli
Theophylact, bishop of Todi 95
Thionville, palace 162–3
Tiber, river 30, 86–7, 106–8, 153–5, 168–9, 171–3
Toto, duke of Nepi, brother of Pope Constantine II 19–20
Tournai, Belgium 227n.1, 233–7, 234f, 241–2
Tours, Saint-Martin's monastery 20–1, 97–8, 111, 117, 119, 138–9, 146–8, 150, 169–70, 195–7, 231–2, 264–8, 313–14, 316–20, 328–9, 339–40
Translatio imperii 324–5, 336–7

Urbis et orbis 145–6, 176–7, 211–12, 323–4
Utrecht 38, 113
Utrecht Psalter 164, 165f; *see also*, Index of Manuscripts

Valla, Lorenzo, humanist scholar (1407–1457) 330–3
Vegio, Maffeo 42–4, 61–4, 69–70, 75, 80–1, 111–12, 131, 230–1, 331–3
Vergil 118, 132, 195–7, 322n.53; *see also* Index of Manuscripts
Verus, Gaius Aurelius *negotiator Britannicianus moritex* 226f, 227–8, 237–8
Vestments 144–5, 162–3; *see also* pallium
Vexillum / banner 98–9, 158, 334–7
Vikings / Scandinavia 112–13, 116
Vine scroll 4–5, 78, 187–9, 188f–189f
Visigothic Spain 153n.44, 308–9, 321–2
Viterbo, Egidio da 48–9
Vitigis, king of the Ostrogoths (536–40) 208
Vulgate, Jerome's Latin translation of the Bible 204–5

Waldo, bishop of Pavia (791–814) 92–3
Wearmouth Jarrow, monastery 267–8
Wilibert, archbishop of Cologne (870–89) 91
Willehad, bishop of Bremen (787–789) 114–15
Winghe, Philippe de 78, 187–9
Witgar, bishop of Augsburg (858–87) 166–7

York 104–5, 112–14, 117–19, 149, 267–9
York Annals see Annals, *Historia Regum*
York Poem see Alcuin
York, archbishop's library 112–14, 118, 267–8, 300
York, archbishops *see*, Ælberht; Eanbald I; Eanbald II; Ecgberht